To: John —

The best sales manager!

Charlie

Media Selling

Broadcast, Cable, Print, and Interactive

Third Edition

Media Selling

Broadcast, Cable, Print, and Interactive

Third Edition

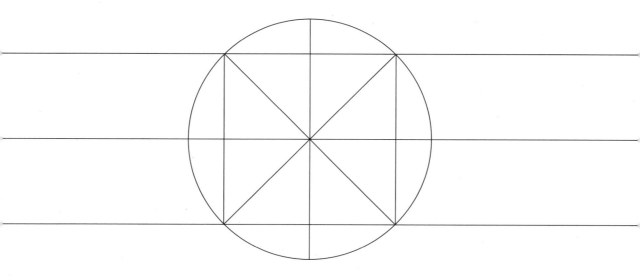

Charles Warner
Joseph Buchman

Iowa State Press

A Blackwell Publishing Company

Iowa State Press
2121 State Avenue, Ames, Iowa 50014

Orders:	1-800-862-6657
Office:	1-515-292-0140
Fax:	1-515-292-3348
Web site:	www.iowastatepress.com

Authorization to photocopy items for internal or personal use, or the internal or personal use of specific clients, is granted by Iowa State Press, provided that the base fee of $.10 per copy is paid directly to the Copyright Clearance Center, 222 Rosewood Drive, Danvers, MA 01923. For those organizations that have been granted a photocopy license by CCC, a separate system of payments has been arranged. The fee code for users of the Transactional Reporting Service is 0-8138-0417-5/2004 $.10.

Printed on acid-free paper in the United States of America

Library of Congress Cataloging-in-Publication Data

Warner, Charles, 1932–
  Media selling : broadcast, cable, print and interactive / Charles Warner
and Joseph Buchman.—3rd ed.
      p. cm.
  Includes index.
    ISBN 0-8138-0417-5 (alk. paper)
    1. Selling—Broadcast advertising. 2. Selling—Advertising,
Newspaper. 3. Selling—Advertising, Magazine. 4. Selling—Advertising,
Outdoor. I. Buchman, Joseph. II. Title.
    HF5439.B67W37 2003
    659.13′068′8—dc22
                                        2003015760

The last digit is the print number: 9 8 7 6 5 4 3 2 1

This book is dedicated to my perfect wife, Julia.

—Charles Warner

Contents

About the Authors

Charles Warner is the Leonard H. Goldenson Professor at the University of Missouri School of Journalism and the author of the first edition of Broadcast and Cable Selling, the classic text in the field. Prior to returning to his endowed chair at Missouri, he was a vice president of America Online Interactive Marketing. He has been actively involved in consulting and training for such companies as ABC, CBS, NBC, FOX, ESPN, MTV, Turner Broadcasting, A.H. Belo, Viacom, and Clear Channel. Before entering academia, he was vice president and general manager of WNBC-AM, WMAQ-AM and WKQX-FM, WWSW-AM and WPEZ-FM, and CBS Radio Spot Sales. Warner attended Dartmouth College, earned his BFA from the School of Dramatic Arts at Columbia University, and earned his MS in journalism from Southern Illinois University.

Joseph Buchman is the co-author of the second edition of Broadcast and Cable Selling. He has taught media management, sales, and marketing at Western Michigan University, Utah State College, and Indiana University. Dr. Buchman earned his BA in marketing at Indiana University, his MS in finance at Purdue University, and his PhD in mass communication from Indiana University. He is currently director of graduate training for The Harmony Institute Training Center, Salt Lake City, Utah.

Mark Chassman is a regional vice president for America Online, leading the company's advertising sales operations in the Midwest. Prior to joining AOL, Chassman had an extensive television career in sales and management. In his last television role he served as vice president and general manager for the Alaskan Television Network running ABC affiliates in Anchorage, Fairbanks, and Juneau. Prior to that he was the general sales manager and director of market development for CBS affiliates in Monterey and Sacramento, CA. He is a graduate of San Diego State University where he received his BA in marketing management.

Ken Foster has 30 years of marketing and media experience, having worked on the agency, media, and client sides of the business. He has written four educational marketing books and taught Marketing Communications and Media Analysis at the University of Utah for 21 years. He served in the administration at the University of Utah for 20 years and was in charge of marketing and public relations until he retired in 2001 to consult with private industry and educational institutions. He has worked extensively with organizations of all sizes across the country in both the public and private sectors.

Phil Frank is group vice president, new business development at Time, Inc.'s Corporate Sales and Marketing Department. Before joining Time, Inc., he was a vice president and national sales manager of AOL Interactive Marketing, a media supervisor at Ogilvy & Mather, and a senior vice president and group media director at Ammirati Puris Lintas. He earned his BA from Lehigh University.

J. William Grimes is a widely known media professional who has been president/CEO of four major media companies, including Univision, Multimedia Inc., Zenith Media, and ESPN (1981 to 1988), and former senior vice president of CBS. He has received the USA Today Sports Executive of the Year and the Gallagher Report's Television Executive of the Year awards. Grimes has taught Media Economics in the Master's Program: Media Studies at New York's New School University since 1997. He earned his BA from West Virginia University and studied law at St. John's University.

Tim Larson is associate professor of communication at the University of Utah and director of their Integrated Marketing Communication Certificate Program. He is also the director of the Telecommunication Sequence at the University of Utah. Prior to joining the University of Utah, he was on the staff of the Wisconsin Governor's Blue Ribbon Cable Task Force. Dr. Larson earned his PhD from the University of Wisconsin.

William Redpath is a vice president of BIA Financial Network, Inc., in Chantilly, VA. Prior to joining BIAfn in 1985, he was an auditor with the Cincinnati office of Arthur Andersen & Co.; assistant financial manager of WISH-TV, Indianapolis; on the internal audit staff of ABC in New York; and a senior financial analyst with NBC in New York. Redpath earned a BA in economics and political science from Indiana University and an MBA from The University of Chicago. He is a certified public accountant (Virginia), a chartered financial analyst, an accredited senior appraiser in business valuation in the American Society of Appraisers, and holds the Accredited in Business Valuation designation from the American Institute of Certified Public Accountants.

Thomas Stultz is the publisher of the *Gwinnett Daily Post* as well as president of the publishing division of Gray Television, Inc. He has held senior management and marketing positions with Multimedia Newspaper Company in Greenville, SC, Suburban Newspapers of Greater St. Louis, and Harte-Hanks Communications, Inc. He began his newspaper career as a reporter in Ashland, KY. He earned his MBA from Georgia State University.

Paul Talbot is senior vice president and market manager for the Infinity Broadcasting radio stations in Phoenix, AZ. Before joining Infinity Broadcasting, he was a director of national sales at AOL Interactive Marketing.

Vincent Thompson is a regional vice president for America Online and leads the company's advertising sales operations in the Southwest. Prior to joining AOL, he was the director of sales for Third Age Media, a dot-com company. He is a graduate of the University of Southern California and has an MBA from Pepperdine University.

Preface

Media Selling is an update and expansion of the updated, 1993, second edition of *Broadcast and Cable Selling*. Media convergence, fragmentation, the growth of the Internet, and the growth of cross-platform selling necessitated the inclusion of all of the advertising-supported media (newspapers, broadcast television, radio, cable television, yellow pages, magazines, the Internet, and outdoor). In the 10 years since the last edition of *Broadcast and Cable Selling* appeared, direct mail advertising rose from the third-largest medium in terms of advertising expenditures to the top position. Direct mail is not included as one of the media covered in this book because the media, as commonly referred to, are news and entertainment media supported entirely or in part by advertising. The content of direct mail is all advertising and it is a component of the direct-response or direct-marketing business, not the media business.

In the updated edition of *Broadcast and Cable Selling*, published in 1993, I included a section near the end of the book on sales ethics. In this new edition, I have decided to move ethics up to the third chapter of the book because I feel that people who hope to have a career in media selling need to know the rules of the game before they begin playing. Another reason I am emphasizing rules and ethics in this book is because the corporate and Wall Street scandals of the last few years have made it more imperative than ever that businesses, including the media, do the right thing, not only to restore the confidence of investors but also to restore the trust of the public, government regulators, and their own employees.

Earlier editions of *Broadcast and Cable Selling* dealt with needs-satisfaction selling, but the professional selling climate has evolved from the needs-satisfaction approach through consultative selling to solutions selling, today's preferred approach by world-class sales organizations. Solutions selling is the approach used in this book. The ground-breaking work of Daniel Goleman and his partners in emotional intelligence has also created a new, highly effective approach to building relationships—always the key to effective selling—and Robert Cialdini's work on the psychology of persuasion and influence has helped us understand the many fundamental psychological principles that direct human behavior. Both of these topics are new in this current edition.

Finally, print, interactive, and outdoor media are included in this book because of the growth of cross-platform selling that is the result of media company consolidation. Huge media conglomerates such as AOL Time Warner and Viacom are now bundling their media together in large cross-platform deals with major national advertisers. Even on the local level, cross-platform selling is occurring more and more often with combinations such as the ABC Television stations and their local Web sites and Infinity Radio and Infinity Outdoor selling on a cross-platform basis. This trend toward more cross-platform selling means media salespeople of the future must be experts in several media.

Focus of the Book

Media Selling focuses on several basic concepts:

- Selling without tricks or manipulation—with authenticity— to build and maintain long-term relationships based on trust.
- The imperative for honesty, integrity, and ethics in selling in this era of corporate misdeeds and erosion of confidence in the media.
- Attitudes control successful sales performance, and attitudes are controlled by using sound goals and objectives to motivate salespeople and help them achieve their dreams.
- Developing emotional intelligence—self-awareness, self-management, social awareness, and relationship management—is necessary for success in selling.
- Understanding the basic principles of persuasion and influence is important for today's media salesperson.
- Solutions selling means selling solutions to marketing and advertising problems.
- Becoming an expert negotiator because a majority of today's media business is conducted through negotiating.
- Understanding the concepts of marketing and advertising in order to develop appropriate solutions.
- Understanding all media is important in an era of cross-platform selling.

Unique Features

- A fully integrated and organized selling system—AESKOPP—that enables salespeople and sales managers to organize and evaluate sales efforts.
- A list of Core Competencies for salespeople that is useful to them and to managers for guiding and evaluating sales performance.
- A strategic selling approach that emphasizes *solving customer problems* by developing *trusting, long-term relationships* using the wisdom of emotional intelligence and the principles of persuasion and influence.
- Definitions of the six steps of selling that focus on discovering and understanding customer needs and wants and solving advertising and marketing problems.
- Tips on organizing, writing, and delivering major presentations to groups at key accounts.
- A thorough section on *negotiating and closing*.
- Tips on effective sales organization systems, To-Do lists, and time management.

Most books on selling tend to assume a salesperson sells a product with a fixed price, and once a salesperson overcomes objections, an order will follow at that price without negotiating. Radio, television, and cable prices have traditionally been negotiated, while newspapers and magazine prices have traditionally been fixed. However, some newspapers' and many magazines' rates are being negotiated more often, especially on a corporate or group basis. Closing becomes a part of the negotiating process and stresses getting commitment rather than trying hard closes, because old-fashioned closing techniques do not work with today's sophisticated media buyers and customers.

Style of the Book

We have tried to write the book in an informal, personal style. All of the authors are experts in their fields, and they have dug into their own extensive experiences to find anecdotes and examples to illustrate concepts and techniques.

Incidentally, we have used the term *salesperson* throughout this book instead of sales representative, account executive, or account manager just to be consistent, since they all mean the same thing.

Media Sales Management

A complete, thorough companion text to *Media Selling*, titled *Media Sales Management*, is available for free downloading on www.mediaselling.us.

Media Sales Management includes chapters on how to hire the best people, training exercises, sales management case studies, an in-depth performance coaching system, a discussion of sophisticated pricing strategies that will increase shares of business, and much more. It is designed to be used along with *Media Selling* in a college course on Media Sales and Sales Management and for working media sales managers and ad directors.

Acknowledgments

Special thanks go to Mark Barrett of Iowa State Press, who has been a superb and patient professional Acquiring Editor; to Tad Ringo for riding shotgun and seeing that the book was published; to Jamie Johnson, Justin Eccles, and Pat Burns, all of Iowa State Press; and copy editor Tracy Petersen and proof-reader Helen Flockhart. Thanks go to a hall-of-fame group of contributors (in order of appearance): William Redpath, Tim Larson, Ken Foster, Tom Stultz, Mark Chassman, Paul Talbot, Bill Grimes, Phil Frank, and Vince Thompson. And thanks to Joe Buchman who contributed four important chapters. The book was guided by the thoughtful reviews of Mike Wirth, Russell Mouritsen, Joyce Chen, and Robert Valentine and I would like thank them for their efforts and encouragement.

Part I

The Marketing/Media Ecology and Selling

Chapter **1** # The Marketing/Media Ecology

By Charles Warner

The media are integral elements of America's economy and of the marketing process that is vital to that economy's vigor. Consumer demand (and spending) is what drives the economy, and it is marketing and advertising that fuel consumer demand. Advertising is a major component of marketing and it is through the media that consumers receive advertising messages about products. If any one of the three elements (marketing, advertising, and the media) is not healthy, the other two cannot thrive. This chapter will examine the interdependent relationships among marketing, advertising, and the media.

What Is Marketing?

In his influential book, *The Practice of Management*, Peter Drucker, "the father of modern management," presented and answered a series of simple, straightforward questions. He asked, "What is a business?" The most common answer, "An organization to make a profit," is not only false, it is also irrelevant to him. If we want to know what a business is, we have to start with its purpose. "There is only one valid definition of business purpose: to create a customer," Drucker wrote.

Drucker pointed out that businesses create markets for products: "There may have been no want at all until business action created it—by advertising, by salesmanship, or by inventing something new. In every case it is a business action that creates a customer." Furthermore, he said, "What a business thinks it produces is not of first importance—especially not to the future of the business and to its success. . . . What the customer thinks he is buying, what he considers 'value,' is decisive—it determines what a business is, what it produces and whether it will prosper." Finally, Drucker said, "Because it is its purpose to create a customer, any business enterprise has two—and only these two—basic functions: marketing and innovation."[1]

Notice that Drucker did not mention production, manufacturing, or distribution, but only customers. That is what marketing is—a customer-focused business approach. The production-oriented business produces goods and then tries to sell them; the customer-oriented business produces goods that it *knows* will sell, not that *might* sell.

Another leading theorist, Harvard Business School Professor Theodore Levitt, wrote an article in 1960 titled "Marketing myopia" that is perhaps the most influential single article on marketing ever published. Levitt claims that the railroads went out of business "not because the need [for passenger and freight transportation] was filled by others . . . but because it was *not* filled by the railroads themselves. They let others take customers away from them because they assumed themselves to be in the railroad business rather than in the

3

transportation business."[2] In other words, they failed because they did not know how to create a customer; they were not marketing oriented. Where would makers of buggy whips be today if they had decided they were in the vehicle acceleration business or in the transportation accessory business instead of being in the buggy whip business?

Levitt cited the problems Detroit's car manufacturers were having in 1960 and would have in the future—they were too production oriented. When American automobile makers researched the needs of their customers, they merely found out customers' preferences among existing products. Japanese automobile makers did the *right* research in the 1970s and gave these customers what they really wanted and still are doing so today, producing the top two best-selling car models.

As a result of the customer-oriented, marketing approach espoused by Drucker, Levitt, and other leading management and business writers, many companies asked themselves the question, "What business are we in?" and subsequently changed their direction. They began to have a heightened sensitivity to customers and began to change the old attitude of "Let's produce this product because we've discovered how to make it."

In today's economy the customer rules and any company that does not put their customers on a pedestal and make raving fans of them will disappear from the business landscape as fast as so many of the dot-coms did.

Some Brief Economic History

From the beginning of the eighteenth century to the latter part of the nineteenth century, America had little or no mass-production capability. People devoted their time to producing agricultural goods, building manufacturing capacity, and developing commerce. They concentrated on inventing and manufacturing products. It was the *era of production.*

By the beginning of the twentieth century, the population had spread out from the East Coast, manufacturing had become efficient, and surpluses had developed. The basic problem shifted from one of production to one of distribution—getting the plentiful goods to people. Thus, in response to the new challenge, businesses developed new distribution systems: mail-order houses (the beginning of Sears, Roebuck and Company), chain stores, wholesalers and distributors, and department stores. It was the *era of distribution.*

When the 1920s came roaring in, the problem changed from one of supply to one of demand. Mass production and mass distribution were in place and an abundance of goods was produced and distributed. The problem now was to convince consumers to buy what was available. Enter the *era of selling,* as businesses attempted to create a demand for the products they had produced and distributed with more intensive selling techniques and advertising. Manufacturers made deceptive and extravagant promises about products, and high-pressure selling tactics were common, especially during the Depression in the 1930s as businesses became more desperate to sell their products.

After World War II, businesses had no trouble selling whatever was made. Consumers released their pent-up demand for goods built up during the years when manufacturing capacity was directed toward supplying the war effort. However, by the 1950s, consumers were beginning to be particular and to demand more choices; they wanted what *they* wanted, not what manufacturers happened to want to produce. The *era of marketing* had begun. Businesses such as IBM and General Electric that recognized the shift in consumer attitudes adopted a consumer-driven approach and survived; those that did not, such as the Pennsylvania Railroad, disappeared.

As has been widely reported, we are now in the *era of information*. Those businesses that can provide, distribute, organize, access, and create information are the ones that are growing rapidly. Microsoft is an information-era company that, by creating popular software, has more market capitalization than General Motors or Ford, both older, production-oriented companies. The Internet is the ultimate distribution channel for information and has become an integral part of most companies' marketing efforts.

The Marketing Concept

The fundamental concept underlying marketing is that of *consumer orientation;* however, just because a business is consumer oriented doesn't automatically ensure its competitive survival. Two other ideas must accompany consumer orientation for the marketing concept to be complete: *profit and internal organization.*

To continue to be sensitive to consumer needs, a business must also stay in business by making a profit. Although Drucker pointed out that profit is not the purpose of a business, profits are still the fuel that keeps the machines of business running; thus, profits are a necessary ingredient in the marketing concept.

To serve consumers, businesses must be organized internally to do so. The efforts of a number of functional areas or departments have to be coordinated so that all of them have the same goal—to create customers by serving their needs.

When the marketing era evolved in the 1950s, many marketing-oriented companies, such as Procter and Gamble, realized they had to change their internal organizational structure to accommodate their change in corporate strategy from production orientation to marketing orientation. They went from an organizational structure based on function (manufacturing, engineering, sales, and distribution) to one arranged by product (Tide, Jif, Crest, and so on).

Thus, a marketing-oriented company will typically organize around its marketing effort and put related functions such as sales, product design, consumer research, advertising and promotion, and customer service under the organizational wing of a marketing department.

The efforts of marketing-oriented departments are directed toward customer satisfaction, and more importantly, customer loyalty. Profit is the reward the business reaps from satisfied, loyal customers.

You might have noticed that we have been using the terms "customers" and "consumers" interchangeably. It is time to clear up that confusion and accurately define the terms. A customer buys a product, a consumer uses a product. Sometimes a customer and a consumer are the same person, for example, when a man buys an electric shaver for himself and uses it. Sometimes they are different people, for example, when a girl says she wants a Gameboy and her mom buys it for her. The customers for Procter and Gamble (P&G) are retailers and the consumers are people who buy Crest. By advertising to consumers and creating demand for Crest, P&G pulls the product through the distribution system. Some manufacturers do not advertise their products but sell them to wholesalers who they hope will sell the products to retailers and, thus, push them through the distribution system. In the media advertising business, the customer is the advertiser and the consumer is the reader, viewer, or listener.

You will find a more detailed discussion of marketing and marketing strategies in Chapter 15, because media salespeople must have a deeper understanding of marketing than is provided in this introductory section to be effective problem solvers and solutions sellers.

What is Advertising?

Harvard Business School Professor Theodore Levitt changed the direction of marketing with his 1960 article "Marketing myopia," and he changed the perception of advertising ten years later with his article "The morality (?) of advertising." Levitt wrote that "In curbing the excesses of advertising, both business and government must distinguish between embellishment and mendacity." He presents a philosophical treatment of the human values of advertising as compared with the values of other "imaginative" disciplines.[3]

Levitt defended advertising against critics who would constrain its creativity, who want less fluff and more fact in advertising. Many critics of advertising come from high-income brackets in business and government whose affluence was generated in industries that either create (advertising agencies) or distribute (the media) advertising, have grown through the use of effective advertising, or have used advertising to promote themselves (politicians). Thus, advertising's critics must look carefully at their own glass houses when throwing stones at advertising.

Levitt also claims that advertising's critics often view the consumer as a helpless, irrational, gullible couch potato, which is far from the truth. As David Ogilvy, the advertising genius and practitioner *par excellence*, wrote to his advertising agency copywriters in his book, *Confessions of an Advertising Man*, "the consumer is not an idiot, she's your wife."[4] Obviously, when Ogilvy made the comment in 1963, most copywriters were men, which is no longer the case.

Levitt, too, believed that "most people spend their money carefully" and are not fooled by advertising's distortions, exaggerations, and deceptions. He writes that rather than deny that distortion and exaggeration exist in advertising, these properties are among advertising's socially desirable purposes. Levitt goes on to say that "illegitimacy in advertising consists only of falsification with larcenous intent." Levitt's thesis is that advertising is like poetry, the purpose of which is "to influence an audience; to affect its perception and sensibilities; perhaps even to change its mind." Advertising, like art, makes things prettier. "Who wants reality?" Levitt asks. When most people get up in the morning and look at reality in the mirror, they do not like what they see and try to change it by shaving, using hair gel, or applying makeup. These things give people hope that they will be better accepted, more attractive and, thus, happier. The goal of the poet, the artist, and the composer are similar to the goal of an ad—creating images and feelings. Most advertising, especially on television, is about feelings and emotions. It is about trying to make people feel good about a product. Levitt writes that "Advertisements are the symbols of man's aspirations."[5] So, Madison Avenue (as the advertising industry is often referred to), like Hollywood, is selling dreams, and dreams and hope are essential to people's well-being.

Furthermore, advertising develops mass markets for goods, and mass production reduces the cost of producing these goods. Thus, advertising is a major contributor to reducing manufacturing and search costs, and, ultimately, retail prices. Products such as personal computers, digital video discs (DVD) players, video cameras, and personal digital assistants (PDAs) steadily come down in price as the market for them grows larger and as manufacturing savings are passed on to consumers in the form of competitive pricing. Consumers get information about these reduced prices through advertising, by the way, not via smoke signals.

Advertising is an important part of the nation's economy, and, as the nation's population increases and products proliferate, advertisers and their agencies will continue to invest more money in the media to reach consumers. You will find a more detailed discussion of advertising and advertising strategies in Chapter 17, because media salespeople must have a more in-depth understanding of the principles of advertising than is provided here to be effective sellers of advertising.

The Media

Advertising is one of the integral elements of the marketing process, just as sales, product design, promotion, and customer service are. We might look at advertising as the mass selling of a product. Where is advertising seen or heard? In the media. What business is an advertising agency in? In the advertising creation and placement business. What business is the media in? *The advertising delivery business.*

When people talk about the media, they are referring to the distributors of news and entertainment content—television, radio, newspapers, magazines, and the Internet. However, newspapers are not in the news business, magazines are not in the fashion business, and broadcast and cable television are not in the entertainment business. All of these media, as well as the other media covered in this book—yellow pages and out of home—are supported all or in part by advertising and are, therefore, in the advertising delivery business.[6] The media are dependent on advertising, and advertising, as an integral part of a larger marketing system, is co-dependent on the media. Without the media to reach large numbers of consumers with an ad or commercial, marketers would have to go door to door and try to sell their goods one-on-one through personal selling or consumers would have to wander from store to store wondering which sold the product they needed—both very expensive undertakings. Advertising agencies would not exist if there were no media to run the ads they created.

The reason marketers and advertisers are dependent on the media is because the media are pervasive and popular with consumers (readers, viewers, listeners) and are their link to the global village. People love and depend on their media—their favorite television program, such as "Friends," their favorite magazine, such as *People*, their favorite country music radio station, or their favorite newspaper, such as *The Wall Street Journal*. Because of this affection and dependency, the media are actually the most powerful business in the country—more powerful than the industries, celebrities, and politicians they cover, expose, and glorify.

It is because of this enormous power coupled with a perception that the media emphasize negative news or sex and violence that people probably have such a low opinion of the media. Americans seem to blame all the ills of society on the media. It is for this reason that we have devoted a separate chapter in this book to ethics. Chapter 3 emphasizes the importance for salespeople to deal with customers ethically, because the reputation of the media is at stake and that reputation needs to be improved.

The role of the media is to expose consumers to advertising, not to guarantee sales or results to advertisers. The media are just that—a medium, a connection between advertisers and customers. There are signs in radio station KOMC/KRZK in Branson, Missouri, for example, that read "Our purpose is to bring our audience and advertisers together." When asked in an interview in a national business magazine what the radio business was all about, Lowry Mays, CEO of Clear Channel Communications, replied, "To help people sell more Fords." These signs and statements reinforce the notion that the media are in the advertising delivery business.

In most of the world's countries, the media are supported and controlled by government; however, the media in the United States are kept free from government control and interference because of advertising support. The mass media from which the American public gets the vast majority of their information and entertainment are free or relatively inexpensive because they are supported by advertising. A daily newspaper that costs fifty cents at a newsstand would cost six or seven dollars were it not for the advertising, plus the newspaper would be much less desirable and useful for consumers if it contained no classified ads, no movie listings, or no bargains for price-conscious shoppers.

Finally, in spite of a love-hate relationship between the public and the media, or perhaps because of it, the media is a profitable industry. Many of the great fortunes in the world have been built in the media. Even if new products do not survive in the marketplace, the media still receive the advertising dollars invested to introduce the product, just as the media get the advertising revenue from losing political candidates. The profit margins in the media are, as a rule, higher than in most other industries, except for the software industry, perhaps. Top-rated radio and television stations in major markets often have profit margins of 50 percent or greater. Newspapers in large markets are usually monopolies or close to it because of joint operating agreements, and profit margins often reach or exceed 30 percent. Popular national magazines often have similarly high profit margins.

The reason for these high profit margins is because in an advertising-supported medium such as radio, television, newspapers, magazines, and Interactive, the cost of adding an additional ad has no or very low incremental costs involved. For example, in television, the time for commercials is baked into most programming, so if a commercial is not scheduled in a commercial pod, a promotion or public service announcement will run. A television station does not expand the programming time if it does not have commercials to run. Thus, at a television station, it costs nothing to add a commercial—there are no incremental costs involved. On the other hand, if an automotive manufacturer sells a car, it has to build one with all of the concomitant costs involved (labor, materials, transportation, etc.). Once a radio or television station has sold enough advertising to cover its cost of operations and debt payment, if any, all additional advertising sold is 100 percent profit.

In newspapers and magazines, which have an additional revenue stream, that of subscriptions, once the cost of operating is recovered, the incremental cost of adding a page of advertising is very low in comparison with the cost of an ad to an advertiser.

What this profitable economic model means for salespeople is that advertising revenue is extremely profitable and, therefore, there is more money to distribute to salespeople in the form of compensation than in less profitable industries. Media salespeople are among the highest paid of any industry, including the advertising industry.

The Media Industry

Table 1.1 shows the number of salespeople in the media covered in this book and the advertising expenditures in those media in 2001.[7] The annual advertising expenditure figures in each medium can be updated on the Internet by going to *Advertising Age*'s Web site (www.adage.com) in the Data Center where you will find Robert Coen's, of McCann-Ericson International, annual media expenditure totals for the current and past years. Coen is the leading estimator and projector of advertising expenditures and the source that we will use throughout this book to remain consistent. We are not covering direct mail, the number-one medium according to Coen's estimates for 2001 advertising expenditures. We do not consider direct mail an advertising-supported medium, rather we believe it is a direct marketing medium. In 2001, according to Coen, direct mail had total revenues of $44.7 billion, edging out the number-two medium, newspapers, by $400,000, or only .01 percent.

As you can see in Table 1.1, there are three times as many salespeople in the radio industry as there are in broadcast television and twice as many sales jobs in the newspaper industry as there are in television. There are three times as many newspaper salespeople as there are magazine salespeople. So, in terms of job opportunities, there are more sales jobs at local radio stations and local newspapers as there are in all of the other media put together.

Table 1.1 Number of Salespeople by Media and Revenue Generated

Medium	# of Salespeople[1]	Revenue[2] $ (billion)	% of Total	Revenue ($)Per Salesperson
Radio	45,000	17.9	7.7	400,000
Local		14.2	6.2	
Newspaper	30,000	44.3	19.2	1,460,000
National		6.6	2.9	
Local		37.6	16.3	
TV	15,000	38.9	16.8	2,600,000
Four networks		14.3	6.2	
National		9.2	4.0	
Local		12.3	5.3	
Magazines	10,000	11.1	4.8	1,100,000
Cable TV	7,000	15.5	6.7	2,285,000
Cable networks		11.9	5.1	
Local		3.7	1.6	
Internet	5,000	5.8	2.5	1,200,000
Yellow Pages	13,000[3]	13.6	5.9	1,046,150
Out of Home		5.1	2.2	
Sub-Total	125,000	152.2		
Total US Ad Expenditures		231.3		

1. Ron Steiner. 2002. Marketing Communications Group, from Mediarecruiter.com. Used with permission from Ron Steiner.

2. Robert J. Coen. 2002. Universal McCann, Media Expenditures, www.adage.com/datacenter.cms?dataCenterId=960. November 23.

3 Barry Maher, author of *Getting the Most From Your Yellow Pages Advertising*. 1997. Aegis Publishing Group. Newport RI. Personal communication with Joseph Buchman November 25, 2002.

In terms of advertising revenue, newspapers ($44.3 billion) are virtually as big as radio, magazines, and cable television combined ($44.5 billion). Eighty-five percent of newspaper advertising revenue is local—individual newspapers in local cities across the country. Keep in mind, too, that newspapers have a second revenue stream, as magazines and cable television do, from subscribers. Subscriber revenue numbers are not included in Coen's advertising expenditure figures. It is clear from this chart that newspapers are the largest local advertising medium by far.

The second largest local advertising medium is radio, with 79 percent of that medium's revenue coming from local advertisers. Local revenues for newspapers and radio are greater than the local revenue for broadcast television, which garners only 32 percent of its revenue from local advertisers. On the other hand, 74 percent of cable television annual advertising revenue is generated by the cable networks (ESPN, CNN, MTV, Lifetime, etc.), whereas 37 percent of broadcast television annual advertising revenue is generated by the four major television networks (ABC, CBS, Fox, and NBC).

If you look at the Revenue Per Salesperson column, you will see that television and cable television have the highest revenue per salesperson. These revenue figures include network, national representative, local television station, and local cable system salespeople. You might want to look carefully at the Revenue Per Salesperson column. There is a rough correlation between the revenue per salesperson and relative pay scales in those industries, keeping in mind that cable and broadcast television revenue is weighted heavily by network revenue and that networks hire only experienced salespeople with proven track records and relationships with major advertising agencies and advertisers, as is the case with large circulation, national magazines. Thus, yellow pages, newspapers, and radio have the best opportunity for entry-level jobs.

As can be seen from Table 1.1, advertisers spend more than $231 billion a year to market their products in the media. Consequently, the ecology of the marketing, advertising, and media elements of our economic system are inextricably bound together and dependent on each other's health, support, and cooperation for survival and growth. Thus, selling for the media, in addition to being potentially lucrative, requires a high degree of cooperation between advertisers and the media.

Test Yourself

1. In the era of marketing, what is the primary focus?
2. Why are consumer orientation, profit, and internal organization important to the marketing concept?
3. What is the difference between a customer and a consumer?
4. Is advertising distorted and exaggerated? If so, what do you think Theodore Levitt might say about this contention?
5. What business is the media in?
6. Why are the media potentially so profitable?
7. What is the largest local advertising medium? The second largest?

Project

Make a list of all of the local media in your market: radio stations, television stations, cable systems, newspapers (daily, weekly, shoppers, suburban, ethnic, etc.), local magazines or journals (e.g., local business journals), outdoor companies, bus or subway posters, yellow pages, and local Web sites that sell advertising. Interview one or two sales managers or advertising directors of some of the media that have revenue in addition to advertising (newspapers subscriptions or a Web site's e-commerce, for example) and get a rough estimate of what percentage of revenue comes from advertising and what percentage comes from other revenue sources. Write some notes about what surprised you in this exercise.

References

Kenneth Blanchard and Sheldon Bowles. 1993. *Raving Fans: A Revolutionary to Customer Service*. New York: William Morrow and Company

Peter Drucker. 1954. *The Practice of Management*, New York: Harper & Row.

Theodore Levitt. 1960. "Marketing myopia," *Harvard Business Review*, July-Aug.

Theodore Levitt. 1970. "The morality (?) of advertising," *Harvard Business Review*, July-Aug.

David Ogilvy. 1989. *Confessions of an Advertising Man 2nd Edition*, New York: Atheneum.

Resources

www.adage.com (*Advertising Age* online)

www.cabletvadvureau.com (Cable Television Advertising Bureau online)

www.editorandpublisher.com (*Editor and Publisher* online)

www.emonline.com (*Electronic Media* online)

www.iab.net (Internet Advertising Bureau online)

www.newspaper-industry.org (Newspaper industry information)

www.oaaa.org (Outdoor Advertising Association of America online)

www.rab.com (Radio Advertising Bureau online)

www.tvb.org (Television Bureau of Advertising online

Endnotes

1. Peter F. Drucker. 1954. *The Practice of Management*. New York: Harper & Row.
2. Theodore Levitt. 1960. "Marketing myopia," *Harvard Business Review*, July-Aug.
3. Theodore Levitt. 1970. "The morality (?) of advertising," *Harvard Business Review*, July-Aug.
4. David Ogilvy. 1989. *Confessions of an Advertising Man 2nd Edition*, New York: Atheneum.
5. Theodore Levitt. 1970. "The morality (?) of advertising," *Harvard Business Review*, July-Aug.
6. HBO is on cable television but is not supported by advertising, but by a monthly subscription fee. Therefore, HBO, and other premium cable services, are not in the advertising delivery business, but in the subscription television business.
7. www.adage.com/page.cms?pageId=906. November 22, 2002.

Chapter **2**

Selling: Perspectives and Approaches

By Charles Warner

The first sale I ever made was for a television station in South Carolina in 1957. The owner of the station had called a local florist and suggested to the proprietor, Mr. Parrott, that his shop purchase a spot next to a popular CBS network program. The owner of the station explained that the Florists Delivery Service was a regular sponsor of the highly rated program and that a lot of people would be watching. The flower shop owner could buy a commercial linking him to the prestigious network program and its national sponsor.

The station owner called me into the sales manager's office and told me to run down the street and sign up Mr. Parrott. I did precisely as I was told. I ran down to the florist shop with a sales contract in my hand and had the following conversation with the hot prospect:

"Hi, Mr. Parrott. I'm Charlie Warner. Mr. Brown sent me down here to pick up an order for an adjacency next to 'Person to Person.'"

"A what?"

"An adjacency—a commercial next to Edward R. Murrow's program 'Person to Person.'"

"Oh, yes. Well, I told him I'd try it. How much is one?"

"Here's our rate card. Would you like an ID or a chain-break?"

"A what?"

"A ten-second or a twenty-second spot?"

"Oh. Let's see, the ten-second one is cheaper. I'll take it."

"Would you like to buy more than just one?"

"No, not now. I'll try it this first time out. How much?"

"That will be $28.44."

"OK."

"Great. Let me fill in this contract here for you to sign. Oh, by the way, there's a charge of $10 for us to make a slide for you."

"A what?"

"A slide. You know, a picture to go up on the TV screen."

"Oh, yes. A picture is extra?"

"Of course. We have to charge for production."

"Oh, a picture is production?"

"Yes. I'll have our promotion man design one and get back to you with the artwork." (Long pause while filling out the contract.)

"Sign here, Mr. Parrott."

"Well, OK, I guess. . . . I never watch television myself. I hope it works."

"Thanks. I'll be back in a few days with your slide."

A station artist made a 35-mm slide, the client approved it, and the brief, static commercial ran next to "Person to Person" on Friday night. I returned to see the florist the following Monday afternoon and had this conversation:

"Hi, Mr. Parrott. Did you see your spot?"

"No."

"Oh, er . . . well, would you like to buy it on a regular basis? I can give you a discount if you sign up for thirteen weeks."

"I don't believe so."

"Why?"

"I didn't get any results. Nobody has called today."

"Well, that's . . ."

"No. I can't afford it anyway. TV is too expensive."

"OK. Well, thanks anyway."

What went wrong with this sale? If you answered "everything," you would be correct. First, the owner of the station was concerned with selling his product, not with satisfying his customer's needs; he was product-oriented, not customer-oriented. He apparently did not inquire about what the customer wanted, or if he did, he did not communicate it to me. The instructions were to "get an order," not to "find out what Mr. Parrott wants and needs." Second, the owner took a very short-range point of view; he was not interested in creating a repeat customer, or in developing a long-range relationship and partnership, only a one-shot sale.

If the owner was initially at fault, I, as a rookie, compounded the errors tenfold. First, I made no attempt to prepare for the call or to consider a strategic approach. Second, I used jargon; I failed to put things in the prospect's language. Next, I did not ask any discovery questions; I just handed the florist a price sheet (rate card) right away. I did not control the interview by using probing questions, and the questions I asked were the wrong ones—ones that easily could be answered in the negative. I did not pick up cues about the prospect's expectations ("I'll try it this first time out").

Instead of explaining the production charges earlier, I presented them as an add-on after a price had been shown. I not only told him to sign a contract for just a small amount but also asked him to wait while I filled it out in front of him. In addition, the client had to ask me what a slide was and I probably made him feel ignorant. Because I was not listening attentively, I did not catch the prospect's doubts (". . . I hope it works"). I failed to try to build a relationship by developing a rapport or being empathetic. I had no skills in understanding objections and then dealing with them. Finally, I *told* the prospect to sign ("Sign here . . .") and I made no attempt to make the customer feel good about his purchase and reinforce his good judgment.

When I eagerly returned the following week, I began by asking the wrong question, got a predictably negative answer (which I did not handle well), and went immediately to a weak close based on a price concession. Finally, I gave up too easily. I realized by that time I had done everything wrong; but even so, I still gave up too easily.

This book is about doing it right, about selling in the media in an in-depth, customer-oriented, solutions-based, partnering approach. This book is for people who hope to begin or who have already begun sales or sales-related careers in the media in small, medium, and large markets. The material presented here represents a distillation of techniques that I have developed and taught with success in a forty-five year career that has included, in addition to teaching at the world's top journalism school, selling, sales management, general management, and consulting and training in media organizations.

Perspectives

This book presents a system that will help you organize your sales efforts and not only get you off to the right start, but will also, if you follow the system, keep you on that track to success. The question most asked by beginning salespeople is, "Where do I start?" The answer is: Start with the AESKOPP system.

A Selling System

AESKOPP is a mnemonic that will help you remember the following elements of successful selling:

Attitude
Emotional Intelligence
Skills
Knowledge
Opportunities
Preparation
Persistence

We will look at each piece of the AESKOPP system more closely in Chapter 4 of this book. First, let's consider some assumptions we will need to make about people and about the field of selling.

Assumptions

Three assumptions form the foundation of the theories and methods proposed in this book.

Assumption 1: People Are Complex and Basically Trustworthy.   Each person is a unique and complex individual who cannot be described adequately by simple, one-word, personality-type labels. People are enormously complicated and understanding them requires much more than snap judgments based on first, or even second, impressions. Understanding people requires emotional intelligence, which will be covered in Chapter 6. It also requires effective communication, effective listening skills, caring, fairness, and respect, which will be covered Chapter 7.

The assumption that people are basically trustworthy gives us a workable model for our actions. Think what the world would be like if we made the opposite assumption—that no one could be trusted. We could not tell anyone the truth and we would have no idea if what people told us was true. We would live in a world as confusing as the following two sentences are:

1. The sentence below is false.
2. The sentence above is true.

In order to have a functioning society we must act on the principle of reciprocity, especially in regard to being straightforward, telling the truth, and trusting people. If we act on the principle that we get from people what we give them and offer the first gift of trust, the odds are good that we will receive a reciprocal gift of trust in return. There will always be an occasional aberration in which someone does not return your trust and tries to deceive you, but that is life—nothing is perfect—and we cannot act as though no one can be trusted. Leon Levy, in his book *The Mind of Wall Street*, suggests that people are either givers or takers.[1] You will meet and have to deal with people who are takers, but it is always best to be a giver and assume others are, too, until you learn differently.

Assumption 2: Selling Is a Worthy Craft.   This statement includes four ideas. First, selling is a craft. Selling contains a body of knowledge and techniques that can be learned, but can only be perfected through practical experience, which makes it a craft. The craft of selling is expressed and exercised primarily through understanding people and is addressed in Chapter 7.

Second, selling is an expression of worthy values—freedom and independence. Selling affords people freedom in dealing with the most complex subject there is, people, and it allows you the freedom to express yourself. Selling also gives you the independence you need to have control over your own actions and work habits and, therefore, to have an exciting daily challenge. In addition to freedom of movement and action and independence to work at your own pace and in you own way, selling also gives you the opportunity to make a lot of money if you are good at it.

Third, selling is worthy because you are helping other people—you are helping them get what they want, helping them to be successful. You help advertising agency buyers get what they want for their clients and you help advertisers get results as they define them and sell more goods. In a sense, you are helping fuel the economy.

Fourth, selling fosters optimism, self-confidence, and the belief in the inherent rationality and goodness of people. Selling encourages, virtually forces, people to have a positive view of the future, of themselves, and of others—to have a healthy outlook on life. You cannot face selling day in and day out if you do not believe in your ability to help your customers solve their marketing and advertising problems. There is great personal satisfaction in helping your customers get results, sell more goods, and be successful.

There is a fifth, and probably the most important, reason that involves selling media, and that is that media sales can be especially rewarding because by selling advertising, salespeople are helping to maintain a free news and entertainment system.

Assumption 3: The Media Are Highly Visible, Important, and Under Attack.   The media are ubiquitous and powerful, and transmit advertising, political, cultural, social, and moral messages (either intended or unintended) to a mass audience. Because radio and broadcast television stations operate on airwaves owned by the public and cable television operates on common-carrier-like technologies, these media are subject to a complicated web of government regulations.

Because of the complex and fuzzy combination of show business and public service, the media will continue to be loved and hated, praised and vilified, regulated and deregulated, and given credit or blamed for everything from keeping our nation free to poisoning the minds of our children. Salespeople in the media must learn to deal with all types of extreme reactions and to accept the fact that they, as representatives of their medium, will have to face these reactions on a daily basis.

The good news is that, as a salesperson, you will usually have easy access to clients because you represent a highly visible medium. The bad news is that your medium will be blamed for everything from a client's sore back to the nation's economy, and you will have to listen to the reasons for your medium's and all of the media's failures in a good-natured way—people tend to lump all the media together as a target for their anger, so it does not matter if you're selling out of home, the Internet, or a newspaper, you will probably get comments about how awful the media are.

The media industry is changing at an accelerated rate in terms of both technological advances and the audience's tastes and needs. As America continues its transition from a production-oriented to an information-oriented industrial system, consumers become more particular and selective. This creates a shifting emphasis for salespeople—from that of selling and getting an order toward one of building relationships and solving problems. Meanwhile, there is less time available for preparation, planning, and negotiating as advertising schedules run for shorter and shorter periods.

In the past, the media enjoyed virtually guaranteed profits, but today the media are becoming increasingly fragmented. Too many media are chasing smaller and smaller market segments and profits are declining, especially during times of slowdown in advertising spending. This means that as the competition for advertising dollars increases, the need for effective salespeople increases, because, to quote an old saw, nothing happens until someone sells something.

The ultimate goal of a business is survival, and profits are critical for a business to survive. Profits are what are left over after subtracting expenses from revenue. There are only so many expenses that accountants and bean counters can cut from a company's budget before cutting through muscle and deep into the bone, thus crippling the business. A more effective way to assure profits is to grow revenue, which requires salespeople, not accountants. Consequently, sales are critical to a company's survival and growth, which is why salespeople are usually the last personnel cuts to be made during a slowdown.

There have never been so many opportunities for competent salespeople in the media; and yet, selling is more difficult, complex, and competitive than ever before. To succeed, you must be better trained, better prepared, and better motivated than in the past, which is why you are reading this book.

With these assumptions in mind, let's consider some of the common questions about selling and define some terms.

Questions and Definitions

People interested in sales careers frequently ask these questions:

1. What is selling?
2. What does a salesperson do?
3. What are the qualities that make a salesperson successful?
4. What does a sales department do?
5. Where do I begin?

We will look at each of these questions in this and subsequent chapters and attempt to find some answers that will guide you to a successful career in selling media.

What Is Selling?

We will use three analogies for selling as we progress through the book: (1) Selling is like *dating* because you have be a good communicator and listener, and you have to be interested in a long-term relationship that leads to partnering to be really good at both dating and selling. (2) Selling is like *sports* because athletic success requires a complex combination of attitude, skills, knowledge, opportunity, preparation, and persistence to be a champion. Team sports is an especially apt analogy because of the unselfish cooperation of a whole team need to win. (3) Selling is like *acting* because to be successful you must learn how to rehearse and how to play your assigned role, even if it is a supporting role, so that you do not attempt to steal the picture from other actors but instead try to make them look good to have a hit movie.

Selling in the media is about creating customers and keeping them. Creating customers and keeping them involves a process by which people help others get what they want. Selling is *not* a manipulative process in which a salesperson gets buyers to do things they do not want to do. In the case of selling advertising in the media, it means helping customers solve their advertising problems. The best way for salespeople to get what they want is to help customers get what they want. Selling is about building trusting relationships, and is guided by three basic relationship rules which will be examined in more detail as we progress through the book:

1. The new Golden Rule of Selling: *Do unto others as they would have others do unto them.* This is a slight twist on the Golden Rule from the Bible, which assumes that everyone likes to be treated the same as you do—not necessarily so. It is better to observe people carefully and discover how they prefer to be treated without making any prior assumptions.
2. *People like and trust people exactly like themselves.* Later, in Chapter 7, I will present some research on communication theory that reinforces the concept that human beings have an affinity for people similar to themselves—call it tribalism or elitism—but it is a reality that salespeople must learn to contend with.
3. *People don't care how much you know until they know how much you care.* In other words, shut up, listen carefully, and give people signals that you care about them as people, not merely as potential sources of revenue.

Buyers.   There are three types of buyers: *prospects, customers,* and *partners.*

Prospects are people who have not bought a product for a variety of reasons, ranging from never having heard of it to disliking it; prospects require *developmental selling.* In the media, prospects might be those people who (1) have never before advertised because they have an established business that they feel does not need advertising; (2) have never advertised because they are starting a new business; (3) advertise but not in your medium; or (4) advertise in your medium but do not use your station, paper, system, magazine, or Web site.

Customers are people who have either decided to buy a product (goods or services) or who have already bought a product and are going to buy it again. Customers require *outrageous service that will make them "raving fans."*[2]

Partners are customers who have joined with a media company to conduct business based on mutual trust and, in a sense, to help each other to be more successful. They do this by cooperating in discovering innovative solutions that connect a partner to a medium's audience in a way that delivers partner-defined results and jointly builds the brands of both companies. As in dating, the ultimate purpose of a sales relationship is to have a partnership based on mutual trust with a long-term commitment to each other.

Products.   Products are either tangible or intangible. *Tangible* products are goods you can see and touch, such as automobiles, personal computers, or cosmetics. *Intangible* products are services that cannot be seen, touched, or tested in advance, such as insurance, banking and financial services, or advertising media time and space.

Tangible products can be experienced and they are usually easy to demonstrate—product features and benefits are apparent before a purchase. However, even tangible products have some degree of intangibility, as pointed out by Theodore Levitt: "You can't taste in advance or even see sardines in a can or soap in a box. This is common for frequently purchased, moderate- to low-priced consumer goods. To make buyers more comfortable and confident about tangibles that can't be pre-tested, companies go beyond the literal promises of specifications, advertisements, and labels to provide reassurance."[3]

Packaging is one common tool used to make the intangible elements of goods more tangible in a customer's mind—for example, putting pickles in a glass jar so purchasers can see the product. Advertising is another tool used to communicate advance assurances that the product is what it says it is.

It is harder to keep customers satisfied with intangible products than with tangible ones. The biggest problem with intangible services, such as advertising time, insurance, or banking services, is that customers are usually not aware of the full range of services they are getting until they no longer get them. Therefore, they rarely appreciate the positives and the negatives tend to be blown out of proportion. This situation means that intangibles require more service and greater efforts on the part of salespeople. From now on all products and services will be referred to as *products,* whether they are tangible or intangible.

Identifying Problems.   The path a salesperson follows in solving customers' and prospects' marketing and advertising problems is that of identifying both those problems and potential opportunities. These problems can be solved by benefits and advantages that your medium can offer and that then can be positioned to appeal to customers according to their needs portrait. Needs portraits will be covered in detail in Chapter 7, but a needs portrait is, essentially, a picture of a customer's most dominant needs and motives.

Generating Proposals.   The final payoff in selling, for both the customer and the salesperson, are solutions to marketing and advertising problems that get results for the customer, then putting these solutions into an arresting, believable, and winning proposal that presents your solutions in the best possible light. Finding solutions to customer problems and proposing them is the most creative and satisfying part of a salesperson's job. You must fully understand your customers' marketing and advertising problems plus have a full understanding of the capabilities of your medium to solve those problems. Creativity is largely a matter of solving problems in new and different ways and presenting them convincingly and dramatically, so if you are a good salesperson, you are a creative problem solver and presenter. And, finally, getting results for customers is personally satisfying and rewarding—you know you helped someone.

What Does a Salesperson Do?

The best way to describe what a salesperson does is to tell you what the objectives are for a media salesperson rather than try to give you a job description or list of tasks he or she does.

Objectives.   The four *primary objectives* of a media salesperson to get and keep customers are:

1. To get results for customers. Results must be defined by customers—for example, increased sales, reduced distribution costs, increased profit margins, increased awareness, improved corporate image. Salespeople must *put customers first*—not themselves, customers. Not their company, customers. If customers do not get results, they will not renew. Thus, salespeople must take a long-term view and create renewable, replicable business.

2. To develop new business. That is, to turn business prospects into customers. Salespeople must continually develop new business not only to replace accounts that are lost each year due to normal account attrition but also to ensure growth. The most important reason for constantly developing new business is to create demand, because it is demand that largely determines the price of media advertising. Salespeople who do not continually seek out new accounts are like sailors who have fallen overboard and are treading water; they get nowhere.

3. To retain and *increase* current business. Servicing business properly to keep accounts satisfied and getting renewals is vital; yet more important is to continually pre-sell and provide clients with solid evidence, reasons, and, especially, ideas for them to increase their investment in your medium. Advertising is not an expense, it is an investment—an investment in future sales and profits. Your best prospects are your current customers, and continually showing them the benefits of your medium and getting an increased investment from them is vital for growth. On every service call, *always* present customers with ideas that will lead to an increased investment and will reinforce the value of their current investment. Remember that advertising is an intangible product that requires more reinforcement, servicing, and reassurance than a tangible product would. Customers require constant attention if you are going to retain and increase current business.

4. To increase customer loyalty. If you are going to put the customer first, get results for the customer, and get all-important renewals, you are going to have to keep customers' satisfaction levels high and increase customer loyalty. It is sort of like being married—you have to work harder after you are married than before in order to keep it on track. Too often, the romance stops after the courtship is over. Like the ex-mayor of New York, Ed Koch, you have to continually ask, "How am I doing?" in order to keep a relationship going and to keep your partner or customer happy and loyal. More and more sales organizations of major companies such as IBM and Hewlett-Packard are evaluating and compensating their salespeople based on levels of customer satisfaction. That means salespeople must not only make a sale, but also, through excellent service after the sale, keep customers happy—provide absolutely, outrageously good service and not only make them happy, but make them raving fans.

Strategies. Strategies are long-term, overall operating concepts and principles that guide actions toward stated objectives. To achieve the preceding sales objectives, salespeople should follow these *sales strategies*:

1. Sell solutions to marketing and advertising problems. Computer manufacturers and retailers learned the hard way that normal consumers did not understand or care about hardware (geeks care, though)—for example, how many memory chips a computer had or how many bytes were stored on a disk. What the ordinary consumer cared about was what the computer did—what writing or accounting or design problems the software was able to solve. By the same token, potential advertisers do not care about a broadcast station's power or antenna height, a cable system' type of commercial insert equipment, or a magazine or newspaper's press size or color-separation ability. What prospects care about is how advertising is going to help them solve marketing or advertising problems. Therefore, salespeople must learn to position their offerings in such a way that they always answer their prospects' question, "What's in it for me," as is covered in depth in chapters 10 and 11.

2. Reinforce the value of advertising and of your medium. In 1978, 60 percent of all marketing dollars were spent in advertising and 40 percent were spent in promotion. In 2001, 50 percent of all marketing dollars were spent in promotion, 50 percent in advertising. The migration of marketing dollars from advertising to promotion hurt the growth rate of advertising over those years. Salespeople who sell advertising must continually reinforce advertising's positive long-term effects and the value of advertising to build brand image. Each medium has its own unique advantages and benefits for advertisers. Salespeople must continually reinforce the benefits of their medium in order to reinforce the value of advertising and stem the migration of advertising dollars to promotion.

3. Create value for your product. A salesperson's most important product is the perception and image of their product that a salesperson creates in a prospect's mind. A kids' toothpaste is (1) a toothpaste that is blue and tastes like bubble gum, or (2) a revolutionary new product that is a glistening, bright, cool, deep blue color that shimmers with flecks of silver, making it interesting, exciting, and fun for children to push out of the easy-to-manipulate dispenser for small hands. Its foaming action in the mouth is new and different—it is thicker and foamier, as if something important is really working in kids' mouths to fight cavities and to make their breath smell great so their mommies will know they really did brush their teeth. When the kids first taste their very own type of new toothpaste that is *not* for adults, they experience a taste sensation unlike any other. It is not toothpaste; *it is bubble gum!* Kids cannot wait to brush their teeth several times a day. They are likely to say after lunch, "Well, I think I'd better go brush my teeth."

Which of the above two descriptions of the new kids' toothpaste creates more value for the product? Which description is more likely to make the sale? The second description creates value for the product, which is positioned according to its benefits to the kids.

You must also create value for your product so you will not have to lower your price to get an order. You will find a much more thorough discussion of the many ways to create value in Chapter 8, because in order to be successful in selling solutions to advertising problems you must be able to create value effectively for your medium and your media outlet.

4. Become the preferred supplier. Salespeople must establish, maintain, and improve relationships with both the customer and the customer's advertising agency. It is a certainty that clients will eventually change advertising agencies, so salespeople *must* establish relationships at the client level. Advertising agencies will often tell you not to see a client, because the client is *their* client. Well, the client is *your* client—the client's name is on the ad or commercial in your medium, not the agency's name. Over the years, newspapers have become the preferred local supplier because they usually give customers more information and better service than other local media do. In order to become the preferred supplier, or a partner, salespeople must provide more and better information and service than any other salesperson from any other medium so the customer will think of them first when they need information or want to buy advertising.

5. Innovate. Every medium must continually introduce new ideas: new packages, new promotions, new community affairs projects, new special sections, and new events. New products such as those mentioned give salespeople a reason to make another call on a customer or agency, they create excitement, and they provide new ways to solve marketing and advertising problems.

6. Help the competition get rich. This strategy seems counterintuitive, but it works. The way to help competitors in your medium to get rich is to raise your rates and to develop new business. You should attempt to increase the size of the total advertising pie in your medium and not obsess about losing any single order or not worry about getting the highest share of business on every order. Sell your medium first and worry about your fair share later. If you do an excellent job of selling your medium, there will be enough for everyone.

Key Functions.   A salesperson has three *key functions:*

1. To create a differential competitive advantage in a buyer's mind. Salespeople who cannot find ways to create *differential competitive advantages* are merely order takers or clerks who wait on customers and process transactions, and they will not last long in the highly competitive environment of media selling.

2. To manage relationships. The relationship must be built on mutual trust and respect. Salespeople must take the long view, just as in dating; do not look at one date, but a whole series of dates. The relationship between a salesperson and a customer does not end when a sale is made; it is just the beginning of the relationship from the customer's point of view. The relationship should intensify over time and help to determine a customer's buying choice the next time around. Thomas J. Peters and Robert H. Waterman, Jr. emphasize in their book, *In Search of Excellence,* that the most important element that the companies they examined shared was being *close to the customer.* Managing a relationship with an account means recognizing that your most important task is building and maintaining a long-term relationship.

3. To solve problems. Salespeople must be creative in solving advertising problems that get results for clients. The goals of a salesperson begin with getting results for clients, and a salesperson's key functions end with solving problems for clients. You cannot get results for clients unless you learn to discover and then solve problems. This is what solutions selling, the basic approach recommended in this book, is.

Related Functions

1. To obtain and process orders. Not only to solve problems and get orders but also to make sure the orders enter the operational system so they can be executed properly and on time.

2. To provide customer service. To be certain that each account's advertising schedules are handled properly and that the billing and production details are correct, to communicate new market information to customers, to communicate new benefits and advantages, to increase revenue from accounts, and to work on establishing long-term relationships. Servicing techniques will be covered in more detail in Chapter 13.

3. To manage accounts. To set objectives for revenue and service, to plan the execution of your management's specific sales strategies as they relate to accounts, and to become knowledgeable about accounts' industries and their business and marketing goals and strategies.

4. To monitor the marketplace. To provide information to your management and other salespeople about competitors in all media—their prices, strategies, content or format changes, management and ownership changes, advertising and promotion strategies, and sales strategies and tactics. Competitive intelligence is vital to your management in determining your company's competitive strategy.

5. To recommend tactics. To recommend pricing changes, new packages, promotions, and changes in selling approaches to your management as a result of what you learn on the street about what your competitors and other media are doing.

6. To cooperate. To help other salespeople in your department learn from each one's experiences (successes and failures); to help the sales department meet its strategic selling objectives; to cooperate in completing reports, expense accounts, and contracts accurately and on time; to help with promotions, parties, and events; and to cover for other salespeople who are absent. Departments in which the mode of operating is cooperative are more productive than those in which the operating mode is competitive, according to Alfie Kohn in his book, *No Contest: The Case Against Competition.*

These are the key and related functions of salespeople. Their responsibility is to demonstrate an intelligent effort in carrying out these functions. In other words, not only must salespeople do what they are supposed to do to carry out these functions, but they must also let their management and their customers know that they are doing it diligently—that they are carrying out their functions and implementing the strategy which management has designed to reach the company's objectives.

What Qualities Make a Salesperson Successful?

The International Radio and Television Society (IRTS) conducted a *Time Buyer Survey* among important media buyers in New York City several years ago. The buyers were asked to name and rank the characteristics they thought were most important for a salesperson to have. The following list resulted from the study:

1. Communication skills—Clarity and conciseness, not oral skills or flamboyance, were ranked as most important.
2. Empathy—Insight and sensitivity.
3. Knowledge of product, industry, and market.
4. Problem-solving ability—Using imagination in presentations and packaging.
5. Respect.
6. Service.
7. Personal responsibility for results.
8. Not knocking the competition.

More recently, a major radio station group commissioned research of advertising time buyers and media executives to find out what they wanted from salespeople. Their results were similar to those of the IRTS study. Here is what buyers wanted from salespeople:

1. Ideas—Especially in the area of added value and how to sell their client's product better.
2. Communication—Clear, concise communication, not long-winded, exaggerated sales pitches.
3. Respect for their time.
4. Run as ordered.
5. Responsiveness—Return calls *fast,* be available at all times, get schedules confirmed quickly and correctly.

Much of the remainder of this book will be spent helping you develop the attitude, emotional intelligence, skills, knowledge, opportunities, preparation, and persistence necessary to become a salesperson who will make raving fans of agency buyers and customers who want the above attributes from salespeople.

In the classic *Harvard Business Review* article, "What makes a good salesman," David Mayer and Herbert Greenberg point out that the two essential qualities for a salesperson to have are *empathy and drive.* Empathy is the ability to feel as another does. Being empathetic does not necessarily mean being sympathetic. A salesperson can know what another person feels without agreeing with that feeling; but, as Mayer and Greenberg point out, ". . . a salesman simply cannot sell well without the invaluable and irreplaceable ability to get powerful feedback from his client through empathy."[4] This attribute will be covered in more detail in Chapter 6. Drive, is a particular type of ego drive "which makes him want and need to make the sale in a personal or ego way, not merely for the money to be gained."

This book can help you learn techniques to improve your empathy and drive, but it cannot imbue you with these two essential qualities—they must come from within. In essence, this means that to be successful in selling, you must genuinely like people and crave being successful.

What Does a Sales Department Do?

The sales department is responsible for the advertising revenue of a medium. The sales department, often referred to as the advertising sales or just advertising department in magazines and newspapers, is responsible for sales planning, which includes setting policy, establishing procedures, and determining strategies. It is responsible for hiring and training salespeople. The sales department communicates appropriate sales information to other departments and passes on appropriate information about other departments to its sales staff. In addition, it is responsible for supervising the activities of salespeople, controlling inventory and sales expenses, and evaluating the performance of salespeople.

There is no standard or right structure for a sales department. Theorists in organizational structure have an axiom that "structure follows strategy," which means that a sales department's structure should reflect its sales strategy, and in most cases, this axiom holds true.

Organizational structures of sales departments range from that of a small-market radio station in which the general manager is also the sales manager to whom three salespeople report, to that of a large-market newspaper in which there is a director of advertising sales (who reports to the publisher), a national sales manager, a retail sales manager, a classified sales manager, category sales managers, and a sales staff of perhaps 150.

Because structure tends to follow strategy, sales department structures do and should alter as the marketplace changes and as sales strategies change in response. For example, many radio and television stations are adding retail sales teams to take advantage of co-op and vendor support opportunities such as newspapers have done for years, or event sales managers to sell heavily promoted events.

Where Do I Begin?

1. **With a non-manipulative sales approach.** Tony Allesandra introduced the concept of non-manipulative selling in his well-organized and thoughtful book of the same name, *Non-Manipulative Selling*, in 1979. Along with sales experts and trainers such as Larry Wilson, Allesandra taught a new form of selling that did not rely on old-fashioned tricks and manipulation techniques. His approach was that of creating long-term customers and managing relationships. The next iteration of selling was the consultative selling approach, which was a further customer-oriented refinement of non-manipulative selling. Neil Rackham's excellent book, *Spin Selling*, best articulates the consultative selling approach. The latest maturation of the non-manipulative, consultative sales approach is a global trend toward *solutions selling*, the ultimate customer-focused approach.

2. **With a systemized, solutions-oriented sales approach**. We devote Chapter 4 to a well-organized, thorough system for approaching sales in today's highly competitive, complex media environment.

Having addressed some of the questions about what media selling is, we will, in subsequent chapters, prepare you to make your first sale, in essence, solving your first problems and getting results for a customer.

Test Yourself

1. What is the difference between customers and prospects?
2. What is the difference between service-oriented and developmental selling?
3. Why is it more difficult to keep customers satisfied with intangible products than with tangible ones?
4. What are the four primary objectives of a salesperson?
5. What are the six primary strategies that salespeople should use to achieve their objectives?
6. What are the three key functions of a salesperson?
7. What are the six related functions of a salesperson?

Project

Make an appointment with the person responsible for purchasing advertising at a large advertiser in your market (not at an advertising agency). This person might be the sales manager of a large automobile dealer or the head of marketing at a large hospital. Interview this person and ask what he or she expects of salespeople from the local media, what attributes he or she would like to see, and what kind of service he or she prefers. Make a list of these answers and compare them to the answers that professional buyers gave in the two surveys in this chapter. Are there any differences? What are they? What did you learn from this exercise?

References

Tony Allesandra, Phil Wexler, and Rick Barerra. 1992. *Non-Manipulative Selling, 2nd Edition.* New York: Fireside Books.

Ken Blanchard and Sheldon Bowles. 1993. *Raving Fans.* New York: William Morrow.

John Phillip Jones. 1995. *When Ads Work: New Proof that Advertising Triggers Sales.* New York: Lexington Books.

Alfie Kohn. 1986. *No Contest: The Case Against Competition.* Boston: Houghton-Mifflin.

Theodore Levitt. 1983. *The Marketing Imagination.* New York: Free Press.

David Mayer and Herbert Greenberg. 1964. "What makes a good salesman." *Harvard Business Review.* July-August.

Neil Rackham. 1988. *Spin Selling.* New York: McGraw-Hill.

Endnotes

1. Leon Levy. 2002. *The Mind of Wall Street.* Public Affairs. New York.
2. Ken Blanchard and Sheldon Bowles. 1993. *Raving Fans.* New York: William Morrow.
3. Theodore Levitt. 1983. *The Marketing Imagination.* New York: Free Press. p. 95.
4. David Mayer and Herbert Greenberg. 1964. "What makes a good salesman. " *Harvard Business Review.* July-Aug. p. 120.

3 Sales Ethics

By Charles Warner

The Sales Executive Council (SEC) is a private, membership-based research consortium serving approximately 300 of the world's largest sales organizations including IBM, Coca-Cola, GE, McGraw-Hill, Microsoft, and Walt Disney. The SEC is a division of the Corporate Executive Board and its mission is to assist executives in enhancing the effectiveness of their sales strategy and operations, from sales productivity and strategic account management to sales training and compensation. The SEC's primary tool is conducting research on sales problems their members face and producing case studies of best practices companies use to solve these problems.

One of the SEC's reports dealt with sales force retention and motivation. In one survey that was a part of this report, it asked 2,500 senior sales executives in major industries worldwide to rank in importance the attributes they felt were necessary to be successful as salespeople and sales managers.[1]

The most important attributes, by far (63 percent inclusion versus 50 percent inclusion for the second-ranked attribute), were honesty and integrity. See Figure 3.1 for details. The SEC conducted this survey in 2000 before the scandals involving Enron, WorldCom, Adelphi Cable, AOL, and Wall Street. One can only guess how high the scores for honesty and integrity would be today.

How does one know how to be honest and act with integrity? What are the rules for honesty and integrity? In business the rules usually come from codes of standards or codes of ethics.

An Introduction to Sales Ethics

"A Hundred Years From Today"
By Victor Young & Ned Washington

Verse

Life is such a great adventure, learn to live it as you go.
No one in the world can censure what we do here below.

Chorus

Don't save your kisses, just pass them around.
You'll find my reason is logically sound.
Who's going to know that you passed them around,
A hundred years from today.

Why crave a penthouse that's fit for a queen?
You're nearer heaven on mother earth's green.
If you had millions what would they all mean,
A hundred years from today.

So laugh and sing, make love the thing.
Be happy while you may.
'Cause there's always one beneath the sun,
Who's bound to make you feel that way.

The moon is shining and that's a good sign.
Cling to me closer dear and say you'll be mine.
Remember darling we won't see it shine,
A hundred years from today.

Sales Ethics in the Advertising-Supported Media

The above ballad, made famous in the late 1930s by Jack Teagarden, has been used by countless young men to woo their dates and to convince them not to wait to give out their kisses (and more), because who would ever know what they had done in 100 years. It was a pitch for a one-night stand, not a long-term relationship. It was probably an effective short-term tactic because two people were not going to live another 100 years and were more than likely able to keep their actions secret if they wanted to.

However, clever short-term tactics are unwise for corporations for two reasons: first, corporations, by charter, are immortal—they last forever—and, therefore, they want to do business 100 years from today; and second, corporations have multiple relationships with customers and suppliers making it highly unlikely that they can keep details of these relationships secret for very

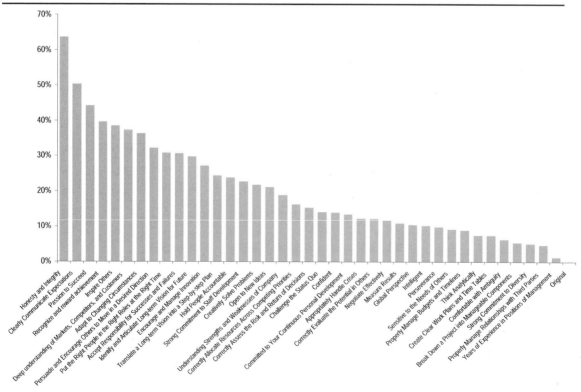

Figure 3.1   Importance ranking of 40 leadership competencies by sales leaders. (Source: Corporate Leadership Council research.)

long. These reasons are especially important for large public corporations that file detailed reports with the Securities and Exchange Commission. Some of these reports contain information on contracts with key strategic partners and are available to the public from www.sec.gov/edgar.shtml.

These two factors are magnified several times with media companies because their revenue depends on maintaining the long-term trust of their advertisers, subscribers, and audiences. Major advertisers provide the lion's share of revenue for most media businesses. Furthermore, major advertisers such as GM, P&G, IBM, and Coca-Cola not only have long memories, but they will also be around in 100 years. It is not smart business to bite the hand that will feed your company in future years. If salespeople lie, cheat, gouge, or over-promise and under-deliver in order to make short-term numbers, they jeopardize revenue far into the future. Simply put, advertisers do not buy from someone they do not trust—they are not looking for one-night stands, they prefer marriage.

There is also a good chance that if you deceive any of these large customers, they will tell others, especially your competitors and the press. The press loves stories about corporate bullies, liars, and cheaters. Witness the coverage of Enron and WorldCom or look at stories during just one week in February 2002, in the *Wall Street Journal* and *New York Times*. The first story that week was about the Enron scandal and how corporate executives were going to have to take more responsibility for the financial dealings of their companies. Another was a story about the advertising agency Ogilvy & Mather, which overcharged the Office of National Drug Control.[2] Finally, there was a story about five investment bankers from Barclays Capital who spent $62,200 on dinner for themselves, no clients, where among the wine consumed were two bottles of Chateau Petrus costing $17,500 and $16,500 each.[3]

In November of that year, WorldCom's MCI division moved up a notch on the list of most infamous companies when *The Wall Street Journal* ran a story with the headline "SBC Claims MCI Is Using Deceptive Marketing Tactics" on the first page of the Marketplace section.[4] The story lists four false statements MCI telephone salespeople made to unwary consumers whom they were trying to switch from local Bell phone company SBC. Those statements were, "MCI bought SBC and customers must switch services;" "Companies are merging into a new venture called 'The Neighborhood by MCI';" "SBC can no longer handle long-distance calls;" and "MCI is taking over some of SBC's calling areas." All of these were lies told by a company in bankruptcy desperate for business.

A year earlier, in November 2001, *Electronic Media* (now *TV Weekly*), the largest and most influential weekly publication in the broadcast and cable industries, ran an editorial condemning the use of Time Machines, a device that digitally compresses time of programs so a television station can fit in more commercials.[5] The editorial lambasted a CBS-owned television station for squeezing in extra commercials. Other stories in *Electronic Media* exposed television station groups, in addition to Viacom-owned CBS's stations, such as Raycom, Granite, and Meredith, which were also alleged to be using the time-compressing device to deceive both audiences and advertisers.

What is happening here? It seems that people either do not know or care about business rules, standards, or ethics. Perhaps they go along with unethical behavior because of group pressure or peer pressure or perhaps they rationalize to themselves that "everyone does it," "it's standard practice in this business," or "no one will know; I won't get caught." Maybe they think, "My manager said to do what it takes to make the quarter," or "If I don't take their money, someone else will." Such callous rationalization of lying, cheating, and stealing is typical sociopathic behavior.

I recently learned of a salesperson for a major media company who forged a client's name on a contract. The salesperson was certain the customer would eventually sign the contract, and the salesperson wanted to start the campaign early. When the advertiser got the first invoice, the surprised reply was, "What's this, we never bought anything or signed anything?" Why did the salesperson forge a signature? Was there pressure from management to close business early or did greediness motivate the salesperson? What was the root cause of this unethical behavior? Of course, being a sociopath or a narcissist clearly can lead to unethical behavior, but people not suffering from these personality disorders sometimes behave unethically. Why?

Reasons People Don't Follow the Rules

There are many reasons for unethical behavior, but here are the four most common. People have a strong tendency to bow to authority and follow orders from higher-ups, giving them the excuse that "I was just following orders." People have a strong tendency to bow to the social pressure and conformity of their peer group, perhaps a leftover tendency from their teenage years, leading to the excuse of "everyone does it." Also, unethical behavior is often due to an absence of clearly defined and communicated rules of behavior, standards, or codes of ethics in a peer group, organization, company, or an industry, particularly among salespeople, allowing people to say, "Nobody told me." Finally, corporate cultures that encourage employees to wink at their company's code of standards or mission statement can justify their actions by saying, "No one will know; I won't get caught," as probably happened with the Time Machine.

While people who bow to authority may have to give up their individual free will and autonomy for the sake of the company, they do not have to turn their conscience and their self-esteem over to someone else. "Just following orders," as we learned in the Nuremberg trials, is not a valid, acceptable excuse for doing the wrong thing. On the other hand, people who cave in to peer pressure to conform negate their own free will and autonomy and hand over their conscience and individuality to the crowd. "Everybody does it" is not an acceptable excuse for breaking the rules or for unethical behavior. An absence of clearly defined standards and codes of ethics can lead to unethical behavior because people can use the cop-out "Nobody told me." This excuse is hollow because ethical behavior is implied and assumed in all of our daily social interactions. For example, we do not go around killing people because nobody said, "Don't kill anyone today." We all know what we are supposed to do and not to do.

Groups, organizations, and companies must create and communicate ethical standards to guard against these abuses and, even more importantly, to follow up with practices and behavior at the highest levels of the organization that adhere to the stated corporate standards. Unfortunately, "Do as I say, not as I do," can be as effective on employees as it was on me as a teenager when my father told me not to smoke cigarettes as he puffed away on one of his forty Chesterfields a day. For example, Enron had a clearly defined code of conduct that it communicated to everyone in the company and posted on its Web site. Enron's top executives obviously viewed this code as public relations, not as a set of rules they should follow, thinking arrogantly and cynically, "No one will know."

Employees of an unethical company whose executives do not follow the rules should strongly consider leaving the company and looking for another job rather than becoming a whistle blower. Tragically, whistle blowers are too often perceived to be "rats" or "squealers" by potential employers rather than as the heroes they are. Leaving an unethical, corrupt company is probably in your long-term self-interest because when the company's ethical problems come to light, your pension fund or 401(k) plan will be worthless if it is invested in company stock and your reputation will be tainted in the job market. Therefore, select the companies you work for very carefully and choose one that will enhance your reputation, not detract from it.

What Are Ethics?

Ethics are clearly defined standards and norms of right and wrong that are expressed as guidelines for behavior. There are three general types of ethical standards. First, most organizations, companies, and professions have written codes of ethics or standards of conduct. An example of published corporate standards are the Values and Principles of A. H. Belo, one of the larger media companies in America, which owns newspapers and television stations in all regions of the country:[6] (See Table 3.1) Next are accepted beliefs and codes of conduct among various social and ethnic groups. Finally, individuals have their own standards of right and wrong that they use to make daily judgments, which are based on a combination of deep-seated personal values and beliefs inculcated from the first moment parents say "bad boy" or "bad girl."

**Table 3.1
A.H. Belo
Corporation Values
and Operating
Principles**

Belo Values	Belo Operating Principles
Integrity	Build common understandings
Excellence	Apply our values
Fairness	Be accountable
Sense of purpose	Practice candor and respect
Inclusiveness	Work as a team

Why Are Ethics and Rules Important?

With heightened press coverage of corporate and Wall Street scandals, the public has become increasing concerned about the ethical behavior of the representatives of our important institutions. Therefore, if ever there was a time when ethical behavior for business and for salespeople was important, it is now. And it is vital to the health and credibility of American business to do the right thing rather than to do things right. Companies should perceive ethical behavior as enlightened self-interest because it preserves a company's long-term reputation, which is its greatest asset.

Five Ethical Responsibilities for Media Salespeople

1. Responsibility to consumers. As defined in Chapter 1, consumers use a product and the consumers of the media are the audiences as readers, viewers, or subscribers.

If a media outlet does not put the interests of its consumers or audience first, the audience will gravitate to sources of information and entertainment that do. It is amazing how most people tend to give their loyalty to those who look after them and have strong values, including strong family values. If a media outlet does not tell the truth, withholds important information from consumers, sells shoddy products, or erodes consumers' values and sense of self-esteem, these consumers will eventually turn to information, entertainment, and opinion sources that provide what they want, and that they find truthful, useful, interesting, and convenient. In other words, they will find someone else to partner with.

Audiences want something in which they can believe. Therefore, the media should not transmit false or misleading advertising. General rules for media salespeople should include not accepting advertising for products that they would not recommend to a relative, not accepting advertising for products that are unsafe, and finally, not linking the sale of news, entertainment, or opinion content to advertising without disclosing the nature of the sales agreement. People do not like to be deceived, especially by the media. Thus, when a medium lies to its audience and loses its credibility, it eventually loses its audience and can no longer be advertiser-supported. Putting the consumers first is at the heart of the marketing concept, and is the essence of ethical behavior in the media.

2. **Responsibility to their conscience.** All salespeople are responsible to themselves for doing what they believe is good or bad or right or wrong and is based on their own conscience or moral standards. John Wooden, the legendary UCLA basketball coach, said that there is no pillow as soft as a clear conscience. Purposely acting unethically will erode a salesperson's self-esteem just as a series of one-night stands does. Salespeople who knowingly cheat to win cannot be truly happy or fulfilled in the long run. By acting ethically, salespeople increase their self-esteem, self-image, and self-confidence and do the same for their company. They develop a long-term perspective, which benefits their mental health and their company as well as the customers and consumers.

Unfortunately, some salespeople and sales organizations are more motivated by greed, making money, or "getting the stock price up" than in building a highly respected personal or company reputation. Such greed inevitably produces cheating, which is a cancer that erodes a person's or a company's reputation and eventually will kill the company. Those who conduct business unethically know they are doing so, but they continue doing the wrong thing because they believe they will not get caught. However, they are playing an ethical lottery in which the odds of being discovered are high, as we saw earlier with WorldCom. Practicing ethical behavior every business day is the only sure way of maintaining a reputation, and self-esteem grows as the result.

3. Responsibility to customers. Customers, the advertisers, do not buy from or partner with media companies and salespeople they do not trust. Thus, media salespeople should concentrate on building trust and managing relationships for the long term, not merely selling for a one-shot deal. For example, AOL Time Warner corporate policy, as articulated by CEO Richard Parsons, currently is to "under-promise and over-deliver."

Customer-Oriented Rules for Media Salespeople—The Don'ts

A. Don't lie to advertisers.
B. Don't sell anything that customers do not need.
C. Don't allow clients to feel like they lost in a negotiation.
D. Don't be unfair to advertisers.
E. Don't sell something customers cannot afford.
F. Don't use bait-and-switch tactics (selling something that they know is not available just to get the money in the door).
G. Don't recommend or accept advertising that is in bad taste or that will harm a client's image.
H. Don't accept false or misleading advertising.
I. Don't give kickbacks (a euphemism for bribes) to customers. Kickbacks often come in the form of unauthorized rebates or other cash payments given by salespeople from their own pockets. Kickbacks are illegal, and there are serious consequences to violating the law, including fines and imprisonment.

Rules for Media Salespeople—The Dos

A. Do represent your clients. Media salespeople's responsibility is to transmit or publish the best possible advertising for their clients and to try to get the clients the best, fairest deal they are entitled to according to a medium's official pricing and positioning policies. Hewlett-Packard, for example, employs customer ombudsmen to represent customers' interests to its sales organizations.
B. Do propose advertising that you would recommend to a close relative. Salespeople should keep in mind that advertising is an investment. When they present an advertising proposal, salespeople should ask themselves if they would recommend it to a relative who is living on the income from the business being advertised.
C. Do keep privileged information confidential. Salespeople must keep privileged information to themselves, including details about advertisers' strategy, budgets, creative plans, special sales, and media plans until the campaign has broken and the information is readily available from outside sources. When a client or advertising agency requests competitive information, salespeople should not give it out before the campaign starts. If salespeople have done their selling job properly, they have sold themselves as solutions providers which implies a privileged relationship, such as that between a doctor and patient. Customers have a right to assume that salespeople are experts whose recommendations are given with their best interests in mind.
D. Under-promise. It is salespeople's responsibility not to promise what advertising by itself cannot deliver. The media can deliver potential exposure to an audience; but the media cannot be certain of generating sales results, so it should not promise results to advertisers. Rather, salespeople should promise only those placements, merchandising, promotions, or tickets to events that they can deliver.

4. Responsibility to the community. The word community has many meanings, but in this context, it is limited to four: (1) The global community, (2) the general business community, (3) an industry community, and (4) a local community.

A.   The global community. Each corporation and individual ultimately has a responsibility to the world community. We owe it to society to act in a way that provides the greatest good for the greatest number of people, enhances the environment, improves the human experience and condition, and, in the words of the Hippocratic oath, does no harm. To answer questions about our social responsibility, we should always ask ourselves the question, "Suppose everybody did this?"[7]

B.   The business community. As members of the free-market business community, salespeople must behave responsibly so that investors, regulators, and the general public have faith in our capitalistic system. All companies have, or should have, published rules, codes, or standards that prohibit unethical behavior such as selling stock based on inside knowledge, shredding documents or deleting computer files to avoid prosecution, and cooking the books to inflate revenue. In business, as well as in society, salespeople must ask: "Suppose everybody did this? Would the regulators, investors, and the public maintain their faith in the free-market system and in business?"

C.   An industry community. The media have a special responsibility to the public, because the media deliver the news to Americans. The public also forms many of their social values, beliefs, attitudes, and opinions from the print, electronic, Interactive, and entertainment media. This enormous power makes it more imperative that the media wield that power responsibly.

As a country, we altered our aggregate opinions about racial prejudice, the Vietnam War, and women's rights while we watched images of these issues mesmerize, indoctrinate, and change us. The advertising messages between these images guaranteed the freedom of the press that bigots, the government, and non-egalitarian people might not want us to have. If any one of these groups had controlled the media, we might not have been exposed to these issues and the truth would not have worked its torturous way into our collective consciousness.

Therefore, media companies and their salespeople have the responsibility of keeping the media and the press free by fueling it with the advertising revenue it needs to remain so. Without a free, advertising- or subscriber-supported media, there cannot be a free exchange of ideas. This exchange of ideas leads to an informed electorate, the foundation of our democracy. As a salesperson, you might say, "The high-minded notion of protecting democracy is fine if you're selling '60 Minutes' or CNN, but I'm selling commercials on a rock-and-roll radio station." But no one program, no one news story, or no one medium is more important; rather it is the free-market, advertising-supported system. By selling within that system, media salespeople are sustaining a market for advertising that supports all information and entertainment content.

Salespeople must be ethical and play by the rules not only because public attention is focused on corporate ethics, but also because attention is intensely focused on the media. The believability of the media in general and journalism specifically has been eroding recently, and advertising has never been at the top of the list in the public's esteem. Thus, the media must attempt to turn around the image, esteem, and credibility of its product (information, entertainment, and opinion) and its supporting buttress (advertising) if the media hope to thrive.[8]

D. A local community. All companies, organizations, and people have a responsibility as citizens to act responsibly and ethically toward their neighbors in the community where they live and work. The simple rule is, "Don't foul your own nest. Don't cheat your neighbor." The local media must first serve their communities, for without local support, local media cannot thrive or even exist. Remember that broadcast media are given licenses based on their promise to serve their communities, so their obligation is not only a moral, social one, but also a regulatory one.

5. Responsibility to a company. Media salespeople represent their companies to their customers and because they are selling an intangible product, they become the personification of, or the surrogate for, their product. Salespeople are often the only contact a customer will have with anyone from a company. Therefore, salespeople have to face the kill-the-messenger attitude many people have about the media. Because of this unique situation, a company's credibility depends on its salespeople's credibility, which to a large degree depends on their personal conduct and integrity. Media salespeople must be law-abiding and respectful of civil liberties and actions or statements that are potentially offensive to others as well as be moderated in their personal habits. It is the responsibility of salespeople to build and maintain customer relationships based on dependability, reliability, believability, integrity, and ethical behavior.

Salespeople must give their job their full attention, being certain not to steal their company's assets, not to waste its resources (which includes efficient and reasonable use of entertainment and transportation money), not to file false expense reports, and not to offer special deals to get business away from others within their own organization.

Salespeople have a responsibility to their company to maximize revenue by getting the highest possible and reasonable rates, selling special promotions and packages, attaining the largest possible and reasonable orders, and reaching the highest possible budget shares. There are times when the responsibility to a company to maximize revenue can come in conflict with a salesperson's duty to his or her customers, to his or her conscience, and to the various communities. When such conflicts occur, salespeople should remember the hierarchy of responsibilities and that their company is at the bottom of that hierarchy, because it is in its best long-term interest to be last. Good companies know that what goes around, comes around; that good karma returns home; that ethical behavior is good business; and that employees are happier working for ethical companies.

Great media companies understand that if they take care of their audience, usage, readership, and ratings will go up, resulting in increased revenue. Also, if advertisers trust salespeople and their companies, most advertisers will pay higher rates for better service from these trusted partners. If salespeople do the wrong thing, it results in lost customers, expensive employee turnover, high lawyers' fees, large court costs, and, perhaps, even time in jail. Unfortunately, many companies set up rewards for salespeople that unwittingly reinforce doing the wrong thing. These include compensation systems that reward getting an order regardless of what's best for the customer, contests that reward selling special promotions or packages regardless of advertisers' needs, and bonuses for making sales budgets regardless of what is reasonable.[9] Beware of CFOs and top management that recommend accounting practices that "preserve a company's assets;" they often have the wrong assets in mind. A company's and a salesperson's most precious asset is an excellent reputation, which is preserved by always doing the right thing.

All large media corporations dream of having a respected publication write something positive about their company. On October 9, 2002, *The New York Times* ran an article in its Business section with the headline, "Viacom is Planning a Multimedia Campaign Against AIDS," which read, in part:

> "Viacom plans to focus its various media properties on a single public service campaign with an AIDS-awareness and education effort. The campaign, scheduled to begin in January, will use unsold advertising time on Viacom's CBS and other television networks, and on its television and radio stations, as well as outdoor billboards, for messages about AIDS. But the company, which plans to announce its plans today, says the effort will go beyond traditional public service announcements to weave messages about AIDS into the scripts of television programs, and possibly films."[10]

Viacom conducted the AIDS campaign not only to serve the public, but also to enhance its own and the television medium's reputation. This example demonstrates how salespeople can enhance their company's reputation by focusing on the five levels of ethical responsibility in the order of their importance. Salespeople can remember these levels by thinking of the Five Cs:

The Five Cs of Ethical Responsibility

Consumers
Conscience
Customers
Community
Company

An Ethics Check [11]

Is it legal?   When salespeople conduct an ethics check, the first question to ask is: "Is what I am considering doing legal?" The term "legal" should be interpreted broadly to include any civil or criminal laws, any state or federal regulations, any industry codes of ethics, or any company policy. If salespeople do not know or have any doubts about the legality of what they are doing, they should ask their boss and the company's legal department.

Is it fair?   Is it rational, as opposed to emotional, and balanced, so that there are no big winners and big losers? Is it fair to all: to both sides, to the consumer, to the salesperson, to the advertiser, to the various communities, and to the company? If the company had an open-book policy, would all of its customers think everyone got a fair shake? Are all customers getting fair rates, placements, rotations, and make-goods? To test for fairness, ask yourself the question, "Suppose everybody did this?"

What does my conscience say?   Salespeople should ask themselves, "How would I feel if what I am doing appeared in the *Wall Street Journal* or the *New York Times*? How would it make me feel about myself? According to my personal moral standards, is what I am doing OK?"

A company's and a salesperson's most valuable assets are their reputations and their relationships with their customers. Reputations and relationships are built by consistently doing ethics checks on the way they do business, by taking a long-term view and not doing anything that would put them in jeopardy, even 100 years from today.

Test Yourself

1. What are the five rationalizations some people use for their unethical behavior?
2. What is a Time Machine?
3. What are the four reasons why people are inclined to behave unethically?
4. What are the Values and Principles of the A. H. Belo Company?
5. What are the Five Cs of Ethical Responsibilities for media salespeople?
6. What are the eight "Don'ts" for media salespeople?
7. What are the four "Dos" for media salespeople?
8. What are the three rules of the Ethics Checklist?

Project

Go to the Web and search the Web sites of several major media companies and see if you can find any statements about ethical behavior, standards of conduct, corporate citizenship, or corporate responsibility. Then, go to the Web sites of major advertisers such as GM, P&G, Ford, GE, IBM, or McDonalds, and see if they have any statements about ethical behavior, standards of conduct, corporate citizenship, or corporate responsibility. What did you discover?

Resources

www.sec.gov/edgar.shtml
http://icarus.ubetc.buffalo.edu/willbern/bestsellers/goodbar/goodbar2.htm

Endnotes

1. "Voice of the Sales Leader." 2001. *Leading the Charge.* Sales Executive Council. Washington, D.C. p.13
2. "Settlement Reached in Overbilling Case." 2002. *The New York Times.* February 13. p. C 10.
3. "Check Please! Take $65,000, Keep the Change." 2002. *The Wall Street Journal.* March 1. p. W 11.
4. "SBC Claims MCI Is Using Deceptive Marketing Tactics." 2002. *The Wall Street Journal.* November 22. p. B1
5. "Editorial: It's not nice to fool Father Time." 2001. *Electronic Media.* November 12. p. 12
6. www.belo.com/about.html November 22, 2002

7. Keith Davis, William C. Frederick and Robert L. Blostrom. 1980. *Business and Society: Concepts and Policy Issue.* New York: McGraw-Hill.

8. Howard Gardner, Mihaly Csikszentmihalyi and William Damron. 2001. *Good Work: When Excellence and Ethics Meet.* New York: Basic Books.

9. Michael Jensen. 2001. "Corporate Budgeting Is Broken—Let's Fix It," *Harvard Business Review,* Vol. 79, Number 10.

10. "Viacom Is Planning a Multimedia Campaign Against AIDS." 2002. *The New York Times,* October 9. p. C 11.

11. Kenneth Blanchard and Norman V. Peale. 1998. *The Power of Ethical Management.* New York: William Morrow.

4

The AESKOPP System of Selling

By Charles Warner

Let's return to that year long ago when I made my first sales call and ask what I did wrong and what my sales manager did wrong. The answer to the first question, what I did wrong, is easy—everything. The answer to the second question, what was wrong with my sales manager's response, is also easy—everything. But "everything" is not a helpful response, so we will put the responses into a context of a selling system to help you understand the elements of a successful sales call and a successful sales system.

To begin with, I did not plan my call properly and my sales manager did not have a framework, or a method for breaking down the sales call into component parts, so that he could coach me about improving my performance on each of the component parts. The AESKOPP system of selling provides such a framework.

The AESKOPP system is a generalization, a simplification of some underlying, universal sales principles and provides a framework for coaching, planning, and evaluating sales thinking and action. It posits that successful selling requires Attitude (A), Emotional Intelligence (E), Skills (S), Knowledge (K), Opportunities (O), Preparation (P), and Persistence (P):

$$A \times E \times S \times K \times O \times P \times P = \text{Success}$$

Notice that each element in the above formula is multiplied by the others. Just as in a mathematical formula, if any one of the elements is not present, then the result is zero success; any element multiplied by zero is zero. Thus, all of the elements must be present for a successful result—creating customers and keeping them.

Before making a sales presentation to a prospect or customer, salespeople should get into the habit of asking themselves the seven AESKOPP questions, and they should also evaluate their overall sales approach and performance by regularly asking themselves these questions. In addition, managers should continually ask these questions about their salespeople and their performance in order to coach them effectively.

The Seven AESKOPP Questions

1. Do I have the right mental Attitude to solve problems and get results for my customers?
2. Do I have the Emotional Intelligence to understand people and build rapport with them?

3. Do I have the Skills necessary?
4. Do I have the Knowledge necessary?
5. Do I have the Opportunities?
6. Do I have sufficient Preparation?
7. Do I have the Persistence to never, never, never give up?

If the answer to all of these questions is yes, you will be successful. Success in the AESKOPP system and in solutions selling is based on your ability to establish and maintain relationships with prospects and customers, to solve advertising and marketing problems for them, and to get results for them (as customers define results). If you do these three things well, you will make lots of sales. However, if you put a priority on closing a sale above all else, you put establishing and maintaining relationships, solving problems, and getting results in a subordinate position. This means that sooner or later your customers will know you care more about yourself and your income than about their problems and desired results.

One of the most widely and publicly reported examples of me-first attitude came during the booming dot-com years of 1998, 1999, and 2000, when America Online's advertising and e-commerce sales division regularly circumvented advertising agencies and called directly on agencies' clients; some of their top sales executives also bashed advertising agencies publicly in industry meetings and forums. America Online pushed companies hard for multi-million-dollar deals and pressed aggressively for quick closes in order to make quarterly revenue numbers. In the advertising slowdown of 2001 and 2002, many advertisers and, especially, advertising agencies, got revenge for their poor treatment by making sure AOL was kept off their advertising schedules. As a result, in the fall of 2002, Yahoo, MSN, and other online advertising sites reported increased ad sales for the previous quarter as America Online reported advertising sales were off more than 40 percent.[1] And, as good as American Online's current salespeople and sales managers are, it will not be easy to erase the perception that America Online is arrogant and difficult to do business with. America Online's revenue decline reinforces the importance of always putting customers first because if you do not, it will come back to haunt you as it did America Online.

The AESKOPP System

In the remainder of this book, we will examine the AESKOPP system in detail. Chapter 5 goes into more depth about attitude and how an optimistic attitude can help you create a positive future. Chapter 6 covers emotional intelligence and provides you with details about how to improve your emotional intelligence. Chapters 7 through 13 concentrate on skills. Chapters 14 through 26 develop knowledge. Chapters 27 and 28 cover opportunities, preparation, and persistence.

Following are definitions of each of the seven AESKOPP elements:

Attitude is having the desire and motivation to be a salesperson and having the proper mind set to do it. If you have the skills, the knowledge, and the opportunities to sell but have no desire to do so, you will not be successful. Chapter 5 presents more details on attitudes and how to control and improve them.

Emotional Intelligence is the ability to understand yourself and others so you can develop empathy and rapport with people and manage relationships successfully. Chapter 6 presents more details on how to increase your emotional intelligence.

Skills are the ability, improved through practice, to use your knowledge of techniques, methods, and tools. For salespeople, it is knowing the techniques of prospecting, identifying problems, generating proposals, presenting, negotiating and closing, and servicing. Chapters 9 through 13 will have in-depth details about these techniques.

Knowledge encompasses the tools of your trade. For salespeople, it means having information about their product, research, marketing and advertising, customers' businesses, and competitive media. Chapters 14 through 26 will give you knowledge about these areas.

Opportunities are the circumstances in which you can use your tools. Even if you have the tools and know how to use them, you cannot accomplish anything unless you have opportunities to put them to use. Salespeople may know how to solve problems and have a storehouse full of product, marketplace, and competitive knowledge, but if they do not make sales calls and find prospective customers, they will lack the opportunities to put their skills and knowledge to work. Chapters 27 and 28 provide you with organizational and motivational tools to increase your opportunities.

Preparation is getting organized to solve customer problems. Even if you have the attitude, emotional intelligence, skills, knowledge, and opportunities to sell, you will not solve problems or make many sales if you forget your presentations and if you do not know anything about your clients' businesses or personalities.

Persistence means never giving up. Salespeople need to continue working on prospects past any initial uninformed "no" they might encounter.

Core Competencies of the AESKOPP System

Each of the seven elements of the AESKOPP system is made up of a group of core competencies—building blocks—that, linked together, lead to successful performance on that element. The core competencies are subject to change, depending on the media selling job involved. Some sales positions, such as in a large-circulation magazine such as *People*, require a high level of knowledge, especially about national advertising, the product, and magazine research, plus very strong relationships with major advertising agencies and advertisers. Other sales positions, such as in a local radio station, might require an understanding of retail businesses, such as an automotive dealership, and skills in negotiating with advertising agencies.

The following is a list of core competencies for each of the elements of the AESKOPP system. These capabilities are what would be appropriate for a mid-size market newspaper, cable system, television station, or radio station salesperson.

Attitude: Honest, positive/optimistic, committed, confident, courageous, competitive, coachable (open/non-defensive), self-motivated, assertive, flexible, cooperative, and nurturing.

Emotional intelligence: Self-awareness, self-management, social awareness, and relationship management (internal and external).

Skills: Communicating (internal and external), listening, understanding people, creating value, presenting (to individuals and groups), negotiating and closing, and servicing.

Knowledge: Financial/economic/business/category, marketing/advertising, market, product, and competitive media.

Opportunity: Prospecting/getting appointments, and identifying problems (discovery).

Preparation: Strategic thinking, creativity/problem-solving, organization, planning, and time management.

Persistence: Determined/never giving up, and follow up.

Rating Your Core Competencies

The next step in effectively using the AESKOPP system is to assign weights that indicate the relative importance of each core competency. Just as the core competencies will change with the type of media selling job, the weights of relative importance of each competency will change. For example, in a mid-sized market newspaper selling job, knowledge of business, economics, and finance might not be important, but such knowledge might be vital for success in selling *Fortune* magazine.

One of the major values of the list of core competencies and weights (see Table 4.1) is that it defines the job of a media salesperson and what it takes to be successful selling media. If you are looking for a sales job in the media, study this list, evaluate yourself, and then develop a plan to improve those competencies in which you lack experience or have a deficit. If you have a job in media sales, we strongly recommend that you study this list carefully and thoughtfully by yourself, rate yourself honestly, then use your ratings as a guideline for self-improvement. But the best use of the core competencies list and weights is to work with your sales manager or ad director to develop one that fits the needs of your selling situation, which you both use as a regular coaching tool.

Note the title "Salesperson Core Competencies." The term *salesperson* is used because it is inclusive of a wide variety of titles that salespeople in the media are assigned by their organizations: sales representative, account executive, account manager, sales consultant, radio marketing consultant, business development director, director of new business, and many more. The preferred title is account executive or account manager, which implies managing customers' accounts, schedules, and campaigns according to what is best for a customer. Also, titles that include "consultant" should be avoided because customers need results more than advice. In this modern age of solutions selling, results generator might be a suitable title. But this euphemism is akin to calling a janitor a maintenance engineer, so account executive or account manager are more appropriate titles. However, in this book, to avoid confusion, salesperson will be used to encompass all titles.

Below are the core competencies list and weights, which reflect my view of what competencies and weights are appropriate for a mid-size market newspaper, cable system, television station, or radio station salesperson.

Table 4.1 shows 48 core competencies in the seven AESKOPP elements. The percentages after each element indicate its relative importance to the selling process. As you can see, Emotional Intelligence, Skills, and Knowledge are most important. In the Desired Level column are ratings that reflect what performance level the average salesperson should be expected to reach and that represent the minimum level of acceptable performance. At the bottom of the table are the Rating Levels: Superior (5), Excellent (4), Very Good (3), Good (2), and Poor (1). The Desired Level scores add up to 124, or an average score

**Table 4.1
Salesperson Core
Competencies—
Desired Performance
Levels**

Attitude (12%)	Desired Level
Honest	5
Positive/optimistic	3
Committed	3
Confident	2
Courageous	3
Competitive	2
Coachable (open/non-defensive)	3
Self-motivated	2
Assertive	2
Flexible	2
Cooperative	3
Nurturing	2
Emotional Intelligence (20%)	
Self-awareness	2
Self-management	2
Social awareness	2
Relationship management	
Internal	2
External	2
Skills (20%)	
Communicating	
Internal	2
External	2
Listening	3
Understanding people	4
Presenting	
Individual	3
Groups	2
Creating value	2
Persuasion	2
Negotiating/closing	2
Servicing	2
Team leadership	2
Knowledge (20%)	
Financial/economic/business/category	2
Marketing/advertising/research	3
Market	3
Product (your medium)	4
Competitors	3
Competitive media	2
Pricing	4
Sales process	4
Contract terms	3
Opportunity (8%)	
Prospecting/getting appointments	4
Identifying problems (discovery)	4
Preparation (12%)	
Generating solutions (research)	2
Strategic thinking	2
Creativity/problem-solving	2
Organization	2
Planning	2
Time management	2
Creating presentations	2
Persistence (8%)	
Determined/never giving up	3
Follow up	3
Desired Level Rating Score =	124
Highest Possible Level Rating Score =	240
Total Core Competencies =	48

Rating Levels: 5 = Superior, 4 = Excellent, 3 = Very Good;
2 = Good, 1 = Poor.

of 2.6, which is a little more than half way between a 2, Good, rating and a 3, Very Good, rating. Thus, a 2.6 is in the middle and, therefore, an average performance. You will also notice in Table 4.1 that there are no 1s in the Desired Levels column because a salesperson must be expected to rate at least a 2, Good, on all 48 core competencies. The desired level of some competencies is 3, Very Good, or 4, Excellent, and salespeople must be expected to master these competencies at that level to be successful.

The most effective way to use this list of core competencies is to download it from the book's Web site (www.mediaselling.us) or copy it from the book. Then, give yourself a rating on each item and chart your ratings against the Desired Level ratings as seen in Table 4.2. Finally, get your sales manager or ad director (if you have a sales job) to fill out the chart with your ratings on the Core Competencies—then you will have an ideal coaching instrument, for yourself and for your manager.

Let's take a closer look at the ratings in Table 4.2 and see what we can learn. Let's assume the salesperson who filled out the ratings, Jane, sells for a radio station in a medium-sized market. First, we can see that Jane and her sales

**Table 4.2
Salesperson Core
Competencies—
Completed Form**

	Desired Level	Sales-person Rating	Manager Rating	Difference
Attitude (12%)				
Honest	5	5	5	
Positive/optimistic	3	2	2	
Committed	3	3	4	+1
Confident	2	2	1	−1
Courageous	3	2	1	−1
Competitive	2	3	2	−1
Coachable (open/non-defensive)	3	4	4	
Self-motivated	2	1	1	
Assertive	2	3	1	−2
Flexible	2	3	4	+1
Cooperative	3	3	3	
Nurturing	2	3	1	-2
Emotional Intelligence (20%)				
Self-awareness	2	2	3	+1
Self-management	2	1	4	+3
Social awareness	2	3	3	
Relationship management				
Internal	2	1	2	+1
External	2	4	4	
Skills (20%)				
Communicating				
Internal	2	1	2	+1
External	2	3	3	
Listening	3	2	1	−1
Understanding people	4	2	2	−2
Presenting				
Individual	3	4	4	
Groups	2	1	1	
Creating value	2	2	1	−1
Persuasion	2	3	3	
Negotiating/closing	2	1	1	
Servicing	2	3	4	+1
Team leadership	2	3	2	−1

manager differed on several items. A score of 124 is the desired level for a salesperson and Jane's manager gave her a 118, or average, which means her glass is half full, which is good, and that she has some areas in which she can improve, which is also good.

What is the overall picture we get of Jane from looking at her and her sales manager's ratings? We discover that she has a better attitude than she thinks she has and that she has excellent emotional intelligence. Yet she lacks confidence and assertiveness, and is weak in skills. Jane is probably a new salesperson who is full of enthusiasm and is eager to learn. She will need coaching and probably will be responsive to it. Jane needs to work on her listening, creating value, and negotiating skills. She will be able to improve her skills over time by presenting to groups. Her sales manager should go on sales calls with her and coach her on these skills. Her sales manager also should ask her to give a presentation to the sales staff at a sales meeting to provide Jane with the opportunity to practice her group presentation skills.

Now for a closer look at Jane. In the Attitude section, both Jane and her manager rated her high on being honest. Both saw that she needed improvement in being positive and optimistic. They know she has a real problem with

Table 4.2
(*Continued*)

	Desired Level	Sales-person Rating	Manager Rating	Difference
Knowledge (20%)				
Financial/economic/ business/category	2	1	1	
Marketing/advertising/ research	3	2	1	−1
Market	3	3	3	
Product (your medium)	4	4	2	−2
Competitors	3	2	1	−1
Competitive media	2	3	1	−2
Pricing	4	4	4	
Sales process	4	4	4	
Contract terms	3	3	3	
Opportunity (8%)				
Prospecting/getting appointments	4	2	1	−1
Identifying problems (discovery)	4	2	1	−1
Preparation (12%)				
Generating solutions (research)	2	3	3	
Strategic thinking	2	3	3	
Creativity/problem-solving	2	2	3	+1
Organization	2	4	4	
Planning	2	4	3	−1
Time management	2	4	4	
Creating presentations	2	1	1	
Persistence (8%)				
Determined/never giving up	3	1	2	+1
Follow up	3	4	4	
Desired Level Rating Score =	124	126	118	
Highest Possible Level Rating Score =		240		
Total Core Competencies =	48			

Rating Levels: 5 = Superior (Top 10%), 4 = Excellent (Top 25%), 3 = Very Good (Top 50%), 2 = Good (Bottom 50%), 1 = Poor (Bottom 25%).

her confidence, which is indicated not only by her own low ratings, but also by the discrepancy between her lower ratings in the areas of being committed and flexible as compared to the higher ratings that her manager gave her. Both rate Jane high on being coachable. Therefore, the sales manager has a potential winner in Jane, who is committed and eager to learn.

Jane's emotional intelligence is a strong area for her and will be beneficial in several ways. It will help her discipline herself to share her ideas and ask for help to overcome her lack of assertiveness. She can use her emotional intelligence to achieve a better understanding of people, their strengths, buying tendencies, and personal needs and wants. Jane's sales manager also recognizes that Jane's emotional intelligence is strong, having given her higher scores in this area than Jane gives herself. These scores probably reflect her lack of confidence in self-management, interestingly an area where her manager feels she excels.

Skills, especially those relevant to internal communication, are an area that Jane needs to focus on. Communication is a common problem among many beginning salespeople, who often do not realize how important it is to keep their managers informed about all they are doing. In addition, salespeople must learn to develop rapport and good lines of communication in all departments of their company and at all levels in their department.

While Jane knows the sales process and pricing well, she needs to improve her knowledge areas, particularly those pertaining to business, marketing, advertising, her product, competing radio stations, and the competitive media. Based on her ratings, her manager might give her books to read on business, marketing, and advertising such as *Kotler on Marketing: How to Create, Win, and Dominate Markets* by Philip Kolter, *The New Marketing Paradigm: Integrated Marketing Communications* by Shultz, Tannenbaum and Latterborn, and *The 33 Ruthless Rules of Local Advertising* by Michael Corbett. Jane's sales manager should encourage her to subscribe to *Business Week*. Her manager might also suggest she listen to her station's three biggest competitors and analyze their programming, on-air presentation, promotions, and commercial loads. In addition, he might have Jane improve her product knowledge by spending a week in the programming department, shadowing the program director, writing promotions, writing and producing some commercials, and answering listener calls to understand her product better.

Finally, in the areas of opportunity, preparation, and persistence, Jane has strengths. She is well organized and persistent. However, she needs to improve her prospecting strategies and her discovery questions skills. Her sales manager should sit with her one morning as she is making prospecting calls and give her tips on her script, prompting her on how to respond to don't-come-see-me stoppers such as "I'm too busy to give you an appointment." Prospecting strategies and methods are covered in detail in Chapter 9.

In three months Jane can revisit the Core Competencies list to evaluate herself again. She would benefit from having her sales manager do the same; then she can compare the two ratings to see the areas in which she has improved and where she still needs additional work. Again, Jane's sales manager should be available to coach her in her weaker areas.

The AESKOPP system of selling provides salespeople with an excellent way to keep track of their strengths and opportunities for improvement (a positive way to say weakness or shortcoming). It is also a valuable tool for managers because by examining the charts of all their salespeople, they will have an excellent snapshot of the department's strengths and weaknesses and who has high potential to become a manager. The AESKOPP system gives you an excellent picture of what it takes to be successful in selling.

Test Yourself

1. What do the various letters in AESKOPP stand for?
2. Do all of the seven AESKOPP elements have to be present for successful selling?
3. Name five core competencies in the Skills element.
4. Name five core competencies in the Preparation element.
5. How can a salesperson use the core competencies rating system to improve performance?
6. Name two ways a sales manager can use the core competencies rating system.

Project

Rate yourself on the 48 core competencies, make a list of the five you need to work on most, and then assign yourself some learning goals, for example, to move your market knowledge rating from a 1 to a 3 in two months by reading Chamber of Commerce materials and Census data.

References

Michael Corbett. 1999. *The 33 Ruthless Rules of Local Advertising*. New York: Pinnacle Books.

Philip Kotler. 1999. *Kotler on Marketing: How to Create, Win, and Dominate Markets*. New York: The Free Press.

Don E. Schultz, Stanley I. Tannenbaum, Robert Lauterborn. 1994. *The New Marketing Paradigm: Integrated Marketing Communications*. Chicago: NTC Business Books.

Charles Warner and Joseph Buchman. 1993. *Broadcast and Cable Selling, Updated 2nd Edition*. Belmont, CA: Wadsworth Publishing.

Resources

www.eqatwork.com
www.eiconsortium.org
http://eqi.org/toc.htm
www.mediaselling.us

Endnotes

1. "America Online Lags as Others Sell More Ads," *Wall Street Journal*, October 24, 2002, p. B1

Part II

Attitude, Emotional Intelligence, and Skills

Chapter 5

Attitude

By Charles Warner

We have been using the word *attitude* in this book in a positive context. You might hear sports commentators say that a particular player has an "attitude," which translated into everyday, non-sports-speak means that the athlete has a negative, nasty, or arrogant attitude. However, the word *attitude* is not a singular noun as in sports-speak, but is an aggregate concept that encompasses all types of mind sets, both positive and negative.

In this chapter we will answer the following questions about attitude:

1. What is attitude?
2. Why are attitudes important in selling?
3. Can I control and change my attitudes?
4. How can I motivate myself to maintain a positive attitude?

What is Attitude?

Attitude is one of the elements in a hierarchical belief system, which consists of four elements: values, beliefs, attitudes, and opinions.

Values are few in number and are deeply felt and strongly held. Values include such things as love of God, patriotism, love of family, freedom, integrity, and equality. People get their values from their parents. These values are so ingrained that they are virtually impossible to change and are a framework around which people live and are willing to die for, as in the case of war.

Beliefs are not as deeply felt or as strongly held as values are, and peoples' beliefs are more numerous than their values. A person may have a basic value of freedom, but this value can manifest itself in different beliefs. People can, and sometimes do, change their beliefs if they are given enough facts, or if a belief is shown to be in conflict with a deeply held value. For example, many Americans' beliefs about the legitimacy of owning slaves underwent a change both before and after the Civil War.

Attitudes are shaped to a large degree by our values and beliefs, but are more numerous and easier to change both in others and in ourselves than values and beliefs are. An attitude is a point of view, either negative or positive, about an idea, situation, or person. We develop favorable attitudes about those ideas, situations, or people that are associated with positive rewards and benefits and unfavorable attitudes toward those that are associated with penalties or dislikes. An attitude is also an outlook on life or a mind-set about something.

An attitude has three components: what you think, what you do, and what you feel.

To change your attitudes you can change the way you think, act, or feel. But changing the way you think and act is easier than changing how you feel, because attitudes, like beliefs, have a strong emotional component despite being supported by varying degrees of fact. Thus, by correcting misconceptions or adding facts, you can change your attitude and those of others. For example, you can learn to like someone about whom you had a negative first impression by thinking about a positive attribute or characteristic and acting friendly at the next encounter, despite lingering negative feelings. Also, acting and thinking positively helps you begin to change the feelings part of your attitude.

Opinions are similar to huge, dark swarms of gnats swirling in our heads, so numerous that we cannot keep track of them. They are easy to wave away and dismiss, only to be replaced by more. People have opinions on everything and their opinions often are based more on feelings than facts. Opinions are usually what people refer to when they say, "I know just enough to be dangerous," meaning, "I know just enough to form an opinion, but I really don't know if it's right or supported by facts."

Why Are Attitudes Important In Selling?

Attitudes are important in selling because performance in a job depends on a person's attitudes and attributes—see definition of attributes later on in this chapter. Performance in selling is like performance in sports; it is a synchronization of mind, body, and action. Many of the characteristics of successful athletes and successful salespeople are similar as is the jargon of selling and sports—both use the terms "superstars," "heavy hitters," and "rookies."

Performance in any endeavor starts with a dream of successful accomplishment. Scientist/philosopher Buckminster Fuller said that people can accomplish anything they can imagine; but first they must have the courage and confidence to believe in their imaginations and to dream. We translate our dreams into objectives and goals, and these objectives and goals are born in our minds as the result of the interaction of our mental attitudes.

You might think that performance comes about as the result of attitudes; to the contrary, we tend to form attitudes because of how well we do things, because of our actions. Research has indicated that performance, which is a series of successful behaviors, often precedes attitudes. In other words, if we do something well, we tend to have a favorable attitude toward it. For example, if you are successful at a job, you are likely to have a favorable attitude about the company for which you work. In contrast, having a positive attitude about your company does not necessarily mean you will perform any better, because what determines job performance is mostly your internal drive or motivation to perform well, not external factors such as a nice work environment or company picnics.

Attitudes represent the mind portion of job performance and, more importantly, performance in selling. Attitudes can be useful in helping salespeople perform better because they can be changed, controlled, and directed from counterproductive attitudes to productive, objective-oriented ones to help improve performance. Thus, your actions can lead to a feeling of success, which, in turn, leads to a positive attitude.

Attributes.   I also included *attributes* in the Attitude section of the list of Core Competencies in Chapter 4. Attributes are somewhat like attitudes in that attributes have a significant impact on job performance, as well. Attributes are inherent talents, characteristics, or qualities of a person. You are born with attributes, but you develop attitudes as you experience life. You can change attitudes, but you can only improve or enhance your attributes. For the purpose of this book, we are combining the concepts of attitudes and attributes into one broad concept—attitude—to avoid confusion and so that the AESKOPP mnemonic is no longer than seven letters.

The following quote explains why attitude is the first element in the AESKOPP system of selling:

> "The longer I live the more I realize the importance of attitude on life. Attitude, to me, is more important than facts. It is more important than the past, than education, than money, than circumstances, than failures, than success, or what other people say or do. It is more important than appearance, giftedness, or skill. It will make or break a company . . . a church . . . a home. The remarkable thing is we have a choice everyday regarding the attitude we embrace that day. We cannot change our past . . . we cannot change the fact that people will act a certain way. We cannot change the inevitable. The only thing we can do is play on the one string we have and that is attitude . . . I am convinced that life is 10% what happens to me and 90% how I react to it. And so it is with you . . . we are in charge of our attitudes."
>
> Charles Swindoll[1]

Attitude control and enhancement in sports is an obvious example of the importance of mental attitude. Experts estimate that sports performance is determined by about 75 percent ability and about 25 percent attitude, with ability consisting of such inherent elements as size, speed, coordination, quickness, and endurance. Attitude is the head, or mind, portion of sports performance. Sales performance is also determined by ability and attitude, but, unlike sports, is split equally between ability and attitude.

While skills and knowledge are vital in selling, the following attitudes from the Core Competencies in Chapter 4 are even more important. Successful media selling requires the following attitudes:

Honesty is technically not an attitude, it is an attribute—it means behaving with integrity and in an ethical, straightforward, morally upright, and truthful way. You trust honest people and feel that their word is their bond. Because so much media business is conducted by verbal agreements and not by signed contracts (contracts sometimes do not get signed for weeks or months after an advertising campaign has started), being honest in media selling is of primary importance, which is why it is listed first.

Optimism. You cannot sell successfully if you do not have a *positive outlook* on life and, thus, have an *optimistic* attitude. Negative people are downers, to themselves and others. Optimism is also directly related to self-esteem and confidence. People with high self-esteem and confidence believe they can affect the future and make things come out right. As Helen Keller said, "Optimism is the faith that leads to achievement. Nothing can be done without hope and confidence."[2] You will see more evidence in Chapter 6, which reinforces that optimism improves sales performance.

Commitment means you have absolutely no doubts and will give everything in support of an undertaking or a cause without turning back. As Myer Berlow, former president of AOL Time Warner Global Marketing Solutions, says: "When you're eating ham and eggs for breakfast, the chicken was involved but the pig was committed."[3] Generals have been known to burn bridges behind their troops to make retreat impossible and, thus, forced their soldiers to be totally committed and to fight for their lives.

Another dimension of commitment is passion for the cause and the task. Louis Gerstner, ex-CEO of IBM wrote in his book, *Who Says Elephants Can't Dance*, which describes his incredible turnaround of IBM, that "personal leadership is about passion."[4] He means a passion for or commitment to winning. Being committed also means that people accept responsibility and hold themselves accountable for their successes and failures.

Confidence is vital in selling. Without confidence, or belief, in yourself, your product, and your offer, you cannot generate the enthusiasm required to reflect a positive image of your product to buyers. All training, all knowledge acquisition, all practice, all planning should be aimed at one thing: that of making you feel more confident about what you are selling.

Courage is a vital attribute for salespeople. Courageous does not mean you have no fear, it means you have the ability to overcome fear. You need courage to stand up to managers and others who might pressure you to do the wrong thing or to be dishonest. You need courage to set out every day to make ten calls when you know you will probably face ten rejections. You need courage to tell your boss the bad news that you did not get an order or a piece of business you had been working on for months. You need courage to be honest and tell the truth to your customers and to your management.

Competitiveness means having a strong desire to win. However, the drive and passion for winning must be channeled into two areas being *self-competitive* and being *externally competitive*. When you are self-competitive, you compete with yourself, pushing yourself to improve. In *Who Says Elephants Can't Dance?* Gerstner refers to this self-competitiveness as "restless self-renewal," or the motivation to constantly improve.[5] Self-competition is a prerequisite for improvement, which the Japanese call *kaizen,* meaning constant improvement in small increments which lead to huge improvements in the long run.

Being externally competitive means having a strong desire to beat the competition, those direct competitors in your medium and competitive media. If you are a television station salesperson, you want to beat the salespeople from other television stations to get higher shares of business and get higher rates, while pulling advertising dollars away from newspapers, radio, yellow pages, and outdoor. Being externally competitive means winning by playing the game fairly and by the rules and not becoming overly competitive either within or out of your own company, which can lead to dishonest and unethical behavior, as described in Chapter 3.

This attitude is probably better described as being *ethically competitive, externally competitive, and self-competitive,* and is exemplified by being a member of a 400-meter relay race team in the Olympic games. You cooperate with other team members on passing the baton as you perfect your own running technique and set increasingly lower lap-time goals, while your overall goal is for the team to win the race.

Coachability means that you are open to feedback and coaching in the form of an evaluation or criticism without becoming defensive. Being open and not defensive is directly related to your self-esteem and self-confidence. People with low self-esteem and self-confidence take almost anything said to them in a negative way, as a criticism or slap in the face. Being coachable and not defensive will help you improve and grow and will make you more valued by your management.

Self-motivation means that you do not depend on others to spark your drive to achieve, but have the discipline and courage to set your own goals and to improve yourself. Being self-motivated means you have a strong desire to work, to do a good job, to achieve, and to improve. Managers often refer to people who are self-motivated and self-confident as being *low-maintenance.*

Assertiveness does not mean being aggressive. It means being firm in expressing your ideas, thoughts, and feelings. One need not be pushy; quiet determination and resolve can result in being heard, included, and recognized.

Flexibility means being willing to change your plans, your attitudes and opinions, and your feelings about people and situations. It allows you to be less rigid, open to new ideas and ways of doing things. Flexibility is an attribute that you were either born with or not, but it can be learned with practice.

Cooperativeness means being a good team member, willing to help others and work toward company goals. The best analogy for cooperation I have ever read is, "We are all angels with only one wing, and the only way we can fly is by embracing each other."

Nurturing means caring for others, wanting to help and mentor. Having a nurturing attitude is vitally important for media salespeople so that they will not forget about their customers after a sale and will care about getting results. This attitude helps salespeople overcome a tendency to hit and run after making a sale. Paperwork and production need to be completed properly, the schedule placed properly, and the customer contacted frequently and serviced after an ad or commercial runs.

Can I Control and Change My Attitudes?

Attitudes can be changed and controlled, but you must have the willpower and discipline to practice relentlessly. Making any changes within ourselves takes self-discipline and practice. Techniques used by sports psychologists can help you control, manage, and change your attitude.

1. Positive framing. This technique is based on the concept that verbal or written communication creates images, or pictures, in our heads that we cannot erase with mere language. If you tell people, "Do not think of a tree" and then ask them what kind of a tree popped into their mind, they will invariably tell you they had an image of an oak, Christmas, or a palm tree. They simply cannot think of a no tree, zero tree, or nothing tree, as instructed. Because we think visually, in pictures, you want to put positive pictures in your and your customers' minds.

Imagine if after losing a basketball game a coach uses a negative frame and says to his team, "Do not miss free throws! We lost the game because we missed too many free throws! You're a bunch of bums!" The team will get a picture implanted in their heads of missing free throws and will continue to miss free throws. On the other hand, it would form a positive image if the coach were to say after losing a game, using a positive frame, "Make your free throws. Free throws win ball games."

Always use positive frames in your inner dialogues with yourself and in external dialogues with others. When you use a positive frame you put a positive spin on things and you create optimism in yourself. An example of a positive frame would be an offer by a gas station of a "cash discount" instead of informing consumers of a "credit card surcharge." Positive framing is a very valuable tool as we will see later in chapters 11 and 12.

2. Visualization and mental rehearsal. To use visualization, mobilize all of your senses and imagine a future sales call, down to how prospects will look and act while viewing your presentation. Visualize your prospects' reaction to your presentation—a big smile and a nod of the head. Next, mentally rehearse your presentation, including how you will overcome objections, and rehearse silently your proposals. Visualize the ideal outcome of your presentation and your reaction when your proposal is accepted. Will you jump up and click your heels? If so, practice this in your mind. Rehearse your presentation word for word, out loud over and over, visualizing prospects' reactions and your responses to their questions. Constant practice of visualization is a key to success and is an excellent confidence booster. While visualization has been referred to as *instant replay,* Spencer Johnson and Larry Wilson, in their best-selling book, *The One Minute Sales Person,* call this technique "The One Minute Rehearsal."

Another dramatic example of the incredible power of visualization was seen in the 40-minute IMAX film set in the 1998 NBA finals. The film featured Michael Jordan explaining what makes him so good; why he demands the last shot of the game, no matter what is at stake. Michael Jordan's rules are:[6]

1. Learn to love the game before you learn to master it.
2. Past failures are irrelevant to the task at hand.
3. If you can visualize winning, you won't fear losing.
4. Strength of heart (attitude) is more important than strength of body.

Visualization also includes the notion of hearing a sound in your head. The great cellist, Zara Nelsova, visualized the phrase "Seamless lines of sound join the eternity between one note and the next . . ."[7] so she could be consistent in her magnificent playing and performances.

3. Do the right thing. Behave ethically at all times. Integrity and honesty are not only good business practices that will help you manage relationships and build trust effectively over the long run, but they are also good for your soul. Conducting business with integrity improves your self-esteem, self-confidence, and health because you know that you are doing the right thing.

Using these three techniques requires mental discipline. Just as the dream of an Olympic gold medal helps athletes push their bodies to their physical limits time and again, they must channel their minds *toward* positive attitudes. Sales success requires the same persistence and mental discipline.

How Can I Motivate Myself to Maintain a Positive Attitude?

People's motivational drive comes more from internal forces than from external ones. While people who fail in sales often blame external elements, such as a company or its management, the vast majority of these people lack sufficient internal motivation to succeed. People who are successful in sales and in most other endeavors crave success and are, thus, high achievers.

High Achievers   People who have strong internal motivation and drive to be successful are high achievers. Research has identified some common characteristics of high achievers:

1. They set goals and objectives.
2. They enjoy solving problems.
3. They take calculated risks.
4. They like immediate feedback on their performance.
5. They take personal responsibility for achieving their goals and objectives.

Looking at these characteristics, we feel solutions selling is an ideal occupation for high achievers, who are more likely to satisfy their needs in sales jobs because of the nature of the tasks required in sales, especially in media sales. Selling requires a continual goal-setting process. High achievers like selling and are motivated by it because it gives them the opportunity to use their self-motivation to work to its peak while satisfying their needs to solve problems, take risks, and receive immediate performance feedback.

Goal Setting: Theory and Practice

Peter Drucker popularized the importance of setting goals and objectives in his classic book, *The Practice of Management*, published in 1954. While there is still some question about who first used the term, Management by Objectives (MBO), it is generally conceded that the initial push came from Drucker, who attributes it to Alfred P. Sloan, the managerial and organizational genius who is credited with building up General Motors.

In the 1960s, Edwin A. Locke published a series of articles that detailed his research on goal setting and on how this motivates people. He not only explained why goals work but also proposed some basic rules for setting them. While Drucker, Locke, and most other goal-setting theorists put their work in a managerial context, these theories also apply to individual goal setting where competence and confidence grow as you get better at your own objectives and goals.

Goal-Setting Theory

Goals and objectives have a significant effect on performance if they have the following attributes: *clarity, difficulty,* and *feedback.* A goal has a time horizon of more than one year and an objective has a time horizon of less than a year. Therefore, one would set several short-term objectives to reach a long-term goal.

Goal Clarity.   *Goal clarity* is the single most important element of setting goals. Goals and objectives must be specific so they can be measured. A general objective of increasing the number of prospecting calls next month is vague, nonspecific, and virtually useless. A more specific objective would be to average two prospecting appointments per day for the next month.

Goal Difficulty.   Increasing the *difficulty of goals and objectives* generally amplifies the challenge, which, in turn, raises the effort to meet the challenge. This concept of goal difficulty creates confusion and is where defining the difference between goals and objectives becomes important. Because *goals* have a long-term time horizon, it is useful to set goals, and, thus, expectations, high. In the best-selling book, *Built to Last,* Collins's and Porras's research shows that one of the things that highly successful companies have in common is that they set BHAGs—Big, Hairy, Audacious Goals. The authors write: "A BHAG should be so clear and compelling that it requires little or no explanation. Remember, a BHAG is a *goal*—like climbing a mountain or going to the moon—not a 'statement.' If it doesn't get people's juices going it's just not a BHAG."[8] One of the 18 built-to-last companies was Merck. Its BHAG was "to become the preeminent drug maker worldwide, via massive R&D and new products that cure disease."[9]

On the other hand, short-term *objective*s set by management should be set to make people feel like winners, a deep-seated need.

Unfortunately, management often sets BHAGs, or "stretches" short-term objectives, believing that they motivate people. Figure 5.1 shows the relationship between motivation and objective difficulty. Setting a very low objective has no motivating effect. On the other hand, setting an objective too high demotivates people because they give up the moment they realize that the objective is unachievable. Working hard to achieve an impossible objective creates cognitive dissonance, so people quit making an effort in order to bring thinking and action into internal harmony.

As you can see from Figure 5.1, the best objectives are moderately difficult, yet provide a challenge because they are perceived as attainable and are, thus, motivating. Contrary to what many managers believe, the trick in setting objectives is to set them on the low side of the moderately difficult peak to ensure that they can be reached with a strong effort and, thus, allow people to feel successful. Unfortunately, too often managers set objectives on the high side of the moderately difficult peak and unintentionally reduce people's motivation.

Interestingly, people with low self-esteem often set unrealistically high goals because they expect failure. Already viewing themselves as losers, they are more comfortable reinforcing this view in advance. Claiming that "the objective was too high" allows them to quit before trying rather than attempting something difficult that they think they are bound to fail at.

The ideal is to set a series of moderately difficult, challenging objectives that get progressively more difficult and challenging as each objective is achieved. This series of realistic, step-by-step, increasingly difficult objectives will lead you to your BHAG.

**Figure 5.1
Goal difficulty and
motivation.**

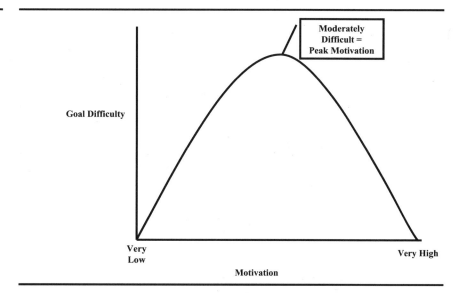

This is an art. It takes work, analysis, thought, and luck, especially when faced with an unpredictable future.

Goal Feedback.   You need to get *feedback,* a reading on how you are doing. You receive feedback from yourself by successfully solving problems and closing sales, by analyzing what you did right, or by failing and analyzing what you did wrong. For example, analyzing statistics about your ratio of total calls to successful calls will give you feedback on how you are doing. We will offer you more specific advice about methods for organizing yourself and analyzing your productivity in Chapter 28. Furthermore, you should get feedback on your goals from your manager on a regular basis. You have the right to know how you are doing and what your manager thinks you can do to improve, but remember, be self-motivated and low-maintenance.

Objective-Setting Practice

Sound individual objectives must be:

Measurable
Attainable
Demanding
Consistent with company goals
Under the control of the individual
Deadlined

Here is a mnemonic for setting objectives—MADCUD. I will provide you with more details about using and prioritizing the MADCUD objectives on a daily and weekly basis in Chapter 28, but for now, here are the elements' definitions:

Measurable. The *measurable* criterion relates to the concept of clarity. Objectives and goals must be specific enough to be measurable, for example, "to increase sales by 15 percent" or "to increase your number of face-to-face presentations from a current average of ten per week to an average of 15 per week." Notice that objectives always begin with "to," which implies an action you are going to take.

Setting specific, measurable revenue objectives is not generally a good idea, although it is common practice. Rather than setting the final objective as a revenue objective, it is more productive to set a series of specific, measurable, smaller objectives that will help you reach a desired monthly revenue level. In the chapter "A Bias for Action" in *In Search of Excellence,* Thomas J. Peters and Robert H. Waterman, Jr. quote the president of one of these successful companies who says he has his managers focus on a few important activity-based objectives. If they have this task-oriented focus, he says that "the financials will take care of themselves."[10]

Attainable. Set moderately difficult but *attainable* objectives. If objectives are reasonable, challenging, and attainable, they are motivating. If people perceive goals to be unattainable, they will not work hard to achieve them. It is important to give time and thought to setting realistic, attainable goals so that when you accomplish them you will feel successful.

Demanding. *Demanding,* like *attainable,* is related to difficulty. As seen in Figure 5.1, an objective has to be not only attainable but also sufficiently demanding to be challenging. High achievers are particularly motivated by demanding goals that challenge them. For high achievers the big payoff is the conquest and feeling like a winner, more so than any money that might be involved.

Consistent with company goals. Individual objectives should be *consistent with company goals and objectives.* For example, broadcast salespeople sometimes work at cross-purposes to their sales departments by concentrating on selling rates that are too low or by "cherry picking" inventory, which means only selecting the highly rated commercial slots or special offers to sell. Such practices would be inconsistent with an overall company goal of maximizing revenue, for example.

Under control of the individual. Another seemingly self-evident criterion for sound objectives states that they must be *under the control of the individual.* Instead of setting a revenue objective, set objectives for the number of calls you will make or for the number of presentations you will give. These are activity goals. Too often, the concept of setting activity objectives is overlooked, especially by beginning salespeople. For example, objectives that would not be under the control of salespeople would be "to increase revenue next month by 25 percent." But what if that next month's ratings on your television station went down 30 percent or last month was the bottom month in a yearlong advertising slowdown? You cannot control ratings, circulation, or the general economy; you can only control how hard you work and your own activities.

Deadlined. Your goals must be *deadlined;* they must have a due date. Without clear deadlines objectives become amorphous. Here is an example of some objectives a radio salesperson might *write:* "Next month I will increase my average rates from last month by 10 percent; I will increase the number of prospecting calls I make in the average week from ten to 15; and I will make 25 percent more face-to-face presentations." These goals are measurable, attainable, demanding, consistent with company goals, under the control of the person, and deadlined. Notice the phrase "a radio station salesperson might *write.*" Objectives that are not written down are worthless. A further way to increase your commitment to your objectives is to give your manager a copy of your written objectives.

Remember to keep your objectives flexible. If they are carved in stone and unchangeable, your objectives can lose their motivating effect, particularly if they turn out to be either too high or too low. In addition, new opportunities might arise that require a priority change.

Take Full Responsibility for Your Cycle of Success

High achievers set goals and objectives, enjoy solving problems, take calculated risks, want immediate feedback on their performance, and take personal responsibility for their own Cycle of Success (see Figure 5.2).

The Cycle of Success is an ongoing cycle of ever-more demanding objectives and goals that lead to ever-increasing success. But just as the AESKOPP formula for success was multiplicative in the sense that if any of the seven AESKOPP elements were not present success could not be achieved, the same is true of the Cycle of Success. All of its elements are inextricably linked.

**Figure 5.2
The Cycle of Success.**

The cycle is your cycle. You own it and must take full responsibility for keeping it moving. What drives it, the motor for this cycle, is your dream. Remember the words of Buckminster Fuller earlier in this chapter, if you can dream it, you can do it. Walt Disney said the same thing, and, in fact, all great people started with a dream of being great.

Your Dream, Your Mission

You cannot win an Olympic gold medal if you do not or cannot dream of winning one. Dennis Waitley in his inspirational book, *Empires of the Mind*, writes about the dreams of accomplished people such as Antonio Stradivari, Andrew Lloyd Webber, Sandra Day O'Connor, Michael Jordan, Jacques Cousteau,

Jonas Salk, and Bill Gates. He suggests writing a personal mission based on your dream to help you realize it. Write it down, keep it in your wallet or purse, and let it drive your Cycle of Success.

Zara Nelsova, the great female cellist, told me of a recurring dream she first had when she was 11 years old. She said that she dreamed that she was in a huge concert hall filled with people and she was on stage playing her cello in a long, white, flowing, silk gown that had a long gossamer train that wrapped around the entire concert hall. She said she heard in her dream this wonderful, beautiful, rich sound coming from her cello.[11] She had that sound in her head and attempted to reproduce it to enraptured audiences throughout the world for more than 50 years. Zara was not only known for her rich, beautiful sound, but also for her impassioned performance and the beautiful gowns in which she performed. She was able to accomplish greatness because of her dream. She lived and played to try to achieve the same exalted performance level on stage that she dreamed about.

Test Yourself

1. What is an attitude?
2. What is the difference between a value and an attitude?
3. What is the difference between an attitude and an attribute?
4. Which comes first, attitude or performance? Why?
5. What is the difference between a goal and an objective?
6. What are the six criteria for sound objectives?
7. What are the elements in the Cycle of Success?

Project

1. Choose a task, such as writing a term paper or a sales presentation, or an activity, such as dating, and write a MADCUD objectives statement that will help you complete the task or activity successfully.

2. Then, write a BHAG for yourself—several years in the future—and write a personal mission statement that will help you focus on and achieve your BHAG, your dream.

References

Peter F. Drucker. 1954. *The Practice of Management.* New York: Harper & Row.

Charles A. Garfield with Hal Zina Bennett. 1984. *Peak Performance: Mental Training Techniques of the World's Greatest Athletes.* New York: Warner Books.

Louis V. Gerstner, Jr. 2002. *Who Says Elephants Can't Dance? Inside IBM's Historic Turnaround.* New York: Harper Business.

Spencer Johnson and Larry Wilson. 1984. *The One Minute Sales Person.* New York: William Morrow and Company, Inc.

Edwin A. Locke. 1966. "The Ubiquity of the Technique of Goal Setting," *Behavioral Science,* Vol. II.

Edwin A. Locke. 1968. "Toward a Theory of Task Motivation and Incentives," *Organizational Behavior and Human Performance,* Vol. 3.

Edwin A. Locke and J. F. Bryan. 1967. "Goal Setting as a Means of Increasing Motivation," *Journal of Applied Psychology, Vol.* 51.

Edwin A. Locke, Norman Cartledge, and Claramae S. Kerr. 1970. "Studies in the Relationship Between Satisfaction, Goal Setting and Performance," *Organizational Behavior and Human Performance,* Vol. 5.

Thomas J. Peters and Robert H. Waterman, Jr. 1982. *In Search of Excellence: Lessons from America's Best Run Companies.* New York: Harper & Row.

Dennis Waitley. 1995. *Empires of the Mind.* New York: William Morrow and Company, Inc.

Resources

www.lessons4living.com

Endnotes

1. www.lessons4living.com/attitude.htm. November 3, 2002.
2.   Helen Keller. 1903. *The Story of My Life*. New York: Bantam Classics, reissue edition 1991.
3. Personal conversation, October 2002.
4. Louis V. Gerstner, Jr. *Who Says Elephants Can't Dance? Inside IBM's Historic Turnaround*. New York: Harper Business. 2002. p. 236.
5. Ibid. p. 214.
6. Ed Adams. "Coach's Eye." *Sailing World*. January 2003. p. 58.
7. Personal conversation with Daniel Gold, nephew of Zara Nelsova. October 2002.
8. James C. Collins and Jerry Porras. 1994. *Built to Last: Successful Habits of Visionary Companies*. New York: Harper Business. p. 111.
9. Ibid. p. 113.
10. Thomas J. Peters and Robert H. Waterman, Jr. 1982. *In Search of Excellence: Lessons from America's Best Run Companies*. New York: Harper & Row Publishers. p. 154.
11. Personal conversation. April, 2002.

Chapter **6**   # Emotional Intelligence

By Charles Warner

When I returned from the final sales call on Parrott's Florist in 1957 as described at the beginning of Chapter 2, my general sales manager asked, "How did it go? Did you close him?"

"No. He said he didn't get any results," I replied sheepishly.

"That's a common objection," replied my sales manager. "You should have asked him a bunch of questions that led him to the answer you wanted him to give you and then sold him sizzle!"

"Sizzle?"

"Yeah, you know, 'sell the sizzle, not the steak!' " My sales manager always spoke in exclamation points. It was his way of showing that he was enthusiastic.

"Enthusiasm, enthusiasm! Enthusiasm is what gets orders! Always sell the sizzle!" And with that, he reached back to his small bookshelf, took out a book, and handed it to me. "Read this," said my sales manager. "It's by Elmer Wheeler and it's called *Sizzlemanship!* It's the greatest book ever written about selling! Memorize it!"

Old-Fashioned Models of Selling

In 1957, books on selling such as *Sizzlemanship!,* Frank Bettger's *How I Raised Myself from Failure to Success in Selling,* and Og Mandino's ode of humility, *The Greatest Salesman in the World,* preached a model of selling that was developed in the 1920s, 1930s, and 1940s, as described in Chapter 1. Books on selling urged the use of techniques and tricks that were relatively successful for products that could be sold in one encounter, that were often low-cost, and for which people could be badgered into buying, often just to get rid of the salesperson.

These outmoded selling models used a simple mnemonic to guide salespeople, AIDA, which stood for Attention, Interest, Desire, and Action. The old-time practitioners urged outrageous, often silly, techniques for getting a prospect's attention. They advocated manipulative techniques such as "sizzlemanship" to get interest and create desire (usually by overselling and overpromising). And they advocated a number of techniques that pressured prospects to act immediately, allowing the salesperson to slam down a one-time sale. While there is nothing wrong with the AIDA mnemonic, these old-fashioned, manipulative, hard-sell techniques, which include the "tell and sell" model, are largely responsible for the bad reputations that salespeople are often saddled with today.

Old Models Don't Work Today

Carl Zaiss and Thomas Gordon point out in their excellent book, *Sales Effectiveness Training*, that old selling models do not work in today's highly competitive, interactive, and sophisticated business environment. This is due to increased competition, the increased need for stronger customer loyalty and long-term relationships, the increased cost of developing new business, and the current trend in business toward solutions selling.

Rather than being seen as the manipulators and hard closers of the past, salespeople want to be perceived as trusted and respected partners who get results for their customers. Unhappy with the pressure and grind of one-shot sales, today's media salespeople prefer long-term relationships.

While many experts on selling have helped shift the focus from the old-fashioned, hard-sell approach to a gentler, needs-based, and consultative approach, four men stand out in the field. They are Larry Wilson with his Counselor Selling Program and training seminars and books, Mack Hanna with his Consultative Selling Program, Tony Allesandra with his book *Non-Manipulative Selling*, and Neil Rackham with his book *SPIN Selling*. While the consultative selling approach has now evolved into a solutions-selling approach, I still recommend reading the Allesandra and Rackham books.

Solutions Selling as the Current Model

Buyers and customers of the media are hypersensitive to the tricks and manipulations of the past. With complex alternatives and problems, buyers need *established and ongoing relationships based on mutual trust*. This is the first step for successful solutions selling and requires *emotional intelligence*.

Emotional Intelligence

The term emotional intelligence was popularized by Daniel Goleman, a Harvard-educated Ph.D. in psychology, in his best seller *Emotional Intelligence: Why it can matter more than IQ*, which expanded on the work of the world-renowned educational psychologists Howard Gardner, Robert Sternberg, and others.

Gardner, Sternberg, and others questioned accepted definitions of intelligence and began to look beyond a number or IQ (intelligence quotient). After exploring the topic thoroughly, they realized that what IQ tests measured was only a person's ability to take an IQ test and was not the enormously complex construct that had been referred to in the past as "intelligence." In his book *The Triarchic Mind: A New Theory of Human Intelligence*, Robert Sternberg wrote about his research that involved interviewing both laymen and professional psychologists concerning their concepts of intelligence. He reported that there was general agreement that intelligence consisted of three facets: *practical problem-solving ability, verbal ability*, and *social competence*.

While Howard Gardner broadly defined intelligence as "the ability to solve problems or to create products that are valued within one or more cultural settings," in his influential book *Frames of Mind: The Theory of Multiple Intelligences*, he identified seven facets of intelligence. These are *linguistic, logical-mathematical, musical, bodily-kinesthetic, spatial, interpersonal*, and *intrapersonal*. In his latest book, *Intelligence Reframed: Multiple Intelligences for the 21st Century*, he added three more facets of intelligence: *naturalist, spiritual, and existential*.

He defined the multiple intelligences as follows: the first two, *linguistic* and *logical-mathematical,* are the ones that have typically been valued in school. *Linguistic intelligence* involves sensitivity to spoken and written language, the ability to learn languages, and the capacity to use language to accomplish certain goals, and is a strength among lawyers, speakers, writers, and poets. *Logical-mathematical intelligence* involves the capacity to analyze problems logically, carry out mathematical operations and calculations, and investigate issues scientifically. Mathematicians, engineers, and scientists utilize logical-mathematical intelligence.[1]

The next three intelligences that Gardner identified are *musical intelligence, bodily-kinesthetic intelligence,* and *spatial intelligence.* Musical intelligence entails skill in performing, composing, and appreciating music and music patterns. *Bodily-kinesthetic intelligence* entails the potential for using all or part of one's body to solve problems or produce products, with dancers, athletes, or mechanics as examples. *Spatial intelligence* includes the potential to recognize and manipulate the patterns of large or confined space. Navigators, pilots, sculptors, surgeons, chess players, graphic artists, and architects are examples of this.[2]

Gardner believes that there are two personal intelligences: *interpersonal* and *intra-personal. Interpersonal intelligence* allows people to understand the intentions, motivations, and desires of others and, thus, relate to and work effectively with others. Salespeople, teachers, religious and political leaders, and actors are examples. *Intrapersonal intelligence* involves the capacity to understand oneself, to have an effective working knowledge of oneself, including one's fears, desires, quirks, and capacities, and the ability to use this knowledge to regulate one's actions and life accordingly.[3]

In 1999, Gardner added three intelligences to his original seven: *naturalist, spiritual,* and *existential.* Those with *naturalist intelligence* have expertise in the recognition and classification of numerous species, of the environment and the ability to categorize new or unfamiliar organisms. *Spiritual intelligence* involves the capacity to think about cosmic, spiritual issues such as the mystery of our own existence and the existence of God. *Existential intelligence* entails the capacity to deal with such issues as the significance of life, the meaning of death, the ultimate fate of the universe, the profound experience of love, and appreciation of and total immersion in art.[4]

Daniel Goleman concentrated his research on the importance of the personal intelligences, which he labeled *emotional intelligence.* Beginning in *Emotional Intelligence,* published in 1995, and in two subsequent books, *Working With Emotional Intelligence* and *Primal Leadership: Realizing the Power of Emotional Intelligence,* Goleman has continued to refine and simplify his construct of emotional intelligence (EI). In *Working With Emotional Intelligence,* Goleman defined *emotional intelligence* as the "capacity for recognizing our own feelings and those of others, for motivating ourselves, and for managing emotions well in ourselves and in our relationships."[5] His most recent book, *Primal Leadership,* lays out an expanded definition that includes four dimensions of EI (See Exhibit 6.1)

How Important Is Emotional Intelligence in Selling?   Goleman makes the case that, contrary to previously held theories, intelligence or IQ might not be an accurate predictor of life success. "At best IQ contributes about 20 percent to the factors that determine life success, which leaves 80 percent to other forces. As one observer notes, 'The vast majority of one's ultimate niche in so-

**Exhibit 6.1
Emotional
Intelligence Domains
and Associated
Competencies**

Personal Competence: These capabilities determine how we manage ourselves:
Self-Awareness
- *Emotional self-awareness:* Reading one's own emotions and recognizing their impact; using "gut sense" to guide decisions.
- *Accurate self-assessment:* Knowing one's strengths and limits.
- *Self-confidence:* A sound sense of one's self-worth and capabilities.

Self-Management
- *Emotional self-control:* Keeping disruptive emotions and impulses under control.
- *Transparency:* Displaying honesty and integrity; trustworthiness.
- *Adaptability:* Flexibility in adapting to changing situations or overcoming obstacles.
- *Achievement:* The drive to improve performance to meet inner standards of excellence.
- *Initiative:* Readiness to act and seize opportunity.
- *Optimism:* Seeing the upside in events.

Social Competence: These capabilities determine how we manage relationships:
Social Awareness
- *Empathy:* Sensing others' emotions, understanding their perspective, and taking an active interest in their concerns.
- *Organizational Awareness:* Reading the currents, decision networks, and politics at the organizational level.
- *Service:* Recognizing and meeting . . . client or customer needs.

Relationship Management
- *Inspirational leadership:* Guiding and motivating with a compelling vision (for media salespeople this would translate into creating value with an inspiring vision for your medium and your media outlet).
- *Influence:* Wielding a range of tactics of persuasion.
- *Developing others:* Bolstering others' ability through feedback and guidance.
- *Change catalyst:* Initiating, managing, and leading in a new direction.
- *Conflict management:* Resolving disagreements.
- *Teamwork and collaboration:* Cooperation and team building.

Source: Daniel Goleman, Richard Boyatzis, and Annie McKee. 2002. *Primal Leadership.* Harvard Business School Press. Used with permission.

ciety is determined by non-IQ factors, ranging from social class to luck.'"[6] A study of Harvard graduates in the fields of law, medicine, teaching, and business found that scores on entrance exams, a surrogate for IQ, had zero or negative correlation with eventual career success.

A study initiated in 1968 by the Stanford Graduate School of Business reinforced the importance of EI for success in business. It conducted in-depth interviews with the members of its graduating class, which examined the students' academic records and grades, their extra-curricular and social activities, and their reputation among their fellow students. The school kept track of the graduates' careers and levels of success with re-interviews in 1978 and in 1988. When the school published the findings of its 20-year study in 1988, it concluded that the only two things that the most successful graduates (top five percent in title, position, and money, for example) had in common was that all of the most successful graduates were in the bottom half of their class in grades and all of them were popular. In other words, relationship skills were more important for success than grades.

A major element of EI and success is optimism. A study of salesmen at Met Life by Martin Seligman revealed that "Being able to take a rejection with grace is essential in sales of all kinds, especially with a product like insurance, where the ratio of nos to yeses can be so discouragingly high. For this reason, about three-quarters of insurance salesmen quit in their first three years." Seligman found that new salesmen who were "by nature optimists sold 37 percent more insurance in their first two years on the job than did pessimists. And during the first year the pessimists quit at twice the rate of the optimists."[7]

Media salespeople sell an intangible product similar to what insurance salespeople sell, but media salespeople do not have quite the same rejection rate, which makes media selling more desirable and satisfying. However, the above research reinforces the importance of optimism in selling. Optimism is defined in terms of how people explain to themselves their own successes and failures. People who are optimistic believe failures are the result of something that can be changed so that they can be successful the next time around. Pessimists take personal blame for failures, blaming them on some inherent characteristic they are helpless to change.[8] Pessimists also often blame their parents or their bosses or even the weather for their failures. Their attitude is that they expect failure; therefore, they create failures and a disastrous future. On the other hand, optimists expect success, and therefore create a successful future.

Do I Have Emotional Intelligence?

Socrates said that all knowledge begins with, "Know thyself." Self-knowledge is the keystone of EI. It is the awareness of one's feelings as they occur. Self-awareness is non-reactive, nonjudgmental attention to one's inner states and feelings. To find out if you have emotional intelligence you have to ask yourself the following questions and answer them honestly.

1. Do I motivate myself to stick doggedly to tasks and practice or am I too easily distracted?
2. Am I critical, condescending, and inhibited or am I socially poised and cheerful?
3. Am I unexpressive and detached or am I outgoing and easily committed to people and causes?
4. Am I prudish, uptight, and uneasy with new experiences?
5. Do I tend to be anxious and handle stress poorly or am I comfortable with myself and how well I handle stress?

(For the following questions, see Exhibit 6.1.)

6. How self-aware am I and how honestly am I able to assess my own strengths and weaknesses?
7. How is my emotional self-control and how well do I control my impulses?
8. How transparent am I? In other words, can people tell I am honest and believe I am trustworthy, that I am not hiding things?
9. Am I flexible and do I adapt easily to change or in overcoming obstacles?
10. Do I have a drive to achieve and to improve my performance to meet my inner standards of excellence?
11. Am I ready to grab the initiative, to act, and to seize opportunities as they present themselves?
12. Am I generally optimistic and do I see the upside in events?
13. How well do I sense others' emotions, understand their points of view, and take an active interest in their concerns?
14. How well do I read the currents, decision networks, and politics in my organization?
15. How good am I at recognizing and satisfying my customers' needs?

16. How good am I at creating value by communicating an inspiring vision for my medium and my product?
17. How persuasive am I?
18. Am I a catalyst for change in my organization?
19. How good am I at confronting problems, conflicts, and disagreements and resolving them?
20. How good am I at cultivating and maintaining a web of relationships?
21. How cooperative am I and how good a team member am I?

Hopefully your answers to these questions placed you more than half-way toward the side of possessing EI, which means that you know you have an opportunity for improvement. This is a positive frame for the concept of deficiency and a good lesson in the use of framing, which will be covered more thoroughly in Chapter 12.

People are sometimes tempted to use personality tests to determine their EI, but most of these tests, developed in the 1960s and 1970s, do not have much value in predicting success, uncovering motivation, and understanding yourself and others. Instead, they attempt to pigeonhole people into types such as "feeling" or "thinking" or "expressive." Most psychological tests are not designed to find EI. Psychological tests are often used by companies to screen job applicants, are designed to diagnose psychological disorders, and are poor predictors of motivation and how people will manage relationships.

Can I Learn Emotional Intelligence?

Goleman feels that emotional intelligence can be learned. In *Working With Emotional Intelligence* he writes: "Unlike IQ, which changes little after our teens years, emotional intelligence seems to be largely learned, and it continues to develop as we go through life and learn from our experiences—our competence in it can keep growing. In fact, studies that have tracked people's level of emotional intelligence through the years show that people get better and better in these capabilities as they grow more adept at handling their own emotions and impulses, at motivating themselves, and at honing their empathy and social adroitness. There is an old-fashioned word for this growth in emotional intelligence: *maturity*."[9]

Some of the things you can do to improve your EI are:

1. Work on controlling your impulses—"There is no psychological skill more fundamental than resisting impulses."[10]
2. Work on developing a positive, optimistic, hopeful outlook and a belief that you are the master over the events in your life and can meet the challenges as they come up, as you learned in the previous chapter.
3. Work on improving your communication and listening skills. Chapter 7 covers more about how to acquire and practice these vital skills.
4. Work on developing a sense of flow. Flow is a state of self-forgetfulness, the opposite of rumination and worry. It is peak performance—athletes call it "the zone"—in which excellence becomes effortless, crowd and competitors disappear into a completely focused absorption in the moment. People "in the zone" are unconcerned about success or failure; it is the sheer pleasure of the act itself that motivates them and makes the task effortless. For more information about flow and how to develop it, you might want to read the inspiring book *Flow: The Psychology of Optimal Experience* by Mihaly Csikszentmihalyi.

How Can I Apply Emotional Intelligence to Selling Media?

Now that you have learned about emotional intelligence and how EI can help you improve your relationships, the next step is to relate EI to selling. Using the three Golden Rules of Selling is the optimum way to apply EI to selling.

Rule 1: Do unto others as they would have others do unto them. Unlike the Bible's Golden Rule, this does not make the assumption others like the same things that you like. Modern psychology and EI indicate that it is better to recognize people's diversity and differences and to value their needs, wants, desires, or preferences. Empathy requires that you find out how others feel, what they like, and what they want, then base your response to them according to how they want to be treated.

Rule 2: People like and trust people exactly like themselves. This rule reinforces the notion that people are most comfortable with other people who are similar, a fact we observe everyday as people gather in groups and cliques. We will cover more about this principle in Chapter 7.

Rule 3: People don't care how much you know until they know how much you care. This rule reminds us that feeling and communicating a sense of caring for another person comes first in any relationship. In other words, you put another's concerns before your own.

These rules should be applied in the following steps:

Step 1: Just before sales conversations or meetings, ask yourself how you feel at that moment and then pause, *exhale*, and proceed. It is important to exhale because when we are nervous or tense, we tend to hold our breath, which tightens us up and makes fluid movement difficult. Exhaling is a sports training technique in which athletes release tension and improve performance. The exhalation technique was highlighted in the 2002 World Series telecasts, when Fox Television showed close-ups of the faces of the pitchers and batters. Before every pitch each pitcher, just before he started his throw to the plate, exhaled visibly. Taking time to recognize your feelings, to relax, and to exhale will allow you to manage your emotions consciously, and to control and use your emotions and your tensions to help you.

Step 2: Sense the mood and the emotional climate of the person or group you are meeting with. Beginning salespeople are usually nervous and anxious when they meet with customers, particularly the first time, and are unaware that customers are probably as nervous, anxious, and uncomfortable as they are. Effective leaders, politicians, and entertainers develop a knack for sensing the mood of a crowd or audience and playing to it. Salespeople must develop similar radar.

Step 3: Set the mood, the emotional tone and climate, for the meeting. Emotion is contagious, so by taking charge and energetically exuding a sense of confidence and enthusiasm (yes, "enthusiasm!" like my first sales manager often repeated) you infect the others with your contagious enthusiasm and positive vibes. Enthusiasm does not have to be the loud, excited, highly demonstrated type we often associate with back-slapping, broad-grinning used-car salesmen, but honest enthusiasm can come through in a restrained, calm, confident way that is in harmony with the emotional state of the other person or people in a meeting.

As Goleman points out in *Emotional Intelligence*, "We transmit and catch moods from each other in what amounts to a subterranean economy of the psyche in which encounters are toxic, some nourishing. This emotional exchange is typically at a subtle, almost imperceptible level; the way a salesperson says "thank you" can leave us feeling ignored, resented, or genuinely welcomed and appreciated. We catch feelings from one another as though they were some kind of social virus."[11] Make sure the viruses you transmit are positive, caring ones.

Step 4: Let the person or people you are meeting with know that you care. The best way to accomplish this step in a first meeting with a person is to begin by being very open about yourself. The goal is to reach out with personal details about yourself to enable the other person to get to know you. At that point you can ask the question, "How about you?" to learn more about the other person. People will normally reciprocate with openness and talk about themselves, their families, their hobbies, and interests. As they are talking, you must search for common interests and associations, such as being married, having children, or loving sports. This is an application of the Golden Rule of Selling, people like and trust people exactly like themselves, and your job is to talk about and emphasize those things in each of your personal lives that are similar. By showing a genuine sense of caring about their personal interests, they will know that you care. After the meeting, write down all the personal details for future reference.

Be prepared to encounter different responses from men and women, for as Goleman writes, men generally ". . . take pride in a lone, tough-minded independence and autonomy . . ." and women generally ". . . see themselves as part of a web of connectedness."[12] These gender differences are pointed out to encourage you to be aware of your own tendencies and to know what you might expect in an initial encounter with someone, to be more like them and to build rapport. You can and probably should change these gender generalizations and initial stereotypes once you have had the opportunity to get to know someone better.

Also, when meeting with a group of people for the first time, it pays large dividends to research their personal backgrounds and interests prior to your meeting. More details about how to prepare for a group presentation will be covered in Chapter 11.

Step 5: Listen with "emotional synchrony," as Goleman calls it. "The degree of emotional rapport people feel in an encounter is mirrored by how tightly concentrated their physical movements are as they talk. . . . One person nods just as the other makes a point, both shift chairs at the same moment, or one leans forward as the other leans back."[13] This type of synchrony is a major way to transmit a "social virus" or emotional state or mood. It also makes you more similar to the other person in the conversation, gets you closer, and makes him or her feel that you care.

Having learned about the importance of emotional intelligence in building relationships in this chapter, in the next chapter you will learn how to put your EI knowledge to work in communicating with and listening carefully to people and understanding what makes them tick.

Test Yourself

1. Why don't old-fashioned sales techniques work in today's media selling environment?
2. How many different intelligences did Howard Gardner identify?
3. What is emotional intelligence?
4. Why is EI more important for success in business and other fields than IQ?
5. What are the four major elements of EI?
6. Why is optimism important in selling?
7. What are the three Golden Rules of Selling?
8. What are the five steps in applying these rules?

Project

Select a week in your life (next week might be good) in which you commit yourself to taking notes on encounters you have with people whose job it is to serve you and be pleasant: waiters in restaurants or retail salespeople, for example. Take notes in two columns. In the first column, note the type of or lack of emotional intelligence you observe in each of the service people you encounter. Did the person try to connect with you? Cause you to leave the encounter feeling put off, angry, dissatisfied, happy, or pleased? In the second column, make notes on your feelings and your ability to control your emotions in reaction to those encounters. You might copy into your notebook the EI elements in Exhibit 6.1 and use them as a guide. At the end of the week, look over your notes and see if you picked out those people who displayed EI and how they were different from those who did not display EI and if you were able to recognize your emotions.

References

Tony Allesandra, Ph.D., Phil Wexler, and Rick Barerra. 1992. *Non-Manipulative Selling, 2nd Edition.* New York: Fireside Books.
Mihaly Csikszentmihalyi. 1990. *Flow: The Psychology of Optimal Experience.* New York: Harper & Row.
Howard Gardner. 1983. *Frames of Mind: The Theory of Multiple Intelligences.* New York: Basic Books.
Howard Gardner. 1993. *Multiple Intelligence: The Theory in Practice.* New York: Basic Books.
Howard Gardner. 1999. *Intelligence Reframed: Multiple Intelligences for the 21st Century.* New York: Basic Books.
Daniel Goleman. 1995. *Emotional Intelligence: Why It Can Matter More Than IQ.* New York: Bantam Books.
Daniel Goleman. 1998. *Working with Emotional Intelligence.* New York: Bantam Books.
Daniel Goleman, Richard Boyatzis and Annie McKee. 2002. *Primal Leadership: Realizing the Power of Emotional Intelligence.* Boston: Harvard Business School Press.
Elaine Hatfield, John T. Cacioppo, and Richard Rapson. 1994. *Emotional Contagion.* New York: Cambridge University Press.
Neil Rackham. 1988. *SPIN Selling.* New York: McGraw-Hill.
Robert J. Sternberg. 1988. *The Triarchic Mind: A New Theory of Human Intelligence.* New York: Viking Penguin.
Carl D. Zaiss and Thomas Gordon, Ph.D. 1993. *Sales Effectiveness Training.* New York: Dutton.

Endnotes

1. Howard Gardner. 1999. *Intelligence Reframed.* New York: Basic Books, p. 41.
2. Ibid. p. 42.
3. Ibid. p. 43.
4. Ibid. p. 43.

5. Daniel Goleman. 1998. *Working With Emotional Intelligence.* New York: Bantam Books. p. 317.
6. Ibid. p. 34.
7. Ibid. p. 89.
8. Ibid. p. 88.
9. Ibid. p. 7.
10. Daniel Goleman. 1995. *Emotional Intelligence.* New York: Bantam Books. p. 79.
11. Ibid. p. 114.
12. Ibid. p. 139.
13. Ibid. p. 116.

Chapter 7

Skills: Effective Communication, Effective Listening, and Understanding People

By Charles Warner

Following is a review of several things we have covered so far.
The three *Golden Rules of Selling* are:

1. Do unto others as they would have others do unto them.
2. People like and trust people exactly like themselves.
3. People don't care what you know until they know you care.

Next, are the *determinants of success* in the AESKOPP system:

1. Establish and maintain relationships with prospects and customers.
2. Solve advertising and marketing problems for them.
3. Get results for them (as they define results).

The most important skill in selling is dealing with other people, and the most important knowledge you can have is knowledge of people and how to build relationships. Understanding your customers' business, your product, and its capabilities are secondary because if you cannot get people to like and trust you, you will never get to the point of being able to discover what their problems are, let alone solve them.

Figure 7.1 shows a schematic conception of all that is involved in building and maintaining relationships.

Communication is the fuel that keeps a relationship going. Without communication, both verbal and non-verbal, a relationship does not go anywhere. The foundation on which the relationship rests, the road on which it travels, is *listening*. Without listening, you do not know where communication is going and there can be no progress in a relationship. The engine that drives the relationship consists of equal parts of *respect, caring,* and *fairness* that must constantly mesh and work hard together. It is kept running smoothly, with a minimum of friction, aided by *trust*, which leads to the final objective of a relationship—that of *mutual understanding.*

A blurb on the cover jacket of Tom Rusk's brilliant book, *The Power of Ethical Persuasion*, reads:

> Maintaining that respect, understanding, caring, and fairness are the foundation of quality in organizations and in personal life, Dr. Rusk shows how to apply these ethical principles in life's most important negotiations: those high-stakes conversations that are threatened by strong emotions and defensive reactions.
>
> In this wise, practical, and insightful guide, filled with lively anecdotes and illustrative conversations, he takes the reader through the three phases of the Ethical Persuasion process, explaining how to listen so that the other person is satisfied that you understand his or her point of view; how to express your own viewpoint effectively; and how then to achieve a mutual understanding.[1]

**Figure 7.1
The schematic
of a relationship.**

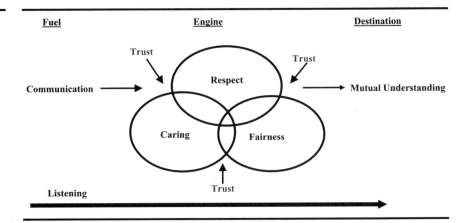

A good way to look at selling is that it is a process of ethical persuasion. I strongly recommend that you read Dr. Rusk's book because it will help you both sell and live better and more ethically.

In *The Power of Ethical Persuasion,* Rusk lists the Five Barriers to Human Communication and the Five Principles of Ethical Persuasion, as shown in Exhibit 7.1.

**Exhibit 7.1a
Five Barriers to
Human
Communication**

1. We all live in unique and private worlds.
2. We tend to react with blame and self-defense.
3. Everyone has difficulty handling strong feelings.
4. Feelings are facts to the person experiencing them.
5. We rarely discuss issues of power openly.

**Exhibit 7.1b
Five Principles
of Ethical
Persuasion**

1. Respect in the presence of feelings.
2. Problem-solving can wait until full mutual understanding is achieved.
3. Listen to the other person's viewpoint first.
4. Restate the other person's viewpoint.
5. Change yourself in a positive direction.

How different this approach of persuading people is from the old-fashioned "tell-and-sell" school of selling that urged "Always Be Closing!" (Exclamation point courtesy of my first sales manager.) This new approach to selling says that in order to sell something, you must understand people, have respect for them and their feelings, establish a relationship based on trust and reach mutual understanding before you try to solve problems, first listen to the other person's point of view, restate the other person's viewpoint, and, finally, change yourself in a positive direction and meet the other person more than halfway. These rules do not include "Always Be Closing," or "tell and sell."

Communication

The model given in Figure 7.2 shows the elements in the communication process. The model is based in part on the one proposed by Claude E. Shannon and Warren Weaver.[2]

**Figure 7.2
The communication
process.**

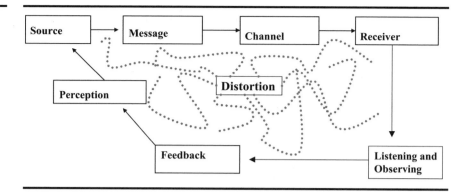

Keep in mind that communication is a continuous *process;* for communication to occur, the feedback loop must be completed. If the source, a salesperson for example, does not make appropriate adjustments in response to a receiver's reactions, the loop is broken and the process stops; instead of being a two-way communication, it becomes a one-way recitation. Let's look more closely at the elements in the communication model in Figure 7.2.

Source

The source is the initiating origin of information in the communication process. The credibility of the source of information is its most important characteristic. Source credibility is multidimensional and, therefore, weakness in one dimension, or characteristic, can be offset by strength in another. Communication research has shown there are seven characteristics that enhance source credibility:

1. **Trustworthiness**: The perception of the trustworthiness of a source by a receiver. Trustworthiness is the first and most important element of source credibility. It usually does not come instantaneously and usually needs to be built up over time. Having experience in a job or profession also tends to add to the perception of trustworthiness, and titles or professional status can enhance trustworthiness. For example, we tend to perceive that pharmacists, doctors, and university professors are trustworthy.

2. **Competence**: The perception of how competent the source is at communicating. Former President Ronald Reagan was known as "the great communicator" because the former actor was terrific at reading speeches and connecting with people.

3. **Objectivity**: Sources are much more credible if they are perceived to be objective, able to see and understand both sides of an issue, position, or argument. Source credibility can be enhanced by the use of a *two-sided argument,* a technique effective with people who are initially opposed to your point of view. The two-sided argument features an *on-the-one-hand this and on-the-other-hand that* approach, always giving the argument counter to your own point of view first. This technique signals that you are objective and candid and have considered the alternative point of view. Recent research indicates that if a sales or advertising message uses a two-sided presentation by beginning with several candid points about a product's weaknesses, subsequent points about the product's strengths are much more likely to be believed. Initial candor is a powerful tool for enhancing objectivity. Salespeople should remember this technique.

4. **Dynamism**: The more dynamic, energetic, and enthusiastic sources are, the more credible they are. It follows that if people are enthusiastic others are likely to say to themselves, "Well, if she believes in it so much, it must be a good product." So my sales manager back in 1957 was not all wrong when he said, "Enthusiasm, enthusiasm! Enthusiasm is what gets orders!" He was right, but only partially right. While there are six other elements that affect source credibility, enthusiasm is a critical element of successful, credible communication as long as it is authentic. Later in this chapter, I will discuss in more depth the importance of being yourself—being authentic.

5. **Expertise**: The more knowledgeable you are and the more you are perceived to be an expert on a subject, the more credible and believable you will be as a source. An excellent way to demonstrate your expertise is by the use of *evidence,* which consists of factual statements from another source, preferably a highly credible one. When your evidence is highly credible, give the source of the evidence before you give the evidence; if not, give the evidence first and then give the source. For example, if you are selling for a television station, indicate your source is the Nielsen Station Index ratings before you show ratings. On the other hand, give product usage information before you mention that it comes from your own internal station research. The credibility of your evidence is vitally important in the long run because content and facts are remembered by a receiver longer than your source characteristics are. In other words, your customers will remember the important facts about your ratings longer than they will remember your competence, enthusiasm, and expertise when you presented them.

6. **Physical attractiveness**: Of course, beauty is always in the eye of the beholder, but communications research has clearly shown that people generally perceive a source of information to be more credible if the source is physically attractive, according the beholder's standards of beauty. This fact probably explains why we rarely see ugly people delivering the news on television and why network television anchors and reporters are often chosen first for their good looks and cute personalities and second for their journalistic expertise. Likewise, one of the criteria for hiring salespeople is that they are reasonably attractive, in both looks and personality. While not all of us are a Julia Roberts, Jennifer Lopez, Denzel Washington, or Brad Pitt, salespeople must always do the best with what they have to work with and pay close attention to their grooming, how they dress, their cosmetic style, and, at the very least, try not to appear unattractive to their customers. Think about it. How many customers have scruffy beards, goatees, green hair, dreadlocks, visible tattoos, or body piercing?

7. **Similarity**: Recall Golden Rule of Selling number two, that "people like and trust people exactly like themselves"? People are simply more comfortable with people like themselves in age, gender, race, cultural background, and tastes and interests. This principle reminds me of the old jazz classic sung by Fats Waller and Jack Teagarden, "That's What I Like About You," in which they sing:

> *Teagarden:* "You got no money. You're too fat. You drink too much gin."
> *Waller:* "But I like what you like."
> *Teagarden:* "That's what I like about you.'

How do you use the seven characteristics of source credibility to enhance your ability to build a relationship and reach mutual understanding? As mentioned earlier, these characteristics are multidimensional and they work together in an intricate and complicated way. Some characteristics might be more important to some people than others are. When choosing someone to date, some people make their decision based on physical attractiveness, others on personality, others on expertise, and others on similarity. You might be robust in some of these characteristics, but not in others. You must observe and listen to the person with whom you want a relationship, understand what characteristics are important to them, and then emphasize your strengths in those areas.

For example, if you are a young female salesperson, you might not be similar to an older male customer from a different cultural background. In this situation, you would emphasize your *competence* in how you present your case, your *expertise* in the medium you are selling, your *enthusiasm* for your product and how it can solve the customer's problems. Finally, you would demonstrate your *objectivity* by using a two-sided argument and presenting some drawbacks of your medium first before presenting its many strengths. These positive attributes can go a very long way toward overcoming your lack of similarity.

Message

The second element in the communication process is the *message.* After establishing your source credibility, you want to work on the strength of your message. Because it is critical that customers comprehend the information you are communicating, what you communicate should be kept relatively simple and easy to understand. *Repetition* is a key factor in the strength of information and its comprehension, and during a conversation or presentation, you must find ways to repeat your important points. For example, regularly summarizing the three major points you are trying to make in a conversation or in either written or oral presentations is an excellent way to repeat your points and make them more memorable. The notion of repeating *three* points is an important one. Just as repetition is effective in advertising, it is also effective in conversations and presentations.

Ordering effects can have an impact on your message's comprehension and make it more memorable. There are two ordering effects: *primacy and recency.* People tend to remember best those elements they see or hear first (primacy) in a conversation, television newscast, or sales presentation and what they see or hear last (recency). Recency effects are especially important when people have to consider carefully and weigh all information in a sequence. Thus, arrange your material with your most important points first and repeat them at the end of a presentation in a concise summary.

Channel

Channel effects are the third element in the communication process. The most effective channel of communication for simple messages is face-to-face, the second most effective is sight-plus-sound (such as film, television, or videotape), the third is sound only (for instance, radio, audiotape, or telephone), and the last is sight only (newspapers, magazines, and all printed materials). However, exactly the reverse is true when dealing with complex messages and material. Thus, complex presentations that contain a large number of facts, statistics, and complicated logical arguments have a much better chance of being comprehended and remembered when they are in writing. The lesson here is that simple messages and presentations that tend to appeal to the emotions are best remembered when presented on video. Complex sales presentations are best remembered when they are in writing, a PowerPoint presentation or comb-bound booklet or both, supplemented by a face-to-face discussion that engages people emotionally and that reinforces the major points of your sales presentations. Always keep in mind the KISS rule—keep it short and simple—and eliminate extraneous points and material from your presentation. In chapters 10 and 11 you will learn more about how to plan, write, and deliver complex sales presentations to both individuals and groups.

Receiver

There are two characteristics of a *receiver* in the communication process that are important—intelligence and self-confidence. People who are not very intelligent and suffer from low self-confidence tend to be slower in comprehending the benefits and advantages of your product, but, on the other hand, they have a greater tendency to accept and to yield to your attempts to persuade them. If you have intelligent and self-confident customers, they are likely to understand the material you present, but will require from you a good deal of source credibility, objectivity, expertise, strong evidence, and message strength to get them to accept your proposal. Remember that while intelligent people might comprehend your points better and faster, they will also come up with a greater number of hard-to-answer counterarguments and objections.

Distortion

Distortion occurs throughout the communication process and can come in a variety of forms, such as interruptions, situational factors (tension or job pressure), lack of attention, inadequate message reception, and intentional or unintentional misunderstandings, to name a few. Anything that confuses a message's meaning and clarity is *distortion*. For example, a customer might say to a salesperson, "I want to be in the newspaper next week. I'll take about any position I can get." *About* is the key word in this message and could create a potentially disastrous number of misunderstandings. To avoid distortion, deliver your written and oral presentations in a quiet atmosphere with as few interruptions as possible. In order to cut down on distortion and possible misunderstandings, make sure you always have leave-behinds of your proposals or presentations so both you and your customers have hard copies. If you make a proposal or reach an agreement on the telephone, always send an e-mail to your customer or buyer confirming the details of what you discussed. Also, send an e-mail after an in-person call summarizing the details of your discussion or agreement. Stating next steps is always vital to cut down on misunderstandings and distortion.

Another reason for summarizing in e-mails is you can use them to fill out call reports or debriefing logs, required by many sales organizations, that use sales force automation software (SFA) such as ACT!.

Listening

Listening is the single most important sales skill because it is the foundation on which relationships are based and is the road to mutual understanding. Listening is the basis for Golden Rule number three, "People don't care how much you know until they know how much you care," which requires that you not only listen but also observe. You are listening to gain understanding of what is being communicated verbally, but we know that non-verbal communication and body language contain a great deal of the meaning of any message; this is why observing is included in listening—you listen for verbal clues and messages and you observe non-verbal messages and body language.

Inevitably, the most effective and successful salespeople are those who have mastered the skills of good listening and observing. Unfortunately, as much as I and other sales trainers and authors such as Larry Wilson, Huthwaite & Company (the firm that teaches SPIN Selling), and Ron Steiner write and teach about the primacy of listening in the sales process and as many times as I have done sales training seminars over the years, I still see too many salespeople nod their heads when they hear about the importance of effective listening and then go right on talking too much, trying to sell as prospects desperately try to get a word in edgewise. Perhaps this unfortunate situation comes about because people who like to talk a lot are attracted to selling and are unable or unwilling to change their behavior. The old-fashioned image of salespeople as glib, fast talkers may be to blame, but as we will see in Exhibit 7.3, the communication process is complicated and entails a lot more than just talking.

In more than 45 years of being a salesperson and managing and training salespeople, the most successful salespeople I have known have been world-class listeners and live by the adage, "Nature has given us one tongue, but two ears so that we hear from others twice as much as we speak." In Exhibit 7.2 you will see what world-class listeners do and what they do not do.

**Exhibit 7.2
World-Class Listener
Dos and Don'ts**

What World-Class Listeners Do:

They Adopt the Proper Attitude. They are optimistic; they tell themselves that they are going to like the person they're calling on and that they are going to have a positive outcome. They are positive, confident, friendly, open, and intensely curious.

They Shut Up and Listen

They Are Conscious of Their Body Language. World-Class listeners are conscious of their posture and how they sit when they listen to someone. They try to make sure their body language indicates they are fascinated and eager to learn more, often leaning forward.

They Respect the Other Person's Point of View. They are able to put themselves in another person's shoes. They see both sides and respect others' views; they don't denigrate or belittle others' views.

They Listen and Look for Emotional Cues. World-Class listeners observe how someone says something and look for clues that reveal underlying feelings. People often say things that try to cover up how they are really feeling. World-Class listeners listen and observe carefully and with empathy and understanding for how the person is feeling. World-Class listeners look for nonverbal clues as to how other people feel and what they really mean to say. World-Class listeners listen for *how* people say something, not so much *what* they say.

They Listen and Look for Buying Cues. They watch very carefully for any little sign or movement that indicates another person has made a decision to agree with them or to buy—a slight leaning forward, a tiny nod of the head, a sudden tension that signals an intent to buy and a desire to begin negotiating.

They Match Speech, Listening Patterns, and Movements to the Speaker. World-Class listeners let the other person set the pace. They talk and listen at the other person's pace, not theirs. They do the adapting and speeding up or slowing down; they don't make other people adjust to them. This type of listening is referred to academically as synchronic listening or listening in synchrony, and it merely means being "in sync" with someone else (not the singing group). By being in sync World-Class listeners show respect for the other person, for their style and even their cultural differences.

They Are Patient. They know that if they listen patiently and courteously to everything others have to say, without interrupting, that others will reciprocate and give them a courteous hearing.

They Pause Often. World-Class listeners pause after someone says something to make sure the other person is finished. Like any good interviewer, they know that a pause often prompts others to talk more—often revealing more than they intend to.

They Listen Actively. See Exhibit 7.6 for details.

They Ask How They Can Help. Once they have gathered information, they don't start selling immediately. World-Class listeners ask how they can be of help.

They Summarize Well. Periodically through a discussion, they pause and summarize the points of agreement. Brief summaries not only make points memorable through repetition, but they also focus the discussion and get it back on track if it has wandered.

They Listen With Authenticity. World-Class listeners are authentic; they don't try to emulate someone else, they are themselves. Others can tell when someone is insincere. Being insincere is manipulative and does not build trust.

What World-Class Listeners Don't Do:

They Don't Listen Judgmentally. See Exhibit 7.6 for details.

They Don't Interrupt and Step on Sentences. The biggest giveaway of poor listeners is that they constantly step on other people's sentences—they interrupt or finish a statement for others. They cannot wait to be heard. These people spend their time during a conversation thinking of what *they* want to say and are more concerned with their need to express themselves than with listening. Poor listeners don't let the other person finish what they are saying, especially if the other person talks slowly. World-Class listeners don't make these errors.

They Don't Think of a Rebuttal. Allied to stepping on sentences is thinking of what the next comment or a rebuttal is going to be while someone is talking. We often have a tendency to do this while we are listening to a speech or lecture to which we cannot respond; we engage ourselves mentally in the game of forming a reply to a particular point. This is a nonproductive game to play. World-Class listeners pay full attention to the speaker and concentrate on listening carefully to every word without thinking of their comeback or rebuttal.

They Don't Respond Too Soon. World-Class listeners let others finish a discussion and make as many points, as many objections as they feel inclined to do. They let people get all the negatives out on the table before responding. By responding too soon, they know they look defensive and may even be interrupting.

They Don't React Emotionally. We learned about the importance of self-management in the previous chapter on Emotional Intelligence and World-Class listeners understand that an excellent time to practice self-control is while they are listening. In Chapter 12 we will go into more detail about negotiating and how sometimes manipulative negotiators will purposely try to get people angry so emotions will kick in and they will make a bad, emotional decision. World-Class listeners know the best way to counteract an attempt to make them angry or to get a rise out of them is to stay calm and never react emotionally—that is the way they turn the tables on others who try to manipulate them.

They Don't Become Distracted. Too often people do not concentrate on looking at the person who is talking; they allow their attention to be diverted to other things. They doodle, look out the window, glance at some attractive person in the next office, or conduct other discourteous and disconcerting behavior. Some people keep their cell phones and pagers on, and, worse, answer them, which gives the speaker the silent message that they are not interested in the speaker.

World-Class listeners focus intently on speakers, look them in the eye, and turn off their cell phones and pagers.

They Don't Respond to Negatives. World-Class listeners know better than to respond too quickly to negative statements because they understand it makes them look defensive and that they might give some credence to the negatives. They ignore negatives and reinforce positive statements or compliments.

They Don't Ask Leading Questions. They don't try to use manipulative questioning and selling techniques or try to trick people into saying things they don't intend to say.

They Don't Take Notes. In 45 years of selling and watching Hall of Fame media salespeople sell, I've rarely seen any of them take notes. They preferred to focus intently on the other person and do their best to build empathy and rapport, which note-taking makes difficult. Taking notes is a distraction from rapport building. Of course, the Hall of Famers are or were all very bright and had memories good enough to remember what was said in a conversation. These great salespeople typically made detailed notes on important calls after a call was over, however. Times when note-taking is a good idea is during the discovery process when you are receiving a great deal of facts—more than can be remembered—and during complicated negotiations over schedules, prices, and contract conditions. By the time negotiating starts, though, you should have built sufficient rapport and know your customer well enough be able to take notes. The rule on taking notes is: Don't take notes unless you have to in order to remember complicated factual details and, even then, keep them as brief as possible.

An article in *Fortune* magazine, "America's Best Salesmen," describes the sales technique of securities salesperson Richard F. Greene when having a breakfast meeting with a prospect.

Greene is an instinctive expert on human psychology, he states in the article. "If you talk, you'll like me," he explains. "If I talk, I'll like you—but if I do the talking, my business will not be served. Now this fellow is the same as everyone else. His wife doesn't listen to him—and he doesn't listen to her. When he goes to parties, the person he's talking to is looking over his shoulder to see what else is going on in the room. Then all of a sudden he goes to breakfast with me. He starts to answer a question. *And he doesn't get interrupted.*" Before the eggs have cooled, Greene has won another client.[3]

Another type of communication that is not shown in Figure 7.2 is *nonverbal communication*. Research has shown that as much as 65 percent of communication between people can be nonverbal. In other words, *how* people say something is often more important than *what* they say. Part of the process of listening entails being sensitive to all the non-verbal, often unconscious, hints people give you about how they feel about you and your medium or product. People's posture and body movement, their facial expressions, their eye contact and movement, their tone of voice and pitch, and their pace of talking usually tell more about how they feel than the content of their messages does. Salespeople must not only develop skills in picking up nonverbal messages but also in using nonverbal communication to give messages.

When selling, look for the attributes and postures described below that might indicate how the other person is receiving your message. Keep in mind that these attributes and postures do not give universal messages that have the same meaning for everyone. Body language, tone of voice, gestures, and facial expressions are unique to each person and communicate consistent meaning only for them. As you get to know your prospects better, you will learn to understand their non-verbal language as well as you understand their words. Exhibit 7.3 shows several pairs of body language clues and their meaning.

**Exhibit 7.3
Non-Verbal Clues**

Closed/Open. Arms folded across the chest keeping you and your ideas out; or letting your ideas in with arms dropped, legs apart.

Backward/Forward. Leaning backward to get away from or be cautious of your ideas; or leaning forward to hear better, becoming more interested.

Rigid/Yielding. Standing or sitting upright or stiff, jaw tight, letting nothing sway them; or yielding, nodding agreement, accepting.

Static/Agitated. Unmoving, no enthusiasm, bored; or excited moving, interested.

Tense/Relaxed. Tight, impenetrable, skeptical, careful; or easygoing, open, casual.

Frowning/Smiling. Hostile, not trusting, unfriendly; or friendly, helpful, caring.

Distant/Close. Uncomfortably guarding their physical space, threatened; or intimate, involved.

Loud/Soft. Speaking loudly, aggressively, energetically, combatively; or softly, submissively, delicately, hesitatingly.

Fast/Slow. Speaking rapidly, not pausing, excitedly, carelessly; or slowly, lots of pauses, carefully.

Use gestures, space, enthusiasm, openness, and other body language to help you emphasize your sales points and to show customers that you care about them and are interested in them, but make sure your gestures are in sync with the person with whom you are talking. Of course, you can overdo the use of gestures. You can become too excited and animated with a shy, inhibited, quiet prospect, for instance. One particular gesture to avoid is finger pointing. This gesture implies "I'm telling you what to do" or "Shame on you" or other authoritarian messages that impedes open communication.

Feedback

To be an effective listener, you have to close the feedback loop in the communication process. You must listen actively and give *responsive feedback*. You must give both verbal and nonverbal feedback, including gestures and expressions, and communicate the appropriate enthusiasm as you actively encourage people to open up. The most important single thing you can do in giving responsive feedback is to *smile*. A smile says, "I like you; I care about you; I'm interested in what you're saying; I'm glad I'm here with you; I approve of you." Nodding your head in agreement is another effective feedback mechanism. Use it often.

Perception

Perception is how people interpret the world around them and try to make sense out of it so they can act. People paint a picture of their world on the canvas of their mind's eye, and, as is the case with real artists, everyone's picture is different. People act based on how they interpret their environment, and all people view their worlds differently, but not necessarily accurately. A television network salesperson may perceive a $2.3 million 30-second spot in the Super Bowl as a genuine bargain, but a customer new to broadcast network television might perceive it to be an outrageous scalping.

What is most important to salespeople is how perception influences one person's view of another. First, salespeople must be aware of these perceptual influences to recognize and to avoid perceptual pitfalls in their own attempt to understand prospects' personalities. Second, salespeople must be aware of these influences because the influences affect how prospects form impressions of them. According to author Richard M. Steers, who has written on the topic of organizational behavior, there are seven influences that color people's perception of others. I have adopted six of Steers's influences in the following list: (1) stereotyping, (2) first impressions, (3) projection, (4) halo effects, (5) selective perception, and (6) ostrichitis.[4]

Table 7.1 summarizes these barriers to perception.

**Table 7.1
Barriers to Accurate
Perception**

Barrier	Definition
Stereotyping	Assign attributes to people solely on the basis of their class or personality type.
First Impressions	Consider first impressions of others to be their enduring traits.
Projection	Ascribe to others those negative traits or feelings we have about ourselves.
Halo Effects	Allow people's dominant traits to influence our impressions of their other traits.
Selective Perception	Systematically screen or discredit information we do not wish to hear and to focus instead on more salient information.
Ostrichitis	Distort or ignore information that is either personally threatening or culturally unacceptable.

Stereotyping.   One of the most common perceptual errors people make is *stereotyping.* People tend to pigeonhole others into a predetermined category or stereotype. For example, we tend to assume that older people are old-fashioned, conservative, and obstinate; and we sometimes assume that salespeople are sly, tricky, and loud. Stereotypical thinking usually has some basis in fact. People tend to compare their own social, demographic, or job groups with others, and thus they generalize and emphasize certain of the more dominant and typical traits. The mistake is to assume that the generalization holds for all individuals.

Salespeople must learn to make stereotypes—their own and their customers'—work for them. Recognize your own tendency to stereotype people, and use stereotypes only during the first few minutes of an introductory meeting to help you in your initial adjustment. Keep an open mind as you get feedback during a sales call and change your original assessment as you observe customers' behavior.

Some customers might harbor a stereotype that all young people are wet behind the ears and lack expertise. You must be able to recognize how customers perceive you, and if they put you into such a stereotypical category, you must work to counteract it. Therefore, if prospects stereotype you as a rookie, it is up to you to change their perception of you from inexperienced and mistake-prone to an expert who is reliable.

First Impressions.   We all have a tendency to make quick *first impressions.* We see what people are wearing, what their verbal style is, and try to guess their approximate age and then tend to make a snap judgment based on this limited exposure. Worse, we tend to stay with this classification and continue to look for clues, behavior, and traits that support this snap judgment.

This tendency creates the classic good news/bad news quandary. It is great news if a prospect has made a wonderful first impression on you and then spends the rest of a sales call reinforcing this favorable perception. It is bad news if somehow you get off on the wrong foot and make a poor first impression.

Learn to play a little game with yourself. As soon as you meet a prospect, ask yourself what your first impression is. If it is negative, pretend that your boss told you the prospect is the greatest person the boss ever met and look for reasons to confirm this view. If your first impression is positive, pretend your boss told you the prospect is a monster and look for reasons to confirm this. In other words, make a conscious effort to overcome your first impression and give yourself time to make an objective, rational judgment.

Always try to make an excellent first impression on your prospects. These initial impressions are typically formed within 15 seconds of meeting a person, so make those few precious moments work for you. Dressing the part of a successful, professional individual is probably most important in molding a first impression. When you realize you have made the wrong first impression, do not try to talk your way out of it. Retreat gracefully and try again another day.

Projection.   *Projection* is a defense mechanism people use to bolster their self-images. They unconsciously see others as a mirror reflecting back their own traits. For instance, stingy, greedy, and mistrustful people are apt to think everyone is the same. The habitual liar believes everyone lies and trusts no one. By being conscious of your behavior and carefully observing other's behavior, you will avoid the trap of projecting your traits onto others and you can see projection in others. Think about projection the next time someone says to you, "Everyone is out to cheat you; you have to be careful." Are you going to trust this person, are you going to believe that this person is not going to try to cheat you? Get in the habit of projecting your own honesty and trustworthiness by trusting others until you learn to do otherwise.

You can take advantage of prospects' tendency to project by matching your behavior to that of your prospects. If you see that a prospect is open, confident, and positive, you should act that way, too. If you see a prospect is mistrusting, skeptical, and cautious, then adopt a conspiratorial approach. Let prospects know you will help them avoid being taken advantage of by others.

Halo Effects.   *Halo effects* can be positive or negative. One trait can color people's impressions of other totally unrelated traits. For example, in a study done by the U.S. Army, a group of officers who were well liked was judged by their subordinates to be more intelligent than less well liked officers. People often attribute a number of positive qualities to celebrities simply because they are well known.

Research has also shown that negative information about people more strongly influences impressions of other people than positive information does. This fact is a good reason to avoid selling negatively (among many other good reasons for not doing it). If you sell negatively and knock the competition, your competitors certainly will do the same in retribution. We will give you even more reasons not to knock the competition in Chapter 8.

To overcome the halo effect, practice describing people in terms of a mosaic of traits, not just a single outstanding one. See people as they really are, and remind yourself that just because customers seem to like you and act friendly does not mean they will necessarily pay their bills on time.

Also, make halo effects work for you. Put your best foot forward from the start, emphasize the strongest point about your medium and your station or publication, and show the best aspects of your personality and appearance by being as attractive, friendly, and knowledgeable as possible.

Selective Perception.   *Selective perception* is the tendency for people to see and hear things they want to see and hear—to seek out those elements in their environment that correspond to and support their previously formed beliefs. Due to the common tendency toward selective perception, it is easier for people to accept information that supports their current beliefs and attitudes than to accept information that is contrary to what they perceive to be true. For instance, people may listen to a newscaster on a local television station because of a belief that the newscaster has similar political inclinations to their own. The success of the Fox News Channel can be explained, to some degree, by selective perception.

People also tend to focus on the information that is most salient to them. Those with accounting backgrounds, say, may be more apt to focus on numbers; those whose interests lie in the arts and show business will tend to focus on aesthetic and creative elements.

People also perceive their products and their companies as better than others, and seek information to support this bias. The tendency toward selective perception can be a salesperson's strong ally when used to reinforce prospects' opinions. In other words, people love others to agree with them and to show how right they are. New car buyers watch automobile commercials more attentively for the car they just bought than they did before their purchase.

Ostrichitis.   Often people tend to ignore or avoid information and, like the proverbial ostrich, stick their heads in the sand. We not only avoid facing events we find unpleasant but also those we feel we cannot handle. Thus, if customers find your heavily numbers-oriented proposal numbingly threatening, they may simply ignore it or dismiss your evidence as irrelevant rather than admit they do not understand it.

You can overcome your own tendency toward *ostrichitis* by disciplining yourself to do the most difficult tasks first: Call on the toughest prospects early, do boring paperwork immediately, and force yourself to hear all feedback, even negative feedback, that your management and customers offer.

Techniques for Effective Listening

In the Introduction to this chapter, I listed the Five Barriers to Human Communication and the Five Principles of Ethical Persuasion from *The Power of Ethical Persuasion*: (1) Respect in the presence of feelings, (2) problem-solving can wait until full mutual understanding is achieved, (3) listen to the other person's viewpoint first, (4) restate the other person's viewpoint, and (5) change yourself in a positive direction.

The concept of restating another person's viewpoint is based on a foundation of some of the earliest and most important communication research conducted by Carl Rogers. In a 1952 article in the *Harvard Business Review,* Rogers wrote under the heading "Barrier: The Tendency to Evaluate" that "we all have a natural urge to judge, evaluate, and approve (or disapprove) another person's statement." He went on further to write, "Although making evaluations is common in almost all conversations, this reaction is heightened in situations where feelings and emotions are deeply involved. So the stronger the feelings, the less likely it is that there will be a mutual understanding in the communication."

Under the heading "Gateway: Listening with Understanding," Rogers writes:

"If you think that you listen well and yet have never seen such results, your listening probably has not been of the type I am describing. Here's one way to test the quality of the type I am describing. The next time you get into an argument with your spouse, friend, or small group of friends, stop the discussion for a moment and suggest this rule: 'Before each person speaks up, he or she must *first* restate the ideas and feelings of the previous speaker accurately and to that speaker's satisfaction.'"

Later in the same article Rogers writes:

So why is this listening approach not more widely used? There are several reasons.

Lack of courage. Listening with understanding means taking a very real risk. If you really understand another person in his way, if you are willing to enter his private world and see the way life appears to him, without any attempt to make evaluative judgments, you run the risk of being changed yourself. You might see things his way; you might find that the he has influenced your attitudes or your personality.

Most of us are afraid to take that risk. So instead we cannot *listen*; we find ourselves compelled to *evaluate* because listening seems too dangerous.[5]

Exhibit 7.4 shows you the *techniques for active, non-judgmental (non-evaluative) listening*, Exhibit 7.5 shows you some *barriers to active, non-judgmental listening*, and Exhibit 7.6 shows *non-judgmental responses*. Like an actor rehearsing lines for a play, a salesperson who wants to master the art of selling must practice active, non-judgmental listening over and over and over until it becomes second nature.

Exhibit 7.4
Techniques for Active, Non-Judgmental Listening

1. **Ask a question.**

2. **Listen to the answer carefully, actively.** For example, wave your hand toward yourself, which gives the message, "Tell me more." Notice what gestures the people you are listening to use. Are they very expressive and do they motion with their hands a lot? Then get in sync with them. Use their gestures. Are they calm and analytical? Do they lean back and ponder things with their fingers intertwined and their chins resting on their folded hands? Get in sync with them.

3. **Respond non-judgmentally.** Non-judgmental listening is non-defensive listening. Don't argue or defend your point of view. Nod, smile, and encourage them to continue talking.
   A. **Develop a non-threatening, non-confrontational approach.** You want people to feel *secure* in opening up, revealing personal information.
   B. **Offer personal information first.** People will reciprocate by giving you personal information.
   C. **Find something you have in common.** Similar interests such as kids, sports, or pets, for example.
   D. **Similar interests create common bonds.** Common bonds create openness, honesty, and trust.
   E. **Vary your responses.** Otherwise your responses become monotonous and recognizable as a technique and not authentic.

**Exhibit 7.5
Barriers to Active,
Non-Judgmental
Listening: Nine
"Nevers"**

1. **Never ask "Why?"** "Why?" questions are challenging to someone. When you ask "Why?" you sound like you doubt what they are saying or are testing them. "Why?" questions send bad emotional vibes.

2. **Never ask leading questions**. Leading questions such as, "Have you stopped beating your wife?" or "Are you still paying those outrageously high newspaper rates?" are challenging and produce frustration and anger.

3. **Never minimize a problem**. This response seems natural, as though you are trying to help someone feel better, that things are not as bad as they seem. However, you are being judgmental and making an assumption that you know more than the person complaining does. Furthermore, you are there to help solve their problems, so the bigger the problems are, the more you can help, so don't minimize problems. Finally, some people love to complain, so do them a favor and let them—"feel their pain."

4. **Never cheer up or reassure**. These responses make you seem happier or more knowledgeable than the person who is speaking. It may be counterintuitive, but telling someone to cheer up maybe unrealistic. It's better to share their misery; develop empathy and demonstrate your supportive feelings.

5. **Never advise or teach**. These responses make you superior and make the other person feel inferior. You may come across as arrogant. You want to be people's trusted friend, not their teacher.

6. **Never criticize or moralize**. These responses are highly judgmental and frustrate and anger other people.

7. **Never argue or defend**. These responses are completely counterproductive and move a conversation backward, not forward. The moment you become defensive, you lose control of the agenda of a conversation and lose rapport and credibility—you are seen as not being objective (and you aren't).

8. **Never be aggressive**. Aggressive responses make you appear competitive instead of cooperative and look as though you are trying to get what you want instead of what the other person wants.

9. **Never respond with "you" statements**. "You" responses are those that begin with "you," such as, "You shouldn't be paying those high rates on other stations." "You" statements appear to be accusatory or seem to be telling other people what they "should" do. Never, never use the word "should" in a response; it is completely judgmental.

Source: Many of the "Never" responses are based on suggestions from Zaiss and Gordon, 1993.

All knowledge, all learning about a customer, begins with a question such as, "How's business?", or "How can I help you?", "What are your marketing goals?" or "How about those Raiders?" Therefore, all effective listening techniques begin with a question. These techniques work in a business or a personal conversation, but it is a good idea to practice them often at the beginning in personal situations, with family and friends, and become comfortable and adept at these listening techniques before attempting them with customers. Here are guidelines and exercises that will help you become a World-Class effective, non-judgmental listener.

Use all of the techniques for effective listening to achieve the goal of becoming a *trusted advisor* to your clients. Keep the concept of being a trusted advisor in the back of your mind as you progress through conversations with customers and always return to the question, "Am I behaving and listening in a manner that my customer believes I am a trusted advisor and am not merely trying to sell something?"

Exhibit 7.6
Non-Judgmental
Response

1. **A non-committal response**. Responses such as "Oh," or "I see," are non-judgmental and non-committal. Responses such as "Yes," or "Right," or "Exactly," indicate you are judging the speaker's responses.

2. **The "I understand" response**. This response takes the burden of understanding on yourself; it is the ideal response because it does not indicate that you agree with or are judging the other person in the conversation, but are, in a sense, honoring them by saying that they have explained themselves well and that you understand. It puts you on their side—you are forming a conspiracy of understanding.

3. **Other "I" statement responses**. Zaiss and Gordon indicate that there are five types of "I" statements:

   A. **Declarative "I" statements**. These types of "I" statements declare your belief, ideas, likes, dislikes, feelings, and thoughts. For example, "Joe, I believe television is the most effective advertising medium by far," or "Charlie, I have put together a campaign that I think will meet your needs; I hope you'll like it." As often as possible and appropriate, use the customer's name in your responses because people love to hear their names; it's also a more familiar type of communication.

   B. **Preventive "I" statements**. This type of "I" statement announces what you want to see happen in the future and increases your chances that others will adjust. For example, "Jane, I would like to start our meeting and end it in 20 minutes because I want to leave time at the end for questions," or "Deborah, I would like to have your answer on my offer by Friday because I must place the order by then to get it in the paper." Note the "because" statements—this word is important because it gives an explanation for what you want someone to do and greatly increases your odds of getting them to do it.

   C. **Responsive "I" statements**. These types of "I" statements respond to a customer's request for something you can't do. It is always best to give an honest answer and take responsibility on your shoulders for not doing something and not put in on the shoulders of someone else, for instance, management. For example, if you responded to a request for lower rates by saying, "Judy, I'd love to, but my sales manager won't let me," you put the burden on your sales manager and indicate you are not in control. Your customer might say, "Well, check with your sales manager and tell her you'll lose the business if you don't lower your rates." You now have to delay the discussion because you have shown you have no power. In this case, it would be much better to respond with, "Judy, I don't want to lower my rates because it wouldn't be fair to my other advertisers or to the station." It's always best to take responsibility for saying "no," and to give an explanation with a "because" statement.

   D. **Appreciative "I" statements**. These types of "I" statements are the easiest to make because they show your appreciation to customers and make them feel good. For example, "Bob, I appreciate your flexibility in adjusting our meeting time because I ran late with another customer," or "Mark, thank you so much for getting back to me in the prompt and concise way you did because it really helped me put together a meaningful presentation." People love compliments as long as they are sincere. In general, you can never be too appreciative too often.

   E. **Confrontive "I" statements**. These type of "I" statements should be used when you have a problem with the statements or behavior of a customer. The customer is not always right and you have rights that at times need to be asserted. It is vital that you do not confront in a blaming fashion, but tell customers how you feel about their behavior. For example, "Paul, you've said that you'd place your schedule 'today' the last three times I've called you. I can't get you in the paper now, and I'm really concerned," or "Emily, the last three times I've called on you, you've kept me waiting for over a half hour. I lost a big order the last time because I couldn't get to an important customer in time. I'm very frustrated." It's important that you not tell people what they have done wrong because you're judging them, but it is important that you tell people how you feel about their behavior and how if affects you.

Source: Zaiss and Gordon, 1993.

90

Exhibit 7.7 provides you with an effective listening exercise that you should practice regularly.

**Exhibit 7.7
Effective Listening
Exercise**

1. **Listen carefully and actively to objections, questions, or statements of your customers.**

2. **Repeat or rephrase their objection.**
   "Let me make sure I understand your position . . . you feel our rates are too high?" Put the burden of understanding on yourself. By repeating or rephrasing an objection, you let your customers know that you are listening and that you heard what they were saying—they like that.

3. **Get their agreement that you understand.**
   "Is that correct?" This is a powerful step in the process because getting their agreement that you understand their objection assures them that you are on their side. You are encouraging them to say "Yes," a habit you want them to get into. If they say, "No," then you must follow up and clarify their objection, and keep doing so until you get it right and they agree that you understand.

4. **Respond with a form of an "I understand" statement (vary your responses).**
   "I understand how you *feel*, other advertisers have *felt* the same way, but they have *found* that our rates are based on market demand and the size of our audience. We have the largest audience in town and the largest number of advertisers of any station in the area, and those advertisers are paying our rates and getting great results." The feel/felt/found responses are incredibly powerful because with the "feel" response you are acknowledging your customers' feelings and respecting them. The "felt" response reinforces and legitimizes their objections so they don't feel silly, out of line, or alone. The "found" response gives you the opportunity to mention the benefits and advantages of what you are offering in the context of the success enjoyed by other advertisers—comforting knowledge for a prospective advertiser.

Practice the effective listening exercise in Exhibit 7.7 as often as you can until you become comfortable with variations on the feel/felt/found technique and are an expert in becoming a trusted advisor. You can download all of the exhibits in this chapter, which appear in one file titled "Effective Listening," from www.mediaselling.us. By downloading these exhibits, you can have them all in one packet to make them easier to study and review. Documents to Go, downloaded from www.dataviz.com, is an excellent program I use that allows me to transfer Word, Excel, and PowerPoint files to my Palm-Pilot-compatible Sony Clié so I can review documents such as the Effective Listening techniques before making a call.

Understanding People

If you are an effective, World-Class listener, that is great, but what are you listening for? Are you listening to find out what makes people tick, to understand them as human beings, or are you listening to them as targets in a business game? In order to understand people we must know what makes people behave as they do.

**The Personality-
Type Approach**

One way we can try to understand people is with a personality-type approach. There are several well-known personality-type descriptive methods; probably the most recognized is the Myers-Briggs Type Indicator (MBTI) which divides people into four classifications and then into two preferences within each classification. The classifications are:

1. How people direct their energy: Extroversion (E) or Introversion (I)
2. How people prefer to process information: Sensing (S) or Intuition (N)
3. How people prefer to make decisions: Thinking (T) or Feeling (F)
4. How people prefer to organize their life: Judgment (J) Perception (P)[6]

Myers-Briggs personality types are then defined by a combination of these four preferences, such as an ISTP (perhaps a journalist) or an ENTJ (perhaps a business executive).

Perhaps the personality-type approach most widely used in business today is the Persogenics style approach, which was developed in the 1960s by Dr. Ford Cheney. The current management of Persogenics claims that their personality profiling method produces more accurate results than Myers-Briggs tests do. The Persogenics approach trains people to identify their own style (by taking a self-administered test) and to identify the style of others using detailed descriptions of the behavior of four types of people. The four types of styles Persogenics identifies are:[7]

1. The Dominant—assertive, outspoken, controlling, task-oriented, driving for results
2. The Expressive—assertive, highly responsive, forceful, demonstrative, people-oriented
3. The Analytical—not assertive, less responsive, task-oriented, disciplined, more interested in information than people
4. The Amiable—not assertive, not forceful, people- and team-oriented, peacemakers

Persogenics suggests that if you follow their program, you can adjust your behavior to match customers' styles. Persogenics suggests that people have a primary and secondary style. Therefore, you might be Expressive/Dominant and a customer you are meeting with might be Dominant/Analytical. With this customer, you would tone down your expressive enthusiasm and focus quietly on a logical, fact-laden presentation with lots of data for the customer to analyze. Persogenics is an excellent system for helping salespeople communicate and build rapport with customers because it builds on the similarity principle. But like any commercial service or system, it requires time, professional training, test taking, and money. The tests and training are not inexpensive, especially for one person.

How can we identify someone's personality type or style without having them take a test or without going through potentially expensive training? And are personality-type and personal style descriptions the best way to understand people?

While personality-type and personal style descriptions are interesting and often fun to talk about, they are a relatively simplistic description of the way people behave. In fact, they almost sound like stereotypes, and as we learned earlier, depending on stereotypes to gain deeper understanding of people can be shallow and foolish. Also, describing how people behave does not give us much insight into why they behave that way, or what their needs and motivations are.

The Needs-Motivation Approach

Why do people behave as they do? What are the underlying reasons for their actions? What drives their personality or style? Psychologists, psychiatrists, and other scientists try to answer these questions to understand, predict, and help people change their behavior. Likewise, salespeople must try to understand, predict, and when necessary and appropriate, alter customers' behavior.

Behavior is the outcome of a process that begins with needs, which impel motives, which lead to behavior. Behavior is the only portion of this process that is observable. We cannot see people's motives or the underlying needs that lead to motives, but we can observe their behavior and try to infer why they act as they do. Needs are not only unobservable but they are also usually unconscious. Even though people act to satisfy their needs, they may not be consciously aware of these needs. Figure 7.3 shows the needs-motivation-behavior process.

**Figure 7.3
The needs-motivation-behavior process.**

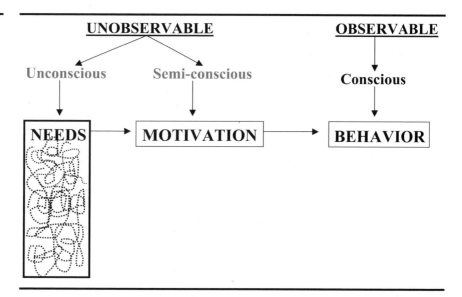

People have multiple needs that are swirling around in their unconscious psyche trying to get recognized and be satisfied. Some of the stronger needs push and impel, or motivate, behavior. Needs are a vague, indefinable itch in the psyche, motives are the semiconscious desire or semiautomatic reaction to scratch, and behavior is the physical act of scratching. Because we can only see them scratching, we infer people have an itch (whereas it might just be a nervous habit). Needs can be uncovered but they cannot be created. People either have a need (itch) or they do not; salespeople cannot create needs because those needs have been formulated early in their prospects' personality development.

It is much more difficult to make a list of motivations, or motives, than to create a list of needs because motives tend to be impelled by the force of a cluster of complex needs that are unique to every person and to every situation. Some people have a small cluster of needs that drives their behavior; other people have multiple needs that interact in a complex way. After we look at the different needs that people have, we will examine more about motivation later in this chapter.

Maslow's Theory of Needs.   Many researchers have contributed to our ideas about human needs. Here, we will take a brief look at some of the major theories.

Abraham H. Maslow's Hierarchy of Needs is the most widely known theory of individual needs and motives. In 1954 he theorized that people are motivated by a desire to satisfy several types of needs simultaneously and that these needs are arranged in a hierarchical manner. Maslow believed that people work their way up from lower to higher ones as each level of needs is satisfied (see Table 7.2).

Table 7.2 Maslow's Hierarchy of Needs (Highest to Lowest)		
Self-actualization	The highest level of people's needs: realization of their unique potential.	
Esteem needs	People's needs for respect from others and a sense of competence within themselves.	
Belongingness and social relations needs	People's needs for closeness, caring, and love.	
Safety and security needs	People's needs for a predictable environment and control over that environment.	
Basic physiological needs	People's lowest level of needs: air, water, food, shelter, sleep, and sex.	

Source: Abraham H. Maslow. 1954. "A Theory of Human Motivation," *Motivation and Personality, 2nd ed.* New York: Harper & Row, Publishers, Inc. Used with permission from Harper & Row, New York.

Subsequent psychological research showed that people are so enormously complex that it is virtually impossible to generalize about any need's hierarchy that fits all people. After the basic existence needs (physiological needs and safety and security needs) are satisfied, one person may feel a strong need for self-fulfillment, another person may feel a strong need for achievement and recognition, and yet another person may sense a huge urge for social acceptance. Thus, Maslow's contribution was to classify needs into theoretical groups and to postulate that people tend to take care of the basic, lower-order needs first.

Salespeople must understand that people do not have simple motivations or needs and that understanding people requires a complex analysis of their unique, individual combination and hierarchy of needs.

Murray's Needs.   Henry Murray developed a needs theory in the 1930s and 1940s that he called the *Manifest Needs Theory,* which has been used subsequently as a starting point for many researchers, sales trainers, and authors. Murray thought people should be classified according to the strengths of various needs and he believed people possessed a number of divergent and conflicting needs.

Murray believed that needs are learned, not inherited, and are activated by cues from the external environment (a sales discussion, for example). He did not arrange his list of needs in a hierarchical fashion, as Maslow did, but his longer list of specific human needs is more useful in describing people and in helping us understand them than Maslow's more generalized list of needs.

Updated List of Human Needs.   Table 7.3 presents a list of human needs I have adapted from a list of Murray's needs (he originally posited 34 needs),

	Need	Brief Description
Table 7.3 **Human Needs**	**Achievement**	Need to overcome obstacles and challenges. To aspire to accomplish difficult tasks; to maintain high standards. To work hard to achieve goals. To respond positively to competition. To put forth extra effort to achieve and maintain excellence.
	Affiliation	Need to form friendships and associations. To enjoy being with friends and people in general, and to accept people readily. To cooperate. To enjoy joining and being with groups.
	Aggression	Need to belittle, harm, blame, ridicule, or accuse another. To start arguments. To be willing to hurt others to get one's way. To have a tendency to "get even." To be overly competitive. To be sadistic.
	Autonomy	Need to resist influence or coercion. To break away from restraint, confinement, or restrictions of any kind. To enjoy being free, unattached, and not tied to people, places, or obligations. To resist authority. To seek independence.
	Competition	Need to be involved in competitive activities. To win. To beat someone else. To do anything to win.
	Conservativeness	Need to hold on to what one has. To refrain from losing what has been gained. To avoid change because it is change. To stick with tradition and past values, beliefs, opinions, and practices.
	Contrariness	Need to act differently from others. To hold unconventional views. To be contrary. To take a stand opposite from others merely for the sake of being different. To argue just for the sake of arguing.
	Control	Need to have control over as many things that affect one's life as possible. To avoid delegating responsibility or tasks to others. To keep work, information, and decision-making under one's control. To control all possible variables in an attempt to make life predictable and free of surprises.
	Cooperation	Need to cooperate. To be a team player. To help others. To be fair. To seek win-win agreements.
	Creativeness	Need to seek and enjoy aesthetic impressions and experiences. Artistic. Imaginative. To enjoy the creative process and building or designing things. To enjoy participating in and experiencing music, dance, theater, or art.
	Defensiveness	Need to defend oneself against any blame or real or imagined belittlement. To justify one's actions. To offer excuses and explanations. To resist probing. To interpret other people's comments, no matter how innocent, in the most personal, negative way possible.
	Deference	Need to admire and willingly follow a superior or another person. To cooperate with a leader. To serve gladly. To defer to others in most things.
	Dominance	Need to seek power. To attempt to influence and control others. To persuade, prohibit, or dictate. To lead or direct. To express opinions forcefully. To try to organize and lead groups. To be political and gain power through political means.
	Endurance	Need to work long hours. Not to give up easily on problems, even in the face of great difficulty. To be patient and unrelenting in one's work habits.
	Entrepreneurism	Need to start something new. To build from the ground up. To take big risks in order to win big.
	Exhibition	Need to attract attention to one's self. To excite, amuse, shock, or thrill others. To be dramatic or funny.
	Impulsiveness	Need to act on the spur of the moment and without deliberation. To make decisions too quickly. To give vent readily to feelings and desires. To speak freely—may be volatile in expressing emotions.

continued

Table 7.3 (continued)	Need	Brief Description
	Insecurity	Need to be emotionally insecure. To have low self-esteem. To seek aid, protection, or sympathy. To constantly seek advice, affection, attention, and reassurance. To be dependent and to feel insecure or helpless. To confide difficulties and insecurities to a receptive person.
	Novelty	Need to seek new experiences. To change for the sake of change. To seek variety and excitement. To prefer things because they are new and/or different.
	Nurturance	To nourish, aid, or protect someone else. To give sympathy and comfort. To assist whenever possible. To give a helping hand readily and to perform favors for others.
	Order	Need to arrange, organize, and put away objects. To be tidy and clean. To be scrupulously precise and orderly. To be interested in developing methods to keep materials and effects methodically organized.
	Play	Need to relax, to amuse oneself. To seek diversion and entertainment. To have fun and love to play games. To laugh and joke.
	Recognition	Need to receive praise and commendation. To receive attention and to gain approval. To crave appreciation. To earn praise. To seek and display symbols of status.
	Risk-Avoidance	Need to avoid failure, shame, or any possibility of loss. To take precautionary measures. To cover up anything that looks like a failure and often to have an unreasonable, obsessive fear of failure.
	Risk-Taking	Need to enjoy taking risks for the hope of big rewards. To gamble on long-shot odds with large payoffs. To court danger, live near the edge. To be a daredevil.
	Understanding	Need to analyze and understand many areas of knowledge. To be intellectually curious. To be fascinated with ideas. To desire to have all the facts and gain as much knowledge on a subject as possible.

combined with a list of Murray's needs adapted by theorist Douglas N. Jackson, and combined with a list by Joseph Thompson. I have added a few needs to those of Murray, Jackson, and Thompson based on my experience.[8] As you read the list of needs, try to visualize a person you know who you think displays behavior that might be driven by one or more of the needs.

Using the Needs-Motivation Approach.   The personality types (ENTJs, for example) and styles (Amiables, for example) discussed previously in this chapter are attempts to describe or paint a word portrait of a person's cluster of needs. For instance, the Dominant-style person who is assertive, outspoken, controlling, task-oriented, and results-driven might be a person who has the following needs from the list in Table 7.3: achievement, aggression, control, dominance, endurance, and order.

So, while you do not need to know the personality type, temperament, or style of people to understand them, you can create your own portrait of them using the 27 colors (needs) in the Human Needs list by careful observation.

Guidelines for Identifying Needs.   Current research has found that, in general, needs tend to be stable over time. As needs swirl around in the psyche, pushing out into the consciousness in an attempt to get satisfied, over time the same cluster of needs tends to appear. However, the rank order of this cluster of needs changes continually. For example, achievement might be someone's primary need one day, but if the person wins a marathon race the next day, that need bubbles down and recognition bubbles up to the top.

Keeping these facts in mind, here are some guidelines for identifying needs:

1. **Don't try to be a psychiatrist**. Your function is to recognize customers' needs and adjust your behavior accordingly. Your job is not to try to change people or tell them what they should do. For instance, if a customer has a high need for dominance and aggression and terrifies employees, it would not be a good idea to tell the customer that the behavior is destructive.

2. **Deal in the present**. The only thing you can be certain about is that peoples' needs swirl around and change in priority. What their primary needs were one week ago may not be the same the next week. Deal with the moment during which you are having a discussion and make adjustments accordingly. Always remain flexible.

3. **Recognize situational influences.** When a customer responds unfavorably to you, it may have nothing to do with you or your presentation but with other external, situational influences. You may be the fifth salesperson the customer has seen that morning, and the customer may be thoroughly frustrated, confused, and bored; or you may be making your presentation during a busy season in which the customer is constantly being interrupted by calls and questions. The customer may be reacting to the frustration and confusion of the situation and not to you. Take these situational influences into consideration when you try to identify needs.[9]

With practice, careful observation, and concentrated listening, salespeople can learn to infer their customer's needs. With careful observation, salespeople can recognize the few dominant needs that seem to motivate their customers' actions. Download the list of Human Needs in Exhibit 7.7 from www.mediaselling.us, print it, and put it in a handy place where you can refer to it easily; also download it to your personal digital assistant (PDA). After making a call, review the Human Needs list, create a needs-based portrait (more about this later in this chapter), and put the portrait in your account file. Chapter 28 will cover account files and sales organization systems. As you get to know your customers better, you can review your account file and your needs-based portrait to verify your observations. If you have perceived your customer's needs correctly, you have gained a powerful tool to position yourself and your product to have a competitive advantage.

For example, when calling on a customer, scrutinize the customer's office. Is it filled with pictures of him or her being chummy with famous and powerful people (such as the car dealer shaking hands with a baseball star or the governor)? This customer has a need for recognition. Position your product so that it appeals to this recognition need: "You and your dealership will both become well known and credible if you do your own commercials," for example.

Does a customer keep you waiting for 20 minutes for a scheduled appointment and then interrupt your discussion by taking phone calls? This customer has a need for dominance. Show respect for and defer to this customer but do not back down easily or seem to be weak. People who have a need for dominance and power over others do not like wimpy people. Position your product according to the customer's desire to beat the competition, to achieve success, to accomplish marketing and advertising goals.

Does a customer ask intelligent, probing questions and want to learn as much as possible about your business? This customer has a need for understanding. Position yourself, your medium, and your product as offering solutions to advertising problems with detailed presentations containing lots of facts and figures.

Is the customer's desk bare: no reports, no folders, or no piles of papers? This customer has a need for order. Position yourself as a tidy, orderly salesperson who takes care of all the little details involved with getting an advertising campaign up and running.

Does a customer talk about goals and challenges? Does the customer use sports analogies or talk in terms of winning or attaining excellence? This customer has a need for achievement. Position your medium and your product as a means for the customer to win, to beat the competition, to achieve success, to accomplish marketing and advertising goals.

A Needs-Based Portrait.   Now that we have identified 27 colors/needs, we can now create a needs-based portrait of someone using a mixture of five, six, or seven colors. The chances are pretty good that if we tried to name our portrait, we would come up with something like The Achiever, The Expressive, or The Idealist—types used by other descriptive systems. Each portrait will be as unique as each person is and much more complex and informative than just the title. But what about motivation?

If you identify a cluster of five, six, or seven needs that seem to drive a person's behavior, then you have enough information to help position your medium and your product to align with those needs and you do not have to worry about motivation. It does not matter why someone does something (greed, pride, lust, love, or revenge, for example); what matters is that you have identified several needs that drive that motivation.

Some people will have a relatively small number of primary needs that drive their behavior, others might have multiple needs. Also, people often have a different cluster of needs and motivation in business than they do in non-business situations. It is important to get to know your customers well enough so that you can paint two needs-based portraits of them because it can be extremely helpful in maintaining relationships.

For example, some people might have needs primarily for achievement, control, and dominance, and those needs drive their behavior. In business situations they might be competitive and stingy. In a non-business, family environment, they might be cooperative, nurturing, and generous. Some people might have needs for achievement, affiliation, cooperation, creativeness, exhibition, recognition, play, and understanding. In business situations they might be friendly, somewhat disorganized team players who crave being well liked. In a non-business environment they might take acting or painting classes for their own pleasure and growth and not care what people think.

Exhibit 7.8 shows how a personal needs-based portrait of a customer might look.

Note in Exhibit 7.8 that Jane Doe's needs are not arranged in alphabetical order, they are arranged in the order of their perceived (by the salesperson) priority. When you identify needs, you are making an educated guess. You know your perception of Jane's needs are not precise and are subject to change, but your intuition tells you that she clearly is not a risk-taker and is very defensive—during the last four times you have called on her, she has consistently behaved in ways that would indicate her risk-avoidance and defensiveness. She always asks for rating guarantees and wants to buy something safe. She reacts

Exhibit 7.8 Customer Personal Needs-Based Portrait	**Customer:** Jane Doe, Dewey, Cheatham, and Howe Advertising Agency
	Personal Needs— Business Situations: **Personal Needs— Non-Business Situations:**

Personal Needs— Business Situations:
- Risk-avoidance *
- Defensiveness *
- Recognition
- Control
- Competition
- Autonomy
- Contrariness

Personal Needs— Non-Business Situations:
- Affiliation *
- Novelty
- Recognition
- Deference
- Play
- Nurturance

* Most dominant needs

very defensively about what she has bought on other stations. You are pretty sure that risk-avoidance and defensiveness are the two needs that tend to be the strongest and motivate her buying behavior.

When you create a needs-based portrait of someone, try to pick out one or two needs that seem to dominate and then try to arrange the rest of the needs you identify in order of priority. This arrangement will help you when it comes to positioning your product.

Personal Needs Versus Business Needs

The needs we have been discussing up to this point have been *personal needs*. There are two types of needs, *personal needs* and *business needs*. *Personal* needs are primarily governed by emotions and could just as well be labeled *emotional* needs. *Business needs* are mainly governed by reasoned, problem-solving behavior and could just as well be labeled *rational needs*. *Personal needs*, as discussed earlier, include the need for recognition, achievement, or dominance. *Business needs* are the reasons people give for their purchases—the rational justifications.

Sterling Getchel, who was an enormously successful advertising copywriter, observed that people buy for emotional reasons and then support their purchase decision with rational reasons. He became wealthy writing advertising based on this belief. Sales trainer and author Tom Hopkins writes that "seldom do people buy logically."[10] At the other end of the heart-versus-head spectrum are those who claim that people are basically rational beings whose behavior consists of a series of attempts to solve problems to satisfy their needs. Even though both emotional and logical needs interact in varying degrees of intensity in all customers at all times, you will be substantially more successful if you assume that personal, emotional needs outweigh business, rational needs in people's decision making by two to one—go with Sterling Getchel.

Positioning Your Product To Align With Personal Needs. As a salesperson, you will be expected to meet and satisfy, for the most part, customers' business needs as a minimum requirement for getting an order. The majority of media salespeople focus on and are adept at satisfying business needs. The big win, the home run, for salespeople is the ability not just to satisfy business needs, but to *position* their medium and their product to appeal to the emotional, personal needs of customers. You want to understand your customers so well that you can position your offers in such a way that your customers will buy because they like you and because your offer meets their personal needs—so they will justify making an emotional decision with logical reasons.

Remember the second core function of a salesperson from Chapter 2 is *managing relationships*. The first step in managing any relationship is getting the other person to like you; the best way to accomplish this, to a large degree, is to understand and then align with their personal needs.

Test Yourself

1. What are the three equal elements that make up the engine that drives a relationship?
2. What is the goal of a relationship?
3. What are the seven characteristics that enhance source credibility?
4. Name two ordering effects and tell what they mean.
5. What are the six barriers to accurate perception?
6. What are the four steps in the effective listening exercise?
7. What are the four personal styles identified by Persogenics?
8. What are the four needs Maslow identified and in what order do they appear in his hierarchy?
9. What do people rely on more to make decisions, rationality or emotions?

Project

Get together with three or four friends and each create a Customer Needs-Based Portrait of a person not in the group whom all of you know reasonably well. Then, compare the portraits you have created and discuss them. How many of you had the same dominant needs? How many had similar lists? If there were differences, what were they? Finally, after the discussion, reach consensus on a single list of six or seven needs.

References

David Maister. 2002. *The Trusted Advisor.* New York: The Free Press.
Tom Rusk, M.D. 1993. *The Power of Ethical Persuasion.* New York: Viking Books.
Carl D. Zaiss and Thomas Gordon. 1993. *Sales Effectiveness Training.* New York: Random House.

Resources

www.mediaselling.us
www.humanmetrics.com
www.persongenics.com
www.dataviz.com

Endnotes

1. Tom Rusk, M.D. 1993. *The Power of Ethical Persuasion.* New York: Viking. Cover jacket
2. Claude E. Shannon and Warren Weaver. 1949. *The Mathematical Theory of Communication.* Urbana, Ill.: University of Illinois Press. Reprinted by permission of the publisher.
3. Monaci Jo Williams. 1987. *Fortune,* October 26. pp. 122-134
4. Material in this section is adapted from Richard M. Steers. 1981. *Introduction to Organizational Behavior.* Chicago: Foresman. pp. 115-122. Used with permission.
5. Carl Rogers. R. and F.J. Roethlisberger. 1952. *Harvard Business Review.* July-August. pp. 105-106
6. www.teamtechnology.co.uk. January 20, 2003
7. www.persogenics.com. January 20, 2003
8. Henry Murray. 1938. *Explorations in Personality.* New York: Oxford University Press. Used with permission; Douglas N. Jackson. 1974. *Personality Research Form Manual.* Port Huron, Mich.: Research Psychologists Press. Used by permission of Sigma Assessment Systems, Inc.; and Joseph Thompson. 1973. *Selling: A Managerial and Behavioral Science Analysis, 2nd ed.* New York: McGraw Hill.

9. Material in this section is adapted from Gary M. Grikscheit, Harold Cash, and W.J.E. Crissey. 1981. *Handbook of Selling: Psychological, Management, and Marketing Bases.* New York: John Wiley. pp. 184-185. Used with permission.

10. Tom Hopkins. 1980. *How to Master the Art of Selling.* Scottsdale, AZ: Champion Press. P. 46.

8 Skills: Influence and Creating Value

By Charles Warner

When I made my first sales call on Parrott's Flowers, the first question Mr. Parrott asked after he figured out what I was trying to sell him, was, "How much is it?" The how-much-does-it-cost question is typically the first one people ask when they are considering a purchase. If they are inexperienced buyers, they often ask the price question defensively because they do not want to go over an arbitrary price limit they have set. If they are experienced buyers, they often ask the price question because they want to react negatively in an attempt to keep the price as low as possible. Experienced buyers also try to convince sellers that they are selling a commodity.

A *commodity* is a product that is interchangeable with other products, widely available, and, therefore, differentiated only by price. Because commodities are interchangeable with other products, meaning there are many substitutes, it is difficult to charge a higher price than other similar products cost. Because commodities are widely available and, thus, a supply surplus exists, it is often difficult to maintain price levels. And because commodities are products that are differentiated only by price, they are sold to the highest bid among low bids. Examples of commodities are wheat, corn, and soybeans, which are typically sold in commodity markets such as the Chicago Board of Trade.

Advertising agency media buyers and price-conscious advertisers naturally want to convince media salespeople that they are selling undifferentiated commodities and, invariably, start price negotiations as quickly as possible and with an extremely low offer. In fact, media buyers' primary objective is to try to lower media prices; therefore, they want media salespeople to believe they are selling a commodity and to sell based exclusively on price.

The hallmarks of weak or inexperienced media salespeople are that they do not know how to position their products effectively, that they readily accede to buyer demands, and that they sell based only on price. The sales pitch of weak salespeople is, "I have the lowest price," a technique that does not add value. Companies do not need salespeople who can sell based only on low prices; employers can hire hourly-wage order takers to handle commodity-like transactions.

World-Class media salespeople do not sell their product as a commodity and they do not lower their rates except in extreme circumstances. One of the main reasons World-Class salespeople do not discount their rates is because lower prices affect their income; less revenue equals lower commissions or bonuses. Instead, they position themselves and their products persuasively and they create value before they mention or discuss price.

In this chapter you will learn more about some persuasive techniques that can influence people, discover why creating value is important, and learn how to create value for your medium, your company, and yourself.

The Psychology of Influence

In 1984 Robert Cialdini wrote an extremely influential book, *Influence: The Psychology of Persuasion.* In 2001 he published the fourth edition of the book, re-titled *Influence: Science and Practice.* Perhaps he dropped the word persuasion from the title because it has a negative, manipulative connotation.

The concept of persuasion somehow indicates that people are persuaded to do something they would rather not do or that is against their better judgment. This book advocates non-manipulative selling; therefore, the concept of persuasion is dealt with gingerly to emphasize ethical persuasion to be consistent with the book's approach to selling. Thus, any attempt at persuasion will be viewed as *influence*, suggesting that people are being tilted or swayed to consciously, willingly do something more suitable for the relationship-based, solutions-selling approach advocated in this book.

Cialdini writes that he began the study of persuasion and influence because he realized that "All my life I've been a patsy."[1] He was particularly interested in what techniques brought about compliance. He studied compliance practitioners and professionals such as salespeople, fundraisers, and advertisers. He studied compliance using participant observation and gained experience in organizations that practiced persuasion techniques, such as encyclopedia, vacuum cleaner, portrait photography, and dance lessons sales organizations—some of the worst examples of manipulative persuasion techniques. Over a three-year period, Cialdini observed thousands of different tactics that compliance practitioners employed to produce a yes, and he found the majority fell into six basic categories. "Each of these categories is governed by a fundamental psychological principle that directs human behavior, and in so doing, gives the tactics their power."[2]

I have modified Cialdini's list of six principles by combining two, liking and authority, and have added one, which I call automatic responses, which was not on Cialdini's original list. I believe this modified list makes it easier to understand, remember, and use the principles of influence in selling situations.

Exhibit 8.1 shows a modified list of the six principles of influence.

Exhibit 8.1 Principles of Influence

1. Automatic responses
2. Reciprocation
3. Commitment and consistency
4. Social proof
5. Scarcity
6. Liking and authority

Source: Cialdini, 2001.

In a footnote to his list of six principles, Cialdini writes:

It is worth noting that I have not included among the six principles the simple rule of material self-interest: that most people want to get the most and pay the least for their choices. This omission does not stem from any perception on my part that the desire to maximize benefits and minimize costs is unimportant in driving our decisions. Nor does it come from any evidence that I have that compliance professionals ignore the power of this rule. Quite the opposite: in my investigations, I frequently saw practitioners use (sometimes honestly, sometimes not) the compelling, "I can give you a good deal" approach. I chose not to treat the material self-interest rule separately in this book because I see it as a motivational given, as a goes-without-saying factor that deserves acknowledgement, but not extensive description."[3]

What we discern from the above footnote are several extremely important ideas: first, that Cialdini's research is based on his assumption that material self-interest is a universal law; second, that at least one tactic can be used honestly; and last, that the "I-can-give-you-a-good-deal" approach is compelling. Thus, the author is implying that when used appropriately, the principles can be an honest attempt to influence someone. But, as you will learn in Chapter 12, a good deal is not necessarily always the lowest price; everyone has their own definition of a good deal.

Let's now look at each of the six principles of influence separately. While you are reading the descriptions, think of ways that you might use them to honestly and ethically influence people.

Automatic Responses.   Being trained in psychology, Dr. Cialdini begins his research by looking at animals, fish, and insects. He writes about the many animals that have instincts that cause them to act in certain *fixed action patterns* that involve intricate sequences of behavior, such as in mating rituals or how a mother wild turkey protects her chicks. Cialdini refers to these instinctual behaviors in animals as pre-programmed tapes and believes that humans, too, have pre-programmed tapes that can trigger unconscious, automatic responses of compliance, sometimes at the wrong times.[4] An example that Cialdini uses to support his thesis is research conducted by social psychologist Ellen Langer and her colleagues, which reinforces the "well-known principle of human behavior that says when we ask people to do us a favor we will be more successful if we provide a reason."[5]

Langer demonstrated this need for a reason by asking a small favor of people waiting in line to use a library copy machine: "Excuse me, I have five pages. May I use the Xerox machine *because* I'm in a rush?" Langer reports that this request *plus* a reason was successful 94 percent of the time, compared to the 60 percent success rate of the request "Excuse me, I have five pages. May I use the Xerox machine?" In another experiment Langer used another because phrase that added no new or even any logical information to a request: "Excuse me, I have five pages. May I use the Xerox machine because I have to make some copies?" The result was 93 percent compliance. There is no logical explanation for the high compliance rate; therefore, a because explanation must trigger an instinctual response that, as human beings, we have been pre-conditioned to make.

There are many automatic responses or *inherent assumptions* that we can use to influence people. Many of these inherent assumptions are culturally based and may not be valid in all circumstances. For example, most Americans have the expensive-equals-good assumption and its opposite, an inexpensive-equals-bad assumption. As Cialdini points out, ". . . in English, the word cheap doesn't just mean inexpensive; it has come to mean inferior, too."[6] Therefore, when we combine this expensive-equals-good inherent assumption with Cialdini's material, self-interest inherent assumption that people want to get the most and pay the least for their choices, our sales tool becomes more powerful when we mix in the concept of *perceptual contrast.*

Exhibit 8.2 shows a letter that is an example of the power of the contrast principle. The letter was suggested by a similar one in Cialdini's book.

Exhibit 8.2
An Example of the Power of the Contrast Principle

Dear Mom and Dad,

I'm sorry I haven't written sooner, but a lot has been going on. You'd better have a good stiff drink before you read further.

First, I'm doing pretty well. The skull fracture and two broken legs I got when I jumped from my dormitory window when my room caught fire after I went to sleep while smoking a joint are all pretty well healed now. I can see pretty well out of one eye, although I do get dizzy spells a couple of times a day.

But there was an upside to the accident. My jump was witnessed by a mechanic at a gas station across the street. He called the fire department and the ambulance. He visited me in the hospital, and because I have nowhere to live, he let me move in with him in his basement room in the Y.

He's a nice man, and even though he is 30 years older, we have fallen deeply in love and are planning to get married. We haven't set a date yet, but it will be sometime before the baby is due. I know you've always wanted to be grandparents, so I know you'll welcome your grandchildren—yes, it's twins. We hope they'll be fine in spite of the fact that I have tested positive for the HIV virus, which I got from Joe. You'll love Joe. He's not well educated, but he's sweet.

Well, now that you've had your drink, I'll tell you that there was no dormitory fire, I don't smoke dope, there was no skull fracture or broken legs, I was not in the hospital, I am not pregnant, I am not infected, and there is no boyfriend. However, at mid-term, I am getting a D in Math and an F in Chemistry, and I wanted you to see those marks in their proper perspective. Things could be worse. By the way, I'm getting an A in Psychology.

Your loving daughter,

Heather

We see the use of the contrast principle daily in automotive sales, retail clothing sales, and real estate sales. An example would be new car salespeople who sell us a $22,000 car and then add on, one at a time, options that seem to be a minor expense when contrasted to the $22,000 price of the car. But the options add up and add up, and soon the car costs $30,000. A real estate salesperson shows prospective buyers three houses that are dumps and then shows them a reasonably clean house that looks spotless in comparison. In the retail clothing business, salespeople are taught to show expensive items first so that subsequent, lower priced items seem like a bargain in comparison. If customers say they are interested in several items, say a suit and some socks, salespeople are taught to always sell the most expensive item first, in this case the suit, then to show them expensive socks, such as cashmere socks. Why? Because cashmere socks, when compared to regular socks, would seem expensive, but compared to what a suit costs, the socks are not perceived to be overpriced. Many people are not perceptive enough to see the effects of the contrast principle working.

Another example Cialdini uses is one from a student who relates that while waiting to board a flight at O'Hare International Airport, the student heard a gate attendant announce that the flight was overbooked. In an attempt at humor, which some airlines encourage, the gate attendant announced that anyone willing to take a later flight would be compensated with a voucher worth $10,000. Because people waiting at the gate knew it was a joke, they all laughed, but when the attendant then offered a $100 voucher, no one took it. Why? Because compared to $10,000, $100 seemed measly. No one took a $200 or $300 voucher either and the attendant had to raise the ante to $500 to get any takers. Had the attendant started with a ridiculous $5 joke offer, there would have been many takers for a real offer of $100 because, compared to $5, $100 would have seemed generous—a good deal.

Thus, the perception of a good deal is based on several things, including inherent assumptions and contrast. The broadcast television networks use these principles of influence effectively when they price their top-rated programs such as the Super Bowl, which is usually announced in July. In July of 2002, ABC announced prices of $2.3 million for the Super Bowl to be played in January of 2003. One reason for announcing pricing in July is to make prices for commercials purchased during the television scatter market, which breaks in September, seem reasonable at $300,000 to $600,000 each.

Used appropriately, the contrast principle is a legitimate method of positioning your offers when selling media. For example, compare the price of your offers to much more expensive prices of competitive media. Or, make your first offer or proposal unreasonably high so that the second one seems reasonable, regardless of its actual value. Or, make your first offer very low and refer to it as cheap, which will imply not only a low price, but low quality, and show that subsequent offers, each more expensive, are better.

Reciprocation.   Noted archeologist Richard Leakey ascribes the essence of what makes us human to the principle of *reciprocation*. The rule of reciprocity is that *we must provide to others the kind of actions they have provided us.* We learn reciprocity as the major motivation for cooperation, which is essential to the functioning of society. It creates a web of indebtedness that allows for the division of labor, the exchange of diverse forms of goods and services, and the interdependence that binds people together into workable units, groups, and cultures.[7] The concept of indebtedness, or *future obligation*, allows people to exchange goods without fear of loss and to build sophisticated systems of aid, gift giving, defense, and trade.

We are taught from early childhood that if someone gives us something, we have an inviolable future obligation to return the gift or favor, no matter how small, and whether or not we asked for the favor. The rule of reciprocity is overpowering. "The rule possesses awesome strength, often producing a yes response to a request that, except for an existing feeling of indebtedness, would surely be refused," writes Cialdini.[8] People who do not reciprocate are held in the lowest possible esteem and are seen as welshers or moochers.

According to Cialdini, a researcher sent Christmas cards randomly to people the researcher did not know, had never met, and who were unaware of who the researcher was. The researcher got almost a universal response. Everyone felt obligated to send the researcher a Christmas card the next year. Probably the most notorious abuse of the rule of reciprocity occurs with the Hare Krishnas when they solicit donations by first giving a target person a gift of a book, flower, or magazine. Even if targeted passerbys are initially repulsed by the look of the Krishnas, when they have flowers given to them or pinned to their lapels, and say, "No, thank you," they are told that the gift cannot be taken back, that, "It is our gift to you." That is when the overpowering rule of reciprocity kicks in and the vast majority of people feel obligated to make a reciprocal gift because refusing it would be against our nature. It is an automatic, uncontrollable response. There are two overwhelming obligations involved: to accept a gift and to reciprocate. So of course, people take the flower and then feel obligated to make a contribution.

We can see the reciprocity rule used in a myriad of circumstances. Waiters who leave a gift of a mint know that it will increase tips, grocery stores that offer free samples of food know that sales will increase significantly, and marketers who give away free samples of their products know trial and future use of a product will increase.

The reciprocity rule works both ways. Not only is there an obligation to reciprocate when someone gives you a gift or does you a favor, but also there is an obligation for the gift-giver to provide an opportunity for the gift receiver to repay the debt or return the favor. A socially satisfactory closure only occurs when a gift has been given and the receiver's reciprocation is accepted. "Thank you" must be followed by "You're welcome."

This rule also applies to concessions, and it is called the rule of *reciprocal concessions*. Imagine that I am heading our college class fundraising drive and I call you up, introduce myself, and then say, "How are you doing today?"

You respond by saying, "Just fine, thanks, Charlie."

"We have a huge fundraising goal this year. Can you pledge $500 because I want our great class to win the competition for raising the most money?"

You decline by saying, "Gee, that's a lot. I just can't afford it now."

"So $500 is a little steep?"

"Yes."

"I certainly understand; a lot of our classmates are in a similar position. Could you give $10? Then we stand a good chance of winning the competition for the highest percentage of participation, and could you volunteer for three hours a week to help me solicit our classmates on the phone?"

How can you not give $10 and three hours of your time, during which you will raise more than $500 using the same technique I used on you: I asked for something, you felt a little guilty but declined. I then came back with a lower request, a concession to my original request, to which you felt obligated to re-ciprocate with a concession—a small gift of money and time.

In Chapter 12 we will show how to use reciprocation tactics to your ad-vantage in negotiating and closing—not unfairly, of course—but to help you counteract people's tendencies toward material self-interest (getting the most for the least amount) and receive a fair price for your product.

Commitment and Consistency.   Cialdini reports on a study of people plac-ing bets on horses at a racetrack. They were much more confident of their horses' chances of winning after placing a bet than before. The same thing hap-pens with voters; they believe much more strongly that their candidate will win after they vote than before they vote. The need for our beliefs to be consistent with our actions lies deep within us and directs our actions with quiet power. As Cialdini writes: *"Once we make a choice or take a stand, we will encounter personal and interpersonal pressures to behave consistently with that commit-ment."*[9]

But in order for people to be consistent, they must take a stand—have something to be consistent about. Commitment comes first. There are several techniques to get commitments. Telemarketers and fundraisers understand the power of commitment when they call and ask, as I did in the conversation above, "How are you doing today?" or "How are you feeling?" If you say, "Just fine," or something similar, you are responding to the apparent concern about you that has been expressed and you will find it difficult to be subsequently grouchy or stingy. Other ways to intensify commitment are to *get people to say yes to small things first*, to give a small amount of money, to volunteer. This works even better if you can *get people to write something down*, put a check in a box, or sign their name to a petition. The third way to strengthen commit-ment is to *get people to tell someone else*. All of these techniques are powerful ways to increase commitment.

One of the best illustrations of the principles of commitment and consis-tency comes from research by psychologists Jonathan Freedman and Scott Fraser. They reported on the results of an experiment in which a researcher, posing as a volunteer, went door to door in a residential California neighbor-hood. They first asked people if they were in favor of driver safety, and, if so, to sign a petition. Everyone signed. Who could be against safe driving? Then the researcher asked if the homeowners would put a small sign on their lawns that read BE A SAFE DRIVER. It was such a trifling request that nearly every-one agreed to it. Two weeks later the "volunteer" returned and said that speed-ing on local streets had not diminished and asked if people would put up a very large, poorly lettered sign that read DRIVE CAREFULLY. The sign almost completely obstructed the view of their houses from the street. Seventy-six per-cent of the people who had put up the small sign agreed to put up the ugly, massive sign. Even the researchers were amazed at how well the consistency principle worked. Once people committed to being involved in a safe driving campaign, they went all out.[10] This technique of getting people to agree to a small request and then to larger and larger ones is called *the foot-in-the-door technique*.

In a follow-up experiment, the researchers went to another neighborhood and asked homeowners if they supported safe driving. If the answer was yes, they showed pictures of the houses with the huge, ugly DRIVE CAREFULLY signs on the lawns, and asked homeowners if they would be willing to put the signs up. Interestingly, only 17 percent said yes, which not only demonstrates the power of the foot-in-the door technique, but also shows the importance of getting the original commitment to safe driving.[11]

The researchers then went to another neighborhood and tried a different procedure. First, they asked homeowners to sign a petition that favored "keeping California beautiful." Naturally, nearly everyone signed it because everyone believes in maintaining the quality of the environment. Two weeks later, the people who signed the "keeping California beautiful" petition were asked to put the big DRIVE CAREFULLY sign on their lawn. The response of the homeowners astounded the researchers; more than 50 percent of those asked said yes. Freedman and Fraser finally realized after examining the data that when people signed the beautification petition, they changed their view of themselves to public-spirited citizens who acted on their civic principles and supported good causes.[12]

If Freedman and Fraser had first gone to homeowners and asked them if they supported safe driving, and, if they said yes, then asked them to put a huge DRIVE CAREFULLY sign on their lawn, the results would have been different. The majority of the homeowners would have refused them. And, if the researchers had returned in two weeks and asked homeowners to put up a smaller four-feet-by-three-feet sign, they might have received more than 75 percent compliance using this *door-in-the-face* technique.

Finally, the technique of making a public commitment is an important one to amplify commitment. For example, if you want to stop smoking, tell everyone you know that you have stopped. Cialdini writes that Chicago restaurant owner Gordon Sinclair lowered his no-show rate for reservations from 30 percent to 10 percent by simply changing "Please call us if you change your plans," to "Will you please call us if you change your plans?" and then waiting for a response. When people responded with a yes, they were publicly expressing their commitment.[13] The pause was the key to this technique. Public commitments work especially well with people with high levels of pride, self-esteem, or public self-consciousness because their egos are involved.

For media salespeople these lessons are important ones to keep in mind when you present proposals and offers. We will discuss some of these techniques in more detail in chapters 11 and 12.

Social Proof.   According to Cialdini, the principle of social proof states that people determine what is correct by finding out what other people think is correct. The principle applies especially to the manner in which we decide what constitutes correct behavior. *"We view behavior as correct in a given situation to the degree that we see others performing it."*[14] Whether it is when to laugh in a movie, how to eat chicken at a dinner party, or whether to help someone lying on a sidewalk, the actions of others is what guides our behavior.

Examples of compliance practitioners using social proof are all around us: street performers who salt their empty fiddle case with a five-dollar bill and public radio and television stations during pledge weeks that constantly give us the names of people who contribute. This technique tells us that "Everyone is doing it, so it must be the right thing to do." Evangelical speakers, such as Billy Graham, seed their audiences with ringers so they will come up and give witness and donations at the proper time. Nightclub owners will keep a long line waiting outside even when there are plenty of seats inside to increase the perception that it is a hot place. Advertisers inform people that their product is "the fastest growing" or "number-one" because they do not have to convince us directly that that their product is good; they need only to tell the public that others think it is good.

Social proof has particularly strong influence under two conditions: *when we view others to be similar to ourselves* and *when people feel unfamiliar or insecure in a specific situation.* In other words, in the first instance monkey see, monkey do, but not when a monkey sees an elephant do it. And in the second instance of monkey see, monkey do, the monkey copies if the monkey is not sure what to do. Therefore, in media selling give evidence of what other people who are similar to a customer have done, and always give evidence or social proof to people who seem to be insecure or lack confidence.

Scarcity.   For media salespeople, the scarcity principle is probably the most important principle and the one they will use most often. Cialdini states the scarcity principle as: *opportunities seem more valuable to us when they are less available.* We are familiar with this principle because we see it operating in everyday life in collecting baseball cards, scalping tickets outside a big game, choosing wine, or in the dating game. Everyone knows that when you tell people they cannot have something, that something becomes even more desirable.[15]

However, there are several interesting corollaries to the basic scarcity principle. The first one is that people are more motivated by the thought of losing something than by the thought of gaining something of equal value. The threat of a potential loss looms especially large under conditions of risk and uncertainty. So, when people are faced with a great deal of risk or uncertainty about the future, they worry about loss and do not think of a possible gain.

For this reason, Cialdini suggests the limited-number tactic is particularly effective. When people are informed that there are only a *limited number* of tickets or shares of stock left to purchase and they are then urged to make a decision quickly, they invariably make an immediate decision and say yes. This tactic is so powerful that unethical salespeople often use it even when it is not true. Keeping with the spirit of this book, we urge media salespeople to use the limited number tactic only when it is true, but when it is true, use it, because it works.[16] You are doing a service to your buyers and customers to inform them that a desirable opportunity such as the Super Bowl, a special newspaper section, or the last episode of a hit television program has only a few slots left. If you have done your job of creating value for the opportunity, they will be motivated by fear of losing it.

In addition to time, *information*, particularly if it is scarce, can be valuable. Businesses know that information is their most valuable resource, and information is more valuable if it is scarce, that is, if very few have it. And having exclusive information is even more precious, more powerful, and, therefore, provides greater opportunities for misuse and corruption, as seen in the insider trading scandals on Wall Street in 2002.

What kind of information can media salespeople use ethically with customers in order to influence decisions? Certainly not inside information about a competitor's advertising before it runs, as we pointed out in Chapter 3. You also cannot lie to customers and tell them that competitors are interested in something the customers are considering if it is not true. Also, do not promise customers exclusive information for their eyes only. On the other hand, it is your responsibility to tell customers if others, particularly their competitors, are considering buying the same thing. The rule is simple; always play it straight and be honest. You must be fair to everyone and make any relevant information available to everyone.

What you can share with your customers is non-exclusive and non-proprietary information that they might not be aware of, information about advertising trends, information in trade journals about new products, or information about new creative approaches that customers would find valuable. It takes time to dig for this kind of information, but it is worth the effort. Give it to customers, and they will appreciate it and you will take a big step toward becoming the preferred supplier.

The final corollary to the scarcity principle is that limited resources become even more valuable when other people are competing for them. Frantic bargain basement shoppers grab up merchandise when they see others competing for the same merchandise and the ardor of an indifferent lover surges with the appearance of a rival, for example. So, when competition does really exist for a scarce resource that you are selling, make sure everyone knows about the competition.

Liking and Authority.   The liking principle is straightforward and comes as no surprise: *we prefer to say yes to people we know and like,*[17] which is similar to the second Golden Rule of Selling, people like and trust people exactly like themselves. Dale Carnegie's book *How to Win Friends and Influence People* was first published in 1937 and became the best-selling self-help book of all time. Even though the book is simplistic, Carnegie's essential point was that the best way to influence people is to get them to like you. This is an effective approach if you are a likable, credible person, but it does not work if you are insincere or not authentic.

Cialdini refers to the principle of authority as *directed deference.* The great power of the authority principle is that for a society to function, we must obey the rules of that society and, therefore, obey its designated authority figures and symbols. Thus, we are trained from childhood to obey the commands and requests of legitimate authority figures: our parents, policemen, firemen, government officials, judges, tax collectors, and presidents.

There are many symbols that communicate authority: titles, clothes, and trappings.[18] Titles are important; they communicate status, prestige, success, power, and authority. When I was a vice president in AOL's Interactive Marketing Division in 1998, I remember the constant battles our top management had with AOL's inflexible human resources (HR) department, attempting to get the regional sales managers and business development (BD) salespeople titles of vice president. The sales managers and BD salespeople used the valid argument that they called on CEOs and senior VPs of marketing and advertising and that these high-level people wanted to deal only with correspondingly high-level executives, not merely salespeople. Although HR held firm for several years, the regional managers and BD salespeople had a simple solution; they called themselves vice presidents on their calling cards. It worked and it became easier to get appointments with top executives. Unfortunately, what this title-consciousness leads to is title inflation and eventually everyone is a senior vice president calling on senior vice presidents. But title inflation is rooted in the basic principle that people do tend to defer to authority.

Clothes are another symbol of authority, status, and power. Clothes, like titles, can trigger mechanical compliance. A policeman's uniform, a doctors' coat, and a pilot's uniform are all symbols of authority. Slightly more subtle, but no less authoritative, are colored shirts with white collars and white cuffs. Add a Hermes scarf or Ferragamo tie and Gucci loafers, and you have an outfit that reeks of authority and commands respect. Trappings of authority such as Rolex watches, huge offices and desks, and luxury cars all add to the cachet of authority and power.

There are two reasons to learn about the principles of influence, offensive and defensive. Offensively, it is a good idea for you to use the principles of influence when it is appropriate in order to influence people legitimately. But be mindful of the *law of instrument,* which was defined by Abraham Kaplan in *The Conduct of Inquiry,* as "give **a** small boy a hammer, and he will find that everything he encounters needs pounding."[19] In other words, now that you know a little about the theory of influence and the power of automatic responses, reciprocity, commitment and consistency, social proof, scarcity, and liking and authority, do not use them as a hammer in every sales situation. However, do use them when appropriate to position your proposals and product effectively to create added value.

I strongly recommend that you read Robert Cialdini's book *Influence: Science and Practice,* study it carefully, and become an expert at using and recognizing the tactics of influence. By being an expert on these principles you can defend yourself against others who use them. Customers and buyers, in their attempt to get more for less, will often use one or all of these principles to get you to give them more, lower your prices, give them better position, say yes to a deal that is good for them quickly, or to defer to their power and authority. The defense against the use of these principles of influence is to recognize them for exactly what they are, stop before you respond automatically, name the tactic ("That's reciprocation," or "The buyer is using social proof to try to influence me,"), and then respond appropriately and rationally.

Creating Value

Creating value encompasses salespeople's main purpose of creating customers and keeping them, their four objectives, their six primary strategies, and their three key functions. In this section you will learn why creating value is important as well as five steps to help you create value.

Why Creating Value Is Important

Creating Value Addresses Sales Objectives, Strategies, and Key Functions. Let's review the sales objectives, strategies, and key functions of a media salesperson.

Four Primary Sales Objectives

1. To get results for customers
2. To develop new business
3. To retain and increase current business
4. To increase customer loyalty

Six Primary Sales Strategies

1. To sell solutions to advertising and marketing problems
2. To reinforce the value of advertising and your medium
3. To create value for your product
4. To become the preferred supplier
5. To innovate
6. To help the competition get rich

Three Key Functions of a Salesperson

1. To create a differential competitive advantage in a buyer's mind
2. To manage relationships
3. To solve problems

Creating Value Addresses Buyer's Needs.   If we review the results of two time-buyer surveys from Chapter 2, as shown below, we see that they provide a virtual road map for creating value. In other words, if you give buyers what they ask for, you will create value. Note in the lists below that of what buyers want, "a low price" is not one of the answers. This fact reinforces the notion that buyers will always ask for a lower price than you first offer, but they do not necessarily expect to get a lower price. It is their job to ask; it is material self-interest at work.

> **International Radio-Television Society (IRTS) Time Buyer Survey of what buyers want:** (1) Communication skills—Clarity and conciseness, not oral skills or flamboyance, were ranked as most important; (2) Empathy—Insight and sensitivity; (3) Knowledge of product, industry, and market; (4) Problem-solving ability—Using imagination in presentations and packaging; (5) Respect; (6) Service; (7) Personal responsibility of results; and (8) Not knocking the competition.

> **Major radio station group buyer survey of what buyers want:** (1) Ideas—Especially in the area of *added value*; (2) Communication—Clear concise communication, not long-winded, exaggerated sales pitches; (3) Respect for their time; (4) Run as ordered; and (5) Responsiveness—Return calls *fast*, be available at all times, and get schedules confirmed quickly and correctly.

Added Value

Please note the phrase "added value" associated with answer (1) in the radio station group buyer survey above. Added value to buyers means additional value that a medium gives at no charge. What buyers want is something free: bonus spots or pages, free promotions, free event tie-ins, free merchandise, or free opening and closing billboards, among other things. The push for added value has become so pervasive in some media, especially radio, that many buyers claim they will not place an order without something free thrown into the deal. To salespeople, a request for added value should not be seen as a problem, but as a negotiating opportunity. In Chapter 12, when we cover negotiating and closing, we will show how to use requests for added value to your advantage by using contrast, social proof, and other principles of influence. However, for the time being, suffice it to say that creating value for your medium and your company does not mean giving stuff away for free.

Creating Value Addresses Companies' Needs.   Creating value also addresses management's needs because if salespeople can create the perception of value for their product and, therefore, keep prices up, they will help accomplish the company's primary goal for sales departments: *maximizing revenue.* Top management of media companies today must look at both the top line (revenue) and the bottom line (profits). Profits are the result of subtracting expenses from revenues, and during the advertising recession of 2001 and 2002 most media companies cut expenses to the bone. The only way for these companies to grow now is to manage the top line and increase revenue, for which they depend on salespeople who sell advertising. Advertising is responsible for the vast majority of revenue for most media companies. Thus, maximizing revenue is management's mantra for media sales departments.

The push for maximizing revenue is understandable, but it creates a dilemma for media salespeople. On the one hand, they must please management (and keep their jobs) by maximizing revenue. On the other hand, they must consider the needs of their customers and follow the tenet of their number-one objective, getting results for customers. How do they resolve this dilemma? By creating value. It is often difficult to create value in recessionary times and to hold rates. The only hope salespeople have of holding their rates is to be creative and innovative in differentiating their product and creating value.

Additional Reasons for Creating Value

Creating Value Reinforces the Value of Advertising, Your Medium, and Your Product. Especially during recessionary times, customers and buyers often look for reasons to cut back on their advertising, for a less-expensive placement in your medium, for less expensive media, or they ask you to lower your prices to keep the business you have. If you call on a customer who is considering cutting back on advertising during a business slowdown, go to www.mediaselling.us, download the presentation "Advertising Strategies in a Slowdown," and show it to the customer. The presentation gives facts, based on research conducted during recessions in the past, that show when companies cut advertising they lose market share, often for five years, whereas competitors who continue advertising gain share. It also shows that market share, once lost, is extremely difficult and expensive to gain back.

Creating Value Enhances Your Credibility and Builds Trust. In the process of creating value you display your expertise, which builds source credibility. You demonstrate that you understand your customers' businesses, their marketing goals and problems, your product, your market, media trends, buyers' and customers' business needs (as indicated in the above buyer surveys), and buyers' personal needs. All of these elements build trust.

Creating Value Can Forestall and Minimize Future Objections, Especially the Price Objection. Before you make a specific proposal that includes prices—if you invest time in creating value for your product—you forestall, or answer beforehand, many potential objections that might come up during a discussion of your proposal. During the creating value process, you justify your pricing.

Creating Value Reinforces Your Solutions-Selling Approach. During the process of creating value, you can persuade customers that you are taking a solutions-selling approach and that you are trying to help them solve their advertising and marketing problems. By taking this approach you are able to show them that your primary objective is to help them get results, not necessarily to sell them something.

Creating Value Helps You Avoid Commodity Selling. By creating value you reinforce your product's worth. An old adage says, "There are people who know the price of everything, but know the value of nothing." In other words, price and value do not mean the same thing, as you will see in the next section of this chapter. During the process of creating value you differentiate your product and its features, benefits, and advantages and make it worth more to your customers so that they will be willing to pay a higher price. In creating value you want to reinforce the inherent assumption that expensive equals good.

Creating Value Helps You Control Your Customers' Expectations. When people contemplate investing in advertising, they do so with the expectation that their business will increase. And because their hopes are high, their expectations usually rise to meet them. In other words, there is a natural tendency for people to expect too much. Part of creating value is creating *realistic value* in the minds of customers, which means lowering your customers' expectations. The lower you can set their expectations, the more pleased they will eventually be with their results, as they define them.

What Is Value?

The Economic Value Formula. The formula for economic value is:

$$\text{Economic Value (EV)} = \frac{\text{Quality (Q)} + \text{Utility (U)} + \text{Service (S)}}{\text{Price (P)}}$$

In order to increase the economic value to a customer, you must increase the value of the numerator in the above equation (quality, utility, and service) and not lower the denominator (price). In fact, if salespeople are experts in creating value and increasing the perception in a buyer's mind of the value of quality, utility, and service, then they can increase the price.

Quality is a subjective concept. Like the concept of beauty, quality is in the eye of the beholder. Perceptions of quality are defined by several attributes of a medium. For example, a magazine might be perceived to be of high quality because of glossy paper stock; beautiful four-color photographs; a pleasing layout and design; and eye-catching, tasteful graphics. A newspaper might be perceived to be high quality because of the upscale demographics of its audience and because of the many Pulitzer Prizes it has won. A radio station might be perceived to be a high quality station because it plays classical music. A television station might be perceived to be a high quality station because its season kick-off parties and presentations are eye-popping, expensive, and include television stars. The more attributes that a medium and its salespeople can promote to create a perception of quality, the higher perceived quality is, the higher prices the medium can charge.

Utility in a media context means, primarily, does advertising in that medium get results as defined by the customer? Customer-defined results vary a great deal by media and by customer. In some cases, results can mean beautiful reproduction and display of four-color ads. At other times, results can mean sales. With some clients, results can mean recall of specific product claims in an ad or commercial. With others, results can mean return on advertising investment as measured by increased stock price. And with other clients, results mean an increase in market share. Therefore, utility means customer-defined usefulness. By understanding a customer's definition of results, salespeople can demonstrate how their medium in general and their specific media outlet can improve results.

Service is a product attribute that is becoming more and more important in our economy. In fact, with many products, especially those that are either highly undifferentiated or are intangible, customers consider service to be the most important differentiator. Also, as an industry matures, customers migrate from being inexperienced generalists to being experienced specialists. Inexperienced generalists are interested in learning more about a product, understanding how to use it, and figuring out how to buy it, and because of the FUD factor—fear, uncertainty, and doubt—will often be predisposed to pay a premium price in order to gain experience. On the other hand, experienced specialists know a product well. They know how to use it and how to buy it, and price and responsive service are most important to them. To experienced specialists, such as agency media buyers, who have multiple substitutes for virtually all mass media, the single most important differentiator, after price, is service.[20]

By emphasizing the importance of quality, utility, and service, salespeople can divert the discussion away from price and get customers and buyers to focus on these other attributes.

In Chapter 27 you will learn more strategies for selling to inexperienced generalists (direct) and experienced specialists (agency).

Economic Value is a Perception.   Every person or potential buyer places a different weight on the relative importance of the quality/utility/service mix and, thus, has a different definition of the value of that mix. Therefore, *value is a perception* that is unique to each individual. Thus, the price people will pay for a product is a result of their unique solution to the economic value formula. For example, a commercial on a local television station news program may be worth $1,000 to one advertiser based on how many adults between the ages of 18 and 49 the newscast reaches. On the other hand, it might be worth $2,000 to another advertiser who wants to have the company's name associated with a station's newscast or sports segment within that newscast, who desires to reach mature, male business decision makers, and who likes an association with sports. Therefore, paying a premium for sponsoring a sports segment that features a brief opening *billboard* such as "Sports brought to you by Warner Ford," makes economic sense to that advertiser.

Value Signals.   Value signals reinforce the perception of value. Here is a list of some value signals:

1. **Company image and reputation.** Does a company's management have a track record of success and a philosophy that stresses dedication to excellence and high business standards? IBM has an excellent reputation, Enron a horrible one, for example.
2. **Media outlet reputation.** *Time* magazine has an excellent reputation; the *National Enquirer's* is not so good.
3. **Ethical practices.** Does the media outlet have a reputation for treating its customers fairly? Is its word its bond? Do advertisers trust it? How many companies want Arthur Anderson to be its auditor?
4. **Awards and prizes.** How many awards for excellence or Pulitzer Prizes has a media outlet amassed? Awards and prizes are the best proof of quality.
5. **Cumulative advertising and promotion.** Coca-Cola is the world's most recognized brand because it has consistently advertised its product for almost 100 years, for example.
6. **Content.** Editorial or programming content. *The New York Times, The Washington Post*, and National Public Radio (NPR) are perceived to have high-quality reporting and content.
7. **Sales promotion material.** Slick, well-designed sales brochures speak volumes about an organization.

8. **Continuity.** The number of years a company has been in business, the number of years a television news anchorperson has been on the air, or the tenure of a magazine editor all impart a perception of value.

9. **Advertisers.** Well-known, prestigious advertisers give a medium credibility and value—they reinforce the idea that "you are known by the company you keep," an example of social proof.

10. **Audience or reader quality and quantity.** High-income readers of *Smithsonian* magazine or the huge audience of a Super Bowl telecast, for example, signal quality.

11. **Price.** The higher the price of a product, the higher the perceived value (expensive equals good). Patek Philippe watches are perceived to have more value than Casio watches, for example.

12. **Management.** The better the reputation of top management and the more visible managers are in the business community, the more competent they are perceived to be.

13. **Production values.** Well-produced newspaper and magazine ads and well-produced radio and television commercials add value.

14. **Sales proposals.** Well-written, problem-solving, and graphically arresting proposals and presentations not only help make a product tangible, they also add value. See Chapter 10 for guidelines for generating winning proposals and presentations.

15. **Salespeople.** One survey asked media buyers what they thought of when the call letters of a radio or television station were mentioned. Seventy-five percent of all buyers gave the name of the salesperson who called on them. Thus, salespeople are the surrogate for the product and can make tangible an intangible media product and add value.

16. **Ideas for added value.** Promotion or event sponsorships and community service project tie-ins can be used to add value—see the list of creating value ideas at the end of this chapter in Exhibit 8.4.

17. **Creative approaches.** Ideas for arresting ads or commercials can add value for direct clients without advertising agencies. Agencies usually do not appreciate suggestions for creative approaches in copy and art because they see creative execution as their prerogative.

Positioning Value

Positioning is creating a unique perception of your product to have a differential competitive advantage in the mind of your customers. As marketing guru Philip Kotler says, "Having a competitive advantage is like having a gun in a knife fight."[21]

When you position your company and your product to have a competitive advantage, a competitor's image is as important as your own image, if not more so, because you are positioning your product against the image of your competitor's medium and product. If you position properly, you can accomplish two things: You position your product to have an advantage and you position your competitors' products to have a disadvantage. For example, AOL's ". . . so easy to use no wonder we're number one" was a brilliant positioning statement. It not only positioned AOL as easy to use at a time when people were terrified of and confused by the Internet, but it is also a clever use of social proof, in that almost everyone wants to be associated with a winner. Furthermore, AOL's statement positions their competitors, other Internet service providers (ISPs), as hard to use.

Other examples of companies' positioning approaches that also position their competitors are those of IBM and Charles Schwab & Co. IBM's television commercial that shows a nerdy salesperson trying sell a "universal adapter" to a group of people positions IBM as a supplier of global Internet and information technology solutions and its competitors as companies that are trying to sell complicated computer hardware and peripherals. When the actor portraying the company president asks the nerdy salesperson if his product works in Europe, the salesperson replies, "You need an adapter." The message is that there are no universal adapters and that IBM is the best company to provide customized solutions.

In magazine ads, Charles Schwab & Co. positions itself as a stockbroker that consumers can trust because the company does not pay its representatives a commission. The ad implies that other stockbrokers are not trustworthy because they pay commissions, a particularly timely approach after the scandals that have plagued many Wall Street firms.

You must clearly establish a differential competitive advantage in the minds of potential customers for your medium, your company, and your product. To do so, you should begin the positioning process by asking yourself the following questions:

1. What position, if any, does my product already occupy in the mind of my customer? Of course, the best way to find out is to ask. In Chapter 9 there is a list of Discovery Questions you can use that will help answer this question.
2. What position do I want to occupy? It must be unique and concise. It must have an easily definable competitive advantage that clearly makes a difference; if it takes too long to explain, customers will not stick around or stay awake long enough to find out how good it is.

Positioning Dimensions.   In deciding what position you want to occupy, you have to look at your competitors and then position your company, medium, and product according to the following dimensions:

1. **The market.** Look at the size and demographic makeup of the local or national market you serve in terms of population and geographic distribution. What is the demographic makeup of the market—that is, what is its racial, age, or educational makeup? For example, Miami, as a local market, has a larger percentage of older people in its population than most markets and San Diego has a larger percentage of younger people. In what geographic area is the largest concentration of high-income people, Hispanics, or large-family dwellings, for example? How do your medium and product address the needs of the market you serve, and what is different and unique about the relationship of your product to its market and its unique dimensions?
2. **The media environment.** How many radio and television stations, cable systems and interconnects, newspapers, billboards, and so on, are there? What is the strength of each? Washington, D.C., is a strong FM radio market but a low-viewing television market (particularly in the early evening); San Francisco is a strong AM radio market and a weak newspaper market; and Seattle has a large cable interconnect, for example. What advantages does your product have in a market's media environment?
3. **The competition.** What is the position and reputation of your competition? Do your competitors have a clearly defined image? Is it different and unique? Analyze them the same way you analyze your own product and look for any edge you might have. Position yourself positively against the

competition, but do not knock the competition. Stating your advantages implies the disadvantages of the competition, so you do not have to name them.

4. **Your competitors' marketing and sales strategies.** Are they appealing to upscale consumers? Are they trying to be price leaders? Do they lower their prices? Do they arrogantly raise prices consistently? Do they sell negatively? Do they advertise and promote aggressively and consistently to keep their audience or readership levels up? Remember, one of your core functions as a salesperson is to create a differential *competitive* advantage; this means that you must know your competition as thoroughly as possible.

When you position your company, your medium, and your product, you should use the right words to paint a positive, colorful picture. For example, you do not sell advertising; instead, you present a traffic-building ad campaign. You do not peddle spots; instead, you offer profit-producing advertising. You do not sell advertising; instead, you sell the opportunity to influence prospective customers. Advertisers do not buy ads or spots; they buy the most effective and efficient way available to generate sales. Always use phrases that color your offer green—the green color of sales and profits.

Five Steps for Creating Value

One of the oldest rules of selling is, "Don't mention price until you are ready to negotiate and close." Before you get into a discussion about price you should position your product to create the perception of value, and the best way to increase the value of what you are selling is to follow the five steps for creating value. As part of the creating value process, it is a good idea to have a general presentation (GP) for your media outlet. Many media organizations have a GP, which is an introduction to their product that reinforces its history; reputation; and combination of quality, utility, and service advantages and benefits—with no mention of price. To see an example of a GP, go to www.mediaselling.us and look at the presentation for the *DeSoto Times*, a small community newspaper.

The five steps of the creating value process parallel a salesperson's six primary sales strategies.

The Five Steps of Creating Value

1. Reinforce your expertise as a problem solver.
2. Reinforce the value of advertising.
3. Reinforce the value of your medium.
4. Reinforce the value of your product (your newspaper, your radio station, or your television station, for example).
5. Position the benefits and advantages of your product.

1. Reinforce Your Expertise as a Problem Solver.   You want your prospects to consider you as a marketing and advertising expert who can use your medium to solve their advertising and marketing problems. In order to demonstrate your expertise, you should demonstrate your broad-based knowledge of national and international economic and business trends as well as economic and business trends in your market, in media and in your medium, and in your customers' businesses. There are two major benefits of having up-to-date information in these areas: You will be welcome at top-management client levels and you will be welcome at all client and agency levels because you provide updated information to your customers and buyers. For example, following is a list of some of the marketing trends that were evident in 2003 and with which you should be familiar:

2003 Marketing Trends

- One-to-one marketing
- Permission marketing
- Mass customization
- "A mass market of one"[22]
- Retail power
- Globalization
- Service sensitivity
- Maximizing touch points
- Consumers concentrate on convenience
- Increasing returns (also known as the network effect, which means that as more people use a product it becomes more valuable and less costly to produce)
- E-commerce
- Business-to-business marketing
- Loyalty marketing (such as frequent-flyer miles)
- Quality control (Six-Sigma programs)
- Higher quality at a lower cost
- The Internet (a disruptive technology)[23]
- Interactivity (television)
- Product placement

Other examples of some of these trends can be found in the "Creating Value for Television" presentation on www.mediaselling.us.

Also, demonstrate your knowledge of marketing and advertising—the goals, strategies, and tactics of not only your customers and their competitors, but also of your own competitors.

Finally, provide to your customers the latest marketing and audience or readership research available. Do not just present reams of data, but put research information in a concise, summarized, easy-to-read format. Customers will appreciate and reward you for your consideration and respect for their time.

Your goal in providing all of this information is to become your customers' preferred supplier—the salesperson and organization your customers would most like to do business with, and, more important, the salesperson they will always call first when they want information. Tom Stultz makes this point effectively in Chapter 18, "Newspapers."

2. Reinforce the Value of Advertising.   In most cases, especially with advertising agencies, you do not have to reinforce the value of advertising. However, occasionally you will find an organization that is not advertising in the mass media. It may be hard to believe, but there are still a few holdouts. For example, it was not until recently that hospitals became major advertisers in many communities. Or, an organization may be investing its marketing dollars primarily in promotion or considering investing less money in advertising and investing more in promotion.

In all of these cases, it is necessary to sell the value of advertising and reinforce the first principle of creating value, that *advertising is not an expense, it is an investment.* You must continually reinforce this concept throughout all of your sales presentations and sales conversations. For example, never ask someone, "How much do you spend in advertising?" Ask, "How much do you invest in advertising?" When you submit a proposed schedule or campaign, never show a total cost, refer to it as a total investment.

Also, as pointed out in Chapter 2, you must reinforce the value of advertising as opposed to the costs of promotions. Remember that in 1978 60 percent of all marketing dollars were spent in advertising, 40 percent in promotion. In 2001 50 percent of all marketing dollars were spent in promotion, 50 percent in advertising. The migration of marketing dollars from advertising to promotion hurt the growth rate of advertising over those years. You must continually reinforce advertising's positive long-term effects and the value of advertising to build brand image and, thus, try to reverse the shift of advertising dollars to promotion. Table 8.1 shows seven problems with promotions that you can discuss with your customers which will help stem the tide of advertising dollars being switched to promotion.

Furthermore, the majority of promotions involve some inducement for consumers to act immediately and purchase a product. Inducements invariably

Table 8.1 The Seven Problems with Promotions	Problem	Description
	1. Short-term effects	There is overwhelming evidence that "the consumer sales effect is limited to the time period of the promotion itself." Contrary to some marketers' belief, there is no residual effect of a promotion. Consumers do not turn into long-term customers. "When the bribe stops, the extra sales also stop."[a]
	2. Mortgage future sales	By encouraging consumers to take action immediately, a promotion brings forward sales from a future period and, therefore, future sales are lower than forecast because of problem no. 1 above.
	3. Encourage stockpiling	Savvy consumers stock up on low-priced promotion items, which cannibalizes future full-price sales and lowers margins.
	4. Train consumers not to pay full price	Price-conscious consumers are aware of continual promotions and wait for them—they become trained never to pay full price which lowers profit margins
	5. Promotions devalue a brand's image	Continual promotions create a low-price, even "cheap," image and often appear to be desperate measures of a sinking brand in trouble. If consumers believe price cuts come from an oversupply, they will often wait for an even lower price.
	6. Promotions are addictive	Marketers become dependent on more and more quick fixes in a vicious circle of more and more promotions at lower and lower prices at shorter and shorter intervals. Unilever describes this circle as "promotion, commotion, and demotion."[a]
	7. Continual use of promotions leads to retaliation	Promotions "fuel the flames of competitive retaliation far more than other marketing activities."[a] Competitors join the price war to defend their position. The long-term result of price wars can lead to the elimination of both retailers' and an entire industry's profit margins.[b]

Notes: (a) Jones, 1990. (b) Srinivasan, Pauwels, Hansses, and Dekimpe, 2002.

involve a price reduction in some form such as rebates, coupons, or free merchandise.

Examples of promotions that have hurt the profit margins of entire industries are the costly rebates American automotive manufacturers offered in 2002. In the first quarter of 2003 Ford Motor Company announced the largest quarterly loss in its history, which Ford indicated was due largely to its rebate policy—it was matching a similar rebate policy by General Motors, which also suffered a huge loss as a result of giving rebates.

These losses due to rebates—essentially a price cut—back up and reinforce the claim that "the cost to a manufacturer of a 1-percent reduction in price is always far greater than the cost of a 1-percent boost in advertising expenditure."[24] Do your customers want to increase sales? Recommend that they raise their advertising investment and do not reduce their prices.

Of course, all of these reasons why cutting prices is not a good idea for customers doubly reinforces why media salespeople should not cut their rates.

3. Reinforce the Value of Your Medium.   In many cases, you may not think you have to sell the value of your medium to a current advertiser who is a heavy user. However, keep in mind that competing media salespeople are calling on your advertisers and doing their best to switch your customers' advertising to their medium. It is a good idea to reinforce the value of your medium, and you can do this in three ways with current advertisers: first, at yearly renewal times, or at mid-year, make a stewardship presentation that shows the ads or commercials an advertiser ran during the previous year, what results they got, and remind them of the excellent service they received from you. Second, ask advertisers for testimonial letters or, better, to participate in a success case study (how to write case studies is covered later in this chapter). By helping you write a success case study, an advertiser's excellent judgment in buying your medium will be reinforced. Third, invite advertisers to your industry's trade association presentations. Associations such as the Television Bureau of Advertising (TVB), the Cabletelevision Advertising Bureau (CAB), and the Radio Advertising Bureau (RAB) regularly make presentations touting their media in cities around the country. It is the job of these associations to sell the value of their media and they do it very well.

You should also make presentations to advertising agencies on the value of your medium if you sell for a medium other than television. Agencies have prejudice in favor of television for several reasons, including that they can spend more money in less time and at less cost to them than in any other medium. I will cover more about this prejudice in Chapter 27 and give you more ideas about how to sell agencies media other than television, but for now, it is enough to say that selling the value of your medium to agencies is important in the long term even though it is not likely to produce an immediate order.

Another reason for reinforcing the value of your medium to both agencies and clients is to attempt to get them to invest more dollars into your medium—increase the size of the advertising pie. You should sell the value of your medium first and worry about your share of the pie later. In many markets, there are radio or television station associations that cooperate in an attempt to get new advertisers into their particular medium and away from another, usually newspapers. For example, a team of television station sales managers will call on a major department store that invests all of its advertising dollars in the local newspapers and try to convince the department store to invest some of that money in television.

4. Reinforce the Value of Your Product.   One of the best examples of a company that positions itself superbly is Patek Philippe, the Swiss watchmaker. Go to the company's Web site at www.patek.com, click on "The Art of Watch Making" link, and then click on the "History" link and see how the company promotes its history, its patents, its customers, and its complicated watches. Notice that while price is never mentioned for any of their watches, some of the famous people who have bought them are listed, such as Charlotte Bronte, Queen Victoria, Madame Curie, and Albert Einstein. After seeing how Patek Philippe positions itself and creates value for its watches, ask yourself if you would like to own one and if you would rather sell these watches as a commissioned salesperson than sell Casio watches.

Just as the Patek Philippe Web site reeks of quality, you want your customers to get the same sense of quality when you talk about your product. One way to create the perception of quality is to repeat the word; to use it in every possible context, such as, "We have a quality newspaper and quality reporters," or "We have a quality production department that produces the highest quality commercials."

Remember, you are trying to position the quality, utility, and service of your product to have a competitive advantage. After quality comes utility, and in the media utility means results. Stress that your medium gets results, and the best way to reinforce this concept is with advertising success case studies. These cases are not only good for positioning the value of your medium with an advertiser who is involved in developing the case study with you, but they are also a very powerful sales tool. An example of excellent success case studies can be seen at www.msn.com. Near the bottom of MSN's home page there is an "Advertise on MSN" link; click on it and then click on the "Case Studies" link on the page you go to. Also, on www.mediaselling.us you will find a paper titled "How to Write an Advertising Success Case Study" and a success case study titled "Aladdin Resort and Casino." Download them and set a goal of writing several success case studies for your medium. You will find case studies are an effective proof of performance and that your medium gets results for advertisers.

Another way to reinforce the value of your product and communicate an image of being responsive to customer needs is to present a *value proposition* to customers. Many of your customers have value propositions that guide them in their dealings with their customers and consumers. Therefore, those customers who have value propositions, and those who do not, will appreciate your value proposition if it is a good one. Here is an example of a value proposition for a television station:

> "We are committed to partnering with our advertisers (and their agencies) by
> providing innovative solutions for connecting them to our audience in a way that
> delivers advertiser-defined results and jointly builds both of our brands."

The above value proposition states that you want to do more than sell your customers something. It means that you want to partner with them, you want to get results for them, and you want to create a win-win situation.

5. Position the Benefits and Advantages of Your Product.   Too often inexperienced media salespeople sell on the basis of the *features* of their product and do not place enough emphasis on *advantages* and *benefits*. Following are the definitions of these elements.

Features are descriptive. They are facts and information about your product and its various parts. The features of a radio station, for example, are its tower, its transmitter, its programming format, its personalities, its coverage, its audience, and its ratings. The features of a newspaper are its presses, its delivery methods, its editorial stance, its comics, its editors and reporters, its special sections, and its circulation. Another example of a feature might be a quarter-inch drill bit. Features describe what you have to sell, but they do not indicate or imply if the features are good or bad or why a customer should care about them. Customers do not buy solely based on product features.

Advantages are comparative. They describe why the features of your product are better. Customers are interested in a feature's advantages and consider these advantages when they make a purchase (or in the case of advertising, an investment) if they feel the features are relevant. Use the contrast principle when you present advantages. Also, you must present the advantages of your product as customers go through each phase of the buying decision process.

In his classic book, *Major Account Sales Strategy*, Neil Rackham describes the *buying decision process*. Rackham suggests that people go through three initial phases when making a buying decision:[25]

> **Recognition of needs.** With consumers, this phase might come when they discover their old car has broken down and they need a new one. With advertisers it might come when they have planned a sale, want to advertise it, and call salespeople and ask them to present schedules. Or, with an agency buyer, it might come when they send out a request for a proposal (RFP) to the media they are considering buying.

> **Evaluation of options.** In this phase buyers ask: "What are my choices?" "Should I buy what I did last time?" "Should I look for alternatives or for a lower price?" It is in the Evaluation of Options phase that product advantages become critical because it is during this phase that buyers narrow down their choices by eliminating those products that are considered less desirable or to be of lower quality.

> **Resolution of concerns.** In phase three buyers look carefully at the few products they are considering and ask themselves: "What happens if the car breaks down; does it have a warranty or service guarantee?" "Which one has the best quality-to-price ratio?" It is in this final stage that benefits are of critical importance, and we will get to benefits shortly.

You must position your advantages so they are clear in your customer's minds when they reach the Evaluation of Alternative phase of the buying process. The best way to accomplish this positioning is *always to show comparative advantages and dramatize them*. Exhibit 8.3 shows four examples of how a television station might display the ratings of an early newscast in a sales presentation. The first four examples are in presentations for station WAAA-TV, the fourth is for station WBBB-TV.

Notice the WBBB-TV proposal. WBBB-TV saw a copy of WAAA-TV's proposal that claimed WAAA-TV had a 50-percent lead over WBBB-TV, which is accurate. However, WBBB-TV showed in its counterproposal that things weren't all that bad—that it only trailed WAAA-TV by 33 percent,

Exhibit 8.3
Example Displays of
Ratings in a Sales
Presentation

Poor WAAA-TV Display of Ratings

	Adults 25-54 Nielsen Ratings WAAA-TV
Early News	6.0

Fair WAAA-TV Display of Ratings (shows a comparative advantage)

	Adults 25-54 Nielsen Ratings WAAA-TV	Adults 25-54 Nielsen Ratings WBBB-TV
Early News	6.0	4.0

Good WAAA-TV Display of Ratings (quantifies a comparative advantage)

	Adults 25-54 Nielsen Ratings WAAA-TV	Adults 25-54 Nielsen Ratings WBBB-TV	WAAA-TV Difference
Early News	6.0	4.0	+ 2.0

Best WAAA-TV Display of Ratings (dramatizes a comparative advantage)

	Adults 25-54 Nielsen Ratings WAAA-TV	Adults 25-54 Nielsen Ratings WBBB-TV	WAAA-TV Advantage
Early News	6.0	4.0	+ 50%

WBBB-TV Counterproposal Display of Ratings (minimizes a comparative disadvantage)

	Adults 25-54 Nielsen Ratings WAAA-TV	Adults 25-54 Nielsen Ratings WBBB-TV	WBBB-TV Disadvantage
Early News	6.0	4.0	− 33%

which is also accurate. The lesson here is to learn to use numbers to compare, maximize, and dramatize your advantages and to minimize your disadvantages.

Benefits are reasons why the features and advantages of your product solve customers' problems. Benefits are what you should concentrate on selling because that is what customers buy—benefits. Peter Drucker explained succinctly that people do not buy quarter-inch drill bits, they buy quarter-inch holes. Every time you state a feature or advantage of your product or proposal, customers ask themselves the WIIFM question, "What's in it for me?" Benefits answer that question. You must never let a customer ask the WIIFM question out loud, you must answer the question by attaching a problem-solving benefit to every feature you mention.

As mentioned before, there are two types of needs: business needs and personal needs. You must position benefits so that they directly address business problems, or *challenges*, and business needs and how your proposed solutions help customers get what they want—achieve their marketing and advertising goals and get results as they define results. There is also a subtle subtext involved that you should master. You must also position the benefits of your product, proposal, or solution in such a way that it appeals to customers' personal needs.

This type of subtle, indirect positioning according to personal needs is where it gets difficult. You can hardly say to a customer, "My proposal to run commercials just before the Super Bowl on my television station will not only help you achieve your marketing goals of reaching the largest possible male audience and locking out your competitors from this valuable position, but it will also appeal to your huge, oversized ego to be in the Super Bowl." Or, "My proposal to run remnant space in my newspaper when it is available will not only help you achieve your goal of making your advertising investments as efficient as possible, but it will also appeal to your obsessive, miserly fear of losing money."

No, you have to be careful and practice subtly positioning your benefits to meet personal needs. Creating a needs-based portrait, as discussed in Chapter 7, is the first step in positioning benefits according to personal needs. The next step is to develop a Benefits Matrix, as seen in Table 8.2. You can download a blank Benefits Matrix from www.mediaselling.us.

You will notice in the matrix that the statements that position the benefits reinforce them in terms of both business and personal needs. For example, in the first row, the "High upside potential" statement could refer to investing in commercials in a Super Bowl telecast that might feature a dramatic match-up that could attract a huge audience. This benefit not only has a practical, business advantage of achieving higher-than-expected reach in an advertiser's target audience, but also a personal, emotional advantage of appealing to the customer's risk-taking nature and greed. The "Buy now, beat the competition" statement also has the practical advantages of investing before all the spots are gone, but it also appeals to the customer's need for domination and competitiveness.

The Home-Run Secret

The most important skill in media selling is being able to subtly position the benefits of your product according to personal needs—without being obvious, as shown in the Benefits Matrix. It is a skill few salespeople have, because it not only requires emotional intelligence, but it also requires a great deal of practice and preparation. Furthermore, this method is not taught in such best-selling sales books as *Spin Selling*, *The New Strategic Selling*, *Major Account Selling Strategies*, *Solutions Selling*, *Non-Manipulative Selling*, or *Consultative Selling*. You have to create a benefits matrix for your key customers and buyers and you have to practice saying the right words to hit their needs and motivations hot buttons. However, if you can master the art of positioning benefits in this manner, it is the biggest home run in selling media and, in fact, in all personal selling.

Two Don'ts in Creating Value

Don't Promise Results.   The first principle of creating value is: *Advertising is not an expense, it is an investment.* The second principle is: *Under-promise and over-deliver.* One of the main things you accomplish when you create value is that you embed and, thus, control your customers' expectations, which is especially vital. Dates turn out badly and marriages fail because of unrealistic expectations. Do not be guilty of setting unrealistic expectations in your customer's minds; it is the fastest way to lose credibility, infuriate a client, and guarantee no renewal. You will have happy customers if you lower their expectations. Then, as their advertising runs, and if they have better results than they expected, you will get an enthusiastic renewal. Conversely, you will have an unhappy customer if you raise their expectations by hinting at or promising results. If they have worse results than they expected, you will get an angry cancellation and possibly even a lawsuit.

Table 8.2   Benefits Matrix

Customer	Business Challenge	Personal Needs	Feature	Benefit	Position the Benefit
Beer	Increasing market share	Risk taker; likes to dominate competitors; motivated by greed	Sports on television	High reach in target audience	"High up-side potential;" "Buy now, beat the competition."
Financial Services	Increase share of mind and share of market	Likes to play it safe; conservative; motivated by fear of loss	News on radio	Ideal environment to improve brand image; credibility	"We're a safe buy;" "No one will criticize you for buying my station— it's number one in news."
HMO	Perceived as hindering choice	Goal oriented; likes to have friends, be liked; motivated by pride.	Health special section in newspaper	Associated with positive concept such as health and wellness; image enhancement	"Help you achieve your goals;" "You'll look good."

Unfortunately, you cannot promise or even predict results with confidence or accuracy because there are many other marketing variables that affect a customers' sales that you have no control over, as seen in Table 8.3.

Table 8.3
Marketing Variables That Affect Sales

Variable	Description
1. **Competitors' offers**	Competitors might offer contests, sweepstakes, rebates, free delivery, cash back on purchases made elsewhere for less.
2. **Competitors' advertising activity**	No matter how much an advertiser invests, if a competitor invests substantially more, especially in the same medium, it's difficult to gain market share.
3. **Competitors' creative approaches**	Competitors' effective and attention-grabbing creative approaches can blunt your customer's attempts to gain market share. Bud Light buried Miller Lite over the years not only with heavier advertising weight but also with consistently brilliant, funny commercials that young men loved.
4. **Customer's backend**	Advertisers may have great creative and sufficient advertising weight, but if their backend cannot process orders efficiently or deliver on time, they lose customers and sales.
5. **Competitors' backend**	If competitors have highly efficient backend systems, they might steal customers with faster delivery cycles and better after-purchase service.
6. **Competitive pricing**	No matter how much an advertiser invests, if competitors' prices are lower for similar quality, it is very difficult to increase sales.
7. **Competitors' innovations**	New, improved product lines and models from competitors can slow your customer's sales.
8. **Purchasing cycle**	No amount of advertising can change a product's historic purchasing cycle. No advertiser can sell bikini bathing suits in the middle of zero-degree cold spells in January.
9. **Interest level, novelty**	Some products are ho-hum products—they have low consumer interest. Household products such as toilet paper and light bulbs do not elicit a lot of interest from consumers. New, novel products such as the Chrysler PT Cruiser create interest. An advertiser with a ho-hum product can see sales fall when competitors introduce exciting new products.

Don't Knock the Competition. The third principle of creating value is: *Don't knock the competition.* Its corollary is: *Don't even mention the competition.* Perhaps the best reason for not knocking the competition is because, as shown in the survey mentioned at the beginning of this chapter, buyers do not like it. Unfortunately, in some highly competitive industries such as radio and magazines, weak, unprofessional salespeople habitually sell negatively. Table 8.4 shows the reasons why not to knock or mention the competition and gives you some ways to deal with competitors when asked about them.

Table 8.4
Knocking the Competition

Why You Shouldn't Knock (or Mention) the Competition	
Reason	**Description**
1. **Buyers hate it**	How would you like it if every conversation you had during a business day were negative, nasty, and mean-spirited? You would become depressed. Buyers feel the same way.
2. **You tear down the image of your medium**	After buyers hear how bad several competitors are, they begin to have a negative impression of the whole medium. Knocking the competition is destructive to your medium.

continued

Table 8.4
(*continued*)

Reason	Description
3. **You waste time**	Customers' and buyers' time is not unlimited; you usually have just a few minutes to get their attention and make a presentation. If you spend time knocking the competition, you waste valuable time. Remember the old adage, "You can't sell what your competitors don't have." You can only sell the benefits of what you have to offer, so get on with it.
4. **You lose credibility**	When you knock the competition, you are not perceived as being objective. Buyers say to themselves, "Of course you're badmouthing the competition; you're trying to sell me something. Why should I believe you?" Therefore, when you knock competitors, you lose credibility.
5. **You lower your image**	Selling negatively puts you down in the gutter with other negatively selling salespeople. Stay above it; refuse to throw dirt. Buyers will appreciate your positive approach and like you better for it.
6. **You can touch hidden sore spots**	You may not know if a customer or buyer has invested in advertising with a competitor (in your medium or another medium), so if you knock a competitor a buyer has invested in, you are insulting the buyer's judgment. When this happens, buyers become defensive and entrenched, and they vigorously defend their past decisions. Also, a buyer may like a salesperson (may even be dating the salesperson) and when you knock that salesperson's medium, you are knocking the salesperson and the buyer will become very defensive and defend their friend's product (and dislike yours). Remember, the media are an intangible product and, thus, salespeople become the surrogates for their products—they *are* the products in the minds of buyers.
7. **You build competitors' importance and image**	Did you ever see an ad in a magazine for Rolex that had a headline, "We're better than a Timex?" *Never* mention the competition below you in rank position; all you do is bring them up to your level. If you mention competitors under you in position, buyers' reactions are, "Why is this salesperson talking about that competitor? What is the salesperson afraid of?"

How to Respond When Asked About Competitors

Response	Description
1. **Compliment competitors**	Use a two-sided argument. The first side is a compliment to your competitors (remember, you do not know who your buyer knows or likes at your competition). By complimenting, you boost the image of your medium and come across as a positive, nice person. For example, if a buyer asks, "I understand *US News* has lowered its circulation base rate. Is this true?" You might respond with something like: "I've heard that, too. It's a shame. *US News* is a solid news magazine with an excellent editorial product and sales staff."
2. **Talk about your strengths**	Do what politicians do; do not answer the question directly, answer the question with information about the benefits of your product. For example, if a buyer says, "WAAA-TV's late news had a 20-percent drop in women 18-to-49 ratings." You might respond with, "My station's late news had a 2-percent increase in that demo even though it was a summer book and viewing levels were down."

continued

Table 8.4 (*continued*)	Reason	Description
	3. **Expose generic weaknesses**	The second side of the two-sided argument is an exposure of your competitor's generic weakness—weaknesses that are not specific to that individual competitor, but to a type or genre of products. For example, in response no. 1 above to the question, "I understand *US News* has lowered its circulation base rate. Is this true?" You might respond not only with, "I've heard that, too. It's a shame. *US News* is a solid news magazine with an excellent editorial product and sales staff," but also with the second side of the argument, "All news magazines are suffering from the advertising slowdown and are looking to cut expenses, and cutting subscriptions is one way to do this. Also, general news magazines are suffering mass circulation erosion because of the proliferation of special interest magazines such as *Maxim*."

Creating Value Ideas

To wind up this chapter, in Exhibit 8.4 you will find a list of creating value ideas. These are just a few of hundreds of ideas that can help you add value to your product, reinforce the perception of quality, utility, and service for your company and your product, and help you become a world-class media salesperson.

Exhibit 8.4
Creating Value Ideas

1. Show audience demographics by ZIP codes.
2. Show Simmons, MRI product-usage data to advertisers.
3. Provide customers with information from their trade journals.
4. Assign category sales specialists.
5. Conduct seminars on strategy for advertisers; for example, "How Retailers Can Use Television," or "How to Use Cable Television to Reach Upscale Viewers," or "How to Get Results Using Newspapers."
6. Offer business breakfasts once a quarter for local business leaders, featuring well-known, expert speakers.
7. Create a buying spectrum graphic that includes your competitors and shows a continuum of values ranging from price to quality, with quality entailing better placement and position and your medium at the quality end of the spectrum.
8. Sponsor a kid's fair or bridal fair at a local convention center or fairgrounds.
9. Develop a system for the sales staff for presenting a predetermined number of speculative ads or speculative commercials per week.
10. Sell production packages to advertisers such as mat services in newspapers or jingle packages in radio.
11. Create SWAT teams of salespeople by category and have the team develop category presentations for the use of the whole sales staff.
12. Have exhibition booths at relevant industry trade shows such as truckers' conventions, retail trade conventions, or Comdex (yearly computer industry trade show).
13. Conduct seminars for advertisers and advertising agencies on how to plan and buy your medium.
14. Conduct creative execution seminars for advertisers and advertising agencies.
15. Offer joint promotions with a charity group, an advertiser, and your company.
16. Sponsor city association luncheons honoring advertisers and advertising agencies and present creative awards.
17. Create fun carnival days to promote your medium at local trade association or civic organization meetings.
18. Offer reciprocal trade arrangements for retail shelf space.
19. In broadcasting, offer remote broadcasts to advertisers; call them marketing opportunities.
20. Distribute magazines and newsletters about your company in both print and e-mail versions.

21. In broadcasting and cable, offer special weeks on the air, similar to a newspaper or magazine advertising section, such as a week featuring furniture styles and values. In print, offer these types of special sections.
22. Develop a "Little Things Mean a Lot" list: top management follow-up calls; thank-you notes and birthday cards in invoices; Rolodex-shaped calling cards for salespeople with business, home, and cell phone numbers and e-mail addresses; framed success letters (on your walls and on your customers' walls); and shopping bags for stores imprinted with your logo and theirs.
23. Develop a total customer responsiveness (TCR) mentality throughout your company, especially by those who answer the telephone. Distribute to the entire staff the "Close to the Customer on the Telephone" paper found on www.mediaselling.us.
24. Provide copy-testing research.
25. Offer premium prices for a guaranteed position or placement.
26. Provide advertisers with several advertising success stories in their category.
27. Provide advertisers marketing research by category.
28. Conduct media auctions for a charity to establish the value of your advertising rates. Donate space or time for the charity to auction off to advertisers, who use it; the money goes to the charity.
29. Look for advertising agency account synergy opportunities for two or more accounts at an agency to share in an idea, promotion, or advertising.
30. Have an area on your Web site on which someone interested in advertising with you can contact you. Also, have access to case studies and other research material on the Web site. See www.msn.com for an example.
31. Conduct shopping mall research among a store's customers, asking them why they shop at competitors' stores.
32. Provide a list by category of your advertisers over the last year.
33. Use Reception Referrals, a system at your reception desk in which you file detailed information about advertisers, the products they promote or stock, and dates of their sales, so if people call and ask about a commercial they heard on your station, the receptionist can give them complete details.
34. Conduct brainstorming sessions. Invite clients to your offices and let the sales staff create ideas for that client; not ideas why a client should purchase your medium, but ideas for promotions, positioning, and slogans, for example.
35. Spend time in a customer's business. For example, bag groceries, wait on tables, or clean up a showroom.

Test Yourself

1. What are the six principles of influence outlined in this chapter?
2. Explain what material self-interest is.
3. Discuss the meaning of the two terms foot-in-the-door and door-in-the face.
4. What is the definition of a commodity?
5. What are the five reasons for creating value?
6. What are the seventeen value signals?
7. Give an example of an advertiser's positioning strategy as seen in an ad or a commercial.
8. What are the five steps of creating value?
9. What are the seven problems with promotions?
10. What are the differences between features, advantages, and benefits?
11. What are the three principles of creating value?
12. What are the seven reasons for not knocking the competition?

Projects

Project #1: Select a week in your life (the same week that you do the project at the end of Chapter 6 would be a good one to choose, then you can combine the two projects) in which you commit yourself to taking notes on encounters you have with compliance practitioners during the week, such as waiters in restaurants, telemarketers, retail salespeople, or fundraisers. Take notes in two columns. In the first column, note which one of the six principles of influence, if any, the compliance practitioner used. In the second column, note whether the attempt to influence you was effective or, if the person did not use a principle of influence, which one might have been appropriate. At the end of the week, look over your notes and see (1) if you identified different principles of influence and (2) if those principles of influence were effective in influencing you and if not which principles might have been used.

Project #2: Go to a local radio or television station, cable system, newspaper, or outdoor company and ask for a copy of a general presentation. If they do not have a general, introductory sales presentation, ask for a copy of a sales presentation to a specific account. Assure them that you are requesting the presentation for a class project and will not show it to competitors. Using what you have learned in this chapter about creating value, critique the presentation—make notes in it on how it could be improved to create more value. As part of this project, craft a value proposition for the organization and include it in the presentation.

References

Tony Allessandra, Ph.D., Phil Wexler and Rick Barrera. 1992. *Non-Manipulative Selling.* New York: Fireside Books.

Michael T. Bosworth. 1995. *Solutions Selling.* New York: McGraw-Hill.

Robert Cialdini. 1984. *Influence: The Psychology of Persuasion.* New York: William Morrow.

Robert Cialdini. 2001. *Influence: Science and Practice.* Boston: Allyn and Bacon.

Jay Conger. 1998. "The Necessary Art of Persuasion." *Harvard Business Review.* May-June.

Mack Hanan. 1999. *Consultative Selling.* New York: AMACOM.

Stephen E. Heiman and Diane Sanchez with Tad Tuleja. 1998. *The New Strategic Selling.* New York: Warner Books.

John Phillip Jones. 1990. "The Double Jeopardy of Sales Promotions." *Harvard Business Review.* September-October.

John Phillip Jones. 1995. *When Ads Work: New Proof That Advertising Triggers Sales.* New York: Lexington Books.

Philip Kotler. 1999. *Kotler on Marketing.* New York: Free Press.

Charles U. Larson. 1986. *Persuasion: Reception and Responsibility.* Belmont, CA: Wadsworth.

Neil Rackham. 1989. *Major Account Selling Strategy.* New York: McGraw-Hill.

Al Ries and Jack Trout. 1981. *Positioning: The Battle for Your Mind.* New York: McGraw-Hill.

Al Ries and Jack Trout. 1986. *Marketing Warfare.* New York: McGraw-Hill.

Jack Trout with Steve Rivkin. 2000. *Differentiate or Die.* New York: John Wiley & Sons, Inc.

Resources

www.mediaselling.us
www.msn.com
www.patek.com

Endnotes

1. Robert B. Cialdini. 2001. *Influence: Science and Practice.* Boston: Allyn and Bacon. p. ix.
2. Ibid. p. x.
3. Ibid. p. x.
4. Ibid. p. 4.
5. Ibid. p. 4.
6. Ibid. p. 4.
7. Ibid. p. 20.

8. Ibid. p. 22.

9. Ibid. p. 53.

10. Ibid. p. 65.

11. Ibid. p. 66.

12. Ibid. p. 67.

13. Ibid. p. 74.

14. Ibid. p. 100.

15. Ibid. p. 205.

16. Ibid. p. 206.

17. Ibid. p. 144.

18. Ibid. p. 188.

19. Abraham Kaplan. 1964. *The Conduct of Inquiry.* Scranton, PA: Chandler Publishing. p. 28.

20. DeBruicker, F. Stewart and Gregory L. Summe. 1985. "Make Sure Your Customers Keep Coming Back." *Harvard Business Review.* January-February.

21. Philip Kotler. 1999. *Kotler on Marketing.* New York: Free Press. p. 94.

22. "A Mass Market of One." 2002. *BusinessWeek.* December 2. p. 68.

23. Clayton M. Christensen. 1997. *The Innovator's Dilemma: When Technologies Can Cause Great Firms to Fail.* Boston: Harvard Business School Press.

24. John Phillip Jones. 1995. *When Ads Work: New Proof That Advertising Triggers Sales.* New York: Lexington Books. p. 53.

25. Neil Rackham. 1989. *Major Account Selling Strategy.* New York: McGraw-Hill. p. 4.

9

Skills: Prospecting and Identifying Problems

By Charles Warner

Solutions Selling

This chapter covers the first two steps of Solutions Selling. You will learn techniques to improve your skills on these two steps and you will learn a system called the Money Engine that will help you organize your efforts for each step.

The Six Steps of Solutions Selling

1. Prospecting
2. Identifying Problems
3. Generating Proposals
4. Presenting
5. Negotiating and Closing
6. Servicing

The Money Engine

The Money Engine is a system for not only getting customers, but also keeping them. It is a system that will help you organize your time and selling and servicing efforts during the above six steps, as seen in Figure 9.1.

The model for the Money Engine was suggested by the Sales Funnel in *The New Strategic Selling*[1] and by Ron Steiner, who runs the annual Broadcast Sales Academy and teaches the Sales Funnel model. You will notice in Figure 9.1 that at the top of the Money Engine there are a number of perpendicular lines.

**Figure 9.1
The money
engine.**

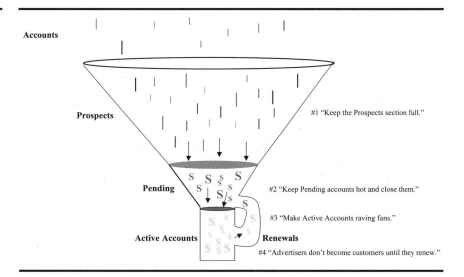

Accounts

Prospects

#1 "Keep the Prospects section full."

Pending

#2 "Keep Pending accounts hot and close them."

#3 "Make Active Accounts raving fans."

Active Accounts   Renewals

#4 "Advertisers don't become customers until they renew."

These lines represent all of the accounts that are on your *account list*, or, if you do not have an account list, all potential advertisers.

Generally, media companies provide their beginning salespeople with some type of account list, which sometimes includes hot prospects and even a few *active accounts*. The Money Engine will help you divide your selling efforts appropriately. If you are not given an account list and have to start from scratch knocking on doors and looking under every rock for someone to call on, the Money Engine model will work well for you, too. In either case, a typical account list might include 100 accounts—sometimes more in small or medium-sized markets and less in large markets or in national media where salespeople call primarily on advertising agencies.

Prospects are those accounts in the top part of the engine. While prospecting will be covered later in the chapter, it is imperative for you to understand the first principle of the Money Engine: *Keep the Prospects section full.*

Think of the Money Engine as a steam boiler that runs a revenue locomotive. You have to keep the top part, the tender, where all the fuel for the engine is stored, filled with prospects to make sure that you continually stoke the boiler fire. Out of a list of, say, 100 total accounts, 80 of them might have reasonable potential. You should spend enough time prospecting to make sure that about 40 of these accounts are bona fide prospects for your medium. Bona fide prospects are those whose target market (women 25 to 54, for example) your medium reaches. In other words, if there is a good fit between your medium's audience or readers and an advertiser's customers, that advertiser is a bona fide prospect for advertising.

Forty is an arbitrary number and in some sales situations, 60 might be a realistic number of prospects, and in others, 10. After a couple of months on the job you will know what an appropriate number is so that you can concentrate your selling efforts on legitimate prospects and not spin your wheels with those who will never buy anything.

The second section of the engine contains Pending accounts. This section is the boiler where prospects, the fuel, are heated up. Prospects become pending when, after you have qualified them, they are in the market to buy and have made a decision to invest in your medium. When salespeople get a request for a proposal (RFP) or a call from an advertising agency buyer to make a proposal, that business is now pending.

This brings us to the second principle of the Money Engine: *Keep Pending accounts hot and close them.* Once an advertiser or an agency buyer has decided to make a buy, you must stay right on top of the situation constantly, cover all the bases, and create a sense of urgency in order to get a commitment. You should shoot for having about 20 accounts pending at any given time, depending, of course, on your situation, medium, and market. In order to always have 20 accounts in the Pending section, you have to strive to keep the Prospects section filled. You should try to achieve a closing ratio of 50 percent with accounts in the Pending section and, thus, move them to the Active Account section of the Money Engine.

The bottom section of the boiler is the Active Accounts section. Active Accounts are advertisers who produce revenue. If you have kept the Prospects section full, and if you have kept Pending accounts hot and have closed 50 percent of them, you should have 10 Active Accounts that are generating money for your company and for you. This brings us to the third principle of the Money Engine: *Make your Active accounts raving fans.* Provide superb service and make sure your Active Accounts get results.

Note that there are accounts in a section of the Money Engine that looks like a handle that goes from the Active Accounts section back up to the Pending section. This is the Renewal section, which brings us to the fourth principle of the Money Engine: *Advertisers do not become customers until they renew* and its corollary: *Always sell for the second order, not just the first.* The second order will come if you under-promised when you were creating value and you over-deliver. In other words, you managed your advertisers' expectations properly and they got better results than they expected. The lower you can set their expectations, the higher their satisfaction with over-delivery will be.

The principle that advertisers do not become customers until they renew is important to remember because there is too often a tendency for salespeople to forget about accounts once they have been sold. Too many salespeople see their job as over once they make a sale. On the other hand, buyers believe a relationship is not a one-night stand and is just beginning when they make a buy. In local broadcasting and cable, attrition rates are often as high as 60 percent from one year to the next, some of it from inattention. Attrition is lower in newspapers, where the inverse is often the case. But whatever the case, it is vital to manage active accounts intensively and give them excellent service in order to reduce the amount of natural account attrition, because it is much easier to maintain and renew an account than it is to create a new one.

Prospecting

Prospecting is *creating opportunities to make a proposal.* The key to successful prospecting is working smart, which means learning how to find the right people to call on and developing an organized system for setting up appointments and presenting to them. You should spend approximately 7.5 percent of your productive time each month prospecting, perhaps twice that if you are just beginning a job or you have no assigned account list.

Prospecting Goals

The first thing to do when prospecting is to get organized and *set prospecting goals.* Set specific, task-oriented goals as follows:

1. Number of prospecting contacts. Set goals for the number of contacts per week and month, which you can make on the phone or in person. The purpose of a contact is to get an appointment. You must keep records of the number of contacts you make each week so you can analyze them later. Your contact goals should be based on how many bona fide prospects you want to have that will, in turn, lead to the number of pending accounts you know you need to have to produce the number of active accounts you want.

2. Number of appointments. You must set goals for the number of appointments you are going to make and complete each week and each month. Obviously, the focus should be placed on completed appointments; contacts are merely the first step to getting an appointment. You should then calculate and analyze on a regular basis, weekly at first, your contact-to-appointment ratio because this tells you how many contacts you have to make to set up your targeted number of appointments. Also, you and your sales manager or ad director can compare your contact-to-appointment ratios with those of other salespeople. If your ratio is low, perhaps you can improve your technique for getting appointments. Every market and medium is different, so you can determine an appropriate contact-to-appointment ratio only by trial and error, but a good benchmark ratio to begin with is 5:1, or five contacts for every legitimate sales appointment.

3. Number of bona fide prospects. When you have an appointment, you begin the solutions-selling process. The first call is an exploratory one, which you begin with an introduction of yourself, your organization, and your product. This introduction might include a general presentation if the prospective advertiser is unfamiliar with your medium or your company. After your initial appointment, you should have a feel for whether or not the prospect is a bona fide one and whether to schedule further appointments. A realistic appointment-to-prospect ratio might be 2:1, so you should set your goals accordingly to acquire the targeted number of pending accounts.

4. Number of pending accounts. You should set goals for the average number of accounts you want to have in the Pending section of the Money Engine each month, which some media companies refer to as a pipeline. You should also keep track of how many pending accounts move into the Active Accounts section of the Money Engine. The ratio of pending to active accounts is your closing ratio, and you must keep track of it. A reasonable closing ratio is 2:1 in competitive situations and probably higher in major markets, especially in television and in newspapers, where there are no viable substitute media.

5. Number of active accounts. Active accounts that run advertising and pay their bills provide commission checks. To determine how many pending accounts and how many active accounts you need to reach the income level you want, use the Radio Advertising Bureau's Sales Commission Calculator: www.rab.com/Sales_Commission_Calculator2.xls. I strongly recommend you try it and use it.

Your eventual success will depend on many variables. These include how many sales you make, the average dollar value of each sale (which, in turn, depends on your rates, the number of spots or ads per average schedule, the length of time the schedule runs), how much repeat business you can build, and how much inventory, or advertising space, is available if you are working in a medium that has a limited supply.

Prospect by Phone

Do most of your prospecting on the telephone. *Cold calls*, or in-person unannounced visits, are sometimes fun to make, particularly on a newly opened business, but they generally have low payoff odds. On occasion, to break the regular office routine, several salespeople can go to a specific area and fan out, making a geographically concentrated series of cold calls. This *gang* technique can occasionally pay dividends, but prospecting is best done alone and on the phone.

If you cannot reach a prospect by phone, write a sales letter or e-mail. Often a brief, well-written, benefit-filled letter or e-mail whets a prospective advertiser's appetite. Always indicate in the letter or e-mail that you will telephone the prospect on a certain day and at a specific time of day. Never leave it up to prospects to call you.

Cold calling is often the only way to see those prospects you cannot reach on the telephone or who have given you the brush-off several times. One broadcast sales organization kept track of the percentage of successful appointments made by phone and by cold calls. The results showed that telephone contacts got appointments 64 percent of the time and that contacts made by cold calling got appointments 92 percent of the time. Nevertheless, the phone is still the preferred method because you are using your time more efficiently.

In no other area of selling is persistence—the last P in the AESKOPP system—more important than in prospecting. You *must* get that appointment, and you should call again and again and again.

Guidelines for Effective Prospecting on the Telephone. Prospecting requires intelligent, effective digging, which is vital if you are going to increase your number of pending and active accounts. To be a successful salesperson you must master the skill of getting appointments over the phone.

Here are some basic guidelines to increase your effectiveness when you are prospecting over the telephone:

1. Write out your pitch in advance. Organize your sales conversation so that you have an effective opening and do not stumble while searching for something to say. Your pitch must be natural, comfortable, and conversational. Do not write something that you would not say in normal conversation. Your pitch must reflect your real personality.

2. Use the prospect's name. This may require a little digging, but it is much easier to get their attention and get them to listen if the first thing they hear is their own name. Use their name immediately and use it often.

3. Introduce yourself and your company. Tell prospects who you are and what company you work for. At this stage, do not ask any questions that could possibly be answered with no. Never ask, "Do you listen to my station?" or "Do you read my newspaper?" or "Have you heard of us?" A negative answer can be embarrassing and would put you on the defensive—a poor starting point.

4. Use a reference. Whenever possible, use the name of a reference you have secured, such as a friend of the prospect you are calling on or a business associate of the prospect. Always get permission to use your reference's name before you do so.

5. State that the purpose of the contact is to set up an appointment. Never try to sell your product to a potential prospect over the phone. Getting an appointment takes a great deal of practice and is by far the most critical step in the prospecting process. You must learn how to arouse prospects' curiosities, excite their interests, and appeal to their self-interest and profit motives. If you are too casual and promise "to drop by" to sell them advertising, you will soon be dissatisfied with your contact-to-appointment ratio.

6. Mention a motivating benefit. Use a phrase such as, "I have a *special reason* for calling you." The term *special reason* is extremely effective in communicating to prospects that you are not just making your rounds but have something unique for them. Make sure you actually have something special and are not over-promising. The worst openings are ones such as, "May I have a few minutes of your time?" (What do you think the inevitable response is?), or "I was wondering if you might be interested in . . .", or "I just happened to be looking in the yellow pages . . .", or, when making a cold call, the equally ineffective, "I just happened to be in the neighborhood." Always mention a motivating benefit—one that you are genuinely excited about.

7. Be quick about it. When introducing yourself and your company and stating the purpose of the call, move along rapidly. Use short sentences and try to follow your opening with a brief question that can only be answered with a yes. People often view phone calls as an interruption and are anxious to get them over with, particularly if they do not know the person on the other end.

8. The word *idea* is magic. People are hungry for ideas. Instead of selling your product, give away ideas and prospects will show their gratitude with orders.

9. Pacing is the key. Over the telephone, you must be enthusiastic and get to the point quickly; however, do not talk too fast. Pause often enough to make sure people understand and absorb what you are saying and have time to respond. Pacing is the key element in getting people to like you over the phone. Your pace should match the verbal pace of the people you are talking to. If they talk rapidly, you should speed up as well. If they talk slowly, poking casually along, then you should slow down to match their pace. Try to synchronize with their pace, tone of voice, and verbal style. Remember, people like and trust people exactly like themselves. On the telephone, become as much like the person you are talking to as possible.

10. Put a mirror on your desk and stand up. Most professional telephone sales trainers recommend that you put a mirror on your desk so you can look at yourself while you are talking on the telephone, because you will be more animated and tend to smile more. You will find that you are much more personable and friendly yourself when you are talking to someone you like. Standing up when you talk also tends to make you more animated and enthusiastic and helps you absorb more details of a phone conversation.

11. Use a headset. If you spend a lot of time on the telephone, as you do when you are calling to set up appointments, it is wise to use a telephone headset. The best ones are cordless headsets that allow you to walk around as you are talking; this keeps you awake and energized.

12. Practice. Record yourself practicing. You might have a colleague play the part of a prospect, then play the recording back and listen carefully to how you sound. Do you have a good telephone personality? If you were a prospect, would you be eager to have you come and give more information? Are you friendly and does it sound like you have a smile in your voice? Are you positive and enthusiastic? Do you sound like a helpful expert? Be critical of your own telephone personality and technique; you can be sure potential customers are.

Following are several examples of prospecting approaches. Keep in mind that these are only examples and that you must develop approaches with which you are comfortable, that reflect your personality and style. You must avoid sounding stiff, unnatural, canned, or rehearsed. The best way to check on how you sound is to record your scripted telephone approach and listen to yourself carefully. Then, ask yourself if you would give you an appointment.

Salesperson: "Hello, Mr. Smith. How are you feeling today? (Pause for an answer.) I'm Charlie Warner from WAAA Radio. I'm not trying to sell you anything over the phone today, but could you use some more store traffic, particularly on Mondays or Tuesdays, your slow days? I would like to make an appointment to see you for a few moments to tell you about an exciting new sales promotion the station has created that I believe can help generate some real excitement, enthusiasm, and *new prospects and traffic* for your store. May I come by tomorrow, say, at 10 in the morning?"

Salesperson: "Hello, Ms. Johnson. This is Charlie Warner from Channel 8. I have just been assigned to your account and I'd like to set up an appointment to come by and introduce myself in person and get to know more about your business. I would also like to update you on some exciting things we are doing for our advertisers. Is tomorrow morning at 10 A.M. good for you?"

Salesperson: "Hello, Mr. Green. I'm Charlie Warner with *The Tribune*. I'd like to share with you an idea that could possibly increase your business more than 200 percent. I can come to your office at any convenient time and show you a layout for an ad that is tailor-made for you. It is based on an idea our advertising people have come up with that is similar to one that was enormously successful for a store just like yours downstate—the ad increased their sales 237 percent! When is best for you? In the morning or in the afternoon?"

13. If you get a yes, reconfirm the time and day and terminate the call. As soon as you get an appointment, reconfirm the time and day and ask the prospect to write it down. Ask, "Do you have your appointment book or personal digital assistant (PDA) handy? I'm putting next Tuesday at 10 A.M. in my PDA. Would you please write the time in your PDA?" People will usually do what you ask. Also, this technique makes you sound like a well-organized professional. Immediately after reconfirming the appointment, terminate the call pleasantly but quickly. Do not stay on the telephone and chat; you might give the prospect another opportunity to think about his or her schedule and to say no. Also, do not call again to confirm the appointment the day of the appointment; it just presents another opportunity for a no. If you have a sales assistant or someone else who could help you, have the assistant call before you arrive and say, "Mr. Jones, Mr. Warner asked me to call and tell you he's on his way and will be on time for his 10 o'clock appointment."

14. If the answer is no, press on. Be persistent; do not give up easily, a mistake many beginning salespeople make. Try to find out in as pleasant a manner as possible why you are being put off. Most prospects' *stoppers (reasons for stopping you from coming to see them)* are not legitimate objections but are merely knee-jerk (reflex) phrases they use to discourage the faint-of-heart. The successful salesperson must learn to move through these initial, brush-off rejections and to get appointments. Getting appointments requires mental toughness and persistence. The natural tendency is to take prospects' put-offs at face value and to accept what they say to avoid being considered pushy. However, pressing on carefully and intelligently is what selling is all about.

Here are some techniques to use to overcome the *don't-come-to-see-me* stopper:

A. Ask *"why"* if the prospect does not offer a reason. Try to get specific objections so you can overcome them one at a time. Write them down so you remember them.

B. Try the *"yes, but"* technique. Always try to find a new way to agree with the prospect and then turn him or her around with a "but:"

Prospect: "I tried radio once and it didn't work."

Salesperson: "*Yes*, I've heard a few people say that. Unfortunately, some advertisers seem to have had a bad experience, *but* on the other hand, some of the most profitable enterprises in your line of business are using it very successfully and often. If I could chat with you for just a few minutes, perhaps I could point out to you why it hasn't worked for you but has for many others."

C. Use the *compliment* technique:

Prospect: "I'm too busy right now. Besides, I'm bothered to death by media salespeople as it is."

Salesperson: "Gosh, Mr. Johnson, I'm really disappointed. You're one of the most important clients I have and you are considered to be one of the best merchandisers in the area. I was hoping to meet you and get your opinion on several things. I won't take up much of your very busy schedule and it certainly would be very important to me."

D. Try the *"if-one-of-your-salespeople"* approach:

Prospect: "No, I don't have time to see you. I've committed my advertising dollars."

Salesperson: "Mr. Johnson, you have salespeople who sell your product, don't you?"

Prospect: "Yes."

Salesperson: "If one of your salespeople came to you and said they were having trouble getting an appointment with a very important customer, what advice would you give that salesperson?"

E. Try the *standing-room-only* technique: This is an honest, limited-supply technique that uses the scarcity principle.

Prospect: "I'm sorry but we're not advertising right now."

Salesperson: "I understand your position, but this special January package is one of the fastest-selling, most efficient packages the station has offered in a long time, and I'd sure hate for you not to at least hear about it. You might really get upset with me if I didn't inform you about such a great deal before it's sold out."

F. Try the *assume-you-want-to-see-me-but-are-too-busy-now* approach:

Prospect: "I'm too busy to see you."

Salesperson: "I know how busy you must be; you're in a tough business. When is the best time to catch you, first thing in the morning or right after closing time?"

Methods of Prospecting

The second thing to do in getting organized properly for this step of selling is to *select a method* of prospecting:

1. By current advertisers in other media
2. By season
3. By category
4. By geographic region
5. By advertisers in your medium
6. By inactive advertisers
7. By current advertisers
8. By business, civic, or social organizations

The obvious first place to start prospecting is in *other media.* Try to find businesses that are advertising but not in your medium. It is generally easier, and thus a more efficient use of your time, to try to sell to prospects who already have an advertising budget than to have to start from scratch with someone and sell them first on advertising, then on your medium, and then on your product.

To prospect in other media, you should know something about their rates so you can estimate advertising budgets. In many larger markets, *newspaper checking bureaus* keep track of ads by client categories. Also, many markets have TNS Media Intelligence competitive media reports (CMR) online that radio and television stations can subscribe to. Each month CMR publishes details of all radio and television advertising schedules that ran the previous month. If your market does not have monitoring services available, you can ask advertisers or their agencies for rate cards of other media outlets in your market and you and your fellow salespeople can monitor other media on a systematic basis.

Next, in your monitoring, you should try to pick out the creative approaches your prospects use, the images they are trying to project about their businesses, and their approximate target audiences for the advertising.

The *yellow pages,* known as the Prospector's Bible, is the place to start because anyone in business who sells a product or service to the public will be in the yellow pages. It is the place to start and to go back to time and again when you prospect in a local market. However, today the best source of prospecting information is the Internet. If you are fortunate to have an auto dealer or two on your list, there are several places you can go to on the Web to get a wealth of information. The Web site for the National Association of Automobile Dealers, www.nada.org, has up-to-date news on auto industry trends and www.hoovers.com is an excellent resource to research companies and industries in general.

If you get a job or work for a television station that is a member of the Television Bureau of Advertising (TVB), its Web site has some industry profiles. The best industry-by-industry profiles I have seen are on the Web site of the Marketing Communications Group, www.tvsalespro.com, but stations have to subscribe in order to access them.

There are other industry associations, such as the National Soft Drink Association, that have informative Web sites (www.nsda.org). If you do not know if a business has a Web site or an industry association, Google it—go to www.google.com and do a search.

If you sell broadcast, cable, or Interactive, *read newspaper ads* carefully, for they are the most fertile ground for other media. Look for a newspaper advertiser's selling points, image, creative approach, and target audience when you examine newspaper ads. If advertisers are continuously getting positions with low reader impact, such as bottom-left, back-of-the-section, or gutter positions (next to the fold), they might be ripe prospects for broadcast, cable, Interactive, or outdoor advertising.

If you sell newspaper, radio, or Interactive, monitor television for commercials for local businesses. Television is the most vulnerable local medium because it is expensive and many local businesses, especially car dealers, over-invest in television.

Prospecting by *seasonal sales patterns* is a productive way to organize your prospecting efforts. Most advertisers have seasonal sales patterns; therefore, advertisers should be contacted anywhere from three to six months before their peak selling seasons begin. A salesperson should find out when advertisers set their annual advertising budgets and make promotion plans and contact them at that time. November is obviously too late to start selling advertising for the Christmas season.

Another way to organize your prospecting is by *category*. Select a business category, such as men's clothing, for example, and begin contacting as many of these businesses as you can. Combine this category method with the seasonal one and choose a category that has a seasonal sales peak coming up. You will find that this category method is an excellent way to become an expert in a particular business category and helps you get referrals. As you get prospects to tell you about their advantages over their competitors, you will also learn how to approach those competitors. You can also go to www.adage.com and look at ad/sales ratios for categories.

Many successful media salespeople have carved out profitable careers by specializing in one or two categories, such as department stores, supermarkets and food, automotive industries, and so on. There are many excellent resources on the Internet for prospecting by category.

Often it makes sense to organize prospecting efforts *geographically*. This is particularly the case in markets that are spread out physically, such as Los Angeles. Isolate an area of town that looks promising and start making phone calls to set up appointments. When you do get your appointments, you will save time and gas money by going to one general area. You can use the Internet to help you prospect in a new geographical area by going to www.mapquest.com and getting a map of the area, which you can download onto your PDA.

You can prospect in *your own medium*. However, this type of prospecting tends to encourage parasitic behavior and leads to hordes of salespeople trying to carve up the same advertising pie, which, in turn, often leads to price cutting and overall lower rates. It is better to try to increase the size of the pie by developing new advertisers whenever possible.

Prospect internally by looking at *inactive account lists*. Go back several years through the files of completed contracts and look for advertisers who were once active but are not currently running. You might be amazed when you ask someone why they are no longer advertising with you and the reply is, "No one asked for my business again." This inactive account would be another easy sale for the disciplined, well-organized prospector.

Furthermore, do not overlook the obvious. Do not forget your *current advertisers*. While serving these customers, think of ways to get them to increase their schedule with you. Sell promotional packages, special events, longer schedules, or more ads, but do not fail to look at them as potential prospects for new revenue.

Finally, you can organize your prospecting efforts *organizationally,* by civil, social, or business clubs or by sports, church, or fraternal organizations. Insurance salespeople often prospect this way, and so can media salespeople.

Referral Prospecting

You should never pass up the opportunity to ask a prospect, a customer, a friend, or an acquaintance to refer you to someone who might be a potential advertiser. The best referrals are from happy customers, so get in the habit of politely asking for referrals, because you have nothing to lose and sales to gain.

Prospecting is where selling begins. Good prospectors can always make a living; they do not have to depend on economic conditions, ratings, circulation, or rates. They can find new customers time and time again, year in and year out. Successful salespeople know how to organize themselves and to plan their time using the Money Engine to keep the Prospects tender full, to keep Pending accounts hot and to close them, and to make Active Accounts raving fans.

Identifying Problems

The next step, after prospecting, in the solutions-selling process is *identifying problems.* This step has two phases: *qualifying* and *identifying problems.*

Qualifying Phase

After you have identified prospects and have made an initial appointment, qualifying prospects comes next. Qualifying is finding the *right* people to call on. According to Mark McCormack, author of *What They Don't Teach You at the Harvard Business School,* effective selling is more a matter of timing and the quality of the doors you knock on than the quantity of doors you knock on.[2]

Qualifying is an important part of the selling process because it is in this step that you *begin your relationship with your customers.* Qualifying is largely a matter of finding out if a prospective customer has the resources to advertise and if there is a fit with your medium so you can get results for the prospect. Qualifying is when you begin to identify needs—both business and personal. You must carefully observe prospects' surroundings and behavior and learn to read the room and their desks.

Learning About Your Prospects.   Harvey B. Mackay, Chairman of the Board of Mackay Envelope Corporation and author of the successful book *Swim With the Sharks Without Being Eaten Alive,* says that knowing your customer is not a cliché, it is the foundation of a sale.[3] In an article in the *Harvard Business Review,* Mackay wrote about a mythical conversation with a salesperson who cannot get a buyer, Bystrom of International Transom, to quit using Mackay Envelope's competitor, Enveloping Envelope. Mackay looks at the account folder with the salesperson and says sternly: "Did you read his desk? Were there any mementos there that told you about him? How many plaques on the wall? What's his alma mater? If he's businesslike with you, what are his aspirations? How does he identify with company goals? You don't have in here a recent article or current analyst's report on his company." Mackay gets up from his desk and gesticulates as he paces to and fro and continues. "How well have YOU shown him that you know and admire his company; that you know how it fits in its industry? Do you know the strengths and weaknesses of Enveloping Envelope in terms of International Transom? Have you emphasized to Bystrom those strengths that we have almost exclusively, such as centralized imprinting?"[4]

You do not want to be in the same position as the hapless salesperson above. Make sure you qualify prospects thoroughly, and read the surroundings, the office, their desk, and their behavior. The first appointment is essential for gathering information about your prospects so you can begin to create a needs-based portrait of their business and personal needs and motivations.

The Qualifying Appointment.   On your first qualifying appointment, it is usually best not to take notes. Taking notes while your prospect is talking is similar to tape recording the conversation; it makes many people nervous and unwilling to open up. It also means you are concentrating on writing and not on the prospect. If you are conducting a lengthy, fact-gathering interview, you might need to take a few notes very quickly, but be careful not to do anything that might reduce the opportunity to establish rapport during the first interview. Immediately *after* you leave the appointment, take detailed notes while the details are fresh in your mind. Follow up the initial appointment with more fact-finding interviews with people who work for the prospect. Learn the prospect's business thoroughly before you make a sales presentation.

Here are your goals for your first meeting:

1. To build rapport instantly: You never get a second chance to make a first impression. You have about 15 to 60 seconds to create a favorable first impression. Prospects will continue to judge you based on this first impression and reinforce their judgment the remainder of the time they know you. Your initial goal from the moment you lay eyes on your prospects is to get them to like you, which requires using the emotional intelligence and influence skills you learned in Chapter 6. You must also use the effective communication, effective listening, and understanding people skills you learned in Chapter 7.

When you shake hands, do exactly what the other person does. If prospects have soft, limp handshakes, you reciprocate. People of this type are not prone to enjoying aggressive handshakes that involve a tight grip, firm squeezing, and vigorous pumping. In contrast, if people grab your hand, squeeze, and pump heartily, follow their energetic lead. Remember, people like and trust people exactly like themselves. As you do when you talk to prospects on the telephone, synchronize with their speech patterns in person.

2. To build trust. The quickest way to build trust with people you do not know well is to find something on which you can agree and then agree 100 percent. In your conversations with prospects, you will touch on a number of subjects, many of which you will disagree on. On the other hand, do not be hypocritical and say something you really do not believe. Keep probing until you find something you can agree on and then say, "I agree 100 percent." Try to compliment your prospect on something specific, which usually gets prospects talking.

If prospects bring up any negatives about salespeople, your medium, or your company, honor them and compliment them for bringing up the point. People will trust you if you show confidence in yourself and your product and are not afraid to deal with negatives, especially if you bring them up. Be totally candid. The two-sided argument is particularly effective at this time. For example, you might say, "There are some problems with using radio, Mr. Jones. You can't demonstrate or show products on radio, but an effective creative approach can work wonders."

3. To become a partner with prospects. You must communicate your desire to become a partner with your prospects in solving their problems and making them successful. Sell yourself as a media expert and an advertising problem solver. By not trying to sell prospects anything while you are qualifying them, you plant the seed that you and your product might become the solution, instilling a sense of cooperation. You are beginning to cultivate a relationship, to build a partnership.

4. To qualify creditworthiness. Qualifying also means that you must check a prospect's credit. There is no future for a salesperson who sells advertising to someone who will not or cannot pay for it. Many small- and medium-market media pay commissions on collections and not on billing. Thus, a salesperson who sells to prospects who have shaky credit ratings is taking time away from selling to prospects who will pay their bills and generate sales commissions.

Checking credit ratings is a task for a business manager and not for salespeople, particularly on the first call. Salespeople, however, should make it a point to know the results of credit checks. If a business office, for whatever reason, recommends getting cash in advance from a prospect whose credit has not yet been established, salespeople should ask for cash in advance very delicately, so as not to risk offending or insulting a potential customer. If a prospect gets upset, a salesperson can blame an overzealous business manager, who is paid to take the heat in situations such as this. This tactic leaves the door open for future contacts. By the way, all political advertising is cash-in-advance, and politicians and those who plan and buy their advertising understand this policy.

Most beginning salespeople find that qualifying is not an easy step to master. One reason for this difficulty is that proper qualifying requires salespeople to be tough-minded and to not waste time with people who are not good, prospective advertisers or with people who are not in a position to make the final decision, no matter how pleasant they might be.

5. To assess perceptual set and readiness. Every person enters every situation with a *perceptual set,* which is a predisposition to perceive things in a certain way. Recall from Chapter 7 how stereotyping, first impressions, projection, and other factors form barriers to perception, and that no one is neutral. People come to any encounter with values, attitudes, beliefs, and opinions about virtually everything. For example, they might not like salespeople in general or they might not care for either female or male salespeople. They might not like your medium. They might not like young people.

It is important for you to ferret out prospects' perceptual sets so you can plan your sales strategy and set your selling priorities. For instance, you may recognize that a particular older male retailer does not seem to care to deal with young people or with females. If you are both, you will have to build source credibility with qualities other than similarity. Thus, you might concentrate on being especially businesslike and try to develop trust through a belief in your expertise and extensive product knowledge.

Readiness is the notion that people will learn what they want to learn and are able to learn. A wide variety of variables, such as educational level, emotions, ambitions, success, past experience, and selective perception condition people's readiness.

A prospect who has had a bad experience advertising in your medium is not willing to learn about what you are offering. You might have to focus your sales strategy on discussing several successful case histories of similar businesses in your medium just to get this prospect to listen to a presentation of the benefits you offer.

6. To get an appointment for a discovery meeting. Remember that the qualifying appointment is not a sales call; it should be a call in which you gain permission to learn more about your prospects' business, to ask a series of discovery questions so you can bring back an appropriate solutions-based proposal.

Identifying Problems Phase

The entire premise of solutions selling rests on the idea that there are marketing and advertising problems to solve. So, once you qualify prospects and find out they have the resources to advertise, and you believe your medium can legitimately help them, the next phase in the solutions-selling process is to get access to prospects' information so you can identify their problems. How do you do this detective work? You ask a lot of the right questions.

There are three types of questions, or probes: *open-end questions, closed-end questions,* and *verification questions.* Start with open-end questions, such as, "Tell me more about your store." You get a lot more information with open-end questions because you are not asking for specific information. Your prospects will often wander off in several directions and sometimes, even, give you more information than they intended. Remember, most people like to talk, so let them.

Closed-end questions are those that ask for a specific answer, such as, "What is your advertising budget?" Think of your questioning technique as a funnel that starts out wide, with open-end questions pouring lots of information into the funnel, and as you learn more, you can be more selective and ask narrower and narrower, more-specific, closed-end questions in order to get the information you want. The reason you start with open-end questions is that they build trust in the relationship, and once trust is established, the prospect is much more likely to give you informative answers to your closed-end questions.

A verification question is an efficient, information-seeking question framed in a way that elicits a yes answer to verify information that you believe is correct. For example, "As advertising manager, you make the final decision. Is that correct?"

Discovery Questions. Ask the 27 Discovery Questions shown in Exhibit 9.1 in a series of interviews with appropriate people in prospects' organizations. Do not try to ask all of them at one meeting—it takes too much time. Spread the questions out over several appointments and among several people, if possible.

Note that the first several questions are ones that you should know the answers to based on your research. This is the perfect situation to use verification questions to make sure your information is correct and to show your prospects that you are knowledgeable about their business and industry.

As you can see from the list, the questions are quite thorough and are obviously not appropriate in every situation. All 27 Discovery Questions might be asked of a major advertiser in a large market or of a national advertiser with a sizeable advertising budget. I suggest using the questions in Exhibit 9.1 as a guideline and that you develop your own list of questions that are appropriate for your market and your medium. (You can download the discovery questions from www.mediaselling.us.)

Finally, the most important questions are follow-up questions. After you get an answer to one of the following Discovery Questions, ask, "Why?" Also, when you are following up, probe for feelings, not just for the company line. If you ask the right probing questions, you can get people to think about their problems from a new perspective and to think more deeply about their problems and potential solutions.

**Exhibit 9.1
Discovery Questions**

1. Before making a call, the following information about a potential customer should be researched. Your first question should be a verification question to confirm that the information you have gathered is correct. For example, "Our research indicates that your revenue is $6 billion a year, your income is $550 million, and that you have 11,000 employees. Are my assumptions correct?"
   A. Size
      i. Revenue (sales)?
      ii. Income?
      iii. Number of employees?
2. In your research, you should also develop a profile of the company and find answers to the following questions. If you can't find the information, you should ask appropriate, closed-ended questions.
   A. How long in business?
   B. Business structure? (Public company, privately held, corporation, partnership, sole proprietor, franchiser, franchisee, e.g.)
   C. Number of locations/outlets?
   D. Distribution channel? (Retail, direct marketing, wholesalers, online, catalogues, e.g.)
   E. Type of product/service? (Impulse purchase, planned purchase, high priced, low priced, middle range, mass consumer, luxury, e.g.)
   F. Peak selling season(s)?
      i. Percent of yearly business at peak seasons?
   G. Business cycle? (Purchase once a day, once a week, once a year, once in a lifetime, e.g.)
   H. Five largest customers?
   I. How has business changed in the past year?
3. Before making a call, the following information about a prospect should be researched. Your next group of questions should confirm what you have learned.
   A. Total marketing budget?
      i. Direct selling?
      ii. Advertising?
      iii. Promotion? (percent trade, percent consumer; advertising/promotion ratio)
      iv. Cause marketing, corporate relations, PR budget?
   B. Total advertising/direct marketing budget in dollars?
      i. Advertising rank in industry? (Who is number 1, number 2, and number 3?)
      ii. National, national spot, and local budgets?
   C. Advertising as a percentage of revenue (sales)–ad/sales ratio.
      i. Ad/sales ratio rank in industry (Who is number 1, number 2, number 3?)
      ii. Advertising rank in industry? ("What competitors spend more in what media?")
4. During the discovery process (which will take several calls at different levels of an organization), you should find answers to the following questions:
   A. "What research do you look at and what does it tell you?" (You need to know the answer to this question so that your eventual proposal doesn't contradict what they believe from their research).

B. Who in the organization will make the final decision?
   i. A single decision maker (CEO, senior VP of marketing, e.g.)
   ii. The key influencers (CFO, senior VP of advertising, e.g.)
   iii. Influencers (Ad committee, consultants, e.g.)
C. What is the organization's decision-making process like? (Fast, slow, consensus, CEO only, consultants, e.g.)
5. "If I could wave a magic wand, and make three wishes come true for your company next year, what would you wish for?" (Examples: Increase profitability, reduce expenses, sell more product/service, introduce new products, increase share of mind (branding), increase stock price)
6. "What are your marketing goals?" Examples:

Introduce new product/service	Create demand
Introduce line extension	Change customer attitudes
Develop/increase traffic	Feature specialty products
Maintain market dominance	Develop seasonal buying
Recapture old customers	Build destination
Expand target market (age, geography)	Build private label
Establish or re-establish image	Increase profit margins
Build brand awareness	Increase response level
Reinforce leadership position	Promote special sales
Promote special events	Increase market share
Increase usage	Move up one market rank
Expand size of pie (market)	Dominate (own) a market

7. "What problems are you having in achieving those marketing goals?"
8. "What are your primary marketing strategies?" (Examples: differentiation, focus/niche marketing, or low-cost producer)
9. "What are your secondary marketing strategies?" (Defense, offense, flanker brand, fighting brand, guerrilla marketing, ambush marketing, e.g.)
10. "What is your current market position?" (Dominant leader, number one, close second, follower, last, e.g.)
11. "Who are you trying to reach—who is your primary target customer?"
    A. "What percentage of your business is done by your heavy users/big customers?" (Example: 85 percent of product bought by 15 percent of customers.)
    B. "Who are your secondary target customers?"
    C. "Who are your most profitable customers?"
12. "Why do your customers buy from you—what is your major appeal?"
13. "What messages or creative approaches have been most successful for you in the past?"
14. "Who (organization) does your creative?"
    A. "Who (organization) does your media planning?"
    B. "What advertising media are you currently using?"
15. "How is your budget allocated among the media you use?"
    A. "Does this allocation reflect current media usage by consumers?"
       i. "How effective are the media you are currently using?"
    B. "How do you track the results/response to your advertising?"
    C. "What advertising problems are you having and which ones are you trying to solve?"
    D. "Are there any perceptions about your brand that you would like to change?"
    E. "What do you want your advertising/direct marketing to do for you?"
16. "What are your advertising goals?" (Examples: Sales/transactions, branding, awareness, information, persuasion, or reminding/reinforcing)
    A. "Who are your three/five biggest competitors?"
17. "Why do your customers buy from each of your major competitors?"
    A. "What strategies do you have to capture share from your competitors?"
    B. "How are you differentiating yourself from your competitors?" (Price, quality, convenience, location, selection, e.g.)
18. "What do you do better than your competitors?"
    A. "What do they do better than you do?"
19. "What do you think of my medium of advertising?"

    A. "Who owns the search terms most valuable to your business and industry?"
       i. "Have you been monitoring your competitors' advertising activity, campaigns, and creative?"
    B. "Are there any specific goals you have in mind for your advertising?" (Low CPMS, promotions, e.g.)
    C. "What advertising/marketing element has produced the best ROI for you?"
20. "What time of year do you (A) plan and (B) buy advertising?"
21. "Are there any co-op dollars available?"
22. "Do you use promotions; if so what kind?" (Sales, rebates, contests, sweepstakes, coupons, free samples, e.g.)
    A. "Is your decision to purchase a medium based on doing a promotion?"
    B. "Do you create your own promotions or do you depend on the media or an outside agency or promotion company?"
23. "What are your criteria for judging the best proposal?"
    A. "What are your metrics for success?"
24. "What do you think of my company?"
    A. "What is the likelihood that you'd buy from us?"
25. "Is there anything I should have asked you, but haven't?"
26. "What are your advertising strategies during the current slowdown?"
27. "What questions do you have for me?"

When you ask your Discovery Questions, the conversation should not be interrogative or manipulative, but should be relaxed and comfortable. In Chapter 6 we wrote that old models of selling don't work any more, which is a major reason why the solutions-selling model evolved. Experienced advertising agencies' media buyers have seen every trick. They know full well when a salesperson tries to manipulate them or tries to close them.

Some salespeople have been trained to ask manipulative questions that lead prospects to a conclusion that the salespeople want them to reach, regardless of what a prospect might want. Even though in Chapter 6 I recommended Neil Rackham's *SPIN Selling* because it contains some useful sales lessons, I do not recommend using the technique of asking the SPIN Selling questions. The mnemonic SPIN stands for four types of questions that salespeople should ask: Situation questions, Problem questions, Implication questions, and Needs-Payoff questions.[5]

Rackham chose an unfortunate mnemonic, unwittingly I'm sure, because SPIN has a pejorative meaning. Spin is a term that means spinning a news story that could be negative away from the underlying truth toward a meaning that is more favorable to the spinner. Spinning news or information is manipulative. Also, the book, published in 1988, was based on research conducted over several years before that, before solutions selling became the modern model for selling, which means that SPIN Selling is an outdated method.

The last two types of SPIN questions (Implication and Needs-Payoff questions) also tend to be manipulative, as Rackham suggests asking them. Using these types of questions is using the Socratic method.

If Socrates was the greatest teacher of all time, how could he be manipulative? In her book *I Only Say This Because I Love You,* author Deborah Tannen writes:

> "The Socratic method, according to philosopher Janice Moulton, is frequently (though not accurately) identified as 'a method of discussion designed to lead the other person into admitting that her/his views were wrong' . . . I use the term *Socratic method* to refer to a style of arguing in which you try to get others to admit they are wrong—and to agree with your conclusion—by getting them

to agree to one after another step along the way, which the Greek philosopher Socrates (as we see in Plato's dialogues) posed a series of questions, the answers to which exposed others' ignorance or uncovered contradictions in their beliefs."[6]

We all know what happened to Socrates—he committed suicide by drinking hemlock rather than be exiled from Athens. Salespeople who try to manipulate and use tricks on savvy customers and media buyers will be exiled. When you ask Discovery Questions, do not ask leading questions; ask straightforward, authentic, non-manipulative questions.

Once you have asked enough questions to identify the marketing and advertising goals, strategies, and problems a prospect has, go back to your office and do a thorough diagnosis of the problems. Come up with solutions that are unique to your medium, and generate proposals that offer your solutions effectively—the subject of the next chapter.

Test Yourself

1. What are the four principles associated with the Money Engine?
2. What are the five prospecting goals?
3. What are the 12 guidelines for effective prospecting on the telephone?
4. What are the eight methods of prospecting?
5. What are the two phases of identifying problems?
6. What are the six goals for your first qualifying appointment?
7. Why is the Socratic method manipulative?

Project

Assume you are a salesperson for your local newspaper. Write a script for a prospecting telephone call to a local business in which you try to get an appointment. Assume the prospect you are calling answers yes to all of your questions. Rehearse reading your script several times, and then record yourself. Play back the recording. Did you sound friendly and confident? Would you give you an appointment? Make notes on how you could improve your telephone technique and try again. Repeat this exercise until you are satisfied that you sound effective, friendly, and confident.

References

Stephen E. Heiman and Diane Sanchez with Tad Tuleja. 1998. *The New Strategic Selling*. New York: Warner Books.

Harvey Mackay. 1988. "Humanize Your Selling Strategy," *Harvard Business Review*. March-April.

Harvey Mackay. 1988 *Swim With the Sharks Without Being Eaten Alive*. New York: William Morrow.

Mark McCormack. 1984. *What They Don't Teach You at the Harvard Business School*. New York: Bantam Books.

Neil Rackham. 1988. *SPIN Selling*. New York: McGraw-Hill.

Deborah Tannen. 2001. "*I Only Say This Because I Love You.*" New York: Random House.

Resources

www.cabletvadbureau.com
www.hoovers.com
www.mapquest.com
www.nna.org

www.nada.org
www.nsda.org
www.rab.com
www.tvb.org
www.tvsalespro.com

Endnotes

1. Stephen E. Heiman and Diane Sanchez with Tad Tuleja. 1998. *The New Strategic Selling*. New York: Warner Books.
2. Mark McCormack. 1984. *What They Don't Teach You at the Harvard Business School*. New York: Bantam Books.
3. Harvey Mackay. 1988 *Swim With the Sharks Without Being Eaten Alive*. New York: William Morrow.
4. Mackay, Harvey. 1988. "Humanize Your Selling Efforts." *Harvard Business Review*. March-April.
5. Neil Rackham. 1988. *SPIN Selling*. New York: McGraw-Hill.
6. Deborah Tannen. 2001. *"I Only Say This Because I Love You."* New York: Random House. p. 80.

10 Skills: Generating Proposals

By Charles Warner

The third step in the solutions-selling process is *generating proposals*. This is the *process of preparation* in which you find an effective match between prospects' problems and solutions that you can provide. Then, you have to present these solutions in an arresting, dramatic, and winning proposal.

To ensure that your solutions and proposals not only address prospects' challenges and needs, but are also ethical, let's review the nine ethical don'ts from Chapter 3:

Nine Don'ts

1. Don't lie to advertisers.
2. Don't sell anything that customers do not need.
3. Don't allow clients to feel that they lost in a negotiation.
4. Don't be unfair to advertisers.
5. Don't sell something customers cannot afford.
6. Don't use bait-and-switch tactics (selling something you know is not available just to get the money in the door).
7. Don't recommend or accept advertising that is in bad taste or that will harm an account's image.
8. Don't accept false or misleading advertising.
9. Don't offer kickbacks to customers.

In 1961, I was fortunate enough to have worked my way from being a rookie salesperson in Spartanburg, SC, to being an account executive for the number-one television station in the country—WCBS-TV, Channel 2, in New York. At the time the station was referred to as the "Big Deuce." It was the Mecca for media salespeople because it was in the number-one media market, it was an owned station of the number-one television network (known as the "Tiffany Network" at the time), and it was, by far, the most dominant television station in New York.

The general sales manager of WCBS-TV, Norm Walt, was notorious in the media and advertising community for insisting that all of his salesmen (there were no women salespeople at that time) create a written presentation for every submission. All of the Big Deuce's business at the time came from advertising agencies, and agency buyers would call the salesmen assigned to them and request avails for one of the agency's accounts. Buyers just wanted to know what times (also called spots) were available on the station and prices for each spot. Other television stations' salesmen often did just that, submit a list of avails and prices and let buyers select what they wanted to buy. Not Big Deuce salesmen.

To buyers' never-ending protestations, WCBS-TV salesmen would come in with thick presentations and proceed to go over every page. Salesmen who did not follow this procedure were fired by the flame-throwing Walt, so everyone slogged through their presentations. The presentations were required to be comb-bound in white plastic, to have a thick, clear plastic outer cover over a deep, heavy-stock, yellow-gold cover page with the famous black CBS eye in the bottom right-hand corner with a tastefully large, white, Helvetica-font 2 over the eye. It was an impressive and tasteful package and it reeked of quality and importance, which, of course, is what Norm Walt wanted.

The presentations had to contain information about the Big Deuce's complete dominance in the market—48 out of the 50 top-ranked spots in the market, for example. The presentations were designed to overwhelm buyers with WCBS-TV's dominance and make them feel they would be lucky to be able to get on the station. Salesmen were chosen for their ability to communicate an image of complete confidence and domination. Most of them crossed over to arrogance.

Salesmen did not offer a list of avails and prices; after creating value for the Big Deuce, they offered packages of spots. Buyers could not buy individual spots within a package, they had to buy the whole package. I offered a package to the buyer for Griffin Shoe Polish that consisted of two Early Morning News spots, seven Late-Late Show spots (after 1:00 A.M.), and one desirable spot, the "7:00 P.M. News with Robert Trout." When I presented the package, the buyer said, "You've got to be kidding! The only spot I want is the news spot. OK, I'll take it to get the news spot."

I jubilantly brought the order back to the station and showed it to Norm Walt who said, "Great order, Charlie. I can confirm all the spots but the 7:00 P.M. News. Go back and get the buyer to accept the change." That was the way it was back then and some salesmen were able to sell that way. I was not good at it.

WCBS-TV designed the whole system to create value and maximize revenue, and it did. But times have changed drastically as the television medium has been fragmented and no one station or network is dominant. Today, buyers are in the driver's seat, not stations or networks. However, the power of an excellent presentation has not diminished.

Proposals and Presentations

This brings up some questions. How excellent is excellent? What is the difference between a presentation and a proposal? How long should a presentation or proposal be?

First, how excellent is excellent? An excellent presentation is one that wins, that beats the competition. If your competitors regularly bring three-page proposals to buyers who have asked for RFPs or avails, you should bring five-page proposals. If your biggest competitor regularly makes unexciting 50-page presentations to major accounts for large, year-long partnership deals, you should create a dramatic, 80-page presentation that blows away the competition.

Never deliver avails, a one-page proposal, or a rate card only, no matter what buyers ask for. You do not want to be merely a clerk who processes transactions. *Always* include qualitative information about your advantages over the competition and benefits. You must create a differential competitive advantage for yourself and your product in order to avoid, if possible, discounting your rates. Your proposals and presentations are major building blocks in constructing a competitive advantage and creating value.

Game Theory

Game theory is currently a hot topic in economics, investing, politics, and international relations. The mathematical genius John von Neumann first developed game theory in 1928.[1] John Nash, the subject of the movie "A Beautiful Mind," won a Nobel Prize in Economics for his refinements to von Neumann's theories. Watching players bluff in a poker game in 1928 inspired von Neumann—father of the modern computer and one of the sharpest minds in the twentieth century—to construct game theory, a mathematical study of deception and competitive strategies.

At its most basic level, game theory posits that players of any game (for example, business, war, negotiating, selling) should not make moves according to the probability of success, but based on the moves of their competitors. So, when you play poker, you do not play the odds of drawing a particular hand or card, but you play according to what the other players' tendencies and moves are. An excellent example of the use of game theory principles was in Super Bowl XXXVII when John Gruden's Tampa Bay Buccaneers whomped the Oakland Raiders. Gruden had been the coach of the Raiders the previous year and knew their tendencies. He knew that Raider quarterback Rich Gannon usually pumped one way, then threw the other way. Because the Buccaneers' defensive backs knew Gannon's tendencies there were a record five interceptions. The Bucs played the game according to the moves they knew their competitors would make.

How excellent is excellent? Excellent is not an absolute term; it is a comparative term that measures how good you are compared to your competitors. Therefore, excellent means excellent enough to win. There are never any excuses for not knowing what kind of proposals and presentations your competitors make, not knowing what kind of proposals your customers like, and not doing better proposals and presentations than your competitors do. An excellent software program, the PROposal Wizard 3.0, will help you with your proposals and presentations. It is available free for 30 days from the Radio Advertising Bureau and can be downloaded from www.rab.com. Many radio stations license the software for their salespeople.

Proposal or Presentation?

What is the difference between a presentation and a proposal? A *presentation* is a structured communication about the features, advantages, and benefits of any one or all of the following elements: your medium, your company, and your product. A presentation can be verbal, written, or computerized. It can be a simple two-minute elevator pitch, a one-page letter or brief e-mail, or it can be a 200-slide PowerPoint presentation accompanied by a 300-page, leather-bound printed book. Presentations can range from being a GP—that is, an introduction to a medium and a company—to a customized, solutions-based recommendation for a partnership deal.

A *proposal* is a formal offer of available space or time and corresponding prices. A proposal certifies that at the time the offer is made, the time or space is available at the price indicated.

Therefore, a presentation may or may not include a proposal. Generally, the first presentation you make to a prospect would be a GP and would not include a proposal. The purpose of the initial presentation is primarily to create value for your medium, your company, and your product. Subsequent presentations might include proposals, but all of them must include some creating-value elements.

Ten good reasons for creating excellent, customized, solution-based presentations:

1. You cannot win without one.
2. You are compelled to do your homework and be thoroughly prepared.
3. They increase your confidence and commitment when you rehearse.
4. They show that you understand your prospects' businesses.
5. They are proof of your professionalism and trustworthiness.
6. They concentrate prospects' focus and attention on your solutions.
7. They provide permanent, tangible, memorable records for prospects.
8. They provide you with a permanent record.
9. They show your management how you sell.
10. They build libraries of presentations and best practices.

How Complex Should Presentations Be?

Figure 10.1 shows the relationship between the complexity of a presentation and the dollars involved.

As you can see from Figure 10.1, the complexity of your presentation should increase as the dollars at stake increase. The dollars involved are relative to your medium and market, so an advertising proposal for a one-week schedule for a few hundred dollars need not be more than five 8½ × 11" pages (but always longer than all of your competitors' proposals and always with some creating-value elements that sell your benefits). On the other hand, a presentation to a major advertiser recommending a large $450 million investment in a partnership that includes not only advertising, but also promotions, events, signage, and personal appearances, for example, might run 200 PowerPoint slides, accompanied by a 400-page hard copy with reams of data attached to it.

**Figure 10.1
Sales proposals and presentations.**

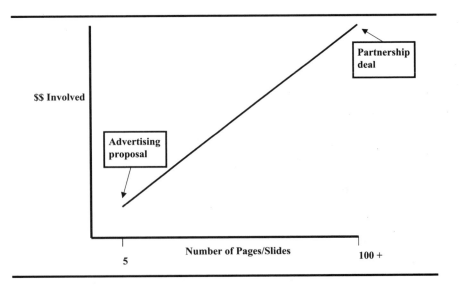

Planning Your Presentation

Begin your planning by determining your target (more about targets later in this chapter) and the presentation's style, then *develop an outline*. You must know what benefits and solutions you are going to present and how you are going to price and order your proposals.

Develop your proposed advertising schedule before you develop an outline and create your presentation because you want your presentation to lead with clear, inescapable logic to an investment in one of the schedules you are going to propose.

Always include at least three proposals in a presentation. Including at least three proposals allows you to use effective ordering effects, such as foot-in-the-door or door-in-the-face. One of your proposals should be large (the optimal order), one (or several) medium, and one small (the minimal order). Target the optimal amount of money you want based on a realistic share of an advertiser's budget or on a dollar amount that you believe is reasonable but optimistic. The medium proposal should be one you would be satisfied to settle for. The small proposal is the minimum order you will accept.

Ordering Tactics for Proposals

The order of the proposals in your presentation depends on the characteristics of your prospect. Normally, you should put the smaller proposal first, then build up to the increased benefits and advantages of each of the larger ones. This ordering is effective because it does not intimidate prospects with a large investment at the beginning. You can build up slowly and logically to the reasons for investing more money and for giving you your optimal order. This tactic is particularly useful with prospects who might not be used to spending much money and with those new to your medium or to advertising. It usually leads to a sale for the medium proposal or even the large one. This first ordering method is known as the *foot-in-the-door* technique; it employs the tactic of getting prospects to agree to a small request or schedule first, then to come back later with a larger one, as outlined in Chapter 8. The first small agreement or order helps them over their initial fear or reluctance.

On the other hand, if your prospects see themselves as important, big-spending clients, then starting with the large proposal can be effective in letting them know that you think they can afford it. You can discuss all of the benefits of the larger proposal and then show how the medium and smaller proposals are not worthy of such an important client.

With some customers, putting the most expensive proposal first makes the following ones look inexpensive by contrast and is an effective tactic with a customer who always complains about high prices. This second method is known as the *door-in-the-face* technique; it presents an unreasonably large initial proposal that is sure to be turned down in order to make the next proposal seem more reasonable. Whichever tactical or ordering decision you make, it should be a conscious one and one that best satisfies prospects' business and personal needs.

Putting Prices in Your Proposals

Break Costs into Smaller Units.   "Just pennies a day" is an example of this tactic. Break your rates or schedules down to the lowest possible unit rate. Show the average unit rate of a schedule instead of the total weekly or monthly or total package price. An average of only $10 per spot sounds to a prospect like an easier amount to handle than $860 per month. Do not show monthly totals, show weekly totals; don't show yearly totals, show monthly totals.

If prospects ask for yearly totals, give them the yearly amount, but also show weekly, monthly, and average rates. Your objective is to minimize the impact of the dollar amount you are proposing. Learn to use modifying words that connote minimization, such as "only" and "just," when you refer to your costs or prices during discussions.

State Costs as Investments.   Advertising is not an expense, it is an investment in future profits. Therefore, on proposals, show "Total investment," not "Total cost."

Determine Your Presentation's Style

Exactly what reaction do you want and what do you want to wind up selling the prospect? This information comes from your targeting and from your analysis of the prospect's needs. Your presentation's style—how you phrase and write your proposals and presentations—will depend on the style preferred by your prospects. Do you need to write very formally with lots of supporting figures for those who like precision and expertise or less formally and more colorfully for a prospect who is impressed by media glitz and glamour? Do you need to write a short presentation for prospects who have tiny attention spans, bordering on attention-deficit-disorder (ADD)?

Your Presentation Outline

After you have determined what solution is best for the client, what you have targeted to sell, and what the best style is, write an outline. You can review it and change it as you complete each step and evaluate it. Here are the guidelines for developing your outline:

1. **Aim your presentation at the right person** at the client or to an agency, a buyer, or top management. Each group will require a slightly different approach, need different facts, and have different needs to be satisfied.
2. **Set priorities for the problems** you are trying to solve and call them challenges in your presentation. Customers don't want to be reminded that they have problems. Concentrate on solving the challenges that are utmost in prospects' minds first.
3. **Be parsimonious with facts**. Do not try to overwhelm prospects with facts; give just enough to win. Some prospects, especially those who must be convinced of your expertise, might need more facts and data, but generally, this is a wasteful, time-consuming approach.
4. **Avoid presenting your proposal's costs (and cost-related statistics) until near the end of the presentation**. Always plan to include qualitative information and to provide facts that create value before you mention price.
5. **Anticipate the competition.** Know what your competitors are most likely to offer and to say about you. Position your strengths directly against their weaknesses and emphasize your strengths; point out, briefly, their generic weaknesses, but do not appear to knock them. Remember game theory and anticipate how complex competitors' presentations are and make yours better and longer, just enough longer to win.
6. **Remember the KISS rule: Keep-It-Short-and-Simple**. Often presentations ramble on with unnecessary detail. Present only as much information as you need to make an important point and to beat the competition. Show just enough to win.

7. **Be honest and accurate**. As you develop your outline, do not include anything that might be an exaggeration, give false information, or use numbers or figures for which you do not give a credible, reliable source. Always double-check your figures for accuracy. Mistakes and inaccuracies in your numbers and writing will destroy your credibility.

8. **Target what you want to sell.** Target the type of order you want to get, which will guide your outline and eventual proposal.

Targeting

Targeting is determining in advance the kind of order you want to get within the framework of an appropriate solution; it is *setting a goal* for yourself for each presentation. Targeting gives you something to shoot at, helps you select your sales strategy, and helps you develop and create your presentation. Your target is your destination and your presentation is the road map.

Targeting is the only part of the solutions-selling process where the focus is on your company's needs. Without a clear, realistic target, you might get so wrapped up in satisfying prospects' needs that you forget about balancing their needs with your company's needs. While you want an order, you want the right order for both your prospect and your company.

Target Selection.   In order to be coordinated with your overall sales strategy, targets should be selected based on the following elements:

1. **A specific opportunity.** In this case, your target is to sell an advertiser a specific opportunity in your medium that is the right solution to their advertising or marketing problem. Examples of opportunities are: special programming (the Academy Awards) or a promotion ("Win a Vacation") in broadcast or cable, a special section in a newspaper (Home & Garden Sunday section), or a special advertising section in a magazine (New Technology).

2. **Price.** In this case, your target is to get prices within a predetermined range. Examples are: in television, to get no lower than $1,300 for an early news spot; in radio, to get an average rate of no lower than a cost-per-point of $125 (you will learn about cost-per-points and cost-per-thousands in Chapter 16, "Media Research"); or in newspapers, to get no less than a bulk line rate of 25,000 lines (you will learn about line rates in Chapter 18, "Newspapers"). In these situations, your primary concern is to sell your product for the highest possible price, regardless of the overall size of an order, the type of order, or the share of an advertiser's budget. A price target might be used in situations such as in broadcasting and cable, where you have limited inventory to sell, or in newspapers, where moving advertisers up to a higher lineage commitment would increase their total investment in the paper.

3. **Size of an order.** Here, your target is to get an order for a particular dollar amount based on what you know advertisers' budgets are and how much investment it will take to get results, as they define and expect them. Examples of size-of-order targets are: in television, a $20,000 per week schedule for four weeks; in radio, a $3,000 per week schedule for eight weeks; or in newspapers, a schedule of three insertions per week for four weeks for a total $15,000. This type of targeting allows you to set goals for each order

based on what it will take to achieve the results an advertiser expects. It also allows you to set minimum order-size goals for yourself so you can manage your selling efforts to achieve your revenue targets. For instance, if you decide to restrict yourself to orders above a certain amount, you can avoid calling on prospects who do not have businesses large enough to support advertising at your minimum level. A combination of price and size targets works well. For example, in radio you might say to yourself, "I want to get an order that is at least $2,000 per week and where I can get an average rate of more than $100 per spot."

4. **Share of budget.** In this case, your target is to get a predetermined share of a customer's advertising budget. This targeting is especially effective when you have abundant inventory available and when getting the highest possible price is not an issue. Used with the other three types of targets, the share-of-budget target can be the most profitable. For example: "I want to sell out the Super Bowl adjacencies at no less than $10,000 each as part of a package that sells for a minimum of $150,000 and that gets 45 percent of XYZ Company's first quarter television budget." This statement gives you a measurable, attainable, demanding, written, and flexible target, as well as a good, solid goal.

Setting size-of-order and share-of-budget targets requires good qualifying. You must know the total revenue of prospects' businesses and their advertising budgets. The type of target you choose will determine your sales strategy, which you must bake into your presentation from the very beginning.

Major Presentations to Key Accounts

At the upper ranges of the sloping line in Figure 10.1—toward the partnership deal end—you should create a winning presentation that will knock your prospects' socks off. And a dynamite presentation does not have to last for an hour-and-a-half, or even an hour. The ideal length for a presentation is 25 minutes, not including time for questions. Therefore, when you write a presentation, write one that the person can comfortably deliver in 25 to 35 minutes.

Here are some tips for creating such a presentation.

1. **Appoint a prep team.** Ask people who have expertise in different areas such as research, marketing, production, and creative to help you create a major presentation and join your prep team.

2. **Preparation.** The prep team should meet in a room that contains flip charts, walls, or white boards on which to write. In this prep room, you will develop a maximum of 11 charts or subject areas and less for some presentations. Pick someone with good, legible handwriting to be the scribe and put information on the charts/areas. The charts are:

   A. *Your prep and presentation team.* A list of who is on the team and each person's role, including the presenters.

   B. *Your purpose.* Concisely state the purpose of the presentation: to introduce a solution and get commitment to pursue, to gain an agency's support, or to close a deal, for example.

   C. *The prospect's objective and challenges.* A chart showing the prospect's marketing and advertising objectives, target consumers, and the challenges (do not call them problems) the prospect faces in achieving those objectives with their target customers.

D. *Your opportunities.* Write down all the relevant opportunities (promotions, packages, etc.) that might possibly be relevant to the prospect or be a potential solution.

E. *Your target.* Determine your target—opportunities you want to propose and your dollar, size, or share target.

F. *An ROI analysis, if applicable.* In Chapter 21 you will learn about an exceptionally powerful sales tool, a return-on-investment (ROI) analysis. An ROI analysis shows what the bottom-line effect is of a one-year advertising investment.

G. *The timetable.* A time-line chart that shows milestone dates for key tasks (deliverables) and who does what and when they do it. Include in this chart tasks such as who does the setup of the room and who prepares and delivers to the site copies of the presentation. Also, plan something special for the setup, such as printed note pads with the prospect's name and logo on them, high-quality pens such as Cross or Mont Blanc to take notes with, small calculators they can take home if numbers are involved. Brainstorm to come up with some creative setup ideas.

H. *The prospect's team.* A chart showing the key people who will be involved in making the decision—the decision maker and influencers who will be listening to and/or evaluating your presentation.

I. *Ideas.* Brainstorm and come up with an *idea pipeline* in five areas:

   i. *The big idea.* A creative or promotion idea that meets the prospect's challenges (solves problems). The big idea may also be a way to spin an existing product element or promotion as a solution.

   ii. *A theme idea.* Come up with ideas for a unifying theme that captures the essence of the big idea and of the presentation overall.

   iii. *Evidence, examples, analogies, equivalencies, and stories.* Think of all the testimonials, success case studies, examples, analogies, equivalencies (definition and example later in this chapter), and stories that might be relevant to support and dramatize your benefits. Analogies and stories are especially effective. An analogy compares your product with something else.

   iv. *Language.* Brainstorm to come up with ideas on the most effective language—phrases and words—to use. You want your language to mirror the jargon, idioms, and slang the prospect and the prospect's target audience use. When Jill Rudnick was head of AOL Interactive Marketing's Marketing Services Department, she crafted a presentation for Burger King, whose target audience was teens. She interviewed several teenagers to discover what language and phrases they used and she wrote the Burger King presentation using their language. AOL Vice Chairman Ted Leonsis made the presentation to Burger King and AOL got the business.

   v. *Wow! opening and closing ideas.* Creative opening and closing ideas plus a memorable and exciting presentation method or style that enhances the impact of a presentation will win big. It may mean opening and closing with a Woody Allen quote, a quote from *The Godfather*, balloons cascading down from the ceiling, a personal appearance by Bugs Bunny, a "Tha', tha', that's all folks" goodbye from Porky Pig, or a final slide of Obi Wan Kenobi "leading us into the future." Do not create a Wow! opening or closing that you are not comfortable delivering.

J. *Deal terms.* In some large deals there are terms and conditions such as payment schedules, exclusivities, content restrictions (no pornography, for example), revenue sharing, or options to renew that are material. Material means that they are deal breakers—not getting these terms would prevent consummating a deal. It is best to put important terms and conditions that are different from standard media contract terms in your presentation and sell them aggressively because you want prospects to know what your terms and conditions are before you get into negotiations. If you spring terms and conditions on prospects after they have agreed to pursue a deal and while you are negotiating, prospects and their negotiators (sometimes lawyers) often become angry and negotiations stall. Introducing deal terms in your presentation will make negotiations go much smoother.

Giving advertisers a deal term that includes the option to renew a contract at the end of a year at the same price originally agreed on is not a good idea because it precludes raising rates or taking a bid from a higher bidder.

K. *A benefits matrix.* Develop a benefits matrix for your presentation.

L. *Your offer and anchor.* When appropriate, have a chart that shows the details of the structure of your opening offer. Pricing your initial offer is probably the most important decision you will make, so spend plenty of time debating and crafting it. You will learn more about opening offers, called anchors, in Chapter 12.

M. *Follow-up.* Brainstorm creative ways to follow up on your presentation. For example, if you give a presentation in your office, as the audience leaves your presentation give them tickets to an opening of a movie. Have a top executive or celebrity greet them and thank them for their time. You could give them a T-shirt or baseball cap with your logo on it, or send something really cool to their offices the day after the presentation. A creative follow-up solidifies the relationship, makes them like you more, makes them feel that you care, reminds them of the terrific experience they had at your presentation, and reinforces the value of doing business with you.

3. **Structure your presentation effectively.** A winning major presentation should have the following eight structural elements: (1) Opening, (2) Theme/Introduction/Purpose, (3) Agenda, (4) Main Body of Content, (5) Success Stories, (6) Deal Terms, (7) Summary, and (8) Conclusion/Next Steps.

A. *Opening.* A relevant quote is a good way to open a presentation to focus, motivate, and even inspire an audience. A carefully chosen quotation can be the theme of your presentation. Here are some good quotes:

Problem solving: "Everything should be made as simple as possible, but not simpler," or "Imagination is more important than intelligence." (Albert Einstein).[2]

Major change: "If there's not a ripple at the bow you're drifting," or "If in the last few months you haven't discarded a major opinion or acquired a new one, check your pulse. You may be dead." (George Bernard Shaw)[3]

Motivation: "When you cease to dream you cease to live." (Malcolm Forbes) "If you can dream it, it is possible." (Buckminster Fuller) "Our greatest glory is not in never failing, but in rising every time we fail." (Confucius) "Failure is only the opportunity to more intelligently begin again." (Henry Ford)[4]

Marketing Strategy: "Never interrupt the enemy when he is doing something wrong." (Rommel) An especially relevant quote: "For every complex problem there is invariably a simple solution—which is invariably wrong." (Lady Wortley Montagu)[5] "The only functions of an enterprise: marketing and innovation." (Peter Drucker).

B. *Theme/Introduction/Purpose.* Near the beginning of a presentation you should state the theme of the presentation. A theme gives a presentation direction and focus. Examples of themes:

"Together into the Year 2004!"

"Making Burger King Number One!"

"A Global Solution for a Global Company!"

"*The Tribune* and AT&T: Partnering for Solutions"

The introduction slide should state the purpose of the presentation, and the presenter's remarks should expand briefly on the purpose statement. An example might be, "The purpose of this presentation is to show how WAAA-TV can provide you with effective and efficient solutions to your two biggest marketing challenges."

C. *Agenda.* The next slide after the introduction should list the main topics of the presentation. Like the old saw says, "Tell 'em what you're going to tell 'em." An agenda tells your audience what to expect, prepares their minds, and sets their anticipation positively to receive your communication. Research shows that people like to know what's coming. An example of an Agenda: 1. The Economy and Competitive Landscape, 2. AT&T's Objectives, 3. AT&T's Challenges, 4. Options in Meeting Those Challenges, 5. Recommended Solutions, 6. Terms and Conditions, 7. Summary, and 8. Conclusion/Next Steps.

D. *Main body of content.* The main body of a presentation should flow logically from one topic to the next and from one solution or proposal to the next. Every feature, every statistic must be accompanied by a corresponding advantage (why it is better) and benefit (how it solves a specific prospect's problem). Numbers without comparisons are ineffective. Dramatic comparisons make the numbers memorable. (See Chapter 8 for examples.)

Make sure to include success stories or case studies that are relevant to the prospect's business and prove that you can get results. Use success stories, case studies, and testimonials in every presentation. Two Web sites that have good case studies are Microsoft's www.msn.com and the Cabletelevision Advertising Bureau's www.cabletvadbureau.com. On the www.mediaselling.us Web site, there is an excellent success case study in the link "Aladdin Resort and Casino Case Study" that was prepared by the Infinity Broadcasting stations in Phoenix and tells a powerful story.

Each section of the presentation (as outlined in the Agenda at the beginning of your presentation) should come to a solid conclusion that points inescapably to the solutions you are offering.

Writing Tips: When you create a presentation it is imperative to start with an outline, then write the presentation following the outline.

After you have written the presentation that follows your outline, edit it to make sure that the headlines are clear, concise, and compelling. Good, short headlines are hard to write, but are the most important single element in a sales presentation—craft them carefully. When you edit your presentation, make sure there is a logical, cohesive flow that leads to an unavoidable conclusion. Make sure you back up each of your benefits with credible, fully sourced evidence. Credible evidence includes testimonials, success case studies, and analogies. Keep numbers to a minimum in the body of the presentation. Instead of raw numbers, always try to use equivalencies. For example, if you are selling for a newspaper in a town near Kansas City, instead of saying that your paper has 73,000 readers, say, "My paper has more readers than a sold-out Arrowhead Stadium holds." This statement makes the number 73,000 more concrete, dramatizes it, and gives your prospects something they can visualize in their minds. Put the dull, raw numbers and statistics in an appendix that you leave behind.

Do not use convoluted or flowery language, but write positively and with enthusiasm. Write clearly, crisply, and concisely and with as few words as possible; ruthlessly edit out unnecessary words. Write in prospects' voice and use their industry language and jargon, not yours. Use simple everyday words. Ernest Hemingway had a small vocabulary of only 800 words, but he used those 800 words brilliantly.

You want to project through your writing that "We're here to make this easy for you." An overly wordy, complex proposal can cause prospects to think doing business with you is going to be too complicated or too hard. You want them to think that you are a salesperson or a team of experienced professionals who know how to make your recommendations work.

When you are satisfied with your presentation, write a script for yourself that contains examples, anecdotes, and stories that reinforce your major points and make your presentation memorable. Most people will remember your stories—particularly if they are good—longer than they will remember your solutions and the facts that support them. Make sure to actually write these stories and anecdotes in your script, because there is nothing worse than coming to a place in your script that reads, "Tell the traveling salesman joke," and you have forgotten the first line.

E. *Success Stories.* Include relevant success stories, testimonials, and case studies.

F. *Terms and Conditions.* Include deal terms.

G. *Summary:* The summary is the most valuable, but often the most overlooked, part of a presentation. The summary ensures that prospects leave with key points you want them to remember. Too many summaries are too long—15 points, for example. Remember the psychological rule of five plus or minus two, which means that the maximum number of things people can possibly remember is seven (Snow White and the eight dwarfs? The nine wonders of the ancient world? Ten card stud?) Five is better than seven and three is ideal. If you can boil your summary down to three key points you want your audience to walk away with, you can be quite confident that those three points will stick with them.

H. *Conclusions and Next Steps*: One of the principles of maximizing a customer's experience is "finish strong." This point comes from the article "Want to Perfect Your Company's Service? Use Behavioral Science," in the *Harvard Business Review*.[6] Your close should be creative, powerful, and memorable.

The conclusion is the close. It tells your audience what you want them to do. If you are offering proposed advertising schedules with prices included in the conclusion, make sure you order them effectively. Do not offer any price concessions or a Clincher Close at the conclusion of your presentation; save these for later, during negotiations. (You will learn about Clincher Closes and negotiating strategies in Chapter 12). At this time, during the conclusion, hand out copies of the presentation, ask if there are any questions, and thank them for their time and attention, their intelligent questions and clarifications, and the opportunity to present your solutions. Finally, make sure to implement the follow-up your prep team has planned.

Create Modular Presentations.   When you write presentations, write them in a modular form—that is, so you can use sections of them again within another presentation. Always keep an eye out for opportunities to write a section of a presentation in such a way that you can copy it and paste it into other proposals and presentations. You repeatedly use much of the information you convey to prospects and customers; this is especially the case with advantages and benefits, value propositions, positioning statements, research information, and competitive media information. Label and save these modular sections as separate PowerPoint and Word files that you can easily retrieve and insert into any presentation, document, or e-mail.

Checklist for Customized, Solution-Based Presentations

Exhibit 10.1 shows a checklist for major customized, solutions-based presentations that are appropriate for key accounts.

The checklist is not only a guide for complex presentations to large advertisers, but also a guide for any type of sales discussion. If you find prospects who have the resources to advertise, and you have discovered their marketing challenges and learned about their businesses, this checklist will help you focus your selling efforts on creating value for your product, dramatizing the solutions you recommend, and getting results for your advertisers.

Exhibit 10.1 Checklist for Customized Solutions-Based Presentations

1. First slide with company's name, logo, and a catchy **theme** that shows you understand its challenges and suggests a partnership
2. Second slide with a concise **introduction** which includes a statement of the purpose of the presentation
3. Next, a list of **agenda** items or a table of contents
4. A list of the prospect's **marketing and advertising goals**
5. A list of the prospect's **challenges** in achieving those goals
6. A statement of the prospect's **current strategy** in achieving marketing and advertising goals (differentiation, focus, low-cost producer, e.g.)
7. A description of the **prospect's primary customers/target audience**
8. An identification of **opportunities that are solutions** to the prospect's problems and challenges
9. Present the **advantages of your solution** over your competition, but **don't knock the competition**.
10. Present **the benefits of your solutions** (schedules, campaigns, packages, etc.) to the prospect's challenges.

11. Show specifically **how the solutions and recommendations will make their business more profitable**. Use an **ROI analysis** if appropriate.
12. Show relevant **success stories and case studies** from similar customers as proof of your ability to perform and get results.
13. Show **terms and conditions** if they are different from standard terms and conditions in your medium.
14. A concise **Summary** of the main benefits and solutions
15. A **Conclusion** or **Next Steps**, both for you and for prospects to implement the proposal and/or to advance the partnership, which is a **call for action or commitment**
16. An **Appendix** containing numbers and supporting information

Test Yourself

1. What is the difference between a proposal and a presentation?
2. How long should a presentation be?
3. What are the four different types of targets?
4. What are the eight elements of an effective sales presentation structure?
5. Give an example of an equivalency.

Project

Who is the largest advertiser in your market? Ask the local newspaper ad department and several local radio and television sales departments. Then select a local medium. Create the first three slides of a PowerPoint presentation to the largest advertiser for the medium you select. Use the Checklist for Customized Solutions-Based Presentations for your guide: a first slide with the medium's name, your name and phone number, the advertiser's logo and a catchy theme headline; a second slide titled "Introduction" with statement of purpose; and last, a table of contents for your presentation.

References

Richard B. Chase and Sriam Dasu. 2001. "Want to Perfect Your Company's Service? Use Behavioral Science." *Harvard Business Review*. June.

Neil Flett. 1996. *The Pitch Doctor: Presenting to Win Multi-million Dollar Accounts*. New York: Prentiss-Hall.

László Mérö. 1998. *Moral Calculations: Game Theory, Logic, and Human Frailty*. New York: Copernicus.

William Poundstone. 1992. *Prisoner's Dilemma*. New York: Doubleday.

Resources

www.charleswarner.us/cseindex.html/gamethry.html
www.gametheory.org
www.mediasellng.org
www.msn.org

Endnotes

1. William Poundstone. 1992. *Prisoner's Dilemma*. New York: Doubleday.
2. Neil Flett. 1996. *The Pitch Doctor: Presenting to Win Multi-million Dollar Accounts*. New York: Prentiss-Hall. p. 201.
3. Ibid. p. 202.
4. Ibid.
5. Ibid.
6. Chase, Richard B. and Sriam Dasu. 2001. "Want to Perfect Your Company's Service? Use Behavioral Science." *Harvard Business Review*. June.

11 Skills: Presenting

By Charles Warner

Presenting is what most people first think of when they think of selling—meeting with prospects, customers, and buyers face to face. But you cannot begin selling without thorough preparation, as you have learned in previous chapters.

Media salespeople present to several different types of people involved in the buying process: prospects for new business, current customers for increases and renewals, and advertising agency media buyers for new and renewal business. In large markets—especially the top 25—the vast majority of media business, with the exception of yellow pages, is conducted with advertising agencies and that involves presenting to media buyers. As markets get smaller, more business—especially in newspapers—is conducted directly with customers and not through agencies. In this chapter, I will refer to prospects, customers, and media buyers as prospects to avoid confusion.

Furthermore, we have discussed selling solutions and putting solutions in the form of proposals that contain advertising schedules and prices. For the first section of this chapter, I will assume all your proposals and presentations are, in fact, solutions of some sort or other, and refer to them as proposals to keep things simple. For media buyers, a solution might well be a schedule that meets their reach goals and demographic targets and falls within their price range.

Presenting is face-to-face selling in front of qualified prospects. Your overall goals in this step are: (1) *To create a differential competitive advantage for your product with an overwhelming weight of evidence*, (2) *to create value for your product*, (3) *to build desire for your proposal*, (4) *to establish conviction that your proposal is the best one*, and (5) *to get a commitment*. Commitment might be taking action and giving you an order, it may be an agreement to recommend your proposal to a client, or it may be having you make a presentation to a board of directors. Just as presentations get longer and more complicated as the amount of money involved increases, getting a commitment and closing a sale takes longer and is more complicated as the amount of money involved grows. Sometimes, with relatively small proposals and renewals, you can get a commitment and close on a single call, whereas with major presentations to key accounts for large partnership deals, it can take weeks, even months to get a commitment.

To accomplish these goals, the sales tactics you use during the presenting step of selling are designed to take prospects up the Sales Ladder as shown in Figure 11.1.

The Sales Ladder is based on the buyer-action theory proposed by Manning and Reece in *Selling Today: A Personal Approach*.[1] Figure 11.1 indicates which of the six steps of selling moves prospects up the Sales Ladder to commitment.

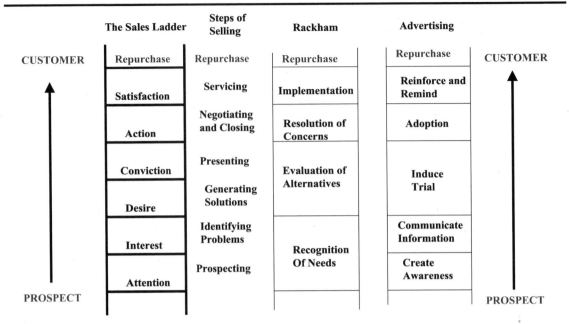

Figure 11.1
The sales ladder. (Source: Manning and Reece, 1990; Rackham, 1989.)

Also, you will see that the steps on the Sales Ladder are parallel to the customer decision process defined by Neil Rackham in *Major Account Sales Strategies*.[2] The Sales Ladder also parallels the objectives of advertising that are covered in Chapter 17 of this book. These parallel models depict the decision process that people go through when they buy, use, and repurchase products. Note, too, that people start out as prospects and do not become customers until they repurchase.

The Sales Ladder is useful in both one-on-one and group selling situations. In this chapter, I am going to divide presenting, negotiating and closing into two dichotomous types, each requiring different approaches, tactics, and skills: one-on-one presenting or presenting to small groups of two or three, and presenting to larger groups of four or more. Typically, one-on-one or small-group presentations are for relatively (relative to the market and the medium) smaller amounts of money and large-group presentations are for substantial deals.

One-on-One Presenting

In an article in the *Harvard Business Review* titled "The Tests of a Good Salesperson," the author, Saul Gellerman, writes under the heading Discussion Focus about what he observed when salespeople made a call, as shown in Exhibit 11.1.

It is important to structure your calls properly so you can take prospects up the Sales Ladder. Call structure allows you to set the agenda for a call and to keep your calls focused on sales.

Exhibit 11.1 **Discussion Focus**	"The first critical factor was what sellers and customers talked about. Who did most of the talking had little importance. Shrewd sellers wanted to discuss which products the customer should order, and preferably at length. In the sales-focused calls, regardless of how much each party had to say about the details of the purchase orders, they spoke mainly about those matters the seller wanted to hear. Sales-focused calls tended to produce the largest orders. The opposite of a sales-focused call was an unfocused call in which most of the conversation involved *anything* but the products that were supposedly on the agenda. Often the customer voiced complaints about prices, delivery, invoicing, or the products themselves. The conversation could dwell too long on irrelevant topics like the customer's preferences among automobiles, baseball teams, or political candidates. The unfocused calls nearly always produced small orders or no orders at all. Customer complaints and excursions into small talk surfaced in virtually all the observed calls. In sales-focused calls, they were dispensed with quickly; the seller found some deft but gracious way to turn the discussion back into the overriding question: What will today's order be?"

Source: Gellerman, 1990, p.65.

Structure your calls as follows to keep them sales-focused:

Call Structure

1. Greeting
2. New Information
3. Opening
4. Recap and Purpose
5. Discussion
6. Summary and Close

Greeting

The purpose of a greeting is to set the tone of the meeting and to build rapport by first being friendly, complimentary, and positive. Keeping in mind Golden Rule of Selling number three, you want to let people know that you care about them before you get down to business.

It is usually best to start out with small talk: a comment about the weather, current news, or a sports event, for example. Appropriately phrased compliments are also a good way to begin; notice the office decor or desk photographs and say something complimentary. You are trying to break the ice and lower prospects' anxiety. Remember, prospects often feel anxious about meetings, too. On the other hand, some prospects dislike making polite conversation. You will know if this is the case from your observations during previous meetings. Limit small talk to one or two comments, such as, "How are you today?" or "Good to see you again." No matter what the circumstances, make your greeting warm and sincere. Whatever your greeting, make it brief so that you can keep the call sales-focused.

New Information

The next phase of a call provides your prospects with some relevant information and, even better, new information, if possible. By giving relevant or new information, you add to your source credibility and your prospects' perception of your expertise. Examples of information you might give are: "I saw a new creative execution your competitor is using. Have you seen it? Do you like it?" or "I saw an article in the *New York Times* about Ann Wintour, the editor of *Vogue,* and the new, more populist approach she is taking. Did you see it?" When you give information, you turn the conversation from a discussion about personal matters as it was in the greeting phase to a focus on business.

Opening

Your opening should be a thoughtful, well-planned statement and not a casual, off-the-cuff remark. A good, solid opening piques your prospects' interest. Your prospects are already interested in what you are going to offer because they agreed to the meeting. You got their attention during your initial meetings when you gathered information in the Identifying Problems and Qualifying steps. During those meetings, you looked for business and personal needs, you made your first assessment of the prospect's intelligence and self-confidence, and you created a personal needs-based portrait (see Chapter 7). You also tried to determine prospects' perceptual set and readiness to hear your information. Your opening should take all of these factors into consideration and hint at the benefits of your proposal.

An example of an effective opening might be: "Mary, I know how much you love Woody Allen movies. Remember when he said in 'Annie Hall' that he'd been going to psychiatrists for 15 years and still wasn't any better? He said he was so desperate he was thinking of going to Lourdes. Well, I've put together a proposal that I think will meet some of your challenges so you won't have to go to Lourdes."

On the other hand, there are times when a planned opening is not appropriate, and you have to ad lib. One of the best examples of a creative opening is one I call The Barbed-Wire Open that I learned from a 25-year-veteran radio salesperson from Fresno named Mark. He told me that he made a call one blistering hot day on a client who owned a men's clothing store. Mark had identified the owner's needs and problems and was returning to sell a radio campaign. He said that when he walked into the store, he knew the call was not going to be a good one. There was about an inch of water on floor, and as Mark slogged toward the owner on soggy carpeting he made the mistake of asking, "How's it going?"

> *Owner:* "How's it going! How's it going! Can't you see it's a damned flood? The damn air conditioner broke. It's 102 degrees outside and 104 in here. There are no customers and it'll cost me a fortune!"
>
> *Mark:* "Gee, this is awful. I've never seen such a mess. You must be furious." He glanced up and saw a strand of barbed wire mounted on a wooden plaque above the back door. "Say, isn't that a Scutt Single-Clip 'H' Plate up there? I've seen pictures of it but never seen a real one."
>
> *Owner* (perking up): "Yes, it's very rare. How did you know? Are you interested in barbed wire?"
>
> *Mark:* "Yeah, I've got a Kelly Thorny common and a Jayne & Hill Locked Staples at home and, of course, some plain old Glidden Square Strand. Say, why don't you close down—you're not going to do any good sweltering in here. Let's go across the street to that cool diner, have a Coke, and talk about barbed wire."[3]

Mark knew his barbed wire, he was authentic, and he knew how to ad-lib. Most of all, he knew how to sell.

Recap and Purpose

The next step in your call structure is to *recap* what challenges you are addressing and then state the *purpose* of the call. Your purpose statement sets the agenda for the call. Here are some examples:

> *You:* "Mary, when you called for avails, you indicated you needed to buy a schedule that reached women 18 to 49, that achieved high reach in a two-week period, and that met your cost-per-point targets. The purpose of my call is to show you how

my proposal meets your parameters and to reach an agreement today so I can book the order before the spots are sold to someone else—demand is running high." (Scarcity principle, deadline, and competition for limited supply.) Or another one:

You: "Since the last time I saw you, Mr. Hernandez, I've thought a great deal about how we might increase your traffic on Mondays and Tuesdays. The purpose of my call today is to show you mock-ups of some ads that I think will get results for you."

Your summary and purpose statements guide prospects into the discussion phase. Your wording depends on your earlier assessment of prospects' challenges and needs.

Discussion

The overall strategy for the *discussion* phase is to move prospects from *desire* for the solutions you present to *a conviction* that your proposal is the best one. The emphasis is on two-way communication in which prospects are partners. They learn through discovery that what you are offering will satisfy their business and personal needs. Their conviction will be stronger if they discover the benefits of your solutions rather than being told directly. Part of prospects' discovery process comes from asking questions or bringing up objections.

Dealing with Objections.   Body builders use the expression, "No pain, no gain." Salespeople should use the phrase "no objection, no sale." To the novice, objections might seem to be negatives and barriers. On the other hand, to the experienced professional, objections are a welcome and necessary part of the discussion process; they are not negatives, they are requests for more information. Prospects do not ask questions and raise objections if they are not interested in what you have to offer.

Dealing with objections successfully is one of the most important skills a salesperson can learn. There are two types of objections: *figurative* and *literal*. A figurative objection is one that does not represent what prospects' words seem to indicate and should not be taken literally. They have no real meaning, but rather represent other, hidden objections, which are often quick initial responses that represent defense mechanisms rather than real reasons. Figurative objections are often used as a buying or negotiating tactic by prospects whose motives are to put salespeople on the defensive and to gain an upper hand.

Literal objections are real reasons why prospects are seriously questioning your proposal, and must be answered with additional information in order to move prospects from desire to conviction. When you deal with literal objections, you should encourage prospects to answer their own objections, which is accomplished through the use of probing questions and restatements and the legitimate use of some of the principles of influence.

Following are several dialogues to help you. These should be used as examples and not as a script. You must sound natural and sincere when you are talking to prospects, not scripted. If you sound rehearsed, you convey the unintended message that you have pat answers that are not unique to their individual objections, and thus you are perceived as being manipulative. You will notice that the following techniques for listening to objections are the same as the effective listening techniques you learned in Chapter 7, but another step has been added—a trial close. Here are examples of some appropriate responses:

Probe to understand. Use open- and closed-end questions to be sure that you hear the full objection or concern and that you and your prospect have the same understanding of it. Discover exactly what the objection is so that you can give a thorough, intelligent answer.

Always listen rather than respond when prospects begin to express an objection, and encourage them to continue. Never jump in with a counterargument. Sometimes a short response such as "Oh?" will provide additional information. For example:

Prospect: "ESPN is pretty good, but it doesn't have enough golf."

You: "Oh?"

Prospect: "Yeah, I like to watch golf and see the great players select their clubs."

You: "Oh?"

Prospect: "Yes, I know it's a personal preference. After all, I'm selling tires to everyone, not just the upscale guys who play golf."

You: "Oh?"

Prospect: "Yeah, my audience prefers auto racing as a sport. ESPN carries auto racing doesn't it?"

You: "Yes. It's the most popular spectator sport in the country." (Social proof.)

Compliment, restate an objection, and get agreement. *Compliment prospects* for raising an objection, for having such good insight. By giving them a compliment, you put prospects in a receptive frame of mind, not on the defensive, and you trigger an obligation for them to reciprocate by listening to your answer. Next, *restate the objection* and then get their agreement that you understand it.

Prospect: "I don't like your newspaper's editorials praising the mayor."

You: "That's a very good point, Mr. Hernandez. I'm glad you brought that up. Let me make sure I understand your point; you do not like the mayor and do not think he's doing a good job. Right?"

Prospect: "Yes, that's right."

Empathize, reassure, and support. Empathize with prospects' objections (how they feel), then reassure them that their objection is not out in left field somewhere (reassure them), and, finally, support your position.

You: "I understand how you feel. A lot of my clients have felt the same way, but they have found that their ads still pull well no matter what stand our editorials take. By the way, why don't you write a letter to the editor; they'll probably print it. You express yourself very well and speak for a lot of people."

Prospect: "That's a good idea. I think I will."

Trial close. Next, get prospects to agree that you have answered their objection and ask for a commitment. You may not get one at this stage of the discussion, but it never hurts to try. The advantage of a trial close early in a discussion is that it elicits either a commitment or another objection, which is what you want.

Using trial closes is a good way to bring out all of the objections prospects have. And once you have addressed them all, you will get a commitment. Let's continue the discussion above:

You: "Great, maybe your letter to the editor will run on the same day as your ad—that would be nice. Shall we go ahead, then?"

Prospect: "Well, before I say yes, I'd like a position up front in the first section."

Your trial close worked. Our prospect has, in effect, said yes, and you are now negotiating for position (and not price). Here is another example:

You: "Channel 32 is the area's top-rated independent television station."

Prospect: "That might be, but I hear that your ratings aren't that good."

You: "What kind of ratings are you referring to?" (Probe to understand.)

Prospect: "The latest Nielsens. The network affiliates have much higher ratings."

You: "In all dayparts?" (Probe to understand.)

Prospect: "I honestly don't know the details. I just know that the affiliates tell me they have much higher ratings."

You: "You seem to be concerned that you won't be able to reach as many people in your target audience on an independent station. Is that correct?"

Prospect: "Yes, that's right."

You: "Of course, you're right. The affiliates do have higher overall ratings in many dayparts, especially in prime time. So I understand how you feel. Your best customers are young women, right?"

Prospect: "Yes."

You: "My station is particularly effective in reaching young women 18 to 49 in early fringe. Here is a rating sheet that shows we have higher ratings among young women in early fringe than all of the affiliates do. If your commercial runs in that time period, you'll be alongside Procter & Gamble, Colgate, Johnson & Johnson and many big national advertisers." (Social proof) "I might be able to get you only one or two in early fringe next week; there is a lot of demand for that time period right now." (Scarcity, competition) "Shall we go ahead?" (Trial close)

Several additional techniques for dealing with objections follow. Each is effective in different situations. However, before you use these techniques, it is imperative to know what objections are common for your medium and product and be prepared to answer them. Ninety-five percent of the objections you hear should not be new to you.

The best sales organizations spend a great deal of time practicing how to deal with objections. Write down the most common objections for your medium and product, then craft intelligent, concise answers. Rehearse the answers repeatedly until you can deal with the most common objections in your sleep and with confidence. Find out from other salespeople in your organization how they answer these objections.

There are several reasons for practicing answers to objections. First, like a hitter in baseball, if you know what pitch is coming, you have an infinitely better chance of hitting it solidly. Second, rehearsing gives you confidence—nothing can puzzle you, and as we know, sometimes prospects throw out objections just to stump you in order to get an edge. Third, by practicing, you can craft answers that are logical and concise, which will allow you to move discussions forward more easily. Exhibit 11.2 shows the most common objections salespeople hear in radio in a large market and at America Online.

**Exhibit 11.2
Objections**

Most common objections heard by radio salespeople:
1. We need to show a picture of our product and radio can't do this.
2. We have multiple locations we need to provide addresses for, which is impossible to do in sixty seconds.
3. We've tried radio and it doesn't work.
4. There are too many stations.
5. Listeners always push the button and go to another station when the commercials come on.
6. We've used the newspaper with great success for years. It's built our business.
7. I don't know if radio works or not. With the newspaper, people cut out the ad and bring it in.

Source: Paul Talbot, Infinity Radio, Phoenix, AZ, February 2003.

Most common objections heard by America Online salespeople:
1. Banner advertising doesn't work.
2. Don't have any money for advertising right now.
3. We only do CPC/CPA (pay per performance) deals.
4. I only do revenue-sharing deals.
5. I can get better deals on other online services.
6. The smaller banners don't work as well as the full-size banners.
7. The click rates were OK, but the conversion rate was poor.
8. I would do a test, but only for a week or so.
9. I'm not concerned with branding. I need sales.
10. Your CPM is too high.
11. We want large rich media formats and AOL's banner sizes are too small.
12. Banners don't work for us anymore, we want integration, and we want AOL to buy our content.

Source: AOL Interactive Marketing, January 2001

Once you have assembled a list of objections for your medium, you can practice using the following techniques to deal with them.

Forestall objections. Forestalling objections means to head them off, to anticipate and answer them before prospects bring them up. Early in your presentation, address the objections from the list of common objections that you have developed. Use a two-sided argument at the beginning of a presentation, which makes you appear to be more objective and candid, and in turn, increases your credibility.

Here's an example of how, during the Recap and Purpose phase of a call, you might forestall an objection you know is going to come up.

You: "Since the last time I saw you, Mr. Hernandez, I've thought a great deal about how we might increase your traffic on Mondays and Tuesdays. The purpose of my call today is to show you mock-ups of some ads that I think will get results for you." (Same Recap and Purpose as above) "You've also mentioned you didn't like our paper's editorial position in regard to the mayor. A lot of people agree with you, especially in the Latino and African-American communities. On the one hand, by advertising in my paper, you'd be supporting a newspaper whose editorial position you are opposed to, which I can understand why you'd be reluctant to do. On the other hand, you know that your customers who disagree with the paper read the paper, if just to get mad at it and reinforce their own views. Plus, your customers who agree with the paper will respect you for running an ad in spite of your opposition. You win both ways. Remember also that you've been a consistent advertiser and have run ads in the past even though you disagreed with the paper." (Consistency principle)

Use "Yes, but..." and compare. When prospects state an objection, first agree with them, then state a benefit that compensates for the perceived shortcoming. This technique works well when it is combined with a comparison with competitive alternatives. For example:

Prospect: "Wow. That's a lot of money to advertise on your cable system."

You: "*Yes*, I can see how that might seem like a lot at first, *but* as a businessman, you know you get what you pay for." (Automatic response, expensive equals good)

Prospect: "There are so many channels on cable, how will my prospects ever see my commercial on only one or two channels?"

You: "*Yes*, there are a number of choices on cable, and I can certainly understand your concern. *But*, because cable is much more selective than broadcast television, you don't have to pay high prices for coverage of down-scale audiences you're not interested in." (You are not knocking a specific competitor; you are pointing out a generic weakness.) "You can be selective. And commercials on any type of television have much more impact with sight, sound, motion, and emotion than advertising on radio or print ads." (Contrast principle)

Use case histories. When an objection comes up, respond by citing case histories of successful advertisers. For example:

Prospect: "I don't want any nighttime spots."

You: "I understand how you feel; a lot of advertisers feel the same way. Nighttime is not the highest-rated time period in radio. However, it is efficient. The Men's Clearance Loft uses nothing but nighttime. In fact, it never runs advertising before midnight. The Loft has been on for three years and has increased its business more than 200 percent. The people there love nighttime radio because they can run a lot of spots and remind people over and over of their low prices. Also, they can afford to dominate a time period in nighttime radio." (Social proof and competition for a resource)

Case histories of successes in a prospect's line of business are particularly effective. Often retailers are very competitive, and if you can sell one of them in a product category, others will follow.

Use "Coming to that . . ." Often in a presentation, prospects will raise an objection that you know you will answer later. Simply tell them you are "coming to that." Also, use this response with minor or figurative objections you suspect are not really material or relevant.

While the general rule with most objections is to deal with them as soon as they occur, sometimes it makes sense to stall prospects, especially when the objections are minor or figurative. If you allow prospects to slow you down too much with nitpicking, you will never finish covering your major advantages and benefits. If an objection is real, literal, or important, prospects will certainly bring it up again. If an objection is literal and you use "coming to that," make sure you do not forget about it and actually come to it later. If you leave a literal, material objection unanswered, it remains a barrier to a sale and it looks like you are trying to dodge the issue.

Pass on objections. There will be times in discussion or presentation when it is best to ignore an objection by pretending a prospect had not mentioned it. Some books refer to this technique as *selling through objections.* This technique is effective when objections are so trivial that they really do not deserve the dignity of an answer. This technique also works with figurative objections. If you suspect that an objection is a reflex response, nod slightly, smile, ignore it, and keep selling benefits. For example:

> *You:* "I can offer you a sponsorship of the new "Green Grocer" segment in our "Sunrise News" program. This is the first day we are offering it, and a lot of supermarkets are probably going to want it. I came to you first."

> *Prospect:* "I don't know how anyone can stand that jerk of a weatherman of yours."

> *You* (smiling slightly): "This sort of exposure should be perfect for your supermarkets because many shoppers are thinking about what fresh produce is available when they go shopping later in the day."

Dealing with the price objection. Finally, you will never be a successful media salesperson if you do not learn to deal with the price objection effectively. If you cannot deal with the price objection, you will find yourself selling a commodity. Commodities are not technically sold, but are bought in a reverse auction where the lowest bidder is awarded the business.

During your discussion, you continually use the word quality to describe your product. You have emphasized value instead of price whenever you can. You have focused on results, service, demographics, and all of the things that create value. You break down prices into smaller units and refer to your proposal as an investment rather than a cost.

When you create value, you try to forestall the price objection, but you cannot forestall it completely. By creating a perception of value you raise the floor of prospects' initial lowball offers (material self-interest). If you can raise the floor of an initial offer by 10 percent and the settlement is in the middle between your initial offer and a prospect's initial offer, then you have managed to raise your price by 10 percent.

The price objection is almost universal. There are a few products, such as a Rolls Royce or a Patek Philippe watch, where price is seldom an issue. The higher the price of these symbols of status and authority, the higher their value is. However, it is rare for the price of media to have status value for prospects. They might want their advertising to be in the Super Bowl or in a prestigious magazine, but they do not generally want to brag that they paid a higher price than anyone else. Therefore, count on hearing the price objection when you are selling media.

Getting a price objection is a good thing. How would you feel, when you finally mention price in your presentation, if a prospect said, "That's a great price"? You would feel terrible because you would know that you have under-priced your proposal. People's perception of a fair price has a great deal to do with their personal needs, motivations, and inherent assumptions. If you have identified these elements well, you will know what reaction to expect when the subject of price comes up. Excellent preparation is the best way to deal with the inevitable price objection.

Welcome the price objection because it signals that prospects desire your product, are convinced that it is right for them, and are ready to take action if an agreement on price can be reached. If you hear the price objection, it is time to summarize and close, which will, more than likely, lead to negotiations.

Conditions. There is a difference between an objection and a condition. An objection might be, "Your price is too high." A condition would be, "Since I saw you last, my insurance rates have gone up so high I have to close my business." You can overcome an objection; you cannot overcome a condition. A condition is a valid reason for not buying or at least for not buying now.

As a general rule, you should discover conditions in the identifying problems and qualifying step, because it is the major function of the qualifying step. You must learn to *recognize conditions* so you do not waste time trying to overcome something that is impossible to overcome.

Even experienced salespeople who are good qualifiers let a condition slip by them in the initial steps and discover they have encountered one in the discussion phase. When you discover a condition that would stand in the way of a sale, you should use probing questions to determine if it is really a condition. Once verified, gracefully and politely stop and cut your losses. Even though you have invested time and effort in a presentation, do not waste any more time, be as pleasant as you can, and leave. After all, the condition might someday go away.

Discussion Phase Tactics

Vary your style. The longer your proposal is, the greater the chances are that your prospects' attention will wander. Following are some ways you can *vary your style* to keep them interested.

Use contrast in your presentation. People notice things that are brighter, bigger, or louder than what has come before, as well as sudden changes in intensity. Anything that is consistently too loud, too soft, or even too in-the-middle will begin to bore. Vary your style; talk louder, then softer. Do not be too emphatic or enthusiastic all the time.

Use movement in your presentation. If you are sitting, get up and walk around for a while, particularly to emphasize an important point. Use gestures to highlight your points.

Also, make prospects move if you can. Have prospects turn the pages of your proposal or hand them a pencil and ask them to make notes in the margins. Ask them to figure a simple math problem for you on the desk calculator to make a point. Movement keeps prospects alert and attentive.

Use novelty. Something is novel if it is fresh, new, different, and unusual. As part of the media industry, you are in the news and entertainment business. Most people love to hear about and be associated with well-known media personalities such as magazine editors, newspaper publishers, and television reporters. Even in many small and medium-sized markets, local television anchors and radio disc jockeys are often important celebrities. So, having lunch or their picture taken with one of these celebrities might be a novel and exciting experience for prospects, especially those who have a high need for recognition or status. (Authority principle)

A few years ago, a national television salesperson in New York was about to make a call on a buyer who had just been discharged from the hospital. The day before the call, the salesperson contacted the people in the offices of the building directly across the street from hers and paid them to hang a sheet out of their windows. On the sheet was written, "Welcome Back, Jeannie!" in huge letters and the sign was unfurled just as the salesperson made the call. The salesperson got the buyer's attention and, of course, got a nice order.

One salesperson in a medium-sized Texas market had been calling on a car dealer trying to crack the account and to get the dealership on radio. The salesperson had done research and knew that the prospect had a four-year-old boy. Each time the salesperson made a call, the salesperson brought along a new Matchbox series toy car. At the appropriate time in the presentation, the salesperson made a point about radio's ability to "move cars," at which time the salesperson produced the toy car and rolled it across the desk toward the prospect. This novelty gimmick became great fun for the prospect as the prospect began to look for the place in the presentation when the toy car would appear. The anticipation riveted the prospect's attention. The car dealer rewarded the salesperson with the biggest share of the dealership's advertising budget.

Use equivalencies to dramatize numbers. One way to help prospects remember the numbers that are inevitably included in a media sales proposal is to use equivalencies. An example of an equivalency would be to tell a prospect, if you were selling for the *Kansas City Star*, "Your ad in my newspaper would reach ten times more people than would fill Arrowhead Stadium where the Chiefs play—ten times more people." Or, "If the Cineplex movie theater in the mall sold out four showings of 'Lord of the Rings' every day for an entire year, not as many people would see the movie as would see just one commercial on my station's 'News 6' at 10:00 PM on Sunday evening." Equivalencies dramatize numbers and make them understandable and tangible.

Narrow down objections and reconfirm. This tactic is also referred to as *questioning down*. Sometimes prospects have some objections that are not easy to overcome with the above techniques and require more discussion and negotiation. The goal in this phase of the discussion is to *narrow down* their objections until they have just one or two. Use trial closes as you go along to make sure you have narrowed down all of the objections to one or two, then *reconfirm* that these are the only objections left. When you overcome the only remaining objections that prospects agree exist, you have made a sale.

Change the basis for evaluation as a last resort. Changing prospects' bases for making purchase evaluations is not always possible or even desirable. However, there will be times in a sales presentation when you find yourself faced with objections that you cannot overcome. Occasionally, it is possible to alter the evaluative basis, or norms, and to change the rules in your favor, but proceed slowly and deliberately. Use well-worded verification questions to let prospects change their own direction. One of the most common alterations in evaluation criteria is to change from efficiency (overall cost and cost-per-thousand, or CPM) to effectiveness (for example, impact, reach and frequency, attentiveness, message recall), or to results (depending on prospects' definition of results). Examples of these alternatives are:

1. Salespeople for independent television stations might try to get prospects to evaluate schedules on the basis of balanced frequency while network affiliate salespeople might try to have schedule evaluation based on reach.

2. Adult contemporary radio stations push the 25-to-54 demographic while rock stations push the 18-to-34 demographic as the primary basis for evaluation.

3. Both radio stations might try to get an advertiser who invests a lot of money in television to evaluate his investments based on a media-mix concept that optimizes total reach rather than just on the basis of the reach of television alone. You will learn more about media mix in Chapter 17.

4. Cable salespeople would try to get buyers to evaluate their audience based on the exclusive, upscale, targeted audiences cable reaches rather than on the basis of ratings, whenever possible.

5. Newspaper salespeople would prefer to have their proposals evaluated on results rather than on price or cost-per-thousand circulation, and would try to change the basis for evaluation accordingly.

Reassure doubts. Prospects may like what you are offering but have some doubts. Doubts are different from objections. When prospects doubt a benefit or an advantage, they have essentially accepted them but remain unsure about how it might apply to their business. The way to handle doubts is with *reassurances* about yourself, your company, and your medium. Prospects need an infusion and transference of confidence from you. The more knowledgeable, enthusiastic, and confident you are about your product, the more reassured prospects will be and the quicker they will accept your point. If they have doubts, they have not moved on to conviction.

Be patient with doubts, do not gloss over them, and do not try to close until they are resolved. Neil Rackham, as you can see in Figure 11.1, the Sales Ladder, refers to doubts as concerns. Rackham makes the point that you cannot resolve prospects' concerns for them, because doubts are their own internal conflicts. They might be political issues, such as how the boss will like it, how it will affect their careers if they make a mistake, or if it is really better than other alternatives. Probe to find the real reason for the doubt or concern and use data and facts to reassure them, but do not pressure them, do not minimize their concerns, and let them work through them on their own. There are times when you will have to back off, and come back another time after they have dealt with their issues.

Evaluate prospects' reactions. As you go through the Discussion phase, you must continually be aware of how your prospects are responding to each point you make. You must listen carefully and *be extremely observant for any possible feedback.* Make a mental note of those benefits prospects respond to most positively so you can use them in a summary later. Watch for signs of boredom or inattention and notice if anything strikes prospects negatively. Look for signs that prospects have shifted from interest to desire and from desire to conviction. Once you see signs of conviction, stop talking and close.

Summary and Close

After you have dealt with prospects' objections and concerns and when you see indications of conviction—body language such as leaning forward or more rapid head nodding—it is time to close, to ask for the order. But first, you should summarize your benefits, which reinforces them. An example is, "Well, Mary, you've agreed that my proposal concentrates on women 18 to 49, achieves high-reach over two weeks, and is very close to your cost-per-point targets. Can we go ahead?"

This last request was a simple trial close that probably will lead to further negotiations, which is one of the purposes of the Summary and Close phase. In the close, you're asking for action, or in some cases, you will ask what the Next Steps are. Next Steps are a form of a close because you are asking for a commitment for action.

Exhibit 11.3 shows an outline of all the steps in a sales-focused call structure and overcoming objections. This outline is also available on www.mediaselling.us so you can download it into a PDA and review it before making a presenting call. I also recommend putting a list of common objections you encounter and your responses in your PDA for continual review and refinement.

Exhibit 11.3
Call Structure and
Dealing With
Objections Outline

1. Greeting
2. New information
3. Opening
4. Recap and purpose
5. Discussion
   A. Dealing with objections
      i. Probe to understand.
      ii. Compliment, restate, and get agreement.
      iii. Empathize, reassure, and support (feel, felt, found).
      iv. Use trial closes.
      v. Forestall objections.
      vi. Use "Yes, but . . ." and compare.
      vii. Use case histories.
      viii. Use "Coming to that..."
      ix. Pass on objections.
      x. Dealing with price objections
         a. Continually talk about quality.
         b. Break price into smallest possible units.
         c. Talk value, not price.
         d. Refer to investments, not costs.
   B. Conditions
   C. Discussion tactics
      i. Vary your style.
         a. Contrast
         b. Movement
         c. Novelty
      ii. Use equivalencies.
      iii. Narrow down objections and reconfirm.
      iv. Change the basis for evaluation as a last resort.
      v. Reassure doubts.
      vi. Evaluate reactions.
6. Summary and close

How to Use Your Proposal One-on-One

When you make presentations to larger groups, you should use PowerPoint or other presentation software, such as PROposal Wizard 3.0, which is available through the Radio Advertising Bureau.[4] But, when you present one-on-one or to small groups, showing people proposals on a computer is often awkward and too impersonal. In these situations I recommend using a hard copy of a proposal.

One technique of handling hard copies of proposals is to put them unfastened into a folder and then to hand each page, one at a time, to prospects. This prevents prospects from jumping ahead and it focuses their attention, especially if they are in a hurry or are impatient. You can control the pace of your presentation and force prospects to stay with you. One of the drawbacks of this technique, though, is that prospects' desks become a jumble of pieces of paper. It can be awkward to try to put all the single sheets back together in order to leave prospects with a complete, well-organized copy of the proposal. When you use the *one-page-at-a-time technique*, bring along an extra copy or two to hand prospects when the call is over.

Another technique is to give a complete copy of your proposal to prospects and ask them to follow along as you go through it. Sometimes you can arrange the physical surroundings so you can sit side by side with prospects. Give them a complete copy and sit with them as you both go over the presentation while they turn the pages, then say, "Here's a proposal I prepared. Let's go over it together. I'll highlight the important points for you. Don't hesitate to stop me if you have any questions." Bring along a couple of highlighter pens; give one to prospects and while you highlight important points, encourage them to do so likewise. Do whatever you can to get prospects involved, to ask questions about the proposal, or to go back and forth in it. Paraphrase the written text as you go and point out the most salient points rather than reading word for word.

Control the physical environment so you eliminate barriers that make developing rapport difficult. In general, you should work as close as possible without violating prospects' social space. Use emotional intelligence when evaluating the proper social space in which to work. By careful observation, you can find ways to connect with them; you will see where their social space is and not invade it. Often, invading someone's social space is a matter of inches, so get as close as you can, but never too close. Be very sensitive to gender differences when evaluating the proper social space in which to work. If you get too close, some people can become offended or take it the wrong way. Always work in what I call professional space.

A third technique is to give your prospects a complete bound copy of your proposal to look over and read while you follow along page by page, so you will be ready to answer any questions. If you use this method, make sure you tell your prospects, "Here's my proposal. Why don't you read it over and I'll answer any questions you have." If you use this technique, do not interrupt. Too often salespeople will go into prospects' offices, hand them a proposal, and then begin making a verbal presentation. The prospect's head bobs up and down as they try to read and listen at the same time. Prospects might also whip ahead to the price page and not hear your well-presented benefits. I do not recommend this technique, primarily because of the latter reason.

Presenting to Groups

When presenting to groups where the stakes are bigger, the proposals are bigger and they become presentations.

Just as it is in your one-on-one calls, it is important to structure your presentations to groups of four or more, which is often in the form of major presentations to key accounts. The primary purpose of a presentation of this type is to move prospects up the Sales Ladder from *desire* to *conviction* to *action*. You should use a PowerPoint presentation because this more formal approach focuses prospects' attention on your solutions and call to action.

Structure your oral presentations as follows:

Structure of a Major Presentation to a Key Account

- Opening
- Theme
- Agenda
- Main body of content
- Summary
- Conclusion and Next Steps

Objectives

Before you begin your preparation for a major presentation to a key account, you must clearly define your objectives. Often, when presenting to groups there will be several presentations during the sales process, and you must set objectives for each presentation. The first one might be a stock general presentation, the second to propose solutions, and the third to show solutions that have been altered to meet prospects' needs and to get a commitment. Initial presentations rarely result in a signed contract. Typically with bigger deals, a commitment leads to further negotiations on deal terms, contract conditions, payment terms, and pricing structure.

Following are objectives for a general presentation (GP). Set similar objectives for each subsequent presentation you make.

Objectives for a GP

1. To create value for your company and your product
2. To create the perception of quality for your company and for your product
3. To build rapport and trust between the prospective customer and the presenting team
4. To get agreement to pursue a partnership and explore solutions and opportunities
5. To get agreement to give you the information you need to come up with meaningful solutions
6. To get agreement on next steps (who does what) and on whom you will be working with from prospects' organizations to gather information

Preparation

Obviously, the first step in preparation is creating the presentation, which was covered in Chapter 10. The next steps are deciding the who, where, when, and how questions.

Who.   Who in your organization should be the person to give a presentation? The rule of thumb is to try to match size and levels. In other words, have your CEO present to CEOs of large companies, your president (or equivalent) present to presidents of large companies, your senior VPs present to senior VPs of large companies, and so forth.

Sometimes there will several people on your presentation team. It might include your CEO, a VP of sales, yourself, and a marketing person. There should be no more than three, or, at most, four people from your organization on the presentation team, and everyone on the team should actively participate in the presentation and not merely be listeners. Too many people overwhelm and confuse prospects. If the leadoff person from your organization is a CEO, president, or senior VP, then the primary salesperson on the account should be present and introduced as the primary contact for the account in the future. The lead should deliver at least one-third of the presentation so prospects can get to know that person. In some situations, with an organization's largest accounts, a CEO might do the entire presentation, talking to an account's CEO and promising the client their continued involvement in the account.

Who should receive a presentation? The first presentation to an account or agency should be to the most senior-level executives that you can gather so you can introduce your organization and get agreement to pursue a relationship. You want to sell to VITO (Very Important Top Officers), as designated by Anthony Parinello in *Selling to VITO,* an excellent book that I strongly recommend.

Where.   If possible, give presentations in your offices because you get the home field advantage and can control the environment and timing. If you give a presentation at a prospect's location or at an agency, make sure you check beforehand to see if there is an LCD projector that will take input from your computer. Also, offer to have food or refreshments delivered. Serve coffee and food before or after a presentation, but never during. Always arrive early to give yourself plenty of time to set up.

When.   You should give your presentation during prospects' advertising planning cycle. You must find this out during your discovery process and give your presentation at the beginning of the process, because it is a waste of time to give a presentation a few months after a major account and its agency have planned their media expenditures for the coming year.

How.   Even if you have given a particular type of presentation several times, and even if you have created a customized, solutions-based presentation before, always *write a script.* Type the script in large type (16- or 18-point bold serif) with only one sentence on a line, in small paragraphs that contain only one point per paragraph, with a space between paragraphs, and with emphasis marked: read up /, read down \, or <u>emphasize</u>. Also, mark where your gestures go in a presentation and rehearse the gestures.

Use the slides in the presentation as the basis for your script, but do not read the slides; *discuss* them and, most important, tell anecdotes and stories and use equivalencies to illustrate and reinforce the points you are making on the slides. A script gives you confidence; it cues you for the anecdotes, stories, equivalencies and gestures, keeps you on track, and helps you avoid wandering off on tangents and rambling.

Rehearsal is imperative, no matter the size of the order. If the situation requires a presentation, then it requires that it be done professionally. In order to make certain that your presentation is better than your competitors' are, you must rehearse. While you do not need the months of rehearsal that a Broadway play does, you need to rehearse once or twice in front of your prep team to make sure your presentation is better than your competitors' are. It is a good idea to try to rehearse in the room where you will give the presentation so you will feel comfortable there. Rehearse walking around the room and talking to empty chairs, especially to the chair in which you want the decision maker to sit.

When you rehearse, keep a mental picture of the physical setup so you will be prepared and be comfortable. You want to *work in as intimate space as possible* to develop rapport with your audience. Practice your movements in a space that is similar to the one in which you will be presenting. Rehearse everything in your script, including your examples, anecdotes, and stories. Rehearse your gestures, too. Time all your rehearsals so you know exactly how long your presentation takes. Use the same presentation aids, such as a laser pointer and a remote mouse, as you will use in the actual presentation. These aids make your presentation look more professional and allow you to move around to make your presentation more energetic and dynamic.

Have plenty of handouts such as relevant articles, pictures of what you are offering and copies of the presentation. But *do not hand out copies of the presentation* beforehand; instead, encourage people to take notes (have note pads available). If you hand out the presentation beforehand, people will look ahead to their area of interest (accountants to the price, for instance) and you will lose control. The time to hand out any printed material is when you have to demonstrate something to make a point. But, it is usually better to wait until the end, because distributing material during a presentation tends to slow down the flow as people look it over.

Know your subject thoroughly. Rehearsal also allows you to hone your knowledge. You are the expert and must have the answers to all possible questions and objections prospects have. It is a good idea to give different areas of expertise to different members of your team. For example, assign operations/production to the person who is an expert in that area, promotion to someone with that expertise, and research to an expert in that field. This arrangement not only relieves pressure on the main presenter, but also introduces other members of your team of experts. Rehearse transitions from one team member to the next to make them fast and smooth.

Understand your audience. Before going into a presentation, you should know in advance your audience's personalities, emotional needs, inherent assumptions, and motivations, especially those of the decision makers to whom you will direct your presentation. You should also have a sense of their attitudes about your company and product.

Finally, plan in advance how you want to arrange the seating. An effective presentation begins with an *effective room setup*. Do not have alternate seating—a member of your team, then a prospect, then a member of your team. Give the prospects the best seats and put them all together in a row or in a circle at the end of a table so they have the best view of the projection screen. Seat the main decision makers in the middle so they are always the center of your attention, although you will include others from time to time. Have your team sit behind the prospects or at the front of the table—your people do not need to have a good view of the presentation. The message you want to convey is that your focus and complete attention is on the prospects. Assign members of your team to watch a member of the prospect's team and take notes unobtrusively of their assigned prospect's reaction to different points in the presentation to give you accurate feedback in a debriefing.

Delivery

Nick Morgan, in a *Harvard Business Review* article titled "The Kinesthetic Speaker: Putting Action into Words," writes, "Sure, presentations are about what a speaker says. But they're also about how a speaker moves. By making adroit use of your body and the space around you, you can create a physical connection with the audience that will earn trust and inspire action." In the article, Morgan writes the Dos and Don'ts of kinesthetic speaking, as seen in Exhibit 11.4.

**Exhibit 11.4
The Dos and
Don'ts
of Kinesthetic
Speaking**

Do...
- identify individuals who can serve as proxies for the whole audience.
- vary the distance between yourself and the audience, moving into the personal space of proxies to recount an anecdote or to make a plea.
- ensure that your physical moves are in harmony with your verbal message.
- prepare your own presentations so your physical moves don't betray inauthentic content.
- read and respond to the nonverbal cues of audience members.

Don't...
- speak generally to the entire audience for long periods.
- repeatedly move back and forth between the podium or slide projector and the screen.
- turn away from the audience to cue up your next slide while speaking.
- fidget away your nervous energy.
- count on the audience remembering more than one or two of your main points.

Source: Morgan, 2001, p.115.

Morgan writes that the alignment of a speaker's movements with his words reinforces the message he is trying to convey. Following are some tips that will make your delivery more effective.

Open.   Before you begin your PowerPoint presentation, make opening remarks that relate to the *theme* of the presentation and that include an *agenda* of what you are going to cover. These should be memorable and demonstrate your confidence and your control of the situation.

Also, opening remarks should deal with questions such as, "Should I take notes?", "Can I ask questions?", and "How long will the presentation take?" Opening remarks should also deal with how to handle questions as they occur in a presentation. One way is to take questions at the end of the presentation, another is to take them at any time, yet another is to take them at specific times during the presentation, or to take only important questions during the presentation and others afterwards. Saving questions until the end will allow you to save time, but it creates a one-way presentation. While you maintain control, you limit interaction and leave some questions unanswered. Worst of all, it hurts the rapport you would like to build between you and the audience.

Taking questions any time during a presentation is very effective if you have relatively loose time constraints, because it gets the audience involved. But keep close track of time. If people ask too many questions you will not finish the entire presentation, so give the problem to them by saying, "Time is in your hands. Our presentation runs 25 minutes and I have built in 15 minutes for questions, but please feel free to ask as many questions as you like, and we can extend the time frame." In this way you alert them to the need to keep track but that you can extend the time if they want.

Taking important questions during the presentation and the rest later is another good tactic. By saying in your opening remarks, "We have allowed time at the end of the presentation for questions, but, of course, feel free to ask any questions that help clarify our presentation," you encourage you audience to save questions while not muzzling them.

Your opening remarks should begin with a sincere "thank you" for giving you the time to make a presentation and should include a tidbit of knowledge about the prospects and their companies that relates to the *theme* of your presentation. For example, before Matt Weisbecker of AOL Interactive Marketing gave a presentation to Panasonic, he prepared himself by reading a book about the company's founder, Matsushita. He opened his presentation with a quote from the company's mission statement that Matsushita had written in 1936 and compared it to AOL's mission statement.

Find out what your audience's interests and hobbies are and relate your opening remarks to them. If you know the decision makers are big sports fans, open with a sports analogy or story that involves their favorite sport or team. Find out what their interests and hobbies are and relate your opening to those interests, if possible. You can also open with an amusing or insightful story, but make sure it is relevant. You do not want your prospects to lose the point of the presentation. *Bridge* your opening story or joke (make sure it is funny and *not off color*) with a statement such as "with that in mind . . ." or ". . . which brings me to the purpose of our presentation." If you cannot make a bridge statement like these, then the story or joke is not relevant and you should not use it.

One of the best opening stories I ever heard comes from James Burke's *Connections* and tells how at the battle of Agincourt a severely outnumbered (six to one) English army defeated the French by using long bows, which the French had never seen. The story highlights how disruptive technology changed forever the way armies waged war and is an analogy of how the Internet changed the way companies conduct business.

In the outstanding book, *Khrushchev's Shoe*, Roy Underhill writes that the features of a presentation or speech that people enjoy most are hands-on experiences.[5] He advocates using your opening to involve your audience in some way, perhaps to get them to perform some action. You might ask, "What is the biggest challenge facing your industry in the next five years?" and then let everyone answer. Or, a favorite of mine is to ask them to write down the five most important people in their company. When they have finished, ask them how many of them put their customers on their lists.

Another way to involve your audience is to ask them to build something. You might open a couple of sets of Lego blocks, dump them on the table, and ask people to build something in five minutes. When they have finished and shared what they have built with one another, tell them that your organization has a number of different packages, programs, and products that they can use to build a solution just as unique.

Your opening remarks give you the opportunity to make a favorable first impression. Therefore, the stronger the opening the better and more lasting the impression. Your opening sets the tone for the entire presentation, so open creatively and use props if you can. Because of the primacy and recency principles, discussed in Chapter 7, people will remember your opening and your closing most vividly.

Main Body of Content.   Table 11.1 contains *delivery tips* for the main body of your presentation. Exhibit 11.5 shows an example of a story that touches an emotional chord.

Table 11.1 Delivery Tips	Tip	Description
	1. Audience expectations	You should have a sense of your audiences' expectations and their preferred style: conservative, formal, and straightforward or informal, humorous, and glitzy, for example.
	2. Poise and confidence	Having poise and demonstrating a sense of confidence are critical for delivering a successful presentation.
	3. Love your product.	Be passionate about it and convey that passion to your audience with your physical movements and gestures.
	4. Be concise.	Don't ramble. Stick to your script and stay within the allotted time. Remember that the ideal length of time for a presentation in 25 minutes.
	5. Remember WIIFM.	Keep in mind that with everything you say, prospects are asking themselves, "What's in it for me?" Therefore, with every feature or advantage you mention, mention a benefit.
	6. Keep jargon to a minimum	In your written presentation you used your prospects' language and avoided jargon, so do not fall into using jargon during your oral presentation.
	7. "We're number one" never sold anything.	What prospects want are solutions, not chest-thumping numbers. Use equivalencies for numbers whenever you can and make sure the numbers you use are relevant to the solutions you are proposing. No one cares if you are number one if you cannot solve their problems.
	8. No negatives	During your presentation never be negative and never knock the competition.
	9. Don't be defensive.	If you get a question, even a hostile one, do not panic. Repeat the question, say something such as "Good point," and answer it concisely, honestly, and directly or put it off until later in your presentation when you have an answer for it. Do not waffle or lose your confidence.
	10. Smile	Inexperienced speakers are often frightened when they present in front of a group and forget to smile. Do not make that mistake; smile as appropriate throughout the presentation.
	11. Establish eye contact with everyone.	Move around and try to establish some eye cotact with everyone, even though you will be concentrating most often on the decision maker.
	12. Vary your voice.	Vary your tone of voice, your pitch, and your volume. Modulate well; you do not want to lull people to sleep with a monotone. Rehearsal helps.
	13. Use people's names.	Direct your points to specific people and use their names: "Isn't this the solution you asked for, Joe?"
	14. Be careful about injecting humor.	Unless you are funny and have a knack for telling jokes and for humor, do not use it. Nothing falls flatter than a poor joke. *Never* insert off-color or inappropriate humor.

continued

Table 11.1 *(continued)*	Tip	Description
	15. Involve the audience.	People learn better when they participate than they do when they just listen. Bob Pittman was the best presenter I have ever seen in action. When he was president of American Online, he would use a variety of questions to get audiences involved. He would often say, "Raise your hands if you ever bought a Cuisinart machine. Now keep them up if you know what closet it's in. Come on now, be honest." Then he would make the point that AOL was not a gimmick, it was an everyday necessity.
	16. Tap into the decision-maker's emotions.	Great speakers such as Winston Churchill and Martin Luther King Jr. were able to touch the hearts of their audiences. They tapped into emotions and feelings, and made these emotions work for them. When you do your homework about your audience in general and the decision maker in particular, find out what their passions are and then find stories that touch their feelings about their country, their business, or its founder. See Exhibit 11.5 for the kind of story that would elicit an emotional response. But remember to match your emotional fervor to the audience's ability to receive the message. (Conger, 1998.)
	17. Keep going.	It takes listeners a long time to catch up to the fact that you have lost your place or gone to the wrong slide. Pause, collect yourself, and keep going. Never say, "I'm sorry" or point out a mistake because your audience more than likely will not notice a mistake unless you point it out. Keep on trucking.
	18. Laugh it off.	If something happens such as a projector breaks or a bulb burns out, so what? Keep on gong. Your audience is with you and wants you to do well, so make them comfortable by handling a crisis with grace and humor without blaming someone—your assistant, the projector, or God. Laugh it off gracefully and keep trucking.
	19. Be yourself and have fun.	Relax and be natural; rehearsals will help a lot to give you confidence and to relax enough to be yourself. You must be authentic because people will know if you are trying too hard or are phony.

Exhibit 11.5
The Firefighter

In January 2002, four months after the tragedy of 9/11, I heard a story that dramatically made a point. A vice president for America Online, where I was working at the time, gave a presentation to the CEO of a key account. When the presentation concluded, the CEO asked for a substantial price concession.

The vice president told a story of a weary New York firefighter who was returning home from working at Ground Zero several weeks after the tragedy. As he trudged along, he saw a homeless man holding a small American flag who asked the firefighter for money for a meal. The firefighter said, "I'll give you $10 for that flag." The homeless man replied, "I may be hungry and homeless, but this is my country's flag. No deal." The weary fireman nodded, stuffed a $10 bill into the homeless man's hand, and went on his way.

The vice president then said to the CEO, "I cannot sell AOL at a discount because I love and respect this company and our product and I will not undervalue or undersell it." The CEO did not mention price again and the VP got a commitment for a sizeable deal.

Summary

Most summaries are too long. I have seen presenters summarize 15 points at the end of a presentation. That is not a summary, it is a novelette. Use the Rule of Three and keep your summary to three points, because that is all your prospects will remember.

Conclusion and Next Steps

Richard B. Chase and Sriram Dasu, in an article titled "Want to Perfect Your Company's Service? Use Behavioral Science" in the *Harvard Business Review*, stress the importance of finishing strong. The authors indicate that of the two ordering effects, primacy and recency, that recency, or the last experience people have in an encounter such as a presentation, is by far the most important.[6] Therefore, not only is it important to have a dramatic, attention-getting opening, but it is even more important that your conclusion is memorable.

Ratchet up your passion in your conclusion. You want to make as an emotional appeal as you can for why a deal between your company and a prospect's company is an ideal partnership. You are asking for the prospect's hand in marriage and you should make your closing remarks worthy of such a union. Widely regarded as the greatest speech in the English language, Lincoln's Gettysburg Address opens memorably with "Four score and seven years ago," but ends unforgettably with ". . . and that government of the people, by the people, for the people shall not perish from the earth." I do not expect you will be able to write as moving, as unforgettable a finish as Lincoln did, but his stirring words are a good place to start when you think about your conclusion.

After your conclusion, ask for *next steps,* which is a nice, polite way to *close and ask for a commitment.* Next steps might include signing a contract or a letter of intent to do a deal, shaking hands on the deal, or having you present to a prospect's board of directors. Whatever the commitment is that you want, never forget to ask for it. It is an unforgivable sin in selling not to do so.

If you get no questions when you are finished with your presentation, you have done something wrong and are in trouble. A friend of mine who used to sell for IBM in the 1970s tells a story about a major presentation he made to the board of directors of a large regional insurance company. At the end of the two-hour presentation when my friend asked if there were any questions, there were none. My friend said he was squirming and did not have a clue as to what to do in the deafening silence. His boss, the regional sales manager, who had been an observer, said, "You didn't do a very good job of explaining the benefits of our solution. They didn't understand. Do the presentation again." My friend panicked for a moment, but did the presentation again as he was told. At the end there were lots of questions and an order followed.

This story points out that presenters must take responsibility for whether or not the audience understands a presentation. If there are no questions at the end of a presentation, it is your fault because you did not explain things well enough. You must take responsibility for clearly communicating the benefits of your solutions, which requires anecdotes, stories, equivalencies, good kinesthetic speaking, and audience participation.

Debriefing

In the first few days after a presentation, the presentation team must have a debriefing meeting. If possible, hold the meeting in the prep room where the charts are still visible. Go over each chart and ask if your preparation was on target and if prospects accepted your ideas and solutions.

Following are the elements on the charts the prep team used in creating the presentation, as outlined in Chapter 10. Use them as guidelines for evaluating your presentation:

1. Your Presentation Team. Were the presenters effective? Who was most effective? In what areas and on what skills could the presenters improve? Give each presenter an honest grade.
2. Your Purpose. Was your purpose on target? How could it be improved the next time?
3. The Prospect's Objectives and Challenges. Did your solutions address them, or were you off target? Did you go deep enough? Did you learn of any new problems?
4. Your Solutions. How were your solutions accepted? Did they thoroughly understand your solutions?
5. Opportunities. Did they like the opportunities you presented?
6. Timetable. Did you give yourselves enough time to create the most effective presentation? Did you plan accurately? Did you estimate how much time each task would take so you will know better next time? How long did the presentation run and was that what you had predicted?
7. The Prospect's Team. Did you analyze their emotional needs and motivations accurately? Did you position your solutions and benefits to meet those needs? Which people on the team responded positively, which negatively, and were there sections of the presentation that they responded to more favorably? Did your people take notes? Who on the prospect's team might be a problem in the future?
8. Ideas. How did the big idea work? How did the theme work? Did it motivate them? Do you need a new big idea?
9. Evidence. What evidence, examples, analogies, and stories did they respond to most positively?
10. Humor. How did they respond to the humor?
11. Benefits Matrix. How accurate was the Benefits Matrix? Does it need to be reworked for subsequent meetings?
12. Your Offer. How effective was your initial offer? Was it too high or too low? How would you structure your offers if you had to do it all over again knowing what you know now?
13. Your Conclusion. How effective was it? Did you offer the right Next Steps? Did you get a commitment?
14. Follow-Up. How were your follow-up ideas received? Would you do anything different the next time? Is there anything more you can do now in the way of follow-up based on what you learned in the presentation?

You cannot learn by your mistakes unless you analyze them objectively. After every presentation be paranoid about losing the order and debrief. The only way to be certain you are better than the competition is to rehearse and debrief more thoroughly than the competition does.

Presenting effectively is a skill that, like acting, requires rehearsal and performance feedback in order to perfect your technique. But it is worth the time and effort you invest, because you cannot be successful unless you learn to present well and with confidence.

Test Yourself

1. What are the four goals of the presenting step of selling?
2. What are the seven steps of the Sales Ladder?
3. What are the six steps in a call structure?

4. What are some techniques for overcoming the price objection?
5. What are three methods of handling proposals one-on-one?
6. What are the 19 delivery tips for making a major presentation to a group?

Project

Write a presentation for a local radio station to a major advertiser. Complete the presentation you started in the project at the end of Chapter 10, using the checklist at the end of that chapter as a guide. Print out the presentation and ask a friend to play the part of a prospect. Give the presentation using both the one-page-at-a-time method and the sit-side-by-side method. See which method you are more comfortable with and pay particular attention to social space and how close you can comfortably work (for you and the prospect). After you have presented your proposal twice, write a script and rehearse delivering the presentation in front of a full-length mirror. Go over the delivery tips in this chapter before you deliver the presentation, and afterward, see how you did. What did you remember to do and what did you forget to do?

References

Richard B. Chase and Sriram Dasu. 2001. "Want to Perfect Your Company's Service? Use Behavioral Science." *Harvard Business Review.* June.

Jay Conger. 1998. "The Necessary Art of Persuasion." *Harvard Business Review.* May-June.

Roger Fisher and William Ury with Bruce Patton. 1991. *Getting to Yes, Second Edition.* New York: Penguin Books.

Neil Flett. 1996. *The Pitch Doctor: Presenting to Win Multi-million Dollar Accounts.* New York: Prentice Hall.

Saul Gellerman. 1990. "The Tests of a Good Salesperson." *Harvard Business Review.* May-June.

Michael Maccoby. 2000. "Narcissistic Leaders: The Incredible Pros, the Inevitable Cons." *Harvard Business Review.* January-February.

Gerald L. Manning and Barry L. Reece. 1990. *Selling Today: A Personal Approach, 4th Edition.* Boston: Allyn and Bacon.

László Merö. 1998. *Moral Calculations: Game Theory, Logic, and Human Frailty.* New York: Copernicus.

Nick Morgan. 2001. "The Kinesthetic Speaker: Putting Action into Words." *Harvard Business Review.* April.

Gerard I. Nierenberg. 1973. *Fundamentals of Negotiating.* New York: Hawthorne Books.

Anthony Parinello. 1999. *Selling to VITO: The Very Important Top Officer.* Holbrook, MA: Adams Media Corp.

Linda L. Putnam and Michael Roloff. 1992. *Communication and Negotiation.* Newbury Park, CA: Sage Publications.

Neil Rackham. 1989. *Major Account Selling Strategies.* New York: McGraw-Hill.

Howard Raiffa. 1982. *The Art & Science of Negotiation.* Cambridge, MA: Harvard University Press.

Thomas C. Schelling. 1980. *The Strategy of Conflict.* Cambridge, MA: Harvard University Press.

James K. Sebenius. 2001. "Six Habits of Merely Effective Negotiators." *Harvard Business Review.* April.

G. Richard Shell. 1999. *Bargaining for Advantage.* New York: Penguin Books.

Roy Underhill. 2000. *Khrushchev's Shoe.* Cambridge, MA: Perseus Publishing.

Bob Woolf. 1990. *Friendly Persuasion.* New York: Berkley Books.

Resources

www.barbwiremuseum.com

Endnotes

1. Gerald L. Manning and Barry L. Reece. 1990. *Selling Today: A Personal Approach, 4th Edition.* Boston: Allyn and Bacon.
2. Neil Rackham. 1989. *Major Account Selling Strategies.* New York: McGraw-Hill.
3. www.barbwiremuseum.com
4. www.rab.com. February, 2003. Free 30-day trial available.
5. Roy Underhill. 2000. *Khrushchev's Shoe.* Cambridge, MA: Perseus Publishing. p. 1.
6. Richard B. Chase and Sriram Dasu. 2001. "Want to Perfect Your Company's Service? Use Behavioral Science." *Harvard Business Review.* June.

12 Skills: Negotiating and Closing

By Charles Warner

Negotiating is one of the most researched and studied topics in business, law, politics, and international affairs. In February 2003 a search on Amazon.com for books on the subject of negotiating came up with 1,276 titles. Obviously, people are buying and reading books on negotiating, so you must assume that your prospects, customers, and buyers have read some of them and possess varying degrees of negotiating expertise. To assume otherwise is foolhardy because the uninformed and unprepared salesperson will lose every time when up against a knowledgeable negotiator. If you are calling on retailers, you must assume they are experts in negotiating because they negotiate every day with their vendors and customers. If you are calling on media buyers, their titles often include the word negotiator, especially at large agencies that purchase network television.

None of the 1,276 negotiating books on Amazon.com were specifically about media negotiating. The majority of the books were about how to negotiate in one-time situations in which long-term relationships were not important and for tangible goods, such as real estate. Negotiating in the media is different from most other types of negotiating and requires special skills for two reasons. First, media negotiating is not about winning at all costs in hard-nosed competitive battles over price and terms. The media does the vast majority of its business with long-term customers and agency buyers, and maintaining relationships with these customers and buyers is vital. Second, the media, especially broadcast and cable, sell a perishable product that if not sold, goes to waste.

Furthermore, all media selling involves negotiating. A negotiation might be a simple three-step process such as, "My price is $100," "I'll give you $90," and "I'll take it." Or an advertiser might negotiate over the position of an ad with a newspaper that will not budge an inch on rates. Television network executives and advertising agency negotiators might negotiate for a $50 million upfront deal. Or a major media conglomerate might negotiate with a major advertiser for a multi-million-dollar deal on all of its media properties, such as the $300 million deal Viacom made with Procter & Gamble (P&G) in May of 2001. But whatever the size of the deal, if you do not learn to be an effective negotiator, your chances of having a successful career in media selling are small, and your chances of being World Class are zero.

Negotiating and closing are included in the same step of selling because the ultimate goal of negotiating is to reach a satisfactory agreement, to close a deal. Therefore, you should look forward to negotiating and not be apprehensive. Why? Because, when you enter into negotiations, prospects have reached the Conviction step on the Sales Ladder. They want to make a deal, and they are ready to take the next step, Action, if they can get what they perceive to be a good deal. It is your task in negotiating to see that customers perceive they get a good deal, which actually should be a good deal for both sides. *An exchange of satisfactions* best describes negotiating. In his classic book, *The Fundamentals of Negotiating*, Gerard Nierenberg writes, "*All parties to a negotiation should come out with some needs satisfied.*"[1]

Negotiating

Rule: Don't negotiate until you've created value and created a differential competitive advantage for your product in the mind of a customer.

Rule: Don't discuss price until you're ready to negotiate and close.

Many inexperienced salespeople make the mistake of negotiating too soon, before they have created value. The first question both experienced media buyers and inexperienced prospects often ask is, "What's the price?" For example, a prospect new to your medium might innocently ask, "How much does an ad in your newspaper cost?" Your response should be, "Well, that's like asking how much a car costs. Are you talking about a Hyundai or a Rolls Royce? The answer is 'It depends.' Let's find out what your needs are and then we'll see what the best type of ad for you would be." If an experienced television buyer whom you have dealt with frequently asks, "What is your cost-per-point?", you should delay the answer until you have had a discussion about the value, benefits, and supply-and-demand issues concerning your product. Even with experienced buyers, always follow the first two rules above.

Some negotiations are not complicated and require minimal preparation. However, because 80 percent of your business will come from 20 percent of your customers, you will find that the majority of your business will involve complex negotiating with your more important customers and agency media buyers. In large markets and in national media such as magazines and network television, virtually all business involves complex negotiating, which requires thorough preparation, as outlined below.

The five elements in the negotiating and closing process are:

1. Your negotiating approach
2. Preparation
3. Maneuvering for dominance and control
4. Bargaining
5. Closing and getting commitment

See the Negotiating and Closing Outline in Appendix D for a summary of the above five elements and the rules of negotiating.

Your Negotiating Approach

Your approach to negotiating should be information-based, relationship-based, ethical, and flexible.

Information-Based.   It is often said that information is power, and in no situation is information more powerful than in negotiating. You should conduct research and gather information about the other side and their competitors, about your competitors, about the other side's cultural background, and about the other side's attitudes and bargaining tactics.

Information about your customers and their competitors. The more information you can gather when you ask your discovery questions and afterwards about customers' goals, strategies, challenges, and business and personal needs (a Needs Portrait), the better chance you have to achieve your objectives in a negotiation. An information-based approach focuses on solid planning, careful listening to discover information about your customers' needs and interests, and recognizing signals the other side sends through its behavior and tactics during the negotiating process.

It is also important to gather complete information about the other side's competitors: the competitors' marketing and advertising strategies, their market positions, their value propositions, their images, and their reputations. As we learned in game theory, your customers' strategies will be determined by their competitors' strategic and tactical moves, so you must have competitive information to position your offers in a way that helps your customers beat their competitors.

Information about your competitors. In the book *The Art of War*, by Sun Tzu, the legendary Chinese general writes, "Spies are a most important element in war, because upon them depends an army's ability to move."[2] For "spies" substitute the modern concept of competitive intelligence, for "war" substitute negotiating, and for "army" substitute the word negotiator. The sentence now reads: Competitive intelligence is the most important element in negotiating, because upon it depends a negotiator's ability to move. Another lesson from Sun Tzu that we must not forget is that "the true object of war is *peace*."[3] Likewise, the true object of negotiating must be *agreement*, not victory.

Intelligence about your competitors is critical to your negotiating planning and to reaching a final agreement: on what prices they will offer, on what concessions they will make, and on what tactics they have traditionally used in past negotiations. Having this information will help you determine your prices, your offers, and your tactics.

Information about the other side's cultural background. The way people approach negotiating and their negotiating style is based on their cultural background. For example, many people from the Middle East conduct business based on haggling over price, which is always negotiable. Some people in America believe in negotiating at every opportunity, others believe that negotiating indicates that they cannot afford something and, thus, do not negotiate to avoid looking cheap.

As an example, I gave a negotiating seminar to a group of magazine salespeople in New York several years ago and made the point that negotiating approaches are culturally based. A woman in the audience said, "Yes, I agree. My family never negotiated for anything." A salesperson sitting next to her said, "Wendy, you grew up in Greenwich, Connecticut. I grew up in the Bronx. My father sold garments on Seventh Avenue and the first two things he taught me were, 'do not eat ham' and 'do not pay retail.'" Neither approach is right nor wrong; both are perfectly valid approaches. It is important for you to acquire information about the other side's approach so you can plan your negotiating tactics accordingly.

The attitudes and tactics of the other side. You might discover in your competitive intelligence research that the person you will be negotiating with tends to be an over-confident braggart who takes great pleasure in belittling others. Bob Woolf, in *Friendly Persuasion,* recommends adopting an attitude of being self-effacing and non-blustering, especially when you have an advantage, or leverage. Woolf suggests that confidence in yourself, your plan, and your offer is vital, but he also recommends that you maintain a humble, agreeable, attitude to keep the other side off guard, especially if the other side is overconfident. Or, you might discover that the other side's lead negotiator has a habit of keeping people waiting for an hour or so before arriving at a negotiating session in order to get the other side angry. Many unethical negotiators will use various bargaining tactics to get the other side angry because they know that when people become angry, their emotional intensity rises and they will make irrational, emotional decisions instead of rational ones. Richard Shell writes in *Bargaining for Advantage* that "You must learn to recognize the hidden psychological strategies that play such an important role in negotiation."[4]

The Influence section of Chapter 8 covers many of these psychological tactics. Some negotiators will try to use the reciprocity principle against you by giving you a small concession and then asking for a big one in return. Sometimes clever negotiators will try to get you over-committed by threatening to buy your competition in the hope that such a threat will create competitive bidding and lower prices substantially. If you do your research on the other side's typical attitudes and its tendency to use various tactics, you can plan your approach to respond accordingly and, therefore, gain an advantage.

Relationship-Based.   Successful negotiating is based on trust. And because media salespeople are selling an intangible service in which a salesperson becomes the surrogate for their product, media selling is all about relationships. As I discussed earlier, to get trust, you must first give trust. However, do not give your trust unconditionally. The first time you negotiate with someone be skeptical. Being skeptical means to delay judgment about people until you learn from their behavior over time that they can be trusted. Initial wariness is important because you might discover over time that you are dealing with highly competitive, unethical negotiators. However, in media selling you will find that the majority of the people you deal with take pride in being fair and honest, especially at large, reputable advertising agencies and clients. But you must establish a bond of mutual trust with these people. Once this trusting relationship occurs, you will find that negotiating is not necessarily contentious and competitive, but can be cooperative, challenging, and enjoyable.

Ethical.   No matter what approach the other side takes, you must retain your integrity, be true to your convictions, and always act ethically—follow the ethical guidelines in Chapter 3.

Flexible.   There is no one best way to negotiate. You must remain adaptable and be able to adjust to the needs of maintaining a relationship, to the urgency of the situation, to the complexities of a large deal, and to whether you are negotiating with a team or an individual. If you negotiate with people on a frequent basis, the rules and patterns of negotiating often become implicit, unstated, and comfortable. They might take advantage of your comfort and change their mood, attitudes, style, and bargaining tactics to catch you off guard and gain an edge. You must be flexible in your approach and tactics, and you must deal with each negotiation based on the situation at the moment and not based on past, comfortable patterns.

Preparation

The side that is best prepared, that has the most thorough, most well-thought-out plan, comes out ahead in every negotiation.

There are ten preparation steps in negotiating:

1. Assess the situation.
2. Asses negotiating styles.
3. Identify interests, set objectives, and determine targets.
4. Assess leverage.
5. Estimate the ballpark, commit to walk-aways, and set anchors.
6. Determine bargaining tactics.
7. Decide when and how to open.
8. Determine frames.
9. Determine concessions and trade goals.
10. Plan your closes.

Assess the Situation.   The first step in planning is to assess the negotiating situation. One of the elements that distinguishes Richard Shell's *Bargaining for Advantage* from other books and seminars on negotiating and makes the book applicable to media negotiating is his concept that there are four basic situations that require different strategies, as shown in Figure 12.1, The Situational Matrix.

Figure 12.1 The situational matrix. (Source: Shell 1999, p. 127. Used with permission.)

| | Perceived Conflict Over Stakes | |
	High	*Low*
High Perceived Importance of Future Relationship Between Sides **Low**	**I. Balanced Concerns** (Business partnership, joint venture, or merger) *Best Strategies:* Problem solving or compromise	**II. Relationships** (Marriage, friendship, or work team) *Best Strategies:* Accommodation, problem solving, or compromise
	III. Transactions (Divorce, house sale, or market transaction) *Best Strategies:* Competition, problem solving, or compromise	**IV. Tacit Coordination** (Highway intersection or airplane seating) *Best Strategies:* Avoidance, accommodation, or compromise

Balanced concerns. In media selling you will run into all four types of situations, but the majority of your negotiating will be in a *balanced concerns* situation in which stakes, such as price, deal terms and conditions, position in a publication, or added value, are as important as maintaining a relationship. Because media negotiating is typically conducted with regular customers who will give you repeat business, you must not negotiate so aggressively and competitively that you win and your customers lose. You must have a balance between getting favorable prices and terms and maintaining a trusting relationship.

Relationship. You will rarely encounter a *relationship* situation in media selling in which maintaining future relationships is such an overriding concern that you will accommodate advertisers with generous terms or large discounts. Because the stakes in a media deal are often public knowledge, as they are in the upfront market or when large contracts between public companies are posted on the Internet, media companies are usually unwilling to give one advertiser a significantly better deal than they would give to another advertiser. On the other hand, many media deals and contracts include a *favored-nation clause* in which a media company agrees to give an advertiser the same low price if the media company ever charges another advertiser a lower price. In a businesses in which most advertisers have many competitors, advertisers and their agencies trust media companies not to give better deals to competitors. Most media companies maintain their integrity and attempt to treat all advertisers fairly.

Furthermore, by overemphasizing a relationship, media companies are subject to relationship blackmail. In an article in the *Harvard Business Review* titled "Negotiation as a Corporate Capability," author Danny Ertel writes:

> Over the years, I have asked hundreds of executives to reflect on their business relationships and to ask themselves which kinds of customers they make the most concessions to, do more costly favors for, and generally give away more value to. Is it their good customers or their bad customers? The vast majority respond, with some chagrin, "The difficult ones, of course. I'm hoping to improve the relationship." But that hope is almost always in vain: once customers find they can get discounts and favors by holding a relationship hostage, why should they change? Without realizing it, many companies have systematically taught their customers the art of blackmail.[5]

It is important not to allow advertisers to blackmail you by threatening to take their business elsewhere if they do not get more than other advertisers get. Do not cave in; treat everyone fairly.

Transaction. In media selling you will occasionally run into a *transaction* situation in which stakes are much more important than relationships. These situations sometimes occur with new customers who try to make a large, one-time deal and negotiate a very low price. But beware of someone who is not a regular customer, whose reputation you do not know, who makes big promises, and who asks for big discounts in return. Always remember that your regular customers are your best customers and vow never to make a one-time deal, no matter how big a promise, that you would not make with your regular customers.

Tacit coordination. You will also find that you will often be in *tacit coordination* situations. Tacit coordination occurs when two people pull up to a stop sign at the same time or when two people simultaneously try to sit in a seat on an airplane. Negotiation is typically quick and unspoken; one person or the other will nod and accommodate the other and move on.

Remember the 80/20 rule applies. Twenty percent of your customers who give you 80 percent of your business will typically be repeat ones who are familiar with your pricing, your terms and conditions, and the added value you offer, if any, and will renew with little or no negotiating involved. In these situations, trust is the key factor. If your clients have learned to trust you to give them the best deal available at the time of the negotiation, they will not haggle—a tacit coordination situation.

In broadcast and cable, where inventory is limited and thus, pricing is based on supply and demand, customers and buyers will usually negotiate to get the best prices available at the time they are making a buy. Some agencies will buy for an account on a weekly or monthly basis and those negotiations will be short and to the point. Your goal should be to develop strong relationships with your customers so they trust you to bring them the best available deals at all times. Mutual trust keeps negotiating to a minimum and makes tacit coordination possible.

An example of tacit coordination is in the annual television upfront market. Agency negotiators initially ask for lower rates than the year before for television network programming, but because their agencies' compensation, to some degree, is based on how much money they spend, agency negotiators' primary interest is not in saving money but buying preferred, high-reach programming in prime time. Therefore, agency negotiators will normally pay reasonable increases except in recessionary years, such as the 2001 upfront, without a great deal of bargaining.

Another example of tacit coordination would be when customers indicate they do not want to negotiate. They might say, "Bring me your best deal and if I like it, I'll buy it," and mean what they say. In such cases, it is imperative that you know the attitudes of your customers before you enter a negotiation and bring these customers reasonable, fair prices and offers.

Once you have determined what type of situation you will be facing in an upcoming negotiation, write it down in the Negotiating and Closing Planner in Appendix E. In fact, you will be writing down a lot of information in a planner, so go to www.mediaselling.us, print out a Negotiating and Closing Planner, and follow it as you read this chapter.

Assess Negotiating Styles.   The next step in preparation and planning is to assess the negotiating style of the other side and to recognize your own negotiating style. Research on negotiating indicates that there are two primary negotiating styles, competitive and cooperative. Author Richard Shell reports that in one study of lawyer-negotiators, who one might expect to be competitive, instead he found that "65 percent of the sample of attorneys exhibited a consistently cooperative style of negotiation, whereas only 24 percent were truly competitive in their orientation. (11 percent defied categorization using these two labels)."[6]

Some of the people Shell uses as examples of highly competitive negotiators in *Bargaining for Advantage* are Donald Trump, Wayne Huizenga, Steve Ross, and Henry Kravis. These famous businessmen appear to fit the personality classification of *narcissist*, as described by Michael Maccoby in his *Harvard Business Review* article, "Narcissistic Leaders: The Incredible Pros, the Inevitable Cons." From my 45 years in the media business, I have come to believe that many of the top executives in the media fit Maccoby's narcissistic label. I have included narcissist in the description of Negotiating Types in Exhibit 12.1 because I believe many of the 11 percent that defied classification in the study mentioned by Shell probably fall into that category, particularly in the media business.

Just as it is vital to know yourself if you are to acquire emotional intelligence to effectively establish and maintain relationships, it is equally important to know your negotiating style if you are to be an effective negotiator. You must

---

**Exhibit 12.1
Negotiation
Styles**

Negotiating Types

Competitors: Favored outcome: "I win, you lose." These people are highly competitive; they focus on winning—often at any cost. They usually put winning in personal terms; they want to beat *you*. They typically pay close attention to the size of their piece of the pie. They are unconcerned about being fair; they want the biggest slice. Winning (and not getting a worse deal than someone else) is everything to them. They often see negotiating as a game and enjoy the process as long as they think they can win.

Accommodators: Favored outcome: "I lose, you win." Accommodators want to maximize the other side's gain; they want the other side to have the biggest piece of the pie. They want you to think they are fair at almost any cost to them. They want you to get the best deal for you—the relationship is the most important thing to them. They are rarely seen in media negotiations.

Narcissists: High probability of an "I lose, you lose" (no deal) outcome. Narcissists do not care about any outcome that does not give them exactly what they want. They want the whole pie. Driven by ego, pride, greed, and selfishness, narcissists are only interested in their own outcomes. They hate to compromise, which means they make threats and demands and then will not negotiate. When others refuse to deal on their terms, which is often the case, narcissists usually turn into fierce, ruthless competitors. This switch is progress because they can be bargained with, although with great difficulty because they use many unethical tactics.

Cooperators: Favored outcome: "I win, you win." Cooperators try to maximize joint gain, build trust, and enhance the relationship. They are concerned about being fair. Cooperators are often problem solvers who can increase the size of the pie.

One of your objectives in negotiations is to train the other side to cooperate by demonstrating that both sides can win, to show them that negotiating fairly and in good faith can produce an outcome that is beneficial for both sides. However, it is very difficult to change a person's negotiating style, so be prepared to be competitive if you have to.

Patterns of Negotiations

Cooperators versus Cooperators: A good combination. If a problem can be solved and an agreement reached, it will be. This often increases the gain for both sides—the pie gets bigger.

Competitors versus Competitors: They understand each other, although there is a higher risk of a breakdown and it consumes more time and resources. However, it is not a bad combination. Rarely is there an increase in the size of the pie; in fact, when competitors try to maximize their own gain or share, the amount of the settlement usually decreases.

Cooperators versus Competitors: A dangerous combination. Most negotiating problems occur with this combination. The two sides do not speak the same language, do not have the same goals, and do not understand each other. Invariably the competitor takes advantage of the cooperator, who winds up with a small piece of the pie.

Cooperators' Objectives	Competitors' Objectives
1. Conduct self ethically	1. Maximize gain
2. Get a fair agreement	2. Win by outmaneuvering
3. Build trust	3. Relationships not important

Cooperator Traits	Competitor Traits
1. Trustworthy, ethical, fair	1. Dominant, forceful, attacking
2. Courteous, tactful, sincere	2. Crafty, rigid, strategic, uncooperative
3. Fair minded	3. Carefully observes opponent
4. Realistic opening position	4. Unrealistic opening
5. Does not use threats	5. Uses threats
6. Willing to share information	6. Reveals information only strategically, gradually
7. Probes opponent's position	7. Willing to stretch facts

Cooperators are quintessential win-win negotiators—they can increase the size of the pie. On the other hand, competitors are win-lose negotiators—they do not care if the pie shrinks, as long as they get the biggest piece. Neither cooperators nor competitors are wrong, they just see the world differently. If you trust a competitor, you will be easily exploited. If you try to be pleasant and get along with or be well liked by a competitor, you will be seen as naive and weak and be taken advantage of. It is imperative to match the style of the other side. When in doubt, be skeptical and assume the other side is a competitor until proven wrong.

---

also be flexible and change your negotiating style to match the other side's style. If you find it difficult to change your style, as many do, select a colleague on your side who matches the other side's style and let that person do the negotiating.

Rule: Match the other side's style (cooperative or competitive).

After you have identified your and the other side's negotiating styles, complete the Negotiating Style section in the Negotiating and Closing Planner.

Identify Interests, Set Objectives, and Determine Targets

Identify interests. Media companies and advertisers set negotiating objectives to achieve their overall, long-term interests. In your negotiating planning process, you must identify both sides' interests before you can set your negotiating objectives, because the ideal outcome of a negotiation is an agreement that satisfies both sides' interests. For example, a beer advertiser might have an interest in acquiring sponsorships for all major league sports in the United States. Before the season begins, the beer advertiser may want to invest in an exclusive sponsorship of the Major League Baseball games broadcast on your radio station, KAAA-AM, and want to lock out other beer sponsors. Let's assume that your station's interests are not to be overly dependent on a small number of advertisers, are not to engage in exclusive sponsorship deals, and are to have several beer advertisers compete for a scarce resource (your baseball broadcasts). Once you have determined what both side's interests are, write them down in the Negotiating and Closing Planner.

Set objectives. Next, you should set your objectives based on your understanding of both sides' interests. Set MADCUD objectives (see Chapter 5) for each negotiating opportunity you have. For example, if you were negotiating for KAAA-AM before the baseball season started, your negotiating objectives would be much different from what they would be if you were a month into the baseball season and had no beer advertisers. Following are some examples of MADCUD objectives in negotiating situations.

Measurable: To get a minimum of a 13-week insertion order for at least three ads a week and to get a no-cancellation contract term.

Attainable: The above measurable objectives must be realistic and reasonable for the advertiser in question and, thus, reasonably attainable—not too much of a stretch.

Demanding: Richard Shell suggests you should set objectives based on your *highest legitimate expectations* (HLE). Research indicates that those who expect more, get more. As we learned in Chapter 5, reasonable but challenging objectives have the greatest motivating effect. Therefore, how you define the concept of more is critical to your success. If by more, you mean your highest legitimate expectations (HLE), your chances of being successful will be much greater.

Consistent with company goals: Too often media salespeople set objectives that meet their own selfish needs and are not consistent with the overall long-term goals and strategies of their companies. For instance, salespeople might set an objective of making a sale regardless of price in order to make the commissions on the sale. Or salespeople might set an objective of getting a sizable order by promising exceptionally favorable positions in a magazine contrary to the magazine's policy guidelines of offering desirable positions only to the largest advertisers. When you set negotiating objectives, always keep in mind that your company's interests, not yours, come first.

Under control of the individual: In a negotiation, you cannot control the other side's attitude or behavior, but you can control your own attitudes and behavior. As in sports, the mental game in negotiating is more important than the physical game. Keep in mind Michael Jordan's rules for winning: (1) Learn to love the game before you learn to master it. (2) Past failures are irrelevant to the task at hand. (3) If you can visualize winning, you won't fear losing. (4) Strength of heart (attitude) is more important than strength of body. Often the strategy of the other side is to get you to lower your confidence and expectations. If you allow this to happen, you will be inclined to lower your rates, give away too much, and settle for much less than you deserve. Control your confidence and expectations during a negotiation and keep them high.

Deadlined: Deadlines in negotiating are based on the scarcity principle—the scarcity of time. When you are selling a non-perishable product such as a house, do not set a deadline for a settlement because having no deadline puts pressure on the other side to settle and increases the fear of losing, which gets more intense over time, thus giving an advantage to the seller.

The opposite is true when you are selling a perishable product such as seats on an airplane, hotel rooms, broadcast or cable time, or a special issue or section of a publication that has a firm closing date. Establish a deadline for settlement, because without one there is no pressure on the other side to settle before the product perishes (goes away). Without a deadline, crafty buyers will wait until the very last possible moment in hopes that sellers will reduce prices significantly rather than see what they are selling go to waste, thus giving an advantage to the buyer.

Setting deadlines on all of your offers counters delaying tactics by the other side. So, when you present a proposal, put a comment line under the one that shows your prices that reads: "These rates are good until December 1," when you know the schedule is planned to start December 7, for example.

Rule: *When selling a perishable product, always set a deadline on your offers.*

Determine targets. You learned about targets in Chapter 10, and you should determine which of these targets is appropriate for an upcoming negotiation. To review, the four types of targets are: a specific opportunity, price, size of order, and share of budget. In the $300 million deal Viacom made with P&G in 2001, Viacom's target was to increase its share of P&G's business. Viacom gave P&G a discount to shift shares from media owned by other companies to Viacom.

Set your objectives and determine your targets for a negotiation and then write them down in the Negotiating and Closing Planner. Furthermore, once you set your objectives and targets based on your highest legitimate expectations (HLE), you must commit to them. The best way to increase your commitment is to write down your objectives and targets and then tell someone about them. For example, say to your boss, "I'm convinced I can get a 15-percent increase over what we got last year from this account, and here's the rate and terms I'm going to get."

Rule: *Make a commitment to your objectives and targets, write them down, and tell someone about them.*

Assess Leverage.   The next step in the planning process is to assess your and the other side's leverage situation to determine who has the stronger and weaker position. Leverage is based on how badly people want something and how fearful they are of losing it. As Bob Woolf writes in *Friendly Persuasion*, "Every reason that the other side wants or needs an agreement is my leverage—provided that I know those reasons."[7]

There are two kinds of leverage: positive and negative. You have *positive leverage* when you have something that the other side wants much more than you want to hold on to it. You have *negative leverage* when the other side is afraid of losing something you have. Both are powerful, but negative leverage is more powerful. Competition for a scarce resource increases negative leverage and often leads to *over-commitment,* which occurs when people invest their egos and a lot of time in negotiating. Their fear of losing after they have invested so much escalates to the point that they often become over-committed and make unrealistically high offers. For example, the television rights for NFL football became so expensive because of over-committed bidding in 1998 that by 2003 ABC, CBS, and Fox were all losing money televising NFL football.[8]

Media salespeople, especially inexperienced salespeople, have more leverage than they realize. Most businesses, except for very small ones, must advertise in order to attract customers, survive, and grow. If a business has competitors, it has to advertise more than its competitors do if it hopes to gain market share. Also, advertising agencies have to invest all the money their clients allocate to advertising because advertising budgets reflect the sales levels advertisers hope to achieve. Their ultimate goal is not to save money, but to get the optimum reach and frequency for the money they have allocated. This need to advertise gives media salespeople leverage if they are selling a medium or a product that is in demand or if they can provide a viable solution to an advertising problem.

Assessing both side's leverage is critical in deciding your overall negotiating strategy and tactics. Once you have a sense of which side has the stronger leverage, there are four tactics that will help you strengthen your leverage or weaken the other side's leverage: a BATNA, tit-for-tat, warnings, and bluffs.

BATNA. A BATNA is the *best alternative to a negotiated agreement.* Fisher and Ury first introduced the concept of a BATNA in their best-selling book, *Getting to Yes.* The purpose of a BATNA is to have at least one viable alternative when you enter into a negotiation. For example, when people ask me how they should ask for a raise, I tell them to get an offer in writing from another company for a job that pays more money than they are currently making. This offer is a BATNA and it provides leverage. Without a competing offer, people who ask for a raise have no leverage and their employer has all the leverage.

In media selling, an example of how to acquire a BATNA would be for KAAA-AM, being aware of the interest of the acquisitive beer advertiser, to offer sponsorships to several other beer advertisers in order to generate interest in its baseball broadcasts before talking to the acquisitive beer company. If KAAA-AM drums up sufficient interest to be certain of an order from another beer advertiser, the station has a BATNA, which increases its leverage considerably with the acquisitive beer company.

Rule: Always go into a negotiation with a BATNA.

Tit-for-tat. The tit-for-tat tactic means that you reciprocate to the tactics, behavior, and style of the other side by matching their tactics, behavior, and style. For example, if the other side pounds the table and threatens to walk out, you pound the table and threaten to walk out. In order to understand the power of tit-for-tat, warnings, and bluffs, let's return to the game theory that was introduced in Chapter 9.

You will recall that John von Neumann invented game theory in 1928 after watching a bluff in a poker game. He reasoned that in order to win in poker it was important not to play according to the probabilities of a certain card being dealt, but to play according to the moves of competitors. Twenty-two years later in a program that was funded by the US Government at the Rand Institute in California, mathematicians, physicists, and other scientists studied, within the context of game theory, the strategic implications of two major world powers, the United States and the Soviet Union, each possessing the horrible destructive power of the atomic bomb.

One of the scientists invented a game called the Prisoner's Dilemma. The game was set up so that the punishments the two prisoners, who were isolated from each other, would receive were a great deal less if they turned in evidence that the other prisoner broke the law (whether the evidence was true or not). The scientists called turning in evidence defecting. The temptation to defect was so strong because of the way the punishments were weighted. Each turned in evidence that the other broke the law and both prisoners wound up in jail for ten years. While in jail, the prisoners met and realized that if they had not defected and had said nothing—in other words, if they had silently cooperated—they would have each received a minor punishment.[9]

When two scientists played a computerized version of the game repeatedly, they found that the best strategy was for each player to cooperate and settle for a smaller reward rather than being greedy (defecting) and going for a big reward. However, occasionally, one of the players would get greedy and get a bigger reward. The players learned that when this defection happened the best strategy on the next move was to defect, or to use the tit-for-tat tactic, which taught the other player to cooperate again on subsequent moves and settle for smaller, but dependable, rewards. The US Government adopted the tit-for-tat tactic as the basis for its policy of deterrence based on the credibility of massive retaliation. In other words, if the Soviet Union built an ICBM with a nuclear warhead, the US would do the same—tit-for-tat.

Eventually, the tit-for-tat policy worked and the Soviet Union, virtually bankrupt from spending on a massive nuclear war machine, agreed to a program of mutual disarmament—cooperation. These lessons from the cold war and from game theory are the foundation for another fundamental rule of negotiating.

Rule: Use tit-for-tat to teach the other side to cooperate.

Warnings. A *warning* is an implied threat. The difference between a threat and a warning is that a warning is a relatively polite statement about what *might* happen. A threat is a more aggressive statement that communicates, "If you do X, I will retaliate by doing Y." Warnings and threats are effective only if they are credible. The other side must share your assumption that carrying out the warning or threat will make them worse off and believe it is not a bluff. President Bush's threat of war against Iraq became credible when the United Nations passed a motion to support a war, when Great Britain's Tony Blair strongly supported the war, and when 150,000 troops were mobilized and put on alert in the Middle East. Unfortunately, Bush's credible threat did not accomplish its purported purpose of motivating Saddam Hussein to disarm; rather it backfired and caused Iraq to intensify its resolve to resist. The war in Iraq is an excellent example of the danger of making credible threats: that they often lead to destructive escalation.

People usually respond with hostility and anger when threatened. In business negotiations, warnings are much more effective than threats. Author Richard Shell writes that using threats in most negotiations is ". . . like playing with fire—dangerous for everyone involved."[10] If you have a strong leverage position, your confident demands can become implied warnings. As an example, station KAAA-AM can tell the acquisitive beer sponsor, "This is our price. We have several offers on the table. The decision is up to you if you want to pay our price and agree to our terms. We'd really prefer to do business with you, but in fairness to everyone, we can't turn down the highest offer." When you warn that you might use your BATNA, be extremely careful and do so politely, self-effacingly, and almost apologetically to avoid unintended consequences and escalation.

Rule: Never threaten; politely warn instead.

Bluffs. A bluff is when you act as though you have a strong position when, in fact, you have a weak position. It takes a great deal of confidence to pull off a successful bluff. Beginners should not bluff. However, in negotiating, just like when you play poker or when you play a team sport such as football, a bluff—or a fake—is an acceptable and sometimes effective tactic. To pull it off, however, you must understand the subtleties and proper timing of a winning bluff. We must once again turn to game theory for answers on how to bluff successfully.

Game theory researchers discovered that the best strategy in playing many games, including the Prisoner's Dilemma, is a mixed strategy of bluffing or defecting occasionally and on a random basis. The logic of this strategy is that if you never bluff, you are too predictable and the other side will take advantage of you because it knows you will be consistent and never retaliate. On the other hand, if you bluff on a regular, predictable basis, the other side will eventually figure out your bluffing pattern and your bluffs become as predictable as Rich Gannon's fakes in Super Bowl XXXVII. Therefore, the best way to keep the other side on the defensive is to bluff occasionally on a purely random basis so the other side never knows what to expect.

An example of a bluff in media selling would be to set your initial offer higher than you are actually willing to accept. If you are dealing with a buyer with whom you regularly negotiate, you must have walked away from business in the past. By doing so, your current bluff becomes credible. Two things can happen in this bluffing situation; either the buyer pays the highball rate or the buyer calls your bluff and says that your price is too high. In that case, you can back down, lower your price and get the business. However, you can only back down on rare occasions, because the buyer will learn that your bluffs are just that, bluffs, and not believe them.

Rule: If you bluff, use a mixed strategy and occasionally bluff on a random basis.

If you bluff on an occasional random basis, a buyer will never be certain whether or not you are bluffing. Bluffs are only for experienced negotiators, not for rookies.

After you have assessed the leverage of both sides and decided which of the above tactics are best suited for your situation and which tactics the other side is apt to use, fill out the Leverage section of the Negotiating and Closing Planner.

Estimate the Ballpark, Commit to Walk-Aways, and Set Anchors

Estimate the ballpark. A *ballpark* is the difference between a buyer's initial offer and your highest legitimate expectations (HLE). Your HLE include not only price but also terms and conditions. Rarely are media negotiations about price alone; they include many other elements such as contract terms, non-cancellation clauses, added value, favorable ad positions, options for renewals, favored-nations clauses, or competitive ad separation. Some of these conditions are often more important than price, and one or more of these elements might be deal breakers for both sides. It is important to know what your deal breakers are and estimate what the other side's deal breakers might be, and plan accordingly.

Just as in Major League Baseball, negotiating ballparks come in different sizes. You want to negotiate in the smallest ballpark possible because it is easier and quicker to reach agreement. The size of the ballpark is determined by the other side's initial offer. Figure 12.2 shows an example of a middle-sized ballpark.

**Figure 12.2
Medium-sized
ballpark.**

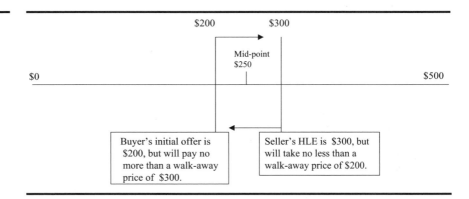

One end of the ballpark is your walk-away ($200 in Figure 12.2) and the other end is the buyer's walk-away ($300 in Figure 12.2). Note that the mid-point of the ballpark is $250, which is the potential agreement point—one that would satisfy both sides.

Rule: Most settlements are close to the mid-point.

You can gain knowledge of the other side's probable initial offer through careful research or by an understanding of the other side's past tendencies and approaches. For example, in Figure 12.2 we will assume the buyer has paid $250 in the past after making a lowest legitimate expectation (LLE) initial offer of $200, so you can assume that the buyer will open again with $200, but will pay more as in the past. Therefore, you should set your HLE at $300 to make sure you arrive at the $250 mid-point, at the minimum.

You will not always find that a buyer's initial offer is a reasonable, legitimate LLE, but is a lowball offer. Many buyers have a rule of negotiating that states: the lower price you initially ask for, the lower price you will wind up with. Therefore, rather than open with an LLE, many buyers open with an unreasonable lowball offer that is way below your walk-away. No matter what the other side's initial offer is, you must clearly define and stick to your walk-aways.

Commit to walk-aways. Without walk-aways, or a firm downside position, you will be nibbled away at by clever negotiators, which is like getting pecked to death by ducks; it takes a long time and is very painful. Walk-away means just that—you will walk away from a negotiation rather than settle for anything less. Your walk-aways must be absolutely firm; you must be committed to them, because having a soft downside position is a prescription for disaster. Read "Selling Magazines to Agencies" in Appendix F for an example of a disaster that occurred to a salesperson who was not committed to a walk-away.

Rule: Always go into every negotiation with a commitment to your walk-aways.

Even though it is vital to have walk-aways, do not focus on them during negotiations. Research shows that inexperienced negotiators have a tendency to focus on their low-end walk-away rather than their high-end HLE because of their aversion to loss. This tendency brings us to another rule of negotiating:

Rule: During negotiations, you must focus on your highest legitimate expectations, not on your walk-away.

Set your anchor. Your HLE, which in Figure 12.2 is $300, should not only be what you must focus on and expect to get, but also should be the starting point in determining your opening offer. Your opening offer is your *anchor*. In negotiating, when buyers first hear a high or low number, they unconsciously adjust their expectations accordingly. Therefore, it is vital that your initial offer anchors the other side's perception of your walk-away and that you open reasonably high. An unreasonably high initial offer to someone with whom you negotiate regularly can kill a deal or destroy your credibility if you drastically reduce your offer later.

It is crucial that you invest time in determining what your optimal anchor should be, because it is the most significant decision you will make in preparation and will be critical to a successful outcome. Anchors include price as well as terms and conditions, so your anchor should include a price that is high enough to give you room to come down to your HLE and include givebacks of terms and conditions that you are willing to concede. By carefully planning your price concessions and givebacks, you can prepare for some effective concession and closing techniques. Figure 12.3 shows the middle-sized ballpark with an anchor of $350.

In the ballpark in Figure 12.3 the mid-point is $250. By setting your anchor, your initial offer, at $350, you move the mid-point between your anchor and the buyer's initial $200 offer up to $275, a 10-percent increase over a $250 mid-point. Ten percent may not seem like much in these examples, but in media deals that involve millions of dollars, 10 percent

Figure 12.3 Medium-sized ballpark with anchor.

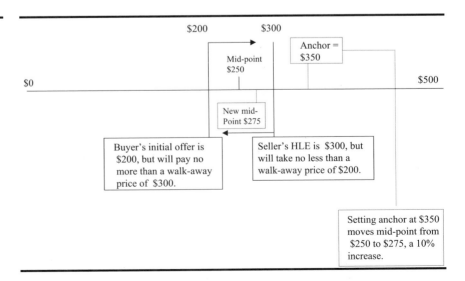

is substantial. In the $300 million Viacom/P&G deal, it would have amounted to $30 million.

Since the other side's initial offer is the basis for your anchor, a lowball initial offer by the other side increases the size of the ballpark because you must increase the relative size of your anchor. Figure 12.4 shows an example of a large ballpark.

Figure 12.4
Large ballpark.

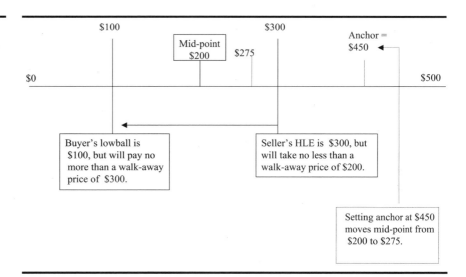

In Figure 12.4, your HLE has remained the same as it was in the middle-sized ballpark in Figure 12.3, but because the buyer's initial unreasonable lowball offer was only $100, the mid-point moved to $200, your walkaway price. Let's assume you don't know what the buyer's upside walk-away ($300) is. Nevertheless, your HLE is $300 and you would like to get close to that if possible. In order to do so, you must raise your anchor to an equally unreasonable $450—tit-for-tat—to move the mid-point to $275, near the settlement you prefer.

Lowball offers often come from inexperienced or unreasonable negotiators or from new customers who are not familiar with your regular pricing, terms, and conditions. In such transaction situations, let the other side open first, remain calm and polite, and set your anchor to move the mid-point close to your HLE.

On the other hand, initial offers from experienced negotiators and regular customers who are familiar with your pricing, terms, and conditions will often be reasonable and be close to current market prices and conditions—a tacit coordination situation. These types of offers will create a small ballpark, as shown in Figure 12.5.

In the small ballpark example in Figure 12.5, the buyer's initial offer is a reasonable $225. Let's assume you deal with the buyer often, are familiar with the buyer's patterns and tendencies, and know that the buyer will not pay more than 10 percent over what was paid on the previous buy, which was $250. Thus, you estimate that the buyer's walk-away is $275 and, therefore, you set your HLE at $275. The mid-point between the buyer's initial offer of $225 and your HLE of $275 is $250, the potential settlement. The chances are that the buyer is counting on a $250 settlement, expecting to

Figure 12.5
Small ballpark.

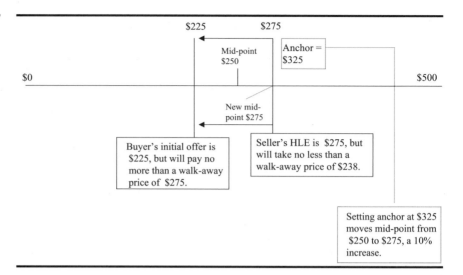

match the previous buy. However, by setting your anchor at $325, you move the mid-point up to $275, or a 10 percent increase over the previous price of $250, and a price the buyer is willing to pay. As you can see, setting a precise, well thought out anchor is crucial to helping you achieve your objectives, targets, and HLE.

Rule: Always have a well thought out anchor.

Determine Bargaining Tactics.   The literature on negotiating identifies a number of bargaining tactics that negotiators use to their advantage. Some are reasonable, and acceptable; others are unfair, unreasonable, and unacceptable. Never use the unacceptable ones and learn to recognize them.

There are several rules suggested in the bargaining tactics in Table 12.1.

Table 12.1
Bargaining Tactics

Acceptable Bargaining Tactics

Tactic	Description/ Purpose	When To Use	When Used Against You, Your Best Response
Auction	Create an auction of competitive bids for a scarce resource—either a buyer for an advertising budget or a seller for a high-demand product.	When you have strong leverage or inventory or a product in high demand. Create a fear of losing in the other side.	Focus on your HLE, never go lower than your walk-away, and signal to the other side that you will walk away and not get into a competitive auction.
Cherry-pick	Pick only the best, most desirable elements of a product or package.	To pick apart a package offering; to negotiate for the most desirable individual elements separately, not as a whole.	When a buyer tries to cherry-pick you, show high prices for the individual units and a lower price for the overall package.
Crunch	In response to a low offer. The rule is, "Whoever gives a number first, loses."	Respond to an offer by saying, "It's not good enough," but don't give a number. Objective is to get the other side to respond with a number that is lower than you hoped for because of the other side's fear of losing.	Don't give a number. If a buyer says, "You're too high," without giving a number, you respond with, "What do you have in mind?"

continued

Table 12.1
continued

Tactic	Description/ Purpose	When To Use	When Used Against You, Your Best Response
Flinch	A sudden, physical reaction that tries to elicit a feeling of guilt, like, "You've got to be kidding!" Response to a low offer.	In response to a lowball offer. Only use occasionally.	Remain calm. Do not react. The other side is trying to get a rise, to shock you. Don't respond.
Good guy/bad guy	The bad guy makes highly unreasonable demands and threats; the good guy's low requests seem reasonable in comparison—the contract principle at work.	In major, complex negotiations. Use your lawyers or management as bad guys (that is what they get paid for); as a salesperson, you be the good guy and offer a reasonable solution.	Make the right comparison. Don't compare the good guy's offer to the bad guy's offer; compare the good guy's offer to your HLE. Keep focused on your HLE
Limited authority	To indicate that a negotiator has limited authority, cannot make a final decision, and has to check with a higher authority—a hint of a pullback in order to gain further concessions.	Use to stall for time, to think over an offer, and craft a counter offer, even if you have the final authority.	Agree to a break in the negotiating process while the other side checks with their higher authority and say, "That's a good idea. I have to check with my boss, too, because I may have gone too far." Hint at a pullback.
Nibble	A negotiator will indicate a strong readiness to settle, but will ask for just one more very small concession . . . then another, then another.	In the last stages of negotiations after many agreements and the other side is overcommitted. Nibble at the last remaining issues. "Can you give me just a dollar more?"	Stop the nibbling with a pin-down close. "I can't give you an additional 2-percent discount, but I will give you a half-percent discount if you give me the order right now with no further requests or changes." Give a small concession you were willing to give anyway to pin down a close.
Price tag	To set a price limit. A buyer might say, "I like your proposal, but I only have $10,000, not the $15,000 you're asking for."	Price tags are buyers' LLE or sellers' HLE, not their walk-aways. Based on the rule that you never get anything you don't ask for, why not ask for your LLE or HLE?	A price tag is a starting point, not a walk-away. Always challenge a price tag and treat it as an opening offer, not a final, walk-away.
Red Herring	To negotiate hard on an unimportant issue, get concessions, then ask for reciprocal concessions on an important issue.	With multiple issues, feign the importance of a minor issue to you, receive concessions, then transfer those concessions to an important issue. Set a reciprocity trap.	Don't fall into reciprocity traps. Don't transfer concessions. Compare apples to apples—concessions on one issue do not apply to concessions on another issue. Commonly used tactic by media buyers.
Silence	To respond to an offer with silence.	Silence, like a crunch, is an attempt to get the other side to respond with concessions—bigger ones than you might have asked for.	The rule is: the first one to talk loses. Respond to silence with silence.

continued

Table 12.1
(*continued*)

Tactic	Description/ Purpose	When To Use	When Used Against You, Your Best Response
Split the difference	To offer to settle at the mid-point.	To get a quick settlement when the two sides are not far apart. Splitting the difference sounds like a fair offer, even if it isn't.	Often buyers will make a lowball offer, then offer to split the difference. Never split the difference when it is in the other side's favor or is not close to your HLE—have patience and keep negotiating.
Take-it-or-leave-it	An ultimatum and refusal to continue negotiations. Forces the other side to make a yes/no decision.	To signal a final offer; often used with the phrase, "A fair, final offer. Take it or leave it."	Leave it unless it is above your walk-away, which it usually isn't. Often a take-it-or-leave-it offer is a bluff, so always call the bluff.
Throw-aways	Issues, terms, conditions, and added value that are part of an initial offer but are intended as concessions later in a negotiation.	Always have throw-aways in complex negotiations. Throw-aways should be issues, terms, conditions, and added value that are of relatively low importance—elements that you would normally give up. By including them in your initial offer, you set them up as concessions later to get the other side to give you concessions you want—the reciprocity principle at work.	Don't fall into reciprocity traps and give away something important to you when the other side makes a concession of minor importance to you. Always work on the fairness principle—trade concessions of similar value or importance.

Unacceptable Bargaining Tactics

Tactic	Description/ Purpose	When To Use	When Used Against You, Your Best Response
Big bait	Make a large initial offer in an attempt to find your bottom and walk-aways.	Never, because it's a hollow bluff or a lie. The user of a big bait has no intention of making good on its initial, implied promise, but is just looking for the other side's rock bottom.	Recognize the tactic and name it. Call the other side's bluff. Say, "This sounds like a big bait to me. Are you willing to sign a firm, non-cancelable contract for the full amount?"
Blackmail	A threat meant to instill fear of loss. Usually a bluff.	Never, because it's unethical.	Recognize the tactic and name it. Call the bluff. Never give in, because it will make you vulnerable to future blackmail and larger and larger demands. Blackmail will continue regardless of what the other side promises. By giving in, you train the other side to blackmail you.
Change of pace	Bring some closure to an agreement with a false promise, then back off, then promise again to get the other side so frustrated it will say yes to anything just to get closure.	Never, because it's unethical.	Recognize the tactic and name it. Have patience. Remain confident in the fairness of your proposal and in your HLE. Do not respond with anger.

continued

Table 12.1
(*continued*)

Tactic	Description/ Purpose	When To Use	When Used Against You, Your Best Response
Deliver garbage	To insult the other side, its product, its management, and everything to instill a fear of losing in the other side. Lowers confidence and expectations.	Never, because it's too competitive and destroys relationships.	Don't catch the garbage. Pay no attention to it. Do not respond, and most important, do not lower your confidence of HLE. Smile and remain silent.
Renege	To take back a previously agreed-upon element in a negotiation. Objective is to instill fear of losing more.	Never, because it breaks a promise, destroys trust, and leads to escalation—tit-for-tat reneging.	Recognize the tactic and name it. Flinch and say, "That's not fair! I have been negotiating in good faith and now you're taking something back." Never agree to reneging by the other side.
Starvation	To keep food and water away from the other side in a lengthy negotiation to try to force a favorable settlement. For example, the side that controls the turf (location) will eat and drink before a negotiating session that begins at 11:00 AM and that will last for several hours, then doesn't provide food or water to the other side.	Never, because it destroys trust and shows lack of respect for the other side. Manipulative.	Name the tactic. Say, "I think you're trying to starve me, so I'm taking a break for an hour to go get something to eat and drink." If the other side objects, say, "Then order in some food. I'm much more agreeable on a full stomach."
Threats	To threaten to take a competitor's offer or to walk out of the negotiating. A threat is like blackmail, often a bluff.	Never, because it destroys trust and discontinues fair negotiations.	Recognize the tactic and name it. Call the bluff and never give in because it will lead to more, larger threats.
Walk-out	To walk out of a negotiation before an agreement is reached; to refuse to negotiate further. Usually accompanied with an accusation of not being fair. Used to instill fear of losing. Invariably a bluff.	Never, because it destroys trust and prolongs negotiations unnecessarily.	Recognize the tactic and name it. Call the bluff. Let the other side walk out. Do not respond emotionally. The other side wouldn't resort to this tactic if it didn't want a deal; therefore, increase your HLE after a walk-out with confidence.

> *Rule: Never split the difference when it is in the other side's favor or is not close to your HLE; have patience and continue negotiating.*

> *Rule: When faced with unacceptable, unethical bargaining tactics, name them and tell the other side the names so the other side knows you are not fooled.*

> *Rule: Never respond emotionally; respond calmly, politely, and firmly.*

After you have assessed the situation; assessed both side's negotiating styles; identified interests, set objectives, and determined your targets; assessed both side's leverage; and estimated the ballpark, committed to your walk-aways, and set your anchors, the next step in the planning process is to determine the most appropriate bargaining tactics from the list of acceptable tactics in Table 12.1 and write them in your Negotiating and Closing Planner.

We have now covered six of the preparation steps. We will pause for a while in the discussion of the negotiating planning process so you can acquire an understanding of the last four steps of preparation: decide when and how to open, determine frames, determine concessions and trade goals, and plan your closes.

Maneuvering for Dominance and Control

Maneuvering for dominance and control is the second element in the negotiating planning process. Each side wants to gain a perceived power advantage or some kind of edge, and they often maneuver to do so. The most common maneuver is for one side to use the authority principle to impress the other with its status, authority, power, titles, and overall importance. Because most people tend to defer to authority and are impressed with status, if one negotiator is perceived to have more status, a more impressive title, or more power, that negotiator has an edge.

Rule: The other side only has the power you give it.

Because experienced negotiators, especially agency media buyers, will usually try to lower your confidence and expectations to gain an advantage, confidence is vital in negotiating: confidence in yourself, your proposal, your company, and your medium. Experienced negotiators will often try to get you to fall for an *authority trap* and indicate that they have the power to give you an order (and, therefore, affect your income). Other authority traps occur when they try to lower your expectations and remind you that their media plans and instructions from their clients will not allow them to pay your asking price. They will also try to instill in you a fear of losing by reminding you that they can get lower prices from competitors or that they can buy another medium. In the face of these maneuvers, you must maintain your confidence and never lower your expectations; always keep your focus on your HLE.

Other maneuvers that crafty buyers use to lower your confidence, reduce your expectations, and get you frustrated and angry (so you will make an emotional, irrational, decision) are: interruptions, hurry-up, delay, keep-you-waiting, and bring-in-the-boss:

Interruptions. Some buyers will continually interrupt a sales discussion or negotiation by taking phone calls, going for coffee, or even making quick calls. Buyers make these maneuvers to fluster, frustrate, and anger you. Buyers know that if you let your ego and your emotions highjack your rationality, you will try to settle too fast just to get it over with and, thus, make a bad deal (for you).

Hurry-up. When they call for avails or give you a request for a proposal (RFP), many buyers will indicate they need it "immediately, if not sooner," in an attempt to hurry you up. Such a request is often followed by, "E-mail me the information by 1:00 PM. I don't have time to see you," or something similar. This maneuver is to hurry you up so that you do not have time to prepare adequately and to instill in you fear of losing if you do not meet the timetable. Of course, if you meet a hurry-up deadline, a buyer will rarely make the buy immediately. They typically use the delay maneuver.

Delay. Once you have made a presentation or submitted your avails or RFP, buyers often delay making the buy for as long as possible. They use this delay maneuver to make you worry about losing the order, hoping you will lower your price to avoid a loss. It is to counter this delay maneuver that you always put a deadline on your offers. Another way to counter the delay maneuver is to call the buyer who uses it and say something like, "I just wanted to let you know that we're filling up fast and those avails (or positions) you wanted may not be available after today. Please give me an order ASAP, because I'd hate to see your client miss out on this opportunity and not be able to run its advertising."

Keep-you-waiting. Often buyers will keep you waiting, knowing that you will become frustrated and angry. Sometimes they will schedule appointments early and make you wait in a reception area with competing salespeople. Buyers use this maneuver because they know that salespeople often put competition on a personal level and, therefore, will lower their expectations and prices to avoid losing to a competitor waiting in the reception area. Remember that fear of losing can be a powerful influence, so do not let fear overcome you when you see a competitor. Be friendly, and increase your resolve to achieve your HLE. When you are waiting in a reception area with competing salespeople, it is sometimes a good idea to psych them out by making a call on your cell phone to the office (no one has to be receiving the call) and say something like, "Hi. I'm stuck here waiting for the buyer. Would you please make sure to book all those orders I got yesterday and call me back when you're through, because I might have to tell the buyer that we have so much business we can't fit him in any more." Boost your confidence and lower the confidence of your competitors.

Bring-in-the-boss. In the middle of a negotiation, sometimes buyers call in their boss and say, "We're getting nowhere, I'm calling in my media director who will make sure you know that you will lose the business if you don't accede to our demands." This is an authority trap; do not fall for it. Do not lower you confidence or expectations. This is a good guy/bad guy tactic designed to intimidate you. Focus on your HLE and keep in mind that the buyer is admitting a desire for the deal by calling in the boss to help.

> *Rule: Check your ego at the door and don't let your fear or emotions get the better of you; patience always wins.*

It will help you maintain your confidence and keep your expectations high if you realize that the other side's maneuvering for dominance and trying to appear to have a power advantage is nothing more than a thinly disguised bluff. After all, who has the power in today's media-dominated world, advertising agencies and their clients or the media? The media are the most powerful communication force in the world. Without advertising carried by the mass media, companies trying to sell their products and services to mass audiences would have to sell them one-on-one to individual consumers. Without advertising, there would be no mass distribution and no mass consumption of products. Modern marketing warfare is conducted by the forces of advertising on the battlefield of the media; this central position gives the media enormous power. As mentioned previously, companies must advertise and agencies must invest their clients' money in advertising, and the media provide advertisers access to both mass and targeted audiences. Media salespeople provide this access, so advertising agencies and their clients are dependent on salespeople to gain access to consumers. Therefore, as a media salesperson, never forget who has the power—you—and use this knowledge to boost your confidence in the face of threats and bluffs.

Experienced negotiators will also try to control the negotiating agenda. They will often come to the negotiating table with a printed agenda and demand that you stick to it. The reason for this is simple, and is expressed by the following rule:

Rule: *Whoever controls the negotiating agenda, controls the outcome.*

The concept is straightforward. If you can control the items you will negotiate about, you can control the shape of subsequent agreements. For example, a media-buyer's one-sided agenda might be as follows:

1. Discussion of price
2. Discussion of discounts
3. Discussion of added value
4. Discussion of positions
5. Discussion of terms and conditions

This agenda will not lead to a discussion, but to a series of demands, beginning with demands on reduced or discounted prices. Once a buyer gets a discounted price, demands for add-ons at no cost will follow. When faced with such a lopsided agenda, discuss it and do not start negotiating until you have reached consensus on a fair, balanced agenda. It is best to hammer out an agreement on an agenda several days before a major negotiation begins.

Or, you can anticipate an agenda similar to the one above, especially if you have previously negotiated with someone. You can anticipate that price will be the first item on their agenda. The first question will be, "What does it cost?" You can reply by saying, "In my price, I factored in the schedule of advertising you requested, our standard terms and conditions, the premium position you asked for, and the added value you requested, so the total, packaged price is $125,000." If the buyer asks for individual cost breakdowns for the premium position and the added value elements, make sure you have priced them so they add up individually to more than $125,000, otherwise the buyer will try to negotiate on each item in the hope of lowering the overall price. By pricing (or packaging) in this way, you take away much of a buyer's negotiating power.

Therefore, as opposed to the buyer's agenda above, an agenda that would be favorable to you would be as follows:

1. Discussion of terms and conditions
2. Discussion of position
3. Discussion of added value
4. Discussion of price

This agenda is better because the final element, price, will depend on agreements on the preceding items. For instance, if a buyer wants a favorable position or a great deal of added value, then the price should go up. Price is not a single element, but is inextricably linked to the other parts of a deal—the more extras, the higher the price. Just like when you buy a car, the final price you pay depends on many factors such as terms (loan), conditions (insurance), and extras (trim, radio, and so forth).

> *Rule: In order to avoid negotiating on each element individually, package all of the elements in a deal so the prices of the individual elements always add up to more than the packaged price.*

Following are several more rules that apply to the pre-bargaining maneuvering for the dominance control phase of negotiating. They are divided into When Rules, Who Rules, Where Rules, and How Rules.

When Rules

> *Rule: Negotiate only after you've created value, early in the customer's planning cycle, and well before your imposed deadline.*

Who Rules

> *Rule: Negotiate at the highest level possible—only with the buying decision maker.*

The bigger the deal, the higher in the organization you should go, because as deals get bigger the decision-making authority level increases and you always want to negotiate with the final decision maker—the boss—if at all possible. The converse of this rule applies to you.

> *Rule: Don't negotiate with your boss present if you can avoid it.*

If your boss is present when you negotiate, the buyer will not talk to you, but to your boss, and you not only lose control of the discussion, but you will also lose control of the account, because the buyer will want to continue to deal with the boss. Furthermore, when bosses (a sales manager, an ad director, a general manager, or a publisher) are present at a negotiation with a salesperson, too often they do not want to look bad or lose the business and will make a bad deal. Some of the worst deals in the media are made by bosses who want to show off to salespeople that they can close and to clients to demonstrate that they have the authority to change terms and lower prices.

On the other hand, there are times when it is desirable to have a boss present in a negotiation. For example, often on a big deal, the other side will want to negotiate at high levels in an organization. Sometimes, you might want to use the boss as the bad guy so you can play the good guy in a negotiation. Often, the boss can impress buyers and put them in an authority trap.

However, whenever the boss is involved in a negotiation, it is critical to come to an agreement beforehand as to the exact role the boss will play. When you negotiate with an account that is assigned to you, you should take the lead in recommending a negotiating strategy. For example, if a boss wants to accompany you on a call and you understand the buyer well enough to know such a call is not appropriate, you might say, "I don't think it's a good idea for you to come on this call. The buyer is very defensive and is intimidated by managers; she thinks they put too much pressure on her. We have a great relationship and she might think you don't trust me. Next week I'll take you on a call on a buyer with whom you can be a great help."

An effective use of bosses is to ask them to join you on a call on a buyer or customer to create value and not to discuss price. Managers can talk effectively about their company's philosophy, upcoming promotions, or community service—things that enhance your company's image and create value. When the buyer asks about price, your boss will say, "I'm not the person to talk about price. I think our product is so terrific that I'll ask too much. You deal with Jane. She will look after your best interests and get you the best deal we can offer. Also, she knows your needs better than I do." This is an ideal one-two approach that uses a boss effectively and keeps the negotiation under the control of the salesperson.

Where Rules

Rule: Negotiate on your own turf if possible.

As professional football, basketball, and baseball teams know, it is always better to have the home-field advantage. If you negotiate in your offices, you control the environment and the room set-up, you can be sure that you have the right equipment, and you have access to your management, to experts, and to information that can help you. There is also a subtle advantage to negotiating on your turf—it is your meeting and your chances of controlling the agenda are better. This rule particularly applies if you have nice turf, if your offices are attractive and reek of glamour (people love the glamour of the media), power, and authority. If you have shabby, unglamorous offices, go to customers' offices.

If customers prefer to negotiate on their turf, which is usually the case with media buyers, do not hesitate to go to their offices. If you go to a buyer's office, take advantage of the opportunity to read the room and learn as much as you can about the personality, needs, tastes, and preferences of the buyer. Sometimes you can move the venue from a buyer's or customer's office to neutral turf. Suggest a meeting at a restaurant over a meal; dinner is best because negotiations can usually be stretched out, which reduces the pressure for a fast settlement.

How Rules

Rule: Negotiate face to face whenever possible.

A lot of media business is conducted on the phone. But when you negotiate on the phone, you are at a disadvantage. You cannot see the body language or non-verbal behavior of the caller, thus substantial communication goes unnoticed and is lost. It is easier to be tough, mean, and competitive on the phone than it is face to face where a buyer has to look you in the eye and deal in person with your potential retaliation (tit-for-tat). It is also more difficult to establish rapport and empathy and build a solid relationship with a buyer on the phone than it is in person. Negotiating face to face gives you an advantage over competitors who do business on the phone or by e-mail.

If you have to deal with a distant buyer on the phone, always be the caller so you are prepared. And if a buyer calls and wants avails or to place a buy, tell the buyer that you will call back. Do not sell or negotiate on an initial call or inquiry. Return the call as promptly as possible, but not before you are thoroughly prepared.

Rule: If you have to negotiate on the phone, you be the caller.

Bargaining

Bargaining is the hand-to-hand combat of the negotiating process; it is where the final agreement or settlement is determined. There are five steps in the bargaining process:

The Bargaining Process

1. Warm-up
2. Open and frames
3. Signaling leverage
4. Making concessions
5. Building agreement

Warm-Up. The warm-up is the opening skirmish in which you test your assumptions about the other side's style, strategy, and tactics. During the warm-up, you listen and observe carefully and do not give away any information that could be useful to the other side.

Rule: Listen and get information two-thirds of the time, give information only one-third of the time.

While you are listening, look for gestures, body language, and grooming that indicate low self-esteem and lack of confidence. Look and listen for clues as to whether the buyer is competitive or cooperative. During the warm-up conversation, start with a positive, complimentary approach. Compliment the person and his or her organization and advertising, but do not go overboard and be wildly enthusiastic. For example, after listening to their opening remarks, you might say, "Because you are a reputable company, we look forward to doing business with you. We would like to have your tasteful advertising in our paper because it makes us look better, and I always enjoy negotiating with you because I learn so much." Do not go overboard, but be positive and complimentary to set the tone for cooperation and an amicable bargaining process.

This approach works particularly well with cooperative negotiators because it signals a desire to cooperate and improve the relationship. Use this approach even with highly competitive people because it will put them off guard and make them over-confident. They will learn how tough you are when they make their first bombastic, outrageous, threatening demand and you use tit-for-tat and counterattack with equal force. When competitors discover that their initial assumptions about you were incorrect, they often become confused and make mistakes. When bullies are challenged, they often give in easily.

Also, before you begin bargaining and during the warm-up, you should have a discussion to verify what you are negotiating about, to get all of the issues on the table. It is important that you observe the following rule:

Rule: Get the other side to state what they want at the beginning, and you tell them what your issues are—get everything on the table.

When they tell you what they want, repeat their requests (or demands) and get agreement. For example, "You would like to run a 52-week schedule of ads in my newspaper at the bulk rate of 30,000 inches and would like the top left position on page two and top right position on page three. Is that correct?" If you get agreement, then you tell them what your issues are. For example, "We'd like your business very much, but those positions you ask for will be difficult to deliver. But, let's see if we can work something out." In Chapter 9 I recommended that it was important to "put important terms and conditions that are different from standard media contract terms that advertisers are used to in your presentation and sell them aggressively because you want prospects to know what your terms and conditions are before you get into negotiations." By including deal terms and conditions in your presentation, you can help this discussion about issues at the beginning of the negotiation.

In larger, more complex deals there might be some terms and conditions that are so vital to you that they are deal breakers—if you do not get them you will walk away from the deal. In these situations, it is important to tell the other side what issues are important to you. When you do so, it is best to include several throw-away terms you can use as concessions later in the negotiation. If you have crucial deal terms that are potential deal breakers, raise the price of your initial offer and then give concessions on that price—lower it to your HLE—in order to secure those vital deal terms. If you do not have throw-away deal terms and corresponding price concessions, you will appear to be inflexible and the deal terms will be seen as unreasonable demands, which could stall and even sink a negotiation.

The other reason for this rule is that you will negotiate based on the other's side's initial requests and if they put additional requests or demands on the table later in the process, it is unfair to you because you will have been negotiating in good faith based on the assumption that all of their issues were on the table. You have been hoodwinked if they ask for more later on. If this should happen, your response should be, "Oh, I'm sorry. I didn't know you wanted a full-page bonus ad every month. You didn't tell me up front. I was basing my negotiating on what you originally put on the table. Now we'll have to start all over again based on this new request."

Before you make an opening offer it is vital to get all the issues on the table so you know the size of the pie you are trying to divide up.

Open and Frames.   We will return now to the ten steps in preparing for a negotiation. Step seven was to determine when and how to open. When you plan your opening strategy, there are two initial questions you have to ask yourself: "Should I open first?" and "Should I open optimistically or realistically?"

Open first? Yes. In almost every situation in media selling, you know what the other side's offer will be. In the identifying problems and qualifying step of selling, you have discovered customers' advertising budgets and have some sense of what they will pay and what terms they want. In the case of selling to agencies, buyers typically send an RFP or call for avails that list the parameters of a buy: price, ratings, demos, dayparts, and so forth.

The only occasions in which you should let the other side open are: (1) those in which you are not familiar with the style or demands of the other side or when you do not know them at all, and (2) when the other side are novices and are unfamiliar with media prices.

Rule: Open first to set an anchor except when you don't know anything about the other side.

When you open, open with an effective anchor. An example of an effective anchor was in 1996 when NBC Television carried the Super Bowl. Traditionally, television networks announce their prices, their anchor, for the upcoming Super Bowl in July. For three prior years each network that carried the Super Bowl had raised the anchor price it announced in July approximately $100,000. In 1995, the price for a 30-second commercial had been $850,000, so the expectation was that NBC would announce $950,000. However, NBC, in a brilliant move, announced that their price for Super Bowl commercials would be $1 million, *but* the price for the last three sold would be $1.3 million. Agency buyers rushed to buy Super Bowl spots for $1 million and NBC announced the first week in December that it had sold all of the available spots in the Super Bowl.

The following year, in 1996, the first year that Fox Television carried the Super Bowl, the network announced in July that its price for the upcoming Super Bowl would be $1 million. Fox did not raise the price because it did not have as extensive market coverage as NBC had. Fox also did not announce that it would raise the price for the last few commercials it sold. The result was that agency buyers waited to place their orders in hopes that Fox would lower its prices. Fox did lower its prices, and wound up selling spots late in December for $750,000 or less. By not having an effective anchor, Fox left several million dollars on the table.[11]

Open optimistically or realistically? In general, open optimistically. In the majority of situations you should open optimistically with the highest price and terms for which there is a supporting standard or explanation that would allow you to make a plausible case for it. In other words, if you can reasonably justify a price and terms, such as basing it on high demand, ask for it. A good rule of thumb is to open at least 15 percent above your HLE price, which leaves room for you to give concessions and still have the potential for getting your HLE. Include at least three additional throw-away terms in your initial offer for the same reason.

In some situations where you are not dealing with an experienced media buyer or regular customer, you can use the contrast principle and open for up to 50 percent higher and then come down to your HLE, which will seem low in contrast. This tactic works best when you are making a presentation that has three proposals, as covered in Chapter 10. For example, if the largest of your proposals is for $75,000, then the second proposal for $50,000 seems much lower than if you opened with the $50,000 proposal.

Opening optimistically brings us to two more fundamental rules of negotiating:

Rule: When in doubt, open optimistically and have room to come down.

Rule: You never get anything you don't ask for, so ask for more than you hope to get.

Optimistic openings work best in transaction negotiating and when you do not know much about the other side.

There are several situations when optimistic openings are not a good tactic and *realistic openings* are better, which leads to the following rule and three corollaries:

Rule: When you know the buyer well, open realistically.
Corollary: Also, open realistically when you have no leverage, when in a tacit coordination situation, and when people say they won't negotiate and mean it.

When you have no leverage, an optimistic opening does not work. When you have a weak position, an overly optimistic open leads buyers to conclusions that you are either bluffing or not too smart—both bad signals to give. When in a tacit coordination situation, you should be realistically optimistic, or close to your highest legitimate expectation. When you are dealing with a person who says, "I won't negotiate; bring me your best price," and you know from experience that the person is telling you the truth, it is best to open realistically with a fair initial offer just above the mid-point in your settlement range.

Experienced media buyers and negotiators, who have read books and attended seminars on negotiating, know the fundamental rules and understand the power of high expectations. Therefore, experienced agency and client negotiators, especially when negotiating for broadcast and cable, will try to lower your expectations every chance they get. They will lower your expectations when they call for avails or send out RFPs. They will say, "I'm in a hurry and have to make the buy today; fax or e-mail me your avails and give me your lowest rates. You have only one shot." In such cases, if you do as instructed, buyers will call back and say something like, "You're too high, lower your rates or you won't get the business." So they lied, in a sense, and are in fact giving you a second shot. Therefore, it is imperative to know your buyers, know what their negotiating tendencies are, and respond accordingly with your opening offers.

When your open, remember the following two rules:

Rule: Get the bad news out of the way early.

Rule: Don't include most of the other side's requests in your initial offer.

The first of these rules comes from the advice of Richard Chase and Sriram Dasu in their *Harvard Business Review* article, "Want to Perfect Your Company's Service? Use Behavioral Science." The authors write: "Behavioral Science tells us that, in a sequence of events involving good and bad outcomes, people prefer to have undesirable events come first—so they can avoid the dread—and to have desirable events come at the end of a sequence—so they can savor them."[12] Recency effects indicate that people tend to remember the last events or experiences in a series of events, so it is effective to save the best, most favorable experiences until last. For example, if your medium requires unusual or onerous terms and conditions, such as asking for cash up front, it is best to introduce these items at the beginning of the bargaining process and get them out of the way.

The second of these rules, about not including most of the other side's requests or demands in your opening offer, is based on the notion that you want the other side to ask for those demands or offers so you can bargain for each request. If you give the other side all they ask for initially, you lose the opportunity to get something in return during the subsequent bargaining and concession-making process, but include a few of their requests in your initial offer to signal some degree of cooperation. Make the other side ask for most of their demands and requests because that way you control your give-backs and concessions.

After you determine when to open and the most effective way of doing so, fill out that section of the Negotiating and Closing Planner

Frames. The eighth step in the planning process is to determine frames and positioning. When you open, *frame* your initial offer positively, as you learned in Chapter 5 ("Free throws win ball games."), and during the bargaining process continue to frame all of your offers positively. Emphasize the value of your offers and their benefits that give the other side a good deal. For example, "The $125,000 package is the best deal we are offering currently. It is a 25-percent discount on the individual elements in the package if purchased separately." Positive framing provides the other side with justifications for making concessions. If you have prepared properly and have a needs portrait of your buyer, you will know the best way to frame your offers. With competitive negotiators who want victory, frame your offers as gains and wins for them-really good deals. With negotiators who fear losing, frame your offers as a way to avoid a loss and emphasize the pain and shame of losing.

Rule: Always frame all of your offers appropriately.

When you have determined how you are going to frame your opening offer and important subsequent offers, fill out that section in the Negotiating and Closing Planner.

Signaling Leverage.   After you frame and present your initial offer and before you begin trading concessions in the bargaining process, you want to signal your leverage, if you have leverage. Figure 12.6 shows how you should act when your leverage is strong and when it is weak.

**Figure 12.6
Signaling leverage.
(Source: Shell
1999, p. 149.)**

How You Want to Act	Your Actual Leverage Situation (As You See It)	
	Strong	*Weak*
Firm	Make confident demands and credible threats. Display your alternatives and leave the decision up to other party.	Emphasize the uncertain future. Bluff (act strong when you are not).
Flexible	Show the other party you are investing in the relationship. Be generous.	Acknowledge the other party's power and stress the potential gains from future cooperation. Appeal to the other party's sympathy. What would they do in your position?

As you can see in Figure 12.6, when you see your leverage as strong you want to act firm, make confident demands, lay out your BATNAs, and leave the decision up to the other side. A particularly strong BATNA will communicate that you have buyers who will pay higher prices for smaller chunks of a package you are offering and want to buy soon in order to get first-mover advantage. If you want to be flexible, show the other side that you are willing to invest in the relationship and be reasonably generous and cooperative. If you see yourself as having a weak leverage position and want to be firm, emphasize the uncertain future—that someone else, even a competitor, could buy your offering and the rates might go up. In this situation, making an early, small concession might be advisable to show your willingness to do a deal. If you want to be flexible when you have a weak leverage position, acknowledge the other side's advantage and frame your offers positively. Appeal to the other side's sympathy and call in some relationship chits. Ask what they would do in your position, and, in effect, throw yourself to the mercy of the court, as lawyers say.

The best way to signal leverage is to show and maintain a high level of confidence. At no time in negotiating can you communicate a fear of losing or a need to close fast. You must be calm, patient, and, most of all, confident. As in a gunfight in the old Western movies, the following rule applies:

Rule: Confidence is everything; whoever blinks first, loses.

Making Concessions.   After you open and anchor the other side's perception of your walk-away, after you frame your initial offers to appeal either to their desire for a win or to increase their fear of losing, and after you have signaled your leverage and firmness or flexibility, you are ready to make concessions, or, better, to make trades. The first three rules of making concessions in the bargaining process are as follows:

Rule: Never begin with a major concession.

Rule: Don't just concede, try to trade; if you give up something, always try to get something in return.

Rule: Give the first concession on an unimportant issue, then get a concession from the other side.

These rules are important because they remind you to begin with a small concession; they also indicate that it is acceptable to give the first concession in order to break the ice and get things started, but give a small, unimportant one. The second rule also reminds you that when you give a concession, always try to get a reciprocal concession before you move on. Sometimes you have to ask for reciprocation by saying, "I gave up on my request for a sixteen-week commitment. Can you give me a higher rate?"

The third rule is important to remember because it gives you a clue as to what is important to the other side. Your first concession will be on an unimportant issue, so you must assume the other side's first concession will be on an issue that is not important. Trading concessions at the beginning of the bargaining process is like bidding in bridge; you are giving the other side signals as to what cards you hold and how strong your position is. Your goal in bargaining is not just to concede, but to trade—to get something in return. If you plan your concessions properly, you can trade small, unimportant concessions for ones that are more important to you. Remember that media buyers usually have to invest all of their client's money, so even though they ask for a lower price initially, it is often not their most important issue.

As you proceed in the process of trading concessions, follow the next two rules:

Rule: Make small concessions and give them slowly.

Rule: Make the other side work hard for everything; they will appreciate it more.

These rules are based on the principle, "What we obtain too cheaply, we esteem lightly."[13] For example, if you open with a price of $100 in the demographic a buyer requested and the buyer says, "That's a little high, but can you give me some added value?" you know price is not the most important issue. The buyer virtually conceded on price and you know added value is more important. In this situation, switch from discussing price to making concessions for added value, starting small and working up slowly to a Clincher Close, which I will discuss later in the chapter.

As you go through the exchanging of concessions, make sure to continually invoke the principle of reciprocity. For example, "OK, I gave you the promotion you wanted, will you give me the price I originally asked for?" Use the reciprocity principle as often as you can. If you feel what you are getting in return for a concession is not fair, say so, as in, "I gave you a valuable promotion and you are not going to give me the price I asked for. That's not fair!" A little outrage in the right places can be quite effective.

As you proceed with bargaining and trading concessions, use an effective concession pattern, which you have planned in advance. Table 12.2 shows six concession patterns.

Table 12.2 Concession Tactics	Which Tactic Is Most Effective?			
1.	25%	25%	25%	25%
2.	0	50%	0	50%
3.	0	0	0	100%
4.	100%	0	0	0
5.	10%	20%	30%	40%
6.	25%	40%	30%	5%

Look at Table 12.2 and let's assume you have planned to give a 15-percent discount in four steps and have some throw-away terms you are willing to concede. But, just considering price, the first pattern is ineffective because all the concessions are of equal value. Therefore, buyers expect the pattern to continue because you have given no signal that you are close to your walk-away. The second pattern is equally ineffective because you say no, then give a big concession, so your buyers expect this pattern to continue and will not believe your no after the last 50-percent concession. The third pattern is awful because you say no several times, and then give a huge concession, so buyers will extend the negotiating interminably because they expect another large concession. The next pattern is also disastrous because you give a huge first concession and then stonewall, so buyers will extend the negotiation and insist on more concessions equally large. The fifth pattern is bad, too, because with each larger concession you raise buyers' expectations, which extends negotiating. The most effective concession pattern is the final one.

Because you are willing to give a total of 15 percent, your concessions would be (1) 3.75 percent (25 percent × 15 percent), (2) 6 percent (40 percent × 15 percent), (3) 4.5 percent (30 percent × 15 percent), and (4) .75 percent (5 percent × 15 percent). All of these concessions are small and you are giving them slowly in four steps. You are beginning with a concession that is 25 percent of your planned total concession, then you move to 40 percent. But from there your concessions get smaller—30 percent and finally only 5 percent, which signals that you have reached your limit. When you give this final concession, you should say something such as, "Well, I can lower my price by $3, but you will have to give me another week on the schedule" (assuming a price of $40). If the buyer cannot give you another week, keep probing until you get something—a larger share of their budget, for example.

As you go through the bargaining process of trading concessions, get small, easy issues out of the way first. If you run into a big issue, set it aside by saying you will come back to it later and move on to settle smaller issues. This tactic uses the commitment principle. As the other side invests increasingly significant amounts of time, energy, and other resources in the negotiating process, they become more and more committed to closing the deal for fear of losing it and wasting their time and energy. As an example: "OK, we've agreed on a promotion and on first position in the newscast, but we're still a little bit apart on price. Let's put the price issue aside for now and see if we can't reach agreement on how long the promotion will run."

Finally, as you progress through bargaining, keep your eye out for what tactics the other side is using. Be aware of all of the tactics in Table 12.1. As Sun Tzu writes, "Do not swallow bait offered by the enemy."[14] Of course your customers are not your enemy, but they will often use tactics, or bait, to try to get an advantage. When you recognize a tactic, name it, do not fall for it, keep your confidence up, and move on.

When you determine the most effective concession pattern for an upcoming negotiation and determine your trade goals, fill out that section in the Negotiating and Closing Planner.

Building Agreement.   Finally, as you go through the process of bargaining, follow the next rule:

> **Rule: Summarize agreements and restate the other side's position on a regular basis.**

Frequently restate the other side's positions during bargaining because, "If they understand you're hearing what they're saying, it reduces stress levels," according to Victoria Ruttenberg, a successful Washington, D.C., lawyer and mediator.[15] You are trying to build agreement brick by small brick; you are trying get the other side to invest time and effort on a series of small agreements so their commitment to the process increases. Perhaps you have put off major issues earlier in the bargaining process; come back to them after you have reached a number of smaller agreements. You will find that large issues are easier to settle after smaller agreements have been reached—the other side's commitment is at its height. During this final stage of the bargaining process, do not get impatient.

> *Rule: Be patient—with patience and hard work in exploring alternatives, you can make the deal better for both sides.*

When you finally deal with the major issue, have patience and explore alternatives—be creative in finding solutions. As soon as you have reached agreement on the major issue, transition smoothly and calmly into your close—stay cool.

Closing and Gaining Commitment

The first rule of closing is:

> *Rule: Expect to close.*

You have planned well, you have bargained intelligently, and your confidence should now be at its peak. You must act as though you deserve the order, as though there is no doubt in your mind that you have the best offer, so ask for a decision—close.

The closing phase can be smooth or a time of high anxiety. It is important to remain cool and confident during the closing phase and not show any worry or anxiety, regardless of the circumstances. Often experienced negotiators save their most powerful tactics for the closing phase. You may think you have reached agreement on all of issues under discussion and have asked for the order, but buyers will introduce tactics they have not used before—a crunch, or a nibble (see Table 12.1). It is common in the closing phase for both sides to use the scarcity principle.

Sellers will use the limited-number approach, the act-now-before-a-competitor-buys-it approach, or the get-in-before-the-deadline approach. Buyers will use the your-competitors-want-a-big-share-and-are-going-much-lower approach and attempt once more to lower your price. This threat may be a bluff or it may be true. According to Richard Shell in *Bargaining for Advantage*, scarcity is an emotional issue; both sides use it to attempt to create the fear of losing in the other side. One side can increase the other side's fear by warning that others are competing for a scarce resource (the seller's offering or the buyer's money). It is always a matter of judgment whether to hold firm or yield to an attempt to push your panic button. Your judgment will be informed by your understanding of the leverage situation at the moment when you must decide.[16] If you know your buyer's tendencies, you will know if they tend to bluff or not and, therefore, whether to hold firm or yield. However, in no circumstances should you go below your walk-away.

If a buyer's apparent final offer is below your walk-away, then always walk away, but do so nicely and not in anger. Say, "I'm sorry I can't go any lower. I'll take your offer back to my management, but I'm not sanguine about their agreeing," which leads to the next rule:

> *Rule: When you walk away, always leave the door open.*

When such a walk-away occurs, you and your management can decide outside the heat of battle whether to go back with another offer. But make sure you wait at least a day—the buyer may call and meet your terms during that day.

In many situations the close will go smoothly, especially if you have used *trial closes* throughout the bargaining phase.

There are five types of closes:

Types of Closes

1. Trial closes
2. Choice closes
3. Clincher closes
4. Last-resort closes
5. Bad, never-use closes

Trial Closes

There is on old saying in selling, "ABC, always be closing." The phrase comes from the old-fashioned, hard-sell school of selling, but as in many rules of thumb, there is a kernel of wisdom in the phrase. In modern selling and negotiating techniques, the always-be-closing concept translates into "use trial closes throughout your presentation and negotiating." Trial closes are an indirect method of testing buyers' temperature. Are buyers cold and need more information, or are they warm and ready to buy? The only way to know for certain is to ask. The worst that can happen is that you discover that they are not ready and they raise another objection. Actually, the main purpose of a trial close is to bring objections to the surface so you can deal with them. If there are no more objections, then you have a deal. Following are several trial closes you can use throughout your presentations and negotiations to test the water.

The Direct Close.   Simply ask for the green light. Always avoid using the words *buy* or *order*. Do not ask, "Will you buy this?" Do not say, "How about it? Could I have the order?" Those words may frighten buyers. "I'll book this right away so you can get on the air by Monday, OK?" or "We'll agree on this price, then. Isn't that fair enough?" are better direct closes.

The phrase "Isn't that fair enough?" is one of the strongest closing phrases you can use. Nobody wants to be accused of implying that someone else is unfair and so will go to great lengths to answer this question positively. Also, never ask a closing question that can be answered with an unambiguous no. The phrase, "I'll book this right away so you can get on the air by Monday, OK?" was used previously. If the buyer says no, then this is an ambiguous no and you make the assumption that they do not want to start on Monday, but do not make the assumption that they do not want to give you the order.

For example, suppose a buyer asks, "Could I run Wednesday through Saturday?" Do not respond with, "If I can schedule it this way, will you give me the order?" because you have, in essence, created an objection when before only a question about how to run the order existed. Instead, say, "Absolutely," thank them for the business, shake hands, and leave. If you cannot run the schedule as requested, say "I'm sorry we can't," explain why, and use another close.

The Assumption Close.   This close is particularly powerful because it is so painless for both a buyer and a salesperson. When you sense that the time has come, that a buyer has shifted gears from desire to conviction, you simply assume that the buyer has made the decision to buy and proceed accordingly. Talk and act as though the buyer has given you the green light. If you are correct in your assumption, the buyer will not stop you, in which case you have the order. If the buyer says, "Hold on. I haven't bought anything yet," then proceed with some probes to find out why the buyer is not ready.

The Summary Close.   This close is an excellent trial close and should be used often. On a regular basis, summarize all the benefits to which a buyer has agreed. Emphasize those benefits in which a buyer has shown the most interest. Present an overwhelming weight of accepted evidence of superiority in your summary. Follow your summary with a statement such as, "Can we go ahead with this plan?" You can also use the Silent Close that follows.

The Silent Close.   Ask for the order with a Direct Close, with a Summary Close, or with any appropriate close and then shut up. There is an old rule used by many salespeople that says after a strong close, "the first one who speaks, loses." You do not have to fill a void with words. Give buyers time to think. Let them become uncomfortable and start talking; if you do not speak, they surely will. When they finally say something, you will either get the green light or an objection, which gives you another opportunity to present a benefit that solves a problem. If you speak first, you let buyers off the hook.

The Pin-Down Close.   This closing technique should be used judiciously. After prospects have expressed an objection, pin them down by asking if you can have the go-ahead if you can overcome their objection. For example, if a prospect says, "I don't like those early news spots," your response would be, "If I can get the sales manager to agree to move them to the late news, may I book the schedule?" You have used a Pin-Down Close. Be careful, though; avoid using this close too often or too early because a prospect might understand what you are doing and use the same tactic against you to get a string of concessions. If a prospect tries to extract another concession from you after a Pin-Down Close, a good tactic is to say, "Hey, let's be fair. You said we could go ahead if I moved those spots."

A good time to use the Pin-Down Close is when prospects try to put off a decision. When prospects say they want to think it over or that they will call you later, quickly isolate their reasons for the stall and use a Pin-Down Close. The *let-me-think-about-it* excuse is the most common one you will encounter, and you must learn to overcome it quickly or you will lose sales. When you get this excuse, pin down the reasons for the excuse, narrow the objection, and then try a Pin-Down Close or a Clincher Close (which you will learn about a little later in this chapter).

Another time when Pin-Down closes work well is when buyers try to nibble you (see Table 12.1). A Pin-Down Close stops a nibble by saying, "OK, if I can get half of your spots moved to the late news, do we have a deal—no further changes?" After a nibble, do not give the other side their full demand; cut it in half, then if you want to, you can go all the way on their demand if half does not work.

The T-Account Close.   Use a lined tablet or any sheet of standard-sized paper and draw a line down the middle of the paper, then cross the T across the paper near the top. Next, in the left top section, write down a buyer's objections and in the section underneath write a list of all the reasons supporting the buyer's objections. Next, write in the right top section your off-setting benefits. Your list should be longer than a buyer's and if it is not, do not use this technique.

For example, if a buyer wants to put off making a final commitment until next month, put "Start Next Month" on top of one column and "Start Now" on top of the other column. With a prospect's help, write all of the objections in the left column, then write all of the reasons to start now in the right column. This technique is dramatic and graphic; it is particularly effective with precise, fact-oriented people. It also gives buyers the perception that you are being objective and fair ("Isn't that a fair list?").

Rule: Use trial closes throughout the negotiating process.

Choice Closes

Choice closes are especially powerful because they build commitment through choice. Chase and Dasu report on an interesting study that found that blood donors perceived significantly less discomfort when they were allowed to select the arm from which their blood would be drawn. The authors write that the lesson from this study is clear: people are happier and more comfortable when they believe they have some control over a process, particularly an uncomfortable one such as giving a salesperson an order. In some cases, the control given over is largely symbolic (as in the choice of arm), or it can be a meaningful, high-stakes decision. The medical profession has long recognized the value of allowing patients to make an informed choice about alternative treatments for cancer and heart disease. Doctors realize there is enormous value in involving the patient in these important decisions. Patients feel less helpless, less hopeless, and, most important, more committed to making the process work.[17] For this reason, increase commitment through choice by offering not just one proposal but possibly as many as three and let the other side choose.

The Choice Close.   The Choice close is one of the easiest closes to use. It is probably used more than any other close, and should be. You have already set up this close by providing three or more proposals in your proposal or presentation. Then, you simply ask prospects which of these options they prefer. When you have the answer, you have the order. "Do you prefer the first, second, or third package I offered, Mr. Franklin?" "The third." "Great, an excellent choice! Thank you. I'll run right back to the office and get this scheduled and e-mail you the confirmation." The buyer might never say yes or "I'll buy it," but the buyer has given assent by making a choice.

When buyers are given a choice, they can make a decision without feeling forced into a corner. Buyers have the reassurance and confidence of asserting their free will and of expressing themselves. Furthermore, after they make the choice, you have the opportunity to reinforce their final decision. Always compliment prospects on their wise judgment.

The Minor-Point Close.   This is another popular, effective, and easier close. With the Minor-Point Close, you attempt to get buyers to choose and approve one or more minor details in an offer; if they agree, you have made a sale. The more minor points on which you can get agreement, the better. "We'll start the schedule next Tuesday so we have time to get the copy in, OK?" or "Instead of billing this to you the first week of the month, we'll send the bill to you a week early so you can be reimbursed more quickly from your client, OK?" When buyers agree to a minor point, they are saying yes the easy way. For example, a buyer who might hesitate if you ask whether you can go head with the $200,000 order for sponsoring baseball broadcasts will probably find it a snap to agree to provide you with artwork for a sponsorship ad in the stadium program booklet.

Clincher Closes

A clincher close is a well-planned close in which you make a final concession on a major request, an important issue, or substantial added value—you hold it back until the end and offer it to clinch the deal. From the beginning, you have your concession or improved offer in your back pocket but bring it out at the end only if you need it to close the deal. For example, you might be negotiating for a major 52-week buy on your radio station. The agency, on behalf of their client, has requested a low rate in return for giving you a firm 52-week commitment, and wants four event promotions (one each quarter) as well as merchandising support for the client's sales force (prizes such as golf clubs and golf balls for sales contest winners). As you have progressed through the negotiation, you have agreed to the merchandising but are 10 percent apart on rate. The agency's final offer has been $225 cost-per-point and they are not budging. You are holding out for $250, the mid-point in the initial ballpark. However, you have not offered the four event promotions even though the other side has continually asked for them, even though you have been prepared to give the promotions. The Clincher Close would be to say, "OK, we seem to be stalled. What if I give you the four event promotions, which will cost us a great deal, and you give me my rate of $250? That seems like a win-win, fair agreement, doesn't it?"

Using Clincher Closes requires detailed planning before the negotiation and great discipline during the process—you lose the power of a Clincher Close if you introduce it too early in the process. Also, use Clincher Closes the first time you negotiate with someone, but not the second time. If you consistently use Clincher Closes with people with whom you regularly negotiate, they will expect them, always hold out for a major concession at the end, and when they receive the concession, they will not appreciate it but instead feel it is their due. With people with whom you regularly negotiate, use Clincher Closes only on an occasional, random basis—use a mixed strategy.

Last-Resort Closes

The "Make-Me-an-Offer" Close.   Real estate and automobile salespeople fully understand the power of this closing technique—it gets prospects to express verbally their commitment to buy. When buyers make you an offer, they are not only committing to buy but they are also giving you the parameters of the final barriers to a sale. This is one of the last techniques you should employ because it typically results in a concession. Even though it is somewhat tricky to do, the best way to handle this close is to get buyers to make you an offer on terms other than price alone, instead, on position or added value. You might say: "I know that you want to be with us and that what I am offering is right for you. Make me an offer that contains an adjustment on something other than price and I'll see what I can do."

The "What-Will-It-Take?" Close.   This is a more desperate version of the "Make-Me-an-Offer" Close. With this close you are vulnerable to lowballing, but often, as a last resort, you will see if the other side goes below your walk-away and how much lower, which is information you can use in your next negotiation, after you walk away. Sometimes you might use this close on a small piece of business when the offer is low and you can walk away to give the other side a clear signal that you will walk away from low offers; it makes your anchor in subsequent negotiations credible.

The "What-Did-I-Do-Wrong?" Close.   Finally, when you have failed to reach an agreement, pack your briefcase, say, "Thank you for your time," and get up and head for the door. Just as you are going through the door, turn to the buyer and say, "Do you mind if I ask you one more question? I respect you and your opinion and feel I could learn something from this experience. Would you mind telling me what I did wrong? Where did I lose the sale?" The chances are good that your prospect will tell you; then, of course, you are in a position to start over (at that instant or on another call, whichever is appropriate).

Bad, Never-Use Closes

The Poor-Me Close.   Salespeople have been known to beg for orders by saying that they will lose their job if they do not get an order or that they must have the money to pay for their child's organ transplant. Do not try to heap guilt on buyers and do not beg to get an order; do not lower yourself or diminish your own dignity. Confidence and self-esteem are vitally important in the selling and negotiating process; do nothing to lessen yourself in the eyes of prospects. Customers admire strength. Begging also puts you in an awful negotiating position.

The Now-You-Have-It-Now-You-Don't Close.   Some unscrupulous salespeople will promise anything just to get an order, knowing full well that they cannot deliver what has been sold. Their strategy is to take an order, then go back to buyers later and say they cannot deliver. They then try to switch buyers into other, lower-rated time slots (in broadcasting and cable), in less desirable positions (in print), or to pay higher rates. This maneuver has a narcotic temptation because it can shut out competitors; however, buyers are not dumb enough to let this work more than once. Nothing destroys your credibility faster than this bait-and-switch technique.

The For-You-Only Close.   Some weak salespeople try only one close and then immediately rely on giving a big concession to make a sale. They promise prospects, "If you give me an order right now, I'll give you the lowest rate possible, lower than anyone else." Salespeople who use this approach sound as though they just came in from an alley where they were peddling pornographic postcards, and buyers tend to show them about that much respect.

Whichever close you decide to use, do not close too aggressively, especially on bigger deals. You can create a sense of urgency with deadlines and limited-supply maneuvers, but the timetable has to be the other side's. Too much pressure can kill a prospective deal. Pressure on your part to close will make the other side suspicious—you will appear too eager for a deal and cause the other side to push for more concessions. As indicated earlier in this chapter, people want to buy, to make a choice. People do not like to be sold or pressured; they are much more comfortable in choosing and controlling the timing of their buying decision. Pressure to close also often strains a relationship, so you must be particularly careful in pressuring people with whom you regularly negotiate.

> *Rule: Don't close too aggressively; always keep the relationship in mind.*

Sales managers, sales trainers, and many sales textbooks often overemphasize closing. You should close only when you are convinced that your customers are committed to your proposed solution and negotiated agreement and that you are convinced it is a fair deal that is right for them. Never push people into buying. Remember, you are managing a relationship for the long haul, and it would be counterproductive to close too aggressively and jeopardize a relationship. However, people have a natural tendency to avoid saying yes, either from fear of losing or fear of not getting a good deal, so you must maintain your confidence that your deal is the right one for them and not signal anything that would give them pause or give them an excuse to hesitate.

> *Rule: When closing, confidence is vital—you cannot signal in any way your fear of losing or need to close fast.*

Confidence is vital throughout the negotiating process, but even more so in the closing phase. There are several things to keep in mind that will enhance your confidence:

> *Rule: Have confidence that you can give the other side a "good deal"—their definition of a good deal.*

People have their own unique definition of a good deal—it is an individualized perception. Your task before or during a negotiation is to discover your customers' personal definition of a good deal, then see that they get it.

Table 12.3 shows a list of some customers' definitions of a good deal and how to respond.

Table 12.3
Types of Good Deals

Definition	Description	Tactic
Got a low price	The perception of a low price is always relative. Remember the salesperson's father's advice, "Never pay retail?" Some people will go to enormous lengths in time and effort to get what they perceive to be a lower price. Often such bargain hunters are called bottom fishers. They will take risks on quality and preemptability (not running an ad and replacing it with another, higher priced one).	Offer bottom fishers low-priced packages of less-desirable, remnant, or preemptable inventory. Identify and keep a list of bargain hunters and call them when you have last-minute, reduced-price inventory. These are people who often know the price of everything and the value of nothing and, thus, will buy hard-to-move inventory. Make sure you emphasize the bargain, low-priced nature of your offering. When you get the order, compliment them on getting such a good bargain.
Got something someone else wanted	The scarcity principle at work. Competition for scarce resources often gets people over-committed and makes something more desirable. Price, discounts, and quality are not important; all that counts is that someone else wants it—especially if a hated competitor wants it. Fear of loss and envy are involved.	During negotiations, make sure people who have a tendency to be envious are aware of your BATNAs and know that their competitors are interested or have made an offer. Be honest, but on the other hand, do not fail to communicate such information. When you make the sale, compliment them for snatching it away from their competitors.

continued

Table 12.3
(continued)

Definition	Description	Tactic
Got high quality at a reasonable price	Many buyers are concerned with quality and service, and do not mind paying for it. For example, many people pay much more for a Mercedes or a Lexus than for a Ford or Chevrolet because of their perception of quality.	Create value from the beginning for these people and continually mention the word quality. When you reach agreement, compliment them for having the excellent judgment to recognize quality.
Got the last one	The scarcity principle at work again. Fear of loss of a scarce and valuable resource is involved.	The limited-supply maneuver works well here. Be honest when you let buyers know that there is only one left and create a sense of urgency due to the competition for it. Price is never the issue, so raise the price for the last one. When you close the deal, compliment them on their ability to make a fast decision.
Got a warranty or guarantee: low risk of dissatisfaction	Some people with low self-confidence, who are risk-averse, and, especially, those who fear making a mistake, feel much more comfortable with guarantees or warranties. Ratings for upfront buys on network television and impressions on Interactive buys are typically guaranteed.	Emphasize the safe, low-risk nature of guarantees. Because guarantees are more important than price, buyers will pay more for guarantees. When you get agreement on a deal, compliment them on being such good, smart negotiators.
Got a discount	To people who crave discounts, the actual price is not as important as the perception that they got a discount. Goods on sale appeal to these people; they will buy more than they need because they cannot resist a "50-percent discount."	Going in to a negotiation, raise the price on your initial offer by 20 percent, negotiate, and then as a Clincher Close, offer a 20-percent discount. When you make the sale, compliment them on being such a good negotiator and being able to get such a large discount.
Got something else free thrown in	There are some people who love to get something for nothing, something free. They will pass up a "50-percent discount" offer, often feeling that it is damaged or undesirable goods, and snap up an offer of "buy one and get one free." Same price, different frame.	With people you have identified as those who like something else free thrown in, as with those who crave discounts, planning is the key. During negotiations, do not concede on price, even though you are willing to come down 15 percent, but as a Clincher Close, say, "OK, if you'll give me my price, I'll give you 15 percent more inventory—a bonus of 15 percent." When you reach an agreement, compliment them for getting something free.
Got a win; feel like they won something important to them	Many competitive buyers and negotiators care more about winning than anything else. In fact, they will not make a deal unless they feel like they have won.	Good planning will do the trick. Use a Red Herring, such as an event promotion that the other side insists on. Say no repeatedly, then as a Clincher Close, say, "OK you win, I'll give you the promotion if you'll give me the order now—before I change my mind or my boss finds out and fires me." When you get the order, compliment them on winning. Make sure you tell them they have won.

continued

Table 12.3
(*continued*)

Definition	Description	Tactic
Got good results from advertising	Many experienced advertisers view advertising as an investment, so it is not how much it costs that matters, but what their return on investment is. Interactive advertising is especially good at showing ROI.	With people who care most about results and ROI, it is vital that you control their expectations from the beginning and always under-promise and over-deliver. By lowering their expectations from the start, you can help ensure results. When you make the sale, compliment them for their sophisticated approach and deep understanding of the ultimate purpose of advertising, and reassure them that your primary objective as a salesperson is to get results for your customers.
Got a good deal compared to other media	In today's media-saturated environment, buyers have a multitude of choices for placing advertising. If they select one over another or in combination with another medium, they typically want to feel that they got a good deal.	When you are in a selling or negotiating situation in which other media are being considered, stress the benefits of your medium, not based solely on price, but based on a wide variety of dimensions. A T-Account Close works well in these situations, where you compare the benefits of your medium to other media. When you reach agreement, compliment buyers on their insight and professionalism.

Note in Table 12.3 that all of the tactics involve complimenting people on their ability to get a good deal and to reinforce their perception of a good deal. Therefore, you have the power when you negotiate to give people a good deal, only if you know what their definition of a good deal is and you can plan your tactics in advance to make sure you give them a good deal.

Finally, it will give you confidence and power in a negotiation if you have no fear of walking away. Good BATNAs vastly increase your confidence to walk away. If you have the confidence to leave if you do not achieve your walk-away, it does you no good unless you signal your confidence in how you act, walk, sit, and talk. Confidence does not mean arrogance, bluster, or threats, but it reflects a firm resolve to make a deal that is fair to both sides.

You are now ready to complete the negotiating planning process by planning your closes. Select several of the above closes that are appropriate for your upcoming negotiating session and fill in the last section of the Negotiating and Closing Planner.

Get Commitment

When one of your closes is successful and you get an agreement, do not be satisfied with an agreement—get commitment. The objective of every negotiation is to secure commitment, not merely agreement. Commitment in closing a deal gives you a deal that sticks and that has incentives or penalties to ensure that both sides perform. Different kinds of negotiating situations call for different types of commitment. In some simple, familiar situations, both side's word and a handshake is good enough, but in other, more complicated situations such as dealing with unfamiliar people or on a large deal, legal contracts and other types of commitment are necessary. According to Richard Shell in *Bargaining for Advantage,* there are four degrees of commitment.[18]

Social Ritual.   The commitment process begins with a simple social ritual such as a handshake, a bow, or an exchange of calling cards. In most buyer-seller relationships in the media both sides feel that their word is their bond, and that they would face loss of self-esteem and their reputation if they went back on their word or did not follow through on a commitment.

Public Announcement.   As the size of the deal increases, social rituals are often not enough to secure adequate commitment and it helps to make a public announcement. Once a public announcement is made, it is much more difficult for either side to back out. These announcements can be made in the form of a press release or a press conference. Just as you increase your commitment to your walk-away by telling your boss and others about it, public disclosures of a big deal bind both sides to an agreement.

Accountability.   Accountability also enhances commitment. One way to finalize accountability is to put an agreement in writing. This type of accountability is commonly accomplished with an exchange of insertion orders (IO) and confirmations between buyer and seller. IOs and confirmations can be by mail, fax, or e-mail. Once IOs and confirmations of the IO are received, the agreement becomes legally binding. Some crafty buyers will reach a verbal agreement then send an IO at a lower price than agreed on, either hoping the receiving salesperson will not notice or will go along to avoid a loss at that late date. Do not fall for this ploy; send back a confirmation that shows your original prices, then wait for the buyer to respond.

Another type of accountability agreement is a non-binding letter of intent (LOI). There might be several details left to be worked out after you have reached an agreement on major points at the end of a negotiation for a big deal. In such a situation, you might ask the other side for a letter that says that they will go ahead with the deal based on the assumption that the final, minor terms can be ironed out. Such a letter is not legally binding, but it significantly increases the other side's commitment to work out the remainder of the issues. Another type of agreement is the exchange of next-step agreement—a list of things both sides must complete to implement an agreement.

Simultaneous Exchange.   In some large, complicated deals, sending back and forth letters of agreement, IOs, or next-steps is not solid enough to secure a firm commitment. In such situations, it might be a good idea to use a simultaneous exchange to seal the deal. In the case of the sale of a home and the subsequent formal closing, the two sides typically exchange the title for the property and a certified check for the required amount at the same time. With extremely large, complex media deals, simultaneous exchange is a good practice.

Whichever form of commitment you use, always follow this rule:

> *Rule: Once you get commitment, say "thank you," shut up, and leave quickly.*

Buyer's remorse usually sets in after someone buys something. You do not want to be present when buyer's remorse occurs. One of the biggest mistakes inexperienced salespeople make is to hang around and chat after they have made a sale or reached an agreement. They are afraid of being considered impolite and ungrateful by rushing off. Forget about being impolite, leave fast. You might want to make an excuse for your quick exit and say, "You've got an excellent deal. Thank you so much for the business. Now I have to run back to the office and book this order before someone else buys the great inventory you just invested in. Goodbye." There is an old saying in sales that the jawbone of an ass slew a thousand Philistines and as many sales have been lost for the same reason because salespeople talk too much after making a sale.

Putting It All Together: Create a Negotiating and Closing Plan

You should fill out the Negotiating and Closing Planner in Appendix E (also available on www.mediaselling.us) whenever you are going into a major negotiation and when dealing with the 20 percent of your customers who give you 80 percent of your business. Also, see the Negotiating and Closing Outline in Appendix D that summarizes all of the strategies, tactics, and rules. It, too, is available on www.mediaselling.us and can be downloaded onto a PDA so you can review it before negotiating.

Once you have created a thorough negotiating and closing plan, and before you enter into a major negotiation, rehearse. An excellent way to rehearse is to get a colleague (salesperson or sales manager) to rehearse with you; you play the other side's role and your colleague plays your role. Rehearsing in this manner is the best way to refine and perfect your plan.

Rule: Always rehearse your negotiating and closing plan.

After you have rehearsed your plan, commit to it—carry it out just as you have rehearsed it. Rehearsal will give you confidence and increase your commitment.

Finally, just as when you make major presentations, debrief after negotiating. Practice makes perfect and debriefing makes it even better, which leads to the final negotiating and closing rule:

Rule: After every negotiation, debrief.

Many of the concepts and the strategies used in this chapter are those recommend by Richard Shell in *Bargaining for Advantage*, a superb book that is applicable to media negotiating and one I recommend you read.

Test Yourself

1. What are the five elements in the negotiating process?
2. Why is knowing the other side's negotiating cultural background important?
3. What are the ten preparation steps in negotiating?
4. What third style do you occasionally find in media negotiating?
5. What are the four negotiating situations?
6. What are the two basic negotiating styles?
7. What is a BATNA?
8. What is the purpose of the tit-for-tat tactic?
9. What is negative leverage?

10. What is an HLE?
11. What is a ballpark?
12. Name six acceptable bargaining tactics.
13. How can you avoid negotiating on each element in a package individually?
14. What are the five steps in the bargaining process?
15. Should you open first?
16. Should you open optimistically?
17. Give an example of a frame.
18. How should you give concessions?
19. Name three trial closes.
20. Give an example of a clincher close.

Projects

Project #1: Pretend your parents can afford to buy you a new car and that you are going to ask them for a BMW roadster. Prepare for your request by filling out the Negotiating and Closing Planner in the Appendix E or on www.mediaselling.us.

Project #2: Go to Appendix A and read "Cost-Per-Point Market Ranks," then go to www.tvsalespro.com and look at the CPP ranks for your market or a television market with which you are familiar and see if you think the television stations in those markets are good at creating value and negotiating to get reasonable rates.

References

Richard B. Chase and Sriram Dasu. 2001. "Want to Perfect Your Company's Service? Use Behavioral Science." *Harvard Business Review.* June.
Jay Conger. 1998. "The Necessary Art of Persuasion." *Harvard Business Review.* May-June.
Danny Ertel. 1999. "Negotiation as a Corporate Capability." *Harvard Business Review.* May-June.
Roger Fisher and William Ury with Bruce Patton. 1991. *Getting to Yes, Second edition.* New York: Penguin Books.
Michael Maccoby. 2000. "Narcissistic Leaders: The Incredible Pros, the Inevitable Cons." *Harvard Business Review.* January-February.
László Mérö. 1998. *Moral Calculations: Game Theory, Logic, and Human Frailty.* New York: Copernicus.
Gerard I. Nierenberg. 1973. *Fundamentals of Negotiating.* New York: Hawthorne Books.
William Poundstone. 1992. *Prisoner's Dilemma.* New York: Doubleday.
Linda L. Putnam and Michael Roloff. 1992. *Communication and Negotiation.* Newbury Park, CA: Sage Publications.
Howard Raiffa. 1982. *The Art & Science of Negotiation.* Cambridge, MA: Harvard University Press.
Thomas C. Schelling. 1980. *The Strategy of Conflict.* Cambridge, MA: Harvard University Press.
James K. Sebenius. 2001. "Six Habits of Merely Effective Negotiators." *Harvard Business Review.* April.
G. Richard Shell. 1999. *Bargaining for Advantage.* New York: Penguin Books.
Sun Tzu. Edited by James Clavell. 1983. *The Art of War.* New York: Dell Publishing.
Bob Woolf. 1990. *Friendly Persuasion.* New York: Berkley Books.

Endnotes

1. Gerard I. Nierenberg. 1973. *Fundamentals of Negotiating.* New York: Hawthorne Books. p. 27.
2. Sun Tzu. Edited by James Clavell. 1983. *The Art of War.* New York: Dell Publishing. p. 82
3. Ibid. p. 7.
4. G. Richard Shell. 1999. *Bargaining for Advantage.* New York: Penguin Books. p. xiii.
5. Danny Ertel. 1999. "Negotiation as a Corporate Capability." *Harvard Business Review.* May-June. p. 6.

6. Ibid. p. 13.

7. Bob Woolf. 1990. *Friendly Persuasion.* New York: Berkley Books. p. 129.

8. Stefan Fatsis. 2003. "Small Ball: NBC Maps a Future Without the Big Leagues." *Wall Street Journal.* January 31. p. A1.

9. William Poundstone. 1992. *Prisoner's Dilemma.* New York: Doubleday.

10. G. Richard Shell. 1999. *Bargaining for Advantage.* New York: Penguin Books. p. 95.

11. Personal conversation with Perry Stein, ex-VP of NBC Sports, November 2000.

12. Richard B. Chase and Sriram Dasu. 2001. "Want to Perfect Your Company's Service? Use Behavioral Science." *Harvard Business Review.* June. p. 82.

13. G. Richard Shell. 1999. *Bargaining for Advantage.* New York: Penguin Books. p. 169.

14. Sun Tzu. Edited by James Clavell. 1983. *The Art of War.* New York: Dell Publishing. p. 35.

15. Hal Lancaster. 1998. "Most Things Are Negotiable: Here's How to Get Good at It." *The Wall Street Journal.* January 27. p. B1.

16. G. Richard Shell. 1999. *Bargaining for Advantage.* New York: Penguin Books. p. 184.

17. Richard B. Chase and Sriram Dasu. 2001. "Want to Perfect Your Company's Service? Use Behavioral Science." *Harvard Business Review.* June. p. 83.

18. G. Richard Shell. 1999. *Bargaining for Advantage.* New York: Penguin Books. p. 197.

Chapter **13** **Skills: Servicing**

By Charles Warner

In Chapter 1 you learned that "There is only one valid definition of a business purpose: to create a customer." In Chapter 2 you learned the definition of selling: "Selling in the media is about creating customers and keeping them." Up to this point, this book has focused on how to create customers. This chapter emphasizes the importance of the last step of selling—servicing—to keep the customers you create, because as you learned in Chapter 2, "Customers require outrageous service that will make them raving fans."

The terms "outrageous service" and "raving fans" come from a book titled *Raving Fans* by Ken Blanchard and Sheldon Bowles, and these terms reflect the increased expectations of consumers for excellent service in addition to a quality product.[1] Before 1990, the four Ps of marketing (product, price, place, and promotion) were taught in colleges and written about in marketing textbooks. But in the 1980s, consumers became fed up with shoddy quality and service from many American manufacturers. Japanese, German, and a few American companies saw a marketing opportunity and began emphasizing the excellent service that accompanied the purchase of their quality products. The best-selling business book of all time, *In Search of Excellence*, published in 1982, urged companies to be close to the customer, and this phrase became the mantra of many companies. Improvement in service by the 1990s raised the expectations of American consumers and post-purchase service became the 5th P of marketing. Today, service is an inextricable attribute of most products, especially with intangible services such as advertising, where the media salesperson's service is what makes the advertising product tangible.

Servicing in the Sales Process

The sales process involves creating customers and keeping them. You know that you have kept your customers when they come back, when they renew. Figure 13.1 shows the Renewal Cycle and how it fits into the sales process.

Note in Figure 13.1 that all of the steps of selling are the same in the renewal process except the first, Prospecting. Prospecting, the act of finding people to sell to, was accomplished when you received your first order from an account. However, as you learned from the Money engine in Chapter 9, advertisers do not become customers until they renew. Therefore, always sell for the second order, not the first. Prospecting is hard, often frustrating work and it is easier to get a renewal for a $100,000 schedule than to prospect and sell a new $100,000 account.

**Figure 13.1
Creating customers
and keeping them:
The renewal cycle.**

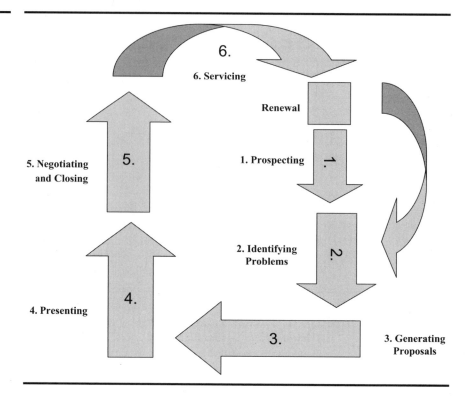

Effective servicing can accomplish the third primary sales objective, to retain and increase current business. Your current customers are your best prospects, and it is easier and more efficient to get an increase of 25 percent (from $100,000 to $125,000, for example) from a current account than prospect and sell a new one. When you sell for a renewal, you have to go through the other five steps of selling because issues and challenges always arise when an advertising schedule runs and you must address them with new solutions. And even while your customers' schedules run, your competitors in your own and in competing media are monitoring your media and trying hard to steal your customers. Your best defense against competitors' attacks is to give your customers outrageous service.

What is outrageous service? Ken Blanchard and Sheldon Bowles define outrageous as substantially exceeding customers' service expectations. Your customers' expectations are determined by three factors: (1) what service they want, (2) what service they get from your competitors (your medium and other media), and (3) what service they have received from your organization in the past. Let's look at each of these factors separately.

What Service Your Customers Want.   Just as you asked Discovery Questions before you got an order, you must ask Servicing Questions after each order you get from a customer (not just after the first one because their needs and wants may change). The first step in providing service that substantially exceeds your customers' expectations is to find out what kind of service your customers want. You already have a good idea, in general, what they want from the surveys listed in chapters 2 and 8 (see page 24). But those surveys are several years old and are based on the views of television and radio media buyers and advertising agency executives. The best thing to do is to ask your customers what they want, to give you a list of items that they believe constitutes ideal service. Asking customers what kind of service they want is an excellent idea for two reasons: (1) it lets them know up front that you care about them, and (2) it identifies a standard, or measure, of expectations so you can know what you have to do to substantially exceed those expectations to provide outrageous service.

Rule: Find out what kind of service your customers want.

What Kind of Service Your Competitors Give.   Immediately after you ask your customers what service they want, the next step is to ask them which media salesperson gives them the best service and what makes their service the best. The reason you ask this question is because the first question will probably produce an extremely high, or even impossibly high, level of service—a wish list. The second question about your competitors' best service lowers the bar of their expectations from perhaps impossible heights to a reasonable height. So, just as with presentations, with service you will know how good you have to be—just good enough to win.

As you learned from game theory, your servicing strategy depends on the that of your competitors. To defend against their inevitable attacks, your strategy must be better because customers will judge your service against the best service they get from competitors, not on an absolute basis compared to their own highly optimistic wish list. By asking customers about the best service they get, you anchor their perception of good service at a reasonable level that you have a good chance of exceeding, providing there are no institutional constraints on your ability to provide competitive service such as extravagant gifts and lavish entertainment. If you discover that your customers' expectations include these types of gifts and entertainment, it is best to control their expectations immediately rather than try to compete inadequately. You might say, "I'm sorry I can't match the entertainment or gift budget of my competition; it's against company policy. But I will try to make up for it with faster response and by providing you with more and better research and promotion ideas." If you are honest, sincere, and follow up on your promises, your customers, except for the few corrupt ones, will be pleased and satisfied.

Rule: Find out which competitor gives the best service and what kind of service it is, then exceed it.

Your Past Service Level.   Your customers' level of expectation is not only set by your competitors, but also by the level of service they have received in the past from your organization. After asking about the best service they receive from your competitors, ask them about the service they have received in the past from your organization. If you are lucky, you will not have to ask this question if a customer answers the question about the best service they get with a reply that it is from you or from your organization. In this case, you have a clear, measurable standard to meet and exceed. If you are not lucky and customers answer the question about your company's service with, "Awful," or worse, you have a serious problem that promises will not even begin to solve. When you run into this problem, all you can say is, "I understand how you feel and I'm sorry for any inconvenience it has caused you. I know the only thing that will change your opinion is action and consistency, not words, so I'll say no more. I'll make no promises except that I will check in regularly to see how I'm doing. Let me try to get off on the right track by asking you what I can do for you right now—in the next few days."

> *Rule: Find out what kind of service customers have received from your organization in the past.*

Exceeding Expectations

As you learned in Chapter 8 about creating value, if you want a happy customer, you under-promise and over-deliver in terms of what results they expect. It is the same with service; you must control your clients' expectations. Do not make any promises about what kind of service you will deliver; action always speaks louder than words. Also, as in negotiating, in servicing, start out small and increase the level of service slowly. If you start out with big perks and entertainment, you raise your customers' expectations. Your level of service must be good enough to be better than your competitors' to be considered superior and does not have to be extravagant or lavish, especially at first.

Also, the vast majority of customers value consistency more than extravagance. The same, consistent, high-level of service with every order, every schedule, every week, every month, and every year is what they prize most.

> *Rule: Consistency, consistency, consistency.*[2]

Systems

Companies that have great reputations for excellent service are driven by excellent systems: mission statements, institutional service attitudes, service standards and policies, service tracking and measurement systems, and service feedback and reward systems. Without a service culture and systems that contain all of these elements, excellent service does not become an institutional priority, but an individual and inconsistent chore.

Mission Statements. Many media companies have mission statements. Some are sincere, but many are public relations documents, such as Enron's, which claim a lofty purpose but are ignored in practice. Few media companies' mission or value statements fail to mention profits, although one of the most profitable, A. H. Belo, does not include profits in its values and operating principles (see Table 3.1). Virtually all media companies' mission statements mention customers in one way or another, but rarely do they put their customers (advertisers) as a top priority; most of them, understandably, put their audience first.

ESPN is one media organization, in addition to A. H. Belo, that gets its priorities right in its mission statement. Note in the last paragraph of ESPN's mission statement in Exhibit 13.1 that employees, customers, community, and shareholders are the order of its priorities (viewers are assumed to be the top priority because of the opening paragraph).

Why are organizational mission statements included in a chapter about servicing advertisers? Because if your company does not have a mission statement or has one that does not indicate or imply that being fair and responsive to customers is important, then you must write a personal mission statement that delineates what kind of a salesperson you want to be and what kind of service you want to provide to your customers. It is more than just setting a goal of providing excellent service. Writing a personal mission statement that includes superior service is making a promise, a commitment, to yourself and to your customers that you will provide service that is better than your com-

**Exhibit 13.1
ESPN Mission
Statement**

ESPN is committed to enhancing its position as the premier sports programmer in the world by delivering a superior product to its viewers, affiliates, and advertisers. We seek to attract and retain the most talented people by fostering an environment for them to thrive in their work efforts as they develop the finest sports program distribution system for both domestic and international markets.

People are the most valuable resource at ESPN. We believe in treating every employee with respect and dignity. We endeavor to support and reward our people for their efforts and we will strive to make ESPN a caring company, cognizant of each employee's personal and professional needs.

Our success has always been dependent upon people working together as a Team. To sustain our success and competitive advantage, we must communicate with one another openly and honestly, assist each other in time of need, and vigorously support the team-building effort.

From the start, aggressive thinking and risk taking have been at the heart of our success. We must constantly practice and encourage these qualities to secure our future. We must feel free to honestly disagree with one another while knowing when to treat mistakes as learning opportunities. In our competitive environment, creative risk-taking can net us huge rewards.

We will continue to maintain our reputation for excellence while ensuring our levels of profitability, as we look for creative ways to deliver the best programming and services within cost-effective practices.

As an organization, we will strive to abide by these Values. We believe that by embracing them, our EMPLOYEES will be enriched, our CUSTOMERS will be better served, we will have a positive impact on our COMMUNITY, and our SHAREHOLDERS will enjoy a healthy return on their investment.

petitors' and that exceeds your customers' expectations. And by writing it down, you increase your commitment.

Institutional Service Attitude. Many media organizations have a culture, an attitude about providing excellent service, that is inculcated throughout the organization. Time, Inc., Condé Nast, and some broadcast and cable television networks are examples of these. Some retailers, such as Nordstrom and Stu Leonard's grocery stores, are widely acclaimed for their outrageous service. Wal-Mart is famous for having greeters at the doors who pleasantly welcome shoppers. As Sam Walton said, "The way you treat your associates is the way they will treat customers." Unfortunately, the majority of media organizations have neither an institutional service attitude nor a management that treats salespeople the way they want salespeople to treat customers.

What do you do if you work in a media company that does not have an institutional service attitude but practices the do-as-I-say-not-as-I-do, get-the-order-regardless style of management? Write a service-oriented personal sales mission statement and vow never to treat your customers as management treats you. You cannot change corporate culture or attitude, but you can change your own culture and attitude. Help yourself to change your attitude and remind yourself of your commitment to outrageous service by pasting Sam Walton's Rule #8 (in Exhibit 13.2) over your desk. It is also available on www.mediaselling.us so you can download it and print it out.

Exhibit 13.2 Sam Walton's Rule #8	Exceed your customer's expectations. If you do, they'll come back over and over. Give them what they want—and a little more. Let them know you appreciate them. Make good on all your mistakes, and don't make excuses—apologize. Stand behind everything you do. "Satisfaction guaranteed" will make all the difference.[1]

Service Standards and Policies.   Some companies have service standards and policies that are based on a customer-oriented approach such as Stu Leonard's, "Our Policy: Rule 1: The customer is always right! Rule 2: If the customer is ever wrong, re-read rule 1."[3] If your company does not have written standards, guidelines, or policies for service, use the Servicing Checklist in Table 13.1 (also available on www.mediaselling.us) as your personal guideline for service.

Table 13.1
Servicing Checklist

1. Ask customers what they want.	Ask what service they would consider perfect.
2. Ask customers what competitors do.	Ask which competitors are best at servicing and what they do that is so good. Use the answer as a benchmark and deliver better service.
3. Set servicing objectives.	After you discover what your customers' expectations are, set specific objectives for giving outrageous service.
4. Always say "thank you."	As soon as you get an order, compliment your customers on their good judgment, thank the person who gave you the order, and, of course, leave quickly. When you return to the office, send a brief handwritten note saying "thank you" again. Handwritten notes are much more personal than e-mails.
5. Review your account list regularly.	Some salespeople review their account list every three days. Do not let a week go by that you do not review all the accounts on your list. Do not rely on your memory because you will forget to call on the grumps and over-call on the sweetie pies.
6. Pre-sell.	Servicing is selling, so always take the opportunity to sell a new benefit or advantage. Your pre-selling will serve you particularly well when a customer or buyer is under pressure to make a buy in a hurry.
7. Make copy, idea, and schedule improvement calls.	In situations where advertising copy can be changed easily, as in medium- and small-market radio, make a copy call, suggest a commercial copy be revised, and recommend a new angle. This recommendation can be welcome in situations where a client has been running the same piece of copy over and over again for months and may be boring everyone, especially the listeners. Furthermore, poor copy is often the cause of poor results for a client. Keep on top of how customers are doing. Is the advertising creating traffic, sales, or other results? If not, is it the copy? Is it the schedule? Change both if necessary, but do not hide your head in the sand and just hope for things to improve. Do something to help your customer. Improvements in schedules, such as moving spots to a new time slot (for example, from daytime to early fringe in television), often allow customers to reach a new audience. Making an unsolicited improvement for your customers can be a wonderful relationship builder. This service should be used rarely (on an occasional and random basis), though, or customers come to expect it.
8. Handle complaints immediately and honestly.	Fast response to client complaints is a must. If your medium has made an error of some kind, customers are probably upset; do not add fuel to the fire with a slow response. If you have made an error, admit it, apologize, and set about correcting the situation immediately. Problems tend to make customers impatient, so do not put them off. Give them status reports if a complaint takes longer than a day or two to be resolved. Do not allow clients to think you have let it slip your mind. Be quick to admit your own errors. If clients have to tell you first, you lose some trust. If you tell them first, you maintain your credibility. Also, if you

---

tell customers first, you are more in control of the proposed solution. For example, if the reproduction of a client's newspaper ad is streaked and muddy, call the client immediately and offer a suitable make-good. Your chances of getting approval are much greater with this method than if a customer calls you.

9. Ask for referrals. There is no better endorsement of you and your medium than a thrilled customer. After you are assured that customers are delighted with their campaign and their results, ask them to refer you to someone else for whom you might be able to solve some advertising problems.

10. Develop case studies. Case studies are more effective than client success letters. Case studies can give specific details on how you solved marketing and advertising problems. Case studies can be used to demonstrate how an organization can marshal its resources and expertise to help customers achieve their specific marketing objectives. In addition, if you develop good advertising success case studies, you will hone your skills of defining and solving advertising problems—the perfect solution-selling approach. Finally, if you develop a case study with current customers, you will find that you will not only cement your relationship with those customers but also that you will come up with additional ideas for them. See "How to Write an Advertising Success Case Study" in Appendix C and on www.mediaselling.us.

11. Ask for feedback. Third-party surveys are best, customer polling by management is next best. If you cannot get either of these, then always ask customers, "How am I doing? Is there anything I could do to give you better service?"

12. Adjust and improve. When you get feedback, use it to adjust your service approach and improve your service until it is outrageous.

Service Tracking and Measurement Systems. Most companies that depend on service for their main income have extensive service tracking and measurement systems. Some media companies have Sales Force Automation (SFA) software programs that track sales calls, including service calls. Management rarely examines these tracking reports, especially those which track service calls, except in some large, national media companies. And when media sales managers peruse call reports, they are usually more interested in the quantity rather than quality. Typically, media salespeople must develop their own system for tracking, measuring, and evaluating all calls, including service calls. These systems will be covered in Chapter 28.

Service Feedback and Reward Systems. If you set servicing standards and goals and attempt to carry them out, how do you know if your customers believe you are providing the best service? You must have a feedback system. You can ask on a regular basis, "How am I doing?", but you will rarely get a candid answer because most people do not like to tell others that they are not doing well. The typical answer to the how-am-I-doing question is, "Fine," which does not give you much useful data. Many companies, including IBM and some premium automobile dealers, have third-party research organizations conduct customer satisfaction surveys immediately after a service encounter or on a regular basis with on-going customers. Some national media companies and a few local ones conduct yearly, third-party customer satisfaction surveys which give invaluable feedback to management about the level of service they provide so they can correct problems and learn what their competitors are doing right and wrong.

If your company does not conduct third-party customer satisfaction surveys at least once a year, then you should encourage your sales manager or ad director to conduct such a survey personally and informally on all of your accounts to see how you, your company, and your competitors are doing. If all else fails, you might consider sending out a survey yourself under the name of a fictitious research company and to a sample of at least 100 customers and agencies (fewer than 100 will give you an unreliable sample because your return rate will probably be around 20 percent). Include a self-addressed return envelope with postage included. The address to which the survey will be returned is the fictitious company's mail box number, which you have rented. This process will ensure you remain anonymous and will give you invaluable feedback. Be prepared for the worst—that you and your management might not be perceived to be the best. It takes courage to find out and face up to your weaknesses. You will find a sample Customer Satisfaction Survey in Appendix B and on www.mediaselling.us in case you want to do one. Make sure you get your sales manager or ad director's approval. If they ask you not to send out a survey, do not send one out; you do not want your management to think you are trying to make them look bad.

More and more global companies have added an incentive payment to their sales compensation plans based on customer satisfaction ratings; 35 percent of IBM's incentive package is based on customer satisfaction. Media companies have generally lagged behind this trend and, unfortunately, few of them include rewards for excellent customer service. However, you can institute your own reward system—a high percentage of renewals at increased rates from raving fans.

Test Yourself

1. What is the purpose of selling?
2. What do customers require? (Hint: Three words.)
3. What step of selling does the renewal cycle eliminate?
4. What is the first rule of servicing?
5. Give two reasons for finding out what kind of service your competitors give.

Project

Project #1: If you are not a media salesperson, contact a local advertising agency media buyer or executive and ask if they would complete a customer satisfaction survey. If you get approval, customize the Customer Satisfaction Survey in Appendix B or on www.mediaselling.us appropriately for your market, make an appointment, and fill out the survey along with the agency person. Analyze the survey and see what the importance of rates and ratings are in your market.

Project #2: If you are a media salesperson, write a mission statement for yourself that includes exceeding your customers' service expectations.

References

Ken Blanchard and Sheldon Bowles. 1993. *Raving Fans*. New York: William Morrow.
Thomas J. Peters and Robert H. Waterman, Jr. 1982. *In Search of Excellence*. New York: Harper & Row.

Endnotes

1. Ken Blanchard and Sheldon Bowles. 1993. *Raving Fans*. New York: William Morrow.
2. Ibid.
3. www.chartcourse.com/articlegoodservice.html

Part III

Knowledge

Chapter 14 Business and Finance

By William Redpath

Accounting Systems

Once a deal for the sale of advertising time is struck and the contract signed, data from that sale is input into a medium's operations, production, or traffic system, depending on the medium. Data flows from these systems into the organization's accounting system. The importance of the proper handling of insertion orders, or sales orders, scheduling of advertising, and monitoring the pace of sales and unsold inventory or space cannot be overstated, for a medium's financial health is at stake. All media organizations must comply with legal requirements such as reporting for tax purposes, or in publicly traded companies for annual reports, and last, but not least, for the career health of sales managers and salespeople.

I know of a television station sales manager who was dismissed after the station ran three Public Service Announcements (PSAs) during local commercial availabilities in a Super Bowl telecast. Unsurprisingly, the station's general manager was watching and was less than amused.

Computers have revolutionized operations, production, and traffic systems. Charles Warner remembers working at radio stations during the 1970s where traffic was handled manually using long, thin cardboard-like strips with advertisers' names and commercial lengths typed on them which were then inserted in chronological order into metal holders. Once the metal holder was filled it was photocopied; the result was a log listing the programs to be aired and the commercials to be aired in them.

Today's systems and the reports they generate make that system look barbaric. Not only do current computerized systems manage data, they analyze it to help management maximize revenue. Revenue management, the application of mathematical and analytical techniques to set prices to maximize revenue on every order, began to be applied in the late 1970s. Revenue management was first applied in industries with inventories that expired with the passage of time, such as airline seats or hotel rooms—much like radio and television inventory. Yield management is considered a branch of revenue management and has been used in the airline industry since the 1970s but is now used in many others, including broadcasting and cable.

A number of companies offer software that integrates the operations of their traffic, production, and financial reporting systems, and also includes revenue management or yield management applications. However, it is my observation and belief that, while revenue management software is now being used more, commercial inventory and pricing analyses are still mostly being done manually by sales management at media companies.

Standard these days are comprehensive data systems that interconnect traffic and operations and the accounting or business office. An accounting system supports all of the other departments of an organization, including sales, just as accounts receivable supports billing of advertising and the collection of receivables due.

The importance of accounting should be obvious. While many people get involved in the media for reasons other than the bottom line, media companies, like any other business enterprise, must earn profits in order to survive. The reason for sales is to bring in the revenue that makes profitability possible. Without accounting, one wouldn't know if the quest for profitability were successful.

Financial Reports

While some small media companies may report their historical financial performance using cash basis accounting, the vast majority, including all that have to report their financial results to government agencies—such as publicly traded companies or financial institutions to which these companies are indebted—use Generally Accepted Accounting Principles (GAAP). While cash basis accounting is acceptable but not mandatory for tax reporting purposes, it is unacceptable for financial reporting purposes.

GAAP are set by the Financial Accounting Standards Board (FASB), a private organization based in Norwalk, CT. GAAP change over time with several new accounting principles issued each year, on average.

GAAP mandates use of accrual accounting, which means that revenues must be recognized when actually earned—in the case of the media, when advertising runs—not when cash is collected. Expenses are recorded when services or goods are used, not when they are paid for.

The general ledger, which lists all accounts in an accounting system, feeds into the financial statements. A complete set of financial statements will include a balance sheet, sometimes referred to as a statement of financial position, an income statement, a statement of cash flows, and a statement of stockholders'—or partners' or members'—equity. Because of its relative unimportance to having a basic understanding of how businesses operate on the financial side, I will not address the statement of stockholders' equity.

Balance Sheet

Figure 14.1 shows an example of a balance sheet. This is the balance sheet for Regent Communications, Inc., a publicly traded radio company, for their 2000 and 2001 fiscal years.

A balance sheet is always a financial snapshot at a single point in time. On a balance sheet, assets always equal the sum of liabilities and owners', or shareholders', equity. If that doesn't make sense offhand, think of it this way. If you have something—an asset—either someone else owns it, and thus, it is a liability, or you own it, and, thus, it becomes equity.

Assets are listed at the top of the balance sheet in Figure 14.1 and liabilities and owners' equity are on bottom. Assets start with Current Assets, which include Cash and Cash Equivalents, which are stable value instruments with a maturity date less than 90 days into the future.

Accounts Receivable are a current asset, as are Prepaid Expenses, assuming the service that was prepaid will be used within one year. Assets are also not supposed to be stated at more than their net realizable value. Therefore, a reserve needs to be estimated for Accounts Receivable that are not likely to be collected.

Figure 14.1
An example balance sheet.

REGENT COMMUNICATIONS, INC.
CONSOLIDATED BALANCE SHEETS
(in thousands, except per share amounts)

	December 31, 2001	2000
ASSETS		
Current Assets:		
Cash and cash equivalents	$1,765	$778
Accounts receivable, net of allowance of $719 and		
$403 at December 31, 2001 and 2000, respectively	9,772	10,639
Other current assets	642	595
Total current assets	12,179	12,012
Property and equipment, net	25,817	20,716
Intangible assets, net	266,420	217,897
Other assets, net	1,940	2,108
Total assets	$306,356	$252,733
LIABILITIES AND STOCKHOLDERS' EQUITY		
Current liabilities:		
Accounts payable	$2,044	$1,672
Accrued compensation	1,000	932
Other current liabilities	3,010	2,298
Total current liabilities	6,054	4,902
Long-term debt, less current portion	87,019	45,010
Other long-term liabilities	75	84
Deferred taxes	4,870	4,317
Total liabilities	98,018	54,313
Stockholders' equity:		
Common stock	369	352
Treasury shares	(6,757)	(7,063)
Additional paid-in capital	270,694	259,386
Retained deficit	(55,968)	(54,255)
Total stockholders' equity	208,338	198,420
Total liabilities and stockholders' equity	$306,356	$252,733

While inventory is certainly a term used in media selling, it is not inventory in the usual sense of the term (i.e., merchandise currently owned by a retailer that is for sale) in the current assets section of a balance sheet. When inventory is accounted for on a balance sheet, it is usually accounted for using the FIFO (First In, First Out) or the LIFO (Last In, First Out) method in terms of recognizing which items to expense and which to retain in inventory. Inventory accounting is usually not an issue for businesses in non-inflationary times.

Long-Term Assets are those that are expected to be used over a period longer than one year, and they usually start with Property, Plant, and Equipment (PP&E), also known as tangible assets. PP&E is stated as cost less depreciation and amortization over the course of its life. Over the lives of tangible assets, depreciation and amortization systematically reduce the assets' net values. Land is not depreciated for financial reporting nor tax purposes because it is not a depreciating asset such as printing presses, for example, which wear out. Land doesn't wear out and need to be replaced.

Sometimes companies list intangible assets as long-term, non-current assets. In the media industries, the most valuable intangible assets include FCC licenses, cable franchises, network affiliation agreements, and customer mailing and subscriber lists.

Program rights are a major intangible asset category for television companies. As with PP&E, program rights are booked when they are purchased and amortized as they are used, when the programs are aired.

Intangible assets are recognized, or booked, only if they are acquired alone or as part of a going-concern business. Self-created intangible assets are not booked if they are developed internally. That is, if a salesperson develops a relationship with a particular advertiser or advertising agency that leads to revenue, that is not recognized as an asset on the books of the station. There can be many valuable self-created intangible assets with a company, but they are never explicitly recognized on the balance sheet. This is part of the tenet of conservatism of financial statements, which will be addressed later in this chapter.

After intangible assets are acquired, they are amortized, almost without exception, in a straight line over 15 years for tax purposes. For financial reporting purposes, intangible assets that have a finite life are amortized (decreased in value), with that amount recognized as an expense on the income statement, year by year, over the useful life of the assets. Intangible assets that have an indefinite life are not amortized but are reviewed each year to ensure their value on the financial statements, also known as book value or carrying value, is not greater than their fair value. If the asset's fair value is less than its book value, its book value must be reduced to be equal to its fair value, with the difference recognized as an expense on the income statement in that year.

Other Assets are other long-term assets that may have significant value, sometimes well above their book value. I once heard a business appraiser at a valuation conference state that he nearly signed a valuation report valuing the equity of a closely-held corporation when it dawned on him to inquire about what was included in the Other Assets of that corporation. The book value of Other Assets was quite low and the assets, therefore, appeared minor in nature at first glance. What he learned was that it was Wal-Mart stock that had been acquired many years earlier. In the interim, the stock had appreciated many times over, so his valuation would have been wrong if he had just assumed that the book value of Other Assets was the fair market value of Other Assets.

Historical Cost and Net Realizable Value are used in financial statements because of conservatism in historical financial statements. With the exception of certain marketable securities, assets are booked at cost and never increased in book value, even if they increase in fair market value. Conservatism is supposed to be an essential tenet of financial statements, even though one might not know it from recent financial scandals involving major corporations. Conservatism brings greater credibility to financial statements so people using those statements can know that claims made on financial statements are reliable and not overstated.

Looking at the bottom half of the balance sheet in Figure 14.1, Current Liabilities are liabilities such as Accounts Payable or Accrued Expenses, goods or services that have been used but haven't been paid for yet and that are to be paid for in less than one year. That also includes the portion of long-term debt that is payable in less than one year, if any. Current Assets minus Current Liabilities equals Working Capital.

Long-term debt consists of loans, notes, and bonds that have maturity dates more than one year into the future. Program payments to be paid in the future are also listed as liabilities, with payments to be made within the next year listed as current liabilities. Magazines' and newspapers' subscriptions are also considered liabilities because subscribers are owed magazines or newspapers in the future.

The Stockholders' Equity section of the balance sheet is at the bottom of Figure 14.1, and it lists the various types of equity of involved, preferred stock, if any, and various classes of common stock, for example. The book values of some of these items may not even be close to the fair market value of those securities. The book value of shareholders' equity can be negative, but, of course, the market value of an equity security cannot go below zero.

In terms of order of interests to be paid off upon liquidation of a corporation, debt has priority over preferred stock, which has priority over common stock. That is why preferred stock is called preferred, even though returns for holders of common stock have been higher over time. Common stock is the residual, or last, claimant on a liquidated corporation and is, therefore, considered riskier than other securities of a corporation.

Income Statement

An income statement, which can be seen in Figure 14.2, covers a period of time such as one month or one year. Figure 14.2 is the public reported income statements for Regent Communications, Inc. for fiscal years 1999, 2000, and 2001.

In internal financial statements, the income statement style I prefer shows revenue and expense categories down the middle, with the past month's actual results, past month's budget, (with plus or minus variance percentage), and past month's budget for the previous year (with plus or minus variance percentage) on the left. On the right, there should be year-to-date actual results, a year-to-date budget (with plus or minus variance percentage) and a year-to-date budget for the previous year (with plus or minus variance percentage). This style is seen by visiting www.mediaselling.us and clicking on "Chapter 14, Internal Income Statement."

On an income statement, revenues are, of course, listed at the top. Revenues are usually listed by category such as Local, Regional, National, Network Compensation, Political, Trade, Production, and Equipment Leasing.

Subtracted from gross revenues in media industry financial statements are advertising agency commissions and commissions paid to national sales representative firms. This reporting is somewhat incongruous, in my opinion, because advertising agencies are agents of advertisers, while national sales representative firms work for the media companies. Local salespeople also work for local media companies, but their commissions are included in sales department expense, which is an expense that is listed below net revenues. Nevertheless, this has been the standard industry accounting treatment of national sales representative expenses for a long time and there is no known prospect of that changing.

Be careful when looking at reported or estimated market revenues in the media, and in radio and television in particular. You need to know if they include trade revenues or not; generally, they don't but sometimes they do. It is particularly important to know when you are estimating the revenue share of a radio or television station within its market. As with anything else, you don't want to compare apples to oranges.

Expenses are best listed by functional departments in income statements, with a more detailed description of expenses by category within functional departments below.

It is important to know exactly what someone means when they use the term Operating Income. In the media industries, that term is frequently used

**Figure 14.2
An example income
statement.**

REGENT COMMUNICATIONS, INC.
CONSOLIDATED STATEMENTS OF OPERATIONS
(in thousands, except per share amounts)

	Year ended December 31,		
	2001	2000	1999
Gross broadcast revenues	$59,339	$48,324	$25,613
Less agency commissions	5,594	4,217	1,759
Net broadcast revenues	53,745	44,107	23,854
Station operating expenses	38,530	30,173	18,325
Depreciation and amortization	13,436	8,602	3,368
Corporate general and administrative expenses	4,857	4,501	2,773
Operating (loss) income	(3,078)	831	(612)
Interest expense	(3,279)	(4,229)	(5,249)
Gain (loss) on exchange/sale of radio stations	4,444	17,504	(602)
Other (expense) income, net	(465)	860	163
(Loss) income before income taxes and extraordinary items	(2,378)	14,966	(6,300)
Income tax benefit	665	0	0
(Loss) income before extraordinary items	(1,713)	14,966	(6,300)
Extraordinary loss from debt extinguishment, net of taxes	0	(1,114)	(471)
Net (loss) income	(1,713)	13,852	(6,771)
Loss applicable to common shares			
Net (loss) income	(1,713)	13,852	(6,771)
Preferred stock dividend requirements	0	(629)	(5,205)
Preferred stock accretion	0	(26,611)	(17,221)
Loss applicable to common shares	(1,713)	(13,388)	(29,197)
Basic and diluted loss per common share:			
Loss before extraordinary items	($0.05)	($0.39)	($119.69)
Extraordinary items	0.00	(0.03)	(1.96)
Net loss per common share	($0.05)	($0.42)	($121.65)

to mean either Operating Cash Flow (OCF), which is the case most of the time, or Earnings Before Interest, Taxes, Depreciation, and Amortization (EBITDA). However, in financial statements among most non-media businesses, the term Operating Income is synonymous with Earnings Before Interest and Taxes (EBIT). Therefore, depreciation and amortization is treated as an operating expense in the financial statements. If depreciation and amortization expense is not given its own line in the income statement, it will have a separate line in the Statement of Cash Flows. It is a reconciling item between Net Income and Cash from Operating Activities, because it is a non-cash expense. Adding depreciation and amortization expense back to EBIT will give you EBITDA.

To get from EBITDA to OCF, corporate overhead expenses (sometimes called management fees), which are charged, for example, by a corporate headquarters to each of its owned media properties, must be added back. The only expenses that should be deducted from revenues to calculate OCF are a station's operating expenses, excluding corporate management expense and depreciation and amortization expense.

Historically, the most recognized profitability measure in the media industry has been OCF, which is all revenues minus all station operating expenses (including advertising agency commissions and sales commissions). OCF is also defined as EBITDA with corporate expense added back.

It is very important to know what OCF is not, however. It is not a measure of true cash flow in the literal sense of the term. OCF is not a profit measure that is recognized in GAAP and it is not equivalent to Cash Flow from Operations that is seen in the Statement of Cash Flows, which is part of a complete set of financial statements.

OCF may be defined differently by different people. Someone I greatly respect defines OCF without including trade revenues or trade expenses. Including them in calculating OCF may change OCF in a given year due to timing differences of revenue and expense recognition, but inclusion of trade revenues and trade expenses is part of GAAP.

There are other problems associated with OCF and EBITDA, so they should definitely not be used as the only measure of earnings of business. Among the problems is that EBITDA and OCF never take into account either depreciation or amortization of a business's assets, capital expenditures for new equipment, or expenditures for purchases of other businesses. EBITDA and OCF also ignore additions to working capital and overstate cash flow in periods when growth of working capital is necessary to sustain a business and nurture its growth.

In analyzing media company financial statements, besides knowing whether they are cash- or accrual-basis financial statements, one should know how trade revenue is treated. In the media industries, advertising time is frequently traded not for cash, but for goods or services. In television, sometimes programs are purchased for a station with no cash outlay, but the program supplier gets to keep a certain number of commercial availabilities to sell to local advertisers within the program. Other radio or television stations may trade the use of a new car for the general manager in return for commercials on the station, without any cash actually changing hands. Financial Accounting Standard (FAS) 63 states that all trade and barter revenue should be recorded at the estimated value of the goods or services received. FAS 63 also states that, as with cash transactions, trade revenue is recognized when earned and trade expense is recognized when a good or service is used. If goods or services are received before commercials are aired, a liability for the advertising must be recognized until the commercial is aired. If the commercial is broadcast before the goods or services are received, an asset must be recognized until the goods or services are used by the station.

Frequently in these financial statements, trade revenues and expenses are listed separately, below the line, that is below the determination of OCF and EBITDA on the income statement. Some income statements will list trade revenues among the gross revenues and list trade expenses among the regular operating expenses. Still other income statements, although a small minority, will make no distinction between cash and trade revenues on the income statement, simply including trade revenues with cash revenues in the appropriate category of gross revenues. Some financial statements (although not GAAP-compliant) don't recognize trade revenues and trade expenses at all. Because trade revenues and expenses can be much higher in the media industry than in any other kinds of businesses, it is important to know how they are accounted for.

Even though its seems obvious that trade involves no exchange of cash, it is important that the terms of trade deals struck by stations with various advertisers are understood by station executives. I know of a television station program director who did not use all of a trade with a local department store. The trade was advertising time in exchange for clothing for news anchors and other on-air personnel. There was a time expiration on the clothing side of the trade. When asked why some of the trade credit went unused, the program director said, "I thought I was saving the station money." Instead, the station was shortchanged some clothing. If you're in charge of affecting either side of a trade deal, be sure you know all the parameters of the deal, as well as how the accounting for the trade is to be handled.

Because trade deals can be easily abused (e.g., merchandise received in a trade can be stolen or services can be diverted to personal, rather than business, use), internal management controls must be in place in the approval process and to ensure the trade deals are implemented and executed properly.

There is a lot of chatter and slang used about margins, profit margins, or cash flow margins, especially in the media industry. A margin is a percentage, or a ratio, with a numerator and denominator. If you don't know for sure what the numerator and denominator are, and I mean not what the numbers are specifically but what they represent, ask. Is the ratio OCF divided by gross revenues or something else? What you may find is that the person dispensing the margin information does not know what constitutes the ratio.

Statement of Cash Flows

The Statement of Cash Flows, as seen in Figure 14.3, is a very important financial statement because this shows the actual cash flows of a business entity. Remember, the term Operating Cash Flow is a misnomer and should not be relied upon for flows of actual cash.

The Statement of Cash Flows is divided into three sections: Cash Flows from Operating Activities, Cash Flows from Investing Activities, and Cash Flows from Financing Activities. Operating Activities are the operation of the business; Investing Activities include things such as capital expenditures; Financing Activities include the raising of cash through the sale of debt and equity securities, or the buyback of those securities, interest payments and dividend payments. It is in the Statement of Cash Flows that one really sees the true cash flows in a business or an entity that owns a business. Cash, after all, is the true lifeblood of a business. Regardless of other assets, revenues, or profitability, if a business doesn't have cash, or cannot raise cash, it cannot function.

One of the most important parts of a full set of financial statements is the footnotes. You should be able to read and understand footnotes because they amplify and elucidate other portions of the financial statements. If you don't understand what you read in financial footnotes, ask the entity's management or their investor relations department. Don't be satisfied with vague explanations that don't make complete sense. Any questions about the financial statements, including the footnotes, should be answered clearly and forthrightly for you, assuming you have a right to know or a need to know—for example, if you are a debt or equity holder. If you are a salesperson looking at financial statements to see if a company is creditworthy or has enough money to be a good prospect, you can ask someone in your own business or accounting department, or ask your company's accounting or auditing firm to help you.

Figure 14.3
An example state-
ment of cash flows.

REGENT COMMUNICATIONS, INC.
CONSOLIDATED STATEMENTS OF CASH FLOWS
(in thousands)

	Year ended December 31,		
	2001	2000	1999
Cash flows from operating activities:			
Net (loss) income	($1,713)	$13,852	($6,771)
Adjustments to reconcile net (loss) to net cash provided by (used in) operating activities:			
Depreciation and amortization	13,436	8,602	3,368
Provision for doubtful accounts	822	725	390
Non-cash interest expense	283	1,579	1,576
Non-cash charge for debt extinguishments	0	1,114	471
Non-cash charge for compensation	491	0	0
(Gain) loss on sale of radio stations	(4,444)	(17,504)	477
Loss on sale of fixed assets and other	160	0	0
Changes in operating assets and liabilities, net of acquisitions:			
Accounts receivable	(328)	(6,249)	(1,481)
Other assets	(107)	(358)	(36)
Current and long-term liabilities	(803)	(2,940)	(372)
Deferred taxes	553	4,317	0
	8,350	3,138	(2,378)
Cash flows from investing activities:			
Acquisitions of radio stations, net of cash acquired, and escrow deposits on pending acquisitions:	(63,450)	(148,940)	(27,533)
Capital expenditures	(3,161)	(1,719)	(1,978)
Net proceeds from sale of radio stations	13,393	2,000	13,999
Proceeds from sale of fixed assets	27	0	0
	(53,191)	(148,659)	(15,512)
Cash flows from financing activities:			
Proceeds from issuance of redeemable convertible preferred stock	0	0	41,754
Proceeds from issuance of common stock	4,068	156,939	0
Proceeds from long-term debt	60,500	48,500	16,500
Principal payments on long-term debt	(18,491)	(28,824)	(26,704)
Payment of notes payable	0	0	(7,500)
Payment for deferred financing costs	0	(1,904)	(427)
Payment of issuance costs	(249)	(11,606)	(2,802)
Treasury stock purchases	0	(7,063)	0
Dividends paid on all series of preferred stock	0	(8,153)	0
Redemption of Series B preferred stock	0	(5,000)	0
	45,828	142,889	20,821
Net increase (decrease) in cash and cash equivalents	987	(2,632)	2,931
Cash and cash equivalents at beginning of period	778	3,410	479
Cash and cash equivalents at end of period	$1,765	$778	$3,410

Financial Information

Historical financial information on all companies that file reports with the Securities and Exchange Commission (SEC) can be found through numerous online services, and at www.sec.gov.

Many radio and television stations voluntarily participate in market revenue compilations. In many, but not all, radio and television markets, an accounting firm or some other entity is hired to survey all the radio or television stations in that market regarding their respective revenues. The survey taker keeps each station's submission confidential, but adds the data for all stations together and then sends the market totals to every station, along with the overall rank number for that station and its rank in various revenue categories. This information illuminates the market revenue situation for everyone and allows management to see objectively how their station(s) stack up versus intramarket competition. In addition, the National Association of Broadcasters (NAB) publishes and sells an annual book on television market revenues for many television markets.

Other historical broadcasting data, including radio and television market revenues, are estimated and published by several firms. BIA Financial Network, Inc. (www.bia.com) publishes several reference books on the radio and television industries, including a unique software reference entitled *Media Access Pro*. BIA plans to publish reference books and software on other media and telecommunications industries in the future.

Each year *Advertising Age* magazine publishes magazine revenue, number of advertising pages sold, and circulation for the top 300 magazines; the information can be found at www.adage.com.

Types of Financial Statements

Financial statements are always the product of management, but they are compiled, reviewed, or opined on by outside accountants. There are essentially four types of financial statements:

1. Internal financial statements. These statements, produced by management, are usually done on an accrual basis but are sometimes done on a cash basis, particularly in smaller companies.
2. Compiled financial statements. These financial statements are developed by an outside accountant or accounting firm based on information supplied by a client. The data is accepted essentially without review or questioning by the outside accountant.
3. Reviewed financial statements. These are financial statements for which an accountant performs some analytical and review procedures, trying to identify major problems that need correction, if any. These procedures are far less than those employed in a full audit.
4. Audited financial statements. This is a full set of financial statements, including footnotes, that includes an audit opinion from an outside, independent accounting firm on whether the financial statements are in accordance with GAAP. Audits are performed in accordance with Generally Accepted Auditing Standards (GAAS). Audited financial statements are mandated by the SEC for any annual financial statements that are filed with the SEC. Companies that have any publicly traded debt or equity must file with the SEC, except for certain very small companies. Also, it is a standard covenant in loan agreements that the debtor give annual audited financial statements to the creditor as long as the loan is outstanding. Business partners or shareholders in closely-held companies sometimes demand audited financial statements as a condition of their investment.

Test Yourself

1. What is the full name of the set of accounting rules used in the United States?
2. Does GAAP mandate cash or accrual accounting?
3. What are the three types of financial statements reviewed in this chapter?
4. What two elements are added together to equal assets?

5. Gross revenues minus what two items equal net revenues?
6. Name some major intangible assets for media companies.
7. What is the difference between OCF and EBITDA?
8. What is the difference between EBITDA and EBIT?
9. What is the difference between operating income (as usually defined in the media industries) and operating income in most other industries?
10. Why is the term "Operating Cash Flow" a misnomer?
11. Is trade revenue and trade expense included in revenues and expenses in GAAP?
12. What are the three sections of the Statement of Cash Flows?
13. What are the four types of financial statements?

Project

Go to the Web site of Viacom at www.viacom.com. Click on the "Shareholder Info" link and then on the "Revenue, EBITDA, and Operating Income" link. Look at the difference between EBITDA and Operating Income. Explain these differences.

Resources

www.adage.com
www.bia.com
www.hoovers.com
www.kagan.com
www.nab.org
www.sec.gov
www.mediaselling.us

15 Marketing

By Tim Larson and Ken Foster

Media salespeople can no longer think of themselves exclusively as print, broadcast, cable, or Internet sales professionals. They are media representatives or marketing communicators, who, although they may work in a specific medium, must have the knowledge and ability to integrate competing media and the 5 Ps of marketing—product, price, promotion, place, and post-purchase service—in order to find, satisfy, and retain customers while making a profit for those customers and themselves.

It is important to understand that each of the 5 Ps in the marketing mix communicate, not just the marketing promotion P represented by such tactics as advertising, public relations, sales promotion, event marketing, the Internet, and personal selling. As a media salesperson primarily focused on the marketing promotion P, you still need to know which of the other 5 Ps need attention when serving a customer and understand that marketing promotion tactics are not always exclusively the answer to a client's marketing problems.

The McDonald's Corporation represents an example in which marketing promotion (which includes advertising) was not the answer to its marketing problem. In 2003, McDonald's was facing a crippling decline in revenue growth and profit for the first time in four decades. Top executives were called together with the creative managers of ten global advertising agencies, and the group was charged with creating some new advertising ideas. "A great brand like McDonald's deserves great advertising," said McDonald's global chief marketing officer. "If you come with a great idea, you'll have the chance to see it adopted globally."[1] This quote makes clear that executives at McDonald's saw the company's problem as primarily involving advertising.

Several marketing experts strongly took issue with that supposition, saying that McDonald's had to reassess its whole business model and positioning, that the company's problem was not anchored in its advertising, and better advertising was not the solution. Its problem was its product, a product that faced considerable consumer dissatisfaction. In other words, the problem was not with the *promotion* P but with the *product* P, not with the sizzle but with the steak.

If you are the media salesperson calling on McDonald's or on any other client experiencing a similar marketing problem, you should be knowledgeable enough about the 5 Ps and the marketing mix to advise your customers that advertising cannot increase the customer's bottom line if the product itself is the problem. To reiterate, resist the natural urge to immediately go tactical with your own advertising ideas for a client when the problem lies with one of the remaining 4 Ps of the marketing mix.

Throughout this chapter, we use the IMC acronym, which stands for Integrated Marketing Communications. IMC is a customer-focused, data-driven, and technology-facilitated marketing communications process easily integrated with the AESKOPP sales concept. IMC also provides a universal framework for coaching, planning, and evaluating sales thinking and action.

In the interest of efficiency, the word *product* is used broadly in this chapter, referring to a service, an idea, a destination, an institution, an organization, an individual (such as a politician running for office), or anything else that can, generally speaking, be marketed.[2]

Integrated Marketing Communication Planning Model

In today's business-to-business (B2B) or business-to-customer (B2C) marketplace, it is important to use IMC strategies to manage profitable relationships. Relationship management involves knowing your customers and your customers' customers. Table 15.1 shows an IMC planning model, which synthesizes the Northwestern University IMC model and marketing author M. Joseph Sirgy's systems approach. It provides a template for you to plan, audit, and monitor a client's marketing communications mix and encourages relationship building up and down the marketing chain.

Each of the seven parts of the IMC planning model in Table 15.1 is discussed below.

Database

The key insight into the database is: information is power and the database empowers you as a media salesperson. IMC planning begins with research. In order to develop and strengthen a relationship with your customers, you must first collect data on your customers' customers. Data are collected in at least four areas: purchase behavior, demographic, psychographic, and category/brand networking, with purchase behavior considered the most useful. This is because conventional wisdom and practice indicate that the best predictor of a future purchase is a past purchase, both of which are quantifiable.

It has always been relatively easy to capture purchase information in business-to-business markets, but now it is nearly as easy in such business-to-customer markets as groceries, where mass-produced goods are scanned to keep track of purchases made by large numbers of individual buyers over a long period of time. Demographic, psychographic, and brand/category data are, in turn, collected to better inform the purchase behavior data.

A database is designed to meet the media client's marketing requirements. There is not one type of database that fits all, but, generally, databases fall into one of three overlapping categories.[3]

1. Historical Data Management System. This involves passive data collection, usually including name, address, lead/sales activity, and promotion effort information. These data are used to develop lead and direct marketing lists. This is the simplest database form, and one not very useful by itself to a media salesperson.
2. Marketing Intelligence Database. This data gathering system builds on the historical system by adding purchase data information that allows the marketer to make detailed marketing decisions about future customer purchasing behavior. A media salesperson could productively use this type of database, but the next type may be superior.

Table 15.1
Integrated Marketing Communications Planning Model

DATABASE	Purchase History	Demographics	Psychographics	Category Network

SEGMENTATION/ CLASSIFICATION/ POSITIONING	•Differentiation or positioning by:
	  •Cost leadership
	  •Low price
	  •Product
	  •Promotion
	  •Price
	  •Place
	  •Service
			•Focus Related/Segmentation by:
			  •Customer benefit/problem
			  •Use or application
			  •User or customer image
			  •B2C
			  •B2B	

CONTACT MANAGEMENT	Manage all information-bearing experiences a customer or prospect has with the brand, the product category, or the market that relates to the marketer's product or service.			
STRATEGIES, OBJECTIVES AND TACTICS	See Figure 15.1 for a systems approach to analyzing marketing strategies and corresponding objectives. See Figure 15.3 for applicable marketing communications tactics and their relative effectiveness in achieving steps in the selling process.			
MARKETING COMMUNICATIONS MIX (5Ps)	Product Price Promotion Post-Purchase Service Place/Distribution			
MARKETING COMMUNICATIONS TACTICS	Mass Media Advertising Direct Marketing Sales Promotion Public Relations Event Marketing Internet Word-of-Mouth (WOM) Personal Selling Others			
MONITORING AND CONTROL	Evaluated from the viewpoint of the media representative, any negative deviations from performance objectives require reassessment and adjustment.			

Sources: Adapted from Don E. Schultz, Stanley I. Tannenbaum, and Robert F. Lauterborn, 1995; M. Joseph Sirgy, 1998.

3. Integrated Business Resource. This type of database drives your customer's business. All customer information sources and functions are integrated, and every aspect of the business is involved. This type of database provides your customers with valuable information about their businesses and drives brand value by helping customers manage relationships, including consumer relationships.

Technology has made database management possible, but there are still a variety of means for managing a database that ranges from low-tech to high-tech. On a small scale, a business card file of historical data is a good start for a database, but should probably be enhanced with additional behavioral information. The larger the list is, the more likely the need for technology to track the information.

Whatever system you use, a database helps you divide your customers' customers into meaningful segments and gives you specific information about who to target in order to achieve a profitable return-on-investment (ROI) for your customers' marketing efforts.

Segmentation

The key insight into segmentation is: it is more important to reach the people who count than to count the people you reach. Using meaningful information from the database, you can identify profitable segments through ROI, lifetime-customer-value (LCV), or other purchase behavior analyses. Segments can be identified by using various positioning factors or by using any number of business-to-consumer and business-to-business variables, but the most meaningful segments are derived from purchasing behavior data. Important information about buyers might include quantities purchased, price sensitivity, seller loyalty, amount of service required, and of course, susceptibility to advertising and promotional messages. Using these data, consumers might, for instance, be grouped into such descriptive buying segments as: Programmed Buyer, Relationship Buyer, Bargain Hunter, and The Chiseler.

Of course, you would have to have a critical mass in any one of these segments, but an ROI analysis, for instance, could reveal the most profitable segments. For example, your behavioral analysis might find that The Chiseler segment is very large, but that the buyers in that segment are so price conscious it is not a profitable segment to market to, that it would cost more in advertising and promotion efforts to attract customers in this segment than you could recoup in sales.

You could discover and test any number of purchase behavior segments using an integrated database system. Purchase or buyer behavior segments could be further delineated by customer demographic, psychographic, and category/networking data.

Contact Management

The key insight into contact management is: every contact a consumer has with your customer's product is an important information-bearing experience. The database also is important in this part of the IMC planning process. You identify all the contacts—also called "moments-of-truth"—the consumer has with the product. This gives you a good indication about how to customize messages for each of the consumer segments.

For instance, if you have a customer who is recruiting students to its college, contacts— "moments-of-truth" or information-bearing experiences— might include parents, peers, and school counselors, all of whom may advise or inform a student's choice. Messages to each of these contacts or segments from your college customer would have a one-look-and-feel component—superb education, fun, great professors—but each message would also be customized to satisfy the specific informational needs of each segment. For example, the students get party information, the parents get safety and financial assistance information, and the school counselors get congratulations for directing the students to the college.

Each time you make contact with your customer or your customers' consumers using the mix of the 5 Ps and marketing communications tactics, it is a moment of truth, and you either put money in the brand-equity bank, or you withdraw it, and your relationship (balance) with your customer and your customers' consumers is positively or negatively affected. Inherent in managing contacts is the timing and orchestration of the customized messages you send to each segment. In our college example, orchestration would involve determining which messages to send, to which segments, using what timing, and in what order.

Strategies, Objectives, and Tactics

The key insight into this step is: don't play Alice in Wonderland. If you do not know where you are going and do not have the knowledge to achieve your marketing communications objectives, you are Alice. You may remember in the story that Alice comes to a fork in the road and asks the Cheshire cat which path she should take. The cat asks Alice where she wants to go, and Alice responds that she doesn't know. With a smile, the cat advises her that it makes no difference which path she takes.

Don't be Alice. Before going tactical with your marketing communications, you need to know where you are headed and what you want to accomplish. Remember the McDonald's example at the opening of this chapter. What are your customers' marketing and marketing communications goals and objectives, and what marketing communications mix involving all of the 5 Ps might be employed strategically to achieve them?

In many cases, your clients may not know where they want to go but also may not know where they are. Suppose you ask a frozen yogurt shop, "Who is your target audience?" The customer replies, "Everyone." Clearly the shop does not know where it is or who its customers are. Suppose you ask, "How is your frozen yogurt different from any other frozen yogurt?" The shop owner replies, "Frozen yogurt is frozen yogurt." Again, no niche, positioning, or unique selling proposition has been identified. It is important to know where you are before you decide where you are going.

Marketing Strategies, Objectives, and Tactics.   Figure 15.1 provides a marketing compass to guide you to Alice's tea party and the best mix of marketing strategies, objectives, and tactics for your customers. The model shows that marketing planning involves selecting among three primary strategies: differentiation, cost leadership, and focus.

Concentrating on a unique and valued one of the 5 Ps is referred to as positioning.

Figure 15.1 Marketing strategies and corresponding objectives. (Source: Adapted from Sirgy 1998.)

MARKETING STRATEGIES

Differentiation (Positioning)

- Product
  - Class
  - Attribute
  - Intangibles
  - Competitors
  - Country of Origin
- Promotion
  - Celebrity spokesperson
  - Lifestyle/ Personality

- Place
  - Distributor
    -Tie-ins
    -Location
    -Service
- Price
  - Relative price

- Post Purchase Service
  - Toll free # or Web contact center
- Seamless & uniform customer interaction
- Customize services & communicate

Cost Leadership

- Low Price
  - Conduct pricing research
  - Set price to value level
  - Communicate to target consumer

Focus Related (Segmentation)

- Position by:
  - Customer benefit or problem
  - User or customer image
  - Use or application

- B2C Segmentation
  - Demographics
  - Psychographics
  - Sociocultural
  - Motivational
  - Consumption

- B2B
  - End use
  - Customer size
  - Geographic
  - Motivational
  - Consumption
  - Channel Type

MARKETING OBJECTIVES

·Brand Awareness ·Brand Learning/Association ·Brand Trial/Purchase ·Repeat Purchase ·Brand Attitude

The differentiation or positioning strategy involves a synergy of the 5 P marketing mix (product, price, place, promotion, and post-purchase service), but with emphasis on a single P. Figure 15.1 shows several possible positioning variables for each of the 5 Ps.

Using a cost leadership strategy involves designing an entire marketing campaign around the single marketing mix element of price. Figure 15.1 shows that if positioning by low price is being contemplated, price research must be conducted.

The focus strategy is used when you want to segment by customer benefit or problem, by user or customer image, or by product use or application.

Which of the three strategies you use depends on your client's overall business goals and objectives, the nature of the product, and which combination of the 5 Ps in the marketing mix are of primary concern.

Marketing Communications Strategies, Objectives, and Tactics.   After determining your marketing strategy, objectives, and tactics, you can use the system of analysis in Figure 15.2 to determine the best marketing communications tactical mix to achieve the highest return-on-investment from your advertising and promotion efforts.

There are four marketing communications strategies: informative (thinker), affective (feeler), habit formation (doer), and self-satisfaction (reactor). These

Figure 15.2 Marketing communication strategies, objectives, and corresponding tactics. (Source: Adapted from Sirgy 1998.)

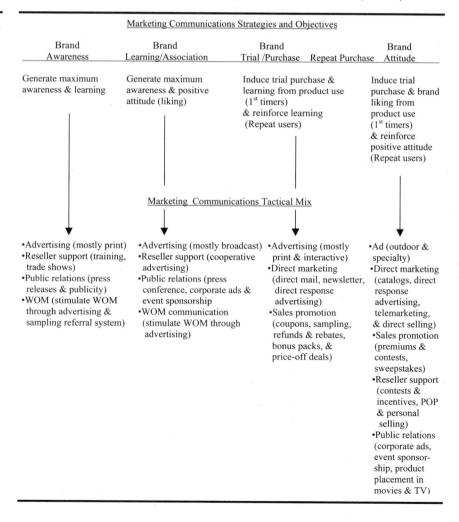

are borrowed from the ubiquitous Foote-Cone-Belding (FCB) advertising planning model. The informative (thinker) strategy is used when you want to educate and inform your client's customers about important costs or benefits and generate maximum awareness and learning. Print and Interactive are good media for this strategy. The affective (feeler) strategy is used when you want to generate maximum awareness and a positive attitude or liking toward your client's branded product. Television and radio are excellent media for this strategy. The habit formation (doer) strategy is used to induce product trials and learning-from-use for first-time buyers, and to reinforce learning for repeat buyers. Sampling promotions are good for this strategy. The self-satisfaction (reactor) strategy is used to reinforce positive attitudes of repeat users. Television, radio, print, Interactive, and outdoor are all good media for this strategy.

The strategic mix of advertising, reseller support, public relations, word of mouth (WOM), direct marketing, point of purchase, sales promotion, and the other marketing communications tactics appropriate for each of the four marketing communications strategies are also shown in Figure 15.2.

Not discussed above is your customer's overall business strategy. It is assumed in using the above marketing and marketing communications models that your customer's goal is to grow their business and that marketing and marketing communications can facilitate that goal. If your customer's overall business goal is to harvest or divest, marketing functions likely are not involved. The objective of a harvest or divest business strategy usually is to maximize profits while minimizing costs. Marketing represents a business expense and takes resources away from this objective. It is important that you clearly identify your customers' overall business goals before you create marketing and marketing communications plans for them.

The Five Ps of the Marketing Communications Mix

The key insight into this step in the marketing communications process is: if you change one, you change them all. If you have ever broken a rack of pool balls, you know you can't move one ball without moving all the others. The same holds true for the marketing mix. Granted, each marketing communications tool and tactic in the mix has intrinsic value, but the value changes in the marketing mix. Change the use-ratio of the tactics and you not only change each one's intrinsic value, but you change the overall communication value of the mix.

The use-ratio of the Five Ps, including marketing communications tactics, known as the marketing mix, varies for each organization. For example, Mrs. Field's, the cookie maker, emphasizes place (distribution) and product in its mix, with very little attention given to promotion or pricing. If you changed the Mrs. Field's use-ratio, you would change the communication value of the entire marketing mix. Mrs. Field's locates its stores in high traffic locations and blows the exhaust of its cookie-cooking ovens into the mall or street to tempt customers. The Five P marketing mix of Mrs. Field's is first and foremost place (location, location, location), then product and, finally, price, with little or no attention given to post-purchase service.

Change that mix and you change everything. For instance, the marketing mix for a typical bank is quite different. A bank also emphasizes location or place, but gives primary consideration to its service, product, pricing and promotion. Change the bank's use-ratio to match the Mrs. Field's mix where distribution is emphasized over the other four Ps, and you may have a run on the bank. Experiment with the marketing communications mix to observe which use-ratio of tactics works best and produces a result greater than the sum of the individual parts.

As was made clear in the McDonald's case at the beginning of this chapter, it is important to remember that all Ps in the marketing communications process communicate, not just the marketing promotion tactics. The following explains this assertion more fully.

Product Communicates

Product lifecycle model. The Product Lifecycle Model (PLC) is grounded in what is called hierarchy-of-effects theory: the PLC principle suggests that every product, service, or idea goes through a series of steps or phases from birth to death, the first being an *introduction* phase. If it survives *introduction*, the product goes through a *growth* phase in which different marketing communications strategies and tactics are implemented. Eventually, the product will *mature* to where still other strategies are required in order to maintain competitiveness. Most products eventually die, but the majority also experience a *decline* phase, in which still other unique strategies apply.[4]

The typical life cycle of a product and the strategies relevant to each phase in the life cycle are shown below. You should note how critical mass media advertising and promotion are in each of the product life cycle phases.

Table 15.2 Product Lifecycle

Introduction	Growth	Maturity	Decline
Raise awareness	Continue awareness campaign	Innovation	Harvest profits
Sell into distribution chain	Relationship sales	Include advertising and promotion	Limit distribution
Target early adopters	Distribution chain coverage	Price to meet competition	Less price sensitivity
Higher price (if new)	Possibly increase advertising and promotion	Line extensions	Less advertising and promotion
Limited distribution	R&D on product innovation		

When a product is first introduced, heavy advertising and promotion efforts are required to keep the product before the public. If a product is successful, then competitors become an issue in the growth phase, and again advertising and promotion are required to differentiate the product from its competition.

Tide detergent, for instance, was introduced in 1948. Since that time it has been marketed as a "new and improved" product every few years in order to elongate its life cycle. So just as in the *introduction* phase, Tide's advertising and promotion reintroduces the "new" Tide product to the marketplace in the *maturity* phase. Only during a product's *decline* phase is advertising less critical. During this last phase, marketers milk the cash cow by cutting expenses related to advertising and promotion. This is done to maintain some profit margin while product demand dwindles.

The diffusion of innovation model. Another marketing model related to how products communicate is Rogers' Diffusion of Innovation Model. Sometimes called the adoption model, this helps you strategize with regard to how consumers adopt new products over a time period.[5] In Rogers' model, only a small segment (2.5 percent) of a target population, labeled *innovators*, is willing to try radically new products. A slightly larger group (13.5 percent), the *early adopters*, lets the innovators experiment for a period of time before they adopt a product, while a two-thirds majority, the *early majority* and the *late majority* of the population (68 percent), represent a critical mass of potential consumers after a product has developed and been branded. Finally, a smaller group (16 percent) of *laggards* is the last segment to adopt a new—maybe at this point old—product.

Your database should contain consumer information telling you where in the Diffusion of Innovation Model consumers reside, helping you to customize messages targeted at the most profitable segments, keeping in mind that the ROI from the people in the *innovator* and *early adopters* segments may be less than the marketing communication expenditures used to attract them. You may nevertheless have to market to these segments, initially by charging higher prices and selling at a loss, in hopes of creating loyal customers when people in these segments move to the *majority* stages of adoption.

To better achieve success, several other general principles are important when introducing a new product or marketing an existing one:

- Heavy and effective advertising and promotion are critical for new brands.
- Besides promoting the brand, effective advertising is also important to promoting the distribution method.
- Effective advertising increases the likelihood of success threefold.
- New products deliver incremental volume for both the manufacturer and the retailer, so the likelihood of co-op advertising and promotion is strong.
- Long-term support is essential: think "*introductory*" for at least two years.
- All products decline; plan for it.

Price Communicates.   As discussed earlier, price in the communications mix has more duties than simply generating revenue for your client. It also communicates. Listed below are some major pricing strategies and how they are likely to be impacted by marketing communications tactics such as mass media advertising. You should be knowledgeable about these strategies in order to advise your clients.

Pricing Strategies

Skimming. Skim the cream from the consumers who can afford a higher price. Lower the price over time. A skimming strategy will use targeted advertising and promotion to reach consumers with high incomes.

Prestige. "You get what you pay for." Set price high to communicate higher quality. Though prestige pricing is not usually advertised, make sure all the other variables of the marketing mix are consistent with a prestige approach. On occasion prestige pricing is advertised to screen nonqualified consumers and to add to the value of the product.

Loss leader. Keep margins low on an item to pull customers into the store. The loss leader approach requires heavy advertising and is very commonly used in the retail business. It is important to integrate in-store signage wherever the loss leader approach is used.

Full-line pricing. Keep margins low on one of your brand products in order to sell the rest of your line.

Volume pricing. Keep prices low to generate more dollar volume rather than dollar margin.

Off-pricing. Communicate the previous price to show savings of the new price.

Odd-pricing. Odd numbers communicate a more real or precise price, lending price some credibility. Volume pricing, off-pricing, and odd pricing also require advertising support.

Penetration. Cover the market with price-oriented product and blitzing promotion. Penetration pricing requires advertising blitz. It is commonly used with a roadblock (when the same slot is purchased on all stations in a market) or other means of obtaining rapid reach.

Competitive pricing. Set prices to match or surpass competition.

Customary pricing. Set prices based on custom; what it has always cost.

Some of your clients may fall into a category of regulated pricing, that is, they do not have control over what the price should be. Colleges and universities are examples: they advertise many of their educational programs and degrees but do not have control of tuition. It is important to ensure that the pricing strategy is consistent with all other variables of the marketing mix. For example as indicated above, if your pricing strategy is prestige, then your promotional material must look and feel prestigious. It makes common sense for all variables of the marketing mix to be consistent with each other all of the time.

Place Communicates.   At first glance, distribution methods may not appear to be associated with advertising and promotion, but it makes sense to consider the marketing communications tactics that can be used at all levels in the distribution process. Simply speaking, distribution means to get the product or service from the marketing organization to the consumer in the B2B and B2C distribution chains.

Your client may be any one of the businesses in the distribution chain—manufacturer, agent, wholesaler or retailer. Each distribution channel has different needs, different relationships with its suppliers and clients, and different laws and rules governing its part in the distribution process. However, each channel partner may be inclined to support advertising and promotion to meet its unique needs. All channel members communicate, not just the retailer. Place communicates and is fertile ground for strategic marketing communications employment.

For some media such as newspapers and broadcasting, it is important to keep in mind that circulation or signal propagation may reach geographic areas that extend beyond the customer's travel range. However, businesses can increase their draw from distant areas if the customers are loyal or are destination purchasers. This is especially true for higher-priced items such as automobiles, furniture, and appliances.

Marketing Promotion Communicates.   Of course, marketing promotion communicates. The possible mix of marketing communications tactics is very broad. However, it is important to know the strengths and weaknesses of each tactic and how each is useful and effective depending on your client's goals and objectives. Figure 15.3 shows how you can employ marketing communications tactics to move the buyer through the five mental steps in the buying process beginning with *Awareness*, followed by progressively more personal tactics: *Interest, Desire,* and *Commitment* to *Action.* This model is known by the AIDCA acronym.[6]

Figure 15.3 AIDCA: Applicable marketing communication tactics and their relative effectiveness in achieving steps in the selling process.

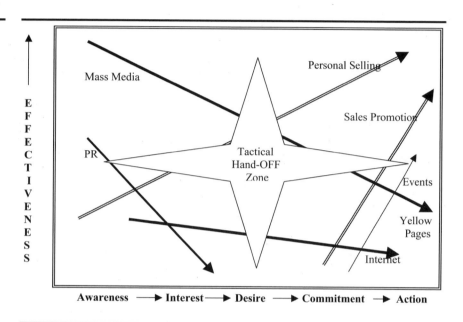

You can see in the AIDCA model that the mass media tactics, with their potentially higher reach, are effective at creating *Awareness* and less effective in creating *Action* (purchase), where more personal tactics are usually needed. On the other hand, note that personal selling, with its fewer contacts and limited reach, is considerably less effective in creating *Awareness*, but more effective in creating *Action*. Several of the other marketing communications tactics and their relative effectiveness in each step are also shown in Figure 15.3. Note that PR helps to create *Awareness* but has little effectiveness as you move toward the *Action* end of the five-mental-step process. Likewise, sales promotion has little effect on the *Awareness* end of the process but is helpful in creating *Action.*

While mass media tactics involve sellers who are looking for buyers, the *yellow pages* involves buyers who are looking for sellers. (When was the last time you browsed the *yellow pages* with no product in mind?) As such, mass media advertising and promotion are used to create *Awareness*, and the *yellow pages* is used to produce behavior more on the *Action* end of the continuum. The effectiveness of event marketing at any AIDCA step depends on the size and purpose of the event.

An important point to be gleaned from Figure 15.3 is that there is a "Tactical Hand-Off Zone" in the AIDCA model. Because no marketing communications tactic is totally effective at every mental step in the buying process, an integrated mix of tactics must be employed. As such, as a media representative you might use mass media tactics to create *Awareness* at the beginning of a schedule or campaign and later hand off the responsibility of creating *Action* (purchase) to more personal tactics, such as sales promotion and personal selling.

The media representative's knowledge of the strengths and weaknesses of each marketing communications tool and tactic and their strategic mix is put to a test in the "Tactical Hand-Off Zone." Some basic knowledge of the effectiveness of each medium, not only the one(s) you sell, will go a long way in helping you develop a relationship with your client and create brand value for your client's product.

Listed below are some common marketing strategies that affect the marketing communications tactical mix:

Seasonality. Seasonal products affect advertising and promotion placement. Though seasonality is often obvious, such as for skis going on sale for winter, there are some products and services that are less apparent. Exactly how far in advance of the buying season media should be placed is product-specific and often debatable. Working with your client, you will know when this strategy is applicable.

Competitive strategies. Some advertisers often run campaigns head to head with competitors. Others choose to fight the competition and "hit them where they ain't."

Market share. To grow market share, you can either steal from the competition or stimulate the entire market to buy more of what you are selling. However, stimulating the entire market may benefit competition as well and is very costly. To steal from the competition requires targeted advertising and an effective message.

Geographic targeting. Marketing that requires geographic targeting, whether national, regional, local, or sub-local, has a direct effect on which marketing communications tactics you will use. For instance, if you are targeting a small geographic area, possibly a zip code, you might not use mass media. On the other hand, it is important to realize that today's population is extremely mobile. A small advertiser might well benefit from mass media placement with extensive reach simply because consumers get around in the new bricks-and-clicks world of technology-assisted e-commerce.

Product strategies. When introducing a new product or innovating an existing one, advertising and promotion support is required. Watch for new product introductions or innovations that are candidates for your medium.

Branding strategies. There are two major strategies for branding: the so-called Ford and General Motors approaches. The Ford approach suggests naming every product line after the Ford brand—Ford Explorer, Ford Expedition, and Ford Taurus. General Motors's products use the secondary umbrella, such as Chevrolet Blazer, and generally ignore the General Motors brand.

Rule of thumb: If the sub-brand benefits from the umbrella brand, use it—Fox News or Sara Lee pastries, for example. When the umbrella brand is not a match, do not use it—Sara Lee luggage is not a match. In either event, you must determine the assistance advertising and promotion can provide branding and recognize the importance of the mass media in the branding effort, especially if the product is new.

Packaging strategies. New labels, a new functional design, a more convenient pouring spout, for example, all require mass media assistance to inform the consumer of package changes.

Sales promotion support. As a media salesperson, you already recognize that the more a potential customer knows of your product, the better your chance of making a sale. You can also use mass media advertising and sales promotion tactics to inform clients about your product.

Event marketing. Events are designed to meet specific needs of targeted consumers and have the capability of demonstrating products and developing brand loyalty. Advertising and promotion support can drive a lot of traffic to an event.

Merchandising. Integration with in-store signage and point-of-purchase (POP) displays can improve turnover rate and gross retail operations. It is imperative for you to work backwards, that is, to go into the store to check out merchandising and then attempt to sell mass media advertising and promotion support to your client. Many studies have shown advertising increases turnover rate for retailers, and the higher the turnover the better the ROI for retail space.

Public relations and publicity. Many marketers depend on public relations and publicity to promote their products. However, advertising and promotion can go a long way to leverage the effect of PR and publicity efforts. Since marketers tend to provide public relations just prior to breaking a mass media campaign, public relations can be an indication of a pending advertising expenditure.

Market research. Many marketers engage in market research prior to initiating a major campaign. It may be wise to provide assistance, even free PSAs, for the research so you keep a foot in the door for the campaign rollout based on the research.

Common sense and good IMC practice dictate that all 5 Ps in the marketing communications mix communicate and must be integrated. Your product communicates by its color, size, sound—listen to a Harley or a Coke, smell—get a whiff of Mrs. Field's cookies, and function—John Deere's "Nothing runs like a Deere." The price you charge communicates—higher price is usually associated with higher quality; lower price with lesser quality and prestige. The place where you distribute your product communicates—Nordstrom's versus Wall-Mart versus the Internet. Certainly, your post-purchase service communicates and either creates a loyal customer and repeat business or drives customers to the competition. And, of course, your marketing promotion communicates—mass media advertising, PR, personal selling, sales promotions, events, the Internet, word of mouth, matchbook covers, whatever—all communicate and have relative strengths, weaknesses, and levels of effectiveness when integrated.

Monitoring and Control

The key insight into this part of the process is that monitoring and control are not actually steps in the marketing communication planning process. Monitoring and control are ongoing, carried on from start to finish of a marketing effort to assess whether the marketing communications plan is meeting your client's performance objectives.

Negative deviations from stated corporate, marketing, and marketing communications performance objectives, as perceived by the salesperson, require ongoing reassessment to discover weaknesses and failures in the plan as it is executed. This allows you to make adjustments at any point in the execution of the plan.

Failure to meet objectives at any level—corporate, marketing or marketing communications—does not necessarily mean your marketing plan is a poor one. In reassessing the plan you may discover the objectives were not realistic, the budget was too small to accomplish stated objectives, or the time allotted to achieve the objectives was too short. With close monitoring and control, timely and salient adjustments can seamlessly be made to the errant objectives, and the execution of the plan can continue uninterrupted.

Test Yourself

1. What are the 5 Ps in the marketing communications mix?
2. Identify and briefly explain each of the seven steps of the IMC planning model.
3. List and briefly explain each of the three marketing planning strategies.
4. List and briefly delineate the four marketing communications strategies.
5. Discuss the use-ratio concept as it applies to the 5 P marketing mix.
6. Discuss the concept of the Tactical Hand-Off Zone in the AIDCA model.

Project

As a media representative, assume you have a light truck dealer as a client. What useful purchase behavior and other data would you collect on your client's customers? Using that data, identify and describe four meaningful buyer behavior segments. Next, suggest and support the best pricing strategy your truck dealer client could use to sell products to people in each of the four segments. Finally, identify the key insight to understanding each segment and write a one-sentence customized message targeting each of the segments.

References

Gary Armstrong and Philip Kotler. 2003. *Marketing*, 6th edition. Upper Saddle River, NJ: Prentice Hall.

George E. Belch and Michael A. Belch. 2001. *Advertising and Promotion: An Integrated Marketing Communications Perspective,* 5th edition. Boston: McGraw-Hill.

Alvin C. Burns and Ronald F. Bush. 2003. *Marketing Research*, 4th edition. Upper Saddle River, NJ: Prentice Hall.

Clarke L. Caywood. 1997. *The Handbook of Strategic Public Relations and Integrated Communications.* New York: McGraw-Hill.

Stuart Elliott. February 4, 2003. "McDonald's stung by a loss, summons a high-level meeting to rework its marketing." *New York Times*, Internet Business/Financial Desk

Rob Jackson and Paul Wang 1994. *Strategic Database Marketing*. Lincolnwood, IL: NTC Books.

James G. Hutton, and Francis J. Mulhern. 2002. *Marketing Communications: Integrated Theory, Strategy and Tactics*. Hackensack, NJ: Pentagram.

Everett M. Rogers. 1983. *Diffusion of Innovations*, 4th edition. New York: Simon & Schuster.

Don E. Schultz, Stanley I. Tannenbaum, and Robert F. Lauterborn. 1995. *The New Marketing Paradigm*. Lincolnwood, IL: NTC Books.

M. Joseph Sirgy. 1998. *Integrated Marketing Communications: A Systems Approach*. Upper Saddle River, NJ: Prentice Hall.

Endnotes

1. Stuart Elliott. February 4, 2003. "McDonald's stung by a loss, summons a high-level meeting to re-work its marketing," *New York Times*, Internet Business/Financial Desk

2. James G. Hutton, and Francis J. Mulhern. 2002. *Marketing Communications: Integrated Theory, Strategy and Tactics*. Hackensack, NJ: Pentagram. p. 4.

3. Rob Jackson and Paul Wang, 1994. *Strategic Database Marketing*. Lincolnwood, IL: NTC Books. P. 27

4. Gary Armstrong and Philip Kotler. 2003. *Marketing*, 6th edition. Upper Saddle River, NJ: Prentice Hall. p. 337.

5. Everett M. Rogers. 1962, 1971, 1983. *Diffusion of Innovations*, 4th edition. New York: Simon & Schuster.

6. M. Joseph Sirgy. 1998. *Integrated Marketing Communications: A Systems Approach*. Upper Saddle River, NJ: Prentice Hall.

16 Media Research

By Joseph Buchman

In 1998, just prior to John Glenn's return to space for the STS-95 mission on the space shuttle Discovery, I had the opportunity to interview the director of one of the National Aeronautics and Space Administration's (NASA) key research projects about the nature of the data they were collecting and the conclusions that could be drawn from it. He told me:

> "You've got to understand. If we have one data point, we'll write in our concluding report, 'Our recent experience has shown that . . .' If we have two data points we'll write, 'A recent series of studies has shown that . . .' And if we have three data points we'll conclude, 'We have shown time, after time, after time, that . . .'"

It is the same with interpreting any set of statistical information. Figures do not lie, but they can easily be misinterpreted by the reader, especially when they are organized and presented in a light most favorable to the source providing them. What my friend at NASA shared is not exaggeration or distortion. One study can show "our recent experience." Two studies are indeed a "series," and three can be described as "time, after time, after time." It is only in the mind of the reader that these and other statements of fact can be distorted into something more. And that is often the case as programmers, salespeople, and managers in the highly competitive media industries attempt to put the best light possible on the statistics collected about their viewers or listeners.

Perhaps you have wondered how three of four radio stations in a market could all claim to be number one, or how several different broadcast network and cable news channels could each claim to have the largest number of viewers. How can "more Americans get their news from . . ." but another channel be the "most influential," and another have the "largest number of viewers." Maybe you have concluded that they all must be lying (or at least all but one of them). By the end of this chapter, perhaps, you will see how they all could indeed be telling the truth. In the movie "Star Wars," Yoda, the last Jedi master, tells Luke that the truth depends very much on his point of view.

The product salespeople sell is advertising space or time, but the product most advertisers think they are buying is the attention, interest, and, ultimately, *action* of an audience. The size of this audience is estimated by ratings services, companies that specialize in the measurement of broadcast, print, Internet, and outdoor audiences. The estimates provided by these companies are based on a small sample of the total number of people who they project are exposed to that media at *any given point in time* or *over some period of time*. In broadcasting, the estimates of listening and viewing based on these samples are commonly referred to as the *ratings*. In the print media, audience size estimates are most commonly referred to as *readership, circulation,* or *exposure*. Outdoor media estimates are based on the number of cars passing a given point over some period of time and are referred to as *showings*.

For almost all media, and especially for the broadcast and cable media, audience estimates provide not only an estimate of the total number of people exposed to a medium, but also estimates of the audience size by combinations of various *demographic variables*. These variables can be sex and age (for example, women 18 to 34 years old) or geographic groups by counties, ZIP codes, and other areas (such as metro counties or *Designated Market Areas* (DMAs). Furthermore, variables can be divided into various qualitative groups (for instance, income, education, or fast-food purchasers), location of exposure (for radio, at home, work, or in the car). Ratings are approximations at best, and wide fluctuations can occur by chance, particularly when audience ratings are broken down into smaller demographic or geographic groups. For this reason, ratings should be used judiciously and with some degree of understanding of the possibility of unexplainable, chance variability from report to report. Only with a thorough knowledge of how the ratings companies analyze audience behavior can you prepare to answer prospective clients' concerns about the accuracy and reliability of these estimates of the audience size of your station, newspaper, magazine, outdoor company, channel, or cable system.

Radio and Television Audience Measurement

Unlike most public opinion polls, broadcast and cable ratings attempt to measure how people actually behave, not how they report they feel, believe, or are likely to behave in the future. This distinction is important because what people claim they like to do or intend to do can differ markedly from their actual listening and viewing behavior. Ratings attempt to provide an accurate estimate of actual media exposure. Knowing what stations and programs people listen to and watch is vital information for both broadcast and cable managers and advertisers.

The broadcast ratings industry has been evolving for more than 75 years. In the early 1930s, radio advertisers decided they needed to know how many people were listening to their commercials, so they formed the Cooperative Analysis of Broadcasting (CAB). This group commissioned the Crossley Company to conduct a survey of station listening. Crossley used a telephone recall methodology in which randomly telephoned individuals were asked to recall the stations they listened to in their household over the past day. In the 1930s, most radio listening occurred in a household or family setting; today's radio ratings are calculated for individuals and not households. New ratings companies have been formed since the '30s, new methodologies have been developed, and ratings companies have made other changes to provide increasingly detailed information to advertisers, advertising agencies, and broadcasters on which to base time-buying, sales, and programming decisions.

There are currently two companies providing radio ratings in the United States, Arbitron and Eastlan, and only one, A.C. Nielsen, providing television and cable ratings. Eastlan, which acquired the Willhight Research Company in July 2000, provides radio ratings for more than 150 mostly smaller West Coast, Alaskan, and Hawaiian markets. The Birch radio ratings company, which provided the only national competition to Arbitron's radio ratings during the 1980s, ceased operations in 1991.

Arbitron uses a seven-day diary methodology. Radio listeners record their daily radio listening in a pocket-sized diary for a period of one week, then mail the completed diary back to Arbitron. Nielsen uses a diary methodology similar to Arbitron's for its local television ratings. Nielsen also uses people meters, which will be discussed later in this chapter, to collect its overnight television ratings information. In 1999 Arbitron began testing a pager-sized, individual people meter for radio as well. Eastlan uses a *telephone-recall* methodology. Listeners are called at random and asked to recall their radio listening for the previous 24 hours to ensure collection of away-from-home listening.

The methodology used by the ratings companies can influence some radio stations' programming, sales, and promotional activities. For example, in markets where Eastlan is used by many local media buyers, some radio stations may engage in contests asking listeners to answer their telephones with the call letters or slogan of the station. In markets where Arbitron is used more extensively, stations may use promotional slogans such as "WXXX—Write it down!" or engage in heavier promotion on Thursdays (when diary keeping begins) or on Wednesdays (when many diary keepers may be attempting to remember their radio listening for the previous week while entering it in their diaries). On a recent business trip, I heard the dominant station in the market air the following promotion: "If you heard the (local NBA franchise) game on the radio last night, chances are you were listening to (call letters of local station) for the entire day." This is a promotion blatantly designed to encourage diary keepers to maximize the amount of time they report listening to the station.

Some stations create promotional items, such as refrigerator magnets, emergency phone number stickers, or coffee or beer mugs, on the theory that most diaries are filled out and most daytime telephone calls are answered in the kitchen. In markets where both Eastlan and Arbitron are available, the ratings that stations choose to emphasize in sales presentations may depend somewhat on the station's format. Stations that attract an older audience, such as easy-listening or talk formats, tend to do better in diary-based ratings than in telephone-recall-based ratings because older listeners are more comfortable recording their listening behavior in a diary than answering telephoned questions from a stranger. On the other hand, stations with young male audiences, such as those with an alternative rock format, tend to do better in telephone-based ratings. Young adult males respond more favorably to telephone questions from a stranger (usually female) than to a request to keep a diary.

Each of the ratings services, Arbitron, Nielsen, and Eastlan, segments listening and viewing into 15-minute time periods—from the top of the hour to 15 after, from 15 after to the half hour, and so forth. To simplify analysis, the ratings companies count someone as listening or viewing if the person reports hearing or viewing a given station for five continuous minutes within a quarter hour. This is why many broadcast stations avoid placing commercials at the quarter hours; they hope to pull their listeners or viewers at least five minutes into the next quarter hour before giving them a reason to tune out. This quarter-hour structure may also affect the scheduling of contest and promotional announcements as stations attempt to retain their audience across several quarter hours. Of course, this assumes diary-keepers are filling out their diaries coincident with their listening or viewing, an assumption that may be questionable at best.

Ratings Terminology

Before discussing how to use ratings information in selling situations, it may prove useful to review some of the fundamental vocabulary of media research. There are six critical concepts to know when attempting to sell radio station advertising time (or to sell against radio as a salesperson for another medium):

1. **Average-Quarter-Hour (AQH) persons**—an estimate of the number of people listening to a radio station (or viewing a television station or cable channel) at a given point in time, say 5:27 in the afternoon.
2. **Cumulative (cume) persons**—the number of people who listened to a radio station (for at least five continuous minutes within a quarter hour) at least once over some period of time (for example, on Monday from 6 to 10 AM). Obviously, people are tuning in and out of radio stations all of the time. Cume persons is the simple tally of all of these different people without regard to the amount of time they may have listened.
3. **AQH rating**—the AQH persons expressed as a percentage of the market population. If WXXX's AQH persons is 20,000 and there are 200,000 people in the market, then WXXX's AQH rating is a 10 *(20,000 ÷ 200,000)*. Note that a 10 rating is really .10, or 10 percent.
4. **AQH share**—the AQH persons expressed as a percentage of all of those people listening to (or viewing) all of the radio stations (or television channels) in a market. AQH share is a measure of how the station or channel is doing against its competition. If, of the 200,000 people in the market above, 50,000 are listening to radio, then WXXX's share is 40 *(20,000 ÷ 50,000)*.
5. **Cume rating**—the percentage of the market population that listened to a given station at least once over a given period of time. If over a week, 40,000 people tuned into WXXX, then WXXX's cume rating would be 20 *(40,000 ÷ 200,000)*. The cume rating is a measure of a station's *reach* or *penetration* into the marketplace.
6. **Exclusive cume rating**—the percentage of people who listened only to your station over some period of time without listening to any other radio station during that time period. For example, if 10,000 of WXXX's cume audience listened only to WXXX, then WXXX's exclusive cume rating would be 5 *(10,000 ÷ 200,000)*. Exclusive cume is a measure of audience *loyalty*.

In television, ratings are based on either the *persons* using television (PUT) or the *households* using television (HUT). Cumes and exclusive cumes are not routinely calculated or reported for television viewing, although similar measures are available in specialized reports sold by Nielsen for an additional fee.

Geographic Areas

Arbitron, Eastlan, and Nielsen each report ratings and shares that are classified by more than twenty standard demographic groups (for instance, women 18 to 49, men 25 to 54) and by three basic geographic areas: the Total Survey Area (TSA), the Designated Market Area (DMA), and the smallest of the geographic areas, the Metropolitan Statistical Area (MSA). Each of these geographic areas is based on county boundaries (see Figure 16.1).

The TSA is the largest of these geographic areas and simply consists of all of the counties around a metro area where a minimal level of television viewing or radio listening is reported for the stations from that metro area. A given county can therefore be included in more than one metro's TSA.

Denver-Boulder

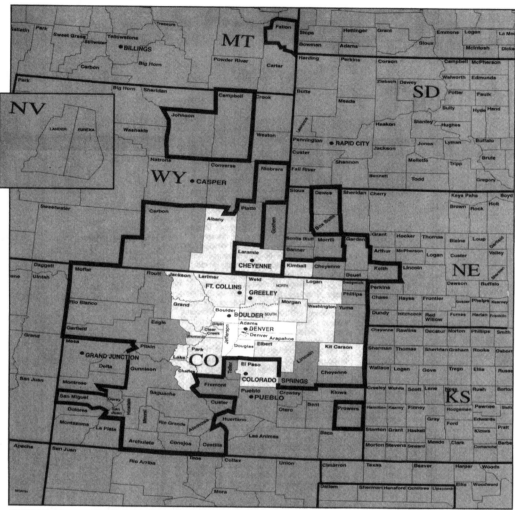

© 2002 Arbitron Inc.   Nonsubscribers to this report may not reproduce this map for any purpose, including but not limited to sales, marketing, advertising or promotional purposes, without the express written permission of Arbitron Inc.

☐ **Metro**   ▨ **TSA**   ▨ **DMA**®

TSA and DMA sampled in Spring and Fall only.
For definitions of the terms Metro, TSA and DMA, see Page M3, Paragraph 1, and Page M7, "Selected Arbitron Terms."

Metro Rank: 22
Market Surveyed: Winter, Spring, Summer, Fall

Station Subscribers to This Report*					
KALC-FM	KBCO-FM	KBPI-FM	KCKK-AM	KDJM-FM	KEZW-AM
KFMD-FM	KHOW-AM	KIMN-FM	KJCD-FM	KJME-AM	KJMN-FM
KKFN-AM	KKZN-AM	KMXA-AM	KOA-AM	KOSI-FM	KQKS-FM
KQMT-FM	KRFX-FM	KTCL-FM	KXDC-FM	KXKL-FM	KXPK-FM
KYGO-FM					

* Station subscribers as of release to print.

Figure 16.1
Total Survey Area (TSA), Designated Market Area (DMA), and Metropolitan Statistical Area (MSA).

The DMA is a television-viewing-based area and consists of those counties where the combined share of all the television stations from a given metro area is greater than the combined shares of the television stations from any other metro area. These county-based viewing levels are averaged on a yearly basis so a given county cannot change DMAs more than once a year.

The counties included in a **Metro area** are determined by the federal government. Arbitron, Eastlan, and Nielsen (with a very few exceptions) simply use the government's metro area definitions. The government's definition of a metro area includes a consideration of the county population, the percentage of that population that commutes to an adjacent county on a daily basis, and other factors.

Of course, each of the audience size measures just described can be calculated for a specific demographic group within a given geographic area (for example, the AQH rating for women 25 to 54 in the DMA, for males 25 to 52, cume persons for the metro, and so forth). Also, television ratings and shares may be calculated based on either people or households. Household-based ratings are most commonly used for television. In the early days of radio, radio ratings were also based on household listening. As technology allowed radio to become a mobile, personal medium, radio ratings shifted from household-based to person-based. The development of multi-set households and portable, battery-operated, flat-screen television sets is likely to cause ratings companies to shift to person-based calculations for television sometime in the next few years. Ratings information will also eventually be available for high-definition television (HDTV) homes and other new technologies as they evolve.

Finally, it is important to note that market size and market rank are determined by the combined populations of each market's DMA counties. A small shift in the viewing level of one or two counties can sometimes create a large shift in the total population assigned to the DMA. This change can have a significant effect on a station's national spot revenues if the population shift causes a change in market rank. For example, if the market's rank changes from market number 103 to market 98, national spot revenues might rise dramatically because many national spot campaigns are purchased to run in only the top 100 markets (while other advertisers might designate a cutoff level of the top 10, 25, 50, or 150 markets). If you have ever wondered why all of the local newscasts in your market were suddenly covering a large number of stories from a small town out in the boonies, chances are they were attempting to attract an outlying county into their DMA to increase their market ranking and, thus, national spot advertising revenues.

If you have trouble understanding any of the above materials, don't worry. We are going to review specific examples of actual ratings company reports. If, on the other hand, you are familiar with audience ratings terminology from prior industry experience or from a good quantatively based broadcast advertising course, you may want to skim some of the following material and concentrate on those terms with which you are less familiar. Arbitron also offers an excellent online ratings tutorial at http://arbitron.colearn.com/arbitronsupport/arblogin.htm

Reading a Television Ratings Report

Figure 16.2 displays a page from the November 2001 Nielsen television ratings report for Chicago.

On the far left-hand side, near the top of the page, find the Tuesday 8:00 PM to 10:00 PM time period. Moving down the left-hand side of the page,

CHICAGO, IL

WK1 11/01-11/07 WK2 11/08-11/14 WK3 11/15-11/21 WK4 11/22-11/28

TUESDAY 8:00PM - 10:00PM

DMA HOUSEHOLD							DMA RATINGS			

Column groups: RATINGS WEEKS / MULTI-WEEK AVG / SHARE TREND / PERSONS / WOMEN / MEN / TNS / CHILD

METRO HH — RTG / SHR

STATION / PROGRAM

R.S.E. THRESHOLDS 25+% (1 S.E.) 4 WK AVG 50+%

8:00PM
STATION	PROGRAM
WBBM	AVG. ALL WKS
	GUARDIAN-CBS
	M JACKSON-CBS
WCIU	CARD SHARKS
WCPX	AVG. ALL WKS
	DOC TUE-PAX
	MYST WY TU-PAX
WFLD	24-FOX
WGBO	DERCH-NACR-UNI
WGN	SMALLVILLE-WB#
WJYS	PAID PROGRAM
WLS	NYPD BLUE-ABC
WMAQ	FRASIER-NBC
WPWR	AVG. ALL WKS
	BUFFY-UPN
	ROSWELL-UPN
WSNS	UGA UGA-TEL
WTTW	NOVA
WYCC	ANTQ RDSHW-PTV
LCLT	PRIME NEWS III
	HUT/PUT/TOTALS*

8:30PM
WBBM	AVG. ALL WKS
	GUARDIAN-CBS
	M JACKSON-CBS
WCIU	ELIMIDATE B
WCPX	AVG. ALL WKS
	DOC TUE-PAX
	MYST WY TU-PAX
WFLD	24-FOX
WGBO	DERCH-NACR-UNI
WGN	SMALLVILLE-WB#
WJYS	AVG. ALL WKS
	PROPHET 3 H
WLS	NYPD BLUE-ABC
WMAQ	AVG. ALL WKS
	SCRUBS-NBC
	FRASIER-SL-NBC
WPWR	ROSWELL-UPN
WSNS	UGA UGA-TEL
WTTW	NOVA
WYCC	ANTQ RDSHW-PTV
LCLT	AVG. ALL WKS
	PRIME NEWS IV
	BLACKHWKS HCKY
	HUT/PUT/TOTALS*

9:00PM
WBBM	AVG. ALL WKS
	JUDGNG AMY-CBS
	M JACKSON-CBS
WCIU	MAD TV
WCPX	DIAGNOSIS-PAX
WFLD	FOX NWS CHCAGO
WGBO	AQ-AHRA TU-UNI
WGN	WGN NEWS
WJYS	FARRAKHAN SPKS
WLS	AVG. ALL WKS
	NYPD BLUE-ABC
	PHILLY-ABC
WMAQ	DATELNE NBC-TU
WPWR	CHEERS
WSNS	UGATEL+FRZ-DS
	UGA UGA-TEL
	FUERZ-DSEO-TEL
WTTW	AVG. ALL WKS
	SCIENTFC-FRNTR
	NOVA
	LIVNG EDEN-PTV
WYCC	AVG. ALL WKS
	CHALK TALK
	ACT OF DUTY
	WARRIOR-WORLDS
	BUFFALO WAR
LCLT	AVG. ALL WKS
	SPORTS PAGE
	BLACKHWKS HCKY
	HUT/PUT/TOTALS*

9:30PM
WBBM	AVG. ALL WKS
	JUDGNG AMY-CBS
	M JACKSON-CBS
WCIU	MAD TV
WCPX	DIAGNOSIS-PAX
WFLD	FOX NWS CHCAGO
WGBO	AQ-AHRA TU-UNI
WGN	WGN NEWS
WJYS	FARRAKHAN SPKS
	Continued...

TUESDAY 8:00PM - 10:00PM

Nielsen Media Research has been advised that a station(s) conducted a special promotional activity. See special notes.

NOVEMBER 2001   210

Figure 16.2
A page from the November 2001 Nielsen television ratings report for Chicago.

287

find the 8 PM listing for WMAQ television. See if you can find the answers to the following five questions:

1. What program did WMAQ air on Tuesdays from 8 PM to 8:30 PM?
2. In the Chicago DMA, was this program more popular with Men or with Women?
3. With which age group was this program most popular?
4. Is this program becoming more or less popular over time?
5. What was the multi-week rating for this program and what does this mean?

Remember that this is one listing, for one show, on one page, of the Chicago 2001 Nielsen ratings report. There are 409 other pages in the report, each with at least 50 other program listings. For this listing the answers are:

1. The show is "Frasier" on NBC (just right of the WMAQ call letters).
2. "Frasier" in Chicago in November 2001 was more popular with women than with men. (At the top of the page, find DMA RATINGS. Under DMA RATINGS, find WOMEN 18+ and MEN 18+ (columns numbered 26 and 35). The DMA RATING for Women 18+ is 9. For Men 18+ it is 7.
3. "Frasier" skews old in this book. (Look under PERSONS and find the highest numbers. Frasier scores a 10 DMA PERSONS rating for 35 to 64 and for 50+.)
4. "Frasier" appears to be stable over time. (Look under DMA HOUSE-HOLD, then under SHARE TREND. "Frasier" enjoyed a 17 share in November 2000, which fell to a 15 share in February and May of 2001, but rebounded to a 17 for this book.)
5. The multi-week rating for "Frasier" is a 12. This means that about 12 percent of the DMA population of Chicago in November 2001 was watching "Frasier."

This book also shows ratings and shares for the METRO area (columns 1 and 2, the two far left columns in the report). Note that the metro audience size measures are based on households, not people. In most cases the metro household ratings and shares and DMA persons ratings and shares will be identical. The major exceptions will be for low-power television stations which do not completely cover the DMA, or for foreign-language stations with viewers concentrated within the metro counties only.

Reading a Radio Ratings Report

Figure 16.3 displays four pages from the Summer 2002 Arbitron ratings report for Denver-Boulder.

These four pages of the 191-page report are the estimates of radio listening by women between the ages of 25 and 49 living in the metro area. Five dayparts are reported. First is the total weekly numbers (Monday to Sunday, 6 AM to midnight), next is morning drive (Monday to Friday, 6 to 10 AM), then middays (Monday to Friday, 10 AM to 3 PM), followed by afternoon drive (3 to 7 PM), and finally late night (7 PM to midnight). Overnight numbers (midnight to 6 AM) are reported elsewhere in the book.

Target Listener Trends

Women 25-49

	Monday-Sunday 6AM-MID				Monday-Friday 6AM-10AM				Monday-Friday 10AM-3PM				Monday-Friday 3PM-7PM				Monday-Friday 7PM-MID			
	AQH (00)	Cume (00)	AQH Rtg	AQH Shr	AQH (00)	Cume (00)	AQH Rtg	AQH Shr	AQH (00)	Cume (00)	AQH Rtg	AQH Shr	AQH (00)	Cume (00)	AQH Rtg	AQH Shr	AQH (00)	Cume (00)	AQH Rtg	AQH Shr
KALC-FM																				
SU '02	37	808	.7	4.7	61	420	1.2	5.2	59	432	1.2	4.6	57	515	1.1	5.8	8	156	.2	3.2
SP '02	46	1026	.9	5.9	71	540	1.4	6.1	77	574	1.5	6.2	67	625	1.3	6.9	12	214	.2	4.7
WI '02	28	831	.6	3.8	41	358	.8	3.7	43	358	.9	3.5	41	463	.8	4.2	6	165	.1	2.8
FA '01	31	915	.6	4.0	46	420	.9	3.7	55	382	1.1	4.3	46	564	.9	4.6	7	173	.1	3.3
4-Book	*36*	*895*	*.7*	*4.6*	*55*	*435*	*1.1*	*4.7*	*59*	*437*	*1.2*	*4.7*	*53*	*542*	*1.0*	*5.4*	*8*	*177*	*.2*	*3.5*
SU '01	31	789	.6	4.3	63	484	1.3	5.7	50	354	1.0	4.3	43	500	.9	4.7	5	136	.1	2.1
KBCO-FM																				
SU '02	95	1381	1.9	12.1	130	850	2.6	11.0	172	890	3.4	13.5	129	963	2.6	13.0	23	302	.5	9.2
SP '02	92	1351	1.8	11.9	131	817	2.6	11.3	172	858	3.4	13.8	120	922	2.4	12.4	25	354	.5	9.9
WI '02	82	1230	1.6	11.1	109	676	2.2	9.8	158	725	3.1	13.0	118	886	2.4	12.1	14	293	.3	6.6
FA '01	71	1084	1.4	9.1	106	644	2.0	8.6	125	575	2.4	9.8	95	715	1.8	9.5	17	349	.3	8.1
4-Book	*85*	*1262*	*1.7*	*11.1*	*119*	*747*	*2.4*	*10.2*	*157*	*762*	*3.1*	*12.5*	*116*	*872*	*2.3*	*11.8*	*20*	*325*	*.4*	*8.5*
SU '01	60	1160	1.2	8.3	86	698	1.7	7.8	96	680	1.9	8.3	85	834	1.7	9.2	19	403	.4	8.2
KBNO-AM																				
SU '02	3	60	.1	.4	3	31	.1	.3	6	34	.1	.5	4	19	.1	.4	1	20		.4
SP '02	17	185	.3	2.2	24	97	.5	2.1	27	122	.5	2.2	5	40	.1	.5	19	65	.4	7.5
WI '02	8	148	.2	1.1	5	40	.1	.5	10	80	.2	.8	7	60	.1	.7	11	54	.2	5.2
FA '01	6	91	.1	.8	7	22	.1	.6	14	51	.3	1.1	6	48	.1	.6	2	20		1.0
4-Book	*9*	*121*	*.2*	*.9*	*10*	*48*	*.2*	*.9*	*14*	*72*	*.3*	*1.2*	*6*	*42*	*.1*	*.6*	*8*	*40*	*.2*	*3.5*
SU '01	10	98	.2	1.4	15	68	.3	1.4	14	66	.3	1.2	12	51	.2	1.3	5	34	.1	2.1
KBPI-FM																				
SU '02	10	356	.2	1.3	6	126	.1	.5	16	169	.3	1.3	16	181	.3	1.6	5	74	.1	2.0
SP '02	10	330	.2	1.3	11	126	.2	1.0	14	152	.3	1.1	14	226	.3	1.4	8	95	.2	3.2
WI '02	10	335	.2	1.4	9	84	.2	.8	14	161	.3	1.1	18	176	.4	1.8	7	87	.1	3.3
FA '01	15	366	.3	1.9	20	144	.4	1.6	24	172	.5	1.9	23	237	.4	2.3	6	118	.1	2.9
4-Book	*11*	*347*	*.2*	*1.5*	*12*	*120*	*.2*	*1.0*	*17*	*164*	*.4*	*1.4*	*18*	*205*	*.4*	*1.8*	*7*	*94*	*.1*	*2.9*
SU '01	18	368	.4	2.5	16	143	.3	1.5	28	154	.6	2.4	26	229	.5	2.8	12	138	.2	5.2
KCKK-AM																				
SU '02	5	51	.1	.6	6	32	.1	.5	8	26	.2	.6	2	18		.2	3	15	.1	1.2
SP '02	2	37		.3	2	19		.2	4	24	.1	.3	2	24		.2		14		
WI '02	1	41		.1	1	15		.1	1	20		.1	2	29		.2		14		
FA '01	1	24		.1	3	5	.1	.2	1	5		.1								
4-Book	*2*	*38*		*.3*	*3*	*18*	*.1*	*.3*	*4*	*19*	*.1*	*.3*	*2*	*18*		*.2*	*1*	*7*		*.3*
SU '01	3	72	.1	.4	3	26	.1	.3	3	13	.1	.3	2	25		.2	1	15		.4
KCUV-AM																				
SU '02	2	30		.3	2	18		.2	4	23	.1	.3		7			2	6		.8
SP '02	5	89	.1	.6	3	23	.1	.3	11	46	.2	.9	7	49	.1	.7				
WI '02	**	**	**	**	**	**	**	**	**	**	**	**	**	**	**	**	**	**	**	**
FA '01	**	**	**	**	**	**	**	**	**	**	**	**	**	**	**	**	**	**	**	**
4-Book	***	***	***	***	***	***	***	***	***	***	***	***	***	***	***	***	***	***	***	***
SU '01	**	**	**	**	**	**	**	**	**	**	**	**	**	**	**	**	**	**	**	**
KDJM-FM																				
SU '02	32	589	.6	4.1	42	304	.8	3.6	58	338	1.2	4.5	43	367	.9	4.3	11	154	.2	4.4
SP '02	34	655	.7	4.4	51	378	1.0	4.4	48	307	1.0	3.8	46	412	.9	4.8	18	199	.4	7.1
WI '02	24	583	.5	3.2	30	329	.6	2.7	38	274	.8	3.1	31	302	.6	3.2	7	164	.1	3.3
FA '01	24	444	.5	3.1	35	231	.7	2.8	39	230	.7	3.1	27	233	.5	2.7	6	64	.1	2.9
4-Book	*29*	*568*	*.6*	*3.7*	*40*	*311*	*.8*	*3.4*	*46*	*287*	*.9*	*3.6*	*37*	*329*	*.7*	*3.8*	*11*	*145*	*.2*	*4.4*
SU '01	22	519	.4	3.0	31	223	.6	2.8	40	264	.8	3.5	29	308	.6	3.1	6	102	.1	2.6
KEZW-AM																				
SU '02	5	113	.1	.6	5	37	.1	.4	6	43	.1	.5	8	55	.2	.8	3	19	.1	1.2
SP '02	6	100	.1	.8	10	59	.2	.9	12	52	.2	1.0	5	52	.1	.5	2	26		.8
WI '02	9	85	.2	1.2	9	43	.2	.8	16	52	.3	1.3	11	46	.2	1.1	2	33		.9
FA '01	6	65	.1	.8	11	42	.2	.9	11	35	.2	.9	7	48	.1	.7	1	19		.5
4-Book	*7*	*91*	*.1*	*.9*	*9*	*45*	*.2*	*.8*	*11*	*46*	*.2*	*.9*	*8*	*50*	*.2*	*.8*	*2*	*24*		*.9*
SU '01	4	66	.1	.6	7	42	.1	.6	8	21	.2	.7	5	40	.1	.7		9		

** Station(s) not reported this survey.   * Listener estimates adjusted for reported broadcast schedule.   + Station(s) changed call letters – see Page 13.   4-Book: Avg. of current and previous 3 surveys. 2-Book: Avg. of most recent 2 surveys.

ARBITRON

SUMMER 2002

Figure 16.3
Four pages from the Summer 2002 Arbitron ratings report for Denver-Boulder.

Target Listener Trends

Women 25-49

	Monday-Sunday 6AM-MID				Monday-Friday 6AM-10AM				Monday-Friday 10AM-3PM				Monday-Friday 3PM-7PM				Monday-Friday 7PM-MID			
	AQH (00)	Cume (00)	AQH Rtg	AQH Shr	AQH (00)	Cume (00)	AQH Rtg	AQH Shr	AQH (00)	Cume (00)	AQH Rtg	AQH Shr	AQH (00)	Cume (00)	AQH Rtg	AQH Shr	AQH (00)	Cume (00)	AQH Rtg	AQH Shr
KFMD-FM																				
SU '02	22	639	.4	2.8	52	330	1.0	4.4	28	278	.6	2.2	27	355	.5	2.7	4	102	.1	1.6
SP '02	19	528	.4	2.4	45	334	.9	3.9	27	186	.5	2.2	27	268	.5	2.8	3	87	.1	1.2
WI '02	22	581	.4	3.0	51	328	1.0	4.6	30	323	.6	2.5	28	343	.6	2.9	3	109	.1	1.4
FA '01	21	552	.4	2.7	45	318	.9	3.6	30	244	.6	2.4	24	295	.5	2.4	3	87	.1	1.4
4-Book	21	575	.4	2.7	48	328	1.0	4.1	29	258	.6	2.3	27	315	.5	2.7	3	96	.1	1.4
SU '01	25	563	.5	3.5	51	361	1.0	4.6	32	204	.6	2.8	30	242	.6	3.3	6	116	.1	2.6
KHOW-AM																				
SU '02	17	322	.3	2.2	37	215	.7	3.1	34	186	.7	2.7	13	137	.3	1.3	4	52	.1	1.6
SP '02	9	221	.2	1.2	17	142	.3	1.5	18	140	.4	1.4	6	82	.1	.6	5	53	.1	2.0
WI '02	16	253	.3	2.2	20	121	.4	1.8	48	179	1.0	3.9	15	112	.3	1.5	2	40		.9
FA '01	13	275	.2	1.7	25	181	.5	2.0	24	192	.5	1.9	15	140	.3	1.5	3	56	.1	1.4
4-Book	14	268	.3	1.8	25	165	.5	2.1	31	174	.7	2.5	12	118	.3	1.2	4	50	.1	1.5
SU '01	10	265	.2	1.4	19	174	.4	1.7	24	141	.5	2.1	6	74	.1	.7	3	35	.1	1.3
KIMN-FM																				
SU '02	48	869	1.0	6.1	89	566	1.8	7.5	89	467	1.8	7.0	56	487	1.1	5.7	7	195	.1	2.8
SP '02	43	856	.9	5.5	87	562	1.7	7.5	76	531	1.5	6.1	47	585	.9	4.9	5	164	.1	2.0
WI '02	48	798	1.0	6.5	79	521	1.6	7.1	86	438	1.7	7.1	58	470	1.2	5.9	12	195	.2	5.6
FA '01	49	806	.9	6.3	77	493	1.5	6.2	79	412	1.5	6.2	69	516	1.3	6.9	10	151	.2	4.8
4-Book	47	832	1.0	6.1	83	536	1.7	7.1	83	462	1.6	6.6	58	515	1.1	5.9	9	176	.2	3.8
SU '01	51	962	1.0	7.1	91	615	1.8	8.3	79	520	1.6	6.8	62	568	1.2	6.7	14	237	.3	6.0
KJCD-FM																				
SU '02	30	571	.6	3.8	24	208	.5	2.0	47	276	.9	3.7	46	334	.9	4.6	14	132	.3	5.6
SP '02	41	583	.8	5.3	55	299	1.1	4.8	81	340	1.6	6.5	56	369	1.1	5.8	11	143	.2	4.3
WI '02	36	480	.7	4.9	52	294	1.0	4.7	62	283	1.2	5.1	39	330	.8	4.0	9	139	.2	4.2
FA '01	18	394	.3	2.3	18	172	.3	1.5	28	199	.5	2.2	29	227	.6	2.9	10	139	.2	4.8
4-Book	31	507	.6	4.1	37	243	.7	3.3	55	275	1.1	4.4	43	315	.9	4.3	11	138	.2	4.7
SU '01	31	496	.6	4.3	33	220	.7	3.0	58	275	1.2	5.0	41	266	.8	4.4	11	135	.2	4.7
KJME-AM																				
SU '02	1	41		.1	3	29	.1	.3	1	18		.1	1	24		.1	1	5		.4
SP '02	5	114	.1	.6	4	33	.1	.3	4	70	.1	.3	7	46	.1	.7	2	33		.8
WI '02	8	112	.2	1.1	11	40	.2	1.0	20	78	.4	1.6	3	52	.1	.3	2	28		.9
FA '01	8	98	.2	1.0	13	68	.2	1.1	12	60	.2	.9	10	44	.2	1.0	2	37		1.0
4-Book	6	91	.1	.7	8	43	.2	.7	9	57	.2	.7	5	42	.1	.5	2	26		.8
SU '01	8	98	.2	1.1	11	85	.2	1.0	11	57	.2	1.0	8	69	.2	.9	3	34	.1	1.3
KJMN-FM																				
SU '02	17	227	.3	2.2	22	131	.4	1.9	22	113	.4	1.7	20	135	.4	2.0	8	62	.2	3.2
SP '02	13	198	.3	1.7	17	119	.3	1.5	22	110	.4	1.8	14	108	.3	1.4	4	43	.1	1.6
WI '02	19	247	.4	2.6	18	119	.4	1.6	35	123	.7	2.9	24	160	.5	2.5	7	80	.1	3.3
FA '01	22	255	.4	2.8	33	185	.6	2.7	39	149	.7	3.1	21	119	.4	2.1	12	115	.2	5.7
4-Book	18	232	.4	2.3	23	139	.4	1.9	30	124	.6	2.4	20	131	.4	2.0	8	75	.2	3.5
SU '01	10	153	.2	1.4	18	72	.4	1.6	13	67	.3	1.1	13	76	.3	1.4	4	64	.1	1.7
KKFN-AM																				
SU '02	1	46		.1	3	20	.1	.3	1	14		.1	1	21		.1		7		
SP '02	6	236	.1	.8	3	19	.1	.3	3	32	.1	.2	5	94	.1	.5	8	120	.2	3.2
WI '02	3	179	.1	.4	6	26	.1	.5	1	18		.1	4	54	.1	.4	6	53	.1	2.8
FA '01	2	129		.3	2	16		.2	2	30		.2	2	16		.2	1	25		.5
4-Book	3	148	.1	.4	4	20	.1	.3	2	24		.2	3	46	.1	.3	4	51	.1	1.6
SU '01	2	70		.3	2	31		.2	3	33	.1	.3	4	51	.1	.4		9		
+KKZN-AM																				
SU '02	1	49		.1	2	20		.2	1	24		.1		6						
SP '02	1	28		.1	5	14	.1	.4	1	20		.1	1	7						
WI '02	1	30		.1		7			2	16		.2	1	14		.1		14		
FA '01	1	56		.1	1	18		.1	3	15	.1	.2	1	15		.1				
4-Book	1	41		.1	2	15		.2	2	19		.2	1	11		.1		4		
SU '01	1	38		.1	7	18	.1	.6		6			1	7		.1		8		

** Station(s) not reported this survey.

* Listener estimates adjusted for reported broadcast schedule.

+ Station(s) changed call letters – see Page 13.

4-Book: Avg. of current and previous 3 surveys.
2-Book: Avg. of most recent 2 surveys.

SUMMER 2002

 ARBITRON

DENVER-BOULDER   I 143

Figure 16.3 continued. . .

Target Listener Trends

Women 25-49

	Monday-Sunday 6AM-MID				Monday-Friday 6AM-10AM				Monday-Friday 10AM-3PM				Monday-Friday 3PM-7PM				Monday-Friday 7PM-MID			
	AQH (00)	Cume (00)	AQH Rtg	AQH Shr	AQH (00)	Cume (00)	AQH Rtg	AQH Shr	AQH (00)	Cume (00)	AQH Rtg	AQH Shr	AQH (00)	Cume (00)	AQH Rtg	AQH Shr	AQH (00)	Cume (00)	AQH Rtg	AQH Shr
KMXA-AM																				
SU '02	9	107	.2	1.2	11	62	.2	.9	20	74	.4	1.6	5	56	.1	.5		6		
SP '02	10	141	.2	1.3	19	91	.4	1.6	16	91	.3	1.3	6	59	.1	.6	2	26		.8
WI '02	10	152	.2	1.4	20	106	.4	1.8	16	102	.3	1.3	6	76	.1	.6	1	17		.5
FA '01	18	131	.3	2.3	45	93	.9	3.6	32	102	.6	2.5	8	68	.2	.8	1	17		.5
4-Book	12	133	.2	1.6	24	88	.5	2.0	21	92	.4	1.7	6	65	.1	.6	1	17		.5
SU '01	5	78	.1	.7	8	51	.2	.7	5	37	.1	.4	7	44	.1	.8	2	21		.9
KNUS-AM																				
SU '02	2	39		.3		7			2	13		.2	8	39	.2	.8	1	13		.4
SP '02	7	61	.1	.9	12	34	.2	1.0	10	34	.2	.8	5	27	.1	.5	5	20	.1	2.0
WI '02	4	78	.1	.5	4	12	.1	.4	6	27	.1	.5	8	39	.2	.8	4	27	.1	1.9
FA '01	3	64	.1	.4	6	37	.1	.5	2	18		.2	3	38	.1	.3	3	15	.1	1.4
4-Book	4	61	.1	.5	6	23	.1	.5	5	23	.1	.4	6	36	.2	.6	3	19	.1	1.4
SU '01	2	76		.3	7	40	.1	.6	2	24		.2	3	50	.1	.3	2	33		.9
KOA -AM																				
SU '02	19	488	.4	2.4	32	233	.6	2.7	22	192	.4	1.7	20	213	.4	2.0	13	86	.3	5.2
SP '02	17	466	.3	2.2	35	261	.7	3.0	21	171	.4	1.7	21	178	.4	2.2	6	95	.1	2.4
WI '02	10	290	.2	1.4	27	191	.5	2.4	12	74	.2	1.0	11	147	.2	1.1	1	20		.5
FA '01	28	690	.5	2.4	52	303	1.0	4.2	56	262	1.1	4.4	23	266	.4	2.3	4	84	.1	1.9
4-Book	19	484	.4	2.4	37	247	.7	3.1	28	175	.5	2.2	19	201	.4	1.9	6	71	.1	2.5
SU '01	17	533	.3	2.4	39	253	.8	3.5	23	224	.5	2.0	20	234	.4	2.2	4	107	.1	1.7
KOSI-FM																				
SU '02	79	1039	1.6	10.1	117	563	2.3	9.9	152	599	3.0	11.9	98	594	2.0	9.9	25	282	.5	10.0
SP '02	70	968	1.4	9.0	92	512	1.8	8.0	149	578	3.0	11.9	93	582	1.9	9.6	18	242	.4	7.1
WI '02	55	894	1.1	7.4	70	483	1.4	6.3	109	489	2.2	8.9	74	540	1.5	7.6	16	220	.3	7.5
FA '01	74	1027	1.4	9.5	107	548	2.1	8.6	152	569	2.9	11.9	92	639	1.8	9.2	27	260	.5	12.9
4-Book	70	982	1.4	9.0	97	527	1.9	8.2	141	559	2.8	11.2	89	589	1.8	9.1	22	251	.4	9.4
SU '01	51	1009	1.0	7.1	82	571	1.6	7.5	100	486	2.0	8.7	68	531	1.4	7.4	9	159	.2	3.9
KQKS-FM																				
SU '02	19	503	.4	2.4	33	199	.7	2.8	20	247	.4	1.6	21	284	.4	2.1	9	184	.2	3.6
SP '02	21	521	.4	2.7	25	286	.5	2.2	25	277	.5	2.0	31	313	.6	3.2	10	150	.2	4.0
WI '02	29	454	.6	3.9	47	284	.9	4.2	46	232	.9	3.8	43	295	.9	4.4	12	122	.2	5.6
FA '01	27	622	.5	3.5	42	325	.8	3.4	39	377	.7	3.1	41	359	.8	4.1	8	155	.2	3.8
4-Book	24	525	.5	3.1	37	274	.7	3.2	33	283	.6	2.6	34	313	.7	3.5	10	153	.2	4.3
SU '01	35	525	.7	4.8	56	264	1.1	5.1	52	290	1.0	4.5	41	338	.8	4.4	14	156	.3	6.0
+KQMT-FM																				
SU '02	38	771	.8	4.9	53	365	1.1	4.5	80	392	1.6	6.3	47	448	.9	4.7	10	197	.2	4.0
SP '02	24	570	.5	3.1	31	278	.6	2.7	39	253	.8	3.1	30	303	.6	3.1	3	97	.1	1.2
WI '02	21	573	.4	2.8	31	253	.6	2.8	35	281	.7	2.9	28	273	.6	2.9	4	126	.1	1.9
FA '01	13	516	.2	1.7	17	245	.3	1.4	19	236	.4	1.5	16	244	.3	1.6	5	90	.1	2.4
4-Book	24	608	.5	3.1	33	285	.7	2.9	43	291	.9	3.5	30	317	.6	3.1	6	128	.1	2.4
SU '01	26	681	.5	3.6	38	322	.8	3.5	49	377	1.0	4.2	31	361	.6	3.4	9	162	.2	3.9
KRFX-FM																				
SU '02	35	637	.7	4.5	66	328	1.3	5.6	49	249	1.0	3.8	39	401	.8	3.9	9	137	.2	3.6
SP '02	29	611	.6	3.7	36	300	.7	3.1	39	264	.8	3.1	44	346	.9	4.6	7	144	.1	2.8
WI '02	22	629	.4	3.0	45	293	.9	4.1	37	247	.7	3.0	23	303	.5	2.4	5	105	.1	2.3
FA '01	26	697	.5	3.3	42	341	.8	3.4	41	280	.8	3.2	32	347	.6	3.2	7	119	.1	3.3
4-Book	28	644	.6	3.6	47	316	.9	4.1	42	260	.8	3.3	35	349	.7	3.5	7	126	.1	3.0
SU '01	26	658	.5	3.6	43	284	.9	3.9	46	280	.9	4.0	31	278	.6	3.4	7	152	.1	3.0
KRKS-FM																				
SU '02	4	102	.1	.5	8	55	.2	.7	5	45	.1	.4	5	56	.1	.5	1	25		.4
SP '02	4	125	.1	.5	13	79	.3	1.1	5	53	.1	.4	5	52	.1	.5	1	26		.4
WI '02	4	170	.1	.5	9	79	.2	.8	5	72	.1	.4	7	46	.1	.7	2	40		.9
FA '01	5	162	.1	.6	17	117	.3	1.4	5	74	.1	.4	4	55	.1	.4	2	39		1.0
4-Book	4	140	.1	.5	12	83	.3	1.0	5	61	.1	.4	5	52	.1	.5	2	33		.7
SU '01	5	87	.1	.7	12	54	.2	1.1	10	65	.2	.9	3	51	.1	.3	1	8		.4

** Station(s) not reported this survey. * Listener estimates adjusted for reported broadcast schedule. + Station(s) changed call letters - see Page 13. 4-Book: Avg. of current and previous 3 surveys. 2-Book: Avg. of most recent 2 surveys.

ARBITRON

SUMMER 2002

Figure 16.3 continued. . .

Target Listener Trends

Women 25-49

	Monday-Sunday 6AM-MID				Monday-Friday 6AM-10AM				Monday-Friday 10AM-3PM				Monday-Friday 3PM-7PM				Monday-Friday 7PM-MID			
	AQH (00)	Cume (00)	AQH Rtg	AQH Shr	AQH (00)	Cume (00)	AQH Rtg	AQH Shr	AQH (00)	Cume (00)	AQH Rtg	AQH Shr	AQH (00)	Cume (00)	AQH Rtg	AQH Shr	AQH (00)	Cume (00)	AQH Rtg	AQH Shr
KTCL-FM																				
SU '02	18	480	.4	2.3	26	243	.5	2.2	31	194	.6	2.4	29	342	.6	2.9	3	82	.1	1.2
SP '02	17	561	.3	2.2	18	192	.4	1.6	23	246	.5	1.8	27	331	.5	2.8	5	131	.1	2.0
WI '02	14	512	.3	1.9	17	225	.3	1.5	20	239	.4	1.6	24	310	.5	2.5	5	130	.1	2.3
FA '01	14	451	.3	1.8	17	215	.3	1.4	27	197	.5	2.1	21	276	.4	2.1	4	111	.1	1.9
4-Book	*16*	*501*	*.3*	*2.1*	*20*	*219*	*.4*	*1.7*	*25*	*219*	*.5*	*2.0*	*25*	*315*	*.5*	*2.6*	*4*	*114*	*.1*	*1.9*
SU '01	10	343	.2	1.4	15	160	.3	1.4	13	132	.3	1.1	15	193	.3	1.6	5	68	.1	2.1
+KXDC-FM																				
SU '02	2	95		.3	2	33		.2	2	60		.2	3	68	.1	.3	1	20		.4
SP '02	8	189	.2	1.0	16	123	.3	1.4	11	85	.2	.9	5	80	.1	.5	3	73	.1	1.2
WI '02	6	157	.1	.8	10	102	.2	.9	6	54	.1	.5	8	77	.2	.8	2	30		.9
FA '01	11	288	.2	1.4	21	147	.4	1.7	13	159	.2	1.0	14	175	.3	1.4	2	51		1.0
4-Book	*7*	*182*	*.1*	*.9*	*12*	*101*	*.2*	*1.1*	*8*	*90*	*.1*	*.7*	*8*	*100*	*.2*	*.8*	*2*	*44*		*.9*
SU '01	6	204	.1	.8	9	96	.2	.8	5	101	.1	.4	10	137	.2	1.1	3	43	.1	1.3
KXKL-FM																				
SU '02	34	638	.7	4.3	53	346	1.1	4.5	66	379	1.3	5.2	35	360	.7	3.5	9	141	.2	3.6
SP '02	28	628	.6	3.6	31	233	.6	2.7	48	335	1.0	3.8	35	330	.7	3.6	9	122	.2	3.6
WI '02	30	605	.6	4.1	45	289	.9	4.1	56	356	1.1	4.6	37	354	.7	3.8	5	104	.1	2.3
FA '01	36	583	.7	4.6	55	292	1.1	4.4	69	292	1.3	5.4	46	343	.9	4.6	7	92	.1	3.3
4-Book	*32*	*614*	*.7*	*4.2*	*46*	*290*	*.9*	*3.9*	*60*	*341*	*1.2*	*4.8*	*38*	*347*	*.8*	*3.9*	*8*	*115*	*.2*	*3.2*
SU '01	38	668	.8	5.3	47	310	.9	4.3	60	339	1.2	5.2	52	419	1.0	5.6	12	145	.2	5.2
KXPK-FM																				
SU '02	10	148	.2	1.3	21	87	.4	1.8	15	112	.3	1.2	3	48	.1	.3	2	28		.8
SP '02	12	287	.2	1.5	19	134	.4	1.6	26	147	.5	2.1	13	127	.3	1.3	1	18		.4
WI '02	19	725	.4	2.6	23	353	.5	2.1	27	369	.5	2.2	30	377	.6	3.1	11	173	.2	5.2
FA '01	23	671	.4	3.0	29	301	.6	2.3	39	268	.7	3.1	35	384	.7	3.5	7	149	.1	3.3
4-Book	*16*	*458*	*.3*	*2.1*	*23*	*219*	*.5*	*2.0*	*27*	*224*	*.5*	*2.2*	*20*	*234*	*.4*	*2.1*	*5*	*92*	*.1*	*2.4*
SU '01	29	712	.6	4.0	29	370	.6	2.6	50	384	1.0	4.3	38	384	.8	4.1	11	189	.2	4.7
KYGO-FM																				
SU '02	60	1082	1.2	7.7	82	680	1.6	6.9	85	612	1.7	6.7	82	717	1.6	8.3	25	291	.5	10.0
SP '02	73	1126	1.5	9.4	110	680	2.2	9.5	98	569	2.0	7.9	91	723	1.8	9.4	25	274	.5	9.9
WI '02	75	942	1.5	10.1	115	626	2.3	10.4	129	582	2.6	10.6	103	674	2.1	10.6	17	226	.3	8.0
FA '01	81	1006	1.6	10.4	140	706	2.7	11.3	127	560	2.4	10.0	107	718	2.1	10.7	21	370	.4	10.0
4-Book	*72*	*1039*	*1.5*	*9.4*	*112*	*673*	*2.2*	*9.5*	*110*	*581*	*2.2*	*8.8*	*96*	*708*	*1.9*	*9.8*	*22*	*290*	*.4*	*9.5*
SU '01	70	1036	1.4	9.7	100	654	2.0	9.1	114	634	2.3	9.9	87	633	1.7	9.4	25	293	.5	10.7
TOTALS																				
SU '02	782	4840		15.6	1182	4245		23.6	1275	4004		25.4	990	4290		19.7	251	2264		5.0
SP '02	776	4905		15.5	1157	4286		23.1	1247	4026		24.9	967	4314		19.3	253	2312		5.0
WI '02	740	4811		14.7	1109	4247		22.1	1219	3900		24.3	975	4336		19.4	213	2199		4.2
FA '01	777	5028		14.9	1238	4494		23.7	1276	3905		24.4	1000	4304		19.2	209	2372		4.0
4-Book	*769*	*4896*		*15.2*	*1172*	*4318*		*23.1*	*1254*	*3959*		*24.8*	*983*	*4311*		*19.4*	*232*	*2287*		*4.6*
SU '01	723	4827		14.4	1099	4149		22.0	1155	3924		23.1	922	4258		18.4	233	2233		4.7

** Station(s) not reported this survey. * Listener estimates adjusted for reported broadcast schedule. + Station(s) changed call letters – see Page 13. 4-Book: Avg. of current and previous 3 surveys. 2-Book: Avg. of most recent 2 surveys.

 ARBITRON

Figure 16.3 continued.

The following four numbers are reported for each daypart:

1. AQH persons
2. Cume persons
3. AQH rating
4. AQH share

There are really only two numbers represented here. Remember the AQH persons is the estimate of the number of people (or in this case, women 25 to 49) who are listening at any given point in time, say 7:31 in the morning. Cume persons are the number of different people tallied over the daypart. Those are the only two numbers reported. Arbitron has saved you from doing some math by also reporting the AQH rating and AQH share. Remember the AQH rating is AQH persons divided by the population of the market (who are women between 25 and 49), while the AQH share is AQH persons divided by the number of people listening to radio (who are women between 25 and 49) in the Denver-Boulder market.

Starting in the far left-hand column, you will notice an alphabetical listing of the call letters of each station in the market. Below each station are the row headings for the five most recent ratings periods (Summer 2002, Spring 2002, Winter 2002, Fall 2001 and Summer 2001), with an average of the past year's ratings listed as "4-Book" before the Summer 2001 listing. The reason for listing these five ratings periods is so seasonal trends can be observed and this book's ratings (Summer 2002) can be easily compared to the prior year's book (Summer 2001). Some station formats tend to do better in different seasons. Looking over these four pages, see if you can find the answers to the following questions:

1. Which station has the highest overall ratings in the current book?
2. Which station has had the highest cume persons in afternoon drive for the past year?
3. Which station has seen the biggest decline in audience over the past year?
4. What's the highest-rated station in the nighttime daypart?
5. Which stations have changed call letters?

Remember, for each of these questions, the answers are based on the demographic of Women 25 to 49 in the Metro area. The answers are:

1. "Which station has the highest overall ratings in the current book?" Clearly, one station dominates this demo in this market. KBCO-FM achieved a 1.9 AQH rating for the Summer 2002 book (follow the SU '02 row to the Monday to Sunday, AQH Rtg column), while its closest competitors achieved a 1.6 (KOSI-FM) and a 1.2 (KYGO-FM). Arbitron estimated 9,500 women 25 to 49 living in the metro area were listening to KBCO-FM on average between Monday to Friday, 6 AM to midnight (follow the SU '02 row to the first column, AQH (00), meaning "hundreds of persons"), while KOSI had, on average 1,600 fewer women 25 to 49 listeners (7,900), and KYGO had 3,500 fewer (6,000.) Over the course of the week in the summer of 2002, Arbitron estimated 138,100 different women 25 to 49 in the metro area tuned into KBCO (see the Cume (00) column). That means KBCO's *reach* into the Denver-Boulder market was more than 25,000 more women 25 to 49, in the metro, than its nearest competitors. (KYGO and KOSI had 108,200 and 103,900 respectively.)

2. "Which station has had the highest cume persons in afternoon drive for the past year?" To answer this question, you must look at the four-book average for cume persons in the Monday to Friday 3 PM to 7 PM column. This is the 7th column from the right-hand side of the page (14th from the left). These numbers are printed in **bold** to make them a bit easier to read. Again, KBCO-FM is the winner with 87,200 different women 25 to 49 tuning in over the course of a week's worth of drive time. As you can see from the column just to the left, about 11,600 of them are listening at any given moment in time.

3. "Which station has seen the biggest decline in audience over the past year?" Another way of asking this question is: "Which station's program director is most likely to be fired?" This question requires you to compare either the AQH persons or cume persons for the Summer 2001 and Summer 2002 books for every station. KXPK-FM stands out in this comparison with a drop of 1,900 AQH persons from Summer 2001 to Summer 2002 (from 2,900 to 1,000), and a drop of 56,400 cume persons (from 71,200 to 14,800). Interestingly, KXPK's morning drive (6 AM to 10 AM) numbers are relatively stable from 2001 to 2002, but they lost significant audience in middays (10 AM to 3 PM), and afternoon drive (3 PM to 7 PM), perhaps due to the loss of a popular program or DJ.

4. "What's the highest rated station in the nighttime (7 PM to MID) daypart?" Here, two stations appear to be tied. Both KYGO-FM and KOSI-FM report 2,500 AQH persons for Summer 2002. Is there a way to break the tie? KYGO-FM reports 29,100 cume persons, while KOSI-FM shows only 28,200. Do those extra 900 cume persons mean KYGO-FM can claim to be number one (at least in late night, metro, women 25 to 49)? Perhaps. But remember, such a small difference could be due to one or two diaries out of the total sample. And larger cume persons are not always an advantage. The ratio between AQH and cume is a measure of the time an average listener spends listening. A smaller cume for a given AQH means a longer time spent listening (TSL) as you will see below. And advertisers may prefer longer TSLs because it suggests listeners are not tuning in and out with each commercial break.

5. "Which stations have changed call letters?" This is an easy one. Note the + sign at the bottom of each page. This indicates that KQMT-FM and KXDC-FM have changed their call letters within the past year.

National Advertisers, Local Advertisers, and Geographic Areas

The Metro area is used most frequently for radio audience estimates by most advertisers. The DMA area ratings can be used to compare television ratings estimates with those for radio. The TSA is rarely used by advertisers because only the most powerful stations in any market have signals that cover the TSA. However, the difference between TSA, DMA, and Metro areas is one reason why more than one station in a market may honestly claim to be number one. A low-power station can dominate the Metro, while its higher-powered competitor can be number one in the TSA. Since the TSA contains many more people than the smaller metro area, the few AM and FM stations that have coverage in the larger TSA (50,000-watt AMs and 100,000-watt FMs) have a built-in advantage over the stations that cover the smaller Metro area, such as Class A FM stations (3,000 watts) and low-power or daytime-only AM stations.

The most appropriate area for salespeople to use in client presentations is determined by the retail trading area of the prospective client's business. A national advertiser, such as McDonald's, Coca-Cola, or Pepsi, with products distributed through retail outlets in every TSA county, will benefit most from buying based on the TSA ratings. On the other hand, a downtown retailer with only one location (for example, a local dry cleaner) would benefit most from evaluating Metro area ratings and generally would not be willing to pay higher prices for additional coverage in the TSA. The extra audience reached in the non-metro TSA for advertisers who have metro-based trade areas is often referred to as *wasted coverage*. Wasted coverage means reaching (and paying to reach) an audience that is not in the advertiser's target market area.

HUT, PUT, and PUR

Time-period ratings are useful to advertisers and their advertising agencies because the AQH ratings of individual time periods (such as morning and afternoon drive) can be added together to get the total rating points that an entire advertising campaign will deliver. If you add up the MSA or TSA AQH persons for all of the stations in a given column in a radio ratings report, the result is another useful statistic: the total of all the people in the geographic area, demographic group, and time period who are tuning in to all of the radio stations combined. This total is the persons using radio (PUR). PUR can also be expressed as a rating (for example, as a percentage of the total population) by dividing the sum of the AQH persons for the radio stations in the market by the market population. PUR percentages are higher for morning drive (6 to 10 AM Monday through Friday) than they are for evenings (7 PM to midnight Monday through Friday). On page 4 of Figure 16.3, PURs are at the bottom of the page in the rows labeled TOTALS. Note how the total number of AQH women 25 to 49 drops from 127,500 for mid-day to 25,100 for evenings. This trend would hold for most other demographic groups as well, with the possible exception of teenagers, who tend to listen to the radio in the evening.

In television, this statistic is known as persons using television (PUT) for person-based ratings or homes using television (HUT) for TVHH-based ratings. Like PUR, HUT and PUT can be expressed as percentages of a universe. HUT percentages are commonly referred to as *HUT levels*. HUTs, PUTs, HUT levels, and PUT levels are reported at the bottom of each time period in the Arbitron and Nielsen television reports. Television HUTs and PUTs have an inverse relationship with radio's PUR. TV HUT levels are highest during evenings (7 PM to midnight) when radio's PUR is lowest, and TV's HUTs are lowest in morning drive (6 to 10 AM) when radio's PURs are highest.

Shares

A *share* is the percentage of all the people tuning in to the medium who are listening to or viewing a particular station. Shares indicate how well a station is doing against its competitors, regardless of how many people from the total base population are tuning in to the medium. Refer to the Nielsen ratings page in Figure 16.2. "Frasier" on WMAQ earned a 17 share (column 2) and a 12 rating (column 1). There is a special relationship among ratings, shares, and HUT levels. If you know any two, you can easily calculate the third number using the following formula:

Rating = Share × HUT level

For Chicago, Tuesdays, 8:00 PM to 8:30 PM, in November 2001, the multi-week average HUT level was 70 (HUT/PUT/TOTALS in column 7). For "Frasier:"

17 share × 70 percent HUT Level = 12 Rating

Also, if you add up the ratings for each of the stations, the result is PUR or HUT level. If you add up the shares for each station, what should you get? You are right if you said 100 percent. Of course, in practice, some of these numbers may not add up exactly due to rounding errors in the report. For example, a 3.7 rating and a 4.4 rating would each be rounded to a 4 rating for publication in the book.

Salespeople use the station's ratings in presentations to advertisers because the ratings reflect the size, demographics, and location of the advertiser's desired target audience. Shares, on the other hand, are used primarily by station program directors to measure how well their station is performing against its competition. Industry standard practice is to refer to a station's rating and then its share without mentioning which is which. For example, you may hear two broadcast executives discussing a station's performance. One might say, "We had an 11/15 in the last book." That statement would mean that the station had an 11 rating and a 15 share. You can be sure that the 11 refers to the rating and the 15 to the share because the rating is always a lower number than the share. That is because a rating is based on the percentage of people in the geographic area, while share is based on the percentage of people in the geographic area who are listening to radio or watching television—a smaller number than the total population.

HUT levels are usually highest on Sunday nights and lowest on Friday and Saturday nights, especially in the summer months (when more people are out doing things rather than at home watching TV). If one program earns a 10/15 on a Sunday, but another earns a 7/31 on a Saturday night, which was the higher rated show? The answer is, just as Yoda suggested, very much dependant on your point of view. For the program director, the Saturday night show was the greater success. A 31 share is unheard of in television today. Yet the salesperson would much rather sell the program with the 15 share on Sunday night because it had the larger audience, even if it did a poorer job against its competition. For example, look at KYGO-FM in Figure 16.3. In the Summer of 2002, in afternoon drive the station had 8,200 AQH persons for a 1.6 rating and 8.3 share. But in late night it had 2,500 AQH persons for a .5 rating and a 10 share! Why? Because the TOTAL PUR dropped from 99,000 in afternoon drive to 25,100 in late night. Even though KYGO has a much smaller audience in late night, it is doing a much better job of programming against its competitors (at least in the women 25 to 49 demo).

Gross Ratings Points

The total of all of the ratings generated by each commercial in an advertiser's schedule is called *Gross Ratings Points* (GRPs). For example, an advertiser who has a target audience of men 18+ and decides to run two commercials in "NYPD Blue" on WLS, two in "Frasier" on WMAQ, and one in "Smallville" on WGN would calculate the total GRPs as follows (Men 18+ rating from column 35):

WLS:	9 rating × 2 =	18 GRPs
WMAQ:	7 rating × 2 =	14 GRPs
WGN:	3 rating × 1 =	3 GRPs
		35 total GRPs

The formula is GRPs = AQH rating × number of spots.

Note that you cannot simply add up the ratings (9 + 7 + 3 = 19) and multiply by the number of spots (19 × 5 = 95 GRPs); nor can you take the average rating (19 ÷ 3 = 6.3) times the number of spots (6.3 × 5 = 31). You must calculate the GRPs for each program and sum the totals to get the GRPs for the schedule.

Gross Impressions

The total of all people reached by the commercials in a campaign is called the *gross impressions (GIs)*. Like GRPs, the total may represent people from a number of different stations or time periods. For this example, let's use the radio persons estimates in Figure 16.3. If an advertiser has a target audience of women 25 to 49 and decides to run 90 commercials in morning drive on KBCO-FM, the total gross impressions created by that campaign would be the 13,000 AQH persons for Summer 2002 (column 5) × the 90 times the commercial would air. 13,000 × 90 = 1,170,000 gross impressions.

Gross Impressions = AQH Persons × number of commercials aired

If the campaign involved airing commercials on multiple stations, then the total campaign GIs can be calculated in the same manner as the television example above. Suppose the advertiser chose to purchase 30 commercials on each of the three highest-rated stations among metro women 25 to 49 in morning drive. KBCO-FM is the highest rated station with 13,000 AQH listeners, KOSI-FM is second with 11,700 and KIMN-FM is third with 8,900. The campaign total GIs would be calculated as follows:

KBCO-FM:	13,000 × 30 = 390,000
KOSI-FM:	11,700 × 30 = 351,000
KIMN-FM:	8,900 × 30 = 267,000
	1,008,000 gross impressions

Note that, as with GRPs, you cannot simply add up the total AQH persons (13,000 + 11,700 + 8,900) and multiply by the number of commercials (90). You must calculate the gross impressions for each station, and then sum the total.

Cumulative Audience

Cumulative audience, or *cume*, refers to the number of unique individuals (or different people) who listen to or view a program during some period of time. Cume is also known as the unduplicated audience. What this means is that listeners or viewers are only *counted* in the Cume Persons estimate *once*, no matter how long they listen or view (so long as it is at least five minutes within a quarter-hour). Cume persons will be important to calculating the number of times a listener or viewer is likely to hear or see a commercial.

Frequency

One of the most important things a prospective advertiser will want to know is, "How many times will a listener to your station (or viewer to your channel) hear (or see) my commercial?" That is a difficult question to answer. Some of the audience may be exposed to the commercial many times—especially those who are the most loyal viewers or listeners. Others, those who tune in and out for a brief time, may only be exposed once, or not at all. However, using the information about the AQH persons, cume persons, and number of times the commercial will air, we can calculate an average frequency for any campaign.

Let's review the KBCO-FM example above. Our advertiser purchased 90 commercials in morning drive. We know that 13,000 AQH listeners are in the audience on average at any given moment during morning drive. Looking in the next column over, we note that over the course of a 5-day week (Monday to Friday) during morning drive, 85,000 different individuals listened to KBCO-FM (Cume (00) in column 6). Some of these 85,000 people may have listened to KBCO during morning drive for an hour or more each day. Others may have tuned in for only a few minutes to catch the latest weather or traffic. But we can calculate the average number of times the average KBCO-FM listener heard our advertiser's commercial using the following formula:

Average Frequency = Gross Impressions ÷ Cume Persons

In our case, 1,170,000 Gross Impressions (13,000 AQH persons × the 90 commercials) ÷ 85,000 Cume Persons = 13.76. This means the average KBCO listener heard our advertiser's commercial almost 14 times.

Advertisers are especially interested in achieving a minimal level of frequency with their campaigns. Until a commercial is heard (or seen) several times over the course of a week, it is unlikely to make an impression. In the same way you have to repeat an instruction to a child, or review a difficult concept several times before an exam, the average audience member needs to hear or see a commercial several times before it is likely to make a lasting impression.

Reach

Equally important, if not more so, advertisers want to know how many total people in a community are likely to be exposed to their commercials. An advertiser may ask, "How many different people in this city are going to hear (or see) my commercial at least once?" Reach is a measure of the number of unique individuals who are exposed to at least one of the commercials in an advertising campaign. The size of a station's reach is equal to its cume audience. Advertisers and agencies often evaluate their commercial schedules in terms of both reach and frequency: how many different people a schedule reaches and how often the average person hears or sees a commercial.

We can now begin to see that the AQH rating is a function of two things: the number of persons watching or listening and the amount of time they watch or listen. Table 16.1 illustrates this concept.

WAAA has 10,000 people who tune in at 6 AM and listen for four full hours (16 quarter hours) without tuning out. WAAA's average quarter-hour audience is obviously 10,000 and so is its cume because no new people were added to WAAA's audience during the four-hour period. This listening pattern (although greatly exaggerated here) is similar to what might occur on the only Spanish language radio station in a market.

Table 16.1
AQH and Cume

	WAAA	WBBB
6AM	10,000 persons	2,500 persons
7AM	10,000 same persons, 0 new persons	2,500 new persons, 0 same
8AM	10,000 same, 0 new	2,500 new, 0 same
9AM	10,000 same, 0 new	2,500 new, 0 same
AQH Persons	10,000	2,500
Cume	10,000	10,000

WBBB has 2,500 people listening during the average quarter hour, but these 2,500 people stop listening at the end of each hour and 2,500 new people begin listening each hour. Over the four-hour period, WBBB has only one-fourth of WAAA's AQH audience, but it has the same cume as WAAA. Just as many different people listened to WBBB, but they listened for shorter periods of time (they listened for only one hour instead of four hours). This listening pattern (again, greatly exaggerated here) is similar to what might be seen on an all-news radio station.

Let's look at the same notion another way in Table 16.2.

Table 16.2
AQH and Cume

	WAAA	WBBB
6AM	10,000 persons	10,000 persons
7AM	10,000 same persons, 0 new persons	10,000 new persons, 0 same
8AM	10,000 same, 0 new	10,000 new, 0 same
9AM	10,000 same, 0 new	10,000 new, 0 same
AQH Persons	10,000	10,000
Cume	10,000	40,000

WAAA still has its 10,000 extremely loyal listeners tuning in from 6 AM to 10 AM with no new listeners joining in. But in this example, we see that WBBB now has 10,000 persons tuning in each hour. In this case, WAAA and WBBB have the same AQH audience sizes, but different cume audiences. If an advertiser bought time from each of the two stations and the stations scheduled the commercials one each hour for the four consecutive hours, what would the advertiser's gross impressions, reach, and frequency be?

First, gross impressions would be the number of spots (4) times the AQH persons (10,000), or 40,000, on both WAAA and WBBB. However, the reach, (cume, or unduplicated audience) on the two stations is quite different. The reach is 10,000 persons on WAAA but it is 40,000 persons on WBBB. The advertiser achieves *four times* as much reach on WBBB as on WAAA, but because people listen for longer periods of time on WAAA, the advertiser achieves four times as much frequency on WAAA as on WBBB. Now, recall the formula for frequency:

Frequency = Gross Impressions ÷ Cume Persons
WAAA frequency = 40,000 ÷ 10,000 = 4
WBBB frequency = 40,000 ÷ 40,000 = 1

Thus, 10,000 people hear the advertiser's commercial four times on WAAA, and 40,000 different people hear the advertiser's commercial once on WBBB.

From a salesperson's point of view, the station that is easier to sell will depend on the advertiser's needs. If frequency of exposure to the commercial message is more important to an advertiser, WAAA would be preferred. If maximizing reach is more important, then WBBB would be the first choice. For an advertiser who sells a product that is not highly differentiated and who has a lot of competitors advertising similar products, or an advertiser selling an impulse item that has a short purchase cycle, frequency is more important than reach. On the other hand, if an advertiser is offering a large discount on an already familiar and popular product, maximizing audience reach is more important than maximizing frequency.

One word of caution: In the preceding formula for estimating frequency (or in any formula that uses cume as a variable), special calculations from the rating companies for cumes will probably be needed. Unless the spot schedule runs on only one station in one time period, special cume estimates must be ordered from the companies that produce the ratings reports. Cumes cannot be added together across stations or across dayparts on a single station because without specialized reports, you cannot determine the percentage of audience that is common to the stations or to the daypart. Thus, it is nearly impossible to estimate frequency for a campaign that runs on multiple stations without a specialized ratings report. Those are usually delivered as part of a computer-based package that can run various optimizations for combinations of stations and spot schedules. You can add average quarter-hour figures and multiply them by the number of commercials in a schedule to determine the gross impressions for any campaign, but you cannot do this with cumes in a ratings report. The cume for each time period stands on its own.

Maintenance

Since ratings are a function of how many people listen and for how long they listen, program and promotion directors in both radio and television do all they can to achieve audience maintenance—to keep people listening or viewing as long as possible so they will be counted in more and more quarter hours. Programmers and promotion people at stations and networks tantalize audiences with promos, such as offering prizes that are "coming up in just twenty minutes" on radio or showing a provocative scene from the program "later tonight" on television. To determine how well a station or program maintains its audience, a standard measurement is needed. Two comparisons are commonly used in the industry: time spent listening (TSL) and audience turnover.

Refer again to Table 16.2. Suppose an advertiser asked you, "How long do people listen to your station?" It should be obvious from the data that WAAA's TSL is four hours and WBBB's TSL is one hour, or you could use the following formula:

TSL = AQH Persons × number of Quarter Hours in the daypart
     ÷ Cume persons

Remember, AQH and cume persons in the ratings report represent quarter-hour-based listening (15-minute time periods), so we will have to calculate the total number of quarter hours in Monday to Friday's 6 AM to 10 AM drive time. That is four Quarter Hours in each hour × four hours per day × five days, or 80 quarter hours per week in morning drive. Now look at Table 16.1 and calculate the TSL for KBCO-FM's Monday-Friday metro morning drive among women 25 to 49.

KBCO-FM (13,000 AQH persons × 80 QHs) ÷ 85,000 Cume Persons
    = 12.24 QHs

Now we will have to convert from quarter hours to hours and minutes. Twelve quarter hours equals 3 hours; .24 of a quarter hour is 24 percent of 15 minutes, or about 3 minutes and 36 seconds. We can round that up to 4 minutes. So, the time spent listening (TSL) by an average KBCO-FM listener is about three hours and four minutes per week. To calculate the TSL on an average day, we will need to divide by 5 (the number of days in morning drive). This can get a bit messy unless we convert to minutes first. Three hours equals 180 minutes, plus 4 minutes equals 184 minutes. Therefore, $184 \div 5 =$ about 37 minutes per day.

A second comparative measure, audience turnover, is closely related to TSL. Turnover is an estimate of the number of times the audience completely changes during the time period being evaluated. Using the KBCO-FM example above, calculate KBCO-FM's audience turnover among women 25 to 49 for morning drive using the following formula:

$$\text{Turnover} = \text{Cume Persons} \div \text{AQH Persons}$$

KBCO-FM's audience turnover is 6.5 ($85,000 \div 13,000$). To keep turnover low, programmers in radio try to keep intrusive interruptions to a minimum and try to keep positive features and familiar music to a maximum. Television programmers try to schedule programs of similar appeal back to back to keep people viewing from program to program.

Ratings Techniques

Three techniques are currently used to gather information about broadcast and cable audiences: telephone recall, diaries, and people meters. Telephone coincidentals and personal interview methodologies have been used by some ratings services in the past and are occasionally used today by the major ratings services to expand the sample size of some difficult-to-measure demographic groups.

Telephone Coincidental

These surveys measure current media use only. This is the oldest rating technique, pioneered by the Crossley and Hooper ratings services, which are no longer in business. Telephone coincidentals were performed by randomly selecting telephone numbers from a directory, calling the numbers, and asking people who answered the phone what they were listening to or watching. The advantage of this technique is that it is relatively inexpensive and fast; results can be given out the next day in most cases. However, this practice has some limitations, which became more and more unacceptable to advertisers. Coincidentals can reflect a respondent's behavior only at the exact time of the phone call. Therefore, they can report only AQH audience estimates but not cume. Telephone coincidentals also cannot measure away-from-home listening (at least not until cellular telephones are universally used). At this time, no major national ratings service uses this technique regularly, although coincidental telephone surveys can be purchased to evaluate special programs or program changes. The major ratings companies sometimes use this technique in their own in-house research as a standard of comparison for diary and meter methodologies.

Telephone Recall

These surveys ask respondents via telephone to recall what they heard or watched recently. This technique was developed to try to overcome some of the disadvantages of the coincidental telephone technique. Eastlan uses telephone recall as did RADAR, a company that measured network radio audiences, until it was acquired by Arbitron in July 1991. Even though the recall technique is subject to some memory loss on the part of respondents, it does have several advantages over the coincidental technique. The recall methodology can measure both AQH and cume persons. The increase in call screening by answering machines, do-not-call lists, and the general dislike of telemarketing in any form has greatly hampered the ability of all research companies to produce telephone-survey-based research.

Diaries

For radio, pre-selected individual listeners are given a *diary* in which they write down all of their in-home and out-of-home listening for a one-week period. Arbitron uses individual diaries that are kept by each member of a randomly selected household for a full week. The diaries are known as open-ended (or unaided) because they contain no preprinted information about time of day or station heard. Radio diaries are pocket-sized to encourage respondents to carry them around to record all of their listening habits. The diaries also contain space for the participants to record demographic information such as age, sex, area of residence, and employment status.

Nielsen's television diaries are slightly more complicated than those for radio because they are assigned to a TV set, not to individuals. All viewing by all people has to be entered, which includes adults, children, and visitors. Television diaries are known as close-ended diaries because each quarter hour of the viewing day is printed on a line. On the back of television diaries, additional information is requested on the number of sets in the household, the number of color sets, family size, and race.

The biggest advantage of diaries is their relatively low cost. Diaries are designed to measure individual, personal listening in radio, both at home and away from home, and how many people are watching a television set.

One of the problems with the diary technique is that it can take up to eight weeks to produce a rating report and get it into the hands of stations, advertisers, and their advertising agencies. Another drawback is that, like any survey technique, diaries have some built-in biases. They tend to favor those radio stations to which people listen for longer periods of time, such as easy-listening, ethnic, and some talk stations. They also tend to favor radio stations with older listeners of a higher socioeconomic status, such as all-news stations. In television, diaries tend to favor network-affiliated stations and news programs.

Meters

Meters were used to measure radio listening as early as the 1930s. As radio became more mobile, radio meter usage declined and the meters were modified to measure television viewing. The major drawback of these early meters was that, while they could accurately measure the channel watched and the duration of viewing, they could not record the size of the audience (remember, early radio and television ratings were strictly household-based) or other demographic information. In other words, meters worked quite well for household-based television ratings but failed to provide the information necessary for person- or demographic-based ratings.

In the early 1980s, a British company—Audits of Great Britain (AGB) — pioneered the development of the *people meter*, a meter that could accurately record channel selection, duration, audience size, and audience demographics. Part of the function of people meters today is automatic (people meters automatically record channel selection and duration) and part is manual (audience size and demos must be entered manually). Nielsen uses people meters in about 65 local markets where they have continuous metered service.

People meters attach to a television set and track every minute that the set is turned on and to which channel it is tuned. Each member of the household is also assigned to a key on the remote control for the people meter. When the set is first turned on, the people meter will ask the viewer with the remote control to enter the code numbers for each of the people in the room. It is also possible to enter additional demographic information about non-family members who may be visiting. The people meter blinks every quarter hour to inquire if there have been any changes in the audience in the room. The information gathered by the meter is stored and sent to a central computer by phone line twice a day. The computer system provides overnight ratings results for subscribing television and cable networks, local stations, and advertisers and their agencies.

Since people meters are mechanical, they are probably more reliable than people recording channel selection in their diaries, especially when channels are changed frequently and during late-night and early-morning dayparts. People meters are relatively expensive, compared to diaries; however, they are becoming the current methodological standard and are gradually replacing diaries in many local markets. People meters are used to generate the overnight ratings for the networks and provide overnight results for local stations as well.

Single Source Measurement and Scanning Meters

In the 1990s, Arbitron and Nielsen both experimented with *scanning meters* that can correlate product purchase behavior with commercial exposure. In Arbitron's ScanAmerica project, people meters were equipped with a wand for recording universal product codes, or UPCs (similar to the scanners used in supermarkets and other retail stores). Individuals in these households were expected to record, with the wand, all of their product purchases that had UPCs. This information could then be used to evaluate the effectiveness of commercials to which household members had been exposed and to provide ratings based on a universe of specific product purchasers (for example, the rating for a show in which the universe was women 18 to 24, living in the metro, who regularly purchased a given brand of shampoo). While the Arbitron ScanAmerica tests were considered a failure, the goal of collecting both media exposure information and household purchase information remains something of a Holy Grail for media research companies. If one company could track both the television commercials you watch and the products you purchase, the data would be as valuable to advertisers as gold.

Passive, Portable People Meters

For the past decade, Arbitron has been developing a passive, portable people meter (PPM) designed to record all radio listening and television viewing information. The meter works by picking up an inaudible (to humans) sound encoded into the radio station's signal, and into the audio portion of the television signal. They also hope to make the device compatible with Internet streaming and, perhaps using some other radio frequency (RF) signal and GPS information, exposure to Outdoor media. Arbitron has tested its meters in England, Wilmington, DE, and Philadelphia and shown that the technology, while extraordinarily expensive compared to diaries, is both workable and more reliable. A.C. Nielsen, which recognizes the PPM as a threat to its television ratings business, has been providing financial support and research data to Arbitron for the PPM tests in return for an option to develop the technology as a joint venture. The PPM is about the size of a standard pager, and is designed to be carried or clipped to clothing. At night it is inserted into a docking station connected to a phone line and the data is uploaded to Arbitron's mainframe computers.

According to information on Arbitron's Web site, the initial PPM trials have demonstrated that:[1]

1. Broadcasters are willing and technically able to encode their audio with no adverse effect on the quality of their signal.
2. Arbitron can effectively recruit a representative panel of consumers for the PPM system.
3. Compliance is high. Participants are willing to regularly carry the meter an average of 15 hours a day.
4. The total radio, television, and cable ratings indicated that the PPM system is capturing television viewing and radio listening that are not being measured by current audience measurement systems, especially among younger demos, men, and for-cable and out-of-home radio and television exposure.

The Ratings Companies

Each of the three major broadcast ratings companies, Arbitron, Eastlan, and Nielsen, survive in a highly competitive and high-cost business. Gone are ratings companies such as Birch, Crossley, Hooper, Pulse, Trendex, and RADAR, and many more that failed to make broadcast audience research profitable. Perhaps they were encouraged to try because of broadcasters' continual dissatisfaction with ratings, but these companies subsequently found, to their dismay, that most station managers complain loudly about poor research but are unwilling to support more or better research financially.

Arbitron

Arbitron selects a sample of households in a local radio market to develop an effective sample base. In the past, Arbitron selected only telephone households to contact, but currently the company is using a technique called an expanded sample frame (ESF) in many markets in an attempt to sample more than just homes with listed telephone numbers. The ESF technique is used in both radio and television by Arbitron and Nielsen and involves random-digit dialing. By programming a computer to generate random telephone numbers for all of the possible combinations available to residences (for example, ignoring business exchanges) in a local telephone exchange and then to dial them, the ratings companies are not relying just on the telephone directories for their samples. This technique has increased the sampling of unlisted telephones, which in some cities can reach as high as 40 or 50 percent of the total active telephone numbers. The ESF technique has also increased the sampling of younger, more transient people—especially the 18 to 24-year-olds—whose numbers may not be in the directories yet.

Placement letters are sent to these randomly selected households when the address is known; for ESF households, a phone call is made first. An Arbitron-trained interviewer then follows up with a phone call to get as many households to cooperate as possible. If the people contacted agree to participate in the survey, the interviewer finds out how many people in the home are over the age of 12; the interviewer then asks that each person record his or her listening habits in a diary for one week.

Spanish-speaking interviewers are used whenever possible in markets with a high percentage of Spanish-speaking people. Special efforts are made to help people with English-language difficulties record their listening habits in their diaries. Arbitron also makes extra efforts to help people complete their diaries in areas that have been identified as traditionally having low diary return rates, such as high density black areas (HDBAs) and high-density Hispanic areas (HDHAs). Also, higher cash incentives may be offered to individuals in these demographic groups, as much as $5 per person.

The day before the radio surveys are sent out, Arbitron interviewers call to remind people that the rating period is beginning. The interviewers call again in the middle of the week to see if there are any problems in filling out the diaries. In spite of all of these precautions, only about 60 percent of the diaries returned are filled out accurately enough to be usable. Arbitron conducts ratings surveys four times each year for 12 weeks in the winter, spring, summer, and fall. In the front of its ratings reports, Arbitron lists radio stations that have engaged in "unusual promotional activity." These activities are often referred to as *hypoing* and consist of unusually heavy promotion, contests, advertising, or disc jockeys trying to influence how people record their listening habits. Most stations claim they promote year-round and that no activity is unusual. Occasionally, however, advertisers and their agencies will re-evaluate a rating position for a station that conducts unusually heavy promotional activity that might have had an impact on the ratings, thus making those ratings questionable.

Eastlan/Willhight

Eastlan uses a telephone-recall methodology. Listeners are randomly dialed and asked to recall their radio listening for the previous 24-hour period. Business and nonworking telephone numbers are eliminated from the sample. One person is interviewed in each household. Eastlan/Willhight interviewers ask probing questions to aid each respondent's recall of away-from-home listening—at work, in cars, at stores, and during sports broadcasts. Among other variables, respondents are asked to identify stations by call letters, frequency, city, format, slogan, and air talent names. Eastlan/Willhight reports its geographic-based radio ratings by ZIP code rather than by the traditional metro, ADI, and TSA areas. Each ZIP code in the market area is weighted to ensure that the number of telephone interviews in that ZIP code is proportional to the percentage of the market population that lives in that ZIP code area.

Nielsen

Nielsen does not measure radio audiences in the United States, but it is the only company that measures nationwide television and cable network audiences. Nielsen calls its local television market ratings reports the *Nielsen Station Index (NSI)* and its network reports the *Nielsen Television Index (NTI)*. Even though Nielsen surveys national cable networks, it does not survey audiences of local cable systems unless a cable channel has high-enough ratings to meet the minimum reporting standards and show up in a regular local television market report. You may also have noticed the Arbitron radio report and the Nielsen television report are formatted quite differently. This is because people watch television differently from the way that they listen to radio. Television ratings reports are formatted to show specific program audiences and the commercial positions, or breaks, between programs. Radio reports are formatted to show broad dayparts. You might notice this effect in your own behavior. Most people can respond with the call letters or slogan of their favorite radio station, but how many people do you know with a favorite television station? On the other hand, many people have a set of favorite television programs but no favorite radio programs. TV audiences tend to be loyal to programs while radio audiences tend to be loyal to stations.

Sampling

Sampling is a complex subject, but because much of the criticism of broadcast and cable research focuses on the size of the samples used by ratings companies, it is worthwhile to develop a rudimentary understanding of it. Perhaps the following analogy will help. Imagine you were to gather all of the media salespeople in the United States into a large stadium and begin by asking for a show of hands for those in television, then for those in radio, then those in Outdoor, and so on. You would soon realize that it was impractical, to say nothing of confusing, to try to count everyone (counting everyone would be called a *census).* The other option is to take a random sample and then infer (or estimate) the distribution by media of the various salespeople in the stadium.

Since to get into the stadium all the media salespeople had to take a number, you begin to choose numbers randomly from a hat. You decide to choose a sample of 100 people. You then offer a free plasma screen TV (or some other universally attractive prize) to all of the people whose numbers have been chosen; they naturally come forward immediately and you ask them which medium they represent. You have just conducted a reasonably good random-sample survey, and you can now infer that—whatever the distribution of salespeople by medium—the odds are pretty good that a similar distribution exists in the total population of media salespeople.

Next, you consider offering a plasma screen TV to 100 more randomly selected salespeople, hoping to improve the accuracy of your prediction. However, being no dummy, you realize that all the plasma screen TVs are costing you a bundle and that you were probably close enough with your first estimate. You remember from your media research class that the standard error of any sample is in inverse proportion to the square root of the sample size. In simpler terms, that means that in order to double the accuracy of your estimate, you would have to quadruple your sample size. You certainly do not feel like shelling out money for 400 plasma screen TVs, so you decide to rely on your first sample of 100.

This mind game is merely a method to make the subject of probability sampling more digestible. For further study and reference, you might consider adding a basic statistics course to your plan of study or reviewing one of the broadcast research texts in the reference section of this chapter. The following is a condensation and summary of the very basic sampling concepts that you should be familiar with.

Definition of a Sample

A sample is a portion of a population from which an inference is going to be made about the characteristics of the entire population. A sample must be selected according to some sampling plan, which includes the sampling frame, type, and size of the sample.

There are two general types of sampling used in generating broadcast ratings: *quota sampling* and *probability sampling. Quota* sampling is a type of non-probability sample in which quotas are set for the number of respondents of various types to be surveyed. For example, quotas may be set for various geographic areas, age groups, or income levels. The aim of quota samples is to try to match the sample to characteristics of a total population. However, since the quotas are not determined on a probability, or random, basis, there is no way of measuring the probable size of the sampling error involved. Quota samples are based on judgment or convenience and may or may not be accurate, but there is no way of calculating how accurate they might be. The ratings services sometimes use this type of sampling when they establish quotas for some hard-to-sample demographics, such as some ethnic groups and young adult males 18 to 24.

With *probability* sampling, every unit (that is, household or person) has an equal chance of being selected; it is also referred to as a random sampling. There are several kinds of probability sampling, such as stratified sampling and cluster sampling, which we will not go into here, but each of them permits one to compute the limits of the margin of error that is attributable to sampling.

Determining Sample Size

The term *sample size* refers to the number of units (again, households or people) actually used to tabulate information. In this sense, the sample size is referred to as an in-tab sample by the ratings companies because not all of the diaries mailed out or returned are usable and only those that are usable become eligible for tabulation to determine the size of an audience. Returned diaries may be deemed unusable if they are postmarked before the end of the survey, have blank pages (diary keepers are asked to check a box on days that they report not hearing a radio), or if it is established that the diary keeper is employed in the media.

Standard Error

The standard error of a rating is the amount of error that can be attributed to the sampling itself. It does not include errors that might occur from the inaccurate filling out or reading of diaries, from printing errors that might occur in a report, or due to station hypoing. A standard error can only be calculated from a probability, or random, sample. The standard error is typically expressed in percentage terms and depends on the size of the sample and of the rating. If you are interested in pursuing the calculation of standard errors further, look in the back of a ratings company report; these reports discuss how to determine the standard error, or possible fluctuations, of any rating in the report, including the confidence level of the rating.

Standard errors are expressed as limits of probable variations, plus or minus a certain percentage from a rating. For example, the standard error for a television station's household rating of 15 might be plus or minus 0.7, with a confidence level of 0.05. The *confidence level* means that 95 times out of 100, the true rating in the total population from which the sample was taken will fall between 14.3 and 15.7. Standard errors can be reduced by averaging ratings across many time periods, across many markets, or across several ratings reports. Average quarter-hour ratings are more reliable (that is, they have a lower standard error) than cume ratings, even though cume numbers are larger. This apparent inconsistency comes about because the more averages that are taken, the more the error due to variations in sampling is minimized.

Some understanding of sampling is important because although advertisers rarely complain about the vagaries of diary or meter techniques, they are often quick to ask how a station can claim to be number one with "such a small sample." Hollywood producers, directors, and stars weep and tear their garments when their network programs are cancelled, and they often blame the "tiny" sample. To avoid as much of this criticism as possible and to satisfy advertisers' desire to have accurate audience information, the ratings companies, the stations, and the networks all go to great lengths to ensure sampling techniques are adequate and reasonable to estimate audience size.

The ratings companies can produce distinguished statisticians who can prove that a national sample of 4,000 people is more than adequate to estimate the ratings for television and cable network programs within acceptable tolerances. These experts also try to prove that a metered sample of 350 to 500 people is all that is needed to get an acceptable estimate of household ratings in local television markets. These samples are acceptable in the sense that advertisers and broadcasters have agreed—through a variety of industry committees, associations, and councils—that the standard error ranges are within acceptable limits to buy and sell time and to make informed programming decisions. Furthermore, over the years when Arbitron and Birch both measured radio audiences, and Arbitron and Nielsen both measured television audiences, the companies were amazingly close in their rating estimates. The same programs came up week after week among the top ten in Arbitron and Nielsen television reports, and Arbitron and Birch (for most formats) had extremely close estimates in spite of very different methodologies. If the ratings services' sampling errors were very large, they should have large differences in their estimates of the ratings much more frequently.

The next time you hear someone complain that a sample is too small, remind him or her that the standard error of a rating is in inverse proportion to the square root of the sample size, not to the size of the entire population. That goes for all samples, regardless of the size of the universe sampled. Thus, a sample size of 400 people is just as accurate to measure ratings in the national population as it would be to measure ratings in the population of metropolitan Chicago. If your doubters do not accept this explanation, suggest that the next time a nurse takes a blood sample of just a few drops, they should each insist on having a couple of quarts drawn to "reduce the size of the sampling error."

Cost Comparisons

If you sell in a small market where ratings are not normally used by advertisers, it may be wise to avoid using ratings. The old adage, "Live by the sword, die by the sword," applies to the use of ratings. It is nice to be number one, but very few stations can make that claim, and usually not for long, so avoid the possibility of eventually having to die by the ratings. If you must use ratings, you will use them primarily to create a differential competitive advantage or to compare your schedule of spots to those of your competitors.

There are two basic types of ratings comparisons: those that involve costs and those that do not. Use the ones that are cost-oriented only if you have to, and then use them as little as possible. As we discussed earlier, you do not want to rely only on price because this tactic limits your ability to focus an advertiser's attention on many of the other important quality elements of your station or system and its programming. You want to focus on value, not on price. You will need to understand cost comparisons, especially in larger markets. Following are several types of cost comparisons:

Cost-Per-Thousand

One of the most commonly used cost comparison techniques is *cost-per-thousand* (CPM). The M is derived from the Latin word for 1,000 and comes from the same root as millennium—1,000 years. The formula used to calculate CPMs is simple:

CPM = Total Campaign Cost ÷ Gross Impressions (in thousands)

Because this is the cost per *thousand*, gross impressions should always be expressed in thousands. For example, if gross impressions were 450,000, use 450. Chances are you will make fewer calculation errors if you follow this technique, and you will be able to do the calculations much faster. However, you may run across a formula that looks like this:

CPM = Total Campaign Cost ÷ (Gross Impressions ÷ 1,000).

Either way, just remember to divide the total gross impressions by 1,000 first. Finally, you may find the formula expressed as follows:

CPM = Total campaign cost × 1,000 ÷ Gross impressions.

You can see how multiplying the numerator by 1,000 would give the same answer as dividing the Gross Impressions in the denominator by 1,000. However, unless you are working this as a formula in a computer, it can make the numbers too unwieldy to manage easily. That is why we recommend just eliminating the last three zeroes from Gross Impressions, and using the simplified formula above.

CPMs are useful for comparing the *efficiency* (a common synonym for CPMs) of commercial schedules on a station or system, on two or more stations in the same market, among media, or among markets. Just like every other ratings measure, CPMs can be expressed for a variety of different demographics, survey areas, and time periods, so it is necessary to label them properly. CPM numbers alone are meaningless; they must be compared to other alternative CPMs in the same demographic area, survey area, and so on. Exhibit 16.1 shows a simple CPM calculation.

Cost-Per-Thousand Reached

This is a CPM based on cume rather than on the AQH. The formula for CPM reached is as follows:

CPM Reached = Total Campaign Cost ÷ Cume of Schedule (in thousands)

To calculate a CPM-reached figure, you must either have a method that estimates a schedule's cume (some personal computer-based programs can estimate

Exhibit 16.1 CPM Calculation

Station	AQH Persons	Number of Commercials Aired	Gross Impressions
KBCO	13,000	90	1,170,000

Cost per commercial: $60.00
Total campaign investment: $60.00 × 90 = $5,400

CPM = $5,400 ÷ 1,170 = $4.62

mixed daypart cumes) or order a special tabulation from a ratings company for a fee. Remember, you cannot add cume figures from a ratings book, so you must get cume estimates from other sources. Many stations have computer software that will estimate a schedule's reach, and some stations have special hookups to the computers of the ratings services and can estimate cumes this way.

Reverse Cost-Per-Thousand

This statistic can be useful in comparing a schedule on your station (whose prices, of course, you know) to a schedule on a station whose prices are unknown. When presenting reverse CPMs, show your schedule and CPMs, then show a similar schedule on a competitive station and indicate the price the other station would have to charge to meet your CPM levels. Reverse CPMs are not a widely used comparison, but they can be useful in certain selling situations, particularly when preventive selling or forestalling an objection is appropriate.

Exhibit 16.2 contains an example of how to present reverse CPMs. Assume your station is WAAA. WBBB's schedule of 31 spots delivers 249,550 gross impressions. To equal WAAA's $3,00 CPM, WBBB would have to charge 24.20 per commercial.

The formula is:

$7.50 (WAAA total investment) ÷ 31 (WBBB number of commercals)
= $24.20

**Exhibit 16.2
Reverse CPM
Calculation**

Station	AQH Persons	Number of Commercials Aired	Gross Impressions
WAAA	10,000	25	250,000

Cost per commercial: $30.00
Total campaign investment: $30.00 × 25 = $750

CPM = $750 ÷ 250 = $3.00

Station	AQH Persons	Number of Commercials Aired	Gross Impressions
WBBB	8,050	31	249,550

The cost per commercial WBBB would have to charge in order to equal WAAA's $3.00 CPM is:

$750 ÷ 31 = $24.20

Cost-Per-Point

Another cost comparison technique often used to evaluate campaigns is *cost-per-point* (CPP), which is sometimes called cost-per-rating-point. The CPP formula is similar to that for calculating CPMs:

CPP = Total Cost of Schedule ÷ Gross Rating Points (GRPs)

CPP calculations are used primarily by advertisers and advertising agencies for media planning purposes, to compare costs among markets and among stations in a market, and to plan on how much they will have to spend to achieve a desired advertising weight in a market and which station is most cost-efficient. Since CPPs are based on rating points (metro persons ratings in radio, or DMA household ratings in television), they will increase as the size of the market increases. For example, a 1 rating represents many more people in New York City than in Bozeman, MT, and thus commands a much higher price (1 percent of New York City's population is much greater than 1 percent of Bozeman's population).

Measuring Audiences

Measuring Magazine Audiences

Mediamark Research Inc. (MRI) is the largest and most often used research company in the magazine industry. MRI's *Survey of the American Consumer* has been conducted continuously since 1979 and reports the demographics, product usage, and media exposure experiences of magazine readers. Monroe Mendelsohn Research (MMR) was founded in 1958 to provide marketing consultation and to conduct custom marketing research surveys for the magazine industry. In 1978, MMR was sold to Walter McCullough, a technical expert on studying the affluent marketplace. The study now measures people who have household incomes of $75,000 or more in all 50 states and Washington, D.C., representing about 22 percent of the US population. MRI and MMR both provide extensive research on the audience of magazines, detailing the composition of their audience as well as the breadth and reach of the audience that reads the magazines (coverage).

Measuring Newspaper Audiences

Newspaper audiences are measured based on a newspaper's circulation and average readers per copy. The Audit Bureau of Circulation (ABC) audits, or verifies, the circulation of the majority of daily newspapers in the United States. Two other circulation auditing companies, Certified Audit of Circulations, Inc. (CAC) and Verified Audit Circulation (VAC), also audit newspaper circulation. Most newspapers make the claim, based on research, that the average newspaper has 2.2 readers per copy.[2] Thus, a newspaper with 50,000 circulation would have an audience of 110,000 readers (50,000 × 2.2). You will learn more about newspaper circulation and audiences in Chapter 18.

Measuring Interactive Audiences

Audience Measurement. ComScore Media Metrix has become to the Internet what Nielsen is to broadcast television—the leading measurement service. Media Metrix is a service dedicated solely to measuring the online audience and to "Detailing the online behavior of people that access the Internet, proprietary networks like AOL, instant messaging and other digital applications. The service delivers the most accurate and comprehensive audience ratings and estimates available today," according to its Web site.[3] Advertisers, media buyers, and Web site content providers alike use Media Metrix to determine which sites and which content attract women 18 to 49 and the best sport sites for kids and people 12 to 24, for example. A complete description of its multiple reports, methodology, and sampling can be found at www.comscore.com.

Media Metrix also provides another useful, sophisticated, and widely-used research tool, @Plan. By using @Plan, media buyers can get a vast amount of target information in six different modules: Statistical Profiling of target markets, such as senior management; Advertising Planning, which determines which Web sites a target market visits and how often; Site Profiling, which profiles Web sites' audiences; Custom Site Comparison, which compares Web sites; and DoubleClick Site Directory, which provides sales and technical information.

A. C. Nielsen Company is also in the Internet ratings business and conducts surveys which are published under the title of Nielsen//NetRatings. This company competes with Media Metrix and provides similar audience information. Nielsen//NetRating's planning tool is called WebRF, which is "the online industry's only comprehensive reach and frequency planning tool from Nielsen//NetRatings and IMS—it gives you sophisticated planning previously available only in traditional media. For the first time, you can access advertising campaign statistics in terms comparable to other media," according to the company's Web site.[4]

Advertising Effectiveness.   Aside from direct response metrics, most effectiveness research is based on the analysis of movement within consumers' brand awareness and purchase intent. The Internet Advertising Bureau (IAB), together with an organization named Marketing Evolution, has conducted several credible studies. In order to distinguish the efforts of online marketing from the other media, they have worked on product launches in which marketers have given 100 percent of the initial media budget to online marketing. This allocation has allowed the researchers to see the direct impact of online marketing without the influence of other media and other variables. Dynamic Logic is a research company that leads the way in online brand effectiveness research. Much of the information about these effectiveness studies are available at www.iab.net.

Measuring Outdoor Audiences

For years, the measurement of exposure to billboards and other outdoor media was limited to simple traffic counts. Roadside meters could count the number of cars passing a given point near a billboard, but no information was available about actual exposure or the demographics of those exposed. In 2002, Nielsen and Arbitron both announced plans to begin tests of systems designed to measure exposure to outdoor advertising. Both systems use GPS to track both motorist and pedestrian exposure to the outdoor media. Small, battery-operated meters were to be carried by a random sample of people, and would report their exact location every 20 seconds. The metered data would then be compared to the known location of outdoor billboards to determine the participants' "opportunity to see" an ad.

Test Yourself

1. What is the difference between a rating and a share?
2. What survey area is used most by advertisers to evaluate radio schedules: TSA, DMA, or metro?
3. What is a HUT level?
4. How are gross impressions and GRPs calculated?
5. What is a cume?
6. What is the difference between reach and frequency?
7. What are the major audience research methodologies for estimating audience size?
8. What are the major ratings companies?
9. What is more important in determining the accuracy of a rating, the size of the population sampled or the size of the sample?
10. How do you calculate campaign CPM and CPP?

Project

Secure a local radio or television ratings book. Select a station to sell for and select a client. Write a schedule proposal that contains 15 spots spread throughout a variety of time periods during a full week. Assume the client has a primary target audience of adults 25 to 54 and a secondary target audience of adults 25 to 49. Use metro ratings and persons for radio, and DMA ratings and total persons for television. Add up the adults 25 to 54 impressions for the 15-spot schedule you select, assume your CPM is $9, and calculate a total investment (cost) for your schedule. Do the same for adults 25 to 49, assume your CPM is $10, and calculate a total investment for the schedule. Next, add up the adults 25 to 54 and the adults 25 to 49 rating points in your schedule and, using the total investments for each schedule (adults 25 to 54 and adults 25 to 49), calculate the cost-per-points (CPP) for each demographic (Hint: Divide GRPs into total investment).

References

A.C. Nielsen Company. *Nielsen Report on Television, 2002.*

Arbitron Ratings Company. 2001. *The Arbitron Radio Listening Diary: Why the Radio Diary is an Effective Research Tool in the Digital Age.*

Arbitron Ratings Company. 2001. *Marketing Solutions & Media Insights: A Guide to Arbitron Information, Software and Services.*

Arbitron Ratings Company. 2001. *Only You Can Prevent Rating Distortion and Rating Bias.*

Arbitron Ratings Company. 2002. *The Portable People Meter: The Electronic Audience Measurement System for the 21st Century.*

Robert Balon. 1988. *Rules of the Radio Ratings Game.* Washington, DC: National Association of Broadcasters.

Roger Baron, Erwin Ephron, and Jack Sissors. 2002. *Advertising Media Planning, 6th edition.* New York: McGraw-Hill.

James Fletcher. 1989. *Profiting from Radio Ratings.* Washington, DC: National Association of Broadcasters.

Jhan Hiber. 1987. *Winning Radio Research.* Washington, DC: National Association of Broadcasters.

Ellen Seiter. 1999. *Television and New Media Audiences.* New York: Oxford University Press.

James G. Webster, Patricia Phalen, and Lawrence W. Lichty. 2000. *Ratings Analysis: The Theory and Practice of Audience Research.* New York: Erlbaum.

Resources

http:\\arbitron.colearn.com
ww.arbitron.com
www.cabletvadbureau.com
www.comscore.com
www.eastlan.com
www.iab.net
www.magazine.org
www.naa.org
www.nielsenmedia.com
www.nielsen-netratings.com
www.rab.com
www.tvb.org

Endnotes

1. www.arbitron.com. February, 2003.
2. Ohio University. Scripps Howard News: *Newspaper Readership Survey Results.* Athens, OH, June 2002.
3. www.comscore.com. April, 2003.
4. www.nielsen-netratings.com. April, 2003.

17 Advertising

By Charles Warner

Advertising is selling (mass selling), so the purpose of advertising is the same as the purpose of personal selling—to get customers and keep them. The way advertising gets and keeps customers is also similar to the way personal selling does it, which is to create value, present effectively, get customers to take action, and then get them to repurchase. In advertising, the creating value function is referred to as building brand image or brand attitude, as Tim Larson and Ken Foster call it in Chapter 15. Getting customers for a national consumer package goods advertiser or a local department store simply means selling products. Therefore, the *purpose of advertising is to build brands and sell products.*

Media consultant Erwin Ephron estimates that approximately 80 percent of national advertising dollars in broadcast television network are invested for brand building, or reminding and reinforcing consumers about brands they are familiar with.[1] This high percentage of ad dollars invested for reminding indicates the importance national advertisers place on building brand image. Great advertising both builds brand image and sells products; good advertising does one of these things well; and poor advertising does neither. But even well-written and well-produced advertising cannot build an image for or sell a bad product, as you learned in Chapter 15.

Advertising and Promotion

Both advertising and promotion are marketing communications and part of the third P of marketing—promotion. However, the objectives of advertising and promotion are different: advertising tells you why to buy a product; promotion tells you when to buy a product. Advertising creates value and builds brand image for the long term and, therefore, consumers will pay more for brands they like and trust. Promotions, as you learned in Chapter 8, are designed to get people to take action and buy a product immediately, usually because of a price reduction, rebate, or discount. Promotions have a short-term effect and eventually hurt sales and profit margins in the long run. Therefore, as you learned in Chapter 8, it is more profitable to invest $1 in advertising than to promote a $1 reduction in price in an attempt to increase volume.

How Advertising Works

Advertising has both a long-term and short-term effect on sales because well-crafted, consistent advertising takes consumers up an Advertising Ladder similar to the Sales Ladder you learned in Chapter 11. Table 17.1 shows the Advertising Ladder.

	Advertising	Corbett *	Marketing **	Sales
Table 17.1 **The Advertising** **Ladder**	Repeat Purchase		Repeat Purchase	Repurchase
	Reinforce and remind	Reminding	Brand attitude	Satisfaction
	Adoption/purchase	Persuading	Brand trial and purchase	Action
				Conviction
	Induce trial		Brand attitude	Desire
	Communicate information	Informing	Brand learning/ association	Interest
	Create awareness		Brand awareness	Attention

* Corbett and Stilli 2002, p. 53.
** See Chapter 15.

In order for advertising to work, it must take consumers step by step up the Advertising Ladder. Every advertising message should have an objective based on the five steps in Table 17.1 that lead up to the sixth step: repeat purchase. As a media salesperson, you must know what advertisers' objectives are (or help them figure them out) in order to recommend an effective solution and an advertising schedule in your medium. To recommend solutions, you must define the problems that accompany the steps on the Advertising Ladder: lack of awareness, lack of information about a product, low share of market, declining sales, low level of repurchase, and so on.

The types of schedules you will recommend depend not only on your customers' advertising objectives but also on their media plans. If you are selling to national advertisers, they will have an agency that creates their media strategy and media plans. If you are selling directly to local advertisers who do not have agencies, you must advise them on the best media strategy and plans to help them meet their advertising objectives.

National Advertising

National advertisers invariably retain advertising agencies to do two things: create and place their advertising.

Creating Advertising. Advertising agency creative departments are responsible for writing and producing advertising in the two top national media—television and magazines. Newspapers and radio are primarily local media, so large, national advertising agencies do not create a lot of advertising for newspapers and radio. Furthermore, highly paid creative people generally do not like to create newspaper ads or radio commercials because they believe these media are dull compared to television and magazines, especially television. Copywriters and agencies do not show prospective clients newspaper ads they have created, they only show their television commercials, or commercial reels as they are called. An agency's, creative director's, and copywriter's resume is their commercial reel, and you will never, ever hear an agency say when showing a reel to a client or a prospective client, "And here is a commercial we did that came from an idea that a salesperson brought us." A media salesperson selling to a national agency does not call on the creative department or creative people at an agency, because it is a waste of time.

Placing Advertising. Agency media departments are responsible for placing advertising; their two basic functions are planning and buying media. Ephron writes, "The purpose of media planning and buying is to enhance advertising's positive effects on sales."[2] In Chapter 27 you will learn more about how to sell to media buyers, but in this chapter you will learn how media planning works, because when you call on media buyers, they will be buying according to a media plan that has been put together by a media planner. In some smaller agencies, the media planning and buying is done by the same person, but in larger national agencies the two functions are separated.

Media Planning

Media planning is essentially deciding which media to buy and how much of each medium to buy to reach an advertiser's target audience while staying within a budget. It sounds relatively simple, but, in practice, it is complicated. Let's look at each of these decisions separately.

Which Media to Buy?   First, media planners analyze which media reach an advertiser's target audience most effectively and most efficiently. The effectiveness criterion is based on the execution the creative department has decided upon. For example, for a mass-marketed cosmetics product that appeals to teenage girls, a creative department might decide that a four-color ad featuring a glamorous teenage model might be the best creative execution, so magazines would be the most effective medium.

Once the most effective media have been selected, planners then consider efficiency. The efficiency criterion is based on media costs, primarily on cost-per-thousands (CPM). CPM is used to judge the comparative efficiency of network television (broadcast and cable), network radio, and magazines. Spot radio, television, and cable and local radio, television, and cable are evaluated based on comparative cost-per-point (CPP) data. Spot means buying on a market-by-market basis. For example, a spot television campaign might include buying the top 100 markets out of a total of 212 television markets in the US.

How Much to Buy?   The next step in the planning process is to figure out how much media can be purchased based on an advertiser's budget. Advertising budgets are determined according to a percentage of sales. Industries have different advertising-to-sales ratios, as seen in Table 17.2, which shows just 10 industries out of 190 industries that are reported on.

The ad-to-sales ratios are available at www.adage.com in the Data Center, in the Marketing/Advertising link, and under the title "Advertising to sales ratios by industry." In Table 17.2, you can see the wide variance by industry, from a low of 0.9 percent to a high of 10.1 percent, of advertising dollars spent

Table 17.2 Advertising-to-Sales Ratios of Selected Industries

Industry	Ad dollars as a percent of sales
Auto rental & leasing	2.2
Beverages	10.1
Biological products	1.7
Blank books, binders	4.1
Book publishing	7.7
Bottled & canned soft drinks, bottled water	6.3
Building mat'l., hardwr., garden-retail	4.2
Business services	6.2
Cable & other pay TV services	7.5
Calculators, acct. machines	0.9

Source: www.adage.com/pagecms?pageID=942. April 2003.

as a percentage of sales. Therefore a typical auto rental and leasing company that had $2 billion in sales would allocate $44 million (2.2 percent) for advertising, whereas a beverage company that had $2 billion in sales would allocate $202 million (10.1 percent) for advertising.

If we take the auto rental company with $2 billion in sales and an annual advertising budget of $44 million as an example, a media planner might go through the following thought process: "I know the client likes television and the creative department believes it has a memorable creative execution. However, because network television is so expensive, we cannot buy enough of it to make an impact. Also, the creative is targeted to business travelers and the majority of business travelers are concentrated in the top 25 markets. I think I'll recommend 70 percent of the budget be spent in spot television in the top 25 markets and 30 percent of the budget in spot cable in those markets on ES-PN and the Golf Channel." Let's assume the auto rental client approves this portion of the media plan.

The next step would be for the planner to look at average CPPs in the top 25 markets for television and cable and estimate how many weeks and how many spots per week in each medium to buy. These two factors will depend on advertising objectives. The planner might go through the following thought process: "The auto rental brand is well known, so I don't have to have a big, short burst of frequency to create awareness or to induce trial. The commercial is persuasive, so I need to reach and persuade business travelers on a continuous basis because business travel is not particularly seasonal. I need to reach them when they are planning a business trip and, therefore, are most receptive to my message. I will recommend a 39-week continuous schedule that runs March through November, I will optimize on reach for $44 million, and I will look at several media mixes."

The preceding paragraph introduces six concepts into planning considerations: reach, frequency, recency, continuous scheduling, optimization, and media mix. As you learned in Chapter 16, *reach* is the number of different people an advertising message reaches over a designated period of time, and *frequency* is how many times the average consumer is reached by an advertising message over a designated period of time. Recency, in terms of media planning, is a little more complicated.

Recency in media planning is a concept that Ephron introduced to media planners in 1994 based on the research of John Phillip Jones. Jones' research was published in his book *When Ads Work*. Up to that time, it was assumed by the media planning community that frequency is what drove sales because people tended to forget advertising messages, so the messages needed to be repeated often. However, Jones' research indicated that a single exposure could strongly influence which brand consumers purchased if those consumers were ready to buy. Recency is the last message consumers are exposed to before they buy and is, therefore, the most effective. Thus, the objective should be to expose advertising messages when consumers are receptive. As Ephron writes, "It is as if there is a window of opportunity for the ad message preceding each purchase; media's job is to put the message in the window."

Since the introduction of the recency planning concept, it has gradually replaced frequency planning as the favored model, especially with package goods advertisers and their agencies. Recency planning means that reach becomes the most important criteria, not frequency.

Continuous scheduling. Jones' and Ephron's research concluded that, because of the concept of recency, it is more effective to advertise continuously than to start and stop with heavy schedules, then cut back for several weeks or months (referred to as flighting) or to load up regular schedules from time to time (referred to as pulsing). The point of continuous scheduling is to always be present in the window of opportunity when a consumer is receptive and in the market for a product.

Optimization means trying to find the best combination that provides the most reach for either the lowest CPM or for a given budget amount. Most of the larger and many mid-sized agency planners use optimization computer programs, called optimizers, into which they input all the data and parameters of a media plan. According to Ephron, "TV optimizers were a response to three powerful forces—*recency planning, fragmentation, and sharp increases in prime time pricing.*"[3] Optimizers produce printouts, called flow charts, which show the best combination of dayparts and media that will provide the optimum reach that is either the most efficient (CPM) or within the limits of a specified dollar amount.

Media Mix modeling is also referred to as marketing mix modeling. Optimizers will always show that the cost of additional reach after a certain reach level has been attained in any one medium is expensive and that a combination of media is the best way to achieve maximum reach at the minimum cost. Figure 17.1 shows an example of how expensive it is to add incremental reach to a network television schedule.

**Figure 17.1
The cost of
incremental
reach.**

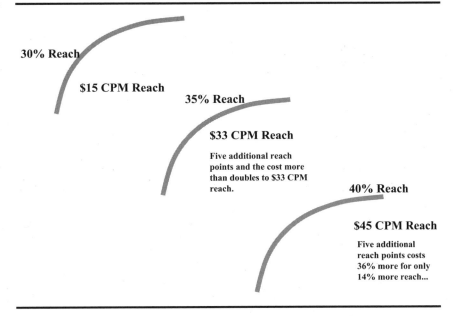

30% Reach

$15 CPM Reach

35% Reach

$33 CPM Reach

Five additional reach
points and the cost more
than doubles to $33 CPM
reach.

40% Reach

$45 CPM Reach

Five additional
reach points costs
36% more for only
14% more reach...

This example is taken from the Media Mix presentation in the Presentations link on www.charleswarner.us. It shows that achieving a 30-percent reach level has a CPM reach of $15, which more than doubles to $33 for just 5 percent more reach; an additional 5-percent reach costs an additional 34 percent. Ephron writes, "Marketing mix modeling finds diminishing marginal response to media weight. As more dollars are spent in any medium, the sales response per-dollar for that medium tends to go down. That's why mixing media is seen as the key to greater advertising effectiveness."[4]

These concepts are explained more fully in Ephron's booklet *From Recency to Fusion: Seven Ideas that Nudged the Business*. This enlightening book is a recent history of media planning by the subject's foremost expert and I recommend that you download it from www.ephrononmedia.com and read it, especially if you are now calling on or hope to call on large agencies with media planning departments that use optimizers.

Selling to Media Planners

If you are a broadcast network television salesperson, there is little reason to call on media planners because most major national advertisers, especially consumer packaged goods advertisers, spend approximately 80 percent of their advertising dollars in television (network and spot) and you would not want to do anything to derail this gravy train. However, if you are selling cable, magazines, radio, or Interactive, you should call on planners and give them media-mix presentations showing that by adding your medium, both reach and efficiency can be increased. In February 2003 *The Jack Myers Report*, a widely read media industry newsletter that often identifies trends, featured a headline that read, "Sellers Shift Focus From Buyers to Planners."[5] The accompanying article indicated that many national sales organizations had realized the benefits of calling on media planners. Several national sales organizations, such as Turner Broadcasting, are armed with their own optimization programs that show their medium can add reach and efficiency to a broadcast network television schedule. The only way to get a medium (other than broadcast network television) added to a media plan is to call on planners with credible research information that shows how your medium can add efficient reach to a television schedule. Do not sell against television, but sell with it—in combination with television—and sell your medium to planners, not buyers. By the time a media plan gets to a buyer, it is too late.

Local Advertising

The purpose of local advertising is the same as that of national advertising, but the local emphasis is generally more on selling products than on building brand image. That means local advertisers generally evaluate the effectiveness of their advertising based more on sales results than on ratings, circulation, CPMs, CPPs, reach, frequency, or branding. Bringing up the concept of optimization, recency, or diminishing marginal response to a local retailer will usually get you nothing but a blank stare, as will a discussion of brand image or branding. However, as you will soon learn, branding is as important in local advertising as it is in national advertising and it is an important concept for you to teach local advertisers.

The other major difference between national and local advertising is that salespeople often have to be responsible for creating advertising—writing copy and either producing or supervising the production of ads or commercials.

The best book about local advertising is Michael Corbett's *The 33 Ruthless Rules of Local Advertising*. I will give you some of those rules in this chapter, but the best way to learn about them is to buy, read, and study the book.

Corbett Rule #6: Know what a new customer is worth to you.

Corbett writes that determining the value of a new customer allows local businesses to manage their advertising expenditures accurately. To calculate the value of a new customer, a business must know several things: (1) How much does the typical customer spend on an average purchase? (2) What is the net profit on an average purchase? (3) What is the average lifetime patronage? (4) How many repeat sales does a customer make? (5) How many prospects will a typical customer refer? (6) How often will that customer base turn over, or how many times will new customers be needed to replace those who leave? (7) What has been invested in advertising to get the current customer base? (8) What is a new customer worth? A business may discover after making all of these calculations that it will be investing more in advertising than will be realized from a customer's first purchase. However, the future profits from repeat purchases and referrals might well compensate for an initial loss on the first purchase.

Corbett Rule #7: Understand the purpose of advertising.

According to Corbett, "The purpose of advertising is to create an equity position in a target market and to reach and motivate a sufficient number of consumers so that a business can realize a specific growth objective."[6] Branding is an equity position, so branding is of critical importance to local advertisers, because, as Corbett writes, "The objective of advertising is to first have an impact on the mind of the consumer followed by or accompanied simultaneously with an impact on the spending of the consumer."[7]

Corbett's Rule #9: Use the most powerful tool in local advertising.

According to Corbett, the most powerful tool in local advertising is a Unique Selling Proposition (USP) or what Corbett calls a Preemptive Advantage. The idea of a USP was developed by the legendary advertising executive Rosser Reeves in the 1950s. In his book *Reality in Advertising*, Reeves defines USP in three parts: "Each advertisement must make a proposition to the consumer. Not just words, not just product puffery, not just show-window advertising. Each advertisement must say to each reader: 'Buy this product and you will get this specific benefit.'" "The proposition must be one that the competition either cannot, or does not, offer. It must be unique—either a uniqueness of the brand or a claim not otherwise made in that particular field of advertising.", and "The proposition must be so strong that it can move the mass millions, i.e., pull over new customers to your product."[8]

Corbett claims that most local businesses have not developed a USP and are not aware of the USP concept, and that without a USP a local business is just one of many similar businesses, "just another store front."[9] But a USP cannot be stated in a worn-out cliché such as "the lowest prices in town" or "the best service in the city" because everyone uses these phrases and nobody believes them. A USP must be a truly unique and different positioning statement and promise.

Corbett Rule #10: If your doors are open, you should be advertising.

And by advertising, Corbett means advertising all the time, not just occasionally, for five reasons: (1) people shop all the time, not just when a business decides to advertise, (2) people move; in some markets as many as 25 percent of the population moves out of the area every year, (3) people forget, mainly because they have been exposed to thousands of advertising messages a day, (4) people often take their time buying, and (5) to establish an equity position in the consumer community. So, what Ephron taught media planners about continuous scheduling works for local advertisers, too, only the words are different. Continuous scheduling means advertise all the time.

Corbett's Rule #12: Think long term.

The notion of a local business saying, "I'll try this for a month and see how it works," will not work. Corbett writes, "Using the media for infrequent, short-term advertising schedules will not get you the same growth benefits you'll get when you advertise with consistency, frequency, and impact. If you advertise from week to week, idea to idea, promotion to promotion, you're usually going to end up disappointed."[10]

Corbett's Rule #26: Use a proven scheduling formula.

By a proven scheduling formula, Corbett means several things, including, "Choose a medium you can dominate," and "Determine if your chosen medium for domination reaches a sufficient number of your target consumers." [11]

If an advertiser cannot dominate an entire medium, such as television, then the advertiser should try to dominate a daypart or a particular type of programming. Corbett recommends radio schedules that run every week for 16 weeks and three out of four weeks thereafter with a minimum level of average frequency of three. In television he recommends a schedule of 250 gross rating points (GRPs) per week and a schedule of two weeks out of every month. Corbett also writes, "If you're advertising with a dominant, consistent schedule, it doesn't matter on which days you run your ads."[12]

Finally, two of Corbett's rules are closely related.

Corbett's Rule #30: Sell something more profitable than low price.
Corbett's Rule #31: Avoid the "sale" syndrome.

The same principle of creating value applies to advertising as well as to media selling—if you create value by emphasizing high quality and excellent service before mentioning price, you can get a higher price. Local businesses that try to compete with national discount chains such as Wal-Mart by offering lower prices are bound to lose in the long run because they can never consistently beat Wal-Mart on prices and they certainly cannot out-advertise these huge corporations. The only hope local businesses have against the big national chains is to create a Unique Selling Proposition that positions their businesses on something other than price—on elements such as quality, selection, service, and convenience.

Corbett's rule to avoid the sale syndrome or habit is closely related to the notion that competing on the basis of low prices is unprofitable. Sales can be useful if used sparingly. Consumers are assaulted by sale advertising day after day in the media and have, therefore, become suspicious of retailers who invent excuses to have a sale. Traditionally, Nordstrom, which is known for high-quality merchandise and excellent service, has only two sales a year which they do not advertise heavily because they do not have to—their shoppers know about them. Regular Nordstrom shoppers eagerly await these bi-annual sales and crowd the stores trying to get a bargain. Nordstrom's increased volume makes up for price reductions. Having a sale means discounting the price of goods, which, in turn, means lowering profit margins. To make up a price reduction of just 15 percent, a retailer has to increase its volume by 80 percent to attain full-price profit levels. To get that kind of increase in volume, a retailer would have to invest in much more advertising, which would wipe out the profit margin of the increased volume. To attempt having sales on a regular basis would merely increase these losses.

Many local retailers say they have no choice but to compete on the basis of price, especially in slow economic times. But of course they have a choice, which is to develop a compelling USP, which is where intelligent local media salespeople can help.

By understanding the advertising objectives of both national and local advertisers, media salespeople can offer solutions to advertising problems—both creative solutions (to local advertisers) and media scheduling solutions.

I have used only nine of Corbett's 33 rules of local advertising because I want to give you just a sample of the wisdom that permeates his book in an attempt to entice you to read it.

Test Yourself

1. What is the purpose of advertising?
2. What is the difference between advertising and promotion?
3. What are the six steps on the Advertising Ladder?
4. What are some of the differences in selling national advertising to large agencies and selling local advertising to businesses that do not have an agency?
5. What is an optimizer?
6. Why is continuous scheduling important?
7. What is a USP and why is it important?

Project

Select commercials for five different products that you see on local television and identify which steps on the advertising ladder they address.

References

Michael Corbett with David Stilli. 2002. *The 33 Ruthless Rules of Local Advertising*. New York: Pinnacle Books.

Erwin Ephron. 2003. *From Recency to Fusion.* www.ephrononmedia.com

John Phillip Jones. 1995. *When Ads Work: New Proof that Advertising Triggers Sales.* New York: Lexington Books.

Resources

www.adage.com
www.charleswarner.us
www.ephrononmedia.com
www.mediaplan.com

Endnotes

1. Personal conversation with Erwin Ephron. October 2002

2. Erwin Ephron. 2003. *From Recency to Fusion.* www.ephrononmedia.com. p. 38.

3. Ibid. p. 14.

4. Ibid. p.3.

5. Myers, Jack. 2003. *The Jack Myers Report.* February 3. p. 1.

6. Michael Corbett with Dave Stilli. 2002. *The 33 Ruthless Rules of Local Advertising.* New York: Pinnacle Books. p. 31.

7. Ibid. p. 31

8. http://www.emediaplan.com/admunch/Biographies/Rosser.asp. April 2003.

9. Michael Corbett with Dave Stili. 2002. *The 33 Ruthless Rules of Local Advertising.* New York: Pinnacle Books. p. 43.

10. Ibid. p. 51.

11. Ibid. p. 125.

12. Ibid. p. 127.

Chapter 18 Newspapers

By Thomas J. Stultz

Newspapers have been a leading source of local advertising since April 26, 1704, when Postmaster John Campbell first published his weekly *Boston News Letter*. The paper's first advertisement was a real estate announcement that sought a buyer for an Oyster Bay, Long Island estate. Reportedly, it was 40 years before the newspaper grew to a circulation base of 300 copies per issue. The spread of advertising grew at a slow pace; it took 20 years for the first advertisements to appear in the higher-profile New York newspapers. In 1724, *The New York Gazette* carried two advertisements—one announcing the sale of a New Jersey farm and the other for a runaway slave.

Surprisingly, the advent of newspaper advertising did not prompt a rapid spread of newspaper publishing in the United States. There were only 70 weekly newspapers in 1790. By 1820, the number of weekly newspapers grew to 422. The number of daily newspapers also rose during that period, increasing from 24 in 1800 to nearly 400 in 1860; however, the biggest push for newspapers came in 1833 when Benjamin Day published *The New York Sun*, the first successful penny newspaper in New York. In four years, circulation of *The Sun* reached 30,000, making it the world's largest newspaper. These penny newspapers were sold by newsboys for a penny, instead of the customary six cents, on street corners in major cities across the United States. Many of these papers relied on sensational articles to appeal to readers and stand out from the other papers being sold on the same street corner. By making the newspaper affordable, circulation began to grow as did the number of newspapers published. In 2001, daily newspaper circulation in the United States totaled 55.6 million copies per day and Sunday newspaper circulation exceeded 59 million copies.[1]

From this auspicious beginning, newspaper advertising has become a major means of communication between merchants, who seek to sell ideas, goods, or services, and the buyers who are looking for these products and relevant price information. Today, approximately half of all available space in the nearly 1,500 US daily newspapers and the more than 9,000 weekly newspapers and free advertising shoppers is devoted to advertising. Advertising now represents between 75 percent and 80 percent of a newspaper's total revenue, providing most of a newspaper's revenues and profits. Advertising is also a critical element for newspaper readership.

A study by the Readership Institute at Northwestern University found that advertising content has great potential to increase readership.[2] This survey of 37,000 consumers across the US found that readers spend more time with a newspaper and read it more completely when it contains advertising content they find interesting. It was clear from the institute's study that consumers rely on newspapers for local store news and that they find this information useful in much the same way they do the local news articles, feature stories, and photos.

While it might be difficult to envision home television viewers turning on the set to see what commercials are being aired, many newspaper buyers rely on their local newspaper for important advertisements to help them plan their weekly grocery shopping and visits to the department store at the mall. It is interesting to note that the late Ralph Ingersoll launched a highly publicized advertising-free daily newspaper called *PM* in New York City in 1940 but folded it in five years when circulation revenues proved insufficient to fund the all-news newspaper.

Daily newspapers are primarily a local medium. In 2001, a total of 1,468 daily newspapers were published in the US with no one single newspaper comprising more than 4 percent of the nation's total circulation. Only 218 daily newspapers have circulation greater than 50,000 and combined, these papers only represent 14.9 percent of the total circulation.[3] Unlike television, which is dominated by four major networks, newspapers remain a very local medium—an attribute that both helps and hinders advertising sales efforts. Advertisers like having the ability to target local markets, and in most cases, newspaper circulation covers the primary retail trading areas most important to retailers. However, dealing with nearly 1,500 newspapers is cumbersome for national chain stores and manufacturers. This makes national advertising programs difficult to implement, especially when compared to nationwide one-order, one-bill services provided by the broadcast and cable networks and broadcast representative firms.

Half a century ago, daily newspapers were primarily published in the afternoon. Of 1,772 daily newspapers published in 1950, more than 80 percent (1,450) were published in the afternoon. In 2001 there were 1,468 newspapers with 692 (47 percent) published in the afternoon. The number of Sunday newspapers has grown from 549 in 1950 to 913 in 2001. While daily circulation of all US newspapers declined from 58.9 million in 1950 to 55.6 million in 2001, Sunday circulation actually increased from 47.7 million to 59.1 million. Consumers spend $10.8 billion annually to read daily newspapers, including the advertisements.[4]

Part of the decline in circulation can be attributed to the increased costs of subscribing to daily and Sunday newspapers, and to selective reductions in delivery to areas outside the paper's primary retail trading zone as part of cost-cutting measures to increase profits. In addition, the merger of morning and afternoon newspapers in previously competitive markets has reduced both the number of newspapers published and total newspaper circulation. As of February 1, 2002, only 45 cities had multiple daily newspapers and 14 of those were operated under common ownership. In addition, 12 of the multi-newspaper cities operated under Joint Operating Agreements (JOA) made possible by the Newspaper Preservation Act of 1970.[5]

JOAs were created to preserve a diversity of editorial opinion in communities where the market no longer supported two competing daily newspapers. Under a JOA, editorial operations remain separate while advertising, printing, delivery, and business operations are combined. It is generally believed that the elimination of competition in newspaper markets results in higher advertising and circulation rates. Duplication of newspaper readership is reduced through consolidations and closings, which some claim makes advertising buys more efficient in single newspaper markets.

In addition to daily newspapers, there are thousands of weekly newspapers—paid and free—alternative weeklies, advertising shoppers, and local magazines and coupon packets competing for print advertising dollars. To offer advertisers increased market penetration, many newspapers publish Total Market Coverage (TMC) products that are distributed free to non-subscribers one or more days per week.

Newspaper executives and advertisers are concerned about the declining newspaper circulation as well as declining readership. Average weekday readership of daily newspapers has declined from 77.6 percent in 1970 to 55.5 percent in 2002 while Sunday readership has gone from 72.3 percent to 63.7 percent in the same period. In spite of this decline in readership, newspapers' reach of 55.5 percent of all adults is nearly 44 percent greater than the reach of an average half hour of prime-time television (38.6 percent) and is more than double the reach of a quarter-hour of all-morning drive radio (22.5 percent).[6] Thus, newspapers remain a strong mass medium with broad appeal to both consumers and advertisers. Newspaper executives are also concerned about the industry's steady decline in market share of total advertising dollars, which has dropped from 27.6 percent in 1980 to 19.2 percent in 2001.[7] Still, at more than $44 billion annually, newspapers garner the largest share of the total media advertising pie. Even though newspapers' share has been declining, the industry has shown year-over-year growth in total advertising revenues for 46 of the past 52 years.

See Figure 18.1[8] and Figure 18.2[9] for details.

Figure 18.1 U.S. newspaper advertising expenditures, 1950–2001 (in billions of U.S. dollars). (Source: NAA 2002.)

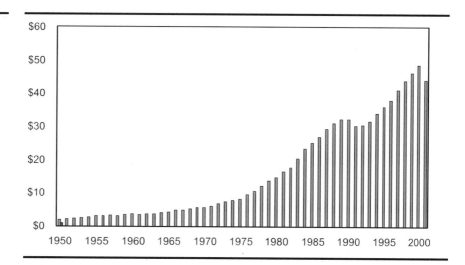

Newspaper Content

Each of the 1,468 daily newspapers is unique in its content because newspapers generally serve different markets, readers, and advertisers. And, the newspapers are written, edited and produced by local news organizations. Newspapers are unique because they totally recreate their products every single day in print. Each day's newspaper is completely different from the one published the day before and from the one to be published the day after. A few newspaper companies have consolidated copy desk functions and some

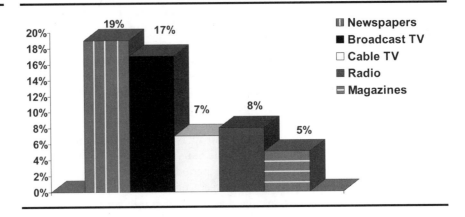

Figure 18.2 Newspapers command the largest share of US media dollars. (Source: NAA 2002.)

reporting assignments, but for the most part, newspapers rely on local staff and operate independently of other newspapers, even those under common ownership. There is a strong movement toward convergence in the media world which may have a significant impact on future newspaper operations. In a converged world, one company would own multiple media outlets (newspaper, television, radio, and Internet) in the same market and use the combined resources to produce the individual products. While this concept is being tested in various markets, a debate rages regarding whether or not convergence will contribute more to product quality, corporate profits, or both. Time will tell.

The content of individual newspapers varies based on the markets served and the size of the newspaper. National newspapers, such as *USA Today* and *The Wall Street Journal*, focus on major national and international news. Metropolitan newspapers such as *The Chicago Tribune* and *The Los Angeles Times* offer very broad coverage with an emphasis on state and national news, politics, and college and professional sports, while de-emphasizing local, community news. Suburban and community newspapers offer highly localized content featuring news about local city and county governments, high school sports, civic group activities, and other information not available in the larger newspapers. Each newspaper offers its own version of business and entertainment news and features geared to the broad national, metropolitan or local, audiences they serve. In order to appeal to everyone in a household, newspaper editors produce a wide variety of material beyond simply covering the news. For example, sports and financial pages are believed to have the most appeal to male readers, while lifestyle, social news, shopping columns, fashion, and food news are produced to attract female readers. Comic strips, school news, high school sports and entertainment news are produced to appeal to younger readers while also appealing to a much wider audience.

In the process of gathering and publishing the news, newspapers serve as a daily record of events. While other media may compete with national and metropolitan newspapers for major political or crime stories, mid-size and smaller newspapers almost exclusively cover the local city council meetings, public hearings, and other local events. The publication of this information contributes to an informed electorate which helps democracy work. The presence of reporters in cities and towns across America also provides a safeguard against political corruption and abuse. Newspapers present news of the preceding day and provide a record of that day's news, business, and sports activities. Newspapers also provide information on upcoming events as well as entertainment. Newspapers carry strong opinions written by their editorial writers or syndicated columnists. These opinions help establish a dialogue on important local, state, or national issues and prompt responses from readers who submit letters to the editor so their viewpoints can be published. This entire process helps unite communities, promote greater understanding, and inform the citizenry in ways that often move them to action.

The typical newspaper is divided into themed sections. While these sections vary from market to market, the most common include Main News, State/Local, National/International, Lifestyle, Business, Sports, and Entertainment. Specialized sections are also published on topics such as Home and Garden, Books, Theater, Movies, Music, Automotive, Real Estate, and Careers. These sections make it easier for the reader to work through a newspaper and provide targeted opportunities for advertisers.

The role of newspapers in society has changed very little since Harrie Davis wrote in 1905, "It is the vigilant sentinel of the masses, the guardian of their rights, the voice of their thoughts, and the bulwark of their liberties. It binds the human race together with a link of friendship, tells men of their fellows, and records the progress of the world in the making."[10]

Today, newspapers are compiled and edited by trained reporters and editors who are charged with selecting and chronicling the day's most important, useful, or entertaining happenings. By doing this work for consumers, the newspaper then becomes a random-access database that offers readers easy, non-linear access to the world's events in a format they can use at their own convenience. Unlike television, which is often viewed passively, a newspaper is an active medium, requiring a hands-on approach to read and use it. Also, television is linear, real time, non-random access, which means that television content (radio, too) comes in linear form, one piece after another, and you cannot skip ahead or skip back. You take the content in the order and time frame in which it is sent.

In order for a newspaper to be influential and successful, it must be trusted by its readers. As a result, newspapers traditionally operate with a strict code of ethics for their journalists. Policies regarding potential conflicts of interest, fairness, independence, and objectivity are found in most newsrooms. In addition to avoiding conflicts brought about by close association with political action groups or acceptance of gifts from news sources, news personnel operate independently of the newspaper sales and marketing departments. The separation is necessary to avoid being asked to provide favorable news coverage for the newspaper's top advertisers. While such a favorable article might offer a short-term benefit to the newspaper financially, it is commonly believed that such coverage would damage the editorial integrity, reputation, and credibility of the newspaper over the longer term. As a result, a higher premium is rightfully placed on the newspaper's credibility than its short-term financial needs. While advertising sales representatives are often asked by advertisers for special news treatment, the separation-of-state policy allows the sales representatives to remove themselves from any potential controversy surrounding advertisers and editors, which best serves the needs of readers. See Chapter 3 for a more detailed discussion of media and sales ethics.

Newspaper Circulation

Daily newspapers are sold to consumers either by subscription or on a single-issue basis. Subscribers receive their papers via home delivery, either through "little merchant" walking carriers or adult motor route carriers. Single issues are purchased out of vending machines or over the counter at various news outlets including, but not limited to, newsstands, street hawkers, grocery stores, and so forth. A number of papers are also available to businesses, hotels and motels, and travelers on a bulk-purchase basis. Regardless of how consumers receive a newspaper, an individual paper's total circulation number is the combined total of paid subscriptions, single-copy sales, and bulk sales. Additional circulation may be added to a newspaper's total distribution through free-sample delivery programs or other bulk distribution programs that may not qualify as paid circulation but have value to advertisers.

Unlike other media that base audience projections on market research sampling, newspapers base their advertising rates and value to advertisers on average circulation or distribution numbers, usually calculated on an annual basis. Newspapers rely on outside circulation auditing firms to provide independent verification of their circulation numbers. Most daily newspapers are audited by the Audit Bureau of Circulation (ABC), which was established in 1914. The ABC has rules and requirements that all of its members must follow to obtain an acceptable audit. The standardization of the auditing process gives advertisers a high level of confidence in a newspaper's circulation claims. In addition, the audits provide advertisers with a consistent format that merges with their own customer databases for more convenient market analysis. Two other newspaper auditing firms, Certified Audit of Circulations, Inc. (CAC) and Verified Audit Circulation (VAC) are also recognized by most advertisers. These audit firms are used primarily by smaller newspapers and weekly publications. In addition to auditing paid circulation newspapers, CAC and VAC also audit free newspapers and advertising publications. The purpose of the auditing process is to give advertisers a high degree of comfort with the numbers presented to them by newspaper sales representatives.

Under audit regulations, newspapers may count as paid circulation any purchase of the newspaper by consumers, as long as the consumers pay at least 50 percent of the cost of the newspaper. For subscribers, that means they must pay half of the regular subscription rates to qualify as paid circulation. Single-copy buyers must pay at least half of the cover price to qualify. Audit rules have been changed recently to permit segment pricing and additional discounting so newspapers can target sales efforts to specific geographic or demographic markets at discounts up to one-quarter of the regular subscription rate. Newspapers are expected to use the additional discounting provisions to attempt to increase penetration in specific markets, for example, apartment dwellers, suburban developments, and minorities. The audits not only provide average paid circulation figures but also record how many of the papers were purchased through discount programs and at regular price. Circulation data for newspapers include the number of copies delivered by various methods—newspaper carriers, dealers or agents, street vendors, over-the-counter, vending machines, and the U.S. Postal Service—for the newspaper's city zone, retail trading zone (RTZ), and areas outside the RTZ. Audit reports typically report circulation by community and by zip code. An audit report will also provide an estimate of occupied households within each of the newspaper's circulation measurement areas to enable advertisers to easily calculate the newspaper's household penetration in the communities or zip codes most important to them.

Only three daily newspapers (*USA Today,* the *New York Times,* and *The Wall Street Journal*) have circulation greater than 1 million copies per day. Most newspapers, 85 percent, have circulation under 50,000 and only 40 newspapers exceed 250,000 paid circulation daily. Daily newspaper circulation has declined since reaching a peak of 62.8 million in 1985. In 2001, total daily circulation was 55.6 million and Sunday circulation was 59.1 million.[11] Because newspapers are such a local medium, advertisers can use one newspaper to serve an individual retail outlet or they can advertise in many newspapers to reach a national audience. This flexibility is one of the major advantages that newspapers have over competing media. Figure 18.3 illustrates newspaper circulation trends.[12]

**Figure 18.3
The newspaper industry today, daily circulation trends 1990–2001. (Source: NAA 2002.)**

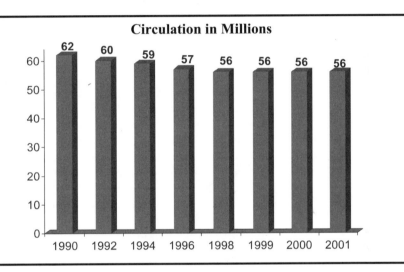

Newspaper executives and audit firms are considering moving the measurement criteria from paid circulation to readership to make the newspaper audience estimates more comparable to other media. ABC and other auditing firms are including readership information on audit reports at an additional cost to newspapers. Some major advertisers have embraced the new emphasis on readership, while others prefer the traditional measurement of paid circulation. For now, audited paid circulation remains the primary method for establishing the size and value of a newspaper's audience for its advertisers.

Newspaper advertising representatives need to know and understand their newspaper's circulation in total and by specific zip code to advise advertisers on how best to use their newspaper. Sales representatives should also know their competition's coverage in their key zip codes and be able to talk about duplication of reach and readership.

Newspaper Readership

So who reads newspapers? More than 120 million adults read a newspaper every day of the week and more than 135 million adults read a newspaper on Sunday.[13] This massive audience regularly turns to newspapers to find out what's happening in the world around them and what bargains are available at their favorite retail stores, malls, and shopping centers. The combined impact of an advertisement in every single daily or Sunday newspaper would equal an audience that is 38 percent bigger every day and 56 percent greater every Sunday than the audience for the National Football League's Super Bowl XXXVI, which aired on the Fox Television Network and earned a 40.4 rating, a 61 share, and an estimated 86.8 million viewers.[14] The daily and Sunday reach by newspapers is even more impressive when stacked up against network television on a non-event week.

For example, the top-rated network television show for a week in 2003 was ABC's "20/20 Special" with pop star Michael Jackson. This top-rated show attracted 27.1 million viewers, according to Nielsen ratings for the week February 3 to February 9, 2003.[15] Daily newspapers deliver nearly five times the audience of the top-rated prime-time television show under normal viewing circumstances. Furthermore, newspapers reach this mass audience on a localized basis. Advertisers can participate in this daily medium and take advantage of its tremendous reach, which can be targeted to just the areas around their stores. Such flexibility makes newspapers a highly effective and efficient buy for advertisers.

Like many mass media outlets, newspapers have seen steady erosion in overall audience over the past 30 years or more as consumers have more choices than ever before. Still, newspapers continue to command a very large and highly desirable audience that produces results for advertisers and value for the readers and communities they serve.

According to the Spring 2002 Competitive Media Index, more than half of all adults, 55.5 percent, in the top 50 U.S. markets read a daily newspaper. Nearly two-thirds, 63.9 percent, read one on Sunday. Overall, more than eight in 10 adults, 81.1 percent, in these same markets read a newspaper during the course of a week. Nationally, more than 55 million newspapers are sold daily, with an average of 2.2 readers per copy, and on Sunday more than 59 million newspapers are sold with an average of 2.3 readers per copy.[16] A similar study by Ohio University-Scripps Howard News Service in June 2002 showed that 50 percent of all adults are regular users of newspapers, where regular use is defined by reading a newspaper four or more days a week.[17]

Newspaper readers are typically better educated and have higher household incomes than non-newspaper readers. Daily newspaper readership by age ranges from a low of 39 percent for adults 18 to 24 to a high of 72 percent of adults 65 and older. On Sunday, readership increases to 49 percent of adults 18 to 24 and 76 percent of adults 65 and older. Men are more likely, 58 percent, to read a daily newspaper than women, 51 percent, but Sunday newspapers garner near equal readership from men, 63 percent, and women, 64 percent. See Figure 18.4 for details.[18]

Readers tend to spend more time with Sunday newspapers. That fact, coupled with the increase in female readership on Sundays, is why so many advertisers prefer advertising in Sunday newspapers.

While daily and Sunday newspaper readers tend to be older, readership remains healthy in all age groups, including among teenagers, where a majority, 54 percent, of teens ages 12 to 17 told researchers they had read at least one newspaper in the last seven days.[19] Among teens 15 to 17, the cumulative reach of newspapers jumped to 70 percent within the past seven days. The Ohio University-Scripps Howard News Service study revealed that 41 percent of all 18- to 24-year-olds are regular users of newspapers.

Figure 18.4 Newspapers reach adults of all ages (% coverage). (Source: Scarborough Research Release 1, February–March 2001. Used with permission.)

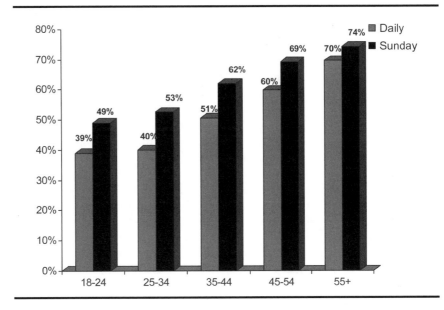

Regular newspaper readership is stronger in suburban markets, 65 percent, than in major cities, 52 percent, and is equal in small cities, 51 percent, and rural areas, 51 percent, according to the Ohio University-Scripps Howard study. Regular newspaper readership is strongest in the northeastern US, 65 percent, and weakest in the western portion of the county, 48 percent.[20]

Newspapers consistently deliver the consumers that advertisers find the most appealing—those with higher incomes, more education, and higher job responsibility. And, even though newspaper readership is weakest among younger audiences, daily newspapers reach a very high percentage, 58.9 percent, of young adults between the ages of 18 and 24 over a five-day time period, and 60.5 percent of 18-to 24-year-olds read at least one Sunday newspaper in a four-week span.[21] This readership pattern argues for frequency advertising programs, instead of large, one-day ads to reach this target audience.

Of course, newspaper readership varies from market to market and depends on each market's demographics, literacy rates, ethnic composition, and competitive alternatives. For that reason, most large and mid-size newspapers conduct their own readership studies on a periodic basis. These studies, conducted by independent research companies that follow established standards of measurement, provide individual newspapers with an excellent look at their readers, non-readers, and users of competitive media including television, radio, weekly newspapers, shoppers, and direct mail. The data collected in these studies is used internally by newspaper managers to identify areas for improvement in content, service, and sales. It is also used externally with both existing advertisers to reassure them of the value of newspaper advertising and with potential advertisers to demonstrate the size of the audience the advertiser is missing by not using the newspaper. It is quite common to find that the newspaper's largest advertiser is also the market's leader in its category or that an advertiser who has reduced its investment in advertising has lost market share since the last survey period. Both trends serve as evidence of the value of newspaper advertising.

This readership research breaks down the market in ways that enable advertisers to analyze the newspaper's reach among various demographic groups.

These breakdowns include household income, age, sex, race, education, home ownership, marital status, and, probably most important, shopping preferences. The studies also track shopping patterns for various shopping centers and malls as well as for individual stores and services. By measuring these variables consistently on a periodic basis, newspapers help advertisers identify trends or market changes that may impact their businesses in positive or negative ways.

Most newspapers provide this proprietary readership data along with other syndicated market demographic information and census data to help advertisers better understand local market trends and conditions. By being a primary provider of this useful information, newspaper advertising representatives become an extension of the advertisers' marketing departments. This information allows salespeople to help advertisers develop successful programs that grow their businesses. Because salespeople are involved in the planning and development of these programs, they often benefit by making sure their newspaper is a significant part of new or expanded advertising programs.

One important finding that practically all market research studies find is that consumers read newspapers for both news and advertising information. The fact that readers regularly and habitually look at newspapers to learn what is on sale at their favorite stores or what special item they can find in the newspaper's classified advertising section makes a compelling argument for newspaper advertising. Readers regularly shop the ads in newspapers whether they are looking for a new home, a new job, or a new stereo system in order to keep up with local price trends.

A 2001 Newspaper Association of America (NAA) study found that nearly two-thirds of consumers, 63 percent, say newspapers are their primary source for advertising or general shopping information. In addition, seven in 10 adults purposely look at newspaper inserts when shopping for a specific item, and 76 percent say they usually check the Sunday advertising inserts just to see what's on sale.[22] Thanks to these consumer habits, newspapers deliver an attentive audience of potential shoppers. Unlike other media that experience commercial zapping or channel surfing, newspaper advertising is welcome, expected, and useful to consumers who are both ready to buy and have the resources to buy the advertised products and services. Many readers buy the paper for the advertising first and the news information second.

In many ways, readers look at newspaper advertising as a shopping mall of information and store news to help them decide where and when to shop.

Newspaper Advertising

Newspaper advertising comes in all shapes and sizes. An effective newspaper ad might consist of only three lines of carefully worded copy and placed in the Merchandise for Sale category in the classified section, or it could be a multipage section printed behind the main news section. Newspapers are organized to accommodate all types of advertising from both big and small advertisers. Advertising in newspapers is typically divided into four categories—classified, classified display, display, and pre-printed inserts.

Classified Advertising

Classified advertisements, also called want ads, appear in small, agate type under indexed headings which identify the type of product or service advertised. Many newspapers also offer bold headlines, color type, and logos in classifieds to help improve the readership of individual ads. These small ads, often numbering more than 1 million per year for large metropolitan newspapers, provide strong newspaper readership and interactivity with readers. Classified ads are usually sold on a per-line basis and appear in the classified sections of the newspaper. These sections generally have 10 columns per page; some papers have six, eight, or nine columns. These small ads inform readers where yard sales are being held, what used cars are for sale, and who is trying to sell their exercise equipment. A number of service businesses also use these classified ads because they can afford to advertise every day. This increased frequency enables consumers to know where to look for contact information when they are in need of someone to trim their trees, mow their lawns, or clean their gutters.

Classified Display Ads

Classified display advertising differs from regular classified ads in several ways. The copy usually occupies more space; it is surrounded by a bold border; and it often features product illustrations, bold type and headlines, and/or company logos. The most common users of classified display advertising are automobile dealers, realtors, and employers or recruiters. By placing these similar advertisements in one section of the paper, newspapers make it easy for readers to comparison shop for this type of service. At the same time, the shopping environment works for advertisers because consumers know where to look for the market's most comprehensive compilation of ads that interest them when they are in the market for a new or used car or truck, a new home, or a new job. Research shows, for example, that new car buyers are very likely to read automotive ads in their newspaper before buying to get information on the models and prices that interest them most. These same buyers continue to read the automotive ads for several weeks after making their purchase just to make sure they got the best possible deal. Consumers have been trained through years of consistent advertising to rely on newspapers for such information. As a result, advertisers know they need to be represented in the newspaper marketplace on a consistent basis if they wish to be successful.

Display Ads

Display advertising (often called ROP—run of paper or run of press) is the term used to describe the bold advertisements found in sections of the newspaper other than the classified section. These display ads usually occupy fairly large spaces, but can vary in size from one column inch (one and seven-eighths inches wide by one inch deep) to a 126 column-inch-page, six columns or 12 inches wide by 21.5 inches deep. Display ads are surrounded by bold or graphic borders and are not placed under specific headers, similar to the classified display ads. These display ads may be promotional, offering price and merchandise information; brand or image building; or a combination of these styles and formats. Advertisers like display ads because they can squeeze a lot of product and price information into each one. This gives consumers more product options to consider. It increases the likelihood that one or more of their advertised items will appeal to potential customers.

Display advertising is often divided into two major categories—local, also referred to as retail, and national, often referred to as general. Newspapers rely heavily on local retail advertising, which is usually sold via bulk annual contracts at the paper's most attractive rates. Local display advertising is sold by the newspaper's salespeople through direct sales calls on local store owners or managers or at regional and national chain store offices. In most cases, an advertiser is treated as a local account if it operates a retail or service outlet within the newspaper's market area. National display advertising has been a declining segment for newspapers. Much of the traditional national display advertising, which consists of manufacturers' product coupons, has shifted away from display ads to coupon ads in the Sunday coupon supplements. These supplements are produced by national firms such as Valassis and News America. They are distributed primarily through Sunday newspapers across the US.

National ads are usually sold by newspaper representative firms. Newspapers charge higher rates for national advertising, which typically comes from manufacturers, wholesalers, service organizations, or political action committees. Publishers justify the rate differentials by explaining that national advertising is usually commissionable to advertising agencies whereas local display ads are usually non-commissionable to advertising agencies. In addition, national advertising representative firms usually take a percentage of each sale, which also increases the newspaper's costs for each national transaction. Furthermore, publishers feel they should reward local advertisers with the most attractive rates because of the consistency of their advertising programs with the newspaper and because most local advertisers don't serve as wide a geographical area as most national advertisers do, and, therefore, don't have as large a potential market. Many advertising executives believe the national rate differential has contributed significantly to the industry's loss of national advertising. However, newspapers that have reduced national rates individually have not typically seen an increase in volume from national accounts. It is more likely that a switch to television advertising by most national advertisers is the culprit and cause of this decline. Broadcast competitors generally do not charge different rates to local and national advertisers.

In addition to local display and national display, newspapers also offer category rates for market segments such as movies and entertainment, electronics, automotive dealer associations, etc. These rates are offered consistently to advertisers who make similar investments within their category.

Newspaper Pricing

Unlike the broadcast and cable media, newspapers are not constrained by limitations on advertising inventory availability—they have what economists call elastic supply. Newspapers can usually add or reduce the number of pages to deal with increases or decreases in advertising volume. While broadcasters sell spots at rates that reflect current market supply and demand economics because of their fixed-inventory constraints and what economists call inelastic supply, newspapers charge established advertising rates that reward advertisers for contractual commitments based on frequency and/or volume (in advertising space or dollar investment).

Newspapers, unlike broadcasting and cable, want to encourage advertisers to buy more and more space because they can easily add inventory—pages. Newspaper advertising contracts are usually sold on an annual basis, although most newspapers reserve the right to adjust advertising rates with 30 days written notice.

A typical newspaper advertising rate card is designed to encourage advertisers to make significant commitments to run well-planned, consistent advertising programs with the newspaper by rewarding them with lower advertising rates based on increased levels of volume or frequency. A newspaper rate card allows advertisers to know in advance what their advertising will cost each and every time they advertise during the life of the contract. It also gives them the assurance that other comparable advertisers are treated fairly and ethically within the framework of the prevailing rate card. This means that advertisers in the same business, running identical advertising schedules, can expect to pay the same rates and have similar opportunities for lower rates based on increases in advertising. While most advertisers would prefer a better deal than anyone else, they do appreciate the fact that they are being treated ethically and equally.

Advertisers also like knowing that their advertising rates are consistent throughout the year. This way, they can better plan and budget their regular advertising and promotion programs. They do not have to worry about costs increasing during their most important seasons and can adjust the size and frequency of their ads to reflect current business trends and seasonal patterns. Larger advertisers negotiate aggressively for preferred positioning within the newspaper, with back pages, color positions, and page three among the more popular positions.

A typical newspaper rate card will offer non-contract rates, Open Rates, for occasional advertisers, annual bulk rates and/or dollar volume contracts for larger advertisers, and various small-space frequency contracts for smaller stores and services. Newspapers often offer special introductory rates to entice non-advertisers to try newspaper advertising. And, many newspapers offer special incentives to advertisers that agree to increase their total investment with the newspaper by significant amounts. Table 18.1 shows a typical newspaper Annual Bulk Rate structure for display ads in a daily and Sunday newspaper with 65,000 circulation.

Table 18.1
Display
Advertising
Annual Bulk Rates

Inches Per Year	Rate Per Column Inch	Minimum Annual Dollar Volume
Non-Contract Open Rate	$ 49.60	
126 Inches Per Year	$ 35.40	$ 4,460
200 Inches Per Year	$ 32.70	$ 6,540
500 Inches Per Year	$ 30.90	$ 15,450
1,000 Inches Per Year	$ 30.10	$ 30,100
2,000 Inches Per Year	$ 29.70	$ 59,400
4,000 Inches Per Year	$ 29.30	$ 117,200
6,500 Inches Per Year	$ 28.90	$ 187,850
9,000 Inches Per Year	$ 28.40	$ 255,600
12,000 Inches Per Year	$ 28.00	$ 336,000
15,000 Inches Per Year	$ 27.60	$ 414,000
20,000 Inches Per Year	$ 27.20	$ 544,000
25,000 Inches Per Year	$ 26.60	$ 665,000
30,000 Inches Per Year	$ 26.20	$ 786,000

As you can see from the rate structure in Table 18.1, newspapers offer contract rates for small, mid-size, and large advertisers. To determine what rate an advertiser should be paying, a salesperson will need to know either the average ad size and frequency or the advertiser's annual budget. For example, an advertiser who wants to run a one-quarter page ad every week, 52 weeks a year, would be running 1,638 column inches per year. To determine the number of annual inches in this case, the salesperson would need to know that a full-page ad is 126 column inches, 6 columns wide by 21 inches deep. Thus, a quarter page ad is 31.5 column inches, 3 columns by 10.5 inches. The salesperson would then multiply the ad size, 31.5 inches, times the number of weeks in a year, 52, to determine the minimum annual commitment. To be on the safe side, a salesperson could have the advertiser sign a 1,000-inch bulk rate contract which would earn the advertiser a contract rate of $30.10 per column inch.

More experienced salespeople will discuss special holiday programs or major sale events when an advertiser might want to increase ad size or frequency. As a result, a more aggressive approach would be to seek a 2,000-inch bulk contract which would earn an advertiser a contract rate of $29.70 per column inch. By signing a larger contract, an advertiser earns a lower rate and gets the benefit of nearly 400 more column inches to help with major sales events. At the same time, salespeople and the newspaper get another $10,000 in advertising revenue from this customer. In this way, the bulk contracts serve as a valuable sales tool to help salespeople increase the business they receive from advertisers by helping them earn lower rates through increased advertising volume.

Newspapers also offer discounts to encourage advertisers to repeat the same ads within a limited time frame. These pick-up rate discounts typically range from 20 percent to 50 percent off the regular price of the ad for increasing the frequency of the ad schedule. Newspapers establish rules for such repeat ads that limit the number of copy changes and the time frame to earn the discounts. Other discount programs encourage advertisers to run ads every day, every other day, weekly, or in large, multi-page units. Many newspapers also offer remnant or stand-by advertising rates. A limited number of remnant ads are sold at lower than normal rates and may or may not be scheduled at the newspaper's convenience. Newspapers use these remnant ads to boost advertising on slower days, fill sections that need to be printed in advance of the main news sections, and balance out the mix of editorial and advertising in the paper's make-up on any given day. A newspaper advertising salesperson should be familiar with all the rate options in order to recommend the most effective program to advertisers.

Color Rates

Advertisers also have a variety of color and positioning options with newspapers. Color ads are available in one color plus black, called spot color, two colors plus black, and process color, or full color. Because the color ads consume more of the newspaper press capacity, newspapers have surcharges that are added to the cost of the advertising space to pay for the additional color ink and loss of press capacity. Because of the uncertainty regarding the number of pages printed on any given day, newspapers usually do not guarantee advertising placement requests from advertisers unless the advertiser is willing to pay a premium rate or negotiates a prime position as part of a regular (usually very large) display advertising contract. Whenever possible, newspapers do try to accommodate positioning requests within the various sections of the paper.

Co-op Advertising

Co-op advertising is another source of revenue for newspapers. Each year national manufacturers set aside billions of dollars to pay for local promotion of their products. Retailers who meet the requirements of the individual co-op programs earn total or partial reimbursement of ad costs from the manufacturers, usually based on the value of the products retailers purchase from the manufacturers. Newspaper salespeople help retailers identify sources of co-op advertising dollars which can then be used by retailers to increase their advertising exposure without increasing their costs. Because manufacturers set aside the co-op advertising dollars when retailers buy their products, the retailers need to use the money they have already invested to increase their store traffic and turn more merchandise through the use of larger, more effective ads. Many newspapers have co-op specialists to assist salespeople in finding and capturing co-op dollars for retailers. Co-op advertising has changed in the past few years. Today many advertisers are taking co-op in the form of discounts on merchandise or in-store placement allowances instead of building up co-op media advertising dollars.

Newspaper Inserts

Newspaper pre-prints, or inserts, are advertising circulars that are not printed as part of the daily or Sunday newspaper but are distributed through the newspaper. Many advertisers, particularly national chain stores, use inserts because they can gain economies of scale by printing millions of copies at a time and shipping them in bulk to the newspapers they select to distribute their advertising messages. Pre-prints also provide advertisers with more options for running full color advertisements and for choosing higher grades of paper. Pre-print advertisers can usually print and distribute more pages of advertising through this method. In addition, pre-print advertising enables advertisers to zone their distribution to targeted areas, usually zip codes, around each of their stores or service areas. By maximizing the space available for product display and targeting the distribution, advertisers feel they can make their advertising investment more effective and more efficient. One weakness, however, is the lead time required for producing these pre-printed inserts. For example, a typical display ad can be scheduled on Thursday for a Sunday newspaper, while a pre-printed insert often must be designed, printed, and shipped weeks ahead of its distribution date. The loss of lead time can make it difficult for advertisers to respond to changing competitive environments. In addition, efforts to centralize and standardize these pre-prints to avoid printer charges for makeovers and changes often result in a loss of autonomy for individual stores or regions which may face different market pressures and preferences.

Newspaper pre-print rates typically charge advertisers based on size of the pre-print, or number of papers; quantity distributed, or thousands of pieces to be delivered; and the annual frequency, or number of times advertisers plan to distribute pre-prints per year. These factors are calculated into a cost-per-thousand rate for each size pre-print. Table 18.2 shows a typical newspaper pre-print rate card.

Table 18.2 Pre-Print Advertising Rates

# Tabloid Pages	Cost-Per-Thousand Based On Annual Frequency					
	1X	6X	12X	24X	48X	96X
1-4	$31	$28	$27	$26	$25	$24
6	$39	$35	$33	$31	$29	$27
8	$43	$38	$36	$34	$32	$30
12	$49	$44	$42	$40	$38	$36
16	$52	$47	$45	$43	$41	$39
20	$55	$50	$48	$46	$45	$42
24	$58	$53	$51	$49	$47	$45
28	$61	$56	$54	$52	$50	$48
32	$65	$60	$58	$56	$54	$52
36	$69	$64	$62	$60	$58	$56
40	$73	$68	$66	$64	$62	$60

Add $4/M for every 4 tab pages above 40.
Zoning available at 10% additional charge.

A newspaper salesperson assisting a pre-print advertiser will need to know the dimension of the pre-prints, the quantity, number of pages, and the frequency of insertion to calculate the cost-per-thousand rate for each preprint. For example, if an advertiser wishes to distribute 16-page tabloid pre-prints to the newspaper's full circulation, say 50,000, a total of 24 times annually, the salesperson will quote a rate of $43 per thousand, or 4.3 cents per piece, based on the advertiser signing an annual contract at that level. In this example, the total cost charged by the newspaper would be $43 per thousand multiplied by the 50,000 ($43 × 50) copies for a total of $2,150 per insertion. It should be noted that newspapers typically price the pre-prints by tabloid page size because most pre-prints are that shape and size. When a non-tabloid pre-print is priced, the newspaper salesperson will need to convert the actual size to a tabloid format for pricing. For example, an eight-page, standard newspaper size pre-print is the same size as a 16-page tabloid. Thus, an advertiser running an eight-page, standard size pre-print would be charged the same rate as an advertiser running a 16-page, tabloid pre-print given the same quantity and frequency levels.

Advertisers who run both display and pre-print advertising with a newspaper may request a dollar volume contract that enables them to leverage all expenditures with the newspaper to qualify for lower rates. Using the rate cards above, an advertiser who invests $150,000 in display advertising and $120,000 in pre-print distribution with the newspaper may seek to have the total annual investment of $270,000 apply to his or her display contract which would enable him or her to earn a 9,000-inch, bulk contract rate instead of a 2,000-inch rate. This type of contract enables the advertiser to either increase volume or reduce overall expenditures.

Newspaper salespeople need to understand the different types of advertising offered by the newspaper and how each is priced. Once they have a full understanding of the newspaper advertising rates and discounts, the salespeople need to become knowledgeable about the specific benefits newspaper advertising offers advertisers and the elements of effective newspaper advertising.

Benefits of Newspaper Advertising

Newspapers remain the dominant local advertising medium for one simple reason: newspaper advertising produces results for advertisers, day after day, week after week, month after month, year after year. Consistency is an integral part of successful advertising. According to the NAA, these are some of the key benefits newspaper advertising offers:[23]

- The majority of all adults, 54 percent, read a newspaper on an average weekday.
- More than six out of 10 adults, 64 percent, read a newspaper on an average Sunday.
- More than seven out of 10 adults, 73 percent, read a newspaper in the past five days.
- More than three-quarters of adults, 77 percent, read a Sunday newspaper in the past month.
- Newspaper usage is strong among emerging markets—teens and Hispanics.
- The newspaper is the most-used advertising source for various store categories.
- Newspaper Web sites are highly rated for being useful and informative.

- Customers for many products and services are also the heaviest newspaper readers.
- The newspaper provides advertisers with unique targeting opportunities.

As noted before, a majority of all US adults read a newspaper every day and practically all Americans read a newspaper occasionally. One of the main reasons consumers read newspapers is for the advertising messages from local stores and services. As a result, newspapers are the favorite advertising medium of the people who seek out newspaper ads to help them with important buying decisions. This receptive attitude toward newspaper advertising is just one reason why newspaper advertising works. Advertising in newspapers is not an annoyance.

Newspaper advertising is available at the reader's convenience. Readers know what types of ads to expect in their newspaper and they can refer to those ads anytime they want to, day or night. Consumers do not need to tune in at a specific time for a newspaper. If readers find an item or advertisement they like, they can clip it out and save it for future reference.

In newspaper ads, advertisers can tell a complete product story with illustrations and compelling reasons to buy. They also can run long or short copy in accordance with their needs and desires. An advertiser can run a full-page ad, a one-inch ad, or any size in between. The ad can be run once a month, once a week, every day, or several times in the same issue. Thus, newspaper advertising is very adaptable and can be designed to fit practically any budget.

Consistent newspaper advertising helps advertisers build a solid reputation in their communities, attract new customers, and remind regular customers that they made a wise choice in shopping with them in the first place.

Newspaper advertising allows advertisers to obtain consistently high reach and frequency. These are necessary ingredients for building and sustaining successful businesses in a thin market where only a small percentage of adults are actually in the market for the goods and services offered by advertisers. For example, in an average week, less than one percent, 0.9 percent, of all adults in the US shopped for major appliances in 1999, and only 78 percent of the shoppers actually bought an appliance.[24] In a market with 100,000 adults, that means only 900 adults per week are shopping for major appliances. If you divided the potential customers evenly among all competitors in a market, it would be clear that each store has a very small pool of prospective customers to draw from in any given week. The key, then, is for businesses to consistently invite these potential customers into their stores by continually telling them why their business is better. The daily frequency of newspapers, along with the flexible ad sizes and frequency contract rates, provides advertisers with direct access to consumers in the thin market when they are coming in and going out of the market.

Newspaper advertising can increase sales and profits. As a result, it should not be viewed as an expense but rather as an investment, as all media advertising should. Smart advertisers realize there are only a few people interested in their products or services at any given time. By consistently advertising in the newspaper, advertisers are positioned to communicate with their best prospects when they are receptive to buy. By increasing sales through advertising, advertisers can actually lower their per-unit costs due to economies of scale which makes the entire business more profitable. Newspaper advertising pays because the newspaper is the advertising source most often used when consumers are seeking information to help them make wise buying decisions. Table 18.3

Store Category	Newspaper	Television
Discount	67%	5%
Department	66	6
Drug	66	5
Appliance	62	6
Home Building Centers	60	6
Home Furnishings	59	8
Sporting Goods	59	6
Office Supply	58	5
Home Electronics	57	6
Computers	45	7

Table 18.3 Consumers' Main Source of Advertising by Store Categories

Source: *Newspaper Advertising of ROP, Inserts & Coupons.* 2001. National Newspaper Association. Conducted by MORI Research, Inc.

shows a comparison of consumer responses when asked to identify the advertising source most often used when thinking of buying from major store categories, according to a NAA 2001 study conducted by MORI Research, Inc.[25]

Elements of Effective Newspaper Advertising

Little has changed over the years since 1923 when Dr. Daniel Starch, a Harvard professor, noted that the "functions of an advertisement are fivefold: To attract attention (the advertisement must be seen), to arouse interest (the advertisement must be read), to create conviction (the advertisement must be believed), to produce a response (the advertisement must be acted upon), and to impress the memory (the advertisement in most cases must be remembered)."[26]

To make their advertising more effective, advertisers often need help with designing their advertising, especially in smaller and middle-size accounts. They need help from their newspaper sales representative to help them find better ways to promote their products and services more effectively. Salespeople should remember that their accounts are not usually experts in advertising. Thus, their job is to educate their customers so their advertisements produce better results. A salesperson's number-one objective is to get results for their customers, as you learned in Chapter 2, and an important factor in generating more results from newspaper ads is finding ways to increase ad readership by using effective layouts and writing good copy.

A professional newspaper salesperson should understand the key elements of good ad copy and layout. Often, a newspaper salesperson may eventually be the person responsible for writing the copy and laying out the ad, especially at smaller newspapers. A creative department usually produces the ads at larger newspapers. Regardless, salespeople need to understand the fundamentals of good advertising copy and layout, so they can advise their clients and potential clients.

One good sales technique is to invest the time to produce a sample ad, or spec ad, which can demonstrate to the advertiser what the newspaper is capable of producing for them. Spec ads also show advertisers that the salesperson is interested in their business and is attempting to share expertise to help advertisers grow their business. Although developing spec ads, either alone or with assistance from a creative services department, takes some time, it is usually very productive in selling advertising campaigns with multiple insertions. If the spec ad helps make the sale, it can turn into months or even years of regular advertising. A number of new digital art and graphics services enables newspaper salespeople to create spec ads quickly by reviewing successful ads from other markets and accessing creative artwork that can be customized for their clients.

Each newspaper should offer training in copy and layout in general with specific procedures for processing advertising materials at that newspaper. For general information, the NAA 2001 Newspaper Advertising Planbook recommends the *AIDA Formula* for creating effective ads. This formula claims that good ads have four things in common: they create Attention, Interest, Desire, and Action—otherwise known as AIDA.

A = Attention Grab the reader's attention with headlines, type, white space and visuals.

I = Interest Make the copy interesting and benefit-oriented.

D = Desire People read ad copy to find out how a product or service benefits them. Make sure the copy answers reader's question, "What's in it for me?"

A = Action Urge the reader to act now—and make it easy to do so.

These four elements translate into successful ad layouts and designs by using attention-grabbing headlines and key benefit statements, dominant illustrations or graphics, readable and complete copy, a compelling offer, and an attractive, recognizable company logo complete with store locations, hours, and telephone numbers. Such ads give consumers the information they need to make intelligent shopping decisions.

Establishing Advertising Budgets

Newspaper salespeople who have earned the trust of their customers will often be asked to help customers develop their advertising budgets. Whether helping prepare an actual budget or simply advising when, what, and how much to advertise, a salesperson needs to understand how to prepare and plan advertising. This planning is another process that takes time on the front end in working with clients, but it reduces the time a salesperson spends with that account on a regular basis, because ads and budgets are planned for the upcoming months.

The budget-planning process begins with an overview of how advertisers' business have performed over the past 12 months and how they expect it to perform in the upcoming year. Wise advertisers should attempt to match their advertising investments with their monthly sales trends or expected sales. The newspaper industry publishes an annual *advertising planbook* that helps salespeople advise their clients on when and what to advertise and how much they should be investing each month based on that industry's sales patterns.

An advertiser and salesperson should record the monthly sales and identify what percentage of the entire year's sales were made each month. In another column, the salesperson should record how much the advertiser invested in advertising each month and what percentage of the entire year's advertising dollars were invested each month. Theoretically, those two items—sales and advertising—should be approximately the same percentage of the year's totals for both categories. For example, advertisers who receive 8 percent of their sales in January should invest 8 percent of their annual advertising in January as well.

This formula ensures that advertisers have a consistent advertising presence in the market while also placing the heaviest advertising investment in the months with the greatest sales potential. It is similar to the notion of fishing when the fish are biting.

By establishing the budget amounts, a salesperson and an advertiser can work together to plan the best items to place each ad, the days to run the ads, and how to track the results of each ad. A salesperson may also want to recommend setting aside some additional dollars for special promotions or opportunities and advise an advertiser to increase spending ahead of the sales curve to build momentum before the biggest shopping seasons.

If newspaper salespeople can become involved in clients' planning and budgeting, they can actually become an extension of the client's marketing and advertising department. Such a relationship places the newspaper salesperson in the best possible position to help clients grow their businesses and to secure a fair share of their advertising for the salesperson's newspaper.

Newspaper Sales Organizations

Newspaper sales departments are organized to serve their various customers and represent their various products, such as classified, classified display, local or retail display, national display and pre-prints. Because each sale involves a different pricing and marketing strategy, most newspapers are organized along these advertising product lines. Naturally, a larger newspaper will have more layers of senior executives and mid-level supervisors than a small paper will. The basic structure, though, will be similar in newspapers of all sizes. The key sub-departments in a typical advertising sales department include the following:

Advertising director or vice president of advertising—This person is the top advertising executive at the newspaper—a position that usually reports either to the publisher or general manager. The advertising director directs all advertising sales and creative and customer service departments, usually including classified, national, and retail departments.

Retail advertising manager—The retail advertising manager manages the local display advertising sales staff and sales, including hiring and supervising direct reports. Retail advertising managers will plan local sales promotions, have input on key pricing decisions, coordinate special advertising sections, and conduct training, and often handle many of the newspaper's major accounts. Depending on the size of the newspaper, retail advertising managers may have local sales supervisors and co-op advertising coordinators reporting to them. The retail advertising manager also works with the advertising director to establish annual revenue and expense budgets and sales initiatives.

Classified advertising manager—The classified advertising manager organizes and supervises the inside telephone sales staff and customer service functions in classifieds and works with inside and outside salespeople selling and servicing existing display accounts and developing new business. Automotive, real estate, recruitment, commercial line, and private party ads usually fall under the supervision of the classified advertising manager. At larger papers, there may be additional inside telephone sales managers; category specialists for recruitment, automotive and real estate; and supervisors for the outside sales teams for each category of classified display advertising. Classified managers recruit, hire, train, and supervise personnel for their departments. They also work with the advertising director to establish budgets and sales goals and quotas and to implement pricing and marketing programs.

Major accounts manager, national advertising manager, co-op advertising manager—These are positions you find at larger newspapers. Major accounts managers direct a team of salespeople who work with the newspaper's largest accounts, which often includes many national and regional retail chains. These accounts demand more attention and a higher level of professional service and sales pressure from newspapers. As a result, the major accounts department attempts to surround these accounts by presenting the newspaper's story and benefits to everyone involved in the advertiser's decision-making process. This intense coverage means calling on local store managers, district managers, regional advertising directors, and corporate officers, for example, to make sure everyone involved in recommending advertising purchases is aware of the newspaper's benefits and its position in its market. The national advertising manager works with the newspaper's national sales representative firm. The co-op manager works with local display salespeople and retailers to find co-op dollars so retailers can stretch their advertising.

The newspaper's sales structure provides the organizational support to care for each type of customer. It also provides excellent career opportunities for professionals who hire in at one level and progress through the ranks. Of all the media salespeople in the market, newspaper salespeople consistently spend the most time with retail clients and decision makers. As a result, they have an excellent knowledge of what is happening in the local market and become a valuable source of information and ideas for all their clients. Generally, newspaper salespeople are the most knowledgeable marketing professionals in their markets.

Account Assignments

Newspaper sales managers have a variety of ways of assigning accounts to salespeople. Newspapers may assign account lists, account categories, or geographic territories to outside salespeople. Each method has it pluses and minuses. Account list assignments give outside salespeople freedom to cover the entire market, prospecting for accounts. Once they make a sale, the account goes on their account list indefinitely. This method makes sure that someone is calling on the best potential accounts because commissioned salespeople aggressively pursue the biggest spenders. However, the account list method often results in duplication of effort as multiple salespeople are calling on the same accounts. In the process, many smaller accounts often get overlooked.

Category assignments make sense when special knowledge or expertise is necessary or where there is a common buying structure in place. Typical category salespeople would serve automotive businesses, realtors, recruiters, entertainment venues, ad agencies, chain stores, department stores, and grocery stores, for example. The advantage of having category specialists is that salespeople develop a depth of category knowledge and expertise that serves advertisers well. Category specialists do not work as well with small local accounts because there are too many of them to effectively cover without wasting a lot of time driving around the market. That's where territorial salespeople come into the picture.

Territorial salespeople are assigned specific geographic areas and every account in their territory is theirs to sell, with the exception of any major or category-excluded accounts. The purpose of the territorial sales structure is to make it efficient for salespeople to park their cars and go door to door soliciting advertising and servicing clients. Because newspapers offer advertising programs for all size businesses and budgets, territorial salespeople consider practically every business in their area a prospect for advertising in the newspaper.

The purpose of all the various sales structure options is to make sure the newspaper is surrounding as many of its potential advertisers as possible with the right amount and type of sales expertise necessary to properly sell and service each type of account. Because the needs of each advertiser vary for a multitude of reasons, most newspapers use a combination of the sales structures. Regardless of how a newspaper operates, it is a salesperson's job to seek more business from existing accounts, while at the same time increasing the number of active accounts by prospecting for and convincing businesses to begin advertising in their newspaper. With slightly more than one-half of the typical newspaper salesperson's compensation based on commissions and bonuses, they have a strong incentive to increase revenues for their newspapers. Newspaper salespeople must also have incentives for signing new accounts since there is usually some turnover with smaller businesses.

Selling Newspaper Advertising

When I worked for Multimedia, Inc., our largest advertiser in the *Greenville News* was a regional department store chain that had not increased spending for four or more years. The company's CEO did not feel any need to increase spending because he knew his firm was far and away the newspaper's largest advertiser. Since his goal was to dominate the market, he felt his 40-percent advertising investment advantage over his closest competitor was evidence that his stores were the number-one shopping destinations in the market and that they were the market's largest and most dominant advertiser.

I was vice president of marketing for the Multimedia newspapers division at the time and was asked by the publisher of our largest paper, the *Greenville News*, if I would head a team that would search for ways to convince this advertiser that he needed to increase his investment significantly. Our team held several planning meetings during which we decided that it would be in everyone's best interest if we approach the department store CEO in a strategic way. We decided to tell the CEO that we had come to the conclusion that our success was dependant upon the retailer's success and that our previous approaches had been wrong. In the past, we had sought ways to get the advertiser just to invest more money with our newspaper. Now, we decided we should try to find ways to help him increase his business in anticipation that an increase in his store sales would also result in an increase in his advertising.

He seemed delighted when we told him of our more customer-based approach and immediately scheduled a series of fact-finding meetings between our team and a team of department store executives. During those meetings we asked hundreds of questions about his business, his customers, his competitors, and his perceived opportunities and challenges. We focused on his goals. When he said, "I want to rip the throat out of my competition," we knew he was committed to remaining the top retailer in our market.

After several of the fact-finding meetings, our newspaper team began to work on a specific proposal that would help him achieve his goals and get our newspaper more advertising in the process.

Our biggest challenge was finding some way to show him that new competition in the market was cutting into his market dominance in ways that resulted in more business for our newspaper. We felt confident we could convince him that his competition was impacting his sales. Our fear, however, was that he would agree that he needed to be more aggressive but since he was already our largest advertiser, he might assume he dominated our medium and would seek to shift dollars elsewhere to gain even greater exposure—exposure that might come at our expense.

Our team carefully analyzed his goals, our market research, his competitors, and all relevant information as we put together some very specific marketing investment opportunity recommendations. As we analyzed his competitors, we made a very important discovery. The department store actually spent more money with the newspaper than any other advertiser in the market, but it did not have the strongest presence in our newspaper. Why? Because several of his competitors had converted from ROP ads to inserts. Since they ran inserts, they had more pages than our leading advertiser and thus, had a stronger share of voice in the market than our top advertiser.

This discovery gave us the ammunition we felt we would need to convince our department store CEO that the competition was actually more dominant in our newspaper than he was. However, it also presented another challenge. What would we do if he agreed with our share-of-voice analogy, which actually showed him as the fourth-largest advertiser in terms of share of voice, and subsequently decided to convert his advertising from ROP to inserts? Such a move could have reduced our revenues from his company by 50 percent or more.

We decided to stress the various benefits of his strong ROP program such as flexibility, timeliness, positioning, tradition, and readership. At the same time we knew we had to find some way to help him fund a more aggressive ROP program so he could regain his position as the market's top advertiser in terms of share of voice. Toward this end, we reviewed all the expenses of his advertising department in an effort to find some efficiencies that might provide the funds he needed to expand his program and increase his market share.

As we got into his numbers, we learned he was spending more than $100,000 per year on photography for his print ads. He was also running similar programs with papers in less important markets. Between those two categories, we realized we could help him fund more promotional advertising space if we could take over his photography services by hiring one full-time photographer dedicated to his account and by becoming his commercial printer to print inserts for the outlying papers.

We then developed a solutions-based sales presentation that recommended he increase his advertising from the $1.4 million annual level to $2.8 million—a 100-percent increase. He liked our proposals and our willingness to be his marketing partner in this manner. However, he felt we were a little too aggressive so he signed a two-year contract for $1.9 million in year one and $2.2 million in year two.

As a result of this cooperative sales effort between a professional newspaper team and a leading department store, the retailer was able to obtain the additional exposure he desired and that he needed to increase his market share in a highly competitive marketplace. And our newspaper was able to get a significant increase from our largest advertiser who had not increased his advertising investment with our newspaper for the previous four years. In addition, the department store's increased aggressiveness enabled us to convince his competitors of the need to be more aggressive, too.

In the process, we all learned the value of listening to our customers and trying to help them find solutions to their problems. We also made some lifelong friends through our more open and mutually beneficial approach to our customer's business.

The Future of Newspapers

With every major new entrant into the media landscape, many observers have predicted the eminent demise of the newspaper industry. First it was radio, then television, direct mail, audiotext and videotext, and now the Internet. All of these entrants were expected to replace newspapers because of the unique characteristics and competitive advantages these up-and-comers offered that newspapers could not—sight, sound, motion, instantaneous access, and depth and breadth of coverage. However, in spite of these threats, newspapers remain a primary source for news and advertising information and the dominant source of local news and information. In addition, newspapers continue to enjoy unusually high profit margins, and they have maintained high valuations in a consistently active merger and acquisition marketplace.

Still, newspapers cannot afford to sit back on their laurels and not realize the rapid rate of change. Newspapers are concerned about the decline of help-wanted advertising since 1991 and publishers are not sure if the decline is due to the country's economic slowdown or if it represents a decomposition of this business through migration to Internet job sites such as Monster.com and HotJobs.com that have both broad general appeal and highly specialized markets.

In addition, newspaper executives are struggling with decisions about declining circulation and market penetration. Many are wondering if the traditional paid circulation model will remain intact or if new measurements for audience penetration and readership might not be more appropriate in the quest to serve both readers and advertisers. These issues are especially sensitive as information becomes more of commodity with increasing amounts of news and information now available free from sources other than daily newspapers.

Newspaper executives are also searching for ways to increase readership and newspaper usage by younger adults and teens, demographics that are highly desirable to advertisers. Several experiments were launched in late 2002 including two highly publicized youth tabloids that were introduced by competing Chicago dailies, the *Chicago Tribune* and the *Chicago Sun-Times*. At this writing, the papers are targeting 18- to 34-year-olds with these tabloids. Their younger-oriented tabloids, *Red Eye* and *Red Streak*, respectively, are being distributed separately from their daily counterparts. While it is too early to tell if the Chicago experiments will be successful, the efforts are an indication that the industry might be waking up to its youth readership problem and that it is willing to take drastic steps to correct it in an effort to ensure the industry's future.

Newspaper executives are also searching for ways to make their popular Internet sites financially successful. Newspaper Web sites are among the most popular on the Web, but newspapers, like most Internet companies, have not yet turned audience acceptance into profitable business models.

In spite of these challenges, newspapers should remain a viable business and an important medium for the foreseeable future. The industry is learning how to reduce and control costs through consolidation, automation, outsourcing, and resource-sharing. Newspapers are using technology to provide better and more efficient customer service. And, most important, newspapers remain the primary vehicle for local news and advertising information.

Finally, while newspapers learn how to attract more young readers, their core readers are part of a generation that is living longer and enjoying more affluence than previous generations. The combination of loyal core readers and the industry's overall profitability should provide the time and the resources necessary for the industry to solve many of its challenges and carve out exciting opportunities for future growth in readership, advertising, and relevance.

Test Yourself

1. What is the significance of penny newspapers?
2. How many daily and weekly newspapers are there in the United States?
3. What is a JOA and how are they usually organized?
4. In 2001, what percentage of total advertising expenditures did newspapers, television, and radio each receive?
5. In the newspaper industry, what do the following sets of initials stand for: ABC, CAC, and VAC?
6. What three newspapers have a daily circulation over 1 million?
7. Which demographics read newspapers (a) the least and (b) the most?
8. What are the two possible meanings of the term ROP?
9. In newspapers, what are bulk rates?
10. Name four benefits of newspaper advertising.

Project

Imagine that you are the owner of a local furniture store that is preparing to open a new store. Your new store will be 50,000 square feet and you know that most furniture stores located in neighborhood shopping centers generate average sales per square foot of $178.33 annually. You've learned that most household furniture stores invest 9.7 percent of sales in advertising and that sales in the fourth quarter typically make up 28.7 percent of the annual total, with 8.6 percent of total sales in October, 9.5 percent in November, and 10.6 percent in December. Given that information, how much should you budget for newspaper advertising in the fourth quarter? Prepare an advertising budget, then use the advertising rate card for display advertising annual bulk rates in Table 18.1 to determine how many column inches of advertising you can purchase. Assuming there are 126 column inches in a full page, how many full-page ads can you purchase and stay within your proposed budget if you assume an annual dollar volume of $336,000 on the rate card in Table 18.1?

Resources

www.naa.org
www.editorandpublisher.com
www.snpa.org
www.inlandpress.org
www.readership.org
www.scripps-research.org

References

Editor & Publisher. 2002 *Editor & Publisher International Year Book 2002*. New York.
Albert Wesley Frey. 1953. *Advertising*. New York: The Ronald Press Company.
Mack Hanan. 1989. *Key Account Selling*. New York: American Management Association.
Mack Hanan. 1999. *Consultative Selling*. New York: American Management Association.
Inland Press Association. 2002. *National Cost and Revenue Study for Daily Newspapers*. Des Plaines, IL.

Inland Press Association. 2002. *Newspaper Industry Compensation Study.* Des Plaines, IL.

International Newspaper Marketing Association. 2002. *Outlook 2003: Positioning Newspapers for Uncertainty.* Dallas.

Otto Kleppner. 1941. *Advertising Procedure.* New York: Prentice-Hall, Inc.

Philip Kotler. 2000. *Marketing Management.* New York: Prentice-Hall, Inc.

Newspaper Association of America. 2001. *NAA 2001 Newspaper Advertising Planbook.* Vienna, VA.

Newspaper Association of America. 2001. *Why Newspapers? They Add Value for Advertisers.* Vienna, VA.

Newspaper Association of America. 2002. *Facts about Newspapers 2002.* Vienna, VA.

New York Press Club. 1906. *Journalism Illustrated.* New York.

Ohio University-Scripps Howard News Service. 2002. *Newspaper Readership Survey Results.* Athens, OH: Ohio University Press. June.

Daniel Starch. 1926. *Principles of Advertising.* Chicago: A.W. Shaw Company.

Endnotes

1. Newspaper Association of America. 2002. *Facts about Newspapers 2002.* Vienna, VA.
2. The Readership Institute. 2002. *Readership Institute's Impact Study of 100 Daily Newspapers 2000-2001.* Media Management Center at Northwestern University. Evanston, IL.
3. Newspaper Association of America. 2002. *Facts about Newspapers 2002.* Vienna, VA
4. Ibid. pp. 4, 13, and 14.
5. *Editor & Publisher Yearbook.* 2002. New York, NY.
6. Newspaper Association of America. 2002. *Succeeding with Newspapers: The Power of Newspaper vs. Competitive Media.* Vienna, VA.
7. Newspaper Association of America. 2002. *Facts about Newspapers 2002.* Vienna, VA. p. 19.
8. Newspaper Association of America. 2002. *Business Analysis and Research.* May. Vienna, VA.
9. Newspaper Association of America. 2002. *Facts about Newspapers 2002.* Vienna, VA.
10. New York Press Club. 1906. *Journalism Illustrated.* New York.
11. Newspaper Association of America. 2002. *Facts about Newspapers 2002.* Vienna, VA.
12. Ibid.
13. Newspaper Association of America. *2002. The Power of Newspaper vs. Television,* Vienna, VA.
14. www.boxofficemojo.com/tv/2002/05.htm. *Primetime Television Ratings.* January 28 to February 3, 2002.
15. Entertainment Weekly's www.ew.com. *TV Chart.* Friday, February 14, 2003. Source: Nielsen Ratings.
16. Newspaper Association of America. 2002. *Facts about Newspapers 2002.* Vienna, VA
17. Ohio University. Scripps Howard News Service: *Newspaper Readership Survey Results.* June 2002. Athens, OH.
18. Newspaper National Network. 2002. Sales Presentation. *2001 Scarborough Research Rel 1.* New York.
19. NAA 2002 Newspaper Advertising Planbook. *Readership Among Teens.* Source: Teenage Research Unlimited, Inc. Spring 2001 study. Vienna, VA. p. 8.
20. Ohio University. Scripps Howard News Service: *Newspaper Readership Survey Results.* June 2002. Athens, OH.
21. Newspaper Association of America. 2002. *The Daily and Sunday Newspaper Audience: Major Demographic Segments, 2002 Report.* Vienna, VA.
22. Newspaper Association of America. 2002. *Facts about Newspapers 2002.* Vienna, VA.
23. Newspaper Association of America. *Planbook 2003: Newspaper Advertising Planbook.* Vienna, VA.
24. Newspaper Association of America. *How America Shops and Spends, 2000 Study.* Vienna, VA.
25. Newspaper Association of American. *Newspaper Advertising of ROP, Inserts & Coupons, NAA 2001.* Conducted by MORI Research, Inc.
26. Daniel Starch. 1926. *Principles of Advertising.* Chicago and New York: A.W. Shaw Company. p. 7.

19 Broadcast Television

By Mark Chassman

For those who grew up as part of the television generation and have a passion for television culture and aspire for business success, there is no more rewarding career than television advertising sales. My career began as a local account executive at the ABC affiliate in Sacramento, CA in the summer of 1988. My training: a Nielsen ratings book, a list of inactive accounts, and a brand-new copy of the local phone directory. This was not the most ideal beginning, to say the least. However, the journey has been nothing but challenging, rewarding, and downright exciting in spite of that inauspicious start.

As with any selling endeavor, a sale in television begins when a relationship is established—a relationship built on mutual trust in which a seller and a buyer come together for mutual gain. With that in mind, a foundation of knowledge that lends to one's credibility with buyers is critical. Today, a broadcast television media salesperson must own consultative and solutions-selling skills and the tenacity to deal with the ambiguous nature of an ever-changing marketplace to succeed. Television salespeople cannot survive on low rates and large audiences as in the past. They must become enablers, marrying the needs of advertisers with the needs of viewers. They must understand both consumers and technology. In today's environment, selling challenges are compounded by audience fragmentation, a term used to describe the growing number of audience subdivisions. Fragmentation makes it more difficult to sell the mass audience reach benefits of broadcast television than it was in the days when the big three television networks dominated media consumption. Accelerated by the proliferation of technology, fragmentation is a byproduct of more devices competing for limited time in the American home. And as a result, cable and pay cable television, VCRs, video games, DVDs, and home computers are eating into time that was once dominated by commercial television viewing. While there are more competing challenges than ever before, there have never been more new opportunities.

As you will discover in the next several pages, the future of broadcast television is bright and the benefits offered to marketers are still the most powerful around. Not only will commercial television continue to be an instrument of mass communication, conveying information and entertainment to the general public, but television's potential for becoming more powerful, more dominant, more credible, and more influential in the digital age has never been greater. The purpose of this chapter is to give you a base of knowledge and insight to build on. Add an account list, a Nielsen ratings book, a brand-new copy of the local phone directory, and a copy of *Media Selling* and you too can be off on a magnificent journey selling television advertising in a market near you.

Brief History

The Federal Communications Commission (FCC) issued the first television station license on July 1, 1941 and opened the door for what would be the beginning of commercial television. By 1948 Americans who lived within range of the growing number of television stations could watch *The Texaco Star Theater* starring Milton Berle (1948), or NBC's *Camel News Caravan* (1948) with John Cameron Swayze, who was required by the tobacco company sponsor to always have a burning cigarette visible when he was on camera. Many early programs such as *Amos 'n' Andy* (1951) or *The Jack Benny Show* (1950) were borrowed from television's older, more established big brother, network radio. Most of the formats of the new programs, such as newscasts, situation comedies, variety shows, and dramas were also borrowed from radio. In 1950 television came into its own with large, national brand marketers when surveys showed that brand recognition levels for television sponsors were higher than they were in radio. The results of these surveys established television as a genuine mass medium, providing sponsors and advertisers with an unprecedented means of reaching and influencing the behavior of consumers. As a result, television program schedules in the 1950s became chock full of programs with titles such as *Kraft Television Theater*, *Colgate Comedy Hour*, and *Coke Time*. As with radio, early programs were produced by advertising agencies for their sponsor-clients and were distributed via the three television networks at the time, NBC, CBS, and ABC.[1]

What came to be called participation advertising was introduced by NBC executive Sylvester L. "Pat" Weaver via the *Today Show*, which made its debut in 1952 with Dave Garroway as host. Also dubbed the magazine concept, participation advertising allowed advertisers to purchase discrete segments of shows, typically one- or two-minute blocks, rather than sponsoring entire programs. As in the case of magazines, which featured ads for a variety of products, a participation program could carry commercials from up to four different sponsors. The concept of discrete sponsored sections imitated magazine's practice of divorcing its editorial content from its advertising content. In theory, the presence of multiple sponsors meant that no one advertiser could control a program.[2]

Although participation advertising met with some initial resistance from Madison Avenue (large, national advertising agencies), many saw this as an ideal promotional vehicle for packaged-goods companies with a cornucopia of brand names such as Procter & Gamble (P&G)—with such disparate products as Tide (laundry detergent), Crest (toothpaste), and Jif (peanut butter). By 1960 the magazine concept dominated television advertising, as it has ever since. Instead of relying on identification with a specific program or program segment, advertisers now spread their messages across the schedule in an effort to reach as many consumers—or at least as many of those within a specified demographic—as possible.

Industry Structure

Networks

Back in the 1950s, during what was referred to as the Golden Age of Television, the commercial television industry came to life, powered by the three major television networks: CBS, NBC, and ABC. A country fascinated with television was limited to watching, almost exclusively, what appeared on those networks. Networks are program distributors affiliated by means of market-exclusive contracts with local television stations. Networks make yearly payments, referred to as network compensation, to their affiliated stations to broadcast the network's programs. Network affiliates then sell geographically targeted commercials to local and national advertisers in the breaks between network programs while the networks retain the right to sell advertising in their programs to advertisers who want exposure across the entire country. Advertisers buy time within a network program to advertise whatever they want to sell, be it a product or an image. With programming and advertising combined, the television program is broadcast to viewers by a local television station.

Today there are seven television networks: ABC, CBS, NBC, FOX, WB, UPN(owned by CBS), and PAX (The Paxson Family Network, the majority of which is owned by NBC). Programming on the networks is designed to appeal to large audience segments within a demographic (for example, Adults 18 to 34, Men 18 to 49, or Women 25 to 54). Networks are often criticized for catering to the lowest common denominator in order to bring together large audiences and, thus, charge high rates to advertisers in their programs. The compensation of television network salespeople ebbs and flows with the demographic ratings tide associated with their network's various programs.

The Upfront

Network television is responsible for the notorious annual *upfront market*, as often mocked in the popular media. The network television upfront is an $8 billion business in which buyers and sellers, in an auction-like fervor often referred to as a "feeding frenzy," come together to negotiate rates for network programs in an upcoming season. The mechanics of the upfront are simple. Advertisers can place their television buys in advance of the season—upfront— or hold back money and buy after the season begins. If advertisers or their agencies buy later in the season, it is called the scatter market. Networks carefully modulate supply—how much inventory is sold upfront and how much is held for scatter. An agency buyer plays the market by betting on demand. If an agency buys upfront for one of its advertisers and the market has overestimated demand, prices will fall in the later scatter market and the upfront buyer will have paid too much. This ritual takes place in May of each year and advertiser dollars are committed in less than two weeks' time. There are billions of dollars committed in the upfront market for the upcoming television season that begins in late September.

Upfront buying is not new. In the earliest days of television everything was sold upfront. Sponsorship discussions between advertisers and the networks started the week after Washington's birthday and by the end of February programs and time periods for the following season had been spoken for. Although it was all upfront, it was different. Negotiations then were low-key and discreet, more like private banking than a liquidation auction.

In the 1950s advertisers owned many of the top-rated shows. The networks wanted to control these programs in order to package them with lower-rated programs, and were looking for a way to break the system of advertisers owning programs. Back then, there was no television season, either. The start date of each program's cycle determined when its new season began. "I Love Lucy" premiered in October and "Dragnet" in January. Then, in 1962, ABC, the third-rated network at the time, came up with the idea of premiering all of its programs in a single week following Labor Day. CBS and NBC joined in and by the mid-60s, the new television season marked the end of summer and the return of kids to school.[3]

The motivation for the upfront came in the 1960s when higher costs and bigger risks of program failure forced advertisers to rethink sponsorship. Program costs rose rapidly when live television production switched to being filmed at the Hollywood studios. The risk of a program failing also became greater as a stronger ABC gave viewers the choice of a third network. These risks meant more shows would fail. The combination of higher costs and higher risk started the advertiser migration from full sponsorship to alternating sponsorship to today's package rotation buying and the upfront market.

By the 1970s the upfront market was strong and the ever-more-confident networks were testing it with steep price increases. When prices went up an incredible 25 percent for the 1975-76 television season, J. Walter Thompson (JWT), the largest television buying agency, decided to sit out the upfront and wait for more sensible pricing. But JWT's timing was bad and their advertisers eventually paid more for poorer programs in the scatter market. That experience left buyers scarred and for the next 15 years the major strategy for buying network was to buy upfront.

Agencies had discovered they were powerless to moderate price increases. Therefore, they began to promote the clout gained from buying for many clients at one time and corporate buying for all of the products of such advertising giants as General Motors and P&G as a way to beat the market by paying less than the average increase. By stressing the need for big dollars to get good prices, buyers became in-house advocates for television. This situation helped the networks capture a greater share of advertising dollars, which increased the demand for television time and helped support ever increasing prices. Today the upfront represents approximately 80 percent of the combined networks' total annual sales.

Another reason that advertising agencies prefer to buy in the upfront market is because the networks guarantee ratings on upfront buys. A rating guarantee means that if, for example, NBC sold a spot in "Friends" and guaranteed it would get a 15 rating, if the program earned only a 12 rating, NBC would owe the advertiser 3 ratings points that it would have to make up later. The first guaranteed cost-per-thousands (CPM) was negotiated by American Home Products with ABC in 1967. It was an informal commitment by the network to protect a buyer who bought as part of the network upfront market and to add free commercials, if necessary, to make up ratings points to get to the negotiated CPM. The networks soon learned buyers would pay a premium for a guaranteed buy and wouldn't be as picky about the programs. The timing was perfect. Despite the celebrity of the Nielsen "Top 10," the television networks were no longer selling shows, they were selling CPMs. To get participation in hit programs at a reasonable price, agencies had to take other, less desirable programs and they had to buy upfront. If agencies agreed to buy that way, the networks would guarantee audience delivery. Guarantees revolutionized the business by reducing advertiser risk. By 1985, guaranteed upfront buys accounted for 85 percent of prime time sales and the phrase "feeding frenzy" began appearing in the press to describe the television upfront.[4]

Agency media buyers soon pressured local television stations to guarantee ratings points for schedules that they purchased. Today some local stations, usually the weaker ones in terms of ratings, will guarantee ratings delivery on purchased schedules.

Stations

There are 1,290 commercial television stations in the United States—573 VHF stations (a signal radius of about 60 miles for Very High Frequency) and 717 UHF stations (a signal radius of about 35 miles for Ultra High Frequency).[5] These numbers are updated annually on the Television Bureau of Advertising's Web site (www.tvb.org, in the Research Central link, in the Market Trends Track link). The majority are network-affiliated stations. These stations use a combination of network programming, local news programming, and syndicated programming, or programs sold to local stations on a market-by-market basis, to fill their schedules. Syndicated programs include game shows, music shows, talk shows, and off-network reruns of past and current programs. Independent television stations are those that are not affiliated with a network and as a result acquire the bulk of their programs through syndication.

DMAs

Broadcast station licenses are issued by the FCC and are licensed to cover a particular area or market. Markets define a trading area surrounding a city or group of cities. Nielsen Media Research calls local television markets Designated Market Areas (DMAs). DMAs include a cluster of counties that are covered by the local television signals in the market area. Every county in the United States is assigned to one and only one DMA. Each DMA is usually named after the biggest city in the market area such as the Chicago DMA (number three) or the Dayton DMA (number 58). However, there are several multi-city DMAs such as San Francisco-Oakland-San Jose (number 5) or Tampa-St. Petersburg (number 13).[6] Each county is assigned to the DMA in which the television stations most watched in the county are located.

In addition to these formal uses of the term "market," there are several other uses for the term in the television business. Some of the common uses are the African-American market, the Hispanic market, or an upscale market. These are market segments that are of interest to advertisers. In all its usages, market indicates a consumer segment that can be targeted by an advertiser.

How Broadcast Television Is Sold

As you learned in Chapter 18, newspaper ads are sold by the column inch, which means that what an advertiser pays for an ad, generally, is based on the size of the ad in that newspaper. Column-inch rates vary, of course, by the size of a newspaper's circulation, so a page in the *New York Times* costs a lot more than a page in the *Des Moines Register*. As you will learn in Chapter 23, magazine ads are sold by fractions of a page, and a magazine's page rate varies with the size of its circulation. The major difference between newspaper pricing and magazine pricing is that newspapers, except in the three largest markets in the country (New York, Los Angeles, and Chicago), typically enjoy a monopoly in their market. These monopolies occur either because there are no competing newspapers or because of a Joint Operating Agreement (described in Chapter 18) with another paper.

The ultimate effect of these newspaper monopolies, as in all monopolies, is that without competition, they can raise prices unrestrained by the threat of competitive pricing or regardless of circulation declines. The magazine industry, on the other hand, is very competitive and the page rates of magazines are based on circulation. In fact, most magazine rate cards include a rate base, which is, in effect, a guarantee to advertisers that a magazine's circulation will not fall below the level stated in the rate base. When a magazine's circulation increases, it will raise its rate base and, thus, its rates. Most magazines' circulation are audited at least annually, so rate bases may or may not go up or down each year. This magazine rate-base pricing system seems a little less arbitrary and a little fairer than monopolistic newspapers' predatory pricing, but, as with newspapers, magazine rates are based on circulation, not necessarily on readership of the publication or on the advertising in that publication. All advertisers know when they buy a print ad is how many total issues of a newspaper or magazine were delivered or purchased at a newsstand.

Newspapers and magazines also try to measure the pass-along audience, and many publications will sell an average-readers-per-copy number to advertisers in an attempt to come up with an audience (readers) for their publication. Most newspapers sell the concept that they have an average of two readers per copy, which seems somewhat reasonable. On the other hand, some magazines claim as many as five readers per copy. For example, you might hear a popular news magazine salesperson saying something like, "Yes, we have an average of six readers per copy. Think of all the copies of our magazine in dentists' offices where dozens of people read them." I suppose advertisers have to take readers-per-copy figures and the notion that all those readers will see and read their ad on faith, which seems to me like having faith that the Chicago Cubs will win the World Series next year.

Another similarity between newspapers and magazines is that, as mentioned in Chapter 18, they have an elastic supply of inventory and can add pages when demand increases. Therefore, print salespeople do not have to negotiate rates based on supply and demand. They generally stick to their rate cards, although in recent years, because of the highly competitive nature of the magazine business, magazine salespeople have begun to negotiate more, primarily with larger advertisers, to get a higher share of their budgets.

Because radio, broadcast television, and cable television's audiences are measured continually, the audience of any program or time period is known with a reasonable amount of precision. Not only is the total audience known, but its demographic components are measured. Rates, or prices, in broadcast television are based on five elements: (1) the size of the audience, (2) the demographic make-up of that audience, (3) the supply of available inventory, (4) the current demand for that inventory, and (5) reach.

Broadcast television is generally priced and sold by dayparts, as seen in Exhibit 19.1.

**Exhibit 19.1
Television
Dayparts.**

Network Television
Early Morning (Monday-Friday)
Daytime (Monday-Friday)
Prime Time (Monday-Sunday)
Early Evening News (Monday-Friday)
Late Evening (Monday-Friday)

Local Television Stations
Early Morning (Monday-Friday)
Daytime (Monday-Friday)
Early News (Monday-Friday)
Early Fringe (Monday-Friday)
Prime Time (Monday-Sunday)
Late News (Monday-Friday)
Late Night (Monday-Friday)

Source: www.tvb.org. Used with permission.

Special programming, such as sports, kids programming, and event programming such as the Academy Awards, is priced at levels that are not tied to traditional daypart pricing, but are driven almost exclusively by demand.

However, daypart pricing is based in large part on audience levels and demographics in those dayparts. Thus, early morning is the least expensive because television's audiences are smallest at that time. Prime time (8 to 11 PM Eastern Standard and Pacific Standard Time, and 7 to 10 PM Central Standard and Mountain Standard Time)is the most expensive because television audiences are the highest then. Even more important, the huge reach of prime time commercials makes them more desirable and in higher demand by large, national advertisers whose products have mass appeal.

Perhaps the most striking difference between selling television and print is that print rates, by and large, are not negotiated, but television is bought and sold almost entirely based on negotiating. Print salespeople will often say that their system is fairer and the process takes much less time because there is little or no haggling. Television salespeople, on the other hand, argue that what an advertiser pays is based on an actual audience, not on the size of an ad, and that an advertiser can take advantage of market conditions and pay based on current supply and demand and, often, get bargains at certain times of the year that are not available to print advertisers.

Therefore, if you are considering a career as a television salesperson, I urge you to pay particular attention to the section on negotiating in Chapter 12 of this book, because it will serve you well.

Benefits and Advantages of Broadcast Television

Ever since television stations began springing up in cities around the country in the early 1950s, Americans have become fascinated with and addicted to watching the tube. As a nation, we get our news, our comedy, our drama, and our sports from television. We are a nation connected with each other by the common experiences we share by watching television. We collectively grieved as we watched the diminutive John-John salute the funeral procession of his slain father and we grieved again as we watched in gut-wrenching horror the news of a grown-up John Kennedy's death in a airplane crash off Cape Cod. We watched in triumph as the Berlin Wall and, with it, Communist domination of Eastern Europe, was torn down. We watched with elation as a guy named Joe made good on his promise as his New Jets team beat the vaunted Baltimore Colts in a Super Bowl game.

No medium of communication has ever dominated a society as television has dominated the American psyche. We live in a society that is defined, by and large, by television. Americans love television, and we watch more each year, as shown in Table 19.1.

As can be seen from Table 19.1, the average television household watches more than seven-and-a-half hours of television daily. Books, movies, CDs, newspapers, and the Internet all compete for people's time, but the clear winner in this competition is television, as seen in Table 19.2. It's no wonder television is the most dominant medium in the country.

Americans not only watch a lot of television, but they *believe* television—it's their primary and most credible source for news, as shown in Table 19.3;

Table 19.1 Time Spent Watching Television

Year	Average Time Spent Per Day Per Household
1950	4 hrs. 35 mins.
1955	4 hrs. 51 mins.
1960	5 hrs. 6 mins.
1965	5 hrs. 29 mins.
1970	5 hrs. 56 mins.
1975	6 hrs. 7 mins.
1980	6 hrs. 36 mins.
1985	7 hrs. 10 mins.
1990	6 hrs. 53 mins.
1995	7 hrs. 17 mins.
1996	7 hrs. 11 mins.
1997	7 hrs. 12 mins.
1998	7 hrs. 15 mins.
1999	7 hrs. 26 mins.
2000	7 hrs. 35 mins.

Source: www.tvb.org. Used with permission.

Table 19.2 Time Spent with Media

Hours Per Person Per Year - 2000	
Television	1,633
Radio *	961
Recorded Music *	263
Daily Newspapers	151
Internet *	124
Magazines	107
Books	90
Video Games	70
Home Video	59
Movies in Theaters	12

* Age 12+, all other 18+
Source: www.tvb.org . Used with permission.

Table 19.3 Television News

Primary Media Sources of News	
Television	69%
Newspapers	37%
Radio	14%
Magazines	5%

News Report Most Credible	
Television	53%
Newspapers	23%
Radio	7%
Magazines	4%

Source: www.tvb.org. Used with permission.

the most authoritative medium, shown in Table 19.4; the most exciting medium, as shown in Table 19.5; the most influential medium, as shown in Table 19.6; and the most persuasive medium, as shown in Table 19.7.

The public's perception of advertising in the various media is critical in the process of selling products and services. Television is clearly the most authoritative, credible, exciting, and persuasive medium for advertising. No other medium can come close to matching television's ability to deliver an advertis-

**Table 19.4
Television as a
Medium**

Most Authoritative	
Television	49%
Newspapers	24%
Radio	11%
Magazines	10%
Internet	6%

Source: www.tvb.org. Used with permission.

**Table 19.5
Television as a
Medium**

Most Exciting	
Television	74%
Internet	9%
Radio	6%
Magazines	6%
Newspapers	5%

Source: www.tvb.org. Used with permission.

**Table 19.6
Television as a
Medium**

Most Influential	
Television	78%
Internet	8%
Newspapers	7%
Radio	4%
Magazines	3%

Source: www.tvb.org. Used with permission.

**Table 19.7
Television as a
Medium**

Most Persuasive	
Television	66%
Newspapers	13%
Radio	8%
Magazines	8%
Internet	5%

Source: www.tvb.org. Used with permission.

er's message using sight, sound, motion, emotion, and color—and deliver these messages with attention-grabbing impact. As a result of this impact, more adults learn about products from television than they do from any other medium, as shown in Table 19.8.

Selling Local Television

Local television salespeople can bring this impact of television advertising to local businesses with a beyond-the-ratings approach and help clients grow their businesses by using television advertising's power to involve people emotionally. Because that's what television does better than any other medium— it engages people's emotions. Television's unique combination of sight, sound, motion, and color grabs viewers' undivided attention. A well-written and well-produced television commercial can elicit people's emotions in favor of a product or service. If viewers love a commercial, they will love the product.

Table 19.8 Television as a Medium	More Adults Learn About Products From Television Than Any Other Medium	
	Television	52%
	Magazines	17%
	Newspapers	15%
	Internet	10%

Source: www.tvb.org. Used with permission.

Static print ads, billboards, or banners don't involve people's emotions like television does, so no medium sells goods and services like television does.

Selling advertising for a local television station differs from selling for a network. In network selling, ratings rule and buying decisions are made on behalf of the client by advertising agencies. Much of the local selling that takes place in small and mid-sized television DMAs is done directly with local businesses. As a result, relationships and creativity become much more important than ratings. Local advertisers like to associate their names and messages with local television news and local events, with the thought that these are what is nearest and dearest to people in their community.

As I mentioned at the beginning of the chapter, my inauspicious start in television sales began with a ratings book, a phone book, and a list of inactive accounts. At the top of my list was a regional muffler chain in the Sacramento Valley. The little I knew about the muffler chain was that it bought a lot of local television time, that it bought a lot of sports programming, and that the owner had a falling-out for some reason with the previous general manager and general sales manager of the station for which I now worked. With that encouraging news, I set out to sell after a pat on the back from my local sales manager and an entreaty to "Get out there and sell!" (Said with the same enthusiasm of Charlie Warner's first sales manager, I'm sure.)

While I had little in the way of media sales training, the one thing I had learned from a neighbor who built his own successful business selling carpets was that selling was first and foremost about serving others; and that service began with listening and was followed by helping others get what they want. So, with that idea clear in my head, I called and left a message for Bob Johnson, the owner of the chain of muffler stores. Twenty-four hours passed and there was no return call. I tried again. I left a message: "This is Mark Chassman with KOVR-Channel 13; can we meet?" No return call. My next plan was to drive to the muffler store where Bob had his office with the objective of getting in front of him, face to face, so I could talk to him about his business challenges. Into the garage I went, looking for Bob Johnson. What I found was an icy reception from one of his local store managers who told me, "Bob is not interested in doing business with your station." And with that rebuff I was shown the door.

With tenacity in my DNA, I drove back to the muffler store the following week. Reminding myself that selling, first and foremost, is about service, and that service begins with listening followed by helping others get what they want, I approached the store manager and again asked if Bob was available. Again, I received a no. This time I probed for some additional information and opened my ears to listen. What I received was an explanation, an explanation that was the key to getting in Bob's door and determining if there were a way

I could be of service to his business. What the store manager told me was that Bob was not available, as he usually was at this time, but that he had left early to coach his teenage son's basketball team. Well, with that little tidbit of information and enough understanding about human behavior vaguely remembered from a psychology class in college, I figured out the key to opening Bob Johnson's door.

The following week I visited at the same time as last with something I knew Bob would value—sharing time with his son. That's right, the service I knew I could offer Bob had nothing to do with selling him television advertising; I could offer something he valued. Off to the muffler store I went with Sacramento Kings basketball tickets in hand. Not just any tickets mind you, but front-row seats, in the seats right up close to the action on the court.

Bob was not in, so I left the tickets in an envelope with a handwritten note that said, "Bob, I'm the new kid on the block at KOVR-13. I'm looking forward to meeting you in the near future to see if there's any way I can be of service to you and your business. No strings attached. I hope you and your son enjoy the pair of front-row seats I've enclosed for next Tuesday's Sacramento Kings vs. Los Angeles. Enjoy, Mark Chassman, KOVR-13." The day following the game Bob Johnson called to thank me. He offered to have me come and meet him in his office.

Our first meeting was mostly about me listening to the problems he had encountered with the previous management of my station. Our second meeting was a discussion about how I might be able to help him grow his business by getting his advertising message in front of young male sports fans. The following week I showed up with an advertising schedule that included commercials in *ABC's* "Monday Night Football" and a season package of spots in "ABC College Football" games. That same day I got an order.

This experience defined, for me, the job of a television media salesperson. Selling in this manner was something I could be passionate about, and it's what I tap into everyday as I remind the salespeople who now work for me what their purpose is and how they should approach their jobs every day—with passion.

Bob Johnson's heart was opened first, then came the opportunity to open his head. The bottom line, in the business of sales, is, "He profits most who serves best." Bob and his chain of muffler stores ended up becoming my largest direct account while at KOVR-13. From this and other experiences, I learned that to be a successful television salesperson you first must bring an unbridled enthusiasm for helping people. Then, you layer in knowledge and skills so you become indispensable when it comes to solving problems for your clients, be they advertising, business, or personal problems.

Selling to Advertising Agencies

As discussed in the selling-direct portion of this chapter, the job of a television salesperson is to turn business prospects, or in some cases suspects, into customers, by getting close and staying close to them. When it comes to serving the wants and needs of advertising agencies, the same rule applies, but the path to success also requires the seller to clearly understand what agency buyers do and how to serve their needs without compromising the needs of your own business.

The first person to really help me understand this concept was a seasoned media buyer by the name of Julie Maxwell, who worked for a well-established and respected media buying agency, Western International Media. Having established a reputation for myself by successfully resurrecting an inactive account (Bob Johnson), I was now thrown into the lion's den of a challenging selling situation when one of our most senior salespeople left to take another job. I was quickly—some might say prematurely—moved to the front lines to handle an agency account; not just any agency account, but the largest buyer of media in our market.

Every day Julie was called on by the best local television, radio, print, and outdoor salespeople in town, so I knew I had to be good to be competitive. My immediate challenge was to earn her trust and respect. Sounds simple, right? But the challenge here, as I learned very quickly, was in serving the needs of media buyers. Julie's first need—a 50-percent rate discount off what she paid the previous year if our station was to receive the same dollar commitment this year. That's right, she wanted more for less. Furthermore, Julie liked to buy the best of our prime time inventory and lots of it, which created even more of a challenge.

Given the fact that in that particular year, inventory, especially prime time inventory, was limited and demand was high relative to supply, selling desirable inventory at a 50-percent discount from the prior year meant that my station would be selling its inventory way too low. While I was relatively new to selling television, I majored in business in college and concluded very quickly that this was probably not a good thing for my career and the profitability of my station. Going back to my foundations of sales training that had taught me "selling was first and foremost about serving others," and that "service began when listening was followed by helping the other person get what they want," I faced my first major selling conundrum. The quandary was: cut my rates to meet a customer's needs or lose a large piece of existing business.

After much head scratching and some conferring with my sales manager, I came to the realization that Julie was testing me. It was a test from a buyer doing her job on behalf of her clients and who was trying to negotiate the best deal possible for her clients. It was also an emotional intelligence test to see how I would react to the initial demands of a skilled media buyer. As mentioned in Chapter 2, "Selling: Perspectives and Approaches," one of the essential qualities of any successful salesperson is empathy.

Empathy means having the ability to see and feel as another does. Being empathetic does not necessarily mean being sympathetic, especially when a demand is not a win for both parties. Julie's offer was not a win for my station or me.

My comments to Julie were, "I understand your desire to get low rates for your clients—that's your job. I will do everything I can to work in your best interests and in the best interest of your clients. But if we cannot find common ground where both of us feel we have gotten a fair deal, then we should not be doing business together." Julie's response to my remarks was an indication that she respected my position. After we negotiated, sometimes heatedly, for over an hour, she gave me a renewal for more dollars than the prior year and at rates with which we could both live.

What I learned in dealing with agency buyers is that selling is a two-way street. It is a process by which a person helps others get what they want and in return both sides receive a fair and equitable deal. Selling is not a manipulative exercise in which salespeople get others to do something that is not in their best interest. This experience with Western International also taught me the most important lesson in negotiating with seasoned agency negotiators: "Always say 'no' to an initial offer, but always say it nicely and come back with a reasonable alternative."

Over the years, I have served hundreds of media planners and buyers at advertising agencies in my efforts to help them and their clients take advantage of the value I, along with the stations I represented, could provide. What I learned from working with them is that, for the most part, they all really want the same thing. They want service-oriented salespeople who value what the buyer's value, respect the buyer's time, and conduct themselves professionally. Being professional means following Chassman's three C's for success in selling television—being candid, concerned, and competent.

Producing Commercials

When television exploded onto the American scene in the late 1940s, nobody—not advertisers, not advertising agencies, not television stations—knew exactly how to make a good commercial. Indeed, the earliest commercials consisted of everything from live demonstrations to the noisy rumble of a studio audience muddling through a rendition of an advertiser's theme song. But if the commercial didn't sell the product, it was useless. Today, along with selling products, television commercials occupy a central position in the landscape of consumer culture. Advertisers commit major resources to finding out how the purchase of a product can fulfill consumer needs and desires, and fulfilling those wants may not have anything to do with the product's use. While television advertising's immediate goal may be the promotion of a specific product or service, its legacy is a standard of values and behavior that turns advertising imagery into forms of commercial expression. Today several genres of television commercials have emerged: testimonial, mini-drama, celebrity endorsement, and demonstration, to name a few. Identifiable characters—Tony the Tiger, the Jolly Green Giant, Mr. Whipple, and countless others—have become cornerstones of the American commercial landscape, building brand identities for their products that have transcended generations of television audiences. More and more, we tend to grade commercials on their ability, if only in passing, to penetrate our popular culture. At their best, we induct them into our collective psyche, muse over them with friends and coworkers, and even add their lingo to our vocabulary.

But the bottom line is that a commercial's success is ultimately judged by only one criterion—its impact on sales or other goals an advertiser might have, such as increased awareness, improved product or corporate awareness, or image.

Over the years the length of television commercials has shrunk, creating a phenomenon some advertisers refer to as on-air clutter. When Le Corbusier wrote, "Less is more," he could have been talking television commercial length. But if clutter has a father, he's an American: Leonard Lavin, who was CEO of Alberto Culver in the 1960s and, in one lifetime, helped launch the 30-second commercial, the 15-second commercial, and the first feminine deodorant spray. Lavin was smart, tough, and understood that paying less was good business. While the cost of producing a 15-, 30-, or 60-second television spot varies, depending upon the sets, special effects, talent, equipment, and crew necessary to pull off a creative concept, the lower production costs of producing shorter commercials helped Alberto Culver save on the overall cost of his advertising. Lavin knew his television budgets were small compared to Proctor & Gamble, Lever Bros., and Bristol Myers, but he also knew he didn't need a full 60 seconds to sell his products. Alberto Culver's budget equalizer would be the 30-second commercial. Back in the 1960s, the networks sold only one-minute commercials, so Lavin became his own time broker. He bought 60s and split them between brands, inventing the piggyback—a commercial announcement by a single advertiser that combines two different and un-related 30-second product commercials.[7]

Today, about 70 percent of network commercials are 30s; the balance are 15s. This decrease in commercial length, from the minute, to the 30, to the 15, is more responsible for the clutter problem than the increase in commercial time. The number of messages per minute of network commercial time has increased from a little over one in the 1960s to two and one-half today. Clutter is the price that advertisers and broadcasters have been willing to pay to keep the price of commercial time down.

Selling Products Direct to Consumer

The blend of entertainment and commercials dates back to a change in federal guidelines in 1984. President Ronald Reagan's Republican-dominated FCC dropped a requirement that limited the time television stations could devote to commercials. That ruling spawned home shopping networks that are 100-percent advertising, along with the half-hour and hour-long infomercials.

Most people have flipped channels onto an infomercial and found themselves still watching 20 minutes later. That's because direct response television spots are specifically engineered to turn passive viewers into active buyers. With infomercials, marketers have more than 28 minutes to showcase all of a product's features and benefits. More than 51 percent of infomercial shoppers polled said there are two reasons they bought from infomercials: (1) The product was not available elsewhere, and (2) they received a complete demonstration of a product that motivated their buying behavior.[8] Generally, such shows are confined to the ghetto of early morning hours on UHF broadcast channels. They look like real programs because they copy the format of television entertainment shows. They often feature guests, a regular host, and, many times, a studio audience. In reality, they are simply paid advertisements featuring compensated actors endorsing products or services. Direct response television advertising is another benefit that marketers, who are looking to reach beyond the limitations of brick and mortar retailing, can use to sell directly to consumers.

Reaching Sports Enthusiasts

The profitability of sports on television has caused professional sports leagues to expand to more and more cities as well as to expand the length of their seasons. Television executives point out that without the money from television, many events would not exist. To accommodate television, sports teams have had to adjust schedules, the pace of games, and games' locations. Professional baseball went from being a sport played mostly in the afternoon to a game that is mostly seen in the evening under artificial lights. Basketball, hockey, and football have added television timeouts to break for commercials.

Television's influence is also responsible for the appearance of on-site banners, logos, and sponsor tie-ins. Arenas and stadiums are covered with billboards. Television networks also sell sponsorships for such things as a halftime report, a kick-off, or being the "official" beer of an event. These sponsorships, of course, added significantly to television's allure to advertisers trying to reach predominantly male audiences, such as beer marketers. The notion that "sports sells beer" is perhaps the most sacred axiom of beer marketing.

Selling sports is one of the most enjoyable selling opportunities in television. Even local advertisers, such as car dealers, invest big dollars in sports to reach a somewhat elusive male television viewer. Unlike the traditional prime-time network fare such as sit-coms, dramas, or reality shows, in which an audience has to be built over time, sports programming comes with an already passionate fan base that consists primarily of men for advertisers to tap into.

Creating Shared Experiences

The big ratings for commercial television come from big events such as the Super Bowl, World Series, Olympics, Academy Awards, and program series finale episodes—the last episode of "Seinfeld," for example. Of the top five most highly rated programs of all time in America, four of them are Super Bowls, including Super Bowl XVI, played in 1982 between the San Francisco 49ers and the Cincinnati Bengals. The program pulled in a 49.1 rating, seen by nearly half of the homes in America.[9] Averaging nearly 80 million viewers, the Super Bowl, on network television, commands more than two million dollars per 30 seconds of commercial time. Watching the commercials and evaluating them has become an important part of the Super Bowl festivities. The Super Bowl held February 3, 2002 was not so super when it came to advertising. A mix of dealing with a sagging economy and competition from the Olympics being held the same month took away from what is normally the biggest advertising day of the year.

The Olympics. The modern Olympics are a combination of ancient ideals and today's commercial reality. For much of the first century of modern Olympic history, financial underwriting by the host cities covered the costs. With the advent of television, sponsorships transformed that idealism. Now, linking with the five-ring logo is good business. Advertising during the Olympic Games guarantees a global audience unmatched in size by any other audience in the world. It's a prime venue for advertisers and marketers, and generates huge amounts of money. Broadcasting companies pay enormous sums of money to buy the rights to televise the Olympics. NBC paid $3.5 billion for the rights to broadcast five Olympics between 2000 and 2008. NBC hopes to make its $3.5 billion back—and much more—by selling advertising spots during these games. It is not possible for every sporting event in the Olympics to be televised, so broadcasters choose certain sporting events based on their appeal to television audiences. For example, it is well known that the figure skating event attracts a large audience of television viewers. One high-rated sporting event that was not a Super Bowl was the women's figure skating final from the 1994 Winter Olympics. It was the third-most-watched sporting event and sixth overall for the entire season with a 48.5 rating. It was so widely watched due to the circumstances involving two of the competitors, Tonya Harding and Nancy Kerrigan.[10]

The bigger an event, the more expensive its advertising; therefore, broadcasters can sell advertising during a women's figure skating event for a large premium. Prime-time, 30-second commercials for the 2002 Winter Games in Salt Lake City cost as much as $600,000 each. The demand for advertising spots is high; by November 2001 NBC had sold 90 percent of its Olympics spots.

Other ways commercial television brings in advertising revenue around major events is through tie-ins. In the winter of 2002 Coca-Cola purchased the rights to be the Olympic Games' official soft drink, and it has also invested in many commercial positions in the Olympics. *Sports Business and Industry Online*'s history of advertising at the Olympics shows that at the 1984 Olympic Games in Los Angeles, Coca-Cola was ranked as the second-leading advertiser—the company spent $29,875,000 on commercials. At the 1996 Olympic games in Atlanta, Coca-Cola spent $73,645,900, making it the number one advertiser at the games. Other tie-ins included "Chevy Moments." These were personal profiles produced by NBC and sponsored by Chevrolet to attract viewers to some of the lesser-known athletes who were not heard of four years before.[11]

Enabling the Political Process

Television advertising has become the weapon of choice for the players in contemporary political arenas. Broadcasters reap a bonanza from fierce competition among candidates, parties, and interest groups for scarce and increasingly expensive airtime in the weeks before Election Day. Candidates, parties, and interest groups in the 2000 federal elections spent approximately $629 million on television advertising. This figure represents an all-time record.[12]

Today, in order to win an election, a candidate must do two things: (1) develop a message that resonates with voters, and (2) deliver that message via television to maximize public acceptance. Ads between programs reach large audiences, built by popular shows, at a fraction of the cost compared to the early days of television when politicians purchased airtime to broadcast entire (and often boring) speeches. Research reports that intensive airing of political commercials three weeks prior to the election can win an election. Today, paying for television ads often takes the better part of a candidate's budget. Supporters of campaign finance reform point to the high cost of television advertising as the principal factor in driving up campaign spending. Some advocate letting candidates have free television time to address voters; others feel this would put limits on how candidates can deliver their messages.

Television in the New Economy

A series of new technologies blurs the face of today's television landscape as penetration grows.

Digital Television

The term digital television (DT) is currently used in many different ways, depending on to whom you are talking. The reason it gets confusing is because digital television in the US combines three new and different ideas. The first idea is that of a digital signal. Broadcast television began as an analog medium. Television stations put up antennas and broadcast analog signals so people could put a pair of rabbit ears on their television sets and pick up channels 2 through 83 free. What they received was a single, analog composite video signal and a separate FM audio signal. Digital television started as a free broadcast medium as well. For example, in San Jose, CA, you can tune in to about a dozen different commercial digital television stations if you have a digital television receiver and an antenna.[13]

The FCC gave television broadcasters a new frequency to use for their digital broadcasts, so currently each broadcaster has an analog television channel and a digital television channel. The digital channel carries digital data that a digital television receives and decodes. Each broadcaster has one digital television channel, but that one channel can carry multiple sub-channels if a broadcaster chooses that option. Broadcasters can create sub-channels because digital television standards allow several different formats.

Broadcasters can choose between SD (standard definition) formats and HD (high definition) formats. Finally, the HD formats of digital television (HDTV) have a different aspect ratio than analog television signals. Analog television has a 4:3 aspect ratio, meaning that television set screens are 4 units wide and 3 units high. For example, a 25-inch diagonal analog television is 15 inches high and 20 inches wide. The HD format for digital television has a 16:9 aspect ratio, a much longer width than its analog counterpart.[14]

Today, most of the benefits of digital television align on the side of the viewer. A clearer and crisper picture makes viewing television a much more enjoyable experience, especially for live sporting events and movies. For advertisers the benefits are still unclear. Until the masses embrace digital television by replacing their old analog sets with new digital ones, the reach of HD programming to consumers will remain limited, and advertisers will continue to question HD advantages.

Interactive Television

Interactive television (ITV), also called enhanced television, platforms and services might reinvent our existing passive television viewing experience and its attendant commercial benefits forever. Telecommunications, cable, satellite, and software companies have been investing millions, even billions, of dollars in new, digital two-way networks to ensure that they own a piece of the broadband digital delivery system which includes data, audio, video, and voice streams. Interactive television investors are hoping that digital network services will bring new revenue streams from enhanced content and the potential for t-commerce, or, interactive commerce on television.[15]

Television, which up to now has been a passive, linear, one-way entertainment viewing experience for millions of people, is now on the verge of becoming an on-demand, participatory, non-linear, infotainment, advertising-targeted, broadband, two-way communications medium. When fully realized on a mass scale, interactive television will transform our current experience with television. For possibly the first time, television will become something a viewer can control and use for information and communications. When this transformation happens, television will not remain a passive delivery vehicle for programming solely from the networks and their affiliates, but will become a platform for opening up new opportunities for marketers to build their businesses.

Companies are developing new business models that reflect complex revenue-sharing arrangements between producers, set-top box vendors, software providers, shopping vendors, Internet service providers (ISPs), and billing vendors and that will bring the full value of enhanced television to life. It is hoped that revenues through tiered subscriptions and new commerce opportunities could bring real growth to today's single-revenue-source broadcasters.

There are many hurdles to overcome, including: advertisers have a lack of knowledge about what ITV is and what platforms are available; advertisers want to start testing but resist due to a low-installed base of ITV set-top boxes; and advertisers and video producers who spend millions on production are concerned that their commercials will be polluted by enhancements. If interactive enhancements are designed to be highly integrated into commercials, advertisers are concerned that viewers will not know what to do. Ad agencies are slow to experiment with new technologies even though advertisers are interested. As you can see, interactive television has a way to go to achieve mass acceptance from consumers and advertisers alike. But the opportunity exists for television salespeople to evangelize and bring new digital tools to their customers who can then profit from the enhanced capabilities of the medium.

Jobs in Television Sales

So you've gotten a taste for commercial television sales. Now you're thinking about a career, or at least exploring the possibility of getting a job selling. Come prepared with both emotional and intellectual capital. Selling advertising is a very different proposition today than it was just a few years ago. Solutions selling is the order of the day and order-taking is out. There is much work to be done after your formal education is over to become a respected player in the television selling profession. Today's buyers of television have many choices. While a strong educational foundation steeped in business, economics, marketing, advertising, journalism, or mass communication can be helpful, ongoing customer-centered sales training is required. Selling television, as mentioned previously, can be very rewarding. Television is show business (entertainment, sports, and news married to advertising) with an emphasis on business. Once you have a job selling television, your compensation can be substantial. Most often, you will be paid a base salary plus commissions on sales.

You can see the compensation ranges for television salespeople in various-size markets in Tables 19.9 and 19.10. Even though these compensation figures are from surveys taken in 1996 and 1999, Ron Steiner, president of the Marketing Communications Group, believes the 1999 compensation ranges probably reflect today's ranges fairly accurately because of the slowdown in advertising in 2001 and 2002 and are less than in 1996 because of increased profit pressures on local television stations.

Table 19.9
Television Sales
Compensation

Account Executives' Compensation - 1996	
Markets 1-25	$119,000
Market 26-50	$92,000
Markets 51-100	$76,500
Markets 101-150	$58,250
Markets 151+	$47,800

Source: Marketing Communications Group. Used with permission.

Table 19.10
Television Sales
Compensation

Account Executives' Compensation - 1999	
Markets 1-10	$95,000
Markets 11-25	$85,500
(Av. of above)	$90,250 (24% less than 1996 USF survey)
Markets 26-50	$71,000 (23% less than 1996 USF survey)
Markets 51-100	$60,940 (20% less than 1996 USF survey)
Markets 100+	$45,700 (14% less than 1996 USF survey)*

* Av. 101-150 and 151+
Source: Marketing Communications Group. Used with permission.

Test Yourself

1. When was the first television station licensed by the FCC?
2. Why were magazine concept programs, introduced by Pat Weaver to NBC, at first resisted by advertising agencies?
3. What is the upfront market?
4. What are guarantees?
5. How many commercial television stations are there in America?
6. What is a DMA?
7. What are the major dayparts sold in local television stations?

8. What medium is considered second most influential after television?
9. What is the most important lesson about negotiating Mark Chassman learned in dealing with Western International?
10. What are Mark Chassman's three Cs of professionalism?

Project

Go to www.tvb.org and browse for information that will help you create a presentation for a local network-affiliated television station in your market for a department store that in the past has put 100 percent of its advertising budget in the market's only newspaper, a morning paper. Create a PowerPoint presentation that sells the medium of television, not a particular station, and do not use ratings.

References

Eric Barnouw. 1968. *The Golden Web: A History of Broadcasting in the United States, Volume 11 1933 to 1953.* New York: Oxford University Press.

Resources

www.bmcommunications.com/tv.htm
www.digitaltelevision.com
www.entrepreneur.com/Magazines
www.itvt.com/etvwhitepaper.html
www.joumalism.indiana.edu/Ehics/isnews.html
www.media.org
http://memory.loc.gov//ammem/ccmphtml/tvhist.html
www.museum.tv/archives.etv
www.nyu.edu/classes/stephens/history
www.tvb.org
www.tvhistory.tv/advertising3.htm
www.upress.utah.edu/books/Barney-Wenn-Martyn.html
http://vax.wcsu.edu/~mccarne /acad/Mendes.html
www.videouniversity.com
www.wsu.edu/8080/~taflinre/tvbiz.html

Endnotes

1. www.tvhistory.tv. October 2002.
2. http://memory.loc.gov//ammem/ccmphtml/tvhist.html. October 2002.
3. Erwin Ephron. "How Television Got the Upfront." www.ephrononmedia.com. October 2002.
4. Ibid.
5. http://www.tvb.org/rcentral/mediatrendstrack/tvbasics/basics4.html. January 18, 2003.
6. http://www.tvb.org/rcentrl/mediatrendstrack/tvbasics/basics4.htm. January 18, 2003.
7. www.alberto.com. October 2002.
8. www.cyberhaven.com. October 2002.
9. www.vax.wcsv.edu. October 2002.
10. www.upress.utah.edu. October 2002.
11. Ibid.
12. www.brennancenter.org. October 2002.
13. www.digitaltelevision.com. October 2002.
14. Ibid.
15. www.itv.com. October, 2002.

Chapter 20 Radio

By Paul Talbot

New York City, August 28, 1922: Rains the night before had broken the heat wave. Fans at the Polo Grounds watching the first-place Yankees play the Saint Louis Browns were sent home early. But tonight there would be an even more dazzling sporting event. Johnny Dundee would defend his World Junior Lightweight Championship against Pepper Martin. Neither the ballgame nor the fight would be heard on the radio. But on that cloudy evening something never before heard would crackle through the city; something that would launch thousands of new careers and indelibly change American business. Shortly after dark on an otherwise uneventful Monday night in 1922, while Johnny Dundee was going the full fifteen rounds with Pepper Martin, the world's first radio advertisement was broadcast.

The advertisement was on radio station WEAF and lasted ten minutes. A real estate development firm had bought a 10-minute block of time to promote its apartment buildings. The program started like this:

> "Let me enjoin upon you as you value your health and your hopes and your home happiness, to get away from the solid masses of brick, where the meager opening admitting a slant of sunlight is mockingly called a light shaft, and where children grow up starved for a run over a patch of grass and the sight of a tree. Friends, you owe it to yourself and your family to leave the congested city and enjoy what nature intended you to enjoy. Visit our new apartment homes in Hawthorne Court, Jackson Heights, where you may enjoy life in a friendly environment."

WEAF had been on the air only a few months when the world's first commercial was broadcast. The station was owned by the American Telephone & Telegraph Company. But it was not America's first radio station. That distinction can be claimed by a number of broadcasters including Pittsburgh's KDKA which broadcast federal election returns in 1920.

When the first advertising was broadcast, the radio itself, the receiver, was hardly the type of device you'd expect to find in millions of homes within a few years. You couldn't plug it in. The early radios required battery power. You could not simply turn a dial to tune in a station. This required the maneuvering of a thin wire, called the cat whisker, over a crystal. Radios didn't have speakers; they required earphones, and an antenna had to be strung up.

On the night its first advertisement was broadcast, radio was the domain of the hobbyist. In the explosion of interest in the device after restrictions of technology were lifted following World War I, broadcast bedlam blotted the airwaves. Stations did not have assigned frequencies.

Five years later the federal government made its first attempt to bring regulatory order to the dial with the establishment of the Federal Radio

Commission (FRC) in 1927. The FRC assigned frequencies, established a broadcasting band between 500 and 1,500 kilocycles, and gave the best-funded stations with the most powerful transmitters the best dial positions which allowed signals to travel farther at night and more clearly during the day. Out of radio's awkward birth, two men emerged who laid the foundations of the broadcasting business that largely remain intact. One was a gruff Russian immigrant who looked like he slept in his clothing. He placed his bets on tubes and transmitters. The other was a debonair American tobacco heir with hundreds of suits in his closet. This man placed his bets on crooners and comedians. Each built a radio network. Each was a visionary. Each was a fierce competitor. And each can take credit as being a founding father of today's media business.

The immigrant was David Sarnoff. Sarnoff's journey from a village in southern Russia to the executive suite of NBC led through the tough New York City neighborhood of Hell's Kitchen where he delivered telegrams. He learned Morse Code, made a name for himself reporting the details of the sinking of the "Titanic," and in 1916 he sent a memo to the president of the Marconi Company suggesting that radio could be used, as he put it, as a "music box." A few years later Sarnoff was the guiding force behind the establishment of the National Broadcasting Company, and the nation's first radio networks that appeared in the fall of 1926.

The tobacco heir was William S. Paley. After graduating from the Wharton School of Finance and Economics at the University of Pennsylvania in 1922, he went to work for his family's Philadelphia-based cigar business, the Congress Cigar Company. Every day the Paley factories manufactured a million and a half cigars, most notably the popular La Palina. In 1927 Paley was a vice president of the Congress Cigar Company when United Independent Broadcasters, a ramshackle radio network which included Philadelphia's WCAU, approached his family for an investment. Paley's father was skeptical, but the family had seen the impact on sales attributable to the "La Palina Hour" broadcast on WCAU.

A deal was struck and in September 1928, William Paley showed up for work at the UIB offices in New York's Paramount Building. The company had sixteen employees. Within a year there was a new name, the Columbia Broadcasting System, and enough new affiliates, radio stations in different markets linked together into one network, for Paley to tell advertisers that his fledgling network was the nation's largest.

Paley and Sarnoff battled through the '30s and '40s to attract the mass audiences that would interest national advertisers. They raided each other's talent and courted each other's clients. Americans loved what these two men put on the air. The first radio show to attract a national audience to tune in at a specific time was "Amos 'n' Andy." It began a 19-year run on NBC in 1929. Radio programmers and producers swept through the nation's vaudeville theaters searching for talent. They found people like Ed Wynn, Burns and Allen, and Jack Benny. In 1900 there were more than 2,000 vaudeville theaters. By 1930, fewer than a hundred remained. The audiences had gone to radio.

Comedy was served up in the easily duplicated structure of the variety show, which featured an announcer, an orchestra, a straight man, sketches, stand-ups, puns, punch lines, and characters which captured the flavor of the audience's diverse ethnicity with exaggerated accents. Every show had a sponsor. Performers wove the name of the product into their scripts. Jack Benny launched every show with the invocation "Jell-O, again."

While radio's largest audiences were delivered by comedians, everything from opera to boxing filled the airwaves. Americans were enthralled. In a landmark 1935 study paid for by the Rockefeller Fund, *The Psychology of Radio* found that for every telephone in the country there were two radios. 78 million Americans were regular listeners. Women liked music, men liked sports, the poor listened more than the well–to-do, and 95 percent of the people surveyed said that they would rather listen to a man's voice than a woman's.[1]

Radio geared itself up to deliver the news in the late 1930s. There was fierce opposition and intense political pressure from newspaper publishers. But as World War II unfolded, an infrastructure was built to report on it. Edward R. Murrow's broadcasts from London, air raid sirens blaring in the background, brought the war into America's living rooms. News became a staple of radio.

World War II was radio's last big story. In 1946 there were nine television stations in the United States. Eight years later there would be 354. By 1950 common wisdom suggested that radio was an unnecessary medium. The popular programs and their stars left radio for television. Radio networks were, for the most part, dismantled. Television captured the nation's fancy, created new stars, and crafted new definitions of leisure.

But radio stations didn't go the way of vaudeville. The opposite took place. In 1948 there were 1,621 AM stations. By 1960 that number had more than doubled to 3,458.[2] Radio still mattered because the medium struck out on a different path from television. Television was a national, mass-appeal medium. Radio evolved into a primarily local medium with segmented audiences. Stations chose formats to deliver well-defined audiences. Television owned the living room but radio owned the kitchen, the bedroom, the car, the back yard, and eventually the beach. The dawn of the transistor in 1954 turned radio into a portable medium. Audiences grew. Revenues rose. And shifting social patterns dealt the medium strong cards as young people and African-Americans turned to radio for entertainment they wanted but couldn't find on television.

Radio has been sold to advertisers since 1922. It has never lost its importance. It has been a vital platform for marketers for more than 80 years. Today the people who sell radio advertising enjoy remarkable opportunities.

Today's Radio Industry

Radio is a local business; in 2001 only 4 percent of radio's total advertising dollars went to national wired radio networks and only 17 percent went to national spot radio, according to McCann-Erikson's Robert Coen.[3] Local radio stations tend to be locally operated, with management, sales, and programming by and large rooted in the local marketplace. Ownership usually isn't. A number of large companies such as Infinity, Clear Channel, Disney, Cox, Emmis, Citadel, and Cumulus own and operate large numbers of stations. Some of these groups own large numbers of small stations in small markets. Some have a smaller number of larger, higher-billing stations clustered in major markets, and some companies have a blend of each. In terms of the number of stations owned and operated, Clear Channel is the largest radio company, with 1,212 stations.[4] This concentration of ownership is largely a result of easing federal restrictions on broadcast ownership.

This ruling paved the way for a business entity to own multiple stations in one market and lifted limits on the total number of stations that one company could own. This deregulation spurred the rise of interest of the investment community in radio. As in other industries where deregulation encouraged economic consolidation, the radio industry, with its emerging economies of scale, became attractive to Wall Street investors. What had been a highly fragmented business quickly became consolidated. And the consolidation of radio has created significant changes and opportunities for salespeople.

Deregulation and Opportunities for Salespeople

The greatest of these opportunities is the possibility that a salesperson may be selling more than one station. Because one company may often own more than one station in a single market, the deployment of salespeople and which station or stations they sell results from a strategy set by management. While the tendency is for individual stations to maintain individual staffs, there are situations in which management may assign a salesperson to a specific account with responsibilities for generating revenue for more than one station. This could be a result of a special relationship the salesperson enjoys with the client, a request from clients to have a single salesperson from the group call on them, or a decision based on a strategy put in place by management.

The degree to which salespeople communicate and cooperate with their counterparts at sister stations differs significantly. This depends, again, on management strategy. In some situations there is a high degree of internal competition in which the salesperson treats a counterpart at a sister station as an actual competitor for revenue. In other situations there is a greater degree of cooperation, to the point that a salesperson will share information about a client and work with the sister stations' salespeople to develop plans to either secure or grow the business for all of the stations involved. Station-based strategies and market-based strategies for maximizing revenues are common.

The consolidation of the radio industry has impacted more than structure. It has prompted organizations to experiment with ways of packaging a number of media assets into one bundle to make potentially attractive offerings for advertisers (cross-platform selling). It has encouraged the emigration of programming from one market into another. Contests, a hallmark of radio promotion, are now often run in a number of markets simultaneously. And behind the scenes, operating expenses are being more aggressively managed as economies of scale are brought to bear on what has historically been a decentralized business.

Radio Station Structure

You'll find much the same structure in most radio stations. As a salesperson you'll report to a sales manager. This may be either a local or a general sales manager. The local sales manager's responsibilities are exactly what they sound like: supervising the local sales department, which in a typical station delivers the majority of the station's revenue. The single most important task a local sales manager performs is to hire the best and most knowledgeable people possible, so you may want to bring this up and sell yourself a bit when you're interviewing. Also, it might be a good idea to bring along a well-thumbed-through copy of this book to an interview.

Other responsibilities include training the sales staff and growing its collective skill level, managing and pricing the inventory of advertising that is available to sell, reporting activities to senior management, evaluating the performance of the sales staff, gathering information from the sales staff to effectively monitor the marketplace and the competition, developing new products to sell, and working with other departments within the station.

The local sales manager may report to a general sales manager, who would typically oversee both the local and the national sales efforts. In situations where there are a number of stations owned by one company in a single market, the sales managers may report to a director of sales, who oversees the sales of the group of stations and sets strategy for all of the company's stations in the market.

The national sales manager works with the station's national sales representative firm. National sales managers spend most of their time on the telephone working on pieces of business that are being negotiated on the station's behalf by national salespeople in cities such as New York, Chicago, or Los Angeles. The national sales manager will travel to these markets to keep the rep firm and important clients informed of the station's activities, such as events and promotions, and market conditions.

The sales department may have a support staff. Sales assistants help salespeople prepare presentations and run research reports. Some stations have research directors who work with the salespeople on presentations that are ratings-intensive.

The sales department works closely with two other departments. One is traffic, the other production. It is the responsibility of the traffic department to make sure that a log is produced each day. The log is a legal document that serves as a record of when advertisements and other program materials are broadcast. Because it is vital that the advertising is broadcast at the time of day the salesperson has told the client it will be on the air, accurate and ongoing communication between the sales department and the traffic department is essential. Salespeople quickly learn that next to their boss, the person in the station who can best help them manage their business and their success is the traffic director.

In some stations, a continuity director reports to the traffic director. It is the function of the continuity director to make sure the produced advertising is in the station before the appointed deadline, that it is properly coded, and that it is in the hands of the production department to be ready for broadcast. Campaigns can often be a bit complicated, with different commercials for different days of the week, or different rotations. Continuity people make sure the advertising runs properly.

The production department typically has three responsibilities, two of which involve the sales department. One responsibility is making sure that advertising produced outside the station is transferred to the medium used to broadcast the commercials, such as a tape cartridge machine or a hard drive. The other is the actual production of advertising that originates with the station and has been produced at the direction of the salesperson. The production director will round up all of the necessary elements, ranging from the voice of on-air talent to sound effects to music in order to produce a professional piece of advertising. The production director's other responsibility, which tends not to involve the sales department, is producing the station's own advertisements, or promos. The promos may deal with anything from a station contest to a weekend's special programming.

Everything that is broadcast by the station is the responsibility of the program director. Commonly known as the PD, this person decides which disk jockeys or personalities will be on the air and when, what music will be played or what kind of talk or news will be aired, what promotions will be run, and what kind of an image the station portrays. It is the PD's objective to get as many people as possible to listen for the longest period of time possible and to have the station positioned in the minds of the listeners so they will remember the station's call letters if they are ever surveyed for the ratings.

Depending on the size of the station, PDs may or may not be performers on the air. PDs may or may not have music directors and promotions or marketing directors reporting to them. The music director decides which songs will be played and how often, based on their popularity.

The business manager tends to all of the financial functions of the station. From managing receivables to processing invoices and preparing month-end profit-and-loss statements and other financial reports, the business manager's day is spent immersed in numbers. Salespeople work with the business manager on two tasks—a new advertiser's creditworthiness and collections. Good radio salespeople know how to read an aging list (a list of accounts that are past due on their payments) and take the proactive steps necessary to make sure the station's invoices are paid in a timely fashion.

The chief engineer has limited interaction with salespeople. The chief engineer is responsible for making sure the station's transmission is in legal compliance, that the transmitter is performing at optimal technical specifications, that the sound of the station is properly processed, and that the studios are properly equipped and maintained.

At the helm of the station is the General Manager (GM). The GM works with all of the department heads to ensure smooth and profitable operations. The GM's most important task is the protection of the license granted by the Federal Communications Commission (FCC) entitling the station to legally broadcast. Without a license there is no station.

The Radio Business Is Competitive, Not Complex

For different reasons, there is no radio station without salespeople. The sales staff is a cornerstone of a station. Most new radio salespeople are daunted by what they perceive to be a formidable learning curve. In particular, they're overwhelmed by the apparent complexities of the ratings, which you learned about in Chapter 16. But in reality, the business is relatively simple.

As a new salesperson, you should remember that you're part of a mature industry where the hardest work is figuring out people, not figuring out industry buzzwords or ratings. It's important to know about the technical aspects of the ratings, but it's essential to know about the people you're calling on. You need to understand their desires, their motivations, their perceptions, and their needs. If you build your career paying more attention to your client's character than your station's cume, if you focus on a prospect's behavior more than focus on your station's broadcast signal pattern, you will prosper. Your true complexities come into play in understanding the type of people you're selling to, not in what you're actually selling. This is hardly the exclusive province of radio. So when you apply the AESKOPP formula and develop your skills in establishing and maintaining relationships with your prospects and customers, identify and solve advertising and marketing problems, and get results for these people, you're covering all the bases. Do not be overwhelmed by imagined complexities of the radio business.

You also need to be aware of the highly competitive nature of the radio business. Just as radio programmers compete for ratings and the loyalty of listeners, radio salespeople compete for business. This competitive environment is unrelenting and is fueled by savvy media buyers who, when negotiating with salespeople, will be quick to remind them that they, the buyers, can buy essentially the same product cheaper from the competition. This threat puts you in a position where you need to know as much about your competitors as possible. When you know their pricing and their inventory situation, you can make more intelligent negotiating decisions. The trap to avoid falling into is thinking the worst of your competition and believing they will always undercut you on price. We are all somebody's competitor. If we all undercut on price, we would all be giving our product away. A healthy respect for the competition and an understanding of what is really happening across the street will benefit you.

With the high degree of competition comes a high degree of fun. Remember that selling radio is more fun than selling newspaper advertising and harnesses more of your creativity than selling television. Your job in radio is inherently more interesting than your competitor's job in another medium. This concept leads to the notion that when it comes to business, you are not just competing against other radio stations, you're competing against other media. You need to understand why radio is inherently better.

The Advantages of Radio

While you should never use negative selling against another radio station, because you are attacking your medium, you should know how to communicate the weaknesses of the media you are competing against. Newspapers, broadcast television, and cable television are each plagued with problems for an advertiser. They are also the home of the budgets you want to target for your station. While the temptation to move dollars from a competing station onto your station is always present and is occasionally acceptable, it does not increase the size of the radio advertising pie in your market. You should remember that in most instances larger financial opportunities present themselves when you work to move dollars from a competing medium. Targeting budgets placed with the newspaper, broadcast television, and cable television is exhilarating, profitable, and something many of your radio competitors aren't very good at. It's also hard work. You need to be patient and prepared. You need to understand the weaknesses of your competitors. Let's start with newspapers.

Radio versus Newspapers

About six times more money is invested in newspaper advertising than is invested in radio advertising. The local newspaper is your primary competitor and it is pockmarked with shortcomings, ranging from unattractive demographics to pricing inefficiencies. Circulation has been on a downward skid for 50 years. So has the amount of time people spend reading the paper. The typical American adult spends 37 minutes a day with the newspaper, but more than three hours a day with radio.[5] Just slightly more than half the people who read the paper read only the first section, which happens to be the strongest section in terms of readership.[6] Less than half the paper's readers even notice a full-page ad. Newspaper advertisers face imposing clutter problems—68 percent of the Sunday paper is advertising. Then there is pricing. As circulation declines, rates increase and advertisers grow resentful and feel trapped by what they often perceive as the only game in town when there is a newspaper monopoly. There aren't too many beloved newspaper salespeople working the streets.

Radio versus Broadcast Television

Broadcast television also has a special knack for upsetting media buyers. Television commercials are often "bumped," or preempted, and not run as scheduled. This can happen for a number of reasons, ranging from being preempted by political advertising to being moved aside to make way for a client willing to pay a higher rate.

But even if every schedule ran exactly the way it was booked, broadcast television has a significant problem with advertisers. In the last 15 years, ABC, CBS, and NBC have lost half their viewers. The three networks commanded a 70-percent share of prime time in the mid-80s. Today it's only a 36 share.[7]

As shares have gone down, unit loads have gone up. Television clutter is highly problematic with a 24-unit spot load every hour.

Television is having trouble connecting with busy people. Forty percent of all viewers are considered light viewers who watch television less than 90 minutes a day. Remember that the average American adult spends more than three hours a day with radio.

There is also the quality of the broadcast television audience. The more money people make, the less broadcast television they watch. Conversely, the more money people make, the more likely they are to be radio listeners.

You might want to remind your clients that the median cost of producing a national television commercial is more than $350,000, and that to effectively compete against these messages on a somewhat level playing field, low budget production won't cut it. Radio, on the other hand, offers highly discrete audiences and highly affordable production.

Sometimes television gets the credit for the job that radio has performed. I remember telling one of my retail clients as we prepared to launch her campaign and put her on the radio for the very first time that someday, one of her customers would come in and say "I saw your ad on TV" when in fact the radio campaign was the only advertising in the market. My client smiled and shook her head in disbelief. But sure enough, a month or so later, she gave me a call: "You wouldn't believe what just happened." Naturally, I did.

Radio versus Cable Television

Cable television is one of the big reasons why broadcast television is being relegated to the media choice of the downscale consumer, but it is not the sole reason. Cable television ratings are largely driven by programming such as wrestling and cartoons, perhaps not the most appropriate environments for an advertiser looking to connect with an interested, affluent consumer.

Cable television audiences are small and they are splintered. There are more choices for the viewer on the cable set-top box than there are for the listener on the radio dial. Ad clutter is even more extreme than broadcast television, with some cable networks running up to 28 units an hour.

Great radio salespeople who understand human nature know that we never want to launch a frontal assault on competitive media, essentially telling an advertiser that they're stupid for spending their money in such a squalid environment. The disadvantages need to be carefully communicated so as to create doubts and in a fashion that sets the stage for a shift in the media mix where radio can be brought into the plan.

National Advertising

I mentioned the role of the national sales manager and the rep firm. Let's revisit this and find out exactly what these people do. Let's say that today is

Monday and that on Friday American Airlines is going to cut all of its domestic fares to $99. Suppose the marketing people at American Airlines know from their market research that 80 percent of their business comes from the top 10 markets, so that's where they'll run 100 percent of their advertising. Because the advertising must be produced and distributed quickly, they decide to use newspapers and radio to advertise the new low fares. The American Airlines marketing people call their advertising agency, give them a budget, and tell them to get radio schedules launched in the top 10 markets on Friday.

Rather than getting in touch with 100 stations (10 leading stations in each of the top 10 markets) for rates and clearance information, media buyers at American's advertising agency will call a rep firm. The rep firm is a sales organization that sells advertising for a number of stations that are its clients. These stations are typically in different markets. The rep firm has salespeople, just like a radio station, that call on the media buyers at large advertising agencies and media-buying firms that place business nationally and regionally.

The American Airlines scenario is typical. The rep firm knows the latest rate and clearance information, which in some instances can change quickly, for all of its stations. So rep salespeople will take rates and clearances for their stations in the markets that are "up," or being bought, to the media buyer at American Airlines' agency. The buyer and the reps then negotiate, and when a deal is struck the reps send the order out to their stations and the business is booked.

A rep's primary contact is the national sales manager, who at some stations may also double as the general sales manager or even the general manager. The national sales manager needs to make sure the rep firm is well informed on the station and the market and that the rep gets quick and accurate information pertaining to specific pieces of business being negotiated.

National business can also be placed on networks. Essentially, there are two types of networks: wired and unwired. A wired network is a traditional network, such as ABC, CBS, or CNN, that links stations with common programming, usually news programs. An unwired network is a collection of stations in different markets with only one common denominator—its stations broadcast a client's advertising. A rep firm sells this group of stations and makes sure the inventory clears, the rotations are proper, the creative is being properly trafficked, and the invoicing is correct.

Local Advertising

Local advertising falls into one of two categories: agency and direct. Agency business comes through advertising agencies. Direct business is created by working directly with an advertiser—there is not an advertising agency involved that handles the creation of the advertising or the scheduling strategy of the campaign. These tasks are a salesperson's responsibility. Skilled salespeople who understand that the most important order they receive is the second order, since this signifies the creation of a customer, will do everything possible to ensure the success of the campaign that has been sold through the first order.

Local advertisers have needs; typically, they are business needs. A restaurant client might tell you, "Dinner business is fine but I need to get more people in here for lunch."

As a skilled salesperson, the only things you need to bring to your first meeting with a direct prospect are a strong sense of curiosity and a business card.

You will ask a lot of intelligent discovery questions similar to what you learned in Chapter 9, you will identify the business need of the prospect, and you will schedule a follow-up meeting to present your solution.

A great first sales call will have you only talking about your station 10 percent of the time and developing an understanding of the customer's marketing issues 90 percent of the time.

When you ask questions to identify these marketing issues, keep in mind there are two schools of thought on taking notes. One says ask for permission and then take copious notes. The other says listen attentively and don't take notes because prospects may feel uncomfortable. They may feel that something they say may be later used in a manipulative fashion to get them to do something they don't want to do. Furthermore, on the first call it's more important to develop rapport with your prospects and show that you care about them and their business than it is to record their every word on a piece of paper. Whatever the case, you can't sell a solution unless you understand what you're selling a solution to and have developed enough rapport so that prospects look forward to having you back.

On your first call you may want to hold off on presenting a media kit or a ratings report. But it's a good idea to have these materials tucked in your briefcase so you can pull them out to discuss them if the client asks.

Local direct advertisers don't care as much about ratings, programming formats, or air personalities as much as they care about making a profitable investment in advertising. They do not have a high degree of price sensitivity. They do have a high degree of results sensitivity.

Radio Programming

Just as magazines target specific audiences by the nature of their editorial content, and just as television networks reach different types of audiences with different programs, radio uses formats to deliver specific audiences.

A 2002 study of formats conducted by M Street Corp. revealed that the most popular format is Country Music, followed by News/Talk.[8]

Radio salespeople should have an understanding of what types of audiences the different formats deliver. All News and Classical Music attract listeners with the highest median incomes. Adult Standards and All Sports attract the highest concentration of homeowners. For broad reach, Adult Contemporary and Country deliver the highest reach of Adults 18 and older. To reach young adults in the 18 to 34 demographic, Contemporary Hit Radio is the leading format.

Regional tastes come into play with format preferences. Country, for instance, has historically failed to deliver sizable audiences in urban markets outside the southern, western, and north central states.

You should also know that variety within a format is commonplace. Some Country stations play music designed to appeal to women in their 30s while others play music for men in their 40s. Some of the songs they play may be the same, but there will be musical-mix differences within the same format, and there will also be differences with the image the station portrays, the style of its announcers, the objectives of its contests, and all the other elements that go into the positioning of a station.

The first week on the job, every new radio salesperson should take their station's program director out to lunch, ask a lot of questions, and learn exactly what the program director is attempting to do. When you have a detailed understanding of the station's programming, how it competes, and the exact niche it is attempting to occupy in the market, you will benefit in two ways. First, you'll be better informed. This information translates into a greater degree of confidence. Second, you'll know exactly what kind of people listen to your station and in turn what kinds of advertisers you can deliver great results for and in what business category you should be prospecting.

How to Get Results for a Client

There is nothing theoretical about results. Advertising must work. It must deliver at least the results the client expects and, preferably, exceed those expectations. So, a sensible first step in ensuring results is a discussion with the client on what can reasonably be expected from a radio advertising campaign.

It behooves a salesperson to carefully manage expectations, as you learned in Chapter 8.

The first thing to keep in mind is that advertising is a risk. Not just radio advertising, but any advertising is as far as one can get from the proverbial sure thing. Smart business people understand this fact. Therefore, never make promises.

Next, have a conversation with a client in which the two of you set some benchmarks for success. If your client is a mortgage broker and makes $2,000 for every new loan processed, a radio schedule that costs $2,000 and generates just two new clients is probably a pretty good deal. You don't want to be the radio salesperson who goes back to the client when the campaign is over, learns that the station created just two pieces of business, and rushes to the conclusion that the results were unacceptable. Only by knowing in advance what defines a win for the client, only by understanding the metrics of the deal, will the salesperson have the knowledge necessary to move forward, renew the business, and create a long-term, satisfied client.

By the way, a good radio salesperson knows that it is a mistake to visit with a new client after the campaign is over and only then to ask how things are going. The better move is to check in after the first week. And don't sell one- or two-week campaigns if you can help it; sell 26- or 52-week campaigns, because continuity is the best strategy for long-term success.

Aside from managing expectations, there are a number of things a good radio salesperson will do to stack the deck in favor of good results. There is nothing wrong or deceitful about stacking the deck. Good results constitute a win for the salesperson and a win for the client.

First comes understanding exactly what the client wants the advertising to do. Results are typically linked to specific objectives. You can't tell how the advertising is working when all the client says he wants to do is, "Get my name out there." This leads us to the notion that in a somewhat simplified context, there are only two kinds of advertising. One is strategic and the other is tactical. The strategic advertisement is designed to get the listener to believe something. The tactical advertisement is designed to get the listener to do something. Know which kind of advertising you're working with.

The advertisement can't be conceived, let alone scripted or produced, unless you and the client agree on its purpose. This concept sounds simple. In reality, it can be difficult. The client may rely on a salesperson to suggest an advertisement's purpose. Only by understanding the client's business can an account executive make a thoughtful recommendation. It may be as simple as getting a listener to call the business to learn about the benefits of refinancing a mortgage.

Creating Radio Commercials

Take note of the word benefits. You have already learned in the material on media sales skills that you don't want to be in the business of selling features. You want to be selling benefits. It is exactly the same with advertising. If you are writing a commercial for an appliance store that's trying to sell refrigerators, don't talk about urethane door insulation. Talk about "Built to use less electricity and save you money." Make sure commercials are wrapped around benefits, not features.

There are five styles of radio ads: jingles, testimonials, drama, humor, and straight information. Each, when properly developed, is effective. The use of jingles prompted one advertising wag to remark, "When you've got nothing to say, sing it." But good jingles have an uncanny ability to penetrate the mind and leave an enduring impression, which is often a good feeling about a product or store. If you have a client interested in a jingle, the production director or the program director at your station can suggest a good producer.

Testimonials are extremely powerful, but only when there is a good fit between the spokesperson and the product. Credibility is important, because it is the ability of the listener to see in his or her mind the spokesperson using and knowing something about the product. Word of mouth is perhaps the single most influential factor when it comes to motivating people to try a product, and well-crafted testimonial campaigns capture the essence of word of mouth.

Drama is often little more than conversation. We've all heard these commercials. A woman asks her husband if he's heard about the new restaurant in town. He says no. She then proceeds to tell him all about it. But realistic conversations are hard to write. Commercials like this are easy to write if the goal is anything short of excellence. But with a few clever twists, a good ear, and production that puts real people and not staged announcers into these roles, these ads are intriguing, informative, and can be quite effective.

Humor is hard work. Humor is also a risky business because if a joke falls flat, the attempt at humor will cast the advertiser in a bad light. To the listener, it's not just a stupid joke, it's a stupid business whose image is impaired by that stupid joke. But just as we all have a primal need for a good story, we enjoy a good laugh, and in the rarefied environments where advertising and humor intersect, great results can be achieved with a clever, memorable, and truly funny commercial.

Then there is the commercial that is straight information. You've heard these and if they strike you as a collection of points hastily strung together to last 60 seconds you're probably correct. Lists of facts about a business in which a benefit is never suggested rarely stimulate a response. That's because these lists of features rarely penetrate our minds. We never really hear radio commercials like this—they don't penetrate our consciousness. For a piece of radio advertising to work, it needs to push whatever we're thinking about right now out of the way so it can command our attention. Only then will the listener consider the message, evaluate its benefits, and be in a position to do business with your advertiser.

One afternoon I was driving back to the station through a hardscrabble part of the city when I noticed the sign that every radio salesperson yearns to see, "Opening Soon."

I had time, so I stopped, went into a trailer, and started chatting with the owner. He had leased a vacant lot surrounded by chain link fencing and was starting an auto auction. He had a very limited budget. I learned that one of his auctions would take place each Sunday night. I knew that we could give him a great rate on Sunday afternoons when demand on our inventory was relatively light. I suggested that he run a campaign with us just to support the Sunday night auction. He understood the benefit of the focus and the immediacy. He also said he would give away a car every Sunday night to one of the registered bidders.

The ad I wrote started and ended with the phrase, "Tonight you can win a free car." The copy was built on the platforms of immediacy, a call to action, and a significant benefit. There was nothing artistic about it. I knew it would never win an award. This piece of advertising was simply a workhorse. The ad ran four times each Sunday between 3 and 7 PM. I never changed the copy. And, of course, it worked like a charm.

The time you take to develop a great piece of advertising is time well spent. You will discover that success is largely a matter of building up a list of active advertisers. The single best way to do this is to get results for advertisers. Developing an advertising campaign is a wonderful creative exercise, and a perfect and profitable means of showcasing your creativity.

See "Writing Copy" in Appendix G for more information about writing effective commercial copy.

Selling to Agency Buyers

Most media buyers at agencies usually want to make good buys. They are receptive to learning more from salespeople about how a station performs in delivering specific audiences, but sometimes they are restricted in how they can make their buy. Whatever the case, it is essential that radio salespeople know their station's audience, understand the strengths and weaknesses of their station, know their station's audience composition, and know how the competitors fare with their audience delivery. But knowing the station and the market is just a start. Knowing the buyer is what matters most.

Great radio salespeople love their buyers. They know exactly how their buyers like to work, and they are highly attentive to both the personal and the business needs of the buyers. They know there are some common themes in what media buyers want from a salesperson—flawless communication skills, integrity, candor, quick turnarounds, accuracy, and consistently flawless execution of booked schedules.

But there's more. Media buyers need to be understood. They need to be respected. They need justification and they need to know why. And media buyers need to know that if there is ever a problem, the salesperson is going to accept responsibility and fix it.

Rate negotiations between a media buyer and a salesperson can be tough and fraught with tension, but the relationship can be wonderful. It is not defined by the tension of the occasional rate negotiation but by a genuine willingness of the two parties to work together, to partner in an effort to do work that benefits the radio station, the agency, and the client. Skilled buyers who are self-confident and self-assured understand this relationship. Less skilled buyers will be hesitant to work toward this type of a relationship.

How Radio Is Sold

When it comes to pricing, radio is a highly negotiable medium. Part of this is due to the notion that most radio salespeople are woefully trained in negotiating if they haven't read Chapter 12 in this book. However, the economics of supply and demand come into play as well.

Most stations in larger markets use some type of a yield management strategy, with the help of software programs, to price their inventory. The higher the demand, the higher the rate and conversely, the lower the demand, the lower the rate. Great sales staffs create demand.

Great sales managers in turn understand exactly how their product should be priced. They use pending reports to have a grasp of what is being offered for sale that has not yet been closed. From an analysis of historical data they understand that there will be greater demand during the middle and final weeks of a month so they will quote higher rates for these weeks. They may also know that more advertisers would like to be on the air Wednesday through Saturday so these days of the week will be priced higher. Different times of day, or dayparts, will attract different levels of demand. They also will be priced differently.

The goal of the station is to sell the highest possible percentage of all available inventory at the highest possible rate. It is the responsibility of the sales manager to anticipate demand, set pricing, take special considerations into account, and help the sales staff maximize revenue.

The tactic most commonly used to support a yield management strategy is packaging. The station wins by building schedules for clients that blend inventory from different dayparts, days, and even weeks to achieve its objectives. The client wins by being in a position to reach broader segments of the station's audience and to enjoy pricing efficiencies.

How to Use Radio Research

Once you start working as a radio salesperson, it won't be long before somebody tells you, "If you live by the ratings, you'll die by the ratings." Ratings are important because in terms of raw dollars most decisions on where to place advertising schedules are primarily based on ratings. The system is simple. The higher a station's ratings, the more business it will attract, the higher the rates it can charge and the higher the levels of revenue it can generate. Another important function of ratings is to help programmers make decisions on their content. Poorly performing dayparts often mean the air personality who hosts those hours may be replaced, the music may be adjusted, or some other change in hopes of attracting higher ratings is put in place.

Agency buyers aren't interested in listening to radio salespeople whine about the shortcomings of Arbitron and the integrity of the data. At the end of the day, blemished as it is, the Arbitron numbers represent the best data for agency buyers and radio salespeople to use.

In a negotiation agency buyers will use the data to make a station look worse than it is so they can try to negotiate a lower rate. The salesperson will do the opposite. There is an abundance of tactics each side in the negotiation will use to support their positions. A skilled radio salesperson needs to know how to mine stories from the raw data, how to establish value from this data, how to rebuff anticipated ratings-based attacks from agency buyers, and in general to have an understanding of the strengths and weaknesses of a station.

When a salesperson calls on an agency and a buyer says, "You went down in the ratings," the salesperson needs to be able to respond with information that counters this negative slant on the new data with something positive, for example: "Yes, our average quarter-hour numbers were off a little but our cume was up . . . we're actually reaching more people now than in the last survey, and look at our weekends; our shares there are up more than 20 percent." Crafting statements like this take time but you can never put yourself in a position where an agency buyer can get away with establishing a one-sided story as the truth. And the truth is that virtually every ratings survey, even those that create ghastly carnage for a station, contains data that a salesperson can use to establish something positive. Optimism is vital—the glass is always half full.

So far we've been talking about the type of ratings that tell us how many people listen, their age, and their sex. This ratings information is called *quantitative ratings*. But in many markets there's an entirely different and additional type of ratings. These ratings tell us about the characteristics of the audience—the educational attainment and household income of a listener, what kind of car they own and plan to buy next, their marital status, even whether they prefer to shop at Target or Wal-Mart, and how much money a week they spend on groceries. These ratings are called *qualitative ratings*.

Because many stations deliver essentially the same numbers of listeners, and because it is the job of the salesperson to create a differential competitive advantage for a station, using qualitative data, if it is available, can make a big difference. If you and your competitor are each trying to get an agency piece of business for a bank where the desired demographic is Adults 25 to 54 and your audience delivery is basically the same, but you can use qualitative data to show that your listeners have higher incomes and higher net worth, thus representing more value to the bank because they will place larger deposits and grow the bank's assets more quickly, you will win. You should also be able to use this qualitative data to secure a higher rate.

If you spend your career looking at ratings to see only how your station ranks against the competition, you squander a wealth of data that can get you pieces of agency business you otherwise would lose. But keep in mind that if you spend your career talking to direct clients about ratings, you're squandering something entirely different—the opportunity to identify a business problem that can be solved by advertising.

Selling Sports on Radio

You don't hear this sort of thing on the radio anymore, but on October 3, 1951, it was all that mattered if you were a baseball fan:

> So don't go away. Light up that Chesterfield. Stay with us and we'll see how Ralph Branca will fare against Bobby Thomson. Thomson against the Brooklyn club has a lot of long ones this year. He has seven home runs. Branca pitches and Bobby takes a strike called, on the inside corner. Branca throws, there's a long fly, it's gonna be, I believe. The Giants win the pennant, the Giants win the pennant, the Giants win the pennant, the Giants win the pennant, the Giants win the pennant.[9]

Russ Hodges made the call as the New York Giants came from behind to beat the cross-town Dodgers and win the National League pennant. His play-by-play descendants aren't inviting their listeners to light up Chesterfields or anything else today, but the fans of every baseball team in America know that just as the book is inevitably better than the movie, the radio broadcast is better than the television broadcast. If you pursue a career in radio sports sales and if you are sufficiently adept at reminding advertisers of this axiom, you'll have a lot of fun and you'll make a handsome living.

Today the sport we almost never hear on the air was the genesis of radio sports broadcasting—boxing.

On the Fourth of July in 1923 in Shelby, MT, Jack Dempsey defended his heavyweight title against Tom Gibbons. Minutes after the last punch, fight fans in New York heard a detailed report of the bout on WOR. This wasn't blow-by-blow, round-by-round live coverage, but the Dempsey-Gibbons fight is regarded as the first sporting event broadcast on radio.[10]

Today there are stations that broadcast nothing but sports. The first was New York's WFAN, which launched an all-sports format in 1987. ESPN has a radio network. Opinionated sports-talk show hosts abound.

The economics of running a sports franchise are closely linked to the economics of broadcasting sports. Today a single play-by-play broadcast may have more than 50 different advertisers. Rights fees have increased dramatically so the amount of inventory sold has expanded commensurately. For years, there would be a single minute of advertising during a basketball time out. Demand has increased this time to a minute and a half. Baseball has gone from one- to two-minute breaks between innings. Between 1955 and 1966 the New York Yankees had two sponsors; Ballantine Beer and Camel Cigarettes.[11]

Over the past 20 years sports programming has been a source of significant economic growth for the radio business. Advertisers have demonstrated a strong thirst for sponsorship opportunities. In the '80s Anheuser Busch went on a spending spree securing a large number of local sponsorships to more effectively compete against Miller and Coors. The strategy worked as Budweiser and Bud Light each gained market share at the expense of the competition.

If you are selling radio sports, you are obviously competing against television. You probably have a number of advantages, the foremost of which would be that the package you are offering consists of broadcasts of every game. On television the rights are typically split between cable, network, pay-per-view, and local stations. An advertiser's investment in radio broadcast rights often provides a bond with the announcer, which approaches something of an implied endorsement. Promotions are easier to execute on radio. Promos the station runs before the broadcast inviting listeners to tune in can include the sponsor's name. And on the radio, tune-out during commercial breaks is less of a problem for advertisers than on television, where zapping is virtually endemic on sports broadcasts.

Selling radio sports is largely a matter of selling the benefits of affiliating a product with the respective team. There is a historic spillover of loyalties from a fan of his team to a product that sponsors the team's broadcasts. In smaller markets, radio salespeople know that finding business owners who are ardent supporters of a team means they have found a good prospect for advertising. The packages that a station or a local network builds will typically include value above and beyond in-game, pre-game, or post-game placements. These packages could range from stadium signage and desirable tickets to awards banquets and team golf tournaments. In any event, advertisers who make a marketing investment in a sports franchise or program are doing much more than making a ratings-driven media buy. They are making an investment in improving the public perception of a business by a positive affiliation with what is hopefully a well-liked sports franchise.

Selling Events

An event might be a concert; it might be a pumpkin patch. Whatever the event, there are opportunities for a radio station to get involved. The station's involvement often leads to selling sponsorships.

This type of business typically falls into a category that radio broadcasters refer to as non-traditional revenue, or NTR. The structure of a deal and the extent of a radio station's involvement determine the economics and the sponsorship opportunities.

Just as sports franchises have developed a lucrative revenue stream by selling signage at stadiums they own or control, radio stations have attempted, with differing degrees of success, to sell on-site exposure at events they produce or promote. This effort can range from a banner inside a concert venue to a booth at a crafts fair. The benefit to an advertiser is the opportunity to have direct contact with a prospective customer in a positive environment and, hopefully, exposure to large numbers of people who fit a particular demographic profile.

There are two major challenges involved with selling events. One is financial and concerns the amount of money a sponsor believes is justified in investing. Measuring the return on this investment is difficult for an advertiser. The second is time. There is both the limited amount of time a sponsor will enjoy exposure during an event, and the often extraordinary amount of time the radio station invests in planning, producing, and selling an event.

Hispanic and Black Radio

Nothing has changed the make-up of radio in the past few years to the extent that Hispanic radio has. There are eight times the number of Hispanic stations than there were 20 years ago. The reason: dramatic shifts in demography.

Hispanics account for about 13 percent of America's population. Looking at this from a different vantage point, America's Hispanics represent the world's fifth-largest Spanish-speaking country. Naturally, Hispanics are served by radio and advertisers look for effective ways of making a connection with this increasingly vital audience through radio.

Because Hispanic population tends to be concentrated in the major markets, so do the radio stations serving them. The audiences are large; the leading stations in Los Angeles, San Francisco, Dallas, and New York are often Hispanic.

Programming is tailored to address different cultural and regional nuances. For the melting pot of New York City, a Bilingual format works well. Regional Mexican formats perform well in California and the other border states. Tejano formats target multi-generational Texans, Tropical formats target Caribbean Hispanics, and Romantica formats provide an international, mass-appeal.

The people who manage Hispanic radio stations suggest that the significance of their medium for advertisers is not as much about language as it is about culture and the links America's Hispanics choose to retain with their cultural roots. They would also point out that Hispanics tend to be heavier users of radio than other media.

America's large African-American population is also served by radio. There are more than 300 urban-formatted stations and a number of formats designed to appeal to different segments. Contemporary Hit and Urban Contemporary target teens. Alternative reaches young adults and older adults prefer Urban Adult Contemporary, Urban Oldies, and Smooth Jazz.

Unique Qualities/Competitive Advantages of Radio

Radio offers advertisers a number of advantages. The most significant of these is the medium's ability to target specific segments of the population. While this can also be achieved on cable television and the much more static, low-impact medium of magazines, the specific characteristics of the audiences radio can deliver to an advertiser can often be more narrowly defined.

For instance, an advertiser who needs to reach a working mother of two young children would be an ideal candidate for radio. Because this woman needs to help get her children ready to leave the home in the morning, she's not watching television, although the television may be turned on and is used as background noise. She does not have time to read the paper, if one comes to the house. But once in the car and on her way to work she is alone with the radio. She may listen to the radio at work, but she's certainly not watching television or reading the newspaper. The radio remains on in her car as she leaves the office to pick up her children and take them to soccer practice. Radio is typically the last medium she is exposed to before making the largest purchase of the day.

Advertisers can study ratings to determine which types of station deliver the largest audience in their targeted demographic. In the case of the working mother of two small children, the target would probably be a woman between 25 and 44. One common mistake advertisers make when determining which radio station(s) to use to deliver a desired audience is in defining the audience too broadly. Advertisers who target audiences with Adult 18 to 49 or Adult 25 to 54 demographics, a fairly common practice, often reach too broad an audience. The advertiser who buys radio against an Adult 25 to 54 demographic should remember that the consumer characteristics of a 25-year-old woman and a 53-year-old man, who are in the defined target, tend to have little in common.

Radio salespeople can help advertisers make more intelligent decisions on which station(s) to include in a campaign and help ensure stronger results, by suggesting that the advertiser look at the demographic epicenter of the target. In the case of a media buy where the advertising agency says it wants to reach Adults 25 to 54, intelligent questions on the part of the salesperson may identify the heavy user of the advertised product as being in a 25-to-34 cell of the demographic. It may turn out that 80 percent of all the purchasing activity within an Adult 25 to 54 demographic takes place in this Adult 25-to-34 cell. This fact means that a good media buy will concentrate on this demographic target cell.

Along with the ability to reach very specifically defined audiences, where radio is surpassed only by direct marketing, both online and offline, radio offers an advertiser other significant advantages. One of these is often perceived as a disadvantage by some prospective advertisers—the fact that radio lacks a visual component.

Radio salespeople are often left with the feeling they have been given an insurmountable objection when an advertiser touts television because of its ability to show a picture of the product. Radio can take on this assignment quite nicely, however. By writing effective copy and by using sound effects and music, a radio commercial can easily engage the imagination. A good radio commercial will actually put listeners to work creating a unique and personal image in their own mind. A television viewer who is in the market for a new sofa may see a furniture store's advertisement. None of the sofas viewed may be appealing. On the other hand, the radio listener who is in the market for a sofa will hear the selection of sofas described. The image of the sofa the listener wants will take shape in the listener's mind. The listener will associate this image with the advertiser and as a result will go to the store and look at the sofas.

This type of theater of the mind often takes place when radio advertising is carefully written and well produced. But when cliché-riddled copy is carelessly thrown together just to get something on the air, radio has been cheated out of an opportunity to do the job it has been performing capably and consistently for more than 80 years.

Local advertisers often believe that "getting my name out there can't hurt." However, in some instances, people exposed to a business's advertising are less likely to buy its product than people who have not been exposed to the advertising if they didn't like the commercial to which they were exposed. Therefore, in radio, as in any medium, good advertising works and bad advertising doesn't work.

Radio is a mobile medium. When transistor radios came along in the 1960s, radio suddenly left the living room and went to the beach. Walkmans took this mobility to a new level in the 1980s. Today, radio reaches us everywhere. Thirty-seven percent of listening takes place at home, 43 percent in the car, and 20 percent elsewhere.[12]

Radio is arguably the most intimate medium. It is alone with a listener in the dark. It is the sole companion for a commuter. Because of the warmth of the human voice and its ability to communicate with intimacy, radio is an extremely powerful marketing tool when the proven fundamentals of advertising strategy are properly applied.

Just as radio can be intimate, it also has the ability to intrude. When someone is alone in their car, driving to a job they don't really like, a radio commercial for a firm which is hiring employees will prove more effective in reaching this potential candidate than a newspaper ad in the help wanted section. The people who go to the help wanted section are looking for a job. Employers know that the best candidates for the positions they have to fill typically are not looking for a job. Instances such as this underscore the importance of intrusiveness. While other media such as television are arguably intrusive, radio's ability to intrude with intimacy and to intrude on a well-defined demographic target gives it special value to the savvy advertiser.

Radio in the New Economy

If we think about radio as most of us know it, something that's on either the AM or FM band, it's probably safe to say that the medium will largely remain as vibrant, as relevant, and as meaningful a part of Americans' media diet as it has been for the past 80 years. Certainly, it will change. Driving the change will be the insurmountable surges of demographic shifts and relentless advances in technology. Radio has traditionally been a harbinger of leading-edge media change. It is where middle-class white teenagers discovered black music on what were called "race stations" in the 1950s. In the 1960s many of the economically undervalued and overlooked stations on the FM dial captured the feelings of a generation whose emerging viewpoints and tastes were all but ignored in virtually every other medium. The 1980s provided substantive media platforms for talk show hosts whose brand of conservative politics paved the way for organizations such as the Fox News Channel.

Radio has a history of being the medium that is on the vanguard of change. But that, too, has changed because of the Internet. A radio station no longer requires a transmitter. And just as the movies redefined live theater and television redefined the movies, it may be a safe bet to say the Internet will, in some ways we have yet to see or accurately conceptualize, redefine radio.

Making a Living Selling Radio Advertising

Radio salespeople work in a medium that offers a variety of rewards. The financial opportunities are potentially lucrative. So are the opportunities to demonstrate creativity, and learn firsthand the lessons of marketing, human nature, and business.

Radio salespeople typically enjoy the opportunity to manage more pieces of the sales and marketing process, from developing a promotional concept to producing the actual advertising, than their counterparts in other media, especially in markets below the top 25, where most of the business comes from agencies. The sales process itself may often rely more on the salesperson's creativity than a more quantitative and numbers-oriented type of sale that tends to exist elsewhere in the media world, especially in television.

One of the benefits of a career in radio sales is the ability to work with a variety of different businesses. This is stimulating, educational, and a virtual guarantee that boredom and complacency will rarely enter into your world. It is not unusual for a radio salesperson to call on a car dealer in the morning, have lunch with a furniture retailer, call on a homebuilder in the afternoon, and stop to see by a nightclub client in the evening.

With tenacity, determination, and a sense of purpose, your first radio sales job may not be hard to get, and it may well be a business more difficult to leave than to enter. You may discover that the friendships you make, the pace at which your business both runs and evolves, and the sense of enjoyment and satisfaction you derive make the radio business one that will stimulate and support you for the rest of your career.

Test Yourself

1. Why did radio evolve from a national to a local medium?
2. What does a program director do?
3. How does selling to an advertising agency differ from selling to a direct client?
4. What do media buyers expect of the salespeople who call on them?

5. If a prospective advertiser told you that television was better than radio because it reached more people, how would you respond?
6. What benefits does sports marketing provide an advertiser?
7. Why is Hispanic radio experiencing such robust growth?

Project

Browse through your daily newspaper and find a large ad. Write two 60-second radio commercials. Write one of the commercials so a radio listener is *encouraged to do something* (a tactical commercial). Write the other ad so the listener is encouraged *to develop a belief* about the advertiser (a strategic commercial).

References

Susan J. Douglas. 1999. *Listening In.* New York: Times Books.
David J. Halberstam. 1999. *Sports on New York Radio.* Lincolnwood, IL: Masters Press.
Radio Advertising Bureau. 2002. *Radio Marketing Guide and Fact Book: 2002-2003 Edition.* New York: Radio Advertising Bureau.

Resources

www.clearchannel.com
www.rab.com

Endnotes

1. Susan J. Douglas. 1999. *Listening In.* New York: Times Books.
2. Ibid.
3. www.adage.com
4. www.clearchannel.com. December 2002.
5. Arbitron/Radio Advertising Bureau Media Targeting. 2000.
6. Media Audit. March 2001.
7. www.cabletvadbureau.com. December 2002.
8. M Street Publications. 2002. *M Street Radio Directory, 11th Edition.*
9. David J. Halberstam. 1999. *Sports on New York Radio.* Lincolnwood, IL: Masters Press. p. 285
10. Ibid.
11. Ibid.
12. Radio Advertising Bureau. 2002. *Radio Marketing Guide and Fact Book: 2002-2003 Edition.* New York: Radio Advertising Bureau.

Chapter 21 Cable Television

By J. William Grimes

In 1948, in the small town of Mahoney City in central Pennsylvania, John Walson, owner of the only general store in town, lamented that he could not sell the hottest new electronics product in America. Throughout the country, television sets were selling in increasing numbers in large cities and suburbs. Television, with its sight, sound, and motion programming from the three networks, was exciting people who lived within the reach of the stations' broadcast signals. But John Walson in Mahoney City had little hope of ever selling this profitable new product because people in his community could not receive the television signals; Mahoney City was too far from the nearest city that had a television station—Pittsburgh to the west and Philadelphia to the east. The problem was further compounded by the pervasiveness of hills and small mountains surrounding the community, which blocked any signal that could approach Mahoney City. Such technical and geographic barriers throughout rural America were excluding millions of people from receiving this new entertainment and information medium in 1948.

It occurred to this entrepreneurial store owner that if he could somehow access the television signals from either distant city and retransmit them into the households of his community, he could begin to sell television sets in his store. To realize his dream he built a large receiving antenna (later called a master antenna) on the top of a high hill in the Allegheny Mountains 30 miles to the east. Next, he purchased cable wire to connect his antenna on the hill to a small building in town. This cable wire, called coaxial cable, was capable of transmitting infinitely more content (text, audio, and video) than normal telephone wires were. From this location, or the system head end as a cable company's central offices are called today, additional coaxial cable trunk wires were strung on telephone poles. Next, separate coaxial wires were strung from the trunk lines into each cable system subscriber's home, thus enabling the television signals of the three Philadelphia television network stations to be distributed in Mahoney City. This new method of distributing *distant signals* of television stations via cable wires into small, usually rural, American towns became known as Community Antenna Television (CATV). Today, it is simply called cable television, or cable.

The vendors of the new coaxial cable, in their sales presentations to cable system owners, stressed an important benefit that at that time had no immediate economic advantage for the cable operators: these cable wires had substantial unused capacity, or *bandwidth*, to deliver more than three channels of television programming into subscribing households. In fact, the earliest coaxial cable had the capacity to deliver twelve channels of video programming. Because there were no other channels except the three networks' stations, and because the cable owners were rapidly building new systems in new communities, negotiating with local telephone companies for access to their poles (pole attachment), and working with banks to obtain the necessary financing, the thought of additional channel capacity or any applications for it was mostly overlooked.

John Walson, the rural Pennsylvania store owner, soon stocked up on RCA television sets. He sold them along with CATV for $3 per month so the customers would have something to watch on their new sets. The biggest expense for the new cable television customer was the one-time $125 up-front connection fee. Some observers called this subscription television because it was the first time people actually paid money to receive television programming. Just as in the magazine industry where people who paid to receive publications were referred to as subscribers, so, too, were those who paid the new cable systems for their television.

The local cable systems sold no advertising during those early years of the cable television industry. The systems retransmitted the network television stations' programming in its entirety, meaning that the stations' network and local advertisers' commercials were seen by cable subscribers—thus increasing the audience outside the stations' broadcast coverage areas. The most significant implication of the growth in cable television subscribers was that the three broadcast networks and their affiliated stations were delivering additional viewers to both their networks and local advertisers.

The cable systems paid no compensation to the networks for their programming nor did the broadcasters pay the cable systems anything for their incremental audience resulting from cable system carriage. In later years these economic issues and others would lead to divisiveness between the broadcasting and cable television industries and to legal initiatives and new government regulations.

Regulation and Legislation

The Federal Communications Commission had been created in 1934 by the United States government to regulate the broadcasting industry—radio and later television. Based on the theory that the airwaves were owned by the American public, the FCC determined that a broadcast station operator, or licensee, must be of worthy character, ascertain the needs of and serve the public interest, and have the resources, both managerial and financial, to successfully operate a broadcast station. After satisfying those requirements the FCC would then grant a license to the applicant to operate a station for a term of seven years and to keep whatever after-tax profits the operator could earn. Achieving these public interest standards would enable the operator to apply to the commission for a seven-year renewal of the license. The FCC later limited the number of stations (licenses) an individual or company could own to seven AM and seven FM radio stations and five VHF television stations. Virtually all of the regulations affecting the broadcasting industry were federal, with FCC oversight.

The regulation of the cable television industry evolved in a very different way. Soon after John Walson's cable system was operating in Mahoney City, scores of other entrepreneurs constructed master antennas and laid cable wires to build systems throughout rural America. Small-town governments, always seeking new tax revenues, soon saw an opportunity to create new income for their communities by taxing the cable systems' monthly subscriber revenues. These taxes created a small but continuous stream of revenue for these towns.

The much larger economic opportunity was realized when communities observed that more and more individuals and new small companies wanted to wire their communities and become the town's cable operator. (It was assumed from the inception of the cable industry that only one cable system could financially operate successfully in a town or city due to the substantial capital expense of building the plant or buying the equipment and wiring the community.) Town governments soon created franchising committees to evaluate the merits of competing proposals and award community franchises.

One increasingly important determinant of the franchising committees was how much up-front cash the applicants would commit to the communities. An important non-financial factor used by communities in selecting their cable franchisee was whether the applicant offered a channel to the community to be used in whatever way the townspeople determined. This channel was referred to as a local access channel.

Thus, the regulation of the nascent cable television industry began as local, unlike the FCC system that regulated the broadcast industry. There were those in Washington, DC, and in the cable and broadcast industries who objected to local control of the cable industry and petitioned the FCC to intervene. In 1956 the FCC issued a landmark opinion in *Frontier Broadcasting v. Coli CATV*, deciding that cable systems were not common carriers and therefore the commission had no jurisdiction over the industry.

Later, both the FCC and the courts held that cable companies could operate in any market (broadcasters had wanted to restrict cable operations to rural areas without total access to broadcast, over-the-air signals) and that cable systems were not in violation of copyright infringement because cable system subscribers were paying for the connection to the content, not for the content itself. While this logic may be debatable, the ruling gave cable systems a chance to succeed economically and enabled millions of people with no previous access to television programming to receive it.

In the ensuing years, the cable industry fended off both legal and congressional lobbying efforts by the telephone, broadcasting, entertainment, and sports industries, which all tried to capture a part of the growing cable system subscription revenues. Many in the cable industry credit the personality power of one of the great cable television pioneers and personalities, "The Mouth of the South," Ted Turner, for turning the industry around.

The Superstation

The year 1975 will be remembered as the year that forever changed the media industry in the United States and, eventually, throughout the world. Prior to that year, only the US government used satellites orbiting thousands of miles above the globe. The Radio Corporation of America (RCA) had won approval from the FCC to launch the first commercial satellite—a space station geosynchronously orbiting 23,400 miles above the earth with the capability of sending 24 channels of television programming back to earth. (Geosynchronous means that as the world turns, so do the satellites, thus enabling the continual reception of the television signals to the same geographic receiver antenna dishes.) Each channel was called a transponder. RCA successfully launched this first satellite in 1975 with one customer, a small pay channel that had existed by mailing videotapes of movies it leased from the Hollywood studios to a few cable systems, which in turn charged their subscribers an incremental monthly fee for the service. The company, called Home Box Office (HBO), agreed to lease one of RCA's satellite transponders for the life of the satellite, which was 10 years.

In order for this new system of distributing television programming by satellite to succeed, a significant amount of capital was required for equipment to send the programming from HBO's studios up to the satellite and to install downlinks at cable systems to receive the programming. In 1975 cable systems were mired in bank debt borrowed to build their systems and few could afford to pay for downlinks at their head ends. HBO, owned by the profitable Time, Inc., devised a financial method to fund the cost of downlinks for the cable systems, thus enabling the systems to receive HBO programming from RCA's satellite and to market the movie channel to their subscribers for $5 per month. HBO's business strategy was to equally share subscriber revenue with the systems and to not accept advertising.

Two years later, in 1977, HBO was still RCA's only customer and its $200 million investment in its communications satellite was looking extremely bleak. Around this time the owner of a money-losing UHF television channel in Atlanta, WTBS, was desperately seeking ways to increase revenues. The station's ratings were continually the lowest in the market and its owner, Ted Turner, could not afford to outbid his competitors for quality entertainment programming. The production of competitive local news was also too expensive. The station, however, did have one valuable programming asset: it had purchased the rights to televise the Atlanta Braves baseball games. Despite the games' high ratings the station still ranked fifth overall and the Atlanta market's television revenues were too low to support five stations.

About this time Turner agreed to meet with a young cable operator from Florida who claimed to have an idea that would increase WTBS' ratings and revenues. The idea was for Turner to lease a transponder on the satellite, uplink the station's programming, and downlink it into cable systems that were now serving nearly 5 million homes. Not only did this plan eventually achieve Turner's financial hopes for his station, which was soon referred to as "the Superstation," but its success also encouraged other programming entrepreneurs to create new and original cable networks. ESPN, USA Network, Turner's CNN, MTV, and others soon followed. Cable systems now had access to a growing supply of non-broadcasting programming. Suddenly, new cable subscriptions were growing at a record pace and Wall Street was courting the cable television industry.

The colorful Ted Turner also turned out to be the cable industry's greatest lobbyist for favorable legislation and regulation. He campaigned tirelessly for Congress and the FCC to relax copyright legislation and, thus, favor cable systems and networks. While pleading cable's merits to one senator he threw himself on the floor, writhing in feigned pain and cried, "The broadcasters are killing me." These histrionics often were successful and Turner became the industry's lightning rod and darling.

While the Superstation sold all of its advertising to local and regional advertisers and, increasingly, to national or network television advertisers, the other new cable networks followed the advertising commercial inventory model created by the broadcast networks with their affiliated stations. That model provided two minutes of commercial time each hour for the cable systems to sell advertising in their local communities. Primarily because the early cable system owners and operators were engineers with little understanding of marketing or advertising, and because of the significant costs associated with advertising insertion equipment and salespeople, few cable systems took advantage of the local advertising sales opportunity. By the early 1980s, however, with the continuing increase in the number of cable networks, improvement of these networks' programming, improvement in audience measurement techniques, and growing advertiser acceptance of cable as a medium, cable systems began to address this important new revenue stream. During the last two decades in the twentieth century the cable system operators have increased their investment in capturing local adverting revenues. In the last few years local advertising has represented the highest percentage of revenue growth for the systems, and in the national television market the cable networks now rival the broadcast networks in ad revenues.

Advertiser Acceptance

In the early years of the cable industry the networks' struggle for advertising revenues was extremely difficult. National advertisers voiced many objections to the cable networks' sales presentations. The most serious negative aspect was that the cable networks were not measured by A.C. Nielsen's National Television Index (NTI). It was not until late 1983, after significant negotiations, that Nielsen agreed that a cable network would qualify for NTI audience measurement if it were available in 12 million households . The broadcast networks vigorously opposed this decision and quietly threatened Nielsen with reprisals. Advertisers, and particularly their ad agencies, also used the poor quality (in their view) of cable's programming, its relatively small universe of subscribing households, and a lack of budget for the new medium as excuses not to advertise on cable.

Nonetheless, cable, with Turner's networks, ESPN, and MTV leading the way, gradually overcame these objections. When the first Nielsen ratings measuring WTBS, ESPN, and USA were released the audiences were infinitesimally small and the combined cable networks' share of viewing was less than 1 percent. But a measured audience it was. The cable networks began to hire more salespeople with experience in selling magazines and radio, salespeople who could sell a concept—the growing cable households and its improving network programming. Interestingly, the more astute of the cable network presidents preferred salespeople who had not been in television because of the ease in selling that medium. In fact, television salespeople were often referred to by cable executives as order-takers who wined and dined agency time buyers but seldom had to write a strategic sales presentation on the merits of their medium and how it might increase their advertisers' sales.

Equally important, the cable system business was now in favor with Wall Street and large institutional lenders, and the pace of new cable system construction rapidly increased. With more new networks, each town and city in the country was now clamoring, "I want my cable TV," a clever takeoff of the successful advertising campaign used by MTV to tell kids to exhort their parents to sign up with the cable system for MTV.

Households with cable rose dramatically during the 1980s from about 10 million to nearly 60 million. Ad agencies began to acknowledge this growth and the enthusiastic sales representatives of the cable networks finally had the ammunition to compare cable's universe to that of radio networks and magazines. Soon, large advertisers such as Proctor & Gamble, Anheuser Bush, and General Motors were beginning to allocate money to advertise on cable networks. At the larger market cable systems the same advertiser acceptance slowly followed as local advertisers recognized the facts about growing subscriber homes and better programming.

The cable networks were also attracting new capital and investment and each began to upgrade the quality of its programming and to schedule more original hours. WTBS added major college football and off-network syndicated programming; CNN opened news bureaus around the world; ESPN featured National Basketball Association (NBA) and National Hockey League (NHL) games, and in 1987 became the first cable network to televise National Football League (NFL) games. MTV wowed kids with a completely new kind of programming—rock-and-roll video clips presented by VJs.

The impact of the new programming was that cable networks' share of television viewing was increasing nearly as fast as households with cable were. And the inventive cable salespeople were having increasing success and were now competing for the large television advertising budgets instead of surviving on the small cable test budgets. By 1987, cable television programming had been tested and the scores were in: it was a winner.

Audience Measurement

Initially, some cable networks did not want Nielsen measurement, fearing low ratings would only confirm cable's weakness and reduce the interest a few advertisers were beginning to show. Attempts by certain networks to hire research firms such as Arbitron, the radio audience measurement company, to do telephone coincidental research on special programs were met with disdain by advertisers and agencies. The cable networks quickly learned an important lesson about media research—advertisers want standardized research for each medium. The idea of two or more companies using different methodologies to measure audiences in one medium was deemed to be not only confusing but also very misleading. Radio had discovered this fact earlier when at one point three different research firms measured the media—sometimes with such dramatic variances in a station's listenership that advertisers lost faith in the medium. When this realization became pervasive the cable networks and their newly formed advertising sales association, the Cable Advertising Bureau (CAB), began their unified efforts to pursue Nielsen's NTI service.

Another important type of research adapted by cable networks, albeit secondary to Nielsen's quantitative measurement, was also gaining acceptance with advertisers—the qualitative profiling research of cable television viewers. Not surprisingly, since cable television viewers had to pay money for their television, the income, occupation, and education levels of the average or composite cable subscriber were higher than those of the broadcast networks' average viewer. As this new qualitative research was being confirmed by more and more studies commissioned by the cable networks, their salespeople had another competitive advantage which they extolled enthusiastically to the advertising community.

Today, local and national advertisers demand research from independent companies that estimate both the audience size and quality of each national channel or network. One of cable's great competitive advantages compared to broadcast networks and stations is that cable delivers an audience composition that provides less audience waste. In other words, because cable networks' programming is targeted to narrower demographic audiences, those audiences do not contain many viewers outside the advertisers' target. A vivid example would be the viewing audience to an America's Cup sailing championship event on ESPN. This event's audience would be 70 percent men, with an average age of 50 and an average income over $100,000, more than two-thirds of whom have college educations and hold prestigious positions.

Industry Structure and Consolidation

By the late 1970s the cable system industry, which was comprised of hundreds of different owners, began to consolidate. New companies were formed to acquire existing systems and petition for new city franchises. As these companies acquired more systems they were referred to as Multiple System Operators (MSOs). Among the consolidators were Time, Inc., HBO's owner; Warner Cable, a division of Warner Communications (today's AOL Time Warner); Comcast, now the largest MSO; and Tele-communications, Inc. (TCI, now Comcast). Before TCI's acquisition by AT&T and then by Comcast, TCI was headed by John Malone, who, more than any individual with the possible exception of Ted Turner, would shake and shape the foundation of the emerging cable television industry. Malone, who possesses a Ph.D. in operational engineering and the mind to quickly manipulate complex financial issues, built TCI into the largest MSO with his intellect, knowledge, and energy.

As in any industry, the key factor driving cable system consolidation was scale economics, meaning the larger a company was (scale) the lower the per-unit cost of necessary goods and services would be (economics). This scale was particularly important in the cable business because of its dependence on a wide variety of equipment and, increasingly, programming. The more systems and subscribers a company had the more negotiating leverage it enjoyed over its suppliers in the form of volume discounts.

The realization of scale economics also affected the industry in another important way: the new MSO leaders were mostly financially trained executives who had skills in corporate capital structuring, banking, and negotiating. A few of the CEOs, similar to John Malone, had both financial and technology training and experience. Thus, the cable industry, through hundreds of mergers and acquisitions, consolidated into fewer and fewer large companies. Today the 10 largest MSOs control 85 percent of all US cable subscribers.

By the mid-1980s the cable networks, while still not profitable, were beginning to be viewed by larger industry companies as valuable assets. Cable network consolidation began with ABC acquiring ESPN from the Getty Oil Company; Viacom acquired MTV, Nickelodeon and The Movie Channel; USA Network was bought by a consortium of Hollywood movie studio companies seeking guaranteed cable distribution for their movies; Lifetime was purchased by a group consisting of ABC, NBC and Hearst Corporation, a large newspaper, magazine, and television station owner; and The Discovery Networks were bought by a group controlled by John Malone's TCI.

Carriage Fees

The idea of consolidation was that the more networks a company owned, the better its bargaining position with the MSOs for programming carriage fees would be. Carriage fees—money paid by cable systems to the networks for the carriage of the networks' programming—were a major change for the industry and would have a lasting impact on cable systems and cable networks as well as broadcast television.

When the cable networks were first formed in the late 1970s the business models they employed were identical to those of the broadcast networks. They would acquire and produce programming and provide it to their affiliates, the cable systems, which would distribute it to their subscribers or audiences. Both parties would promote the programming and, importantly, similar to the model of broadcast television, the cable networks would compensate the systems for their distribution and generate all their revenues from the sale of advertising. By 1982 it became apparent to the cable networks that their advertising revenue estimates were greatly exaggerated and not achievable. The result was increasing operating losses with little hope of ever reaching profitability.

That year ESPN was paying its cable system affiliates five cents compensation per subscriber per year. While this may seem like a modest expense, the cost to ESPN, with 12 million subscribers, was $720,000 and growing rapidly as the systems added thousands of new subscribers every month. With escalating programming costs and anemic advertising revenue, even a major company such as Getty Oil could not be expected to fund ESPN's operating losses year after year.

As president and CEO of ESPN, I met with my executive vice president and the company's chief strategist, Roger Werner, to discuss the future of ESPN. Roger is a brilliant thinker with an MBA who sold vacuum cleaners door to door before joining Gillette's marketing department and later becoming a consultant at the prestigious McKinsey & Company. Roger and I devised a plan that we unveiled in the fall of 1982. ESPN announced that as MSO and system carriage contracts with ESPN expired we would no longer pay compensation. Furthermore, ESPN would charge the system companies 10 cents per subscriber per month, or $1.20 per year, per subscriber. At that time, MSOs were charging an average of $15 per month for only 12 channels of television programming while not only not paying anything for the programming but also collecting monthly fees from the networks. The MSOs charged subscribers a minimum fee that included cable delivery of local television stations, WTBS, and a group of advertising-supported cable networks such as ESPN, MTV, CNN, USA, and Lifetime. This minimum was referred to as basic cable—the basic tier. Pay or premium cable referred to the channels such as HBO and Showtime, in another tier, that subscribers paid an incremental monthly charge to receive. These premium channels were commercial-free.

After 18 months of intense and often heated negotiations with each MSO, all agreed to pay ESPN a monthly subscriber fee averaging five cents per subscriber per month. The actual monthly fee was a bit higher, but ESPN provided a discount to systems that agreed to advertise ESPN programming on other channels using local advertising inventory of other cable networks. This new business model, or partnership, changed the industry forever because as other networks followed ESPN's lead in charging a carriage fee, all the cable networks' subscriber revenues greatly increased and soon exceeded their growing advertising revenues. Much of the new profits that the networks were now generating were reinvested in new programming, which enabled the networks to increase both the quantity and quality of their programming.

This was indeed a new partnership because the subscriber fees paid by the MSOs to the networks led to better programming which created the rationale for cable operators to raise their prices and add new subscribers. The result was a substantial increase in new revenues and profits for both MSOs and cable networks. Further, this new partnership motivated the MSOs to begin upgrading their system facilities, thus creating more channels for new cable networks and to begin making substantial investments in people and equipment to sell local advertising aggressively. Thus, in the mid-1980s the MSOs embarked upon a concerted effort to challenge newspapers, radio, and television stations for their share of local advertising. It has taken the systems much time, investment, and effort, but today local advertising represents local cable systems' fastest growing revenue stream, and the systems are continually taking shares of the market from local television stations.

Cable Network Programming and Sales Strategies

Doubters of the viability of the cable industry—and there were many in the late 1970s when cable networks were being founded—based their dire predictions of cable's impending demise on two assumptions. The first was that there was a surfeit of television programming already available to all Americans from the broadcast networks (by this time numerous UHF, or low signal stations, were also being approved by the FCC). The second was that the networks had monopolized all available programming and there was nothing left for cable networks to acquire or produce. This latter concern was trumpeted by the broadcast networks that wanted both Madison Avenue and Wall Street to hold pessimistic views on the cable networks' business prospects. In the trade press, at industry conventions, and in investment banking meetings, broadcast television executives initially ignored cable completely, as if it were not in existence. Soon after, however, the broadcast networks were unleashing a barrage of negative, anti-cable comments at every opportunity.

Attack by Broadcasters

This negative strategy and behavior by broadcasters has occurred in many industries where either new technology or new regulation has helped usher new competitors into profitable, well-established markets. In the mid-1980s I recall lamenting the networks' attacks on cable to a very successful entrepreneur who had founded two companies that competed with the legacy leaders in their markets. Arthur Jones, founder of Nautilus, Inc., the exercise equipment maker, responded to my concern in these words: "When a new company enters a market dominated by established competitors the first response by the incumbents is to ignore the company, to act as if it does not exist. Step two is to vitriolically criticize the management, the business plan, and the product and take every opportunity to tell everyone that it is a loser. The final response, when the new company has become a success, is to emulate it, copy its product benefits, mimic its sales presentations, and hire its people." These observations by Mr. Jones not only alleviated my fears a bit but also turned out to be prophetic.

Management pundits often refer to this type of change in a market dominated by established firms and assisted by changes in technology, regulation, legislation, and, even, at times, the lack of available capital as *market disruption.*

Cable Network Programming Strategy

With the doubts about cable's ability to find programming, what strategies did the cable networks employ? Before a strategy can be deployed in business, a thorough understanding of market information must be garnered and analyzed. The cable networks adapted this approach and the results pleasantly surprised them. There were libraries of movies not only from Hollywood but also from around the world, and, better yet, the broadcast networks had licensed only a small percentage of these films. USA Network was successful, in part, by programming feature films, for example. More news could always be produced with investments in bureaus and journalists, as had been done by CNN, MSNBC, and FOX News. Thousands of college sporting events were not being televised by the broadcasters, and fishing, auto racing, and yachting were available—a fact ESPN and the regional sports networks took advantage of. Already-produced films about animals, history, and geography existed in large quantities, which the Discovery Channel and A & E took advantage of. The list could continue, but the point is that a large supply of programming did exist and not all of it was expensive.

Having learned that the programming existed and could be acquired, the cable networks next learned that to differentiate from and compete with the broadcast networks it would be strategically smart to program each channel with programming of similar genre or type. This would provide the viewer with a clearer understanding of the networks' programming position. More importantly, the networks would be able to approach advertisers with whom their target audience was compatible. Most importantly, the networks could offer to many advertisers a high composition of the desired target audience. Consider the alternatives for an advertiser seeking to buy an audience of men 18 to 34: a sports event on ESPN might have 1 million total viewers, and as many as 60 percent to 70 percent of those viewers might be men 18 to 34. The same advertiser could buy a similar type program on CBS, which might deliver 2 million viewers, but a lower percentage would be men 18 to 34. Thus, ESPN's audience composition would be better—less waste—making ESPN, in this example, more competitive with a broadcast network even when its total audience was much smaller.

The confluence of the programming strategy—scheduling programs of the same type so the viewer knows the channel will always provide some kind of sports (ESPN), news or information (CNN), or youth lifestyle (MTV) —and the advertising sales strategy of selling audience composition proved to create a great deal of economic value for the cable networks.

Cable Network Sales Strategies

Soon the cable networks were using a new and effective strategy that would also add value, although it was adopted reluctantly. The idea was to emphasize to advertisers the significant CPM differential between the broadcast and cable networks. During the early days each cable network was forced to price their audience on a cost-per-thousand (CPM) much lower than their broadcast competitors because of a smaller household universe, lower viewing levels, and a greater supply of commercial inventory. The economic theorem of supply and demand states that if the supply of a product increases and the demand for it remains the same, prices will go down. This price drop is what happened in the television industry in the '80s as more cable networks came into existence, each with 10 or more commercial minutes an hour to sell. Advertising agencies quickly recognized the growing supply of commercial inventory and, via negotiation, drove down CPMs for both broadcast and cable networks.

ESPN, recognizing that CPMs necessarily had to decrease, turned this seeming disadvantage into sales positive. It actually trumpeted lower cable CPMs and used this lower price directly against the broadcast networks. The sports network noted in all its sales proposals, "ESPN will sell you a thousand men for half the price of ABC, CBS, and NBC." The cable networks in the aggregate had a massive supply of commercial inventory and in the earlier years could afford to discount prices because of lesser advertiser acceptance, lower households, and ratings within those households. Today, while most cable networks' CPMs sell at a small discount to the broadcast networks, some networks (again, ESPN as an example) actually often receive a CPM premium from advertisers.

An important reason why certain cable networks at times receive a higher CPM than broadcast networks do relates to another sales strategy successfully implemented by the cable networks. As mentioned earlier, the cable networks began to boast that cable households had higher incomes than non-cable households. The clear implication was that cable subscribers had greater purchasing power and were therefore better prospects to buy most consumer products advertised on television. Research confirmed this fact for cable networks in total while showing that certain networks had significantly higher audience income than their broadcast competitors. In a research study released in November 2002, CAB found that total income today in homes with cable is nearly four times that of non-cable homes.[1]

Today, cable television programming and advertiser acceptance are at or near parity with that of broadcasters. The cable networks are more profitable than the broadcast networks primarily because of income from subscriber fees from the MSOs and lower operating expenses. The business strategies developed in the early days of the industry to address revenue sharing with the systems, demonstrate media effectiveness to advertisers, and control operating expenses have contributed to a robust future for cable companies and their employees.

Industry Suppliers and Associations

Suppliers

An industry is a collection of companies with similar products competing for customers. Industries also consist of suppliers that specialize in making necessary components or inputs used by the industry companies to produce their products.

The cable television industry depends heavily on equipment and new technology to upgrade its system facilities. The industry has used coaxial copper cable in much of its cable wires but increasingly purchases glass fiber optics from suppliers such as Corning Glass and Lucent. Firms such as Scientific Atlanta and General Instruments manufacture the set-top boxes that enable subscribers to decipher the programming. The cable system industry also has suppliers that provide ad insertion equipment, traffic and billing hardware, interactive software, consulting and training, and research and marketing services.

An increasingly important group of suppliers to the cable industry are the firms that supply national and regional advertising sales representation. As the cable systems focus more on advertising sales and assemble their own local sales staffs, they also are growing more dependent on the contributions of their national and regional sales representation firms.

The largest cable sales representative firm is National Cable Communications (NCC). Based in New York with sales offices in 14 cities, NCC represents systems with access to 60 million cable households in nearly 200 markets. NCC's stated mission on its Web site is "to market the strategic value of spot cable advertising to national agencies while simultaneously developing leading technology which positions spot cable as the easiest to execute."

In striving to achieve its goal, NCC is also the largest provider of electronic invoicing in all media. Its site claims that "more than 80 percent of NCC's cable system affiliates are delivering electronic affidavits." This leading supplier also has a subsidiary, Cable Link Interconnects, which contributed to the creation of several large market cable system interconnects. A cable interconnect is created when different systems in different geographic areas of a market are linked together to enable advertisers' commercials to be presented simultaneously on any number of the systems. NCC is a good example of a supplier company that has created a growing number of products and services for its customers in the cable system industry.

Associations

An important measure of the strength of any industry is the number and quality of its trade associations. A trade association is a non-profit organization consisting of skilled people whose mission is to support certain objectives and interests of the industry and its companies. Judging the cable television industry by this measure, most would agree that it is very successful.

Since all industries are subject to some government regulation, they all benefit from an organization that maintains good relationships with elected officials and regulators. For the cable television industry that organization is the National Cable Television Association (NCTA), located in Washington, DC. The NCTA also represents the industry's interests on all proposed legislation and regulation affecting cable television and persuades officials to propose legislation or regulatory changes that would positively impact the industry—changes that would enhance the competitive position of the industry's firms and provide them with greater freedom to operate. In addition to the NCTA, which concentrates on national legislative and regulatory matters, the cable industry supports numerous state and regional trade associations which have similar objectives.

The Cable Television Advertising Bureau (CAB), with headquarters in New York, is supported by all MSOs and cable networks, and is responsible for ensuring that advertisers and agencies across the country are well informed about the benefits and competitive advantages of cable advertising. CAB employs experienced media sales and marketing people who use research and advertising case studies to demonstrate why cable should continue to attain a larger share of advertising budgets. Visiting the CAB Web site (www.cabletvadbureau.com) will acquaint you with the wide array of sales activities in the cable industry and with the latest statistics on cable television's national penetration, demographics, and advantages as an advertising medium. Local market information on MSOs, interconnects, and more can also be found on CAB's Web site.

The Cable Television Association for Marketing (CTAM) is dedicated to helping cable systems improve consumer marketing and has become more important to the industry as it competes vigorously with direct satellite-to-home companies for subscribers. Visit its Web site at www.ctam.com. As the need for new products and their reliance on new technology has become more evident, CableLabs (www.cablelabs.com) was created in Denver to develop technologies that would lead to the creation of new cable industry products such as cable modems, telephony over cable, interactive TV, and real-time multimedia services.

As the largest sector of the communications industry, with $77 billion in total 2001 revenues, the cable television business needs the support of strong supplier companies and leading-edge trade associations. The fact that the cable industry is also the fastest-growing media sector is additional evidence that the performance of its key suppliers and trade associations are contributing solidly to the industry's success.

Satellite Direct-to-Home Competition

The great growth for the cable television industry began in the early 1980s, driven by access to capital that enabled the operators to build new system franchises and cable networks to produce original programming. Even as new systems were being built throughout America, there were many rural areas that lacked sufficient population and density of homes to justify the investment in a system. However, people in these remote areas had no less desire for television than their distant neighbors did.

The companies that manufactured the satellite receiving antennas for cable systems recognized that if they could produce a receiver dish that people would purchase and locate on their property, these companies would have access to a new market. Soon they produced a consumer satellite antenna receiver and, although these new dishes were six feet in diameter and often an obtrusive sight on a property, people bought them. Despite a high installation cost and the fact that local television stations could not yet be offered, by 1990 more than 2 million large dishes were dotting the landscape of rural America.

In 1994 Hughes Aircraft Company launched four high-powered satellites 23,400 miles above earth. The power of these satellites was such that more than 200 video channels could be downlinked into 18-inch receivers.

In 2003 the direct-television industry, consisting mainly of the Hughes service (now called DirecTV) and EchoStar provide serious competition to the cable system industry and together have 17 million subscribers. DirecTV, in addition to offering 225 channels including pay-per-view events, sports season subscriptions (for example, every NFL game for $200 per season), and local television stations in the top 40 markets, offers three nascent services for which the company has high hopes.

First, there is DirectInteractive which enables the subscriber to use the remote control to access sports scores, weather, games, and some product purchasing, all while watching television. It may represent the first movement toward the convergence of the computer and the television set.

Next, is High-Definition Television (HDTV), which is a new format of television production based on the increase in information in the signal (more pixels, for example) that results in a higher-resolution image on the screen. Recently the first all high-definition television network, HDNet, debuted on DirecTV. Each day it features 16 hours of mostly sports and movies. HBO has also launched a high-definition television channel which presents their most popular programming in the high definition mode. To receive this new form of television, consumers must purchase HDTV-compatible sets or special enabling components for their current sets and producers must use special equipment.

The third new product that DirecTV is beginning to promote is high speed Internet access, called DirecTVDSL. The service costs $40 per month and competes in the field of high-speed data access with cable modems and telephone companies' DSL service. The user of DirecTVDSL need not be a two-telephone line customer nor a subscriber to DirecTV's television service.

The direct satellite-to-home business, led by DirecTV and EchoStar, has become an important competitor to the cable industry. As a result of the competition, companies work harder to supply new services their customers want at increasingly lower real costs while simultaneously improving customer service. The winner is the consumer.

Cable Industry Performance Metrics

To measure how a company is performing compared to its competitors or how an industry is faring against other industries, it is important to look at key operating and economic statistics. These are often referred to as metrics and in this chapter you will see that the cable industry, by nearly every metric, is becoming the most powerful media industry in America.

Total US households in 2003 were estimated by the A.C. Nielsen Company to number nearly 107 million.[2] The word household in this context has an economic meaning: a discrete dwelling unit where one or more individuals live. The total US population is approximately 280 million.

Cable systems in 2003 have an aggregate of about 75 million subscribers.[3] The direct satellite-to-home companies claim 17 million customers.[4] While adding the two competitors' subscribers would equal 92 million, Nielsen estimates that cable network programming is received in a total of 86 million homes. That would indicate that direct satellite-to-home companies add a net 9 million households to the cable networks' universe while the remaining seven million households subscribe to both cable and direct satellite. Remember that the broadcast networks distributed to households via cable and terrestrial, over-the-air signals are available in virtually 100 percent of the nation's 105 million homes.

According to Cable TV Facts and Nielsen, in 1986, cable networks' programming was available in 50 percent (45 million) of all homes. Its share of all television viewing that year was 10 percent.[5] Today, as previously observed, cable network channels are delivered into 86 million households while, importantly, the cable networks' share of viewing has grown to 41 percent in 2001. Another perspective on the surging success of cable programming is the increase in the hours per week of viewing. According to Nielsen, in 1989, US households spent a little less than 15 hours per week watching cable networks' programming. By 2001 the time spent with cable networks had increased to 29 hours and 49 minutes.[6]

In early 2002, Nielsen reported that for the first time ad-supported cable networks' share of viewing on a total-week, 24-hour basis had exceeded that of all broadcast television networks and stations (note that this excludes the pay channels such as HBO). The ad-supported cable networks received 44 percent of the audience while broadcast fell to 41 percent (down from 47.5 percent only one year earlier). The remaining 15 percent was spent with pay channels. [7]

The key drivers of cable's viewing share-of-audience increases are the rise in the number of cable networks now available to households and the substantial increase in investment in programming. More than 50 cable networks are received in at least 35 million households and that number ramps up each year. With cable systems and direct satellite-to-home services adding additional channel capacity, there is no indication that cable networks' viewing share will decrease. According to Paul Kagan & Associates, a highly-respected media industry research firm, in 2002 all cable networks spent a combined $7.6 billion to acquire and/or produce programming. Ten years earlier that number was $2 billion.[8]

At this point we have reviewed the number of homes cable programming reaches as well as the audience increases and the reasons for these increases. Now let us examine another metric of cable television's performance, one that influences many advertisers to allocate a greater percentage of their budgets to cable advertising: the affluence of cable households. As mentioned earlier, it is logical to believe that households with cable have higher incomes because cable is pay television and thus has an associated cost to consumers. Scores of qualitative research in recent years have confirmed this premise. Following are two recent highlights from research firm MRI Doublebase: (1) average US Household (HH) income in 2001 was $51,899; non-cable HH income was $41,626 and cable HH income was $56,172; and (2) product expenditures by cable HH exceeds that of non-cable HH by 10 percent or greater in out-of-home dining, auto insurance, tires, and furniture, to name a few.[9]

It is clear that the sales message that cable networks and systems present to both national and local advertisers is increasingly strong. That message essentially is that more households are subscribing to more cable programming, ratings and audience shares continue to rise, and cable households are more affluent than homes without cable programming. It is also clear that a portion of cable's advertising revenue's growth is coming from budgets that used to go to broadcast television networks and stations.

According to Robert Coen of McCann Erikson, the nation's most respected estimator of media advertising expenditures, the cable industry increased revenues at an average yearly rate of 13.6 percent between 1996 and 2001. This increase was the largest of any medium in the same five-year period. This 13.6 percent increase includes the advertising recession year of 2001, when cable revenue increased .5 percent over the previous year, broadcast television was down 13.3 percent, newspapers were down 9.8 percent, magazines were down 10.3 percent, radio was down 7.4 percent, and the Internet was down 11.6 percent—largely due to AOL's big slide.[10]

The cable networks, with $12 billion in ad revenues in 2001, garnered 32 percent of the national television revenues. With a current 44 percent of the viewing versus the broadcast networks' 41 percent, it can be expected that the cable networks will continue to take share of market from the broadcast networks and that their growth rate should substantially outpace that of broadcast networks as it has during the last five years.

In local advertising sales, the growth opportunity for cable systems is even greater than it is for local television stations. In recent years the MSOs have invested heavily, completing local market interconnects, acquiring state-of-the-art ad insertion and billing systems, and hiring more local sales representatives. With the tremendous disparity between audience share and revenue, and with the heavy investment, local cable advertising revenues are poised for great growth. And as we shall see, new interactive and household-addressable technology, which is nearly ready for market rollout, creates an even rosier future.

Selling Advertising and Cable Television: A Personal View

The various skills and disciplines that contribute to the successful selling of any advertising medium have been specified and discussed in this book. Nonetheless, throughout a career selling advertising for yellow pages, a trade magazine, and radio stations, working for a radio national sales representative firm, and managing salespeople at cable networks and systems, newspapers, television stations, syndicated television programs, and Internet sites, I have developed some opinions over the years about the media sales profession. I'll discuss one unique concept in the following section.

First, it is true that successful salespeople must be more knowledgeable about their product than about any of their advertisers or their agencies. That is because only with substantial knowledge of the strengths and of the weaknesses of your media can you supply your client with the best counsel on how to best buy it. To provide this counsel and have it accepted does not usually come so quickly and it is not dependent on product and market knowledge alone. From the beginning, the successful salesperson must earn the trust of a client. To do that usually means demonstrating and sustaining honesty and responsibility—doing what you promise a client you will do. It sounds simple, but many salespeople don't quite live up to it day after day. Consistently good behavior wins trust. If I were CEO or sales manager of a media organization, I would insist that all of my salespeople read Chapter 3 of this text and I would hold them to the ethical guidelines outlined in the chapter.

Ascertaining what your client really wants to achieve is sometimes not so obvious as you might think. As president of ESPN in the early 1980s, I received a call one day asking if I would like to meet with the founder of Nautilus, the exercise equipment maker. It was an October day that Arthur Jones arrived in my office, and we spent two hours together. He said he had 1 million dollars to spend but that he had to spend it all by December 31. Instead of asking him why, I extolled the unique benefits of adverting on ESPN—how we could expand Nautilus' market and the extraordinary number of commercials that I would provide for his $1 million. Finally, he looked at me and said, "Young man, your enthusiasm for your network is obvious, but you do not understand my need to spend all the money by year end, do you?" I fumbled and muttered that it had to be because he had an unusually large inventory of equipment and therefore wanted to maximize holiday sales. He looked at me and said, "Never assume what a client wants. Always ask, because customer knowledge is the most important asset a salesman can possess. Mr. Grimes, I must spend the 1 million dollars by December 31, or it will have to be counted as income and I will have to pay federal income taxes. Spending it on advertising, it becomes an expense and the $1 million will be deductible. Never have I owned a company that paid our government a penny in tax. Taxes are against my religion!"

Arthur Jones either liked or pitied me, but he wanted to spend his money with ESPN. Had I asked why he needed to spend that much money (in those days) in such a short time, I would have learned why and the sales call would have ended an hour and a half earlier. More importantly, I would have looked a lot smarter in my new client's eyes. Arthur Jones *both* liked and pitied me but enough of the former to endure the additional time spent to teach me a lesson not forgotten.

Also important is the knowledge of the market, and that means not only knowing your direct media competitors but also having a thorough understanding of other competing media properties in your geographic market. Being aware of changes in the daily newspaper's circulation and demographics is essential when selling for a radio or television station. Knowing the fundamentals of existing market and competitive research that enables you to quantify and qualify your medium's audience to the client is a necessity. Research on the client's business, while often overlooked, can be of crucial competitive importance, as you will see later.

Selling Advertising as a Return on Investment

At one point in my career, when I was responsible for a group of television stations and newspapers, I began one day to reevaluate all I had learned about selling advertising. The economy was weak in many of our key markets and advertising budgets were not increasing. Thus, driven by a desire to preserve my comfortable employment, I began to seek a more intelligent way to sell advertising than packaging the best combination of CPMs, reach, and frequency. To begin, I made the assumption that the most interested person at any client company should be its owner or chief executive. Next, I asked my sales managers and myself why companies advertise and why should they. The simple answer was that companies advertise to acquire and maintain customers for their business. Then I recognized that attracting new customers was not an economically sufficient reason. What company needs new customers if it loses money because of the cost of attracting them? The profit that a company achieves from the new customers generated by an advertising expenditure on my stations and newspapers must exceed the cost of the advertising. Note that I said profit, not sales.

It then occurred to my increasingly excited team of television and newspaper sales managers that the cost of advertising is a business expense to companies and that the same money spent in advertising its products or services could also be spent—or better, invested, as you have learned elsewhere in this book—on other projects or assets that could increase a company's profits. For example, the company could hire more people, it could open new stores or offices, it could buy other businesses, or it could simply take the money allocated for advertising and return it as a dividend to its shareholders.

Then it became clear to us all that advertising expenditures were indeed a business expense, but more importantly, an investment. When companies make investments of capital they expect a return on their investment (ROI). I had never spoken to CEOs or owners about their ROI expectations from advertising. However, I was now a CEO myself and had learned quickly that if I wanted to invest company money in a new project, develop a new product, or make an acquisition, I had to demonstrate an *expected return on investment* to my board of directors. Therefore, our advertising clients must have some expectation of the economic return on the money they invest in advertising with our stations or newspapers.

At last we sensed a breakthrough. What if we could demonstrate to the client some estimated ROI that he or she might find believable—an ROI estimate both believable and financially acceptable? Would that not lead to making the client very happy? And would that not lead to even more advertising? Wouldn't that help me keep my job as a major industry player? From that revelation I was determined to develop an ROI model for a large client of one of our stations or papers. To do that, I needed lots of information about that company's business, then I would need to test the ROI model with our salespeople.

The prospective client we selected was a large supermarket chain in St. Louis where we owned the leading television station. To gather the necessary information about its business that could not be found through our researching efforts at the station, I called the company's CEO who arranged for a meeting with his senior managers. In preparation we read the company's annual report and gathered as much information from local market sources that we could. At the beginning of the meeting I told the client that we were not there to talk about our station but to learn about their business and determine whether we could help improve profitability. "No media peddler has ever said that to me," the CEO stated. "Ask your questions."

First, we learned that the company owned 11 supermarkets in the St. Louis market which generated $200 million in sales and that its market share was 25 percent. Total sales annually in the market were therefore $800 million. The company's management also said their market share rank was third among the six competing supermarkets. Its operating, or pre-tax, profit margin was 3 percent (about average for the supermarket industry), which meant that after paying all operating expenses—cost of goods sold, salaries and benefits, rent, and marketing costs—the company had 3 percent of revenues remaining before paying taxes. We were also told that the lifetime of a customer of the company was a little over three years— that the supermarket chain's customers remained loyal customers for that period of time. Finally, and importantly, we learned that the shares of the company's stock were selling for 12 times the company's pre-tax profits.

We thanked management for the information and assured them that we would use it in confidence and that we would return with a recommendation to invest in advertising on our station only if we believed we could increase their profits and their shareholders' value. Note the words "invest," "increase," and "profits."

Back at the station, I asked our team the key question: did we believe that with a substantial expenditure of advertising on our station over a sustained period—at least a year—that our supermarket chain client could increase its share of market? And, if we believed that our station could grow the supermarket chain's business enough for it to have a positive and competitive ROI, could we convincingly present this to the client? Our salespeople, citing success stories of how several station advertisers had experienced solid market share increases, stated strongly their belief that with an expenditure of $1 million over the course of the year and by maximizing the commercial placement of the client's schedule and taking a solid creative approach, the supermarket could attain a 2-percent market share increase. With each market share point worth $8 million in total sales in the market (1 percent of $800 million total market supermarket sales) and with our client's 25-percent market share, that meant each share point increase was worth $2 million in sales for our client. It seemed to me that we could make a strong case that our supermarket client could likely receive a compelling ROI with his investment on our station.

We decided to build our ROI model on the client gaining a 1-percent market share increase—not the 2 percent our people felt achievable—because it would obviously be more believable to the client. With the 1 percent of market sales worth $2 million annually for our client, we now had to estimate what the incremental costs associated with our recommended program would be. First, there was the $1 million in additional advertising invested by the client on our station. We then assumed that for the 11 stores to generate $2 million in additional sales, it would not require much additional operating expense. It seemed unlikely that the stores would have to stay open more hours a day. Therefore, essential non-personnel costs such as rent, lighting, and heating expenses would not increase. We did build into our model $200,000 for several new checkout counter personnel and another $300,000 in miscellaneous expenses since we did not know as much about the supermarket business as our client did and because we wanted as few of our assumptions challenged by the client as possible.

Table 21.1 shows how the economics of our ROI program for our client looked.

Table 21.1 Advertising Return-on-Investment Analysis			
A. Investment in TV advertising=	$1,000,000	
B. Investment in 8 check-out personnel=	$ 200,000	
C. Miscellaneous expenses=	$ 300,000	
D. Total investment=	$1,500,000	D = A+B+C
E. 1% market share increase realized from TV advertising=	$2,000,000	
F. Increased pre-tax income=	$ 500,000	F = E-D
G. ROI=	50%	G = F/A

A 50-percent return on investment was almost 17 times the 3-percent ROI the supermarket chain was currently receiving on its shareholders' investment. Therefore, we knew the client—if he accepted our assumptions in our ROI model—would acknowledge that the ROI was more than acceptable. But I knew that there was one more vital piece of missing information that our client would find even more appealing.

Because we had learned that the equity value of the company was currently based upon a multiple of 12 times the company's pre-tax profits, we could now provide a believable estimate for the increase in the enterprise value of the supermarket chain company. This information is readily available for all publicly traded companies and can be determined for private companies relatively easily by any person trained in finance. Therefore, multiplying $500,000 (the incremental pre-tax profit the investment in advertising with our station produced) by 12 (the pre-tax multiplier the stock market had placed on the company's share price) resulted in an increase of $6 million in the market value of our supermarket chain. Assuming—and we did not look into this—that there were 50 million shares outstanding, the price per share of the company's stock would increase about 12 cents. This is the kind of information that CEOs like to hear. See Table 21.2 for the potential effect of the advertising investment on share price.

Table 21.2 **ROI Impact on** **Share Price** **Analysis**	A. Return on $1,000,000 advertising investment=	$ 500,000	
	B. Equity value of company multiple=	12	
	C. Increase in company market value=	$ 6,000,000	C = A×B
	D. Outstanding shares of stock=	50,000,000	
	E. Increase in value per share=	$.12	E = D/C

We added one more assumption to our ROI model that gained the attention and approval of the client's management team. We assumed that half of the incremental sales revenue, or $250,000, generated by the advertising on our station would come from current customers spending more money per shopping visit. The other half we assumed would come from new customers. Since the client had told us before that new customers remain with stores an average of three years, we then estimated that our advertising program would also add $250,000 more in profits during the two years following the advertising campaign on our station, even if the $1 million advertising investment was not continued. This additional pre-tax profit also increased the already high ROI on the $1 million investment and it would positively impact the share price in the following two years as well.

It is important to note here that we did not attempt to persuade the client to allocate any of his current advertising budget to our $1 million-investment ROI proposal. We believed that if we proposed any of the dollars the client was currently spending on media in St. Louis, including investment on our station, were re-allocated, he may well argue that his current share of market sales could be offset to some degree. We knew that our ROI proposal had to be judged on its own merits as a new and incremental investment opportunity and to suggest switching any of its current advertising investment to our proposal would lead to a debate on existing market share and possibly upon existing relationships the client may value.

Two meetings later, we had the sale. Two wonderful other things happened. The salespeople had reason to believe that advertising on our stations or in our newspapers meant a lot more than cost-per-thousand and cost-per-point. Advertising was a very valuable investment made by a company, and discussing ROI with senior management was a smart way to build a really deep relationship with a client. And that leads to the next wonderful thing that happened: the CEO of the supermarket chain wrote and said, "Never before have I worked with media people who knew something about business, finance, and corporate value. Your team was a combination of the best consulting firm and investment banker we have used."

The Competitive Advantages of Cable TV Advertising

Advertising on cable television has many of the benefits of other media and certain unique advantages.

First, it has the sight, sound, and motion of television, which of course, it is. For most consumer products, the unmatchable power of sight, sound, and motion is acknowledged to drive sales more than any other medium.

As with magazines, cable's segmented programming attracts viewers with highly desirable demographics. ESPN, as an example, has a high percentage of men viewers in its audience. This high male audience composition results in less waste audience for an advertiser for whose products men are the primary buyers.

Cable also shares radio's ability to inexpensively add frequency to an advertising schedule. Increased frequency occurs because when buying advertising on one station in radio or one channel in cable, audiences remain loyal to the narrow genre of the programming. As a schedule of commercials air on that channel, frequency builds because many of the same people view for longer periods of time and return the next day and next week to the same channel. These channels have loyal viewers.

Cable advertising also adds reach to an advertising campaign that consists of only broadcast television. There are still some advertisers who spend most of their advertising dollars in broadcast television. Because such a campaign would under-deliver in cable homes, the broadcast campaign would likely reach a lower audience than planned on and the audience it would reach would have, in general, lower income levels than a similar schedule on cable would. Allocating some of a broadcast-only budget to cable would offset some or all of this loss and improve the overall demographics of the buy. See the CAB Web site (www.cabletvadbureau.com) for specific examples of how reach is added to a broadcast television advertising campaign by the substitution of some cable for broadcast in the schedule.

An advantage of cable television advertising that only weekly newspapers or direct mail can claim is the delivery of an audience in a small geographic area or trading zone. In most markets there is more than one cable system head end, which means that the television commercial can be distributed to subscribers in more than one smaller geographic subset of a market. Thus, in New York City an advertiser who wants to reach only consumers in Queens County can do so without having to buy advertising on the cable systems in the four other boroughs. This geographic targeting of consumers is increasing throughout the country as cable systems add new technology. The result is that the advent of these smaller trading zones is providing cable television with a new competitive advantage for advertisers. Smaller geographic audience delivery also is enabling cable systems, for the first time, to compete effectively with small weekly newspapers, direct mail, and penny savers (free weekly newspapers).

Another more generic advantage of cable as an advertising medium is that its commercial unit cost is invariably lower than that of its broadcast competitors. This is particularly true in local cable sales where the systems have not attracted nearly the share of advertising revenue that their share of viewing should dictate. Therefore, not only is the system's commercial price significantly lower than that of the market's television stations on a dollar basis, but its cost-per-thousand viewers delivered to the advertiser are also much lower than those of broadcast stations.

I mentioned earlier that cable reaches households with higher incomes than broadcast television does. This advantage translates into a cable household spending more money on virtually every advertised product and service, and, thus, those households are much more attractive to advertisers, especially those of upscale products such as Mercedes, financial services, or premium wine.

The Future of Cable Television Advertising

To better understand what lies ahead for cable television advertising we must look at its changing technology. At the beginning of this chapter we learned that the early cable systems, using broad bandwidth of copper coaxial cable wires, had the capacity to deliver more content—video, audio and text—than was available to them at the time. Just as satellite technology's arrival in 1975 dramatically changed the cable industry, another technology breakthrough occurred in the '90s that would have an equally dramatic impact— the deployment of fiber optics.

You will recall that the early cable systems delivered programming from their head ends through coaxial cable into subscribers' homes. Fiber optics is another form of distribution of content but instead of using wires, it consists of a number of tiny strands of optically pure glass, each of which is capable of delivering hundreds of video channels over distances much longer than coaxial cable. These fiber optic strands are coated with a jacket that protects them from damage and moisture.

During the last decade the cable industry has replaced coaxial trunk lines with fiber optics and has thereby created a new cable system configuration or network. Called HFC for Hybrid Fiber Cable system, this combination of coaxial cable and fiber optics is enabling cable to deliver more services to the home. It works this way: the information, including video and audio channels, Internet data, and telephony capabilities, is sent from the cable head end down the main streets or thoroughfares of a city through bandwidth-rich fiber optic trunk lines. These trunk lines branch off the main distribution routes into nodes, or information centers, each of which addresses only 200 to 500 households. Prior to HFC, the same coaxial line would have served all households in the market and had the negative effect of reducing bandwidth of coaxial and deterioration of the signal quality. This technology means that households in each node can receive, for example, different commercials in the same programming than households in the adjacent neighborhood node.

HFC also enables the delivery of data via the Internet at high speeds and high quality because fiber optics are much more effective than coaxial cable at carrying the data through the main trunk lines of the market and coaxial cable is much faster from the trunk line to the home—"the last mile"—than telephone wires. Cable systems in some markets such as San Diego are also using HFC to provide telephone service for their cable subscribers. In that market Cox Communications provides cable television, high-speed Internet access, and local and long distance telephony—all on one bill and at a discount to its customers.

An even newer technology than fiber optics, the advanced software contained in the coming generation of new cable set-top boxes, will soon have a large impact upon the media and advertising industries. It will enable: (1) Internet Protocol (IP) Telephony, a newly-developed system of converting voice into digital packets over the Internet and converting the message back into analog voice at the receiver end at lower costs than today's analog phone line telephone system; (2) multimedia conferencing, which allows people to engage in video conversations with many others from their homes; (3) interactive gaming, which will permit many simultaneous players competing at "twitch speed;" and (4) Video-on-Demand (VOD), a long-awaited service which provides the viewing of any movie at the moment the consumer wants to view it. Additional server capacity in the home, in addition to the new set-top boxes, will permit VOD in cable households soon.

What do these technology enhancements mean for Cable television's ability to better compete with other media for advertising revenues? Three advertising-related applications from the new set-top boxes are of interest. First, and most significant, multiple television commercials in one network slot will be sent simultaneously within the programming throughout the cable systems. The network or systems with knowledge of the demographics and buying preferences of each household will be able to select which of the many commercials for the same advertiser will be seen in each specific household. The advantages of precision customer targeting and the resulting advertising effectiveness will greatly benefit the advertiser, making cable ever more competitive.

The new cable technology also enables the uplinking of cue messages that alert the advertising equipment located in cable system head ends that a basketball game, for example, has gone into overtime. It then, in real time, automatically selects and inserts correctly-priced commercials to run in the nonscheduled overtime portion of the game. This capability will save cable sales managers many headaches because they will have pre-selected alternative commercials, already priced, prior to the telecast, so there is no worry of calling the system or network about what commercials to insert and then later how to price them.

Because the technology favors digitizing all content, the set-top box and head end equipment also permits the real-time insertion of digital commercials into digital program streams of live network feeds. This process means that at the last instant before a commercial is scheduled to run in a cable program, the advertiser could select a different commercial and, through its agency, for example, alert the network digitally and select a different 30-second commercial.

The future of set-top box addressability raises the question of audience measurement. When this new technology is pervasive in cable households, will advertisers, ad agencies, cable networks and systems, and broadcast networks and stations need Nielsen to estimate viewing audiences? Will Nielsen's NTI people meter universe of 6,000 households be even remotely able to compete with cable's 70 million+ households, each with its own people meter installed within the set-top box? Furthermore, will current audience measurement—the number of people estimated to be viewing a channel or program—even matter when advertisers will know exactly how many people in each specific home saw their commercial? With call-in phone numbers to buy the advertised product and virtual coupons for the advertised product printed out from the set-top box, advertisers will know how many sales were generated from each commercial.

The speed at which technology is affecting television's ability to provide advertisers with more applications to better communicate with its customers is rapidly increasing. Because cable television has built a content distribution system that has infinitely more bandwidth than any other medium, its growth in subscribers, viewing, and advertising expenditures will be the envy of all media. Those of you seeking a career in media selling will have the opportunity in cable television to better use your own imaginations to develop new advertising solutions for your clients' advertising and marketing challenges.

Test Yourself

1. What does CATV stand for and why is it important in the history of cable?
2. In the early days of cable, how many channels were offered and what programming was on those channels?
3. What federal agency regulates broadcasting but not cable?

4. What type of regulation is there for local cable systems?
5. Who was the "Mouth of the South" and why was he important?
6. What programming service was the first to go up in 1975 on the RCA satellite?
7. Who changed the business model of the cable network business by first charging MSOs a carriage fee?
8. What is an ROI analysis?

Project

Visit or call your local cable television company and find out what packages they offer for different tiers of programming and services (including digital, if available) and what the monthly charge is for each package. Include telephone service, a broadband Internet connection, and digital if they offer it. Then, call DirectTV and EchoStar and gather the same information. Compare the prices, number of channels, and different types of programming and services.

Resources

www.cabletvadbureau.com
www.nielsenmedia.com
www.sbca.com
www.kagan.com
www.adage.com

Endnotes

1. www.cabletvadbureau.com. November 3, 2002
2. www.nielsenmedia.com. January, 14, 2003.
3. www.cabletvadbureau.com. January 12, 2003
4. http://www.sbca.com/mediaguide/factsfigures.htm. January 14, 2003
5. www.cabletvadbureau.com. January 14, 2003
6. ibid.
7. ibid.
8. www.kagan.com. January 14, 2003
9. www.cabletvadbureau.com. January 14, 2003
10. www.adage.com/pagecms?pid=600. January 14, 2003

22 Yellow Pages

By Joseph Buchman

"Television ads get attention; yellow pages ads get the sales."[1]

In 1881, the Chicago Directory Company, whose primary business was the publication of local business directories, published its first telephone directory for what was then the Chicago Telephone Company. This phone book is generally acknowledged as containing the first example of telephone directory advertising, the medium that we know today as the yellow pages. The Chicago Directory Company eventually became the R.H. Donnelley Company, one of the largest independent marketers of yellow pages advertising in the United States. R.H. Donnelley publishes more than 175 different directories with a total circulation of more than 15 million.

The origin of the term *yellow pages* appears to go back to 1883 when a printer in Cheyenne, WY ran out of white paper for a local directory and substituted yellow. In 1909, the Saint Louis phone company produced the first yellow pages with coupons. Today, more than 6,500 different directories are published each year to serve virtually every home and business in America.[2]

Prior to the development of the Internet, the only media that could claim to attract potential buyers *immediately prior to a sale* were point-of-purchase displays and the yellow pages. Since the early 1900s, the yellow pages have offered a unique and highly valuable environment for influencing product purchases. Even today, no other advertising media can so exclusively target its advertising messages to only those who are about to buy. For this reason, the yellow pages are known as a *directive medium,* as opposed to newspapers, television, and radio, for example, which are *reactive media*. The yellow pages *direct* predisposed buyers where to find a product *after* they have made up their minds that they need or want it.

Today the yellow pages advertising industry generates more than $15 billion in revenue and has seen explosive growth since the breakup of AT&T in 1984. The late 1980s saw the entry of dozens of competing publishers, but by the late 1990s the industry was again dominated by the Regional Bell Operating Companies (RBOCs). Today, local phone company publishers account for just over 90 percent of yellow pages advertising revenues while the independents, such as TransWestern, McLeod, and Yellow Book account for about 9 percent. Local carriers are anticipated to remain the dominant force in yellow pages publishing, due to their ability to package local phone service, Internet access, and yellow pages advertising.

Because the yellow pages offers almost 100 percent penetration in nearly every market in the United States, and because more than 85 percent of yellow pages advertising revenue is derived from local businesses, the downturn in national advertising associated with the economic recession has not appeared to slow the growth of yellow pages as an advertising medium.

A Directive Medium

While there are exceptions to most every rule of advertising, it is the very rare yellow pages reader who is just looking through the book for fun or for its entertainment or educational value. Some people may use the yellow pages from time to time to get a sense of the ethnic or religious diversity of a community (by looking at listings under "restaurants" and "churches," for example). Other readers may be salespeople for business-to-business marketing firms or radio or television stations looking for potential clients. For these readers, the yellow pages is often called the "Prospector's Bible," because of its usefulness in developing a list of prospective advertising clients. But for the most part, advertising messages in the yellow pages are seen only by consumers with a high motivation to purchase a product or service within the next few hours or minutes. No other medium can make this claim so effectively.

Think about your own behavior when faced with a broken furnace, sudden travel emergency, backed-up plumbing, or a toothache; where do you turn for information? If you have water pouring into your basement, are you going to run to the television to wait for the next plumbing commercial, grab the local paper to look through the classified or display advertising, or log onto the Internet to search for the nearest plumber? For information about products or services that can solve immediate or emergency needs, the yellow pages are impossible to beat.

Yellow pages advertising is also an effective medium for reaching the newest residents of a local community. Few other media can reach prospective customers so soon after they move into a new city. This is especially important in communities with a high population turnover such as college towns, tourist destinations, and those near military bases. Again, imagine your own behavior shortly after moving to a new town. Where would you first seek information about the closest movie theater, hardware store, dry cleaner, Tibetan restaurant, dentist, or pizza parlor? With a far smaller group of contacts, friends, and family than long-term residents, new residents really have only one place to turn. The yellow pages are extremely valuable in shaping the early purchase decisions and ultimate retail outlet loyalty of the newest residents of any community.

Many job seekers, when interviewing for a position in a new town, will take a copy of the yellow pages home with them to ease the transition should they accept an offer. Knowing this, most yellow pages publishers provide the major hotel chains with extra copies. By the way, your local library probably has a collection of yellow pages directories from around the United States and overseas. It is a great resource for researching a local community before going there for a job interview or some other business or recreational purpose.

Yellow pages advertising targets potential customers who are *seeking information for a known product or service*. Unlike television, radio, or other print media, yellow pages advertising does not work well at all in changing customer loyalty to brands, generating initial brand awareness, or introducing new products or services. This is because top-of-the–mind awareness, brand recognition, and the like are the result of frequency of exposure to advertising messages. Brand recognition requires frequent exposures which cost a great deal of money and can generally be afforded only by larger businesses. Herein lies the relative importance of yellow pages advertising for small businesses that need a much more targeted and directive marketing approach than mass advertising media can provide. The yellow pages also work extremely well for infrequently needed, highly specialized products and services that would seldom be advertised in most other media, such as tree stump removal, cosmetic surgery, and chimney sweeping.

For these reasons and the relatively limited amount of competition in yellow pages publishing, yellow pages advertising is both extraordinarily expensive and extraordinarily valuable. Yellow pages was a virtual monopoly until a few years ago. A career selling yellow pages advertising can be lucrative, but it may also require frequent travel away from home. While many of today's yellow pages sales representatives are able to work out of central call centers, traditionally, yellow pages advertising salespeople lived out of a suitcase, moving from town to town as each community's book was closed and sent to the publishers.

Yellow pages advertising in any given book is sold only once a year, in a relatively short window of time before each edition closes. When calling on prospective clients in some small towns, yellow pages salespeople may only be present for a day or two. In other words, a yellow pages salesperson may have only one chance each year, sometimes as short as 48 hours in any given location, to sell each prospective client their one yellow pages ad for the year.

Because of this schedule, yellow pages advertisers will expect their salespeople to help them design the most effective display ad, to place it in the most effective listing, and to review with them all other possible headings where they might want to advertise as well.

Look around the location where you are reading this chapter now. How far away is the nearest yellow pages? If you can find a copy nearby, look to see how old it is. Even when the new book hits the streets, it may take several months or more for the average household to throw away (or recycle) all their old copies of the yellow pages and begin using only the new edition. It seems people are always finding a three-year-old copy of the yellow pages around their homes and no one in the house seems to know where the new ones have gone.

Yellow pages advertisements are purchased for a full year at a time. For core book advertising, the advertising purchased from the local phone company, the monthly cost of an ad is added to a business's telephone bill. Governmental regulations prevent the phone company from disconnecting a business phone for non-payment of yellow pages advertising. Therefore, the only way for the business to stop the monthly bill for its yellow pages ad (which can be as high as $2,000 per month for a display ad in a medium to large market), is to ask the phone company to disconnect its business phone. That's why independent publishers, and increasingly the telephone companies, sometimes demand full payment for the year's worth of yellow pages advertising in advance.

Because yellow pages advertising is sold in year-long increments, it lacks the *immediacy* of other print, broadcast, cable, and Interactive advertising media. In other words, a yellow pages display ad designed today needs to be accurate and effective as long as two years from now. Specific information about products and pricing is rarely mentioned in a yellow pages ad, and there is never anything about special sales, discounts, or one-time-only offers. This is also a reason why local businesses are loath to change their phone numbers.

Competing media salespeople use this lack of immediacy against the yellow pages. On the other hand, yellow pages sales representatives emphasize the *durability* of their product. Compared to advertisements in the other *ephemeral* media—they disappear almost as soon as they are aired or run in the local paper—the yellow pages go on and on and on. More than 7,000 different yellow pages books are published each year. That means yellow pages salespeople are making their final calls for nearly 30 yellow pages books across the nation each day.

National Campaigns

While national advertising accounts for only about 15 percent of total yellow pages revenue, those campaigns are vital to some industries. Selling a client a national yellow pages campaign can be very difficult due to the large number of publishers, their almost Byzantine (and sometimes secret) pricing strategies, and the differences in the books' size of the paper, number of columns, color printing options, and geographical areas served.

Today about 10 companies account for the bulk of yellow pages publishing, but there are dozens of smaller but viable regional publishers as well, including specialty directories and ethnicity-specific directories. The only effective way for an advertiser to purchase a national advertising campaign in the yellow pages is with the assistance of a certified marketing representative (CMR)—the yellow pages equivalent of a national spot or rep salesperson.

If a national advertiser is unhappy with a campaign that is running in any of the ephemeral media, the campaign can usually be pulled overnight or changed within a few days. However, problems with an existing national yellow pages campaign will take more than a full year to change because the new ads roll out from market to market and as each market's book hits the street. When national advertisers decide to change their toll-free numbers, brand names, or slogans, that can be accomplished in most other media within a few days. However, in the yellow pages, the old number, brand name, or slogan will live on for up to 18 months.

Local Campaigns

Yellow pages sales representatives spend most of their efforts on relatively small local businesses such as attorneys, restaurants, automobile dealerships, physicians, and the like. In almost all markets, two or three different yellow pages publishers compete for this business. Some publishers offer only one version of the book, while others may offer highly specialized or targeted directories. When more than one publisher of a yellow pages directory competes for broad coverage in a market, the books are said to be overlapping. The most common forms of specialized books are business-to-business, senior (or "silver"), college dorm or military base housing, neighborhood (covering specific suburban areas within a large city), non-English language (Hispanic or Asian), and gay community directories. The silver pages, proved to be a dismal failure in most markets and are seldom published any more.

Yellow pages salespeople may be expected to sell the core book in a given area, to sell the core book as an overlapping book in an adjacent area, and to sell a number of specialty directories. Yellow pages sales reps must guide their prospects and clients to the most effective combination of advertising possible.

Seldom, if ever, is a strategy of buying all the books in a market in the client's best interest. Most yellow pages consultants recommend a strategy of placing the bulk of their client's yellow pages advertising in the book with the largest circulation, and never buying in more than two books in all but the very largest markets. In practice, over the past decade this strategy has had the effect of reducing the number of viable overlapping and specialty books to two or three per market.

Yellow Pages Advertising Options

Yellow pages books are published in three basic styles:

1. Five-column books (mostly Pac Bell and GTE in California)
2. Four-column books
3. Three-column books

To make their book more valuable to users, most publishers offer every business a free listing in the yellow pages. Unfortunately, those free listings are derisively referred to as the "squint-and-print" listings. The first upgrade from a print-and-squint listing is the purchase of a bold listing, then an additional line or two under the free listing. Some publishers require a minimum ad size of one-half per column inch, while others require a minimum of three-fourths of a column inch. Some books allow for an additional single color (usually red), others offer full-color printing (with yellow as the background), and still others offer the option for a white background. Display ads can run from a small, one-column box to a full page, or even double-page ad.

Research by The Thomas Register shows that the biggest display ad on a page outpolls a single line listing by more than 40 times.[3] It is important for yellow pages salespeople to be well-versed in every option available to their clients, not only in their company's book, but also in each of the competing books offered in their market as well. Years of tenure in a yellow pages book by the advertiser will determine the placement of the display ad. For most publishers, advertisers who have been in the yellow pages for the most consecutive years will have the first choice for the placement of their ads. When an advertiser moves to a different sized ad, their tenure starts over.

Scoping

Before a directory can be assembled, a publisher will scope it. Scoping is the process of determining the geographic area and listing content of a directory. Each publisher has its own scoping criteria. Generally, business listings, in addition to the white pages listings, will receive one free listing in the yellow pages.

In a study published in the *American Journal of Small Business*, researchers found that even when a customer knows the name of a specific business, but not its phone number, two-thirds of the time he or she will look it up in the yellow pages rather than in the white pages. That means 66 percent of customers who use the yellow pages to look up a specific business phone number will also be exposed to advertising for many of the company's strongest competitors.[4]

Copy Strategies

Writing copy for yellow pages advertising requires a different perspective than that of almost any other advertising medium. Copywriters for the broadcast and print media know they must attract the attention or interest of their prospective viewers, listeners, or readers. They use attention-getting techniques such as bright colors, fast movement, and loud sounds. The yellow pages audience (if it can be thought of as an audience) is already actively looking to make a purchase. Therefore, such attention-getting strategies are not necessary. Instead, yellow pages salespeople tend to emphasize copy points that are not designed to get attention, but to close the sale.

One traditional formula, still used by many today to evaluate effective yellow pages copy, is RASCIL: Reliability, Authorized provider, Specialty, Completeness, Illustration, and Location.

Price, detailed product descriptions, comparisons to competitors, and appeals to ignore other advertising are all prohibited in almost all yellow pages books.

Alan Saltz of Guaranteed Marketing suggests this scenario for developing yellow pages advertising copy:

> Imagine a customer is standing in front of you and six of your competitors. Each of you gets the chance to make one quick statement to get the customer to choose you. Now, would that ever happen? Um, no. *But* . . . the similarities between that situation and your yellow pages ad are striking. Your ad needs to stand out among your competitors, grab attention, and *keep it*.[5]

The yellow pages are the ultimate cluttered advertising environment. Potential clients can quickly compare dozens and sometimes hundreds of businesses and their offers within a few minutes.

Barry Maher, one of the nation's premiere yellow pages and general management consultants, developed the following Ten Commandments of Yellow Pages Advertising, which are directed at yellow pages advertisers:

The Ten Commandments of Yellow Pages Advertising

First Commandment: Thou Shalt Not Whip It Up. Many yellow pages ads are whipped up in the few minutes the salesperson has left after trying to sell you a bigger ad. Ask—no, insist—that your directory publishers develop an ad for you that justifies the cost. If they can't or won't, have the ad produced yourself.

Second Commandment: Honor Thy Headlines. The first piece of ad copy that readers see—the headline—has to be powerful enough to drag them away from all those competing ads. Never use your company name as your headline unless it really is that powerful—unless it really is the most important *selling* copy in the ad.

Third Commandment: Honor Thy Illustration. Nothing can turn a mediocre yellow pages ad into a great one faster than the right illustration. If your picture isn't worth a thousand words, find one that is.

Fourth Commandment: Remember All Key Selling Points. You have to include *all* the hard, factual information potential customers need to make a decision to call or drop by, be it about image, market niche, type of cuisine, specialties, additional services, pricing, quality, speed, hours, location, credit cards—whatever it might be.

Fifth Commandment: Thou Shalt Not Overburden the Eyeballs.   Your ad is competing for visibility and readability with every other ad under the heading. If it's difficult to read, it isn't going to be read. You've got to refine your copy until you can provide all the information directory users want and need in an ad that's so uncluttered and inviting that reading it becomes automatic.

Sixth Commandment: Thou Shalt Not Forget Placement.   Unfortunately, ad size is important. All things being equal, bigger ads get a greater response. They also get the best placement—closest to the front of the heading. And placement can be even more important than size.

The good news is that all things are seldom equal. The biggest ad under the heading is not always the most effective. And a well-designed, visually appealing ad can make up for a lot of size, especially under a smaller heading where all the ads are on the same page or two. It's much more difficult, of course, to compete with ads on an earlier page. That page may never even be turned.

Always consider placement when you're deciding on ad size. Have your salesperson show you where the size you're considering would fall in this year's directory. That should give you an approximate idea of the position—relative to the competition—you'd have next year. Sometimes going up a single size and spending just a few more dollars will move you much closer to the front of the heading. Sometimes you can cut back in size without losing much at all in the way of position.

Seventh Commandment: Remember, Position over Color.   Color *is* eye catching. It's also expensive. If the money you'd be spending is approximately the same, you're far better off significantly improving the size and placement of your ad than the color.

Eighth Commandment: Thou Shalt Track.   Perhaps the surest way to waste money is to advertise in a directory no one's using. Always make your salesperson *prove* value, especially when you're considering an independent (non-phone company) directory. If he can't, don't put any real money there. Instead, try something small, perhaps even a simple in-column ad or even just a listing. Track your response—survey your customers to discover how *they* discovered *you*—and next year you'll have your own proof. One way or the other.

Ninth Commandment: Thou Shalt Not Squander Yellow Pages Dollars in the White Pages.   You bought that costly new in-column ad in the white pages because . . . ?

If you're Albany Emporium and you're in the midst of seven white pages of Albany this and Albany that, you do need something beyond a bold listing to make it easier for your customers to find you. Or perhaps you're Ralph's Refrigeration, and Randal Refrigeration Service usually falls on the same page, and you want to siphon off a few of their calls.

Otherwise? If your customers are looking for you alphabetically in the white pages, they will find you. And call you. You don't have any competition in the white pages. A bold listing is sufficient. Save your hard-earned advertising dollars for the yellow pages.

Tenth Commandment: Never Rely on Faith for Your Yellow Pages: Get a Proof.   Always insist on getting a proof for your display ad. Remember the small error one publisher made in an advertiser's ad, turning "Dan Hadley, therapist" into, "Dan Hadley, the rapist."[6]

Measuring the Effectiveness of Yellow Pages Advertising

Before the advent of non-telco publishers, AT&T was able to fairly easily determine the effectiveness of different sized-yellow pages advertising. In a series of classic experiments, a specific local business was given a series of different sized ads in different copies of a single edition of the yellow pages in a community. In other words, in some of the books the business had a simple, in-column listing; in others the business had a very small display ad; and in yet others the business had a large display ad. Each ad contained a unique phone number (different from the other two ads) that was then rerouted to a phone line at the business after going through a counting mechanism at the phone company. The yellow pages directories were distributed randomly throughout the community, with about one-third receiving the smallest ad, one-third the medium ad, and one-third the large ad. In this way the telephone company could determine the effectiveness of the different-sized ads based on actual telephone calls placed by real customers.

One such experiment was for Neff Plumbing in Youngstown, OH. In that study the in-column listing generated 241 calls, the one and one-half-inch ad generated 443 calls, and the large display ad generated 1,382 calls. More surprising was the finding that more than half of the calls were from old customers who had looked up one of Neff Plumbing's new phone numbers in the yellow pages listing.[7] Even an advertiser's most loyal customers are not likely to remember the advertiser's phone number, and more than half of them are likely to look for the number in the yellow pages. Once there, they will be exposed to many of the advertiser's competitor's ads. That's why it is vital for an advertiser's yellow pages ad to stand out from all the others.

Types of Yellow Pages Books

The Core Book   The core book was the yellow pages directory published by the local phone company back when there was a monopoly on publishing phone books. For this reason, core books were distributed based on the technical determination of the local calling area within a community, rather than on actual shopping behavior. Today, the biggest book is likely to be published by the company that was once part of the local telephone monopoly, but they are more likely to distribute it to a geographic area determined by shopping patterns rather than what had been the local calling area. The telco-published books are still the dominant books in most markets, and for this reason they are still called the core book. The core book, because it is owned by the local phone company, usually will allow advertisers to be billed monthly, starting with the date the book hits the street. In most cases the advertising bill is just added to the business's phone bill. Non-telco publishers sometimes require advance payment. Because they are independent publishers, they may need the up-front payment to cover the cost of printing and distributing the book.

The Neighborhood Book

Neighborhood books are published in larger cities in an attempt to provide an alternative for businesses with small local retail trade areas. Imagine you own a dry cleaning company in Los Angeles. Chances are, no matter how good your advertising campaign, few prospective customers will drive past more than one or two other dry cleaners to reach your front door. For this reason, advertising in a core book would generate perhaps as much as 95 percent wasted coverage. Neighborhood books provide what can be a more effective and less expensive alternative, *if the books are actually used.* Remember, it will not matter how many books a yellow pages publisher prints if consumers find the core book more valuable.

Neighborhood books also create problems for clients who have a large retail trade area. Those clients are faced with a choice of advertising in the core book and each of the neighborhood books, in essence doubling or tripling their expected yellow pages advertising expense, or of losing exposure to those areas where the neighborhood book is effective. Of course, this is almost impossible to determine prior to the first edition or two of a neighborhood book.

Yellow pages salespeople must advise their large retail, trade area clients about the best strategy. In some cases they may not have a clue either, other than to point out how similar books have done in comparable markets. Most often, yellow pages clients will choose to advertise only in the core book, or dramatically reduce the size of their ads (and thus their useful information) in the neighborhood books. When this becomes common practice, neighborhood-book households are likely to find the neighborhood book less valuable and either burn it as kindling, or not be able to find where they have hidden it in the house, even when they are looking for a neighborhood business. This is referred to as the difference between the book's *coverage*—the number of copies distributed in a given area—and its actual *usage*—readership. Thus, many publishers of neighborhood books will authorize their salespeople to cut prices for larger ads when experiencing client reluctance. More than in any other advertising medium, it is in the yellow pages publisher's interest to have advertising that contains useful and detailed information. Once the book is established as the preferred book, ad rates may rise dramatically.

Another advantage of the neighborhood book for clients with smaller retail trade areas is that they can advertise "free delivery" or "free pick-up" without having to include a map (which would be the case if they were to use those incentives in a core book.)

Overlay Books

Overlay books occur when two or more yellow pages publishers decide to cover the same geographic area. They can also occur when the publisher in a nearby city decides to include the other city (or part of the other city) in the next edition of their book. The greatest weaknesses of overlay books are their lack of targeting and excessive wasted coverage.

Specialty Books

Specialty books include business-to-business directories and those published for college dorms, the elderly, women, gays, Hispanics, and Asians. In my office, for example, I have a copy of the "Cable Television" yellow pages, with listings for every cable television system in the US, and yellow pages ads for program suppliers, consultants, and equipment manufacturers nationwide. Indeed, some historians trace the development of the yellow pages back to

England in the 1600s, long before the invention of the telephone, when the first business directories, with addresses only, were produced.

Online or Internet Yellow Pages

Want to find a manufacturer of calliopes (steam-powered showboat organs), a bed and breakfast with a view of an active volcano, or all the indoor sky diving locations in Tennessee? I know there's one in Pigeon Forge. One of my sales classes at the University of Tennessee met there one day to "overcome fear." Obviously, this is where the Internet, whether in the form of a yellow pages type of site or a simple Google search, has become an effective alternative to a printed directory.

Compensation and Training

Traditionally, yellow pages salespeople were paid strictly on a commission based on an advertiser's increase, or overage, from the previous year. That commission produced a tremendous incentive for yellow pages reps to attempt to sell larger and larger ads each year. Simply taking an order for a continuation of the same size ad resulted in zero compensation to a yellow pages sales representative. In the days before deregulation, when the local phone company held a monopoly on yellow pages advertising, this sort of high-pressure sales approach was tolerated. Today, most yellow pages salespeople are paid on a combination of base salary and commission. Financial incentives are still offered to encourage selling larger ads, but it is more of a carrot than a stick. In markets with two or more competitive books, compensation may be geared to simply keeping current accounts.

Because of the pressure to constantly increase the size of yellow pages ads, or to add expensive new features such as color, other media salespeople attempt to convince their clients to shift yellow pages advertising dollars to their station or channel. Both the Radio Advertising Bureau (RAB) and Television Bureau of Advertising (TVB) offer research pointing to the value of moving to a smaller yellow pages ad and investing the dollars saved into radio or television. This is typically a difficult sell, because the clients who choose to do this will lose their tenure in the book and will face extraordinary pressure from the yellow pages rep.

Yellow pages salespeople are among the best trained of all media salespeople. Six-week training courses are offered with an oral final exam in front of previously certified yellow pages sales managers and supervisors. Yellow pages salespeople and advertisers are also more aware of what their competitors are actually doing than most media salespeople. While they may or may not know their competitors' radio or television schedules, it is much easier for them to see what their clients' competitors are doing in the yellow pages.

Test Yourself

1. What are the differences between the core, overlay, and specialty books?
2. How does the way yellow pages salespeople are compensated affect the methods they use to sell the book?
3. What is the RASCIL formula?
4. What percentage of yellow pages advertisers are local? What percentage are national? How does this affect yellow pages revenues during economic recessions?
5. What is scoping?

6. What is meant by "tenure in the book?"
7. Why is yellow pages called a "directive medium"?
8. What copy points that are commonly used in other media generally not included in yellow pages advertising?
9. Why is yellow pages said to be more durable than other media?
10. Why have neighborhood books generally been less successful?

Project

Go to your largest local library and ask to see their yellow pages section, which is usually located in the reference collections. Pick 10 yellow pages directories at random. Notice whether they are core, neighborhood, specialty, or overlapping books. Also note which company published each directory. Write a report comparing and contrasting the differences in the books.

References

Avery M. Abernethy and David Laband. 1999. *The Influence of Price, Population, and New Residents on the Purchase of Service Marketer's Yellow Page Display Ads.* Journal of Advertising Research 39, 5: pp. 15 to 26.

Karen V. Fernandez and Dennis L. Rosen. 2000. *The Effectiveness of Information and Color in Yellow Pages Advertising.* Journal of Advertising, 29 (Summer), pp. 59 to 73.

Thomas Foster. 1995 *Turning Yellow Pages to Gold* T&E Publishing: Largo, FL.

Barry Maher. 1997. *Getting the Most from Your Yellow Pages Advertising: Maximum Profits at Minimum Cost.* Newport, RI: Aegis Publishing Group.

Resources

www.buyyellow.com
www.barrymaher.com
www.max-effect.com
www.yellowpagesima.com
www.yellowpagesprofit.com

Endnotes

1. Maher, Barry. 1997 *Yellow Pages Advertising: Maximum Profits at Minimum Cost.* Newport RI: Aegis Publishing Group. p. 31.
2. Yellow Pages Integrated Media Association 2002 Industry Revenue Forecast.
3. Yin, Sandra. 2002. "The Reach of the Yellow Pages." American Demographics. November 2002, Vol. 24, Issue 10. p.24.
4. Ibid.
5. "How to (Legally) 'Steal' Business From Your Competition 'Armed' With a Yellow Pages Ad." http://www.yellowpagesprofit.com January 22, 2003.
6. Used with permission from *The Ten Commandments of Yellow Pages Advertising* by Barry Maher. Barry can be reached at *www.barrymaher.com;* Box 1104, Helendale, CA 92342; (760) 962-9872; or barrymaher@barrymaher.com.
7. Jackson, Ralph W. and A. Parasuraman. 1986. *The Yellow Pages as an Advertising Tool for Small Businesses.* American Journal of Small Business, 10 (4), pp. 29 to 35.

Chapter 23 Magazines

By Phil Frank

Magazines and newspapers, together, represent two of the oldest media in the world. Going back to the 1860s, magazines and newspapers played a vital role in the history of advertising. Since that time, magazines have been documenting the events, opinions, and emotions of the world.

Magazines are incredibly personal, with 17,500 magazines dedicated to a wide variety of interests.[1] If you have a hobby or an interest in something, there is a magazine for you. When a reader and magazine come together, it's a different relationship than a person has with a television program, a radio personality, or a Web site.

Magazines arrive in people's mailboxes, on their doorsteps, or in their shopping carts because people have made an effort to get the magazines and pay for them. The fact that readers pay for magazines is a fundamental difference between magazines and most other media. This transaction creates a relationship built on trust. Readers trust that the editors of a magazine will provide them with a quality product that appeals to their tastes and interests and is worthy of their investment.

Selling advertising in a magazine can be fulfilling because, if you enjoy reading a particular magazine, you'll have conviction and a sense of satisfaction when you sell advertising in it.

The magazine business is also quite challenging because it is highly competitive. Marketers are selective when they invest their money and they choose only a limited number of magazines in which to buy advertising. Most marketers cannot afford to surround a reader with ads in multiple publications, and, thus, competition for limited advertising budgets is intense. Therefore, it is imperative that good magazine salespeople position their books to have top-of-mind awareness in an advertiser's mind to get their fair share of limited budgets. Because of the competitive sales environment, it is also vital for a successful magazine salesperson to have a strategic understanding of an advertiser's business and to cultivate strong personal relationships.

The people who work in magazine sales need to be more than effective, smart negotiators; they need to be creative in how they position their product to a variety of advertisers. They need to think strategically to develop winning ideas that distinguish themselves and their product in the marketplace, and they need to be flexible enough to alter their approach as many marketers face the impact of a sagging economy.

A Brief History of Magazines

In the late 1800s magazine were read by only a few people because at the time, they were expensive to produce and distribute—there was no mass transportation at the time—and they appealed primarily to an upper-class audience.[2]

Magazines at that time were small, soft-cover books that carried stories of limited appeal because they had a European, aristocratic approach. The masses were reading newspapers and weekly tabloids. In the 1800s the magazine production process was expensive and technologically limited; printing 100,000 copies took a very long time. And until the United States Congress created second-class mail in 1879, the post office would only carry magazines a short distance, and it was quite expensive.[3]

In 1883, a Scott named S.S. McClure dropped the price of his general interest magazine, *McClure's*, to only 15 cents. It became very successful and widely read. Not long after, a rival publisher lowered the price of his magazine to 10 cents from 25 cents. This set off a new age in magazine sales, as everyone realized that dropping cover prices could lead to increased circulation.[4]

However, magazines still looked and read like books. There were no headlines or continued stories and pictures were confined to small sizes, but the design and production of magazines would soon change. In the 1890s, sketch artists were employed by magazines and assigned to cover events and stories. The artists sent back dramatic and romantic interpretations of the world. As one historian pointed out, the drawings of the Civil War were far from the reality of gruesome events.[5]

The first photo interview was conducted in the early 1900s, and started what would later lead to significant changes in editorial approach and design. New technology also was developed, which changed the look of the printed page, and advertising agencies now saw real possibilities for new forms of advertising layouts.[6]

In the late 1800s magazines carried mostly small-sized classified advertising, but new magazine and advertising designs and layouts were suddenly attractive to advertisers, and the economy of producing magazines underwent massive changes. By the 1930s, magazines were starting to bring in more and more advertising dollars, and this surging revenue made it possible to sell magazines to readers at below production cost. Thus, publishers could lower cover prices and increase readership. Magazines no longer were selling to merely readers, they tried to attract a steady and returning audience for advertisers.[7]

Advertisers soon realized that full-page ads with slogans, headlines, and logos allowed for a different language in selling their products and services. The best magazine designers came from advertising agencies, and they reshaped editorial content to bring readers to the ads. From the 1930s on, advertising continues to strengthen its grip on publishers.[8]

The design revolution continued in the 1940s and 1950s, led mostly by fashion magazines. Bleed photographs—photographs or art that extend to the edge of the page—were developed and several influential art directors refined magazine design by using big pictures, experimenting with headlines, and jumping the gutter—running pictures or headlines across the centerfold of a two-page spread. *People* magazine, launched in the early 1970s, positioned itself as a general-interest magazine that celebrated celebrity—it was one of the greatest launches in magazine history.[9]

There have been continual changes in magazine design and technology since the 1970s, and the medium has grown because of its innovative approach to finding more and more areas of interest so people continue to justify paying for more magazines than ever before.

**The Current
State of
Magazines**

New trends are developing in the way magazines are produced and delivered. Production is growing more sophisticated, allowing advertisers to insert two or three different versions of an ad to selected editions, such as regional editions, of a magazine. New editorial segments continue to be developed, and readers are still intrigued by attractive, up-to-the-minute design. Editors are continually being challenged in their approach by other media, and they are looking for ways to stay original, unique, and relevant.

Editorial

**Editorial
Diversity**

The primary difference between magazines and other media is that there is a magazine for many of the diverse interests of a huge number of people.

It's hard at first to realize the vastness of the editorial universe, but think about the working mother for a moment and the many different aspects of her life. How many different magazines might be of interest to such a woman?

- She works and has an interest in the business world: *a business magazine*
- She likes to get away from her job and travel: a *travel magazine*
- She's a mother: a *family magazine*
- She shops for many things for her home: a *home magazine* and a *food magazine*
- She likes to keep up with the world: a *news magazine*
- She likes movies and music: an *entertainment magazine*
- She takes her appearance seriously: a *fitness magazine*, a *fashion magazine*, and a *beauty magazine*

That makes 10 areas of interest that she spends time and energy on each week, and there are many, many magazines to help satisfy those interests.

Magazines offer readers information in subjects and areas of their lives that reflect their values and aspirations, which is one reason why the average reader spends 45 minutes reading each issue of a magazine.[10]

There is literally a magazine for everyone. The chart below outlines the actual number of consumer magazines from 1991 to 2001.

**Table 23.1
Number of
Magazines**

Year	Total Magazines
1991	14,256
1992	14,870
1993	14,302
1994	15,069
1995	15,996
1996	17,195
1997	18,047
1998	18,606
1999	17,970
2000	17,815
2001	17,964

Source: Magazine Publishers Association, 2002.

As readers crave to be entertained and informed, magazine editors and publishers look for opportunities to fulfill these needs. Each year the magazine industry works to bring new magazines to the market, filling the narrowest of interests and the broadest of topics. In 2001, 293 new consumer magazines were introduced to satisfy the needs people feel to be informed and entertained. The launches spanned approximately 40 different interest categories, as shown in Table 23.2.

Table 23.2
New Magazine
Launches by
Interest Category,
2001

Miscellaneous	40	Media Personalities	3
Metro/Regional/State	39	Aviation	3
Crafts/Games/Hobbies	25	Fitness	3
Sports	19	Gay Interest	2
Computers	13	Bridal	2
Home Service/Home	13	TV/Radio/Communications	2
Sex	12	Religious/Denominational	2
Children's	12	Dogs/Pets	2
Black/Ethnic Interest	11	Gaming	2
Fashion/Beauty/Grooming	9	Literary Reviews/Writing	2
Fishing/Hunting	8	Nature/Ecology	2
Music	7	Military/Naval	2
Automotive	7	Political/Social Topics	2
Business/Finance	5	Women's	1
Teen	5	Photography	1
Epicurean	5	Science/Technology	1
Arts/Antiques	5	Dress	1
Health	5	Camping/Outdoor	1
Men's	4	Babies	1
Travel	4	Gardening	1
Pop Culture	3		
Comics/Comic Technique	3	**TOTAL**	**93**
Entertainment/Perf. Arts	3		

Source: Magazine Publishers Association, 2002.

Some launches, such as *ESPN—The Magazine, O, In Style, Maxim,* and *Teen People* quickly become regular features on the newsstand, while others, such as *Rosie, Talk, Yahoo! Internet Life,* and *Industry Standard* get a lot of publicity but eventually fold for one reason or another. The success or failure of a magazine often has a direct link to the general psyche of the country, the economy, people's current tastes and fads, and the rise and fall of certain industries.

Editorial Is the Brand, the Product

For advertising salespeople, a magazine's editorial content, combined with the audience it attracts, is the product they have to sell. The editorial content (referred to as simply editorial from now on) is the beginning and end of a magazine's success. It's the editorial that distinguishes one magazine from its competitors. For example, *Time* magazine's editorial is far different from that of *U.S. News & World Report*. It is the editorial that readers pay to have delivered to their homes or purchase on a newsstand. It's the editorial that draws a certain type of reader to a magazine, thus creating a demographic profile that salespeople use to attract advertisers interested in reaching that particular demographic.

It's the editorial that can be the catalyst of a successful magazine or the cause of its downfall. Editorial becomes the brand of a magazine, and editorial is the stimulus for growth in readers and, in turn, advertising pages. Marketers who want to reach those readers will want to be associated with the magazine's brand. In time, certain advertisers and their brands become so closely associated with a magazine that the two brands seem to meld together. Think of sports magazines and a beer advertiser or beauty magazines and a cosmetic advertiser. This close association leads to some sensitive issues regarding editorial and advertising.

Advertising to Editorial Ratio

Nearly all magazines contain both editorial and advertising. It's advertising that keeps subscription and newsstand prices reasonable. While editorial and advertising both inform and entertain, magazine staffs work hard to keep a reasonable ratio between these two elements. To readers, if editorial and advertising are not in a suitable balance, it can have one of two effects: (1) alienate readers because there is too much advertising, or (2) not deliver enough revenue to keep the magazine alive because there is too much editorial. In consumer magazines in 2001, the percentage of advertising to editorial was 55 percent editorial to 45 percent advertising, a ratio that has remained relatively stable for a decade.[11]

Balancing editorial and advertising is a science and an art, and sometimes there are exceptions to the average 55/45 ratio. The exceptions can be found all over the newsstands, but when they are executed in an intelligent way, imbalances are hardly noticeable. In bridal, car, and computer magazines, the advertising-to-editorial ratio can swing all the way to 80/20 because readers are often as interested in the ads as they are in the editorial.

In developing and maintaining the correct ad-to-editorial ratio, magazine editors and publishers, who run the business side of a magazine, tend to work quite closely together and focus on readers' interests. However, they fall on different sides of the fence when it comes to final editorial control.

Editorial and Advertising: Church and State

"Church and state" is the phrase magazine people use to describe the hard line that exists between the editorial side of a magazine and the business and advertising side. The separation can be fuzzy at times, but it boils down to maintaining the integrity of the relationship between the editors and the readers of a magazine. Just as church and state should be independent of one and other in our form of government, so should the editorial and the advertising sides of a magazine.

As an example, imagine if you're reading an article in *BusinessWeek* about home mortgages and inside the story there is a favorable mention of a particular bank; then, smack in the middle of it, there is an ad for the same bank mentioned in the story.

Finally, imagine that this bank is one of the magazine's largest advertising clients; would you think the mention in the story was a coincidence? Could the editor have been influenced to write a favorable story about the advertiser in the magazine? If you, or readers in general, perceive that the editorial of the magazine is not objective, you stop reading it.

Editors and publishers are in agreement on the issue of the editorial's integrity and credibility. Editors need to maintain the objectivity and credibility of the magazine by keeping the readers' faith that the writers are independent. Publishers occasionally become angry when editors write critical articles involving advertisers, but a responsible publisher realizes that this objectivity is the very reason readers trust the magazine's editorial.

The biggest outcry comes from advertisers. It's not uncommon for an advertiser to ask a salesperson if some editorial pieces can be created to frame their advertising in a beneficial way. This response to such a request should be an automatic "No" for a salesperson, but often money clouds a publisher's judgment and there is a face-off with the editor. In the end, editors typically win, and, hopefully, advertisers understand.

This issue hits at one of the two core responsibilities of the editors, which are to not compromise on editorial integrity and always to keep readers' best interests in mind.

Audience

A magazine's audience starts with its circulation and grows as original readers pass an issue along to other readers. This second part of a magazine's audience is aptly labeled the pass-along audience. Circulation comes from two sources, subscriptions and single-copy sales, or newsstand sales.

Subscribers

A magazine gets subscriptions when readers agree to pay an upfront fee to have the magazine sent to an address. Consumers usually receive a discount over the price they would pay if they were to buy the same number of issues one at a time at a newsstand. Subscribers also purchase the convenience of having the magazine delivered to their homes or offices. For the magazine, there are two advantages: (1) they have made a guaranteed sale of their magazine well into the future, and (2) they grow their audience in a way that creates greater stability over time.

In 2001, 84 percent of all consumer magazines were sold by subscription, a percentage that has been growing steadily over the last 10 years. In addition, there hasn't been a major change in the last 10 years in the total number of consumer magazines sold. [12] Therefore, as media planners wonder where to invest their dollars, they can consider magazines' stability, particularly in light of the media fragmentation that has occurred over the last 10 years, led by cable television and the Internet. Stability is an important consideration for someone charged with the responsibility of investing millions and millions of dollars in advertising.

Single-Copy Sales or Newsstand Sales

While subscriptions represent the stable part of a magazine's circulation, single-copy sales demonstrate the vitality and level of interest in a magazine. Single-copy sales are an important measure for a media buyer to study, because this piece of data provides a gauge of a magazine's editorial strength, the appeal of its graphics design, the relevance of its cover story, and its overall ability to compete in popularity with other magazines that fit into a similar category.

Good magazine buyers take many other factors into consideration as they evaluate the health and strength of a magazine's total circulation. For example, magazines that are more established should not have to rely too much on newsstand sales to keep their circulations strong. On the other hand, a successful launch of a new magazine should result in a high number of newsstand sales, demonstrating that it is gaining momentum early in its life, and helping to convert many of these single-copy purchasers into subscribers over time.

Qualified Circulation

The practice of qualified, or controlled, circulation is more common in business-to-business and trade magazines. This is a circulation strategy in which publishers actually give magazines away free, but only to people who meet certain qualifications. A magazine about the software industry may want to give its magazine away to product engineers, for example.

Because a limited number of readers have to qualify to receive the magazine, the magazine creates an attractive audience for advertisers who want to reach qualified buyers.

Establishing and Growing a Rate Base

Advertisers and media buyers establish an agreement that magazines must deliver a guaranteed number of readers on an issue-by-issue basis. This guarantee on the actual number of people who receive the magazine, either by subscription or by buying a single copy, is known as a magazine's rate base.

Magazine publishers use the rate base to set their advertising rates on the basis of CPMs, which become guarantees of the number of readers that an advertiser will reach. Magazines set and adjust their own rate bases, but, naturally, they try to grow them so they can, in turn, raise their advertising rates.

Additionally, a magazine's circulation is affected by its age. As I mentioned earlier, a magazine that has been published for 50 years or so, such as *Sports Illustrated,* will probably not see huge changes in its audience size or rate base because the audience has matured and leveled off. In fact, magazines that have been around for many years and that are consistent in maintaining their rate bases demonstrate that they maintain their relevance to their readers. However, for a younger magazine that is still developing and has yet to achieve its potential audience level, rate base increases are common and actually cheered on by media buyers as a sign of popularity.

Magazine publishing companies are experts at pricing their magazines. They decide on the price of a single copy based on several factors, which include: (1) the frequency of the publication, such as weekly as in the case of *People* or monthly in the case of *Architectural Digest*; (2) the editorial category and the audience it will attract, such as an upscale or mass appeal audience; (3) the number of competitors in a magazine category; and (4) the perceived value to a reader.

Circulation managers at magazines continually look to build and grow their audiences. They typically look for interesting promotional opportunities; some magazines will give away merchandise such as clothing, appointment books, or chances to travel in order to induce people to subscribe. Or they may try to partner with a retailer—for example, a grocery store, a pharmacy, or a more specialized store—that will bundle the sale of a subscription with that of their own goods.

This practice of building circulation and raising rate bases has recently undergone scrutiny and some challenges. For example, recently, a consumer advocate group was able to stop Publisher's Clearing House from selling subscriptions to potential readers via sweepstakes. Sweepstakes and contests were a consistent source for new subscribers, and recent restrictions of these practices have put even more pressure on circulation managers to use other methods to replace those subscribers no longer available through the use of sweepstakes.

Rate Base Audits

Magazine publishers and agency planners and buyers use a third party to monitor the rules by which a magazine can raise its circulation, and thus its rate base, to avoid any questionable practices. The monitoring entity is known as the Audit Bureau of Circulation (ABC). One of the ABC's most important jobs is to question any suspicious activity in rate base growth, which can include continuing to send issues to people who have cancelled or counting subscriptions that have been sold at deep discounts as full price.

Revenue from Circulation

The average magazine draws half of its revenue from advertising and half from circulation. It's easy to see how publishers see their advertising sales team and their circulation sales team as equally important. This 50/50 split hasn't changed much in the last few years, and even as the economy leaps and dives, the ratio has remained steady. The ratio of 50 percent advertising revenue, 36 percent subscription revenue, and 14 percent single-copy sales revenue has remained the same since 1997.[13]

The circulation business is a $10 billion industry in its own right. Circulation managers are facing many challenges in the early part of this decade as editorial departments continually look for openings on the newsstands and the opportunity to develop new magazines. Good circulation directors tend to be aggressive with both new and old magazines, and will often run a series of short-term promotions to increase single-copy as well as subscription sales. They know that if they can recruit subscribers, there is a good chance that the magazine will be able to hold them for a long time, which will help sustain and grow revenue far into the future.

Audience

There is a saying in the real estate industry, "Location, location, location." Many advertisers would say that for media companies it should be, "Audience, audience, audience." While decisions on where to spend media dollars are not always one-dimensional, audience size does play a big role.

For the most part, advertisers want audiences to be both targeted and large. Magazines deliver in both ways. With just one issue of a magazine, advertisers can reach tens of millions of consumers, and magazine readers have demographics that are much more desirable than television audiences or even consumers on the Internet.

Magazine Reach

Many media planners and buyers make the argument that network television is the best medium for reach; however, with the fragmentation of audiences and programming success of subscription-only cable networks, this argument is not as airtight as it used to be.

A large number of magazines can compete with top-rated network television programs on the basis of audience accumulation and reach. Many magazines deliver larger audiences than most cable networks and top-ranked Web sites.

Pass-Along Audience

You may wonder how magazines can achieve this reach, particularly if the circulation numbers of the top 25 magazines are, for the most part, under 5 million.

Magazines are portable and consumers can read them at home or away from home. Most issues of most magazines are also read by more than one person. This extra audience is referred to as the pass-along audience, as I mentioned previously.

Depending on the quality of the editorial and the interest category, some magazines have a pass-along audience that reaches more than 10 readers per copy. This occurs when a magazine is delivered to home or office and several

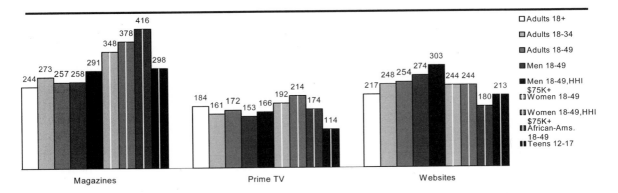

Figure 23.1
Gross rating points of top 25 magazines, prime TV shows, and Web sites. (Source: Magazine Publishers Association 2002.)

different people pick it up and read it. How many people actually read an issue of a magazine at a doctor's office, a friend's home, a barber shop, or a library? This is largely how magazines accumulate the massive reach that makes them very competitive with other media. Table 23.3 shows the many locations in which magazines are read.

Table 23.3 Magazine Reading by Place		
In Own Home		84%
Out-of-Home		76%
Doctor/Dentist Office		34%
In Someone Else's Home		29%
At Work		27%
At a Newsstand/Store		25%
Beauty/Barber Shop		13%
At Library/Club/School		8%
On an Airplane		6%
Business Reception Room		6%

Source: Magazine Publishers Association, 2002.

Reach Development

Because it's nearly impossible for two people to read a magazine at the same time, the accumulation of the full audience, which includes subscribers plus the pass-along audience, takes some time. A few media buyers and planners argue that the amount of time that it takes to build reach makes readership less desirable because an ad loses its relevancy.

This suggestion is only somewhat valid because different magazines accumulate their full audience in shorter periods of time than others, making these magazines as valuable as other media, if not more so. For example, weekly magazines such as *Time, BusinessWeek, US,* and *TV Guide* accumulate their audiences very quickly because another issue comes out in seven days, and the assumption is that readers read the issues of these magazines during the week they are issued. In fact, a media buy of three to four weeklies provides more reach at more efficient CPMs than the top 10 newspapers in the country. The same magazines accumulate more reach than nearly every Web site and all cable networks, and compete very closely with prime time network television programming.[14]

General Profile of Magazine Readers

Magazines, in general, offer an audience that is younger, more affluent, better educated, and more empowered than other media. Heavy magazine readers also are a very loyal group, and consume less television than the general population. These characteristics make the average magazine reader very desirable for advertisers, especially when compared to the average television viewer. Table 23.4 shows some demographic comparisons between magazines and television.

**Table 23.4
The Average
Magazine Reader
vs. Average TV
Viewer**

	Heavy Magazine Readers	Heavy Television Viewers
Average Age	43	48
Average Household Income	$69,495	$53,245
Average Value of Owned Home	$193,572	$159,286
Index - Graduated College +	120	76
Index - Household Income 75,000+	119	76
Index - Employed	109	84
Index - Professional/Manager	117	72
Index - Top Management	116	77
Index - Use Internet 3+ Times a Week	121	85

Indexes are based on total US population.
Source: Magazine Publishers Association, 2002.

Advertising

Production of a Magazine

Magazine production is an art unto itself. First, there is the physical production of the book, then the quantity produced, and finally the frequency of publication.

In terms of the physical production, there are two methods of binding. The first is called saddle stitch. In this method, the pages are laid on top of each other over an arm, the way a saddle lays on top of a horse, and then fastened together, or stitched, with staples. The second method is called perfect bound. This method employs gluing the pages to a spine, much the way many books are bound.

Perfect-bound production is largely used for magazines that carry a substantial number of pages in one issue, because staples are not large or sturdy enough to pierce and hold a large bunch of paper. It's typically easier for perfect-bound magazines to handle advertising on heavier stock than it is for saddle-stitch magazines. However, saddle-stitch magazines offer publishers a more efficient way to customize different versions of the same issue to reach specific subscribers.

Pricing

Magazines are largely priced the same way other media are. Pricing is based on cost-per-thousands (CPMs) and is measured on the basis of circulation. Magazines that have mass appeal tend to have lower CPMs, typically in the range of $7.50 to $25. Other magazines, which reach special-interest audiences, have higher CPMs. The CPMs of some of the smaller, more specialized magazines are usually in the range of hundreds of dollars, and can easily surpass $500. Yet, media buyers and advertisers know that other media have waste coverage and cannot put advertising in front of special interest and highly desirable demographic groups as accurately as magazines can. In contrast, the

CPMs for direct mail catalogues can be as high as $3,000, so a $500 CPM for a highly targeted magazine seems like a bargain.

For an example of the importance of pricing in selling and negotiating magazines to agencies, read "Selling Magazines to Agencies" in Appendix F.

Research

Several syndicated research companies provide vital information to magazine sales teams and media buyers, including Mediamark Research, Inc. (MRI) and Monroe Mendelsohn Research (MMR), which are similar to the Nielsen ratings in network television.

To demonstrate how important research is and how it can be used to pinpoint a target audience, the following example shows how I used research when I was a media supervisor at Ammirati and Puris, an advertising agency. I once had a client who produced a product that kept fruit fresh for a long time and was good for either canning, preserving, or serving fruit. The product worked well and fruit salad wouldn't get that brown tinge on it in an hour. Through research, we learned that our target audience was primarily women in the southeast United States. In fact, we found women in that region who canned more than 15 jars of fruit each month—a small audience of heavy users—and we were able to find several magazines that reached just this target audience.

Buyers look at both demographic and psychographic research. There are many studies that help a buyer understand the psychographics, or lifestyles, of their target audience, such as aspiring vs. comfortable or settled vs. adventurous; and their interests, such as, cars, jazz, local politics, or nature hikes. Magazines are particularly suited to delivering desirable demographics in a way that addresses the interests and psychographics of a target audience.

Positioning an Ad in a Magazine

Media buyers are often taught to find the medium that reaches their audience, then buy it at the best price they can negotiate. Once a buyer has selected a magazine on those two parameters, the next discussion is typically about the position an ad will receive inside the book. Depending on how image-conscious an advertiser is, this part of the discussion can play a major role in negotiations.

Publishers realize the importance of position and charge extra for the most desirable spots in their books. The most desirable positions are determined according to two main factors: (1) visibility, which has to do with the way readers actually read a magazine, and the assumption is that most readers read from front to back, and (2) adjacency to desirable editorial.

There are three or four positions in a magazine that are considered more visible than others: (1) the first ad inside the front cover, called the second cover, (2) the page on the inside of the back cover, called the third cover, (3) the back cover itself, called the fourth cover, and (4) the page opposite the table of contents (TOC).

Other key positions are based on how close to the front of the magazine an ad is located. Advertisers that are positioned more forward are more likely to be seen, simply because most people read a magazine from front to back. For the most part, the front of the book is read more than the back. Good publishers and editors work hard to spread the more widely read editorial throughout the magazine in an attempt to have readers go through the entire book.

Another desirable position is adjacent to a specific editorial that may have particular interest to a specific segment of a magazine's audience or ties well into an advertiser's creative execution. For instance, in a sports-oriented magazine, a financial advertiser may remark how they are the leader in performance among their competitors, and the magazine may list statistical leaders in a sport. Thus, the ad and the editorial have some synergy and may provide added exposure for an ad.

In some instances, desirable editorial position occurs when single copies of magazines are bought largely due to their covers. In those cases, advertisers may want to secure a position adjacent to the cover story editorial on the theory that readers will spend time in that part of the magazine, thus increasing their ad's exposure.

Ad Units

Many different types of ads appear in magazines; currently 22 ad sizes are measured for effectiveness. These range from a single black and white page to larger units using color, called four-color ads. The position, appearance, and size of an ad are reasons why some appear to be more ubiquitous and memorable than others. Table 23.5 shows the impact of various size magazine ads.

Table 23.5
The Impact of Magazine Advertising by Type of Unit

Ad Type	Recall Index
Page 4-Color Ad (P4C)	100
Fourth Cover Position (P4C)	120
Second Cover Position (P4C)	112
Third Cover Position (P4C)	90
Second Cover Position (4C Gatefold)	145
Inside Spread (4C)	130
Inside Spread 2 Color (2C)	110
Inside Spread Black and White (B/W)	95
Vertical 2/3 Page (4C)	81
Horizontal 1/2 Page (4C)	72
Vertical 1/3 Page (4C)	60
Horizontal 1/3 Page (4C)	60
Vertical 2/3 Page (2C)	60
Vertical 2/3 Page (B/W)	60
Horizontal 1/2 Page (2C)	56
Horizontal 1/2 Page (B/W)	56
Horizontal 1/3 Page (2C)	47
Horizontal 1/3 Page (B/W)	47
Vertical 1/3 Page (2C)	42
Vertical 1/3 Page (B/W)	42
Page 2C	78
Page B/W	74

Source: Magazine Publishers Association, 2002.

Advertisers continue to find new size and shapes of ads to put in magazines. Larger ads and more creative sizes and shapes help advertisers' messages achieve greater impact. The various sizes tend to be given names that make it interesting for the production people to try to understand, such as French doors, double Dutch, half-page flap, eighth-page gate, and tabs.

Marketing Extensions

More and more advertisers are asking publishers to provide some kind of extension for their advertising campaigns or marketing strategies. These extensions can be included in the cost of the advertising or, in the case of larger-scale extensions, a publisher may ask for and receive incremental revenue.

These marketing extensions are referred to by several names, including merchandising and added value. In the current competitive magazine marketplace, publications often give advertisers 1 percent to 2 percent of their advertising spending for marketing extension, such as reprints of their ads to be used in direct marketing or as collateral sales material for an advertiser's own sales force.

What's happening more often is that magazines are creating larger and larger extensions, such as hosting seminars, setting up entertainment events, and conducting sweepstakes. These programs are usually offered to the advertiser for an incremental investment, which is often highly discounted from the true value of the extension.

As clients and agencies undergo downsizing and the window of opportunity for a truly groundbreaking and successful product launch is getting smaller and smaller, marketers are continually looking to their media partners to develop concepts to cover a wide spectrum of marketing responsibilities.

This increased demand for media companies to develop broader and broader marketing extensions and cohesive programs has been spurred on by the slow economy and its effect on both marketers and advertising agencies.

Marketers are reducing their staffs and, thus, are reducing both manpower and intellectual capital in their organizations. They are also reducing their number of agency relationships and consolidating the work with one or two agencies, instead of having specialists work on different aspects of their marketing communications.

Advertising agencies are consolidating their buying functions, which is providing them with greater and greater clout in negotiating for lower prices. As a result, magazines must develop ideas for which they can charge premiums. Agencies are being pressured by their clients to deliver efficient costs; a strong return on investment; and new, high-impact creative ideas. At the same time, agencies have to reduce their staff size, which lessens their ability to provide marketing support, and, in turn, results in a rising demand for media companies to provide additional services and more in the way of added value.

Working with Both Advertising Agencies and Clients

Good magazine salespeople cover both agencies and clients because they can learn a great deal from both about how to craft the most effective solutions. And combining the information that they get from each and using it wisely typically distinguishes the good salespeople from the rest of the pack.

Agencies are paid to analyze media and make investment recommendations based on the overall marketing objectives and strategies of their clients. The clients that magazine salespeople typically call on are brand managers who are paid to keep their products fresh in the minds of consumers and help build equity in a brand and its product. It's this equity that creates and sustains long-term loyalty among their customers. In other words, agencies have a great deal of information about specific advertising campaigns, while clients have large-scale information about the overall marketing direction of a brand and know about market conditions and strategies and the competitive landscape.

Traditionally in magazines, brand managers, advertising directors, senior vice presidents of marketing, and even CEOs see salespeople from major national magazines, particularly those that cover their industry, such as *Car and Driver*, *PC World*, and *Travel and Leisure*. Over the years, no other media, with perhaps the exception of the major television and cable networks, have had access to top management, and this access is one of the great advantages of selling for national magazines.

Magazine Advantages Over Other Media

Magazines have access to top management at both agencies and clients because they are important national media and because magazines are unique in many ways, ranging from their physical characteristics to the way readers respond to advertising.

Effectiveness of Print Advertising

Magazine advertising is a core resource to some of the world's largest marketers. Magazines have the reach, demographics, immediacy, efficiency, creative platform, and ability to either communicate with a mass audience or target a narrowly defined group of people, all of which marketers find advantageous.

Magazines have proven effective for both building brands and selling products, generating awareness and building momentum for an extremely diverse mix of companies for years and years. Millard Brown International, a global research firm that specializes in advertising tracking and awareness studies, conducted a study that reveals the power and efficiency of magazines in generating advertising awareness. Figure 23.2 shows the results of that study.

Figure 23.2
Share of advertising awareness and spending in 113 brands, averages across 22 categories. (Source: Magazine Publishers Association 2002.)

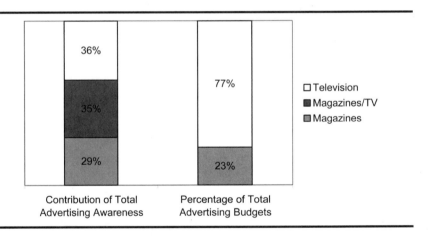

The study covered 1996 and 1997 and revealed that dollar-for-dollar, advertising investments in magazines produced significantly higher advertising awareness levels than television. The media multiplier concept of two media working in tandem to produce better results than either one alone was strongly supported in this study. More than one-third of the total advertising awareness achieved by the 113 brands measured was a result of both magazines and television. However, in the study, 77 percent of the brands' advertising budgets were invested in television and only 23 percent in magazines, which resulted in an awareness-to-cost index of a sub-par 92 for television and a whopping 278 for magazines—a much better return on investment.

In addition to being cost-efficient, magazines, in terms of targetability by interest, are highly competitive with the Internet and cable television. The Internet currently has in the neighborhood of 3 billion Web sites, which is growing daily, compared to about 17,500 consumer magazines. There are often thousands or even millions of Web sites on one topic. For example, a Google search for the term "interest rates" returned 3,490,000 results. This fractionalization makes it exceptionally difficult to place advertising in order to achieve reach quickly.

With cable television, more than 300 channels are currently available. Even the most popular channels typically average only a 1.0 rating in prime time. Magazines not only provide the diversity of cable, but also higher reach.

Magazines and ROI

There is an old saying in advertising: "I know my advertising is working, but I'm just not sure where my advertising is working." In the late 1990s and early part of this century, marketers, more so than at any time in recent history, began to stress that advertising needs to generate a return on investment (ROI). The Internet was a major catapult for ROI because it provided specific feedback, immediately, on the productivity of an ad in terms of response rates.

Today it's common for marketers to hold their ad agencies to ROI goals and in turn, agencies try to hold media companies to ROI goals as well. ROI has become such an important element of advertising that marketers now have their finance departments attend meetings in which ad agencies try to win a company's advertisement assignments, for example.

Therefore, media has to show, in one form or another, that they can help with sales and produce ROI on the dollars they receive. Many studies have shown that dollar-for-dollar, magazines are more effective than television at generating advertising awareness and product sales, as can be seen in Figure 23.3.

**Figure 23.3
The impact of magazine advertising.
(Source: Magazine Publishers
Association 2002.)**

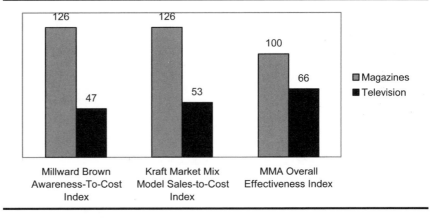

The three studies in Figure 23.3 show that magazines are more likely to have a much higher index of awareness to cost, a much higher index of sales to cost, and higher overall effectiveness. More details about these studies and other magazine effectiveness research can be obtained at www.magazines.org/resources/research.html.

Relationship with Readers/ Audience Involvement

Magazines and newspapers are media that consumers pay for on a regular basis. No one pays to watch the NFL or "Late Night with David Letterman" on television.

You may pay your cable company to get 300 channels, but not specific programming. No one pays to listen to his or her local radio station; you simply get a radio and turn it on. No one pays to surf CNN.com or Yahoo; you pay your cable company, phone company, or an Internet service provider (ISP) to get access to the Internet, but, for the most part, you're not paying to go to a specific non-porn site.

With print, consumers turn over money for every magazine or paper they want to receive and read. This transaction is fundamental to understanding the relationship magazines have with their readers.

It's not uncommon to hear someone ask, "What are your favorite magazines?" The variety or lack of variety in their magazine choices can be an interesting insight into someone's interests. The answer may be, "I subscribe to magazines X, Y, and Z, and on occasion I'll pick up magazines A, B, and C." Magazines are very personal for their readers, providing the information and entertainment that is most relevant and interesting to them.

The relationship between a reader and magazine, represented by the transactional nature of the relationship, is very much built on trust. If readers pay for an issue, they expect value. If the value they expect is delivered, then readers return and pay again, expecting the magazine to deliver again. If that trust is broken on a consistent basis, readers don't return.

For advertisers, this relationship is certainly an excellent context in which to communicate. Readers of magazines are committed to their decision on what to read and what not to read. They carry issues of magazines to work and even while they are on vacation. Because of this relationship, readers tend to interact with advertising in a very different way as well.

Furthermore, magazine readers have to be actively engaged with a magazine for advertising even to be seen. If a reader is not turning the pages of a magazine, nothing happens. However, if a television viewer or radio listener wanders away, losing all interaction with a broadcast, the broadcast continues and advertising runs with nobody there to receive it. Figure 23.4 shows how consumers respond to magazines compared to other media.

Figure 23.4 Consumers respond to magazine advertising. (Source: Magazine Publishers Association 2002.)

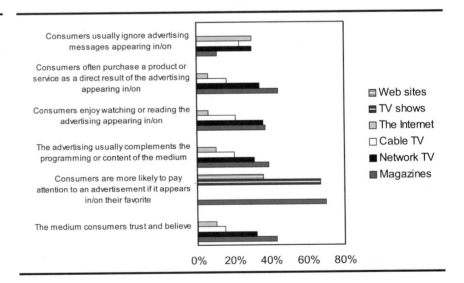

Consumers usually ignore advertising messages appearing in/on

Consumers often purchase a product or service as a direct result of the advertising appearing in/on

Consumers enjoy watching or reading the advertising appearing in/on

The advertising usually complements the programming or content of the medium

Consumers are more likely to pay attention to an advertisement if it appears in/on their favorite

The medium consumers trust and believe

0% 20% 40% 60% 80%

- Web sites
- TV shows
- The Internet
- Cable TV
- Network TV
- Magazines

Uniquely Creative

For several reasons, magazines offer advertising agencies' copywriters and art directors a rare opportunity—to tell a story or explain something in more than 60, 30, or 15 seconds. There is no limit on the time someone can spend accessing the contents of a magazine. This type of access is referred to as *random access* because readers can access a page as often as they like and whenever they want, on a random basis. Radio and television offer *linear access* because listeners and viewers cannot go back or skip forward to hear or view just those parts of the programming that interest them. Because of this type of access, print ads have the opportunity to expand the way they communicate with a reader.

Try to explain, or sell, something to a friend in 30 seconds—the average length of a television commercial—it's hard. Thirty seconds is not a long time; you can't give much information in 30 seconds, so copywriters for television concentrate on trying to get viewers to make an emotional connection with a brand by making them laugh, cry, lust for it. For copywriters, magazines give them more liberty to explain product benefits, make competitive comparisons, give more information, and define a brand.

Magazine advertising also can be fun. There are many entertaining, creative platforms for an ad. Whether it's putting a sticky note on an ad, creating suspense with consecutive pages, or using pop-ups, magazines offer much more than a one-dimensional piece of paper to work with. On the other hand, a straightforward, full-page ad in a magazine provides the space to tell a good, informative brand story.

Context for Advertising

Magazines provide excellent opportunities for marketers to place their ads in an environment that is relevant to, complementary to, and in harmony with their advertising message. This concept is referred to as context. Having an ad appear in an environment that is relevant to the advertising message or to the product is good context.

Because there are a multitude of magazines that cover a vast array of interests, marketers have a wonderful opportunity to take advantage of the special, complementary context that magazines can provide for their messages.

Magazines in the New Economy: Competition

Competition in magazines is fiercer than ever as the country wades through the longest recession in the history of advertising spending.

Unfortunately, magazines were first to be hit by the advertising recession. They began to see ad dollars fall in late 2000, and as many people are forecasting, magazines will be the medium that takes the longest time to recover when the economy picks up.

Many magazines are also fighting to maintain their profitability levels, or to maintain any profit at all. New magazines are being launched and while some fail, and others are quite healthy and are putting their older competitors in a position of high risk.

Both of these elements have a positive side, as well. The recession will have its impact on many titles, but world events and an ever-changing culture in the United States have brought relevancy and readers back to magazines. The competition of one title versus another is always healthy and keeps editorial staffs sharp and up-to-date on how consumers digest information and what information they want.

The interesting part of the recession is that as magazines face competition from television, the Internet, and other media, the cooperation between these different media is also on the rise and will help minimize many of the competitive threats. For example, there is a *People Weekly* segment in NBC's "Dateline," and CNET and *Fortune* are cooperating on a technology review feature each week. Many of Time, Inc.'s prestigious titles are also available on AOL.

Making a Living Selling Magazine Advertising

Jobs and Roles Most magazines have similar structures in their sales operations. The various departments and the jobs within them are the following:

Sales. Sales, the front line of any media company, can be the most rewarding role, but it is also the most demanding. The typical sales organization for a magazine consists of the following jobs, starting at the top: publisher, associate publisher, regional manager, office manager, senior account executive, junior account executive, and sales assistant. **Typically, magazine salespeople right out of school start as sales assistants or junior account executives.** As people enter and move up through the ranks of a sales division, they find they're spending time with fewer and fewer clients and more time on managerial issues. However, publishers and their primary associates do not sit in their offices all the time. Publishers often travel across the country to call on a magazine's largest accounts.

Account executives typically make multiple sales calls each day. Most will start with a breakfast meeting, then schedule other calls throughout the day. In the span of a week, an account executive will make between 10 and 25 calls, depending on the location and availability of their clients.

Magazines are very dependent on relationships. The medium is not like a commodity, as much of television and radio are, and it faces fierce competition every day. Therefore, it's important to be in sync with clients every step of the way and build and maintain very close relationships.

Sales Development. The sales development group works very closely with sales to create strategically oriented proposals that capitalize on the inherent assets of a magazine and its effectiveness in elevating a marketer's message. People in this group need to have a strong marketing background and be able to understand advertising objectives and translate all of these elements into creative solutions that can sell an advertiser's product.

In recent years, sales development teams have been spending more time on sales calls with their salespeople. It's important that this group understand the opportunities and priorities of their clients, and they are often asked to help sell the architecture and core elements of the proposals they develop.

A sales development job has less pressure than a sales job does, because compensation is typically not tied to achieving a sales goal. As a result, salaries and total compensation are usually lower than those of salespeople.

Marketing. Some magazines combine sales development and marketing teams; however, the responsibilities are distinctly different. The focus of marketing/events centers on making sure the magazine and its editorial and audience are well understood in the advertising marketplace.

Marketing people work directly with their research departments to help understand the make-up of a magazine's audience. They also work directly with editors to help position a magazine's content in a unique way. Marketing staffs help develop a positioning story and value proposition for sales teams that will help salespeople position the magazine to maximize their opportunity to sell ad pages.

Research.   Research departments at magazines are taking on more diverse responsibilities than ever before. The Internet has been a primary cause of this change. Historically, research departments studied data that was delivered by syndicated research firms; today they are more proactive and are asked to provide analyses of a magazine's audience as well as the direction and trends of the marketplace and their advertisers.

Research departments work closely with sales departments to study historical trends of individual advertisers or categories of advertisers. They look for positive momentum or downward trends, either of which can signify opportunities for growing revenue. These departments also develop capsules of information on advertising prospects that help salespeople approach their clients with knowledgeable background information on their company and their industry.

If a magazine has just been launched and its audience is too new and too volatile to be measured by syndicated research, it is the responsibility of a research department to develop a prototype of its audience. The prototype is developed by selecting other magazines with similar editorial, circulation, and demographic appeal. Prototyping a magazine's audience can be very interesting because it involves trying to create a personality for a magazine based on what little available data there is.

Finance.   The finance group at any magazine is important to every salesperson because it helps develop the pricing component of every sales proposal. The finance department has an interesting perspective of a magazine. Because finance people work with every salesperson, they know the ins and outs of each deal and can be extremely helpful and even creative in pricing a deal. Often, pricing is not as simple as studying history to see what prices an advertiser has paid in the past or forecasting future growth for certain accounts. Pricing also involves figuring out the production costs that a magazine may assume for special creative units as well as other production costs. Overall, this team makes sure that every proposal that goes out the door brings revenue to the bottom line of the magazine.

A career in magazine sales is one of the most interesting, rewarding, creative, and satisfying of all. Whether you sell for a city magazine, a trade magazine, or a national, mass-consumer magazine, you'll find selling for one of the oldest advertising media is both highly competitive and extremely satisfying—you can find a magazine that fits your greatest interests and passion and can therefore sell a product that you love to intelligent, interesting people.

Test Yourself

1. When was the first mass-appeal magazine sold for 15 cents?
2. Give an example of the number of different magazines, by interest category, a working mother who has an interest in her business, the world, her family, her children, travel, and her appearance might subscribe to.
3. Approximately how many different magazine titles were there in 2002?
4. How many new magazines were launched in 2001?

5. What is the advertising-to-editorial ratio in the average consumer magazine?
6. Explain what is meant by the phrase "church and state" as it applies to the magazine business.
7. What percentage of the total revenue of an average consumer magazine comes from subscriptions?
8. Explain the difference between a saddle-stitch and a perfect-bound magazine.
9. Give three reasons for magazine's effectiveness as an advertising medium.

Project

Purchase a copy of *Teen People* magazine and read it carefully, noting all of its editorial features and advertising. Then, create a PowerPoint presentation for Pepsi-Cola, recommending that it make a major, year-long investment in *Teen People*. This investment will require shifting some dollars out of network and cable television. Don't be concerned with any cost figures; your task is to get Pepsi-Cola to reduce its television expenditures and invest in *Teen People*. Rely heavily on information about magazines' effectiveness you will find in *The Magazine Handbook*, available at www.magazine.org/resources/research.html.

References

Samir Husni. 2002. *Guide to New Consumer Magazines.* New York: Bowker.
Art Kleiner. 1979. "A History of Magazines on a Timeline,." *Co-Evolution Quarterly.*
Magazine Publishers Association. 2002. *The Magazine Handbook.* New York: Magazine Publishers Association.
Oxbridge Communications. 2003. *National Directory of Magazines.* New York: Oxbridge Communications.

Resources

www.adage.com/datecenter.crm
www.magazine.org/resources/research.html
www.mediafinder.com

Endnotes

1. Magazine Publishers Association. 2002. *The Magazine Handbook.* www.magazine.org/resources/research.html
2. Kleiner, Art. 1979. "A History of Magazines on a Timeline." *Co-Evolution Quarterly.*
3. Ibid.
4. Ibid.
5. Ibid.
6. Ibid.
7. Ibid.
8. Ibid.
9. Ibid.
10. Magazine Publishers Association. 2002. *The Magazine Handbook.* www.magazine.org/resources/research.html
11. Ibid.
12. Ibid.
13. Ibid.
14. Ibid.

24 Interactive

By Vincent Thompson

One of the tenets of marketing guru Jay Levinson's work has been the concept that successful marketing requires an assortment of weapons. If Levinson is correct, then the Internet is the most sophisticated marketing weapon to date. However, in the minds of most marketers the medium is still unproven, non-standardized, measured differently than other media, and difficult to implement. While scores of brilliant people are working to solve these barriers, they still exist to one degree or another because of one simple fact. The Internet—and Internet marketing—is new. So why market online? Because the online experience is one of the greatest innovations of our time and represents the most fertile environment ever made available for marketer and consumer interaction.

The Birth of a Medium

Most historians agree that the birth of the Internet occurred in 1969 when computer scientists from the government and universities linked large mainframe computers together for the purpose of sharing data and distributing information over a computer network. This groundbreaking work came from a desire to ensure the safety of government data during natural disasters or war and to allow university researchers the ability to share information. Prior to this project, networks were set up like phone systems, with information traveling through vulnerable centralized hubs. With the invention of the distributed network, information could be simply routed along any of the networks' many connections until it found its way to its final destination. Aiding in this concept was the use of packets, which allows for small chunks of digital data to be sent into the network independently and then reassembled at their final destinations. Once the initial computers at the University of California-Los Angeles and Stanford University were connected in 1969, other universities followed suit and with each addition the network gained more power and provided more value to its users.[1]

Over the next five years scientists developed cornerstone technologies such as e-mail, the ability to access the network remotely, and the ability to host multiple chat sessions. Born as the Arpanet, the main long-distance backbone was paid for and maintained by the National Science Foundation (NSF). The NSF had an Acceptable Use Policy limiting any commercial use of the Internet and encouraging researchers to only exchange e-mail or share files with people in their fields of expertise.[2]

It was e-mail that first demonstrated the incredible value of the medium. Suddenly phone tag was decreasing and the challenges that time zones played in the realm of communications were falling by the wayside. Researchers were communicating more and the benefits were obvious. Some within the research community argued that the Internet should be commercially available so business could share in these new efficiencies, but computers were still extremely expensive and the Internet needed another wave of innovation before their case became apparent.[3]

That time did come, however, in 1993 when Tim Berners-Lee, a researcher at the CERN atomic research center in Switzerland, developed protocols which allowed computers to better communicate over the Internet and allowed any computer on the network to browse another's content. Soon a Web browser followed and the World Wide Web was born.

A student at the University of Illinois, Marc Andreessen—who later co-founded Netscape—and his friends took the Web to a whole new level by introducing a browser with the ability to view graphics while running on the ubiquitous Windows platform. This innovation, combined with factors such as the rising popularity and falling price of the personal computer (PC) and the government's decision to lift the Acceptable Use Policy and stop subsidizing the Internet, created tremendous momentum.

In 1994 the Internet became a commercial medium and entrepreneurs sprung up all over to harness the power and opportunity provided by the Internet. Internet service providers (ISPs) grew out of small fan clubs or non-profit endeavors and morphed into large-scale businesses. Between 1993 and 1996 the number of Web sites one could visit grew from 130 to more than 150,000.[4] Today there are more than 3 billion Web sites—so many, in fact, that the largest search engines can only search 20 percent of what is on the Web. In Robert Reid's book *Architects of the Web*, he profiles the core innovations that defined the World Wide Web in its earliest days and still play a key role today.[5]

According to Reid, those core innovations are:

HTML and the Internet browser. HTML gave us the language to program Web pages. It tells the browsers how to display content, where to put pictures, and what backgrounds should look like. Browsers recognize all of these commands and bring the pieces together for us.

Java. Java gave us the opportunity to run little computer programs within the HTML content. It allowed programmers to animate many Web applications such as mortgage calculators, registration forms, and booking engines.

Streaming audio. A company named Real Audio provided a way for us to send music, and later video, over the Internet in a stream of packets that assemble on computers and provide users with a constant image or music stream.

VRML: The Web in 3-D. Virtual Reality Modeling Language (VRML) gave us the opportunity to render 3-D images on the Web, making visual applications more appealing and powerful.

Advertising measurement. I-Pro was the first company to measure the Web in such a manner that advertisers and programmers could understand it and how people used it.

Content sites and merged media. *Wired* magazine and C-Net came along with custom content designed to inform the users and build a relationship

with them unique to the online world. Users would not only read content
but they would also participate in creating their own content through message boards and chat rooms.

As the online world and the Internet gained popularity with consumers in
the late '90s, exuberance for the Web skyrocketed. Anyone coming in touch
with the medium could see the value of doing things online and the influence
that this new medium could have on business. Suddenly, everyone wanted a
piece of the action and investors began throwing their money at Web-based
businesses. Authors spoke of the "new economy" and those involved felt they
were at the epicenter of a revolution. Each month, a new business category
gained popularity online and immediately followers jumped into the game.
Businesses that originated solely as online businesses were called pure-plays or
dot-com businesses. Businesses that had physical locations and created online
sites earned the moniker of click-and-mortar businesses. On Wall Street investors made large bets that the pure-plays would displace the traditional
offline category leaders and bet against traditional firms without Internet presence. It was the new economy against the old and the old guard raced to join
the game, only adding to the Internet frenzy. During this phase of incredible
expansion dot-com jobs and dot-com dreams filled the heads of many recent
college graduates and many mid-career employees as they sought wealth in the
form of valuable stock options from dot-com start-ups.

The Promise of Online

Business people bought into the premise that online made things more efficient. Retailers didn't need stores. Banks didn't need branches. Brokerage houses did not need brokers; you could trade your own stock. Everyone hates the
car-buying process, right? Why not sell cars online? How about Christmas
trees and hams? Why not sell them online? What about hardware or pet food
or sports scores or the yellow pages? Hey, wait a minute, how about a bride
from Russia? It seemed like any thought or need that one could have suddenly had taken the form of a funded business plan and a destination on the Web.
Many believed that Universal Record Locators (URLs), or domain names, as
they are called, such as Etoys.com, or Pets.com were prime real estate. Some
well-respected Los Angeles entrepreneurs paid an estimated $7.5 million in
stock for the rights to Business.com. As hysterical as things became, and as
high as the valuations spiraled, the time came for Newton's law of gravity and
reality to take hold. Many of the dot-coms simply imploded. Short of cash,
they sold their assets and sent their employees home. Many hard lessons were
learned in the dot-com era. While some of the lessons can still be argued, in
general, we learned the following about consumers and the online universe:

Efficiency and price are not the only drivers of success. Adding convenience and cost savings does not guarantee success. For instance, Pets.com
did not make it as a pure-play Internet company. Consumers weren't ready
to abandon their habits. Some even enjoyed the process of shopping at the
local pet store. Now a part of Petsmart, Pets.com serves a valuable role in e-
commerce but not in the way imagined. Pets.com did not replace pet stores,
it simply added to the convenience and experience. Amazon.com, the Web's

biggest retailer, has built a large brand and a thriving business, but it did not replace the bookstores in my neighborhood. What about the other thousands of dot-com sites? Most didn't make it, and most failed to do what people in offline stores do every day by selling things to us and creating desire. The Web has yet to replace the salesperson who tells me how nice my sweater looks after trying it on. All of that just said, clothing is a category that is working online. The Gap, Banana Republic, and Old Navy have made their online businesses work, but it started with customers buying basic clothes they know and understand and the business has built from there.

Most consumers expect Web content to be free. With the Web came communities and the ability to find people with similar interests and passions. If you were a punk rocker in Utah you could connect with punks in Great Britain. Community sites flourished as users contributed to message boards and participated in chats. Editors began to believe that E-zines, or online magazines, would allow them to publish content with lower costs and reach highly targeted groups. Content sites were born and investors raced to support them. The value of these sites was measured by the number of visitors and by the potential to sell advertising. What publishers learned, however, was that content was very expensive to create. The typical dot-com content site was burning anywhere from $500,000 to $1 million a month, and users were unwilling to pay for the content as if it were a magazine. At the same time, advertisers were not buying enough to fund the businesses. For online marketers there quickly became a glut of advertising inventory, which meant these online publishers could not recover their costs and many folded. Paid content is currently gathering steam, but not on the scale initially imagined.

I'm not as interested in it as you are. While to the early adopter it seemed we were all nuts for not jumping into online banking, the fact is, for many of us we just didn't care enough or didn't have the time to take on what business people were asking of us. Is online banking more convenient? Will it help my life? Sure, but I just don't have the time to figure it out right now, thanks anyway. Make sense? We could all eat better and exercise more. Just because it makes sense does not mean you can count on consumers to do it.

The Cs of the Online World

America Online (AOL) popularized the following words starting with C as a way to look at and understand the online world. Here are the eight Cs from one of AOL's latest presentations:

Connectivity. Tapping into the network. In order to access the vast online databases and content, people need a connection either via phone lines or through a cable company to an ISP.

Content. A key driver to the Web's success, content represents anything one could put online that is not advertising, such as words, pictures, video, music, and tools such as calculators. Technically, advertising could be content as well; however, few in the industry refer to it as such.

Community. Community is people coming together online with like interests or a bond, such as family. Community interaction is usually facilitated online by e-mail, chat rooms, bulletin boards for posting messages, and custom Web pages such as AOL's Hometown or Yahoo's Geocities.

Communication. These are tools that connect people such as e-mail, chat rooms, and instant messaging. Online communications are now the preferred method for many communications and a large part of users' time online is spent engaged in communications.

Commerce. Three models of commerce are dominant on the Web: (1) Business-to-consumer, such as Gap.com and Amazon.com. (2) Business-to-business. We often aren't aware of this activity because these companies are not marketing to us but to other businesses. Sometimes they trade in raw materials, other times in specialized items such as aircraft parts. (3) Consumer-to-consumer. This model has been a smashing success for eBay. Initially, eBay was a business for collectors and it still is, but now the site sells both used and new products and even facilitates the sale of hundreds of cars per hour.

Controls. With the vastness of the Internet and the lack of regulation, many have expressed concern about the types of content available to children. While companies on the Internet have tried to self-regulate, users have found most of these efforts inadequate. Therefore, most ISPs, such as AOL and MSN, have taken an interest in giving users the control to block certain types of content from appearing in their Web browsers or their mailboxes and those of their children. The two largest online services, AOL and MSN, see such controls as a key feature of their service offerings.

Customization. One of the great features of the online world is the ability to customize. Many online service software providers and Web browsers allow users the opportunity to set preferences and design the experience in a way most suited to their liking. You can change colors, determine which mail to accept, and decide how others will see you online with custom icons for chat rooms and custom art for e-mail signatures. Opportunities to customize the online experience are endless and this customization is unique to the online medium.

Convenience. The growth of the online universe has been largely attributed to convenience. E-mail is more convenient and, therefore, it is a huge hit. Booking travel is more convenient, and therefore it is a hit. Convenience is all about making things seamless and easy for consumers.

The Internet Today

In 2003, more than 633 million people around the world access the Web. In the United States alone, 162 million Americans access the web and the average user spends 58 minutes online per day.[6] In fact, a high percentage of television viewers spend time multitasking—watching television and being online.[7] Today, the online medium has earned its place at the media table, as can be seen in Table 24.1.

According to the AOL/Roper Cyberstudy, American's find the Internet the best place to: shop, conduct research, talk with family, find old friends, communicate with workmates, or make a considered purchase.[8]

Medium	% of At-Work Users	% of Non-Work Users
Internet	34%	26%
TV	30%	44%
Radio	26%	18%
Magazines	6%	7%
Newspapers	4%	5%

**Table 24.1
U.S. Media
Consumption by
At-Work and Non-
Work Users by
Media Type, 2001**

Source: eMarketer. "Online Advertising Report." May, 2002. Used with permission.

If they were stranded on a desert island and given the chance to have one technology such as a phone, a television, or a computer connected to the Internet, 68 percent of Americans would choose an Internet connection, which means that the dream of AOL founder Steve Case has come true.[9]

In 1990, Case challenged his then small organization, America Online, to make online as ubiquitous as the telephone or television but even more valuable. In March of 2003 AOL had more than 35 million members worldwide, Microsoft's MSN had more than 8 million, and Earthlink had more than 3 million. AOL's largest competitors, back when Case started AOL, CompuServe and Prodigy, have gone away. CompuServe, the first commercial online service, was acquired by AOL in 1997. At the end of 2002 153 million people were online and 10 million more were expected to come online in 2003.[10]

The revolution has come and gone. Online, dot-com, and the Web are all part of the lexicon and are accepted as part of everyday life.

The Internet: Looking Ahead

The key drivers that brought forth the Internet and aided in its popularity are still hard at work today. We are marching toward a vision created many years ago and which is becoming more and more real as computer technology is being added to everything and everything is being added to the network. Ultimately, the cattle gate on your ranch will have a chip in it so it can tell you the last time it was opened. Your refrigerator will scan your groceries as you put them in and take them out and by networking with your personal calendar will make sure to supply you with a grocery list displayed on your tablet computer as you arrive at the grocery store; that is, if you still enjoy shopping. If you don't enjoy shopping, your appliances will do the ordering online. Your computer will know that you have diabetes because of the health profile your doctor beams to your personal digital assistant (PDA). And while you are at work, your computer will scan the Internet and television networks for good diet advice.

Today many Americans are installing home networks; many are wireless. Television sets connected to hard drives are gaining popularity with devices such as TIVO, and cell phones are starting to take pictures, carry entire address books, and beam music files. Suddenly, devices are talking to each other, and your phone is acting like your television set, your television set is acting like your computer, and your laptop is acting like your camera. It is called convergence.

Business and the Web

We introduced the concept of pure plays, businesses that exist only online, and mentioned the idea of bricks-and-clicks, businesses that have physical locations as well as an online presence. Understanding these business models and their relationships with consumers will help prepare you to be an Interactive solutions seller.

Benefits the Web Provides to Business

1. The ability to inform, educate, and transact with customers 24 hours a day, 7 days a week.
2. The ability to collect data on customer's behavior (observed) and preferences (shared).
3. The opportunity to test offers and products.
4. The opportunity to offer better customer service.

Successful Businesses Online

E-Commerce. Many of the pure-play retailers have failed. Today's biggest online e-commerce success stories are sites that are attached to big national brands such as Target.com, Walmart.com, and Gap.com. Amazon.com and Buy.com are exceptions. Both sites aggregate a large number of products and attempt to sell them at a discount. Amazon.com and eBay have the largest brand recognition and the greatest chance for long-term success. Many niche commerce sites are flourishing because they give consumers access to products that are hard to find—for every imaginable item, you'll find a commerce site. Look to this category for new and innovative ways to sell consumers more and more products and more diverse products. Amazon uses artificial intelligence to build profiles of its customers' past purchases and make recommendations about similar products for them. This type of creative merchandising will also help grow the online e-commerce category.

Community and Commerce. eBay developed a site for collectible enthusiasts that has become a commerce mecca. Today, shoppers using the site participate in more than $1 billion in transactions a month. If you need it, someone is likely selling it on eBay. eBay users have formed a self-governing community with rules and order established and maintained by the users.

News and Content. Tens of thousands of people pay for the online version of *The Wall Street Journal. The New York Times* and the *Los Angeles Times* offer their content free, as does CNN.com, one of the largest content sites on the Web. Why don't all sites charge for their content? Publishers struggle with this dilemma daily. First, the goal of the site must be determined. By offering content free, sites generally get more traffic, and more traffic usually means a greater opportunity to sell advertising and a larger forum to promote the offline version of their content. Epicurious.com is one of the Internet's largest sites dedicated to food. The site is free and houses thousands of recipes. Epicurious.com makes money by charging companies for the placement of their products.

Online Gaming. The gaming sector is exploding as is evidenced by Sony's success with Everquest.com, which has many thousands of paying customers. The games channels on major portals, and sites such as AOL Games and Yahoo Games are flourishing and all projections for this sector are bullish. Look for gaming to play a much larger role in the way we communicate and to provide new and innovative ways to advertise. Sites such as Microsoft's X Box Live and Sony's Everquest.com are building large paid audiences. In addition to gaming for pure entertainment's sake, gaming-for-profit sites proliferate the Web. While regulation has kept gambling offshore, legislation may one day allow American companies to offer online gambling.

Financial Services.   In the financial sector you'll find the Web used as a powerful customer service tool. You can do your banking 24 hours a day, seven days a week (24/7) on sites such as Citibank, and you can trade stocks without a broker on E-trade.com or Schwab.com. You'll also find sites that aggregate offers and facilitate transactions between buyers and sellers. Lendingtree.com will help you find the lowest mortgage by giving mortgage bankers the chance to compete for your business.

Matchmaking.   The Internet has served as a good place for matchmaking. While eBay brings buyers and sellers together and Monster.com matches job seekers with employers, Match.com plays a matchmaking role and will work tirelessly to help you find the love of your life.

Travel.   The Internet is not only a place for research but it's a place to transact. There are travel sites such as Orbitz.com, Travelocity.com, and Priceline.com, as well as several niche brands such as the Alaska Travel Saver.com.

Auto.   The automotive category has two types of online players: (1) manufacturers, such as GM, Ford, and Toyota, which primarily use the Web to educate the public about their products and special offers and send them to their dealer network, and (2) lead re-sellers who usually provide product information and comparison tools while qualifying leads and sending them off to a local dealer. Lead re-sellers usually have relationships with dealers in which the dealer pays the lead re-sellers for each qualified lead.

The Birth of Internet Advertising

It was the summer of 1994 and the Web had become a commercial environment. However, few knew about it and the controversy over how the Web should be used dominated the conversations of those who were knowledgeable. Should sites accept advertising? Should content be free? Time Inc.'s Walter Isaacson was rolling out Pathfinder, an assemblage of some of the prestigious and popular Time Inc. content on the Web and freely accessible to all. *The New York Times* launched @times.com, and in San Francisco's South of Market district, in the depths of *Wired* magazine's accounting office, sat a cubby hole filled with designers cranking away on what would become HotWired.com.

HotWired.com would be a hip site that examined technology and its implications on society, just as its sister publication had, but without moving content from the printed media online. HotWired.com would stay away from shovelware, as they called re-purposed content from print, and create its own fresh content for the Web. *Wired* founder Louis Rossetto, HotWired CEO Andrew Anker, and their first hire, Jonathon Steuer, all knew that advertising was going to be the primary revenue stream in their business plan. When it came time to execute, none of them really had any preconceived ideas about what online advertising was. Prodigy had tried advertising on its online service and was vilified by its users, but this was the Web, a pristine environment without advertising and without standards. Nevertheless, HotWired.com included advertising in their business plan and moved ahead.[11]

Thinking about the relationship between advertising and editorial in the print world, the HotWired.com team decided that ads would ride along with content and that users who clicked on the ads would be directed to advertisers' Web sites. After some debate, they settled on what they believed to be their primary advertising vehicle, a 468×60 mega-pixel unit floating at the top of each page. They could have called it a spot, a billboard, a Web click or many things; instead they called it a banner, and today it remains the most common form of Internet advertising. However, that situation may change, as many marketers today believe the traditional 468×60 banner unit is too small to work for branding and some users have become immune to the size. Many marketers believe that consumers simply move past banners and don't stop to read them. Thus, there has been a push for larger ad units and ads with more interaction in them. Now, larger ad sizes that include interaction and moving graphics enliven the Web. These exciting new ads are called rich media.

When it came time for the HotWired.com team to determine pricing, they decided to charge a set fee per banner per month. They did not charge for individual impressions. The idea of charging for impressions by the thousand came from traditional media buying practices and soon after became the standard Internet pricing model.

The Web as a Place for Marketers

With the Web beginning to percolate, marketers started taking notice. In the advertising industry's trade magazines and at their conferences the Internet began making its way into the conversations. Those who considered themselves trend watchers and early adopters headed to San Francisco's Silicon Valley, the South of Market area, or New York's Silicon Alley to check out the phenomenon. Others chose to dismiss the medium immediately and get back to business. At the National Association of Broadcasters (NAB) conference in 1996, I remember sitting in a presentation and hearing a radio station owner tell the audience that he felt the Internet was headed the way of the CB radio. He said he'd remembered all the claims made about CBs as a new way to communicate and when the world got together on CB radios all they could really talk about was the weather and share alerts about highway speed traps: "Smokey on highway 68; over and out good buddy." For those who did see the future and the promise of the online medium, there was a lot of discussion about the following benefits for marketers.

The Ability to Brand, Inform, and Sell within the Same Environment. Historically, marketers used different marketing weapons to accomplish their goals. For instance, television was always considered the best branding medium, and brochures and newsprint the best way to inform. For selling products or services, you needed a sales force to sell on the phone or in person. While the early Internet marketers were not recommending discarding the other channels, they were making the point that the online world seemed to be the best place to do it all.

Myer Berlow, a gifted agency executive, was AOL's first advertising sales executive and the man who led AOL's Interactive Marketing division from its inception through the AOL Time Warner merger. Myer used to give the following example: Let's say you're a car dealer and you're trying to sell Mercedes. You run some television spots in order to create interest. These spots probably cost you about $15 per thousand impressions. Because of these television commercials, some customers come in and look around. Your salesperson tells them a little about the cars and puts a brochure in their hands to read at home. That brochure cost you about $3 or $3,000 per thousand. Next, it's time to transact. You've invested in a beautiful building with a terrific receptionist who can make latte for your customers while you do the paperwork. What does all of that cost? Five hundred dollars a sale or $1,000?

Now let's look at the online ad unit. Instead of running on television during a golf match that is supposed to have an audience of well-to-do people hopefully interested in a car, we'll run your ad in our luxury auto area and we'll only charge you for the people who visit that area and see your ad. Of those people who are interested in cars, some will want more information. If they want more information, they can click on your ad and will be directed to your Web site, which is just like a brochure, except they didn't have to go to the dealership and you didn't have to pay for printing. If you have a user-friendly site, they'll likely register and tell you more about themselves and their interests than they ever would tell your salesperson in the dealership. Now, it's time to purchase and for those who clicked through, you've given them a chance to custom-order the car of their dreams.

So online has given you the ability to sell your brand to the appropriate audience, inform them, and transact. Did we mention that while you pay $15 per thousand for branding, $3,000 per thousand to inform, and several hundred thousand dollars per thousand to sell cars, that we can do it all for the low price of $60 per thousand? Are you beginning to see how people became so excited about marketing on the Internet?

Pull vs. Push.   Until the Internet came along, all content was determined by producers, editors, directors, and publishers packaging up their best estimate of what the public's tastes were and pushing it via a daily newspaper, a television station, a radio station, or a magazine. With the Internet, users are in charge. Web sessions are entirely controlled by users. They will pull up what they are interested in either by browsing around or by using search engines such as Google or Yahoo. So instead of waiting to watch a television special on the band U2, people can go online and download their music, read about their lives, watch their videos, and print pictures of the band. No longer are people sitting around and waiting for a particular part of a television program in which a song they like is played.

Online Is a Personal Experience.   Unlike television or radio, where the ads need to scream at you to get your attention, online ads are literally 18 to 24 inches from your nose, occupying a good part of your view. The Web is also a private place, giving users the ability to look at products and ads they may be embarrassed to look at in print for fear someone could see what they are reading. The Web provides a whole new forum for sensitive health issues, research, or anything private.

Online Allows Users to Customize Their Relationship with a Brand. Scott Bedbury, known for his marketing roles at Nike and Starbucks and giving the World "Just do It" and "Frappuccino," has said, "A great brand is a story that's never completely told."[12] As marketers work hard to give their brands meaning and create stronger connections to their consumers, the Web is a perfect incubator and laboratory. Consumers can download screen savers, take company logos, and *skin* their music players with them, as well as build fan sites and interactive chat areas with other fans. For marketers this can be quite good or quite bad. When consumers are leading the brand story, they can take it in a direction good for profits or they can trash a brand in forums and chat rooms in a matter of days. Should marketers take the risk? Most trend-oriented brands do, and have found that the Web accelerates the inevitable.

Online and Opportunity to View.   Kent Volandra, who worked at Prodigy in the online service's early days and ran Interactive advertising for Initiative Media in the late '90s, illustrated for me the concept of Opportunity to View within the online universe. Kent said that essentially all media is purchased on the concept of Opportunity to View. When an advertiser buys advertising time on television, the advertiser is not guaranteed viewers, but rather is guaranteed the opportunity for viewers to see an ad. An advertiser can buy an ad in the newspaper on page four of section B, and, hopefully, the reader will turn to page four of section B and read the ad. The difference with online is that you only pay when your ad is served up on a page, and pages are only served up seconds after prospects click a mouse. For every ad they buy online, advertisers can be assured that prospects were staring into their screens waiting for the content and the ad to appear.

Leveling the Field.   On the Internet, it's hard to tell the difference between Wal-Mart and Wall's Mart. Businesses of any size can look like equals. This leveling effect provides a great advantage to smaller businesses, provided they can out-market and out-service their larger competitors. Unlike traditional national marketing, which gives an edge to large companies due to cost barriers, online can be purchased in small increments and, thus, give the smallest businesses the opportunity to compete.

Online Extends the Customer Relationship.   In 1997 Martha Rogers and Don Peppers penned the bestseller *The One-to-One Future*. This book served as a lightning rod for the marketing community by demonstrating the value of focusing on share of customer as opposed to share of market and by highlighting the methods leading edge marketers were using to facilitate one-to-one marketing relationships with their consumers. Relationships in which marketers, by gathering as much information as they could about their customers, could present the most appropriate and salable opportunities. By giving customers relevant value, customers would be more willing to share information and marketers could deliver better products allowing the relationship to grow and grow. The Internet quickly became the perfect vehicle for one-to-one marketing.[13]

Customers could fill out their profiles, respond to offers, and share opinions while marketers could gather data, study their preferences and behaviors, and find ways to please them. Marketers could send newsletters with helpful tips and give customers incentives such as coupons and special offers. For marketers, this all made great sense and for a moment it seemed every company wanted these types of relationships with customers.

Everybody but Consumers.   I remember a friend telling me he had no interest in having a relationship with his toothpaste. For some companies, establishing a relationship with customers was difficult; for others with strong brands and users desiring a relationship, it would be easy. Nike, yes; Preparation H, maybe not. As the interest in one-to-one marketing swelled, the customer relationship management (CRM) business boomed.

The CRM industry came about to provide end-to-end solutions, mostly software based, to help manage relationships. The Web played a key role in collecting e-mail addresses and personal data. The primary method for e-mail address collection online is usually through contests or promotions; people enter their e-mail addresses to win something. During this contest registration process, a publisher or marketer usually offers a newsletter subscription. E-mail addresses, if properly managed and re-marketed to consumers, can spell gold for many companies. Then, suddenly, when it's time to launch a new product, marketers can send a note to many of their best customers. These one-to-one relationships have changed marketing significantly as many companies, who never knew who their customers were, now have a chance to have a relationship with them.

Customer Service.   The Internet has enabled customers to gain information as never before. Running Windows? Get one of dozens of updates this year at Microsoft.com. Broke a piece on your baby stroller and the company is in Italy? No problem; order it online and download the schematic for installation. Many sites now offer live support; simply log on, open a chat window, and begin typing. The company saves long distance charges and the user can get a text record of the conversations and instructions for later use and get links for more information.

The Ability to Measure and Track.   With increasing clutter and the overall effectiveness of advertising dropping, in the last decade marketers have been looking for proof about the effectiveness of their advertising. Early Internet pioneers quickly positioned the Internet's ability to track consumer's actions as the greatest benefit of the online medium. With the Internet, marketers know every impression served and every ad clicked on. By placing a cookie on a user's computer when an ad is viewed, marketers can actually see if users saw an ad and if they came later to visit the advertised site. Tracking was and still is very powerful for marketers. With an investment in online advertising, marketers can now do what they could never do with their offline media—they can quantify their investments. This fact has done a great service to the industry as well as a great disservice. The quality of measurement and the role it plays in determining the medium's value is central to any discussion on Internet advertising. Some believe the medium's value is limited to that which can be measured. Others believe Albert Einstein's, "Not everything that counts can be counted, and not everything that can be counted counts."[14] The debate over the value of tracking metrics is still being waged.

The Evolution of Online Marketing and Today's Online Marketing Tools

Once the 468 × 60 banner was born, smaller units were referred to as buttons. Many of these buttons were 120 × 60 or 60 × 60—the numbers referred to the number of mega-pixels on the computer monitor that the ads covered. Units that did not contain graphics, but instead were lines of clickable text, were referred to as text links. Banners, buttons, and text links were quickly adopted by many sites and became the first standard units of the industry. Uniform ad sizes have been an important part of the industry's growth, because they have allowed marketers to make uniform size ad units for submission and viewing on many sites. But were these early standard units the best or just the first? As the industry struggles to determine the value of an online ad unit and how to best measure it, either by click-through, sales, or brand recall, the publishing community has continued to experiment with new sizes and new technologies that will make online advertising more effective.

Internet publishers and marketers have learned a great deal since the first banner appeared on HotWired.com. Several new ad sizes have been introduced, most of them much larger than standard-sized banners, and experts agree that ad units will likely vary greatly in the future. Unlike television or radio, it is doubtful that Internet marketers will find a one-size-fits-all solution such as the 30-second television spot or 60-second radio commercial.

Online Tools

Following is an overview of the most popular online marketing vehicles today.

Standard Ad Units.   Standard ad units usually refers to units that are fixed or animated in nature and occupy spaces defined by pixel size such as 468 × 60, 234 × 30, or 160 × 600. The current collective wisdom is that bigger is better. C-Net's chairman, Shelby Bonnie, pushed this evolution to larger sizes and challenged the industry to follow the lead of C-Net with fewer ads and larger units. Soon after Bonnie led the way, the Internet Advertising Bureau (IAB) published a list of Standard Units, which included many larger units. Many Web sites now offer the larger units, and marketers are applauding.

Some of the terms used to describe these standard units are:

- 468 × 60 = Banners
- Anything smaller than 468 × 60 = Buttons
- 160 × 600 or larger = Skyscrapers or Towers
- 250 × 250 = Big Boxes

Content Integration.   It is not always easy to tell what is editorial and what is advertising on the Internet. Some online publishers simply wholesale content slots to third parties. Sometimes these third parties supply the content. Sometimes the content is objective; other times it is pure advertising disguised as editorial. Most marketers have found that including advertising within the content is good for their business, yet at the same time understand that the force driving the effectiveness of these placements is users' trust in the content. Proper content integration includes good journalism and full disclosure. If the content a consumer is reading about Alzheimer's comes from a drug company, that is acceptable as long they let consumers know. Consumers would hate to learn that there were some non-traditional treatment methods that are as effective but that did not find their way into the content because the content was paid for and written by an advertiser.

Sites usually charge more for content integration. This integration may take several forms, such as the ability for a sponsor to have the following:

Inclusion in an article. Text and links recommend a marketer's site. Sometimes such a recommendation takes place in a sidebar and sometimes these links are included in the editorial. These placements can be paid, free editorial, or part of a value-added offering in conjunction with an advertising buy.

An integrated mini-site or information center. An integrated mini-site is often a sponsored content area that links from an editorial page and contains articles and utilities. For example, a health Web site may offer a mini-site on sexual health for college students linked from a sexual health area. This mini-site may contain special articles written by, or from the perspective of, a college student and may include a chat area and links to student health services. This area may be provided or sponsored by a pharmaceutical firm or public health agency.

The complete responsibility for programming an area or channel. America Online and several large portals, such as Yahoo, have sold the opportunity to program content areas or channels to outside firms. For example, a large part of AOL's Health Channel is currently programmed by WebMD, and the majority of AOL's Games Channel is currently programmed by Electronic Arts. Often in these arrangements, the company that is programming the channel receives the rights to sell or share in the sale of advertising and to create customer relationships with users.

Search Advertising.   The majority of online users do not simply wander or browse the Web aimlessly, but actively search it with the help of search engines such as Google, Yahoo, or many others. Users also use search engines within shopping destinations to find products. Search advertising presents a powerful marketing opportunity because marketers can place advertising in front of prospects while they are expressing an interest and potential need. Search advertising takes several forms. Many publishers have banner inventory on the top of each Web page and can serve banners for advertisers only when users request certain terms. For instance, a dog food manufacturer can buy the search term "pet food," and whenever this term is input by a user, the manufacturer's ad will appear along with the search results. Many search engines also allow sponsored integration, thus giving the sponsor what looks like a typical link within the general search returns. Usually these links are denoted in some manner as sponsored or featured links. If you'd like to review the types of search offerings and learn more about search advertising, visit Google.com, Yahoo.com, Overture.com, and Search123.com.

Pop-Ups and Pop-Unders.   In addition to the ads served within Web pages, Internet users are faced with ads that appear on their screen, either covering or appearing below content. These types of ads are highly intrusive and are the least favorite among online users. At the same time, some marketers find them to be powerful marketing devices. If the product or service being advertised is desired by the user, then the pop-up may actually be a welcome piece of content. For example, if my music site knew that I'd bought a Rolling Stones album and served me a reminder about Rolling Stones concert tickets going on sale, I'd welcome the intrusion. However, if while at work, I received a pop-up selling discount auto insurance, I might be rather annoyed. I may not have a car, and when I do get insurance I may actively disqualify the firm that annoyed me. Marketers using these more intrusive methods must consider users' reactions to the intrusion and the potentially negative effects. Most intrusive advertising is for products not looking to brand themselves with users or hoping to develop long-term relationships, but from direct marketers looking to sell a product in a one-time-only transaction.

E-Mail Marketing. A huge industry has blossomed to help marketers sell their products via e-mail relationships with consumers. Consumers receive two types of e-mail: (1) unsolicited e-mail, referred to as spam, which is hated by everyone, and (2) opt-in e-mail that the user has requested. In most cases, consumers receive opt-in e-mail either as an e-mail newsletter or as a single e-mail notification of product releases, events, or promotions. Contests, access to sites, or special content is the most common way for marketers to get users to opt-in to an e-mail program. E-mail marketing is quite effective if properly targeted and executed. As with all marketing, clutter reduces response rates, and in the field of e-mail marketing this is a key issue along with the debate related to spam and rights of mailers versus recipients.

Promotions and Contests. Creating promotional events and contests are powerful ways to get users to know a brand and to take a specific action for a reward or the potential for a reward. Often, if a promotion or contest is structured properly, marketers can get users to have several interactions with their brand. For instance, an auto manufacture may run a "sightings campaign" in which users are encouraged to visit the auto company's Web site daily to see the car in a new environment. With each visit, a consumer can enter to win additional prizes. Promotions and contests can be as creative as a marketer chooses. The benefits of contests to marketers often extend for years if a marketer is wise in their collection of user data and re-markets to its data bank of customers' names.

Affiliate Networks. Rather than paying for advertising and hoping sales will follow, many marketers have turned to offering bounties or commissions for referrals. Amazon.com has more than 1,000 affiliates who agree to place an Amazon.com logo on their Web sites. Each time a product is purchased by someone who clicks through to Amazon.com using the link, Amazon.com agrees to pay the Web site publisher a portion of the transaction. While it seems that everyone would do business this way, there are some drawbacks. For example, marketers such as Amazon.com have less control over the environment in which their ad appears. They must watch out for objectionable content, and some brands simply refuse to be marketed next to competitors or in cluttered environments with brands of less stature. Also, only a minority of the online universe is going to purchase in this manner. Therefore, while many companies have taken advantage of affiliate networks, few have looked to affiliate groups as their only source of Web traffic and sales. To learn more about affiliate marketing you can read articles at www.channelseven.com or visit the sites of affiliate marketers www.befree.com or www.linkshare.com.

Rich Media. The term rich media generally refers to any advertising or content application that does more on the page than just lay there as a static placement. Rich media includes, but is not limited to, animation, 3-D treatments, on-screen video, and ads that have utilities built into them such as forms for submission or calculators. Rich media executions usually take one of the following forms:

> **In-the-banner executions.** These are ads in which all the animation, video, or rich elements begin and finish within the constraints of the banner dimensions.

Out-of-the-banner executions. These ads begin in the banner and may either expand the banner area when clicked on or rolled over, or begin in the banner and then fly out over the page and return to the banner later. For example, a recent Dodge truck ad showed the truck driving out of the banner across the page of content, then driving back into the banner.

Beyond-the-banner executions. These executions do not occur in any set area; they simply execute on the page. Sometimes the ads appear or float across pages and other times they cover entire pages until clicked on.

Benefits and Drawbacks of Rich Media.   Rich media has proven to have greater click-through rates and higher recall among users. When properly targeted and executed, users appreciate the technology. As with other ad vehicles, when rich media advertising is distracting and poorly executed, users get turned off. Rich media usually costs more to execute, approximately $1,000 to $5,000 per creative unit, while more standard units fall in the $500-to-$1,500 range. Of course, online ad creation, like all ad creation, has a dramatic range in pricing based on the execution and the cost of talent involved in building it. Beyond the creative costs, rich media usually has higher advertising and serving costs. Sites usually charge more for any ad unit that blocks content and rich media usually needs to be served by a rich media provider who will charge a serving fee, which ultimately comes out to a small percentage of the overall ad costs. Another barrier is the fact that not everyone can see rich media on their computers. Many rich media applications require fast processors and a computer program or plug-in to be installed. Realizing this barrier, many of the top-line rich media manufacturers are working with software and computer suppliers to pre-install their plug-ins, thus eliminating the need for the user to do so.

Learning about Rich Media.   While all online technologies are evolving at a fast clip, rich media is among the fastest. The best way to familiarize yourself with these technologies is to read online ad industry trades such as www.channelseven.com and visit the sites of the rich media providers mentioned below. Most providers offer galleries of their work so you'll be able to see the technologies in action and conceptualize new opportunities.

Rich Media Sites

www.viewpoint.com
www.eyeblaster.com
www.pointroll.com
www.unicast.com
www.eyewonder.com

Measuring Online Advertising

Before initiating any online advertising campaign, clients, agencies, and publishers need to agree on the goals of the campaign and discuss expectations. With different goals come different forms of measurement. Following are the most common types of measurement:

Types of Online Advertising Measurement

Impressions Delivered.   This is the amount of impressions actually served to an online user. Usually an ad is recorded as being served the moment the users' browser calls for the ad to be rendered onto a page.

Click-Through.   Of those impressions served, click-through is measured by how many users performed an action by clicking on the banner or link.

Conversion.   Of those who click through on one ad, conversion is measured by how many completed an action desired by the marketer, such as the purchase of a product, enrollment for a newsletter, or the participation in an online game. Conversion percentages are arrived at by matching a marketer's data with the publisher's data or relying on a third party to serve the ads and track users' behavior online. Third-party ad servers accomplish this tracking by using small computer programs called cookies. Cookies also allow for latent conversion tracking, which allows marketers can ask, "How many people viewed my ad, didn't click, but decided to visit my Web site later?" Marketers tracking latent conversion have found these numbers to be quite high. In some cases, as many as five people visited a site later for every one person clicking through immediately. This tracking technology has given some support to those arguing in favor of the Web's ability to brand.

Brand Recall.   While some products are best suited for direct marketing and direct marketing measurements, the majority of brands advertised rely much more heavily on brand metrics. You may buy Ron Popeil's Rotisserie on television or buy it online with a call or a click, but it is unlikely you'll buy a Cadillac that way or decide to switch your homeowner's insurance that way. Because of these challenges, marketers look to brand recall research to measure if users saw an ad, if they remember the marketing message, and if they were influenced to the point of changing their buying intentions or taking action. Dynamic Logic, the leading firm for this type of research on the Web, conducts its research by showing an ad to users and then asking them several questions about their awareness of the brand and purchase intentions. Later, Dynamic Logic contrasts the users' answers against the answers of a control group who didn't see the ad. By looking at the two sets of data, marketers can determine if the ad influenced their target consumers.

Interactive Pricing Models

While most advertising is sold on the basis of CPM, the Internet has allowed for experimentation with pricing models. With CPM, a publisher sells inventory for what the market will bear and advertisers take the risk that the investment will yield sales. The other models are based on the premise that a publisher risks inventory and does not receive payment until the user performs an agreed-upon action. Following is a list of the most common performance-based deals:

Performance-Based Pricing Models

CPC—(Cost-per-click) Marketers only pay for users who click.

CPA—(Cost-per-acquisition) Marketers only pay for customers who are acquired after clicking on an ad. Often at question is whether the marketer will pay the same rate for someone who is a new customer and someone who is an existing customer. Another question is whether the payment to the publisher should be based on a one-time purchase or on a customer's lifetime value to the marketer.

CPR—(Cost-per-registration) Marketers only pay for customers who come to them as a result of clicking on an ad and register at their site.

CPT—(Cost-per-trial) Marketers only pay for those who agree to try their product.

Most major Web site publishers are not willing to assume the risk up front that they will get paid on a performance-based deal, especially for inventory in heavy demand. However, many publishers have been willing to try performance-based models for inventory that is in low demand or once they have established a marketer's response rate and can predict return on investment with some certainty. Often marketers and publishers will agree on a hybrid deal in which a marketer guarantees a certain minimum to the publisher plus the opportunity to share in any upside if sales exceed baseline projections.

It's important to remember that pricing models are fundamental points of negotiation, and in negotiation each party wants to increase the upside and limit risk. Once two parties are in business together, if willing, they can share results and negotiate with a solid base of knowledge.

Learning More About Online Advertising

Several organizations and trade publications exist to educate the industry, spur debate, and share innovation. Channelseven.com provides many good articles by industry contributors, as does ClickZ.com. The Internet Advertising Bureau (IAB) provides a host of resources and access to some excellent research at www.iab.net.

Making a Living Selling Interactive Advertising

There are many opportunities today to sell online advertising, and with the industry projected to grow, there will be many more to come. Many online sales jobs do not come with the security of traditional media sales jobs, yet many do come with the opportunity to earn substantially more money. Many believe online media to be the fast track for learning and career growth.

Following are some typical jobs in an online sales department. You will find these titles vary from company to company, but the responsibilities are similar.

Interactive Sales Jobs

Account Executive/Sales Representative.   These roles are for media salespeople dealing directly with clients and agencies. Some companies have inside sales forces using the telephone to sell such products as online directories and search. Most account executives receive a base salary plus a commission based on attaining a revenue goal. Account executives need to be much more than ad peddlers. It is essential that they are students of marketing and provide real expertise in helping their partners achieve their marketing goals.

Account Manager.   Account managers exist in organizations that support customer service above and beyond the normal service of a salesperson. Account managers take responsibility for ensuring that agreements are met and that online schedules are implemented and tracked properly. The online medium is extremely complex; getting banners up and running and served properly and checking click-throughs daily and weekly to see that partners get agreed-upon results is a huge task. Account management personnel work very hard to make customers happy. Most people who work in account management are not paid based on commission, but many do have bonus plans.

Sales Coordinator.   These roles are usually entry-level positions designed to provide assistance to account executives or account managers. Coordinators usually help create advertising plans, sales presentations, scheduling, and much more. A sales coordinator's role provides a tremendous opportunity to learn the business by getting a broad view of the organization and the sales process while playing a key role on a sales team.

Planner/Sales Strategy/Solutions.   In some sales departments the role of creating advertising packages and ideas for clients is staffed with media experts, called planners. In some companies this group is called sales strategy or business solutions. In other companies, the system for pulling together media plans is automated or the role of strategy is left to the manager and salesperson. The creation of media plans and ideas is an extremely important role because effective, creative plans differentiate a company in the market. Planning and sales strategy are rewarding positions for creative people with knowledge in this area.

Operations Specialist.   The role of an operations specialist can consist of processing contracts, trafficking ad copy, implementing campaigns by scheduling impressions, and pulling reports, or it can be defined more narrowly with other job titles dedicated to this process. Regardless, there is a great opportunity for those who like working with systems and supporting sales organizations in a non-selling role.

My Career Path and the Role of This Book in It   When I began my career in local television advertising sales, my boss gave me a copy of Charles Warner's *Broadcast and Cable Selling*. I read it cover to cover and referred to it often along with a half-dozen other books that gave me a foundation in that business. Not only is it important to learn consultative selling, but, if you want to be successful, it is essential that you learn to think like a marketer.

Several years later, while working at a dot-com company called Third Age Media, I wrote a guest column in *Electronic Media* about how the Internet offered an incredible opportunity for creative salespeople. Soon after the column appeared, I got a call from an executive recruiter who asked if I would be interested in interviewing for a job with AOL as the western sales manager for their Interactive Marketing Division. A few days later I found myself sitting across from Charles Warner, who was a vice president at AOL brought in to consult with management and build the sales force. He had read my article and of course I had read his book. What a thrill, I thought. Even if I didn't get the job it would be a real pleasure to meet Charlie Warner. Of course, things went much better than I hoped. He autographed my copy of his book and gave me a job.

What can you learn from my experience? First, always thoroughly prepare for a job. Second, if you want to get noticed or promoted, get prospective employers' attention by getting published somehow, appearing on a panel at an industry conference, or making contacts at trade shows. The point is to do something out of the ordinary—more than just a good performance on the job—to get noticed. Finally, read as much as you can about your calling—sales. Become an expert and demonstrate your expertise to prospective employers.

I have found Interactive advertising to be incredibly challenging and gratifying. I go to work each day with the knowledge that I'm helping to build something great, something that adds tremendous value to people's lives and something that grows our economy and helps raise our standards of living. My wish for you is that through continuous learning and application you gain the same sense of fulfillment that I have while delivering the power of an incredible medium to marketers and consumers.

Test Yourself

1. What is purpose of the browser?
2. How does Java help us?
3. What are the eight Cs of the online world?
4. What is rich media?
5. Why is it important to agree with your client on how success will be measured?
6. What are the various pricing models for interactive advertising?

Project

Print a Web page and circle the areas that you think are supported by advertising. Then, call the sales department at that Web property, inform them of your research, and inquire about the availability of the units that you have circled. Also explore with them ways that advertising may be incorporated into text or pictures that appear to be news.

References

Scott Bedbury. 1997. *"What Great Brands Do." Fast Company*, August.
Ward Hansen. 2000. *Principles of Internet Marketing*. South-Western College Publishing.
Sam Hill. 2002. *60 Trends in 60 Minutes*. New York: John Wiley & Sons.
Jay Conrad Levinson. 1993. *Guerrilla Marketing, 2nd Edition*. New York: Houghton Mifflin.
Robert Reid. 1997. *Architects of the Web: 1000 Days That Built the Future of Business*. New York: John Wiley & Sons.
Martha Rogers and Don Peppers. 1997. *The One-to-One Future: Building Relationships One Customer at a Time*. New York: Doubleday.

Resources

www.befree.com
www.channelseven.com
www.clickz.com
www.eyeblaster.com
www.eyewonder.com
www.google.com
www.iab.net
www.linkshare.com
www.marketingterms.com
www.overture.com

www.pointroll.com
www.search123.com
www.unicast.com
www.viewpoint.com
www.yahoo.com

Endnotes

1. John Cassidy. 2002. *dot.con: The Greatest Story Ever Sold.* New York: Harper Collins.
2. Ibid.
3. Ibid.
4. Ibid.
5. Robert Reid. 1997. *Architects of the Web: 1000 Days that Built the Future of Business.* New York: John Wiley & Sons.
6. eMarketer. 2002. "North America Online." www.emarketer.com. February 2003.
7. Ibid.
8. AOL/Roper Cyberstudy. 2002.
9. Ibid.
10. www.emarketer.com. February, 2003.
11. Robert Reid. 1997. *Architects of the Web: 1000 Days that Built the Future of Business.* New York: John Wiley & Sons.
12. "What Great Brands Do." 1997. *Fast Company.* August. v.10. p. 96
13. Martha Rogers and Don Peppers. 1997. *The One-to-One Future: Building Relationships One Customer at a Time.* New York: Doubleday
14. http://aolsearch.aol.com/dirsearch.adp?query=Albert%20Einstein's%20quotes

25 **Outdoor**

By Joseph Buchman

Outdoor media are often called the "mother of all media" because examples can be found in the very earliest records of almost all human history. Early outdoor media in Egypt and Greece were used to advertise local businesses, promote political candidates and, all too often, to offer rewards for the return of runaway slaves. Today Egyptian obelisks still carry, for those who can read them, advertising messages more than 5,000 years old. Modern outdoor media include traditional posters and painted billboards; transit advertising on taxis, buses and even police cars in some cities; backlit bulletins on airport terminal walls; and a variety of other media.

Full-color painted advertising dates at least as far back as Pompeii, where richly decorated walls promoted local businesses. In 1796, the lithograph printing press allowed for the mass production of illustrated posters, and the outdoor media developed its first standard size—one determined by the limitations on the length and width of paper that could be printed. In the 1800s in Great Britain, outdoor posters were very popular because, unlike newspapers, they were not subject to taxes. Posters were also more creative and could be displayed more quickly than newspaper advertising. However, because the display areas were not privately owned, they often suffered from competitors posting their ads over the top of each other within hours, or even minutes—a practice still found in the US today, with flyers for political campaigns posted on telephone poles or other public display areas.

Eventually, poster companies developed standards that ensured exposure of a message for a fixed period of time. In order to offer desirable locations, billposters began to purchase locations to put up their own structures. This also prevented the practice of competitors slapping their posters over the top of existing ads. Late in the 1800s, wooden boards were installed in strategic locations by enterprising companies who then leased them to advertisers for posting bills, which is how the word billboard originated. While Mail-Pouch Tobacco advertising can still be seen on barns throughout the Midwestern United States, today's billboards are available in full-motion, video-quality, electronic displays.

Radio and Outdoor Media

Today, outdoor media account for about 2 percent of all advertising expenditures in the United States. When Clear Channel merged with Jacor in 1999 it created not only one of the largest radio station companies in the United States, but also the largest outdoor advertising company in the world. Today

Clear Channel controls more than 1,200 radio stations and more than 730,000 billboards and other displays in 25 nations.[1] Radio companies have been buying, and merging with, outdoor companies at full speed for the past several years. The trend started in 1996 when Infinity, before it merged with CBS, bought Transportation Displays. That was followed by Clear Channel's 1997 purchase of Eller Media and Universal Outdoor. In 1998 Chancellor Media bought Marlin Media and Whiteco to create Chancellor Outdoor. CBS strengthened its outdoor interests when it purchased Outdoor Systems in a deal valued at $8.3 billion. Today, the top outdoor companies are either owned by or have alliances with radio companies, and command more than half of the total outdoor revenue.

Outdoor Media and Television

While the 14-foot × 48-foot billboard remains the standard, advances in printing have created new outdoor media options such as city bus wrap-a-rounds, animated features, and cutouts. In early 2003 a new form of billboard was introduced in the San Francisco area that has caused some to predict that the outdoor media has begun a transformation into something very much like large outdoor television screens.[2] These billboards are actually large video displays that can change their message depending on the percentage of car radios tuned to a particular format. Electronic equipment placed along the highway can monitor passing cars and determine which stations they are tuned to. This data is analyzed by a computer that associates the stations' formats with known listener profiles. The video screen billboard can then change its message to appeal to the largest percentage of drivers. For example, it can display one ad when most passing vehicles are tuned to country stations, but another for rock-and-roll or news/talk. These new outdoor video screens can also allow advertisers to include animation and change their messages based on time of day or local weather conditions. 7-Eleven stores are equipped with LCD screens at their cash registers that update shoppers on the local weather, winning lottery numbers, missing persons reports, and in-store specials.

The Outdoor Audience

The available audience for outdoor billboards along major highways is growing as more than 125 million Americans commute to work each day. According to the US Department of Transportation, over the past 30 years the number of cars on US highways has increased by 47 percent. The amount of time any given driver or passenger is exposed to outdoor media is increasing, too, both because of traffic congestion in major metro markets and because of an increasing number of billboards.

While billboards (both painted and 30-sheet poster-sized) account for the bulk of advertising dollars spent on outdoor media, other forms are beginning to offer attractive options to advertisers. Outdoor media can be classified as either stationary or mobile, and as either indoor or outdoor. Stationary-outdoor media are by far the most common, and include painted billboards, poster billboards, and transit shelter and platform advertising (for example, bus stops). Mobile-outdoor media include bus boards, taxi displays, banners pulled behind airplanes, balloons, and displays on vans or trucks. The latter can be seen in many large cities, and look much like giant, two-sided, flat screen television sets; some even include audio. Stationary-indoor media include billboard-sized displays, which are often backlit, in airport terminals, convention and visitor's centers, and malls. Several companies, including the appropriately named Johnny Ads, display advertising above urinals and on the inside doors of toilet booths in public restrooms. They promise no wasted coverage as the only 100-percent guaranteed gender-specific advertising media. Even Little League is in the outdoor act; fundraising information for Little League teams indicates a regulation Little League baseball field has "over 40 4 × 8 sheets of plywood which could be made available for rent."[3]

In nations where the electronic media have yet to fully develop, outdoor media are even more prevalent. Video vans are especially popular in India while mobile sound trucks are often used in Haiti where literacy rates are extremely low.[4]

Outdoor media delivers the lowest CPM impressions of any measured medium, can be used to target specific geographic areas, can be combined with other media to create frequency at a very low cost, and reaches those who may avoid advertising in other media. Traditionally, outdoor media were limited to no more than three to five words, required a relatively long production lead time (one to three weeks), and have been subject to opposition in some communities. Improvements in outdoor advertising technology are driving much of its growth. Faster turn-around times for replacing both painted billboards and poster bulletins is both less expensive and more efficient than ever before and many of the new technologies could revolutionize the industry if they prove economically and technically viable. See Table 25.1 for the estimated 2002 revenues for out-of-home media.

Table 25.1 Estimated 2002 Revenues for Out-of-Home Media (in millions)		
Billboards (painted and poster-sized)	$3,000	
Mobile transit and shelter	$ 625	
Indoor (retail and mall)	$ 550	
Stadium/arena	$ 350	
Airport terminal	$ 100	

Source: Veronis Shuler, 2002. *Communications Industry Forecast, 2001*. July. Estimates rounded.

Outdoor Media Research

In 2001 the Arbitron company conducted a study titled *Outdoor Media Consumers and Their Crucial Role in the Media Mix,* in which just over 2,000 individuals were surveyed by telephone about their outdoor media exposure.[5] The study showed that outdoor media in the United States reach the entire socioeconomic range of Americans. Outdoor media also reach consumers not exposed to or only lightly exposed to newspaper and local television news. The Arbitron study also found that the average American's one-way commute is 27 minutes and that the heaviest commuters spend nearly two hours a day getting to and from work. As anticipated, those with the longest commutes also tended to have the highest incomes. This group is also the most difficult to reach with newspaper and local television news. The greater the time spent driving, the greater the time spent with outdoor media and radio. The Arbitron study concluded, among other findings, that:

> ". . . heavy commuters and people who drive a lot of miles have attractive socioeconomic profiles, including higher incomes, higher education, and high presence of children. Those who drive a lot of miles and have long commutes are significant consumers of outdoor media. These consumers are harder to reach with such media as local TV news and newspaper."[6]

Posters vs. Painted Billboards

Most outdoor advertising is sold in three categories of sizes:

1. The painted bulletin or superboard (14 feet tall × 48 feet wide), located along major highways
2. The 30-sheet poster (14 feet tall × 24 feet wide), usually along city streets
3. The eight-sheet poster (about 6 feet tall × 12 feet wide), located closer to street level

While 14-foot × 48-foot painted billboards offer the greatest visual impact, poster boards, both 30-sheet and eight-sheet, provide several advantages, including lower cost. In fact, the CPMs for outdoor posters make them one of the least expensive of all advertising media.[7] Poster boards are also available in many strategic locations within metropolitan areas, while the painted superboards are usually limited to placement alongside major interstates. Poster boards can target specific geographic areas within a market more easily than any other media. In addition, paper stripes, called snipes, can be pasted over the basic poster to provide additional visual impact.

The 14-foot × 48-foot superboards, despite their cost, have their fans, as well. Superboards provide the largest, and some would say strongest, visual impact of all the advertising media. Recall of a superboard ad can be twice that of a standard 30-sheet poster.[8] Special cut extensions and 3-D additions, some as large as a small car, can be structurally attached to superboards. Some outdoor bulletin locations can be purchased by advertisers on a multi-year basis, usually for signs that give directions.

Exposure Duration

The average exposure duration to a billboard is about four seconds,[9] which limits effective copy to no more than six words. On busy rural interstates, three or four words may be the effective maximum. In congested urban areas, up to 10 words may remain effective. Bright, high-contrasting colors are the most effective combination not only during daylight hours, but especially when lit at night. Most billboard contracts are sold in one-year increments, and include rotation to three or four sites over the course of the year. Painted billboards are physically removed and touched up before being moved to new locations, which can create a few days of down time. Thirty-sheet and eight-sheet poster billboards, however, require new paper every few months due to ultraviolet fading and other weather effects.

Transit Advertising

Transit advertising is generally available only in the largest markets in the United States and abroad, or those with some form of viable mass transit system. The most popular forms of transit advertising are street level advertising (about 6 feet tall × 4 feet wide), which are usually posted on bus or transit shelters or other locations where pedestrians congregate, and busboards. Busboards can be sold in five locations on the bus— the street side (king), the curb or sidewalk side (queen), the back of the bus (tail), the front of the bus, and inside the bus. New painting techniques allow the bus to be wrapped in the advertisement, which gives the advertisement the appearance of covering both sides, the back, and the windows.

In 1999, Lycos, the Internet site, became the first company to advertise on fully animated video ads on the tops of taxi cabs. These taxi-top video screens were developed by Vert, Inc., a wireless media company based in Somerville, MA.[10] The ads displayed on the Vert system changed as the taxi moved from block to block, based on a GPS system incorporated into the display. A wireless connection delivers the ad content to the display in real time, and can include live weather and stock market quotes. This allows advertisers to take advantage of micro-geographical targeting technology to drive advertising messages where and when they want them, down to specific zip codes, neighborhoods, or even specific intersections.

Riding the Boards

Riding the boards is a phrase used to describe the process of actually driving by a series of billboards, either when salespeople are selling to prospects, or when advertisers check out the actual location of the advertisements they have purchased. Not every outdoor bulletin location is created equal, but most outdoor companies will sell them as if they are all equal. The two key elements that maximize the value of an outdoor advertising location are:

1. The length of read time when driving an average speed for the location under average weather conditions, and
2. The number of other visual distractions at that location.

A billboard averages a two- to five-second read time in non-commute traffic.[11] Exposure demographics can also be estimated by simply observing the cars passing the billboard's location. Some areas have more upscale commuters, and others will lower social and economic status depending on the neighborhood. It's also important to ride the boards at night to check for proper lighting to see if read time is reduced, or if there are other visual distractions. Some boards get better at night while others get worse.

Measuring Outdoor Exposure

The Traffic Audit Bureau (TAB) is an independent audit company that certifies each board's daily effective circulation (DEC) count. Outdoor companies also rate their boards in gross ratings points (GRPs), or what they sometimes refer to as "showings." A package of boards with a 50 showing, for example, is one that generates daily exposure opportunities equal to 50 percent of the market population—equivalent to a 50 GRP. A premium is usually charged to clients who want to cherry-pick locations. The price for each board is based on the following three factors:

1. The size of the board
2. The DEC, GRPs, or showing numbers
3. The cost of illumination (sunset to midnight, or all night).

Some boards may be sold at a premium price for exceptionally good read times, or at a discount for above-average clutter or low read times. Often, the latter locations are sold to national advertisers who have no way of determining the quality of the location of the actual board. The price for outdoor advertising also depends on the quantity of boards purchased, the length of the contract, and whether they will be painted, or made of paper or vinyl. Paper lasts for 30 days, but is very inexpensive to produce. Vinyl lasts for six to 12 months. Although vinyl is initially more expensive, it can be cheaper than paper if the board is to be shown for 10 months or more.

Determining Outdoor Advertising Effectiveness

In 2001, Sensory Logic, a commercial research firm, conducted a series of tests to determine the effectiveness of outdoor advertising. Among the variables they examined were four attributes that they concluded were key to successful outdoor advertising:

1. Stopping Power: Color contrast, bright colors with good saturation, and an easily perceived distinction between foreground and background.
2. Readability: Integrated graphics, short copy lines, and varied font sizes.
3. Communicating the Message: Relating the offer to familiar ideas and situations, avoiding excessive brain-teasing, and providing large-sized depictions of the product.
4. Memorability: Using an anchoring image to help the viewer relate to the product or situation depicted, and creating a meaningful picture.[12]

In 1999, the Outdoor Advertising Association of America commissioned Perception Research Services to conduct a series of studies to measure how consumers observe and react to outdoor advertising. The study found that children were more likely to notice outdoor visuals, whereas adults were more likely to read outdoor advertising copy, and that more than 25 percent of respondents stated that the outdoor advertising would influence their purchase decisions.[13]

In 1998 the J. Walter Thompson company's Media Research Group conducted a study for the Fox television network to explore the effectiveness of outdoor media at reaching children. The study found that outdoor advertising was not effective at introducing a new brand or character to children, but was effective at reinforcing perceptions of familiar brands and characters. The study also found that children were likely to remember the location of billboards depicting their favorite television characters, especially when they were placed near parks, schools, or other locations where children congregate.[14]

In 1999, Elizabeth Tucker, a researcher at the University of Texas, conducted a study to determine the effectiveness of an outdoor advertising campaign in Austin, TX. She used a 100 showing of 30-sheet posters with the black on white copy "Calvin Coolidge was the 30th President" and a smaller font "www.calvincoolidge.com" in the lower left corner. Prior to the poster display, a random telephone survey was conducted to ascertain the percentage of Austin residents who knew Coolidge was the 30th president of the United States—one out of 350 respondents (0.3 percent) indicated Coolidge was the 30th president. Following a two-month-long showing, 18 percent of respondents were able to identify Coolidge as the 30th president. Over the two-month period, more than 36,000 unique hits, or about 5 percent of the Austin population, were recorded on the calvincoolidge.com Web site.[15]

In another study conducted for the OAAA, researcher Erwin Ephron proposed these three laws to maximize the effectiveness of outdoor advertising:

1. Don't pig out.
2. Don't skip meals.
3. Eat a balanced diet.

His first two laws emphasize the importance of a continuous advertising placement strategy over one of scheduling in flights. Ephron states:

"The workings of these (first) two laws teach the advertiser that more weeks of advertising are a better choice than running heavier weight for fewer weeks."[16]

Ephron's third law emphasizes the importance of placing advertising in multiple media. He points out the *diminishing marginal utility*, or declining return-per-dollar of excessive advertising that is placed in only one medium.

Knowledge Networks, founded in 1998 by two Stanford University professors, has conducted media-mix research which concludes that optimal media buying requires the use of at least four of the five measured media (television, radio, newspapers, magazines, and online) together. For television, radio, and print media, the audience size is a measure of the number of people seeing the program, listening to the station, and subscribing to or reading the publication. These are all measures of an opportunity to see the commercial or print ad, and are not measures of exposure to the ad itself. Passive people meter technology, and some current Nielsen meters, may be able to measure actual exposure to television and radio commercials, but these data have yet to be used in media buying. In the same way, the number of cars or pedestrians passing by a billboard measures an opportunity to see the ad, not actual exposure to the ad itself.[17]

Design Issues

Most outdoor companies offer artwork in-house, but often clients complain about what they perceive as its poor quality. Those who do so tend to hire graphic designers with little background in the outdoor media. Graphic designers tend to design outdoor advertising with far too many words and too many distracting visual elements. For effective outdoor advertising, keep it as simple as possible, with no more than five to seven words. Fonts should be as large as possible with no shadows, no screens, no gradations, no outlines; just 100 percent ink coverage. Ample spacing should be provided between each letter and each line of text. Do not use all caps.

Never use gray, pastels, or mauve colors. Use bold, sharply contrasting colors that accentuate the other. Most outdoor designers recommend using one of the following color combinations:

Black on yellow
Yellow on black
Red on yellow
Yellow on red
Black on white
Red on white

Recent technical advances have improved the production quality of outdoor advertising, including the use of vinyl for long-term displays and the development of computerized air-brush painting for exact photographic replication on both posters and superboards.

The Regulation of Outdoor Media

Outdoor media are subject to a wide variety of federal, state, and local regulations designed to address a variety of social concerns. In 1965, the US Congress passed the Highway Beautification Act which limited the (at least initial) placement of outdoor billboards along the new interstate highway system. In 1998, the attorney generals of 46 states reached agreement with the tobacco industry to ban all cigarette advertising from outdoor media. Prior to that, critics claim, Joe Camel and other youth-appealing cigarette icons were intentionally placed near public schools and other places where children were likely to congregate. However, the ban on billboard tobacco advertising did not have a negative impact on the revenues of outdoor advertising companies. Tobacco advertising often had premium locations with 10- to 20-year contracts so they were paying discount rates for the space. The major outdoor companies resold the space formerly committed to tobacco for as much as twice what the tobacco companies had been paying.

Other groups have attempted to restrict the light pollution caused by well-lit billboards at night, or reduce the "visual pollution" of daytime billboards. Others have pointed out the legitimate safety hazards created by some especially visually engaging mobile media. Some cities and states have proposed extending the ban on outdoor cigarette advertising to include alcohol. Other government regulations limit the size and location of outdoor media. China and many European countries have banned tobacco advertising on billboards, and in the US many other companies cannot post billboards within 500 feet of any place where children tend to congregate. The Outdoor Advertising Association of America also has a voluntary code of principles, which restricts the placement of ads for age-restricted products near locations where children may congregate and the over-saturation of urban neighborhoods with billboards.[18]

Advantages and Disadvantages of Outdoor Media

Advantages

1. Geographic targeting. Unlike any other medium, outdoor can be purchased in a specific location, as well as by zip code, neighborhood, city limits, county, or region.

2. Efficiency. Outdoor has one of the lowest CPMs of any medium.
3. Visual Appeal. While some find all outdoor advertising offensive, others are impressed by the size, bright colors, lighting, and creativity of super bulletins, posters, and back-lit indoor displays.

Disadvantages

1. Limited message capacity. Most outdoor advertising is limited to three to five words.
2. Waste coverage. Although outdoor can be targeted geographically, it does not target demographic characteristics such as age, gender, and income as effectively as other media.
3. Social attitudes. As mentioned earlier, some consumers find all outdoor advertising to be offensive and some communities have oppressive restrictions on outdoor advertising.

Test Yourself

1. What is the maximum number of words that can be used on a billboard for peak effectiveness?
2. What is the average commute time in the United States?
3. What are the dimensions of a painted superboard?
4. What are the dimensions of a 30-sheet poster billboard?
5. What are the two key elements that maximize the value of an outdoor advertising location?
6. What are the four keys to successful outdoor advertising?
7. What are the three main advantages of outdoor advertising?

Project

Ride the boards in your local community. If you live near an interstate, produce an inventory of all the outdoor advertising on at least a 10-mile stretch of the highway. If you live near an urban center, compare this interstate to the type of outdoor advertising found in the core downtown area. If you live in a rural area, produce an inventory of all of the outdoor media options available in your community. If possible, contact a local outdoor company and ask to speak to a salesperson. Conduct an interview with the salesperson about the career opportunities in outdoor advertising sales.

Endnotes

1. http://www.hoovers.com. February 2003.
2. Louis Brill. *LED Billboards: Outdoor Advertising in the Video Age.* http://www.signindustry.com. February 10, 2003.
3. http://ifpaa.org/IFPAANews2001.html. February, 2003.
4. http://www.primeoutdoors.com/others.asp. February 2003
5. Arbitron, Inc. 2001. *Outdoor Media Consumers and Their Crucial Role in the Media Mix.* September 2001.
6. Ibid. p. 7.
7. http://oaaa.org/outdoor/facts/. February 2003.
8. Ibid.
9. Arbitron, Inc. *Outdoor Media Consumers and Their Crucial Role in the Media Mix.* September 2001. p. 3.
10. http://www.vert.net. February 2003.
11. Arbitron, Inc. *Outdoor Media Consumers and Their Crucial Role in the Media Mix.* September 2001. p. 3.

12. Sensory Logic Inc. November 2000. *"Success in Outdoor Advertising."* Report for the Outdoor Advertising Association of America.
13. Perception Research Services. June 1999. *Outdoor's Power To Entice.*
14. J. Walter Thompson, Media Research Group. May 1998. *Fox Kids: Outdoor Study.*
15. Elizabeth Tucker. September 1999. *The Power of Posters: Examining the Effectiveness of 30-Sheet Posters: The effectiveness of 30-sheets are measured via ad recall and ad recognition.* Outdoor Advertising Association of America.
16. Erwin Ephron. October 2001. *Outdoor and the Natural Laws of Advertising.* Outdoor Advertising Association of America.
17. Ibid.
18. http://www.oaaa.org/government/codes.asp. February 2003.

26 Media Comparisons: Advantages and Disadvantages

By Charles Warner

As you learned in Chapter 9, one method of prospecting is to approach current advertisers in other media. Because there are few businesses that do not advertise in one media or another, the vast majority of your prospecting will be conducted by monitoring other media and then selling the advantages of your medium. And, because your best prospects are your current customers, you will encourage them to invest less in other media and to invest more in your medium. In this process, you have to be careful not to disparage customers' judgment for buying another medium. It is best to focus on the concept of media mix and how your medium can add reach, frequency, improved targeting, impact, or all of these elements to an advertising campaign. However, while recommending a media-mix strategy, you must never knock the competition, either in your medium or in other media. This rule exists because all advertising is good and all media have advantages in certain areas. Instead, you sell the advantages and synergies that can come from combining media.

With the increased fragmentation and segmentation of media—more cable channels and networks, more Web sites, and the decline in newspaper circulation and broadcast television viewing—mixing and combining media is the best way for advertisers to get more for their advertising dollars, especially more reach. To understand the media mix concept more thoroughly, go to www.charleswarner.us/indexpresentations.html and read the presentation "Media Mix and the Natural Laws of Advertising" by Erwin Ephron.

Cross-platform selling will steadily increase in the next decade, and in order to participate in this trend salespeople will have to be experts in all media and sell them bundled together as an effective advertising mix. Media giants Viacom and AOL Time Warner are currently practicing this media-mix, cross-platform selling approach.

Following are lists of advantages and disadvantages of the eight media covered in this book. When you view the lists, keep in mind that you should not focus on the disadvantages of other media, but on the advantages of your medium and how it can add to the effectiveness of a media mix. To give you some ideas of which media to go after to get a larger share of budgets allocated to them, see Table 26.1.

As you can see from Table 26.1, television gets the largest share of adults' (ages 18 to 49 and 18 to 65) time and the largest share of total and national advertising dollars. Newspapers receive a substantially higher percentage of total dollars than time people spend reading them in an average week (19.2 percent versus 5 percent). This disparity indicates that newspapers are vulnerable to competitive media attacks if the argument that media dollars should be al-

Table 26.1
Media Time and Money Allocation

Medium	Percent of Average Time Spent Weekly, A 18-49 (Hours)*	Percent of Average Time Spent Weekly, A 18-65 (Hours)*	Percent of Total Advertising Expenditures**	Percent of National Advertising Expenditures**
Newspapers	5% (2.82 hours)	5% (2.82 hours)	19.2%	2.9%
Television	48% (29.36 hours	50% (29.94 hours)	23.5% ***	17.0%
Radio	32% (19.46 hours)	30% (19.08 hours)	7.7%	1.4%
Magazines	3% (1.68 hours)	3% (1.68 hours)	4.8%	4.8% ****
Interactive	12% (6.93 hours)	12% (6.93 hours)	2.5%	2.5% *****

* Statistical Research, Inc. Media Scan. Fall 2000. America Online sales presentation.

** Robert J. Coen. 2002. Universal McCann, Media Expenditures. www.adge.com/datacenter.cms?dataCenterId=960. November 23.

*** Ibid. Coen's Broadcast TV and Cable TV estimates are added to arrive at a "Television" estimate.

**** Ibid. Coen does not give local and national estimates because magazines, even city magazines, are considered to be a national media.

***** Ibid. Coen does not give local and national estimates for the Internet. Local is a small percent of total Interactive advertising.

located according to how much time people spend with each media holds up. This is a rational approach and one I recommend.

Some media, such as television, are considered to have more impact than some others. However, if you give television credit for having greater impact and reach and for being more memorable, you still have to ask how much more valuable these advantages are. Are television's advantages worth 10 percent or 20 percent more of an advertiser's budget than the percentage of time spent with the medium? Is television worth almost 50 percent more money than time spent as is currently the case? Probably not.

On the other hand, radio gets 32 percent of adults' time spent with all media but only 7.7 percent of total advertising dollars and 6.1 percent of local advertising dollars.[1] Therefore, radio, using time-spent dollar allocation logic, should get a considerably higher share of advertisers' dollars. The same rationale holds true for Interactive, which gets only 2.5 percent of dollars and 12 percent of time spent.

Newspapers

If you sell for a medium other than newspapers, be careful not to criticize newspapers too much, especially to local retailers who have been relying on newspaper advertising for their survival and growth. The best way to go after newspaper money is to sell your medium in combination with newspapers. Recommend smaller ads and less frequency, but do not recommend omitting newspaper ads entirely.

Broadcast Television

Both American viewers and advertisers are in love with television, and with good reason. Television moves products and service, it embeds brands in people's minds, and it creates an emotional bond between consumers, advertisers, and ideas. Television garners the biggest share of major national advertising dollars because it works—or at least major advertisers and their agencies are

Table 26.2 Newspapers	Advantages	Disadvantages
	Credibility: One of the oldest, most highly regarded media. Loyal readers,high degree of credibility, familiarity, and acceptance.	**Decreasing Circulation:** In most cities, circulation reaches less than 50 percent of all households. Nationwide, newspaper circulation has been declining steadily for decades.
	Visuals: The combination of text, graphics, and pictures can show products and create a visual appeal that reinforces a message.	**Increased CPMs:** As circulation has declined, newspaper rates continue to increase, thus increasing CPMs, which are among the highest in the media.
	Mass Audience: Newspapers reach a large audience in a market with one exposure.	**Passive:** Newspapers provide information once a consumer is in the market for a product, but they do not build awareness, aid in branding, or create product demand. Used mainly for price comparisons.
	Ad Variety: Newspapers offer a variety of ad sizes that allow advertisers to match budgets to ad sizes.	**Clutter:** A typical daily newspaper is more than 60 percent ads, not counting free-standing inserts. Ads often appear next to or on top of competitive ads, encouraging price comparisons. Little or no product separation.
	Upscale Audience: Newspapers generally reach an older, upscale audience, including homeowners.	**Browsers:** Most people do not read all sections of a paper every day, only those they are interested in. Even the most read sections are seen by only one-half of the people who buy a newspaper.
	Long Copy: Newspaper ads have the ability to communicate lengthy, complex,or detailed information and descriptions.	**Low Ad Readership:** Even if people read a newspaper section, on the average only 42 percent of readers will recall noting a full-page ad.
	Couponing:, Advertisers can track responses by use of coupons.	**Older Readers:** People in younger demographics rarely read newspapers, especially 18 to 24.
	Random Access: Readers can access an ad when they want to, at their convenience, and pore over it. Readers control the amount of ad exposure.	**Increased Competition:** Interactive is attacking one of newspapers' stronger ad categories—classifieds, especially recruitment advertising. eBay is now the country's largest used-car dealership.
	Portability: Newspapers can be read anywhere: on a train, on the beach, in any room in a house.	**Low Targetability:** Difficult to reach many high-potential target segments efficiently.
	Shelf Life: Newspapers can hang around for days or weeks and be accessed again and again.	**Poor Production:** Even with the addition of new and improved newspaper color printing technology, it is difficult to make some products, such as food and new , cars appealing in newspaper advertising.
	Lead Time: Advertisers can place orders with a relatively short lead time—not as long a lead time as magazines, outdoor, or television.	**Declining Couponing:** Despite increased coupon face values, coupon redemption has been declining for years—too many coupons, too little interest.

Source: Radio Advertising Bureau, 2003.

convinced that it works. Changing their minds is like pushing a huge rock up-hill; it is incredibly hard work and it takes a long, long time. The best way to get a piece of a television advertising budget is to go slowly and try to get a little bit at a time. Cable television struggled for 15 years before it made significant inroads on broadcast television, especially network, budgets. If you are selling against television, you have allies such as radio, newspapers, and magazines—all make television their primary target. Use a media-mix approach and show advertisers that despite television being an excellent reach medium, it is quite expensive to add reach after about 35 percent reach is achieved because of diminishing marginal response to media weight. See www.charleswarner.us/indexpresentations.html, "Media Mix and the Natural Laws of Advertising" by Erwin Ephron for a more thorough understanding of the media-mix concept.

Radio

Radio continues to slog along unglamorously as an efficient advertising workhorse. Radio is efficient, builds frequency, and is a great medium for consistently reminding people about their favorite brand, store, or automobile dealer. It is also an excellent hamburger helper—radio can beef up impact, efficiency, and reach when combined with another medium. Radio's greatest advantage is its recency—the last advertising consumers are exposed to when they are ready to make a buy and before they make a purchase. For more information on how radio can work effectively with other media, go to www.rab.com, the Media tab, and the Media Facts: A Guide to Competitive Media.

Cable Television

In March 2003 cable television networks had a larger audience in prime time than the seven broadcast television networks combined (ABC, CBS, FOX, NBC, PAX, UPN, and the WB).[2] Even though direct-broadcast satellites (DBS) have captured more than 17 million subscribers and are eating into cable television viewing slightly, cable continues to capture a bigger share of national advertising revenue. In 2001, according to Robert Coen, cable television had the largest growth over the previous year of any medium in a recessionary year.[3] Cable offers more targeted programming to a more affluent audience than broadcast television.

Yellow Pages

In the recessionary year of 2001, which was an especially bad year for advertising, yellow pages was the only medium other than cable television to enjoy increased revenue over the previous year.[4] This increase, even though slight, attests to the stability of yellow pages. However, for local media such as newspa-

	Advantages	Disadvantages
Table 26.3 Broadcast Television	**Sight, Sound, Motion, Emotion:** The most powerful medium. Combines visual appeal with the ability to touch viewers' emotions. Well-executed television commercials can grab and hold attention like no other medium. Excellent for creating awareness, branding, and reminding.	**Declining Audience Shares:** Television's most watched time period—prime time—ratings and share of viewing have been steadily declining, thus decreasing the medium's reach.
	Reach: Television is ubiquitous; 98 percent of American homes have a television set. Television, especially prime time TV and big events such as the Super Bowl and Academy Awards, can reach more than half the homes in America with a single program. No medium has the reach of television.	**Increased CPMs:** As ratings have declined, rates have not been lowered correspondingly. Television requires large budgets to make an impact—not for the small businesses or the faint of heart.
		Linear Access: Unlike in print, viewers cannot go back or forward to view a commercial again; when it is gone, it is gone. Commercials have no shelf life unless recorded on a time-shifting device such as TiVo.
	Mass Audience: Television is the most mass of all the mass media. It reaches virtually everyone.	**Clutter:** Commercial clutter has increased substantially in recent years. Some television commercial and promotional pods contain as many as 17 individual units, thus causing people to record programs so they can skip commercials. (*zapping*)
	Time Spent: People spend a great deal of time with television. The average home watches almost 30 hours a week, on the average.	
	Young Audience: Baby-boomers (34- to 50-year-olds) and 18-to 34-year-olds grew up with television, watch it, and love it. The medium continues to attract younger viewers, who are desirable targets for most advertisers.	**High Production Costs:** The average national television commercial costs more than $350,000 to produce. Small advertisers cannot compete.
		Channel Surfing: People watch TV with a remote in their hands and surf when commercials come on. Personal video recorders such as TiVo also make it easy to skip commercials.
	Competitive Separation: Television provides more competitive separation than newspapers and the yellow pages.	**Viewing Decreases as Income Increases:** The lightest television-viewing households are in the top third of incomes in the US. Heavy viewing is in lower-income households and by older people (65 +)
	Intrusive: The most intrusive of all media. Viewers have to make an active effort to avoid commercials.	

Source: Radio Advertising Bureau, 2003.

pers, radio, local Interactive, and television, large-sized yellow pages ads are a good target for additional revenue because larger sizes are expensive and not that much more effective than small listings. Yellow pages advertising is particularly vulnerable to attacks from Interactive, electronic yellow pages, which can provide precise tracking of who accesses an ad, listings that can be customized by users, and real-time updates.

Table 26.4 Radio	Advantages	Disadvantages
	Personal, the Theater of the Mind: Even though radio is only a sound medium, it is a very personal medium. Radio can involve and excite people's imaginations with scenes and stories that would be impossible to put in a television commercial. Radio is second only to television in its ability to emotionally involve people.	**Sound Only:** You cannot show or demonstrate a product or its package and label on radio. Although the human voice is personal and warm, many advertisers believe they need a picture of their store, product, or themselves to sell their products.
	Frequency and Reach: Radio is an inexpensive medium and frequency can be purchased efficiently. Radio is also even more ubiquitous than television. Because of radio's extensive penetration, it can extend the reach of any other medium.	**Increased Clutter:** Though not as cluttered as television, in the last several years radio has become more cluttered with not only more commercials in an hour but also with more commercials appearing in a single commercial break, which limits a commercial's impact.
	Low Production Costs, Fast Closing: Lowest production costs of all media. Some of the most effective commercials cost nothing and are read by on-air personalities. Commercial copy can be added or changed on a same-day basis if need be.	**Linear Access:** Unlike in print, listeners cannot go back or forward to hear a commercial again; when it is gone, it is gone. Commercials have no shelf life.
	Efficient: In terms of CPMs, radio's are the lowest of any medium except outdoor. Radio offers both reach and frequency efficiently.	**Fragmentation:** In some markets there are more than 60 radio signals competing for listeners' attention and advertisers' money. Even though radio as a medium can deliver reach, in many markets to match the reach of a newspaper or a television station, 10 or 20 radio stations have to be purchased, making it difficult to buy.
	Imagery Transfer: Studies show that by airing the audio portion of a well-crafted television commercial, radio can stimulate the mind to recreate the visual image originally placed there by television, which costs a lot less than it does on a television screen.	
	Competitive Separation: Radio provides more separation than newspapers and the yellow pages.	
	Intrusive: Not as intrusive as television, but more intrusive than print or outdoor.	
	Targetability: Similar to magazines in ability to target a wide variety of age, interest, lifestyle, and gender groups. Especially effective at reaching hard-to-reach teens, minorities, and ethic groups.	
	Portable: Radio is everywhere. There is more radio listening in cars than there is at home. You cannot read a newspaper or magazine, watch cable or broadcast television, or surf the Internet while driving a car, but you can listen to radio and look at billboards—an excellent combination of media.	

Source: Radio Advertising Bureau, 2003.

**Table 26.5
Cable Television**

Advantages	Disadvantages
Sight, Sound, Motion, Emotion: The same qualities as broadcast television, the most powerful medium. Combines visual appeal with the ability to touch viewers' emotions. Well-executed television commercials can grab and hold attention like no other medium. Excellent for creating awareness, branding, and reminding.	**Small Audiences:** Because cable gives viewers so many choices, cable audiences are fragmented and much smaller than those in broadcast television.
Continued Growth: Cable now reaches two-thirds of US television households and continues to take audience from broadcast television.	**Inaccurate Local Numbers:** As many as 12 percent of homes get television programming from DBS or other delivery systems, so local cable ratings are not as stable as cable network ratings.
Inexpensive: Compared to broadcast television, cable CPMs are low.	**Clutter:** Commercial clutter has increased substantially in recent years. Some cable television commercial and promotional pods contain as many as 12 individual units, thus chasing people to record programs so they can skip commercials.
Targetability: Cable can subdivide its audience into more easily targeted segments than broadcast television. Most homes have a choice of more than 50 channels, and that number is growing. Cable is the choice medium of: sports, music, news, food, and travel.	**Linear Access:** Unlike in print, viewers cannot go back or forward to view a commercial again; when it is gone, it is gone. Commercials have no shelf life, unless recorded on a time-shifting device such as TiVo.
Upscale, suburban: Because cable is a subscription medium, it tends to reach upscale households in major markets and their suburbs. Cable households generally are better educated and have higher incomes.	
Competitive Separation: As with broadcast television, cable provides more competitive separation than newspapers and the yellow pages.	
Intrusive: Television is the most intrusive of all media. Viewers have to make an active effort to avoid commercials.	

Source: Radio Advertising Bureau, 2003.

Magazines

Magazines are a highly targeted medium, with magazines devoted to almost any human endeavor you can think of. However, with increased time spent on the Internet and other media, time spent with magazines has declined in recent years, and has the lowest time spent of the major measured media (see Table 26.1.). For national media such as broadcast television, cable, radio networks and, especially, Interactive, magazines are currently a vulnerable target.

	Advantages	Disadvantages
Table 26.6 Yellow Pages	**Ubiquitous:** Almost every home in America (97 percent) and business has a copy of one yellow pages book or another. **Usage:** The majority of adults say they check the yellow pages for a phone number or address at least once a week. **Reference Tool:** The yellow pages serve as a directorial reference for consumers who had already decided to buy a product. **Targets Consumers In the Market:** Yellow pages advertising targets consumers who have made a decision to buy a product and usually where to buy it.	**Inflexible:** Most yellow pages directories are published only once a year and advertising must be created and placed well in advance. Changes cannot be made to reflect new locations, phone numbers, and such. **Ad Clutter and No Separation:** The yellow pages are all advertising, and ads and listings appear alongside competitors, where shoppers can compare. **No Branding:** Yellow pages do not brand and do not create awareness. Poor production quality leaves little room for a quality approach or creativity. **Inconvenient:** Yellow pages directories are usually big and bulky, especially in major markets, and they are often out of date, so more and more people are going to the Internet for their shopping information.

Source: Radio Advertising Bureau, 2003.

Interactive

After the implosion of the dot-com speculative bubble, the Interactive medium's incredible advertising revenue growth curve plunged. According to Robert Coen, in 2001, Interactive revenue had an 11.6-percent decline over the boom year of 2000[5] and the Interactive Advertising Bureau (IAB) estimated it declined another 17 percent in 2002.[6] However, in the last quarter of 2002, Interactive revenues grew 2.3 percent and were expected to grow at an even greater rate for the full year.[7] Interactive will have the highest percentage growth over the next decade of any medium, aided by cross-media optimization studies (XMOS) such as the IAB's study with Kimberly-Clark and Colgate-Palmolive.[8]

Table 26.7 Magazines	Advantages	Disadvantages
	Wide Readership: According to the spring 2001 Simmons data, 89 percent of adults say they read one or more magazines.	**Competition:** There are nearly 18,000 magazines, which creates too many choices for consumers. Many magazines do not survive their first year of publication. Established magazines are expensive for this reason.
	Targetability: There is a magazine for every conceivable interest. Advertisers can target demographically or by product affinity, lifestyle, interest, or hobby,.	**Time:** The average person spends only 3 percent of media time weekly with magazines.
	Portability: Magazines are even more portable than newspapers because they are smaller. Magazines can be read anywhere except, hopefully, the car.	**Expensive:** Magazines are the most expensive, on a CPM basis, of the major media. And even though magazines can be purchased on a regional or spot (market-by-market) basis, to do so is extremely expensive.
	Content Relevance: Advertising can be placed near relevant editorial material to heighten the interest and readership.	**Inflexible:** Because lead times of six weeks or more are common, ads must be prepared long before publication dates, which limits flexibility to adapt to market conditions.
	Regionalizing: Magazines can be purchased on a regional, city, or even ZIP-code basis.	
	Advertorial: An in-depth advertising message can be created to appear more like editorial copy than an ad and can present complex information.	
	Production: Most magazines are printed on glossy stock that can reproduce for color advertising beautifully. There are many exciting and arresting creative opportunities in magazines.	

Source: Radio Advertising Bureau, 2003.

Outdoor

Billboards reach everyone who can read—they are highly visible and virtually inescapable, and new technologies are making outdoor advertising more noticeable and exciting. Never a high-growth medium, out-of-home advertising will continue to be an important medium, especially on the highways and for tobacco and liquor advertisers.

Table 26.8 Interactive	Advantages	Disadvantages
	Direct Response: Through the interactive media, advertisers can reach highly educated, affluent, and younger consumers who can purchase with a mouse click.	**Low Awareness:** Internet and interactive users pay less and less attention to banners every year.
	Interactivity: Interactive allows customers to communicate directly with advertisers and tell them what they like and do not like, and what they will buy.	**Inexperience:** Many advertisers and agencies have yet to learn the intricacies of the interactive medium—how to use it, how to buy it, and how to design effective creative.
	Information: Advertisers can provide information to consumers before they buy a product. More than 60 percent of the people who buy a new or used car research it on the Internet.	**Spam and Pop-Ups:** Spam has rendered e-mail marketing almost useless. Software can block annoying pop-ups.
	Immediate: Consumers do not have to wait for a brochure to be sent to get information. Advertisers can change offers and prices in real time in response to competitive pressure.	**Hard to Buy:** Difficult for many advertisers to understand. Hard for agencies to make a profit buying interactive. Some Interactive companies, such as AOL, are very difficult to do business with.
	Tracking: Interactive technology allows advertisers to measure exactly how many people saw which ad and how they responded or bought.	
	Optimization: Interactive advertising ad-serving technology can serve demographically, geographically, and lifestyle targeted ads to specific consumers.	
	Branding: New research indicates that the interactive medium is not only an excellent direct-response medium but is also good for branding. New interactive, rich-media ad technology make branding more effective than previously.	
	Efficient: CPMs in interactive are generally lower than other media, except out-of-home, primarily due to a glut of inventory.	
	Add Reach: Advertising dollars invested in Interactive can add reach to any other media investment. Along with radio, the ideal media-mix component.	

Source: Radio Advertising Bureau, 2003.

Table 26.9 Outdoor	Advantages	Disadvantages
	Brevity: Outdoor is effective for conveying brief messages and simple concepts.	**Brevity:** Message capacity is limited to five or seven words at most—cannot deliver more than a simple message and cannot show benefits or advantages.
	Low Cost: Out-of-home's CPMs are significantly lower than any other medium by a factor of 10 or more.	**Low Recall:** Commuters behind the wheel and other potential customers are exposed very briefly and such conditions as rain and fog can limit readability and recall.
	Directional: Billboards can be used to point directions to businesses.	
	Geographically Targeted: Billboards can be placed in high-traffic areas and transit ads can be placed where people commute. Also, an inexpensive way to reach minorities or ethnic groups that might be grouped in certain locations.	**Lack of Effective Measuring Tools:** Unlike other media, out-of-home has no reliable method to measure its audience or effectiveness. CPMs are based on street or highway traffic, not on exposure.
	Bonus Showings: Billboard operators do not pull down a board when a contract is up or until the board is sold to another advertiser, so sometimes free showing can last for months.	**Inflexible:** Ads must be ordered 28 days before they go up, and once up cannot be changed, in most cases.
		Ugly Image: Because of growing environmental concerns, many communities have limited the volume of out-of-home advertising.

Source: Radio Advertising Bureau, 2003.

Test Yourself

1. What are six advantages of newspapers?
2. What are four advantages of broadcast television?
3. What are five advantages of radio?
4. What are four advantages of cable television?
5. What are four disadvantages of yellow pages?
6. What are four advantages of magazines?
7. What are five advantages of Interactive?
8. What are five disadvantages of outdoor?

Project

Assume you are selling interactive advertising for a local Web site in your market. Write a presentation to a local advertiser who invests all of its advertising dollars in the local newspaper, recommending a switch of some percentage of that budget onto your Web site. Use the data in Table 26.1 and in the media-mix presentation on www.charleswarner.us/indexpresentations.html in the presentation "Media Mix and the Natural Laws of Advertising" by Erwin Ephron to craft your recommendations.

Resources

www.cabletvadbureau.com
www.charleswarner.us
www.ephrononmedia.com
www.iab.net
www.magazine.org
www.oaaa.org
www.rab.com
www.tvb.org
www.yellowpagesprofit.com

References

Radio Advertising Bureau. 2003. *Media Facts: A Guide to Competitive Media.* www.rab.com.

Endnotes

1. Robert J. Coen. 2002. Universal McCann, Media Expenditures. www.adge.com/datacenter.cms? dataCenterId=960. November 23, 2002. Table 26.1 shows radio with 1.4 percent of national revenue; subtract this number and Coen's reported .3 percent from 7.7, and you get 6.1.
2. www.cabletvadbureau.com. April 2003.
3. Robert J. Coen. 2002. Universal McCann, Media Expenditures. www.adge.com/datacenter.cms? dataCenterId=960. April 2003.
4. Ibid.
5. Ibid.
6. www.iab.net April 2003.
7. Ibid.
8. Ibid.

Part IV

Opportunities, Preparation, and Persistence

27 Opportunities: Direct and Agency Selling

By Charles Warner

In their *Harvard Business Review* article "Make Sure Your Customers Keep Coming Back," F. Stewart DeBruicker and Gregory Summe identify two types of buyers: inexperienced generalists and experienced specialists. In media selling, examples of inexperienced generalists are smaller customers, often retailers and others you call on directly, or who are new to advertising in a medium. Agency media buyers are an example of experienced specialists. DeBruicker and Summe point out that selling strategies with these two types of customers must be different.

Inexperienced generalists typically do many jobs in their businesses. For example, a small, owner-run retailer might keep the books, set up displays, and do personal selling as well as place advertising. If this retailer, who we will call Jane, is unfamiliar with radio, for instance, she wants to know how to buy it, schedule it, write copy, and best position her store to appeal to her target customers. Jane is more interested in expert marketing and advertising advice and results (selling more goods) than in price; therefore, salespeople must provide expert advice in those areas in which she needs help.

Experienced specialists typically specialize in one activity. For example, an agency media buyer does only one thing, placing media buys, and is an expert in that activity. If this buyer, who we will call John, is making a television buy in a market, he is interested only in price and service—fast, responsive service. John is not interested in marketing or advertising advice or in advice about writing effective copy, and he is interested in a different type of results—ratings, circulation, CPPs, and CPMs.

As inexperienced direct accounts gain experience, their needs shift from asking for marketing and advertising advice to asking for responsive service and competitive prices. However, one thing direct accounts, especially retailers, will always focus on is sales results, which will always be more important to them than ratings, circulation, or research data. In the following sections of this chapter, you will learn more about strategies for calling on direct accounts and on agencies.

Salespeople who sell the Interactive medium find that the majority of their prospects at both direct accounts and agencies are inexperienced in the medium and need expert advice. Unfortunately, as in other media, after salespeople go to considerable effort and invest a lot of time in teaching customers about their medium, the clients become experienced and more interested in price. Therefore, the selling strategy must change accordingly.

Direct Selling

Direct accounts are those who do not retain an advertising agency, so media salespeople call on the principle owner, the CEO, or director of marketing. Most direct selling, particularly in local media, occurs with retail businesses. The selling tips that follow are for calling on retail businesses, but they also apply to calling on the majority of direct accounts.

The Retail Business

Retailers bridge the gap between manufacturers and consumers, and advertising plays an important role because retailers sell their goods and services in a highly competitive environment. Few businesses that start up survive; two out of every three new retail businesses will fail within one year. Changes in the nation's demographics and lifestyles have caused many of the more traditional retailers to rethink their strategies. Single-brand loyalty has declined, and mass-marketing techniques have been developed to accommodate the proliferation of new products. Consumer groups that used to share homogeneous tastes have now splintered into many groups, all demanding different products to meet their different and changing needs.

Retailers have had to change their ways of doing business to satisfy and attract consumers who are generally older, better educated, more cynical of product claims, and more demanding of quality. To entice these consumers, advertising and promotion have become more important than ever before; retailers now use new media technologies such as the Internet and new media combinations such as Interactive, catalogues, and data-based marketing.

In the current marketing era, there is a proliferation of commodity products that depend on massive advertising and promotional support to get shelf space, then move off those shelves. Hundreds of new products come out weekly as marketers try to please demanding consumers and find profitable new market segments.

Introducing new products is an expensive process. The average cost to introduce a new consumer product nationally is approximately $60 million, and Microsoft budgeted $350 million to introduce version 8.0 of its MSN in 2002. Even with intense advertising support, new products have a rough time; only about 50 percent make it.

Retailers must keep pace not only with the changing demands of their customers but also with the number of products and the discounts, rebates, and promotions associated with these products. At the same time, they must create an image for their stores and create traffic for the brands that are advertised by manufacturers and are typically available at many other retail outlets. This results in an ambivalent relationship between manufacturers and retailers. Manufacturers, also known as vendors, want consumers to buy their brands, but they do not care where they buy their products; retailers want consumers to shop in their stores, but they do not care which brand they purchase.

However, retailers and manufacturers are dependent on each other, to the frustration of both, as in most co-dependent relationships. Manufacturers are frustrated that they spend virtually all of their money and effort on 95 percent of the marketing process (getting a product on a retailer's shelf), but their fate is out of their control at the store level during that last five percent of the process, in which the purchase commitment is made. Retailers are frustrated that they spend so much time, money, and effort to find a location, build a store, stock it, hire sales personnel, and display merchandise only to have manufacturers give their lines to competing retailers to sell. Retailers and manufacturers have different goals, but they must cooperate as part of the marketing system that gets products to consumers.

Getting products off a manufacturer's shipping department shelves, off a wholesaler's warehouse shelves, and off a retailer's shelves and onto the consumer's shelves is an enormously complex marketing process of which advertising is only a relatively small part, as you learned in Chapter 15.

Retail/ Development Selling

Retail is a broad category for which there is no standard definition; stores (hard goods, soft goods, food), services (insurance, banks, dry cleaning), entertainment (theaters, clubs, VCR rental), and restaurants all normally come under the general classification of retail. In this book, all types of retail establishments and sellers of services are referred to as *stores*. The most appropriate way to differentiate between types of accounts is according to their orientation—results-oriented or numbers-oriented. For example, those that are results-oriented should be designated as retail clients, *or accounts,* and have development-oriented salespeople call on them. A retailer may have an advertising agency that buys according to the dictates of a store owner who cares only about results and who directs the agency to buy in a particular pattern that has proven to be successful in the past. This kind of agency and account should be called on by a retail/development specialist.

Many seasoned sales managers and ad directors suggest their retail/development salespeople tell retailers, "CPMs don't buy things, people do. Retailers want to see people in their stores, not ratings." The development-oriented salesperson must be patient and not always seek a fast sale, a quick close, a high share of budget, or a high price. These tactics are best suited for a numbers-oriented agency selling situation. It may take much longer to sell to a retailer who is trying to fit advertising into a complex marketing and merchandising mix than to an advertising agency that is merely trying to make an efficient media buy.

Many media outlets in larger markets (newspapers and radio and television stations, for example) sometimes split their local sales efforts into two divisions: *agency* and *retail.* This distinction is made because the two types of clients have different needs. Advertising agencies do the media buying for a variety of clients, including retail clients. To standardize and quantify their media evaluations and buying efforts, and to justify their decisions, they use ratings and efficiency evaluations: CPM (cost-per-thousand), CPP (cost-per-point), reach and frequency, and so on. Thus, advertising agencies are typically ratings-oriented and require a service-oriented salesperson who understands ratings and is experienced in operating in a numbers- and negotiation-oriented selling environment. Retailers, especially inexperienced generalists, need a salesperson with a development-selling orientation.

Media buying may be the responsibility of a number of different people at a direct account, depending on the business size and organization. Buyers of media range from a store owner to the director of merchandising to the advertising manager to the merchandise buyer in a store department. According to the organizational rule of thumb that structure follows strategy, the amount of emphasis a media organization places on its agency or retail selling efforts depends to a large degree on two things: the size of the market and the relative rank position of a medium versus its competition. The larger the market and the stronger the rank position, the greater the weight that is typically given to agency selling efforts because the majority of advertising is bought by agencies in large markets. On the other hand, the smaller the market or the weaker a station's ratings position, the greater the need to emphasize a retail or developmental selling strategy.

Newspaper selling is mostly retail/development selling because rarely are agencies involved.

A Five-Step Approach to Direct/Retail Selling.   Direct/retail selling also requires thorough, intensive servicing because direct accounts and retailers need to be reassured, they need attention, and they need a multitude of details to be handled. Telephone calls about when their commercials, ads, or banners will run must often be made, co-op records must be kept, notarized affidavits of performance must be provided, last-minute copy and schedule changes must be made, and so on.

Step #1: Identify seasonal patterns. Look at a calendar of seasonal sales patterns for various businesses and concentrate on two or three categories that will have peak seasons in four or five months. Retailers normally plan their promotion and advertising budgets from four to six months in advance; some plan a year in advance.

Step #2: Select target accounts. The next step is to select several of the larger accounts in these categories as *target accounts*—ones on which you will concentrate—then go about qualifying them and identifying their problems. You want to focus on your most profitable opportunities.

After you have made the initial calls, research the accounts by looking at their past media usage. In many markets newspaper-checking bureaus publish information on what advertising has run in the newspaper in the past year. If you are targeting newspaper advertising and if your company does not subscribe to such a monitoring service, you can go to the library and scan past issues of the newspaper to get a feel for the amount of advertising a target account used. As part of your discovery process, you might ask how much money or what portion of the advertising budget an account invested in each medium. You might ask a retailer's competitors in the same category about that retailer's media mix, spending, and advertising strategy. Another advantage of prospecting and identifying problems by category is that you become familiar with or even a semi-expert on a business and its competitors.

Step #3: Write a retail presentation. Once you know enough about your target accounts, you should write a retail presentation which will demonstrate to your target accounts that you not only understand the retail business but also have some solid recommendations on how to use your medium most effectively. Once you write such a presentation, you can easily adapt it for other retailers. See www.charleswarner.us in the "Presentations" link for a sample retail presentation, which can be adapted for any media calling on retailers.

Step #4: Sell ideas that solve problems. The standard prototype of the ultimate loser as a salesperson is someone who shuffles into a store and asks timidly, "You don't want to buy anything today, do you?" The best way to avoid being this kind of loser is to sell retailers ideas that help them solve their advertising problems: promotional ideas, event ideas, contest ideas, special package and section ideas, copy ideas, and so on. Make an appointment with a retailer after you have completed your identifying-problems step, then stride in and announce, "I've got a special reason for calling on you today—a terrific promotion idea that will help you maximize inventory turnover on several of your high markup lines!"

It is always best to approach retail prospects with something extra to offer, such as a promotional slogan or special event that has some excitement and urgency about it. Standard offerings have a way of turning sales calls into boring, ho-hum exercises in futility, but promotions, special packages and sections, and copy ideas help give you a very distinctive, differential, competitive advantage and make it easier to close, too. Remember, retailers do not care about ratings, circulation or impressions; they will only listen if you can help them satisfy *their* needs, solve *their* advertising problems, or help *them* identify a meaningful marketing opportunity—all aligned with getting results.

Promotions. Promotions are designed to create traffic at a retailer's location by generating excitement and increased awareness for a store or a product. A promotion can be as simple as a radio disc jockey giving away a pair of local movie theater tickets to the 10th caller or as elaborate as MTV giving away an island. Thousands of promotions have been run by media in cooperation with advertisers and retailers; industry trade organizations such as the RAB, TVB, MPA, NNA and CAB have documented many of them in their sales promotion literature and on their Web sites.

The term promotion covers a variety of situations that are over and above supplying advertising time and that promote the increased involvement with advertisers' products. Promotions typically involve the dual promotion of a medium and an advertiser; a medium contributes a schedule of advertising (which usually includes the advertiser's name) to create audience involvement in the promotion, and the advertiser buys a schedule and contributes prizes. The combination of the two schedules creates a synergistic effect that benefits both the medium and the advertiser.

Some promotions last for months, such as with an ongoing bumper-sticker campaign in which people pick up the stickers at an advertiser's stores. Others involve only a single event, such as disc jockeys wrestling in Jell-O at a shopping center. Others are tied in with a charity, for example, an air guitar contest (pretending to play without a guitar) in which the $5 entry fee goes to the Special Olympics and the winners receive prizes donated by a sponsor or traded out by the station.

A properly conceived and executed promotion can generate substantial excitement and extra exposure. However, before a promotion is offered to a sponsor, salespeople must get the approval and assured cooperation of all the departments in their company. Make sure the details are worked out before offering a promotion, for poorly executed promotions are sure to turn away clients and make it virtually impossible to get them back.

Special packages and sections. Various media can create a variety of attractive opportunities for retail advertisers, such as year-end football packages that include professional football playoff games, college post-season bowl games, and the Super Bowl. These packages can offer certain, primarily male-oriented, advertisers an excellent vehicle to reach their target audience. Theme packages, such as back-to-school packages that run in late August and early September, or January New Year's packages, can offer substantial savings to advertisers.

A special package should be offered to a retailer as a sale item that is a good deal, because, after all, retailers are accustomed to the notion of sales and deals because that is how they do business. A good deal does not necessarily mean a cut in price; it can also mean an outstanding value—a high quality at a reasonable price.

Newspapers and magazines often have special sections that are especially effective. Sections such as Home and Garden, Home Decorating, Spring Lawn Care, or New Electronic Products can be special offerings to retailers as well as big revenue generators for a publication.

Special packages and sections can give salespeople a reason to call on an account by saying, "I just wanted to keep you up to date on some excellent values we have available for a limited time." Every call made with a special package or section is a potential for an increased investment.

Copy ideas. Salespeople can also get increased advertising investments and renewals from an account by suggesting new copy themes and approaches to retailers who have not retained an advertising agency to do this job for them. Sometimes salespeople can suggest copy ideas to a retailer's agency, but such attempts are usually unwelcome. Agencies are paid to create copy and do not normally take kindly to salespeople who offer advice.

Recommending commercial copy ideas can be a risky proposition because it is hard to tell in advance the kind of copy approach a retailer will like. You must proceed carefully, especially if the merchant is particularly fond of the copy approach currently being used. Merchants sometimes write their own copy, so be extremely cautious about criticizing the creative approach of current advertising. One of the best ways to approach customers with a new copy idea is to play commercials for them or show them ads or banners that other businesses have used successfully. Another is to create a commercial or an ad especially for the client's business on a speculative basis, called *spec spots* or *spec ads.*

Most media trade organizations such as the RAB, TVB, CAB, NAA, MPA, and IAB have libraries of effective ads and commercials in a variety of different business categories, both local and national, that have generated results. A salesperson can take several of these commercials or ads to clients and give them ideas for a number of different approaches. Creating spec ads is an excellent method of arousing a prospect's interest in an idea—an idea that can only be implemented by purchasing or increasing an advertising investment, of course. Many schedules have been sold by enterprising salespeople who sold a copy idea first and then a schedule to go along with it.

Writing copy. In large markets, salespeople are seldom expected to write commercial copy. In small- and medium-sized markets, however, salespeople often write copy for their clients. Most of the advertising placed in large markets is through agencies or by experienced retailers who have their own advertising departments. This fact does not necessarily mean that the copy or creative approach will be good or effective; it just means that it is someone else's responsibility to create it. Many large- and medium-market radio stations, cable systems, television stations, and newspapers designate a person or department to create and produce commercials and ads. If you find yourself in a situation where it is your responsibility to write copy for an advertiser, though, see "Writing Copy" in Appendix G and re-read the copy writing tips in Paul Talbot's Chapter 20 about radio, or the advice about writing newspaper ads in Tom Stultz's Chapter 18.

Step #5: Present an ROI analysis. The most powerful case you can make to a targeted direct account for investing in your medium is a thorough, realistic ROI analysis, which you learned how to do in Bill Grimes' Chapter 21; see Tables 21.1 and 21.2. Present an ROI analysis to the top executive of an account; if the account has an agency do not show it the ROI analysis because an agency will ask exactly the wrong question, "What's the CPM."

Co-Op Advertising

Cooperative, or *co-op, advertising* began in the early 1900s when retailers asked manufacturers to cooperate with them in advertising efforts. Stores requested that the manufacturers help them by underwriting part of their advertising costs; thus the tug-of-war began. Vendors wanted to help the retailers (their customers) sell more of their product, so co-op advertising seemed reasonable. Retailers felt it was only fair for manufacturers to help pay for advertising because retailers were spending most of the money to let consumers know what was available and where they could buy it. However, as mentioned previously, stores wanted *traffic* and vendors wanted *brand identification*. This dichotomy has kept the co-op partnership an uneasy one, with a long history of mistrust and abuses on both sides.

One of the conditions that led to the growth of co-op advertising was the way newspapers sold advertising. Most newspapers charged more—up to 50 percent more—to national advertisers than to local advertisers. Furthermore, most newspapers offer substantial volume discounts which large local retailers could earn because they advertised a great deal more than national manufacturers normally did. Thus, by having retailers place the advertising and take advantage of their much lower rates, vendors could reimburse them for a percentage of the advertising and save money.

For example, say an ad in a newspaper cost a national advertiser $1,000. That same ad at local rates with large earned-rate discounts might cost a local merchant $500. If the manufacturer agreed to *co-op* 50 percent of the store's ad featuring the vendor's product, then the manufacturer would pay $250 for what otherwise would have cost $500 and the retailer pays only $250 for advertising valued by the retailer at $500. Most local advertising that features brand-name products involves co-op advertising support from vendors.

The Robinson-Patman Act. Years ago, dominant stores pressured vendors for favorable co-op arrangements that gave them a competitive edge over smaller retailers. Congress stopped this practice in 1936 by passing the Robinson-Patman Act, making it illegal for a vendor to offer to one customer a co-op plan that was proportionately different than that offered to another customer in a given geographic area. This law is policed by the Federal Trade Commission (FTC), which has issued guidelines on what vendors and retailers can and cannot do with co-op advertising. Thus, if a vendor offers co-op advertising support or allowances to one retailer in an area, it has to offer the same deal (proportionately) to all competing retailers in the area.

How Co-Op Works.   Most co-op plans offered by vendors are based on how much a retailer purchases of the vendor's product. A co-op plan might reimburse a retailer for up to 50 percent of the cost of an ad (at the retailer's earned rate) featuring the vendor's product; the upper limit on the total amount reimbursed would be 10 percent of the total value of the vendor's product that was purchased. So, if an auto parts store purchased $10,000 worth of Champion spark plugs, Champion would reimburse the store 50 percent of the total advertising cost, up to a maximum reimbursement of $1,000.

There are almost as many different co-op plans that manufacturers offer as there are manufacturers, and they change their plans regularly to fit their marketing strategies. Some vendors offer 100 percent co-op, some 50 percent, and some 25 percent. Some offer it on 1 percent of purchases, some on 10 percent of purchases. Others do not offer co-op based on a percentage of purchases, but they offer an advertising allowance of a specific dollar amount on each item purchased, such as $150 per automobile. Others offer co-op only in newspapers, which was typical until the late 1970s. Some offer it in all media, some only in radio or television. For example, a motorcycle manufacturer's co-op plan makes co-op funds available only for radio because the company found that retailers used newspapers almost exclusively for their advertising and the vendor wanted to force the retailers to use a more diverse media mix that included radio.

Newspapers were favored as a co-op vehicle in the past largely because they were the traditional advertising vehicle for retailers. It was also quite easy to provide a *tear sheet* of a newspaper ad and prove to a vendor that the ad ran in the proportion that was agreed upon. With the help of the RAB and TVB, proof of performance for co-op advertising in the broadcast media was greatly simplified in the 1980s. Today, most manufacturers include broadcast and cable in their co-op plans, but few include Interactive.

For retailers to receive reimbursement from a vendor, they have to submit a bill and proof that an ad or commercial ran: a tear sheet from a newspaper or a notarized affidavit (bill) from a station or cable system. It is illegal for the retailer to submit false bills to vendors and for the media to help them submit fraudulent bills. The practice is referred to as *double-billing*, and the FCC has either fined, issued limited license renewals, or revoked the licenses of several radio stations for engaging in double-billing schemes with advertisers.

To make matters even more complicated, a retailer can run several co-op products in one ad or commercial. For example, a home improvement store might run a springtime radio campaign offering four products—a garden hose, grass seed, fertilizer, and a spreader—to homeowners. In such a case, each of the four vendors would co-op 25 percent of the schedule, each according to their own co-op plans.

How Retailers Obtain Co-Op Funds.   To obtain co-op funds from vendors, retailers go through a number of steps:

1. Retailers keep track of all their purchases from a vendor, and the co-op advertising allowance percentage is applied to these purchases to build up advertising allowance credits, called *accruals.*

2. Retailers obtain and keep on file a copy of each vendor's co-op plan, which gives details on how to go about applying for co-op funds and about the types of media and advertising copy the vendor will support.

3. When the accruals become large enough, the retailer buys the advertising according to the vendor's guidelines. Strict adherence to the vendor's guidelines is important so the retailer can be reimbursed.

4. After the advertising runs, the retailer submits a co-op claim (a copy of the media's bill for the advertising), along with some proof (tear sheet or affidavit) that the advertising ran in the prescribed manner.

5. The vendor double checks that the advertising ran according to its published co-op plan and policy.

6. Once the vendor is assured that the co-op advertising ran properly and that the retailer accrued sufficient funds to pay for the advertising, a check is sent to the retailer for the amount of the vendor's participation. Retailers may not deduct co-op allowances from vendors' merchandise invoices, but they must go through the process of making the claims as outlined above.

Sometimes the process of checking the tear sheets and affidavits and sending out reimbursement checks can take several months. Many manufacturers hire third-party companies, such as the Advertising Checking Bureau of Chicago, to audit their co-op plans and to see that retailers get prompt reimbursement. Co-op advertising is a tremendous administrative undertaking for both the manufacturer and the retailer, but it is also one of the most effective ways possible to communicate information about products to consumers.

Caveats

There are several things to be careful about when you call on retailers or direct accounts. Sometimes direct accounts will ask you to give them a 15-percent discount off your rates because they do not have an agency. Do not do this for two reasons: (1) if agencies find out about it, they will be furious and try to blackball you and shut you out of agency business because your are, in a sense, encouraging accounts not to hire agencies; and (2) you usually have to write copy, pick it up and deliver it, and, generally, provide more service to a direct account than you would if it had an agency, so it does not make sense to give a discount when you have to do more work. Agencies perform valuable services, such as writing copy, for which you should be delighted to pay because it saves you time. Even though you get higher billing credit for direct accounts (because your medium remits 15 percent to agencies), you can make more calls if you do not have to write copy or service accounts as thoroughly as an agency would. It is also better, in the long run, to have an agency involved and to write copy for an account because if results are poor, you can always blame the copy (often justifiably), which you cannot do if you write the copy yourself.

Occasionally a retailer or direct account will ask you to recommend an advertising agency. The natural tendency is to recommend an agency on your account list or a friend on whom you call, but always recommend several agencies (a choice of three is best) for two reasons: (1) if other agencies on your list find out you recommended someone else, they will be justifiably upset and might stiff you on future buys, and (2) if the client does not like an agency you recommend, the client will blame you. If asked to recommend an agency, say, "Here is a list of three agencies that I think could do a good job for your size and type of account. You pick the one you like best."

On the other side of the coin, sometimes agencies will ask you to send them clients to solidify your relationship with the agency. Do not do this because if you have other agencies on your list and they find out you are favoring one agency over another, you will be in trouble. Whenever you are asked for recommendations from agencies or direct clients, always keep in mind the rule from Chapter 3 on ethics, and be fair.

Agency Selling

Advertising Agencies

Advertising agencies came into existence in the 1880s when they sprang up as sales representatives for newspapers and magazines. As sales representatives for the media, they kept a 15-percent commission on the amount of money advertisers spent with them in the media they represented. Thus, an advertiser might spend $1,000 for ads in a magazine and the agencies would keep $150 and give $850 to the magazine. As time went on, the agencies got close to their advertisers and began to create advertising for them and decide in which media to place it. The agencies maintained the practice of keeping 15 percent of the amount the advertisers spent in the media. The structure of the advertiser-agency-media relationship was set and has remained virtually unchanged to the present day.

Agencies also make money by adding a 15-percent commission to the material, services, and production they purchase for a client, a practice that is referred to as *grossing up* a charge. For example, if an agency purchases $850 worth of photography for a client, it would gross it up 17.65 percent (or multiply $850 by 1.1765) and charge the client $1,000. (You may recall from basic high school algebra that you cannot take a 15 percent discount off the price of some product and then multiply the discounted price by 1.15 to get the original number; the two values will not be equal. For example, 15 percent less than 100 is 85, but 1.15 times 85 equals only 97.7.)

Fee Arrangements. Advertising agencies are service businesses and their expenses are mostly for people: copywriters, artists, media buyers, media planners, account management people, and so forth. Advertising agencies have to do virtually the same amount of work to produce an ad in a small newspaper as for one in *The New York Times* or to produce a commercial for a local television station in San Francisco as for one on the NBC Television Network. Therefore, if a client needs a great deal of work done and is not buying enough media to produce sufficient commissions to compensate the agency adequately for its efforts, the agency might charge the client a fee. The fees are typically based on the following: (1) a monthly retainer fee against which media commissions are credited, (2) an agreed-upon charge per hour for work performed, or (3) a complex formula related to the amount of work the agency performs for a client as a percentage of the agency's total overhead. The fee arrangement is growing in popularity, as both agencies and clients perceive it to be more equitable than the straight 15-percent commission on media purchases and more in line with the actual amount of work done for a client. By 2000, almost 70 percent of the advertising agencies in the country worked on some type of fee arrangement other than a straight 15-percent commission. One reason that the fee arrangement is preferred by many advertisers is that they do not want their agency's income to depend on how much money they spend in the media. Advertisers want to make sure the agencies place their money as efficiently as possible and that the most effective, not necessarily the most expensive, media are purchased.

A trend that has developed in recent years is that more agencies are merging with each other or are being bought out by large, international, publicly owned conglomerates. This trend has put pressure on agencies to produce higher profits. As the push for bottom-line performance has increased, some advertisers have become concerned that the more expensive and easily purchased media, such as network television, might be favored over the less expensive media, such as radio and Interactive, which are more time-consuming to purchase.

Agency Structure.   Advertising agencies vary in size from large conglomerates with more than 25,000 employees in offices throughout the world and media billings in the tens of billions of dollars to local, one-person agencies in smaller towns.

Basic Functions.   The work in the typical agency is broken into three basic functions: *account management, creative,* and *media.* These functions are supported in larger agencies by plans groups and by research, production, traffic, and accounting departments.

The account management function is carried out by account executives, account supervisors, and management supervisors, who are the primary contact people between the agency and its clients. The account management team usually solicits the clients and services them once they are signed up.

The creative function is handled by artists, copywriters, and creative directors (or supervisors) who create advertising. Typically, the account executive presents a client's advertising problem to the creative group, normally an art director and a copywriter, who will mull it over and recommend an overall campaign or a single ad or commercial approach. Ideas are often the result of brainstorming among the agency's art directors, copywriters, account people, and media people. The account executive then presents the idea to the client. If the client accepts the approach, the creative people write detailed storyboards (for television) and arrange for the production of the commercials.

The media function is carried out by media planners, media buyers, and media directors (or supervisors) who evaluate and place advertising. Planners recommend what media and how much of each should be used. Media buyers select which networks, stations, newspapers, magazines, or Web sites to buy; they are the people on whom media salespeople typically call. However, in recent years, planners have become more important in the evaluation process and salespeople, especially magazine salespeople, have been calling on planners more often.

Media departments are organized in various ways, depending on the agency. Some are organized by product, and buyers buy all markets around the country for a certain product or brand. Other agencies organize on a regional basis and have buyers specialize in buying one or more markets for all of the agency's products. Most larger agencies have gone to this regional approach because they feel it gives them more in-depth knowledge about the constantly changing rates, ratings, and circulation data in markets; it also gives them better leverage in negotiating, particularly if they buy for a number of products. Furthermore, large agencies usually have buyers who specialize in a particular medium: network television buyers, spot television buyers, radio buyers, print buyers, and Interactive buyers, for example.

Support Functions.   The support functions in larger agencies are handled by a number of groups.

The plans group (sometimes called the *strategy group*) consists of the top account, creative, and media management people who meet to discuss the overall long-term strategic plans the agency will recommend to each client.

The research department keeps up-to-date on economic, population, media, advertising, marketing, and other relevant research information and provides it to the account management, creative, and media departments in an agency.

The production department produces ads and commercials by overseeing all the myriad details that go into getting advertising in front of viewers, listeners, or readers.

The traffic department ensures that the right ads or commercials get to the right newspaper, magazine, Web site, or television or radio station at the right time, with instructions on when, where, and how often to run them.

The accounting department bills clients, pays media, does an agency's payroll, and produces financial reports.

To complicate matters further, some agencies' media departments serve as the *agency of record* for large multiple-product advertisers, such as Procter & Gamble (P&G). The giant consumer-products company has dozens of products that each invest millions of dollars in advertising. To keep track of all of its advertising for all of its brands and to make sure that it is taking advantage of all possible media discounts, one agency is designated as the agency of record. This agency gathers and coordinates all the information about all media buys from all of P&G's various advertising agencies.

House Agencies.   Some advertisers in local markets establish their own in-house advertising agencies. Instead of paying a 15-percent commission to an outside advertising agency, they want to keep the money within their own company. Such advertisers hire people to fill the creative and media buying functions and produce and place their own advertising, usually under a separate agency name. Often the savings realized from house agencies do not offset the disadvantages of having less than superior advertising execution. Full-service agencies can support top creative and media people with the income from several accounts, whereas house agencies typically do not have the funds or diversity of interests to attract excellent people.

Boutiques.   A *boutique* is an agency that sells various agency functions on a piecemeal, or modular, basis. Some boutiques sell only their creative services, some specialize in doing only media planning and buying, and some do only research. Boutiques often can offer advertisers topflight talent they might not otherwise be able to afford. For example, a highly regarded art director and a top copywriter in a large agency may get tired of the bureaucratic environment and decide to set up their own small creative boutique to serve just a few clients. Of course, if the boutiques produce excellent advertising, they soon grow larger. Many successful large agencies started out as boutiques. Clients of boutique-type agencies usually deal with several agencies, each with a specialty, simultaneously.

Trade Deals and Buying Services

One of the characteristics of broadcast time is that it is instantly perishable; lost revenue from an unsold spot can never be recovered. Many years ago, enterprising entrepreneurs discovered they could make a profit by bartering goods for unsold time on radio and television stations at a very favorable exchange rate and then reselling the time to advertisers.

Here is how a typical barter arrangement, or *trade deal,* might be made: entrepreneurs form an advertising agency, sometimes referred to as a *barter house,* and contact radio and television stations. They then negotiate to give the stations something of value in return for time. A barter house might send a catalogue of merchandise (television sets, stereos, athletic equipment, or whatever) to a station. The merchandise is offered at full price—at retail cost or above.

The barter house then negotiates with the station for time, often referred to as a *bank* of spots, at a favorable exchange rate—for instance, $2 worth of spots for every $1 worth of merchandise (a two-for-one trade deal). Stations willing to make such an arrangement would run the spots for which they have contracted with the barter house only if they have no paid advertising to fill up their time. Thus, the station is able to get something of value in return for the commercial time that would have had no value.

The barter house builds a bank of spots on as many stations in as many markets as possible, then calls on advertisers, offering to sell them advertising at large discounts on the stations with which they have contracts. They might have gotten the spots at a 50-percent discount from the two-for-one trade deal. They then resell the spots to advertisers at a 25-percent discount off the station's rate card, with the understanding that the spots might not run at the best times, namely, only in unsold time periods. The barter house makes a tidy 25-percent profit on this resale. It also makes money on the other end by buying merchandise in volume or otherwise heavily discounted and trading it with a station for spots based on the full price of the merchandise.

Several barter houses became successful at convincing advertisers they could place their media schedules for less, and they persuaded the advertisers to let them handle their media buying. The barter houses soon discovered that by taking tough negotiating stances and acquiring extensive market and station knowledge, they could often outperform media departments at traditional agencies. In the late 1960s, the general function of these services changed from being primarily barter houses to being boutique-type *buying services* staffed by professional media directors, planners, and buyers who did not handle barter and who performed a straightforward media-buying service. Media-buying services typically operate on a fee basis, with incentives built into their fees for bringing in media buys at targeted rating-point levels for less than the allocated budget.

Television Bias

In most large- and medium-sized agencies, there is a bias in favor of television in general and network television in particular. A typical large national advertising agency might place 40 percent of its total US media dollars in broadcast network television, 25 percent in spot television, 16 percent in cable, 10 percent in magazines, 4 percent in radio, 2 percent in newspapers, 2 percent in Interactive, and 1 percent in out-of-home. Account people try to sell the benefits of letting their agency handle the advertising for large users of network television because if clients can afford the networks, they will generate large commissions or fees. The media department likes to buy network television because it can spend and administer huge amounts of money with fewer people. Because the size of each order is so large, two or three people can easily spend and keep track of $50 million on the television networks. The same amount spent in radio might keep a media department of 10 people busy most of the year.

Moreover, creative people do not get higher-paying jobs by producing beautiful newspaper ads; they move up the ladder to become highly paid creative directors by developing a reel of award-winning television commercials.

Finally, agencies keep accounts by doing what their clients want, and clients are typically enamored with the traditional national media, especially with network television. Agencies may recommend new creative approaches or nontraditional media, but they normally do not push very hard if their client is not disposed toward what they are recommending.

Agency-Media Relationships

Agencies depend on the media for their existence. Their incomes are based on how much time or space they buy; conversely, the media depend on agency buying decisions for much of their incomes. As a result, agencies and media continually perform a ritualized, arm's-length waltz: agencies try to buy at the lowest rates possible, and the media try to sell at the highest rates possible. This is a good example of an ambivalent, love-hate relationship.

A further complication is that agencies tend to be defensive because of the tenuous nature of agency-client relationships. Although clients and agencies have contracts that normally spell out the financial details of relationships, rarely is a long-term commitment involved. Agencies continue to serve their clients because of the advertiser's trust, faith, and, too often, whims. Agencies sell a service even more intangible than media advertising—their abilities to create good advertising and place it efficiently and effectively. There are few ways to measure the creative and buying effectiveness of an agency. For example, did sales go up because the advertising was great or did the client cut prices? Did sales go down because of a poor ad campaign or was the product awful? It is often easier for a client's product managers to blame their agency for their failures than to blame themselves.

Advertisers might drop an agency for a number of reasons: advertiser personnel changes (a new person at the client wants to make a change), new personnel at the agency (the client does not like an agency's new creative director), agency plunder (agencies target other agencies' clients), or competitive media grumbling (a disgruntled salesperson from a medium goes to a client and criticizes an agency). The precarious and insecure nature of the agency business tends to bring out several personal traits and needs in agency personnel: defensiveness, risk-avoidance, recognition, affiliation, and contrariness. Salespeople who call on agencies must learn to deal with the complex needs and behaviors of agency people, particularly media buyers.

Media buyers are in the bottom echelon of an agency's media department. They are typically overworked, unappreciated, and underpaid. They are the agency's infantry troops slogging through mountains of media research and media proposals. There is little wonder that buyers tend to be defensive, given the pressure under which they work. They are particularly touchy about salespeople going to their clients.

Calling on Clients.   Some media salespeople, especially those from magazines and television networks, frequently make sales calls on both the advertising agency and the agency's clients with the blessing, or at least the grudging cooperation, of an agency. Generally, the larger the agency, the more secure it is in its relationship with clients, or at least so it seems because the loss of one client does not threaten the agency too much. The higher the position of a person in the agency hierarchy, the less that person usually objects to media salespeople calling on the agency's clients because they hope the salesperson can convince the client to increase an advertising budget. However, a secure relationship is more the exception than the rule, and buyers, who are far down on the organizational ladder, normally do not like salespeople calling on their clients, especially if it is to complain about a buy or to make waves of any sort.

If you feel it is necessary to stir things up to get your message across to a client, and a buyer has told you not to call on the client, then sell your way up through the agency's media department (through the associate media director to the media director to the vice president in charge of media). All along the way, tell your medium's story; tell the agency why you want to see their client and exactly what you are going to tell the advertiser. Someone higher up will finally give you permission to see the client because he or she will realize that, in the final analysis, the agency cannot keep you away if the client agrees to see you, plus, you might get the client to invest more in advertising.

The secret to getting agencies' permission to call on their clients is to keep the agencies involved all along the way and to go over your presentations with them so they will be assured you are not going to make them look bad.

Ratings: The Security Blanket.   As mentioned previously, agency selling is numbers-oriented selling, as opposed to direct/retail selling, which is usually results-oriented. Since an agency's performance is difficult to measure, anything that has a number associated with it is eagerly grasped as a measurement device. Ratings are used as a tool to evaluate an agency's media-buying performance. This process is called a *post-buy analysis*. An agency's broadcast media buyers make decisions based on ratings information that is three months to one year old at the time the buy is made. When the ratings for the time period that the advertisements ran are published, agencies compare the actual audience size, CPMs, and CPPs to those that they had projected at the time the buy was made. This analysis is usually done on a computer, which also checks all the advertising that actually ran against invoices. This process of *posting* is used, more than any other variable, in evaluating the performance of agency media buyers, most commonly in broadcast and cable advertising. When stations or networks fail to earn the ratings projected in an original buy (that is, they fail to *post)*, agencies may pressure for make-goods, sometimes referred to as audience deficiency announcements (ADAs). In many cases stations, networks, and Web sites offer ratings or impressions guarantees and will schedule ADAs to meet their guarantees. However, this is not always the case. Remember, an agency is not going to pay a station, network, or Web site a higher rate because it exceeded pre-buy estimates. Salespeople should point out that an occasional failure to post is balanced by other occasions when the medium outperformed initial estimates.

In broadcasting and cable, ratings are also invaluable when planning how much media to buy and approximately what to pay for it. For example, planners set a rating-point goal and a budget based on cost-per-rating-point (CPP) estimates for a market. Next, the agency gets a client's approval of the plan (sometimes called a *pre-buy analysis),* and it is turned over to a media buyer to execute. If a buyer can bring in the campaign on budget for the desired rating points or, in the case of print, circulation, the agency and the buyer have a way of quantifying their performance to the client. The agency and the client feel secure with the numbers because ratings are tangible evidence of the fact that the agency performed its service and exercised its buying judgment. Therefore, do not expect agencies and their clients to give up their security blankets. You have to play the game using their rules, and their rules emphasize numbers, not results.

Still, if agencies and their clients take refuge in the security of numbers and make their media buys based on ratings and circulation, you might well ask how a salesperson makes a difference and emphasizes quality. It is because numbers are so absolute and finite that salespeople *can* make a difference. In fact, in a numbers-oriented selling situation, salespeople are the only difference, because a 10 rating is a 10 rating is a 10 rating. Buyers continually need reassurance that what they are buying will turn out to be what they hoped for. In their hearts, they know that CPMs or CPPs do not walk through doors and buy products, but that people do. They know that ultimately they will be judged by their clients on the overall effectiveness of their advertising campaigns. If they buy very efficiently in media that have the wrong demographics or to which no one pays attention, then their campaigns will not be successful. Therefore, agency buyers depend on media salespeople to keep them thoroughly informed about the various media: demographics, attentiveness levels, programming and content changes, rate changes, personnel changes, and anything that will help them evaluate the media better and make better buys.

Remember also, in the case of broadcast and cable, ratings, and in print, circulation, are based on past, not current or future, performance. Effective salespeople challenge the wisdom of basing media-buying decisions solely on old data. They provide information on what their medium is doing *now*—information that may serve to make the old numbers obsolete.

Qualifying Agency Buyers. When calling on buyers, just as with any prospect, you should be sure to qualify their *personal needs first.* Business needs will change from buy to buy and from client to client, but a buyer's personal needs will remain relatively stable and, if you are lucky, predictable. Furthermore, when instructions to make a buy come from clients, a buyer may be in too much of a hurry to spend much time with you. When a buy comes down and a buyer requests avails or sends out an RFP, you should already understand enough about the buyer to know what sales tactics will work best.

Since the majority of your business from agencies will come from requests for avails or RFPs, agency selling is primarily a service-type sell and not a developmental-type sell. Agencies sell your medium for you; your job is to compete for existing dollars already allocated to your medium. In return for their sales efforts to clients, you must sell to them on their terms with efficient and effective CPMs and CPPs.

Determining Flexibility and Autonomy. In addition to qualifying an agency buyer's personal needs and creating a needs portrait, you must qualify the degree of *flexibility* and *autonomy* a buyer has. Some agencies and clients give their buyers virtually no discretion in making a buy and insist that they stick to the parameters given in the media plan. Other agencies give their buyers a great deal of leeway. Typically, a media plan will outline an overall rating-point goal and a budget for a market, but the selection of individual media outlets will be left up to the buyer. Some plans outline reach and frequency targets, some outline the number and types of media outlets and number of spots or inserts per outlets, and other plans merely give a budget and leave the rest to the buyer.

Normally, more experienced buyers who have demonstrated time and again that they can buy efficiently are given more flexibility to use their discretion in making a buy.

Once you have ferreted out the amount of discretion a buyer is allowed, it is your task to work with the buyer within the parameters set by the media plan and within the boundaries of the buyer's flexibility. Your ability to balance the needs of the agency with the needs of your company will determine your success in agency selling. For example, can you balance an agency's need for a good CPP with your station's need for a high share of budget?

Agency buyers reward salespeople whom they feel are working for them to get the best buys and the most out of a particular medium. Your ability to convey to agencies that you are working hard for them is the critical element in augmenting your product, in creating a differential competitive service advantage, and in becoming *the* difference.

Getting the Parameters of a Buy.   Once a buy is up (a buyer has called you with an RFP), you must get complete information about the upcoming buy. These buying parameters define the *business needs* of the buyer. You should develop a list of advertising agency Discovery Questions similar to the client Discovery Questions in Exhibit 9.1 in Chapter 9.

Call Timing.   Try to be either first in line *(primacy)* to see the buyer or last *(recency)*. First is best under three conditions: (1) your buyer is very intelligent and self-confident and you are confident your proposal is so good that it will make all subsequent proposals by other salespeople look poor by comparison; (2) you are so confident of your ability to give such a dynamic, superior sales presentation that all others will pale in comparison; or (3) you have an especially timely offer that is in such demand that you want to get in first. In the latter case, you are really doing an agency a favor by giving them an opportunity to buy a high-demand opportunity for their client. Most salespeople generally prefer to be last in line because it gives them the opportunity to ask how their proposals compare to all the others and the chance to make last-minute competitive adjustments. The best timing is to be both first (with a dynamite proposal) and last (to make competitive adjustments), which requires having a better relationship with a buyer than competing salespeople have.

Agency Selling Tips

Show Up for All of Your Appointments a Little Early.   It is not good form to be late or to be sweating and out of breath when you get into a buyer's office. By showing up about ten minutes early and being announced to buyers, you also let them know that you are there, which puts pressure on the buyer to hurry up and finish with the salesperson they are seeing, probably your competitor. Another reason for showing up early and lingering a little while after your presentations are over is to *get to know the salespeople who are competing against you.* Remember, you are going to position your medium to have a differential competitive advantage, and sometimes that advantage can be positioned in terms of a competing salesperson. For example, if you know that one of your competitors is extremely aggressive and tends to browbeat buyers and close quite strongly, you might counter by urging the buyer to look carefully at all proposals and not be pushed into making a decision. If the buyer then resists and the competitor pushes too hard, the buyer might become annoyed and shut the competitor out of the buy.

Buyers are usually very busy, particularly when they are making a buy. Respect their time and learn to tell your story quickly and efficiently. This tactic will also help you focus on your most important benefits. Many salespeople refer to such a sales story as an *elevator pitch*, or a concise, two-minute oral presentation that summarizes your medium's value proposition and major benefits. Develop and rehearse your elevator pitch. Also, try to think of creative, memorable ways to make your elevator pitch more tangible by using props and leave-behinds.

Be Honest, Accurate, and Dependable.   Never offer anything you cannot deliver. If you make an offer, you should be able to get a subsequent order confirmed by your sales manager. Agencies do not have time to play cat-and-mouse games. If demand is strong and something you are offering may be sold soon, give buyers an accurate assessment of demand and how long your offer is likely to be good. When you get an order, take accurate notes, book the order immediately, and get back at once with confirmations. If you cannot confirm at least 75 percent of what was offered, you probably did not do your job well initially, did not keep the buyer informed about the availability of what you offered, and did not suggest enough substitutes.

Get Competitive Information.   As soon after a buy as is practical, ask the buyer to give you competitive information about what else was bought (naturally, you got an order). One of your functions is to *monitor the marketplace,* and one of the best ways to do this is to uncover schedules and rates of competing outlets in your medium. Getting accurate information on street rates can help your management set pricing strategy. Your ability to get competitive information will vary depending on the agency. Some agency buyers will give competitive information as a matter of course, others will not give any information, and others will lie. There is a common phrase in the television business that "buyers are liars." This phrase comes about because many buyers, in an attempt not to make salespeople look bad—especially in broadcasting and cable—will inflate the share they tell each salesperson they received due to pressure from salespeople's management to find out what share of the business they got. Share information from buyers is inevitably inaccurate. Similarly, rate information from buyers is often inaccurate because they are trying to drive down prices and they will act accordingly. How accurate the information you get from a buyer depends entirely on how good your relationship with that buyer is. The best way to establish a trusting relationship is to create a tacit agreement: "You don't lowball me, and I won't highball you."

For further insight into agency selling, read "Selling Magazines to Agencies" in Appendix F. The author of the piece, Phil Frank, wrote Chapter 23 and is a former media supervisor at Ogilvy and Mather and a senior vice president and group media director at Ammirati Puris Lintas advertising.

Test Yourself

1. Define a direct account.
2. What is the difference in orientation between retailers and advertising agencies when they invest in the media?
3. What are the five steps of direct/retail selling?
4. How do retailers obtain co-op funds?
5. Why do agencies have a bias for television?
6. What is a trade deal?

Projects

Project #1: Look at the Retail Presentation in the "Presentation" link on www.charleswarner.us and write a schedule proposal for a local retailer in your market.

Project #2: Read "Writing Copy" in Appendix G and write three newspaper ads and three radio commercials for a local retailer, each with a slightly different approach (you are writing three versions so the copy does not get stale when it runs and so you can give the retailer a choice).

Project #3: If you are a salesperson in the media, do an ROI analysis for your largest target account.

References

F. Stewart DeBruicker and Gregory Summe. 1985. "Make Sure Your Customers Keep Coming Back." *Harvard Business Review*. January-February.

Charles Warner and Joseph Buchman. 1993. *Broadcast and Cable Selling*. Belmont, CA: Wadsworth Publishing.

Chapter 28 Preparation and Persistence: Organization and Time Management

By Charles Warner

There is an old joke that you have heard a thousand times, but it bears repeating in this chapter about preparation and persistence. A young person stops a passerby on Fifth Avenue in New York and asks, "How do I get to Carnegie Hall?" The stranger answers emphatically, "Practice, practice, practice." Notice the passerby did not say "practice" once, but three times, which not only emphasizes the need to practice, but also to be persistent. Preparation and persistence, the last two elements in the AESKOPP system, go together hand-in-glove.

The twist in the above joke is that the passerby thought Carnegie Hall was a goal rather than a destination. However, to either achieve a goal or arrive at a destination, you need directions. You need a plan for your journey toward your goal of being a successful media salesperson, perhaps even being a world-class, champion salesperson.

As a young boy, Tiger Woods set a goal of being the greatest golfer who ever lived, which he eventually achieved. How? Practice, practice, practice. Tiger's practice routines are legendary. He will practice a six-foot putt 100 times; however, he will not just practice the putt, but practice it 100 times without missing. In a *Time* magazine article, Dan Goodgame wrote:

> He has become, over time, eerily calm under pressure and an obsessive student of the game who reviews videotapes of old tournaments for clues about how to play each hole. He works hard at building his strengths and honing his shots. But what is most remarkable about Woods is his relentless drive for what the Japanese call *kaizen*, or continuous improvement. Toyota engineers will push a perfectly good assembly line until it breaks down. Then they'll find and fix the flaw and push the system again. That's *kaizen*. That's Tiger. It's also Tiger's buddy, Michael Jordan, who worked as hard on defense as offense and in his later years added a deadly fallaway jumper to his arsenal. No matter how good they say you are, Michael tells Tiger, "always keep working on your game."[1]

Later in the article, Dan Goodgame writes about how Woods decided to rebuild his swing after he won the Master's tournament in 1997. His coach, Butch Harmon, told Woods that it would not come quickly, but, as Goodgame writes, ". . . Woods didn't hesitate. He and Harmon went to work in a *kaizen* sequence of (1) pounding hundreds of practice balls, (2) reviewing tapes of the swing, and (3) repeating both the above."[2]

The *kaizen* sequence emphasizes the importance of creating a Spiral of Disciplined Preparations that you can repeat over and over again—with persistence—to achieve more and more success, as shown in Figure 28.1.

Note in Figure 28.1 that as you go along the path and implement the elements of Set Objectives, Plan, Organize, Perform, Measure, Evaluate, and Adjust that

**Figure 28.1
Spiral of disciplined
preparation.**

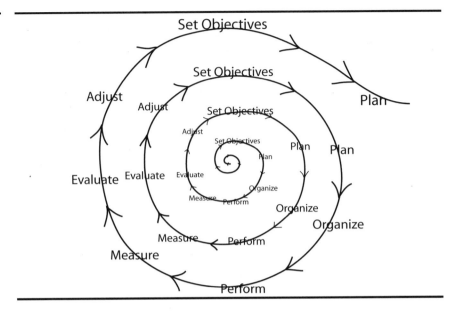

lead to Set Objectives, and each Set Objectives element is larger—you are raising your performance bar each time in a continual spiral of improvement.

Because of all you must try to get done in each of the six steps of selling, as a media salesperson you have to keep a lot of balls in the air. To help you manage this juggling act and help you keep everything straight, you need well-organized systems for each of the elements in the Spiral. You will learn in the remainder of this chapter a number of systems and rules that will help you.

Preparation

Set Objectives

Remember that goals have a longer time horizon than objectives—long-term goals, short-term objectives. Goals are set for longer than a year in the future, objectives for a year or less. The first objective you must set is how much you want to earn in the coming year. Then, work backwards to see how much revenue you must generate to achieve your income objective. In most radio and television stations, salespeople are paid on some sort of commission system, so there is a direct relationship between their income and how much revenue they generate. In most television and cable networks, magazine, newspaper, and Interactive sales organizations, salespeople are paid on the basis of a salary plus an incentive for reaching an individual or an organizational revenue goal. Whatever the makeup of your compensation system, you must estimate the revenue you need to generate in order to achieve your desired income level. To arrive at that income, you must set objectives for activities in each of the six steps of selling. When you have set your objectives, you must then develop plans to achieve them.

Plan

Yearly Plan. Begin each year with a yearly plan, as shown in Figure 28.2, which is a yearly sales plan for a radio station salesperson. All of the examples in this chapter are for radio salespeople because there are more radio salespeople than in any other media, thus the examples are applicable to more media sales jobs. However, all of the examples are applicable to all media selling situations and can easily be adapted for any medium.

Figure 28.2
Yearly plan.

Priority	Yearly Objectives Year: *2004*	Due Date	Date of Follow-up			
A	*Increase billing by 15% to $2.,543,000*	*12/31*				
A	*Select 7 new target accounts*	*1/15*				
A	*Spend more time on A and B accounts*	*12/31*				
A	*Increase average order size by 25%*	*6/31*				
B	*Improve closing skills --- up to 33%*	*6/31*				
B	*Improve prospecting skills – contact/appointment ratio up to 70%*	*4/1*				
B	*Get Torres Cadillac on 52-week schedule*	*3/15*				
B	*Get 20% more money from Davis Toyota*	*2/15*				
B	*Get 25% more money from Coca-Cola*	*5/1*				
C	*Improve research knowledge*	*3/1*				
C	*Write a retail presentation*	*2/1*				
C	*Practice presentation delivery skills*	*5/15*				

Monthly Planner

Priority	Monthly Objectives Month: *March*	Due Date	Date of Follow-up		
A	*Write J. C. Penny presentation*	*3/9*			
A	*Set up J.C. Penny breakfast meeting*	*3/2*			
A	*Work out with PD details of Coca-Cola promotion*	*3/5*			
A	*Write Coca-Cola presentation*	*3/9*			
B	*Take Torres to basketball game*	*3/16*			
B	*Make baseball presentation to Davis Toyota*	*3/23*			
B	*Collect from Sub Shop, Jones Motors*	*3/28*			
B	*Follow up on Men's Shop promotion*	*3/30*			

Weekly Planner

Week: _3/3-7_

MONDAY	TUESDAY	WEDNESDAY	THURSDAY	FRIDAY
9:30 – Quincy's - pitch baseball	*8:30 – Sales meeting*	*8:30 – Finalize and rehearse Coca-Cola presentation*	*7:30 – Breakfast – Coca Cola marketing group – pitch renewal*	*9:00 – In office – prospecting on the phone*
10:30 – Torres Cadillac – presentation - renewal	*10:00 – BBB Agency - presentation*	*10:30 – Martin Motors - service*	*10:30 – Torres Cadillac - presentation*	*10:00 - Prospecting*
11:45 – Sub Shop collection	*11:45 – Engine Re-builders - qualify*	*11:00– Cutler Cutlery – discovery*	*11:45 – Sub Shop - collection*	*11:00 – Prospecting*
Lunch: *Davis – baseball sponsorship*	**Lunch:** *John Doe - promotion idea*	**Lunch:** *CCC Agency – pitch baseball*	**Lunch:** *Mary Martin - get Kolb's buy parameters*	**Lunch:** *Open*
2:15 – Smith Honda – pitch news	*2:00– Black Ford – new schedule*	*2:15 – Doobie Bros. – spec spot*	*2:30 – Henry's Harley's – renewal*	*2:15 – Open*
3:00 – The Mall – service- results of weekend sale.	*3:00 –Bower Jewelers – service*	*3:00 – The Mall – renewal*	*3:30 – Newbie's – discovery*	*3:00 – Rill's Restaurant – pitch weekend package*
4:00 – Morton's – spec spot	*4:00 – Able Agency – spec spot*	*4:00 – Open*	*4:15 – PermaPress – pitch copy idea*	*4:00 – On phone – make appointments for next week*
5:00 – Jones Agency – pitch movie schedule	*5:00 – Harry the Hat – pitch baseball*	*5:15 – Fletcher Furniture – pitch special weekend package*	*5:00 – Jones Agency – close on movie schedule*	*5:00 – On phone – make appointments for next week*
	7:00 – Dinner BBB Agency – pitch baseball		*7:30 – Dinner Widmer Brothers – pitch special weekend package*	*6:00 – Office – paperwork and week's wrap-up.*

Daily Planner

Priority	To Do *Monday, March 3*	Deadline
2	*Make McDonald's appointment for 4:00 Wed.*	*12:00*
1	*9:30 Quincy's baseball pitch*	*9:30*
2	*Work out with PD details of Coca-Cola promotion*	*5:00*
1	*10:30 Torres Cadillac –renewal pitch*	*10:30*
1	*12:30 Lunch: Les Escargot – Davis - baseball*	*12:30*
1	*2:15 Smith Honda – news pitch*	*2:15*
1	*3:00 The Mall – check results*	*3:00*
1	*4:00 Morton's – spec spot*	*4:00*
1	*Jones Agency – pitch movie schedule*	*5:00*
3	*Write Barney's IO*	*6:00*
3	*Check on Doobie Bros. spec spot for Wed.*	*6:00*
3	*Write Mall renewal pitch*	*7:00*

Note in the Yearly Planner in Figure 28.2 that the yearly objectives are prioritized A, B, and C. There are no D priorities; if a priority is not an A, B, or C, you should not bother with it.

Monthly Plan. Begin each month by filling out a Monthly Planner, as shown in Figure 28.2. Set your monthly objectives so that: (1) you keep on track to accomplish your yearly goals and their due dates, and (2) you keep your Money Engine heated up. As you remember, the Money Engine has four sections: Prospects, Pending Accounts, Active Accounts, and Renewals (see Figure 9.1). The example that was used in Chapter 9 for keeping the Money Engine fueled was: out of 100 accounts on your list, 80 should have reasonable potential, 40 should be bona fide prospects, 20 should be pending, 10 should be active accounts if you consistently have a 50-percent closing ratio, and you should be working on renewals for all 10 active accounts if all 10 are legitimately renewable.

You must look at your account list, decide which type of account in the Money Engine needs attention, enter the activities into your Monthly Planner, then prioritize them.

Weekly Plan. The most important element in your planning system is your weekly plan (see the Weekly Planner in Figure 28.2). Weekly Planners are much more effective than call reports because Weekly Planners focus on the future rather than report on past activity. Call reports are typically exercises in writing fiction and are typically used as policing systems by management, which does not sit well with or motivate salespeople (they get the message that management does not trust them). Planners, on the other hand, focus on planning. During the week, you must continually work to set up appointments for the next week, or weeks, so that by the end of the week your Weekly Planner for the next week is 90 percent full. This system forces you to be organized and to be conscious of how many calls and what type of calls you will make.

On Friday evening or over the weekend, go through the following steps in filling out your Weekly Planner for the upcoming week:

1. Examine your previous week's Weekly Planner to see if there is any unfinished business to be carried forward.
2. Fill in information about any additional calls you made during the previous week.
3. Fill out the Key Account Call Tracker (see Figure 28.3) based on the calls you made the previous week.
4. Look over your appointment calendar and schedule all your appointments for the coming week in your Weekly Planner. Always include the purpose of the call or type of call in the Weekly Planner. Never make or schedule calls that do not move a sale forward or have a specific servicing purpose.
5. Look over your Monthly Planner and see what type of accounts need attention and what activities need to be undertaken and put both on your To-Do list (To-Do lists will be covered later in the chapter).
6. Examine your To-Do list and enter items that need to be accomplished during the upcoming week on the appropriate days in your Weekly Planner.
7. Give a copy of your Weekly Planner to your sales manager or ad director, and keep a copy for yourself.
8. Keep all of your Weekly Planners in a folder and evaluate them at the end of the month.

**Figure 28.3
Key account call
tracker.**

Key Account Call Tracker

Account	3/1	3/8	3/15	3/22	3/39	Month	4/5	4/12	4/19	4/26	Month	5/3	5/10	5/17	5/24	5/31	Month	Qtr.
Abbey	R*		S		I	3												
Bud	S			I	U	3												
Cartier	U	S		U	I	4												
Denny's	I			I	U	3												
Eckert	IP		I			2												
Ford	N		NG		S	3												
GM	NG		S			2												
Hoyt	R			I		2												
IHOP	R					1												
Jack's	S		I		R	3												
K&K	S			N	NG	3												
Liberty	S		U			2												
Mazda	U			NG		2												
Nissan	I		R		S	3												
Orrey	N					1												
PepBoys	NG		U			2												
Quill	S		U		S	3												
Royal	NG			U		2												
Sam's	S			NG		2												
Turbo	R		S	S	S	4												

* Call Type: I = Idea, IP = Identify Problems (every six months), N = New schedule, NG = Negotiation,
PE = Presenting, R = Renewal, S = Service, U = Up-sell

Monthly Analysis

1. Too many calls on Turbo and Cartier, not enough on Orrey and IHOP.
2. Too many service, not enough idea calls.

In the Weekly Planner in Figure 28.2, notice that that the 32 calls that have been scheduled (including lunch and dinner) are of different types: pitching copy ideas and spec spots, pitching baseball sponsorships and a special week-end package, pitching for renewals, collecting, discovery, and qualifying. Notice there are open slots so the unscheduled times can be filled in when new opportunities occur during the week. The week is not over-schedule—a good practice to follow. Also, note that a whole morning has been set aside for making prospecting calls and part of Friday afternoon has been left unscheduled so that calls can be made to set up appointments for the following week.

Daily Plan. As you make appointments for upcoming weeks, enter them into your appointment calendar system. Most media salespeople use PDAs such as a Palm Pilot, a Clié, some type of organizer-cell phone combination, or an appointment booklet. Whatever system you prefer, have only one system and use it to guide you each day and as the basis for filling out your Weekly Planners and Daily Planners. See the Daily Planner in Figure 28.2. Follow these steps when you fill out a Daily Planner each morning before 9 AM (after 9 AM, you should be doing scheduled tasks or on the street making scheduled calls):

1. Look at your Weekly Planner and enter all appointments for the day in your Daily Planner.
2. Look at your appointment calendar and enter any new appointments you have made that are not in your Weekly Planner.
3. Look at your To-Do list and transfer items that need to be completed that day to your Daily Planner.
4. Fill out any Business Opportunity Reports and Business Disposition Reports that need to be completed because of the calls you made or information you received the previous day (see Figure 28.4). Update your Business Pending Tracker (see Figure 28.5) with information from the Business Opportunity Reports. It is important to do these three tasks daily,

**Figure 28.4
Business opportunity
report.**

BUSINESS OPPORTUNITY REPORT

Account: *XYZ Toyota*
Product: *Autos*
Agency: *K&K*
Buyer: *Mary Smith*
Salesperson: *Charles Warner*

Date of Request: *9/23*
Rating Service: *Arbitron*
Primary Target Audience: *A 25-54* **Secondary Target Audience:** *W 25-49*
Schedule Starts: *10/28*   **Schedule ends:** *12/1*
Evaluation Basis (Metro, DMA, TSA): *Metro*
Number of Weeks: *5*   **Weekly reach goal:** *30*
Weekly market budget: *$5,600*   **Weekly frequency goal:** *4*
Market CPP Target: *$95*   **Dayparts:** *AM, PM, WE*
Target number of spots per station: *15*   **Target number of stations:** *5*

Other: (Merchandising, promotions, co-op, affidavits, contests): *Request merchandising, will buy without it.*

DISPOSITION

Won: ☺ **Lost:**

Order ($/spots/dayparts): *$1,500; 15 spots, AM, PM, WE*

CPP: *$100*   **Share of budget:** *25%*   **Avg. Rate:** *$100*

Stations ($/spots) CPP, Share of Budget:

WBBB – 18%
WCCC – 17%
WDDD – 20%
WEEE – 20%

---

because if you let them slide, you will never catch up. Be disciplined and get in the habit of filling out Business Opportunity Reports and the Disposition Reports at the bottom of the Business Pending Report, and updating your Business Pending Tracker daily.

5. Do not over-schedule yourself—no more than 12 To-Do items or appointments in a day.

When you schedule your Daily Planner be tough on yourself. Do the hardest things first if you can. If you have several top-priority calls to make during the day, begin with the most difficult ones and save the easiest ones for late in the day if you can. If you do the task that is most fun last and reward yourself, you will have something pleasant to look forward to.

Organize

Organize Your Accounts.   You have two types of accounts on your account list: *assigned and unassigned*. Assigned accounts and agencies are those given to you by your management and those for which you are responsible; unassigned

Business Pending Tracker
Charles Warner
10/7/2003

Account	Wk$	Demo	Wks	Up Date	AM	Day	PM	WE	NT	10/14	10/22	10/28	11/4	11/11	11/18	11/25	12/2	12/9	12/16	12/23	12/30	1/5	W/L	Reason
Warner Bros	$1.0	A12-34	2	9/30	1	1	1		1	1														
20th Cent Fox	$2.0	M18-34	1	9/30	1	1	1		1		1													
ABC Ford	$10.0	A25-54	8	9/23	1		1	1					1	1	1	1	1	1	1	1			W	
XYZ Toyota	$28.0	A25-54	5	9/23	1		1	1				1	1	1	1	1							W	
Courtsy Chev	$12.0	A25-49	6	9/16	1		1	1			1	1	1	1	1	1							W	
Dixie Lexus	$6.0	M25+	4	9/23	1	1	1	1			1	1	1	1									W	
Big Wheel Tires	$4.0	A25-54	3	9/30	1		1	1			1		1	1									W	
Joe Cadillac	$5.0	A25+	9	9/16	1		1					1	1	1	1	1	1	1	1	1			W	
Mary Mattress	$2.0	W25-49	4	9/30	1		1	1	1			1	1		1	1							W	
Belk's	$5.0	W25-54	1	9/30	1	1	1	1	1						1								W	
					10	5	9	8	5	1	4	5	7	6	6	5	2	2	2	2	0	0		

Daypart columns: AM, Day, PM, WE, NT. Disposition columns: W/L, Reason.

Total $ '03 = 390 *   **Total $ '02 = 305 ***

Total # '03 = 10   **Total # '02 = 7**

Av. # Wks '03 = 4.3   **Av. # Wks '02 = 6.4**

Won '03= 8, Lost= 2 (80%W)

Won '02= 5, Lost= 2 (71%W)

* Weekly $ X No. Wks.

Figure 28.5
Business pending tracker.

accounts are those you develop yourself through prospecting. Both types of accounts should be classified as A, B, or C accounts. Accounts classified as A are *key accounts*, or those 20 percent of your active accounts that generate 80 percent of your billing. Accounts classified as B are *target accounts*, or those that you have not yet sold but have the potential of being key accounts. Accounts classified as C are medium-sized accounts that are currently active or have reasonable potential. You must have a system for organizing the information on your accounts in order to prospect, sell, and service them. Systems can vary from simple index cards to complex computerized systems, but whatever system you use, it must be an easily accessible database that contains the information as seen in the Account File in Figure 28.6.

**Figure 28.6
Account file.**

Account: *J. C. Penny*   **Agency:** *BB & B*   **Products:** *Various*
Buyer: *Jane Doe*

Address: *700 Main St.*   **Address:** *333 Oak St.*
Fairfield 20202   *Fairfield 20202*
Phone: *322-8000*   **Phone:** *433-7654*

Decision Maker: *Harry Hoyt, Store manager (X – 8001, harry@jcp.com), Mary Sanders, Advertising Manager (X – 8002, mary@jcp)*

Needs Portrait: *Harry – Personal/Business: Achievement, competition, control, impulsiveness, order, risk-taking*
Personal/Non—business: Conservative, nurturance, play, recognition,
Mary – Personal/Business: Risk avoidance, defensiveness, recognition, control, autonomy, contrariness
Personal/Non-business: Affiliation, novelty, recognition, deference, play, nurturance

Business Needs: *Huge newspaper schedule. Use radio as supplement. Demos: Adults 18+, women 25-54. Sale and promotions oriented*

Competition: *Wal-Mart, Target, Sears. Wal-Mart and Target outspend substantially in TV, Sears outspends substantially in newspapers. None uses much radio.*

$ Potential: *$200,000*   **Type:** *B (Target account)*

Contact Date	Contact Type	Pending	Order
1/17	PO *		
1/20	IP		
1/30	IP		
2/8	IP		
3/2	PE		
3/9	PE	$150,000	
3/16	NG		$145,000

* PO = Prospecting, IP = Identifying Problems, PE = Presenting, NG = Negotiating and Closing, S = Servicing

Organize Your Desk. It is vital to keep your internal materials well ordered and accessible. When you are in a hurry, and salespeople are often in a hurry, you do not want to have to shuffle through a pile of randomly arranged papers to find the latest rate information or a copy of a sales presentation. You should be able to see the top of your desk every morning when you come to work. Put information in folders that you can reach easily when you are on the phone. I prefer colored folders with a different color for each subject such as: Active Accounts, Weekly Planners, Prospects, Management, and so forth. The Management folder is for notes of things you want to talk to management about. Do not waste time and interrupt yourself and your management with each individual question that might come up (unless it is urgent); save items so you can talk to management about several at a time. Put your phone, if it has a cord, on your left if you are right handed so you can hold the phone with your left hand and write with your right hand and the phone cord is not trailing across the desk as you try to write. Keep an $8\frac{1}{2}"\times11"$ spiral notebook so you can make notes when you talk on the phone and attend meetings. Put the following information in separate folders:

Sales promotion materials and presentations are the tools of your trade. Make sure you keep them up to date and in folders nearby so you can get to them in a hurry when you are preparing a proposal or presentation, rushing out to make a call, or talking to someone on the phone.

Rate information and special packages or sections must be kept current on a daily basis. Check with your sales manager or ad director regularly to see if new inventory has become available, rates have changed, or new packages or sections have been designed and released.

Inventory records also must be continually maintained. Put the latest information in a folder and keep it at your fingertips for quick reference when you are on the phone. Develop a good relationship with the operations department so you can always find out the latest information on what is available to sell. Your income depends on how much you sell, which, of course, depends on what is available.

Active account information must also be current. Keep a copy of the current Insertion Order (IO) or contract for each account in a three ring binder or accessible in an automated, computerized system. When you fill out an IO or contract, put a copy in the binder or enter it into a system such as Integrated Radio Systems (IRS). Enter new IO or contract information daily.

Organize Your Briefcase.   Carpenters and mechanics have their toolboxes; you have your briefcase. It is as important to you as any worker's toolbox. Your briefcase is not only a necessity but it also has become a symbol of a salesperson, so make sure your symbol reflects the image you want to convey to your customers. Equip yourself with an attractive, functional briefcase. It should contain a good calculator and a laptop computer with a wireless card so you can send and receive e-mail from anywhere. Keep several copies of current research information, sales promotion materials, and success case studies in your briefcase. Also, have extra batteries for your cell phone, laptop, and other electronic devices in your briefcase.

Organize Your PDA and Laptop.   I strongly recommend that you invest in a color-screen PDA such as a Palm Pilot or Clié, not only to use as an appointment calendar and address book, but also to store important documents that you can review before making calls. While you are waiting in a reception area to see a buyer or a client, it is handy to be able to fire up your PDA and review your Negotiating and Closing Planner, or when you are in a prospect's office to refer to the Discovery Questions on your PDA. A software program called Documents to Go will allow you to transfer Word, Excel, PDF, and PowerPoint files onto your PDA. The program is available on www.dataviz.com.

Organize your laptop so you can easily find presentations that you show to buyers and customers. I recommend that you keep all of your presentations on your desktop and not in separate files that you have to search for and open. Also, download onto your laptop the documents, presentations, and forms such as "Advertising Strategies in a Slowdown," the Checklist for Presentations, and all the blank forms from this chapter. All of this material is available on www.mediaselling.us.

Organize Your Knowledge Acquisition. You should keep folders or three-ring binders on your desk for each competitor in your medium and for each competitive medium. In these folders or binders, you should place the latest rate information (if you can obtain it), sales promotion material, and research information. You can usually pick up this material from clients and agencies if you have managed relationships with them properly. Keep these competitive folders updated. When you are on the telephone with customers who inform you that they are considering buying from one of your competitors, it helps enormously to have an abundance of information about that competitor at your fingertips; it helps you in create a differential competitive advantage. You should regularly monitor the content of your major competitors and put brief handwritten notes into the proper folders about any major shifts in programming, content, advertising strategy, and management. You want to be a market expert in order to gain source credibility with your accounts, so you must keep your information current.

You should also have folders or binders for the following knowledge areas: (1) market information such as population, demographics, demographic trends, business conditions, and the like; (2) Customer-helpful information such as relevant material from general business publications such as *Business Week, Fortune, Forbes, The Jack Myers Report,* and *Advertising Age;* (3) publications specific to your key accounts' industries such as *Automotive News;* and (4) publications specific to your industry such as *Editor and Publisher, Folio, Radio, Inc.,* or *Television Week.*

You should always have your computer on your desk turned on and connected to the Internet so you can go to a company's Web site when you talk on the phone to a customer. When you talk on the phone to an account, you should have its Account File on your screen, either in a file generated by an automated software system or in a file you have generated (blank file available on www.mediaselling.us).

Organize Your Community Activities. It is not only good citizenship but also good business practice to become involved in community activities. It is helpful to become part of a network of relationships with business executives, community leaders, and consumers. Get involved in organizations such as Rotary Club, League of Women Voters, Kiwanis, Knights of Columbus, Boy Scouts and Girl Scouts, or various church groups.

Manage Your Money. The two most important resources you have are *money* and *time*. You must set up systems to organize and manage both. Let's begin with money. First, keep track of where your money goes. Buy a good record-keeping system for appointments and expenses if your organization does not supply you with such a system. If you do not write down your expenses daily, you will forget most of the details about them and will not be able to get full credit for them. If you are ever audited by the Internal Revenue Service, you will need to produce a *daily expense record* in addition to receipts as proof.

Second, budget your expense money, then look over your *weekly expense record* to see if you are on budget. Be stingy with yourself; save your money for important clients and plan your calls geographically to save both time and gas. Even if your company allows you to use some of its trade deals with local restaurants, treat these deals as though they were cash, and do not waste lunches on friends or other salespeople. Be sure to take prospects and customers to lunch and dinner at nice restaurants. It is better to invest your expense money in fewer but more memorable, quality meals—you are creating value with meals and entertainment, too.

Next, always fill out expense reports weekly. If you let them go longer than a week, they will become even more burdensome and time-consuming. If your organization does not reimburse you for your business and entertainment expenses, you must know exactly how much of your own money you are spending so you can budget it, spend it in the most effective manner, and get proper deductions for your expenses when you pay your taxes.

If your company reimburses you for all or part of your expenses, keep the same accurate weekly records as you would if it were your own money and submit your expense accounts weekly. The longer you wait to fill out your expense reports and turn them in, the more interest-free money you will be lending to your company. It is best to handle your expenses in cash rather than on credit cards unless you have two credit cards, one for business and one for personal use. If you have just one credit card that charges interest on unpaid balances and you put business expenses on it, you will invariably wind up paying interest on business expenses.

Another tip based on my personal experience: do not get in the habit of taking cash advances from your company to finance your business expenses. You will regret it. You will more than likely spend the cash not only on business expenses but also on other things, too, unless you can possibly remember to keep your own money in one pocket and the business's in another pocket; then when you go to bed, to put the money from one pocket on the left-hand side of the dresser . . . forget it. Do not take cash advances for expenses or you will find yourself paying back money to the company for which you cannot account—a painful experience.

Manage Your Time.   The other resource you must control is your *time*. Time is a salesperson's most important resource, even more important than money, because you must have time to make the calls and presentations that result in sales. It is easy for salespeople to find a million excuses to have coffee with acquaintances, to linger longer than is necessary with friendly customers, or to knock off early to get back to the office to do paperwork. After several days of rejections without getting an order, it is a natural tendency to want to hang around the office and not to go out and face prospects and more rejections. Remember: no opportunities, no sales; no objections, no sales; no rejections, no sales. You must organize your days, weeks, and months to take advantage of every minute of the workday. You must manage your time to maximize face-to-face contacts with prospects and customers.

The first rule in time management is:

Rule: Develop the proper attitude about time.

Just as you must learn to control and manage your emotions, attitudes, and money, you must learn to control and manage your time. Restructure your thinking so that you see time as an opportunity to gain a competitive edge. Time is a finite, non-expandable resource of which everyone has exactly the same amount. Every salesperson on your staff and on every sales staff in every medium has a maximum of 24 hours a day, not a millisecond more or less, so no one has an edge in the amount of time available to use. You create your competitive edge by how well you manage the time available to you and to everyone.

Because time is finite and ticks away at the same rate for everyone, when you say to yourself something like, "I didn't make that call on Coca-Cola today because I didn't have enough time," stop and think how illogical you are being. There cannot be "enough" or "too much" time—everyone has the same amount. The problem is not that there is not enough time, the problem is that you did not effectively manage the finite amount of time available to you. Furthermore, once time passes by, it is irreplaceable. It cannot be saved, made up, or overspent; so, you must use what you have wisely.

Rule: *Time can only be used or wasted.*

The next rule in managing your time is:

Rule: *Know how much your time is worth.*

Calculate how much your time is worth to you. As we did at the beginning of this chapter, figure out how much you want to earn in a year and then break that amount down into weekly, daily, and hourly amounts. Put a note with the hourly figure (such as "$68 per hour," which is $136,000 yearly) in plain view at your office desk so you can see it daily, particularly when you are on the phone, to serve as a reminder of how much income it costs you each hour you spend in the office not making calls.

The next rule of managing your time is:

Rule: *Know where your time goes.*

Peter Drucker, in his classic book, writes that managing time is a three-step process: recording time, managing time, and consolidating time.[3] In order to know where your time goes, you must record your time by keeping a minute-by-minute log of everything you do for three days every six months. Keep your notebook with you at all times for these three days and write down absolutely everything that you do. It is imperative that the time log be complete and accurate. The reason to keep a time log is that the perceptions we all have about how we spend our time are incredibly inaccurate. Things that we like doing seem to go fast, and things that we dislike doing seem to go slowly, so we invariably misjudge how much time we spend on each type of task. It is impossible to estimate how much time you spend on each activity in your daily routine, so you must write it down. If you are to manage your time, you must first know how you spend it, and the time log is the only useful tool to use for recording activity.

Your time log should have five columns and should look like the example in Figure 28.7.

When you have finished your time log, analyze it to see if you are doing the right things. Fill in the Improvement column on your time log after you have asked yourself the following questions:

1. Am I doing the right things at the right time? Did I do things I did not need to do? Could they have been done outside the office?

**Figure 28.7
Time log.**

Time	Activity	Time Used	Priority	Improvement
8:00 am	Read paper	20 min.	2	Read at home.
8:20 am	Got coffee	10 min.	3	Bring it with me.
8:30 am	Planned day	15 min.	1	Do night before.
8:45 am	Did paperwork	30 min.	1	Do in the evening.
9:15 am	Drove to call	15 min.	1	Start earlier.
9:30 am	Called on Coca-Cola	45 min.	1	

2. What could be done better, faster, simpler, in less detail?
3. What interrupted me? How often, how long, and how important were the interruptions? How long did it take to recover and get back on track?
4. What contacts did I make with others? How important were the people? Were the communications important? How long did they take?

Most time logs reveal that interruptions are the biggest time wasters and that the biggest source of interruptions is ourselves. We interrupt ourselves because we allow our attention to wander, we want to be friendly, we need to socialize, and we tend to place a low value on our own time. Analyze your time log carefully, then use the following tips to help you manage your time more efficiently.

Rule: Consolidate your activities.

Here are more time management rules.

Rule: Do one thing until it is finished.

The most important lesson you can learn about time management is to do one task at a time and not to leave it until you are finished. Concentrate and do not interrupt yourself; do not get up and go for coffee or talk to your friend at the next desk. When people interrupt you, tell them you will get back in a few minutes when you are finished with what you are doing. If you are interrupted by someone you cannot put off, make sure you go back to the task you were working on immediately after the interruption. Go back, and back, and back until you finish it.

Rule: Use chunking.

Set aside large chunks of time in which to do your non-selling tasks, preparations, and follow-ups. Part of the trick to sticking to a task until it is finished is to plan your time efficiently. It is very inefficient to stop and start tasks. It takes you a few minutes to get mentally prepared, organized, and into the task you are doing; for example, you line up your pens, arrange the stapler, rearrange your desk top, find paper clips, turn on your computer, think about how to start, think about how to begin, and think about how to commence. If you are interrupted, you have to begin the mental process all over again, and that wastes time. A job that takes 15 minutes to do working straight through without interruptions will take half an hour if you are interrupted for only one minute three or four times while you are working. Thus, it is vital that you plan your time so that when you have tasks that take large blocks of time (15 minutes or more) you set aside chunks of time to do these tasks during parts of the day when you are least likely to be disturbed.

For instance, if you have to complete the paperwork on several orders, estimate how long this task will take you (say, half an hour) and set time apart in tomorrow's schedule for half an hour of uninterrupted time. Before or after normal office hours is best for paperwork. You should be calling on customers between 9 AM and 5:30 PM. Most salespeople find they can maximize their selling time by doing their paperwork and generating presentations at home at night or in the morning before they get into the office and by planning for large chunks of continuous time in which to do their work.

Rule: Write everything down.

Write down the important details of every conversation in your spiral notebook. (I prefer spiral notebooks because I can keep them on file and refer back to them.) Never trust your memory for anything, and write down everything you have to do. At the end of the day (at home is best), you can look over your notes and transfer information to your To-Do list. You can transfer the notes on accounts onto your To-Do list, into your Account Files, or into a folder if the notes are extensive and important for future reference. Taking good notes is a major time-saving device because you know where to find information and you will not have to rack your brain to remember things.

Rule: Plan every hour of your workday.

In no area of selling is self-discipline more important than in planning your time. You must plan every hour of your working day, every week, every month, and every year. Time management experts estimate that every hour you spend in planning saves you three or four hours in execution. By failing to plan, you plan to fail. Do your daily plan for the next day the evening before or in the early morning of that day. Indecision and procrastination are huge time wasters. The best way to overcome a natural tendency to be indecisive about what to do, and to avoid procrastinating about doing it, is to plan carefully every hour of your day and then to work this plan relentlessly.

Rule: Set priorities for everything and do first things first and second things not at all.

When you make a plan, put a priority on everything according to its importance. As Peter Drucker said in his book *The Effective Executive,* "Do first things first and second things not at all."[4] Set priorities on the basis of the 20/80 principle. In time management, this means that 20 percent of your activity will produce 80 percent of your results. Set priorities to concentrate on your key and target accounts.

Rule: Set a deadline on everything.

When you fill out your Daily, Weekly, and Monthly Planners, you must put a deadline on every task (you probably remember the importance of deadlined goals from Chapter 5). Unless you have a deadline, your tasks are immeasurable intentions instead of measurable objectives. The classic example of an indefinite, immeasurable, and useless objective is the use of the phrase "as soon as possible." "As soon as possible" may mean the next hour, the next day, or the next week depending on who defines what is possible and whose priorities are being used. Plans and To-Do lists are virtually worthless unless they contain specific deadlines for each activity.

Rule: Do not attempt to do too much.

We all tend to be unrealistic about how much we can get done; we tend to be optimistic. You are probably aware of Murphy's first law, "If anything can go wrong, it will." Murphy's second law is "Everything takes more time than you think." Salespeople are especially optimistic by nature and in their overall outlook, which is good for most things. However, this tendency can work against you when you are planning your time. Not only does over-planning mean that you will not get some things done but it also means that you are apt to get discouraged and depressed about how much you are not getting done. Just as you must control your customers' expectations, you must control your own expectations about how much you can get done so you will not feel frustrated and unsuccessful. When you hear people say, "I never have enough time and I'm always behind," it probably means that their expectations for what they can get done are too high. This condition can lead to stress and low self-confidence, which can be disastrous. As in any objective-setting situation, you want to set moderately difficult but achievable task-completion objectives to give yourself a sense of success and confidence when they are achieved.

Rule: Be flexible.

Your task-completion objectives and daily schedules must be flexible. Unforeseen opportunities will always occur, so you must be able to adapt. One way to build in flexibility is to purposefully avoid filling your schedule so that, in a sense, you are planning for interruptions and a little serendipity. If you have established your priorities properly, you will set four or five calls or tasks to be done in a day; therefore, if a top-priority item comes along unexpectedly, you can move some of your second-priority items to the next day.

Rule: Bunch your tasks.

Consolidate, or bunch, your tasks so that you schedule a group of similar things together to be done at the same time. For instance, you might set aside 4:45-5:30 PM to return phone calls or set aside 7:45-8:30 AM on another day to get some reports and paperwork out of the way. You can bunch service calls by making six or seven in-and-out calls in a morning or you can bunch calls by geographic area. Always be on the lookout for efficient ways to bunch your activities and tasks, which is a way to execute the third of Drucker's steps in time management, consolidate time.

Rule: Remember Parkinson's Law.

"Work expands so as to fill the time available for its completion," economics professor C. Northcote Parkinson noted while observing large bureaucratic organizations in which everyone seemed busy but little was getting accomplished.[5] In other words, if there were seven people in a bureaucratic organization and the work that had to be done could be done by one person, the six other people would find ways to keep busy by inventing systems, controls, hierarchies, and paperwork.

Applying this principle to individual time planning reveals that it is temptingly easy for you to keep busy and to fill time. You can find a thousand tasks that have to be done in the office on a rainy day. The colder it is outside, the longer it takes to generate each presentation and the more time it takes in the office to rehearse them. The problem in time management is not filling time or doing things but doing the *right* things. When you make your daily plan and write down things to do, ask yourself, "Does this *have* to get done?" Be ruthless with yourself and eliminate all frivolous time wasters. Ask yourself, "How much money am I making by doing this?" and "Am I moving the sale forward on this upcoming call"? The most important time you have is face-to-face time with your clients and prospects, so, maximize it.

If you use this cost-benefit analysis technique in planning your time, when you come to items such as dropping by to see a friend or taking time off to pick up tickets for next Saturday's football game, you will know what the costs are (because you have figured out what an hour is worth to you) and you will be able to make an informed decision. By the way, workaholics often do not get a lot accomplished; they are dedicated to keeping busy, so they tend to invent activities to fill time. Plan your time so you *work smart* and get the right things done. If you manage your time properly, you can normally get your work done in eight or 10 hours each day and have plenty of time to be a well-rounded person and devote time to community service and to your family or other interests.

Rule: Focus on activities that get results.

Too many sales planning and reporting systems focus on activity for its own sake, not on activities that get *results*. For example, a reporting system that only keeps track of the quantity of calls a salesperson makes focuses on activity, not results. Your job is creating customers, and the outcome of creating customers is getting orders. Thus, you must focus on getting the right orders from the right customers (your key and target accounts that pay their bills).

Effective systems must include all of the selling elements that lead up to results, not just one or two activity elements. Some sales managers or ad directors still insist that salespeople fill out activity-oriented call reports. It is counterproductive to argue or to try to teach them how it should be done by saying, "Charles Warner says in his book, *Media Selling*, that activity-focused call reports are useless." Do not tempt fate or jeopardize your job; keep quiet and fill out the reports neatly and turn them in on time, two critically important factors for those who use call reports (they rarely read them, but they want them to be neat and on time). However, make sure you use your own results-oriented systems that you are learning about in this chapter.

Manage Your To-Do Lists. To-Do lists that contain a large number of things you intend to accomplish are virtually useless unless they are prioritized and deadlined. For To-Do lists to be useful, they must be part of a time management system that begins with yearly and monthly objectives and they must be updated on a weekly and daily basis. You may find that your initial To-Do list contains just your objectives and the immediate tasks that are required to achieve those objectives, and at the beginning of the year it may be two pages long on your appointment calendar or To-Do system (on your computer or on your PDA). I do not recommend keeping To-Do lists in spiral notebooks because To-Do lists need to be updated weekly at a minimum, which can be done easily in a software system such as Palm or Outlook, which saves time from having to hand-write an updated list every week.

Following are rules for To-Do lists.

Rule: Prioritize all To-Do list items.

People usually compile To-Do lists by adding items to the bottom of the list as they occur to them, and, therefore, the items are not ordered according to priority. Priorities should be set on a first-, second-, or third-level basis. If you have anything less important than a three, you should not be doing it. To make matters worse, most people cross off items on the list as they do them, thus making the list hard to read and even more disorganized.

Rule: The longer your daily list is, the worse it is.

When people look at a To-Do list, the longer it is, the more they get discouraged, so they play little unconscious tricks on themselves. To make themselves feel better and more successful, they choose a number of minor list items that they can accomplish in a hurry and for which they can give themselves feedback for achievement. To correct this tendency, you must use a Daily Planner and move only those items from your To-Do list and appointment calendar onto your Daily Planner that are important and that you know you can complete.

How you feel about how much you get done is not based on how hard you work but on how long your daily To-Do list is. If you put 10 items on your Daily Planner and complete all of them, you will be happy and feel successful, as though you accomplished a lot. If you put 12 items on your Daily Planner and complete 10 of them, you will be depressed and feel unsuccessful, stressed, and as though you did not accomplish much. It is up to you how successful you feel; you can control it by the length of your daily To-Do list.

Rule: Do the nastiest, hardest things first.

People also tend to select from their To-Do list the easiest or the most fun things to do. Picking the smallest, easiest, and most enjoyable tasks may satisfy our personal, short-term needs for achievement, but they are really excuses to procrastinate and put off harder and, often, more important tasks. These types of rationalizations disregard priorities and thus are self-defeating for achieving objectives.

Perform

The next step in the Spiral of Disciplined Preparation is to perform the daily tasks and activities on your Daily Planner. Do not waste time; stay on schedule. In his *Harvard Business Review* article, "The Tests of a Good Salesperson," Saul Gellerman identified three factors that differentiated top-performing salespeople from mediocre salespeople: discussion focus, time management, and staying power.[6]

You learned about the importance of discussion focus in Chapter 11. Gellerman says that the top-performing salespeople he observed did several things to manage their time effectively. First, they did not wait more than 20 or 30 minutes for a scheduled appointment with a customer, as many salespeople did, because they realized it was a signal of low regard, low interest, or a negotiating ploy. Waiting also signaled that a seller was willing to be put off in a like manner during future calls. Top-performing salespeople also knew that they had to get on with their scheduled appointments and spend time with promising customers. By staying power, Gellerman meant that top-performing salespeople stuck to their schedules and slogged on relentlessly, regardless of multiple rejections or weather. These stars "hunted for a quick sandwich and then headed for the next customer. Weaker sellers lingered over lunch, cussed the fates that had ordained that day to be so unrewarding, and eventually reentered the fray with low expectations."

Gellerman's message is clear: When you perform your daily tasks, finish all of your scheduled tasks and do so with relentless discipline.

Measure

You must measure your performance so you can evaluate it, adjust it, improve it, and set higher objectives. Even though your billing is certainly an important measure of your performance, it is not the only one that tells you how well you are doing. There are several things other than billing that you should measure:

1. **Key account contacts**, which you track with the Key Call Account Tracker Report in Figure 28.3. You do not need to track all of your calls because that would take too much time, but you need to focus on your 10 or 20 key accounts that give you 80 percent of your billing. Update this report daily and give a copy of it each week to your management.

2. **Pending business**, which you measure by filling out a Business Pending Report (Figure 28.4) daily (and giving a copy to management daily) and transferring the information from the Business Pending Report into a Business Pending Tracker (Figure 28.5). Give a copy of your updated Business Pending Tracker to management every week. Many media organizations refer to business pending reports as a pipeline. Some sales organizations want pipelines for all pending business, some just for pending business on target accounts, and some just on pending business over a specified amount, $100,000 for example. Regardless of organizational requirements, you should keep your own pipeline on all pending business. If your company does not have automated computerized programs that compile these pending business reports, or pipelines, for you, you should do them by hand.

3. **Business lost.** Once a month do a summary of your business disposition reports (at the far right of the Business Pending Tracker in Figure 28.5). Summarize why you lost any business and to whom. All salespeople hate to fill out business disposition reports and often fail to do so to avoid the pain. However, do not be defensive but be candid in this summary because you want to know the reasons for losses so you, and especially management, can make any necessary adjustments. Business disposition reports are like cod-liver oil—bitter to take, but they help you get better. Figure 28.8 shows a monthly Business Disposition Summary (the information which you get from the Business Pending Tracker).

4. **Business closed**. A business-closed report is the most fun of any report; all salespeople love to fill them out when they close business and love to send

them to management. Some companies call these reports business-booked reports. Update this summary daily and give it to management at the end of the week. These reports also measure your progress toward your two main objectives—your revenue and income objectives.

Figure 28.8
Business disposition summary.

Salesperson:
Week:

Account	$	W/L	Share	Reason	Stations
Warner Bros		L		A12-24 demo ($1,000)	WBBB WCCC
20ᵗʰ Cent Fox		L		M18-34 ($2,000)	WBBB WCCC
ABC Ford	$2,000	W	20%		
XYZ Toyota	$,7,000	W	25%		
Courtesy Chev.	$4,000	W	30%	Merchandising	
Dixie Lexus	$2,000	W	33%		
Big Wheel Tires	$800	W	20%		
Joe Cadillac	$5,000	W	100%	Baseball	
Mary Mattress	$1,000	W	50%	WE package	
Belk's	$1,000	W	20%		
Speedway		L		M 18-34 ($3,000)	WBBB WCCC
Pepsi-Cola		L		A12-34 ($30,000)	WBBB WCCC WDDD WEEE WFFF WGGG

Month: **Analysis**

Lost young demo business: Warner Bros., Fox, and Speedway.
Lost Pepsi – big piece of business. Bought six other stations that cut rates significantly. Do not pursue business or cut rates because we have lion's share of Coca-Cola business at higher rates.
Won Courtesy Chev. Due to merchandising – only cost 1% for merchandising.
Won Joe Cadillac because of baseball – only buys sports and pays good rates.
Won Mary Mattress becsue of WE package. The package worked well; need more special packages to pick up similar business.

Evaluate

If you want to create more customers one month than you did the previous month, you are going to have to continually improve your performance—*kaizen*. The elements in the Spiral of Disciplined Preparation will help you improve. The next step toward *kaizen* is to evaluate the information (measurements) you have gathered, as Tiger Woods does when he watches videotapes of his golf matches and you do when you debrief after giving a major presentation or going through an important negotiation.

Table 28.1 shows an Evaluation Schedule that indicates the performance elements you should evaluate and when you should do so (daily, weekly, monthly, quarterly, or yearly).

All of the forms and reports listed in Table 28.1 are available as blank forms on www.mediaselling.us.

Adjust

The next step after evaluating all of your performance elements is to adjust, to correct any problems you have discovered—like Tiger Woods or a Major League Baseball player, to adjust your swing and make it better. Your adjustment should include a set of improvement objectives, as shown in the Improvement Opportunities Chart in Figure 28.9.

**Table 28.1
Evaluation
Schedule**

Report	When You Complete	When You Give to Management	When You Evaluate
Yearly Planner	Beginning of year	Beginning of year	Yearly
Monthly Planner	Beginning of month	Beginning of month	Monthly
Weekly Planner	End of old week	Beginning of new week	Weekly
Daily Planner	Daily		Weekly
Key Account Call Tracker	Daily	End of week	Monthly
Business Opportunity Report	Daily	Weekly	Monthly
Business Pending Tracker	Daily	Weekly	Monthly
Business Disposition Summary	Weekly	Monthly	Monthly
Time Log	Every six months		Every six months
Core Competencies	Quarterly	Quarterly	Quarterly
Improvement Opportunity Chart	Quarterly		Quarterly

Is all this necessary? You may ask, "Do I really have to go through these planning, organizing, measuring, and evaluating steps? Can't I just get out there and sell?" The answer is, no, you do not *have* to. You might be able to improve your performance without filling out all these reports and doing all of the analysis. If you are doing well and writing orders, you may feel you do not need help. On the other hand, even when things are going well, you might not know why you are being successful. It is wise to keep records so if you have a slump you can compare what you are doing to when you were performing well.

Just as Tiger Woods looks at tapes of every hole he plays, by constant analysis, evaluation, and detailed improvement plans, other champion athletes are able to lift their performance with similar disciplined preparation. Champion salespeople are no different. Remember, sports performance is more dependent on natural talent than is sales performance. Thus, in sports, a talented Major League Baseball hitter might be able to raise his performance by 15 percent from .280 to .322, or by 25 percent to a league-leading .350, by improving his techniques. However, a weak .230 hitter may have an impossible time trying to improve his performance 15 percent because of a lack of natural ability.

However, most salespeople can reasonably expect to improve their performance by at least 15 percent and perhaps 25 percent over the course of a year by using the systems in this chapter. If you can improve your performance by 25 percent each year for three years, if you are on a commission system, you can potentially double your yearly income.

By administering these systems, you will be more objective about your performance, something few salespeople are, and the systems will help you make a thorough evaluation of your sales activities. Administering these systems takes about a half-hour each day, an hour at the end of each week, two hours at the end of each month, and three hours at the end of each quarter—less if you keep up with everything on a daily basis—all of which time is well invested considering the potential results. Your performance should improve slowly but steadily, and you could well become a top-billing professional. At least 80 percent of all media salespeople do not perform this type of detailed measurement and evaluation each month, but they are the ones who typically do only

		This Month: September		
Figure 28.9 Improvement opportunity chart.	**Performance Measures**		**Opportunities for Improvement**	**Competencies to Concentrate On**
	Average order size:	$3,000	*Larger orders—pitch recency theory and continuity.*	*Preparation: Generating solutions (research).*
	Average number of orders per week:	6	*Make more prospecting contacts to fill up the Prospecting section of the Money Engine to increase my pipeline.*	*Opportunity: Prospecting*
	Average length of schedules:	4.3 weeks	*Pitch recency and continuity. Talk to sales manager about offering a 6-week discount.*	*Knowledge: Pricing*
	Average number of spots per order:	15	*Pitch Week End Packages and bundle in more WE and nighttime spots in all proposals.*	*Preparation: Strategic thinking.*
	Average rate:	$100	*Open higher in negotiations and ask for higher rates on proposals.*	*Skills: Negotiating and closing.*
	Average share of budget per order:	25%	*See above to get higher rates. Don't lower rates to get a higher share—25% is fine if rates are higher. Have BATNAs for all proposals.*	*Skills: Negotiating and closing.*
	Average number of contacts * per week:	45	*Up contacts by 50%. Set aside more time during week.*	*Skills: Prospecting, getting appointments.*
	Average number of appointments * per week:	20	*See above and below.*	*See above.*
	Contacts/Appointments ratio:	44%	*Practice phone techniques. Write a new phone script and rehearse it.*	*See above.*
	Average number of presentations * per week:	10	*If appointments go up, presentations will go up.*	*Skills: Presenting*
	Closing ratio (orders/ presentations ratio):	60%	*Prepare more thoroughly for negotiations*	*Skills: Presenting, negotiating*

* Contacts = prospecting call trying to set up an appointment. **Appointments** = A qualifying, identifying problem, or servicing call, not a call on which you expect to get an order. **Presentations** = A call on which you present something (an idea, a promotion, or a proposal) and on which you could possibly or expect to close a sale. A presentation call could be a negotiation.

20 percent of the billing. Be one of the few who manage their time well, who analyze their performance regularly, and who are invariably among the 20 percent who bill 80 percent of the revenues and make 80 percent of the money.

Persistence

The great hitters in Major League Baseball know that when they are in a slump they must keep swinging the bat. A major factor in their success is their confidence. They know that they can hit, that their grips and stances are right, and that they will get their hits if they watch tapes of their at bats, adjust, and keep swinging.

These top performers also know that no player can be totally consistent all the time and that every player is subject to streaks. Top performers have longer hot streaks and shorter slumps than do other players, but they are still relatively inconsistent from day to day, although over a season they tend to perform close to their lifetime averages. Top performers are realistic about these streaks and have the mental discipline to wait them out, to be patient, and to keep swinging. Patience is not only a virtue but it is also a necessary ingredient of successful performance.

Salespeople are like Major League Baseball players in that they are also subject to hot streaks and slumps. The way out of slumps is the same for salespeople as it is for baseball players—to keep swinging. Be persistent and disciplined in your work habits. Have confidence in your ability, and do not let negative thinking get the best of you. Give yourself positive feedback, practice visualization and mental rehearsal, and take the high road by doing the right, ethical thing and your slumps will get shorter and shorter and you will be more and more successful.

Persistence means never giving up and continually slogging along on the journey toward *kaizen* and your ultimate goal to which the Spiral of Disciplined Preparation will take you.

Test Yourself

1. What are the seven elements in the Spiral of Disciplined Preparation?
2. What is the first objective you must set?
3. What are the four types of planners?
4. Which planner is most important?
5. What should you do with accounts classified as D accounts?
6. Give three areas for knowledge acquisition.
7. When should you file expense reports?
8. If you should do first things first, when should you do second things?
9. What is chunking?
10. What is wrong with long to-do lists?

Project

Write a list of all of things you want to get done next month, then order these items according to priority on a one-, two-, or three-level basis and set deadlines for them. Next, prepare a daily planning guide for what you will do tomorrow, complete with priorities and deadlines.

References

Peter F. Drucker. 1966. *The Effective Executive*. New York: Harper & Row.

Alex McKenzie. 1975. *The Time Trap*. New York: McGraw-Hill.

C. Northcote Parkinson. 1957. *Parkinson's Law*. New York: Ballantine Books.

Stephanie Winston. 1983. *The Organized Executive: New Ways to Manage Time, Paper, and People*. New York: W. W. Norton.

Endnotes

1. Goodgame, Dan. 2000. "The Game of Risk: How the Best Golfer in the World Got Even Better." *Time*. August 14. www.time.com. April 2003.
2. Ibid.
3. Peter F. Drucker. 1966. *The Effective Executive*. New York: Harper & Row. p. 25.
4. Ibid. p. 24.
5. C. Northcote Parkinson. 1957. *Parkinson's Law*. New York: Ballantine Books. p. 15.
6. Saul Gellerman. 1990. "The Tests of a Good Salesperson." *Harvard Business Review*. May-June.

Part V

The Future

29 The Future of Media Selling

By Joseph Buchman and Charles Warner

By now you should be aware of the importance of a winning *attitude* and the need for *emotional intelligence* in selling. If you have read this book carefully and practiced its lessons, you should have developed some *skills and knowledge* and you should know the importance of seizing *opportunities, effective preparation,* and *persistence.* You are now well on your way toward a successful career in media selling. Yet one more element is required, and that is the flexibility to adapt as the media industry changes. Without this flexibility, you will suffer the same fate as the dinosaurs, or the same tragic fate as a typical *formula-based* manipulative media salesperson from the 1960s. "Difficult to see, always in motion is the future," Yoda said in "Star Wars Episode IV: The Empire Strikes Back."[1]

While it may be folly to attempt to predict the future, it is a greater folly to assume things will always remain as they are. Your future success will be greatly enhanced by developing a disciplined monitoring of your external environment, your competition, governmental regulation, social trends, the economy, and new technologies, then determining strategies to react quickly to the most likely changes.

From 1968 to 1972 NASA sent nine Apollo spacecraft on the long voyage to the moon. Yet when each of those nine spacecraft fired its engines for TLI (Trans Lunar Injection), they were not aimed at the moon, but at an empty point in space. NASA did not aim for the moon, they aimed for where they knew the moon would be at the time the Apollo spacecraft arrived. If they had aimed for the moon, it would have been long gone by the time they got there. Do not reach for the stars, reach for where the stars will be.

Chances are, as you have been reading this book, you have been considering a career in media selling. But even if you are considering some other career, just like that Apollo spacecraft, it is vital for you to shoot at some target in the future that may appear to be an empty void now, but will become a richly rewarding opportunity by the time you are prepared to be at the peak of whatever career you choose.

Each generation of media salespeople has been faced by this challenge. In the early 1920s, when the print media dominated, the new unproven medium was radio. By the late 1940s it was television. Prescient radio salespeople in the 1960s began moving from AM to FM stations, or into cable television. In the 1990s Web-based media, interactivity, and broadband seemed filled with limitless opportunities. Today, major media companies are combining to produce such media conglomerates as AOL TimeWarner, Viacom, NBC Universal, and News Corp., and these conglomerates are bundling their various media together and selling cross-platform, multi-media deals. To compete in the future, salespeople must be experts in all media so they can participate in this cross-platform selling evolution, not revolution, for it will take another decade for cross-platform selling to mature.

Environmental Scanning for a Media Sales Career

Jack Myers writes in *The Jack Myers Report* that "The traditional walls that have been built around buyer and seller relationships are being torn down by seller and buyer alike."[2]

Some predict all print media will be replaced by text displayed on handheld foldable screens. Others claim to foresee advertising-supported broadcast television replaced by paid broadband wireless streaming video, outdoor billboards replaced by in-car video and audio displays, and radio by commercial-free, satellite-delivered subscription music services. Yet these predictions are revolutionary, rather than evolutionary, and while valuable for long-term planning, seldom prove completely accurate in the long-term, or immediately useful in the short-term. Rather than base your future career on some, however seductive, idealized vision of the future, it may be valuable to examine some of the large-scale trends that currently carry sufficient momentum to affect the media sales environment over the next 10 years or so. It will also assist you in practicing the kind of routine environmental scanning that will be necessary in your career. The task of seeing further than 10 years into the future will be entirely up to you.

Media Outlooks

Television Outlook. Selling television will shift from strategies based on price to buying based on value. In the past, in a four- or five-network universe with nearly ubiquitous programming, price (CPPs/CPMs) was the primary purchase decision point. By the early 1990s, however, a national television buy began to involve the evaluation of more than 60 viable cable networks. Into the next decade, television salespeople will not only be required to approach advertising agencies with their proposals, but also to call directly on clients. Value, or return on investment (ROI), will become the key sales decision point as advertisers seek closer ties to the network's programming by means of product placement and sponsorships.

Broadcast television network sales jobs will continue to be the most prestigious and sought-after media sales positions, with cable television networks sales jobs catching up within a few years. As you learned in Bill Grimes' Chapter 21, growth in cable will be substantial; there will continue to be more sales opportunities in cable television than broadcast television, especially at the local level, where entry-level sales jobs will increase.

Newspaper Outlook. The death of the newspaper industry has been regularly predicted (mostly by broadcast and cable executives) over the last decade, but its demise, like Mark Twain said about a newspaper account of his death, has been greatly exaggerated. As you learned in Tom Stultz's Chapter 18, newspapers' vital signs continue to be vigorous and newspapers will not lose their number-one ranking in local advertising revenue for decades. Therefore, opportunities for sales jobs in newspapers will continue to be excellent. Although, traditionally, newspaper sales jobs have not paid quite as well as those in broadcasting, they are more secure, less competitive, more service-oriented, and more numerous than in any other medium except local radio.

Radio Outlook.   Although radio listening has been declining slightly in the past several years, probably due to song swapping and news on the Internet and mp3-file listening, advertising revenue for radio will continue to grow faster than the overall economy. This growth rate is due to the fact that advertisers are increasingly looking for less expensive alternatives to television, and radio is often the first place they look. Radio industry consolidation also has led to the increase in the number of industry sales jobs as large owners decrease the size of back office, support, and programming personnel and increase sales staffs. There will continue to be 50 percent more sales jobs in radio than the next medium, local newspapers. And because many of those jobs are in small and medium-sized markets, there are many more entry-level sales jobs in radio than in any other industry.

Magazine Outlook.   Buying decisions will shift from value to price. Whereas television purchase decisions are increasingly determined by value, intense competition in the magazine industry has resulted in a shift away from value, back to decisions based on price. With several print titles each offering the same kind of targeted audience, buyers have increased negotiating power over magazine salespeople. Therefore, negotiating will become more prevalent and negotiating skills more important in magazine selling. The recent economic slowdown affected the magazine industry more seriously than other advertising-supported media and recovery will take longer. Many of the lavish perks offered by top national magazine chains such as Condé-Nast and Hearst have been pared back, and commissions and bonuses have not been as large as in the past. However, the number of jobs selling magazines should remain steady—in fourth place behind radio, newspapers, and broadcast television. While challenging and glamorous to sell, large national consumer magazines offer few entry-level positions. It is better to start selling in small trade magazines and move up.

Advertising Agency Outlook.   Advertising agency consolidation will demand value-added selling. In the mid 1990s about 40 advertising agencies represented about 70 percent of all national television advertising. By 2003, only four advertising agency holding companies controlled almost 70 percent of all national advertising. Two of those agency holding groups, Interpublic and Omnicom, are headed by former network television sales executives, which is also serving to break down the traditional relationships between buyer and seller. As these consolidated agencies gain more clout in buying media and demand more added value, team-selling will increase, which will present increased opportunities for promotion, research, and marketing specialists. These specialized jobs are an excellent way to prepare yourself for a sales job.

Cross-Platform Selling Outlook.   The headline on a May 7, 2003 article in the *Wall Street Journal* read, "Clear Channel Battles TV Networks: Radio, Outdoor-Ad Firm Makes Cross- Platform Bid for a Part of Fall Spending."[3] Such cross-platform selling efforts by large media companies such as Clear Channel, Viacom, and AOL TimeWarner will increase because advertisers will demand cross-platform deals. Advertisers want these deals because they are easier to buy and because big advertisers can use their clout to get lower prices. The first major cross-platform deal, between Viacom and P&G in 2001, set the standard for these bundled deals to be sold at a discount. AOL TimeWarner initially hoped to sell cross-platform deals at a premium because of a purported synergy among their media properties, but met with agency and client resistance. Future cross-platform deals will be highly complex and take a long time to put together and close, but they will offer opportunities to salespeople who are experts in all media.

Social/Cultural Environment

Television Viewing.   Television will become an increasingly personal media experience. Traditionally, radio was the personal medium because after the advent of television listening largely was experienced by one individual to one radio, while television remained a group experience. However, by 2003 the average US household had two or more televisions. Television sets are also finding their way out of the home and into the workplace and cars. Television sets in the backs of front passenger seats can be found in many family-targeted vans, but the latest accessory is a television screen for the steering wheel. The device is supposed to be turned off while the car is in motion, allowing viewing only when parked or stuck in traffic. This increased fragmentation of viewing will mean smaller and smaller mass, high-reach media opportunities for advertisers.

Workplaces are increasingly awash in television sets. Financial institutions have sets tuned to Bloomberg or one of the other financial channels; government offices and embassies worldwide have CNN; veterinarians have Animal Planet; day care centers show Disney; and it is virtually impossible to find a bar without ESPN. Other businesses have put together custom reels of their own commercials to play over television sets in their lobbies, public areas, and even elevators. JetBlue, one of the most successful airline start-ups in history, even offers free live broadcast television at every seat. This trend will mean more sales job opportunities in narrowly targeted media.

Reality Programming.   Reality programming will include reality advertising. What initially was termed product placement—the paid use of an advertiser's product within a television show or motion picture—has today become known as product integration. Where past television program development was based on creating plot and character devices designed to attract a large audience, which could then be sold to any national advertiser, increasingly programming itself is being created to enhance the value of the products used within it. Marketers are looking for a program environment not only friendly to their product, but one in which the program itself can become, in effect, one extended commercial. This trend will lead to a less number-oriented, more conceptual type of sell—more qualitative, less quantitative—and, thus, more opportunity for creative selling and creative salespeople.

Women in Management.   More and more women are moving into sales and general management. Today more than half of radio salespeople are women and the best of those will move on to sales and general management positions. In early 2003, the Most Influential Women in Radio (MIW) released a study indicating about one-third of radio stations had women as general sales managers.[4] That was a significant increase from 1995, when only about one in four radio stations had women as sales managers. However, from 1995 to 2003 the percentage of women who manage radio stations remained at about 15 percent and, although slightly more than 50 percent of radio formats are targeted to women, only 10 percent of radio stations are programmed by women. Over the next decade, the percentage of women in management positions will double. According to Joan E. Gerberding, president of Nassau Media Partners and a spokesperson for the MIW group, "The radio broadcasting industry is inching its way toward gender parity."[5] Also, in 2003, two of the three largest magazine companies, Time, Inc. and Hearst, had women presidents. The opportunities for women in sales in the media has never been better, and it will continue to improve.

Minorities in the Media.   The percentage of minorities in media sales jobs has not grown perceptibly over the past decade. Most media companies continue to seek minorities for sales positions, so the opportunity for minorities is excellent.

Aging Baby Boomers.   As baby boomers age, target demos shift up from the 25-to-54 demo to the 35-to-64 demo, affecting the nature of radio formats, print media, and television programming. The baby-boom generation now begins to experience the inevitable effects of aging, but with the added benefit of a longer life span than their parents' generation thanks to advances in health care. This trend brings good news to middle-aged and mature salespeople, because they can have extended careers in selling media that are targeted to mature audiences such as themselves.

Competitive Environment

Specialized Skills.   Ed Erhardt, the president of ESPN/ABC Sports Marketing and Sales points out:

> "There are multiple decision makers in every segment of the advertising and marketing mix. Sales organizations need people whose skills are relevant to each of those constituencies."[6]

No longer is a media buying decision made simply between a salesperson and a media buyer. Today promotion experts from the media need to be involved with promotion managers from the client. Top creative people may be expected to meet with top management from major accounts, especially if the product is to be integrated within the program. Top managers from the media organization may be expected to contact senior managers at both the agency and advertiser. Increasingly, a media salesperson's job will be orchestrating these contacts so the sales message remains focused and void of conflicting messages.

As buying decisions become more complex, more specialized sales and sales-oriented jobs will be available. Entry-level jobs such as coordinator, planner, or strategy specialist are good places to begin a climb up the sales career ladder.

Integrated Marketing Teams.   Teams will support traditional salespeople. Sales forces are transforming into integrated marketing teams and include individuals who were not traditionally seen as members of the sales force. Indeed, at some level, *every* member of a media organization is part of the sales force. According to Jack Myers, in the 2002 upfront market, virtually every media buyer was charged with the task of negotiating some value-added promotional service, in return for their purchase of basic commercial inventory.[7] This type of selling requires the involvement of promotion, marketing, and merchandising experts.

Segmentation and Fragmentation.   Segmentation of audiences and fragmentation of advertising media will continue. With media now including broadband Internet streaming, paid satellite car radio, and 50+ channel cable systems, to name just a few examples, fragmentation will continue and increase in the decade ahead. The mass media, with very few exceptions, are no longer mass. Those exceptions include events such as the Super Bowl, the Olympics, or times of national or global tragedy or war. Advertisers will intensify their quest for ever more narrowly defined and efficient market niches with less wasted coverage. Many will even seek to create new media opportunities with more narrowly defined appeal. Many elements of the broadcast, print, and cable media are responding by focusing on narrower target audiences. FOX created FOX Family, ESPN created ESPN News, NBC created CNBC, and CNN created CNNFI.

The increase in the number of media available to advertisers in any given campaign will continue to create a vastly more complicated selling environment, and competitive pressure on buyers and sellers will continue to intensify. Media salespeople will become more important as buyers seek advice and reassurance from salespeople they trust. Salespeople increasingly must deal with the creative, qualitative side of the business. More segmentation and fragmentation means more sales jobs, plus, it allows salespeople to seek jobs in media that are aligned with their own interests, such as sports, world news, or financial news.

Clutter.   Increased clutter diminishes the value of broadcast and cable advertising. A 2002 study by the American Association of Advertising Agencies (AAAA) showed record amounts of commercial and promotional television clutter on the major broadcast networks. Clutter during morning dayparts was just over 18 minutes per hour, almost 21 minutes during the soaps, and just over 17 minutes in local news. Prime time clutter has been holding steady at about 16 minutes per hour. The study showed that 11 of 19 measured cable networks also posted increased clutter in November 2001 versus the previous year. The report also noted that among 35 selected syndicated programs, over 18 minutes per hour were devoted to non-program (commercial and promo) clutter.[8] Continuing clutter will cause advertisers to look elsewhere for opportunities with more impact and measurable results in Interactive and direct mail. Sales jobs in Interactive will become more attractive and more plentiful because of this and other trends.

Broadband Penetration.   Increased broadband penetration levels have begun to create viable Internet alternatives to cable channels. By 2005, one in four US households is predicted to have broadband access. With additional broadband access at work and on college campuses, some streaming video services will reach an affluent, highly educated, and technology-savvy audience sufficient to attract major advertisers. Improved online audience measurement and ad serving will allow advertisers to purchase specific demos and dayparts. Jobs selling Interactive will increase in number, importance, complexity, and pay levels as broadband penetration expands.

Technical Environment

Commercial-Avoidance Technologies.   Consumers will embrace commercial avoidance technologies such as TiVo, and new products from Intel, Microsoft, and SonicBlue will offer personal video players (PVPs) that can skip commercials. Walkman-sized video players that can reproduce 70+ hours of video on 4-inch LCD screens will soon appear in stores. Increased processing power, equivalent to that of a desktop computer of just a few years ago, will be integrated into all media electronic devices. Some of this technology will allow consumers to avoid spot commercial breaks entirely, and, thus, product-placement opportunities will increase as will sales jobs in this area.

Videogames.   Videogames will develop as an alternative advertising vehicle. In 2002 a company named WildTangent, based in Redmond, WA, designed online *advergames* for Toyota, DaimlerChrysler, FOX television, and Nike, among others. Their advergame Corolla Joy Ride, which promoted the 2003 Toyota Corolla, attracted 425,000 unique visitors in its first month. The game/ad allowed users to choose their favorite car model and color, then relayed that information back to Toyota while telling players the location of the nearest dealership. According to the WildTangent Web site:

> With the wide range of entertainment choices available to audiences today, film and television production studios are finding it increasingly difficult to create buzz about a new TV show or film. To extend the power and reach of traditional marketing campaigns, WildTangent can quickly create an interactive game closely tied to your feature film or TV program. In addition, you can drive increased revenues by integrating sponsorship and product placement opportunities into the game. In fact, in-game sponsorships often cover 100 percent of game development costs. Finally, while most TV and film-based games have several free levels, you can further capitalize on your property's value by selling additional game levels to consumers.[9]

Sales jobs in this interactive video game field will increase and be attractive to technically oriented people.

Television's Digital Conversion.   Television's digital conversion will reach critical mass. The FCC has required all television sets sold after July 1, 2007 to include digital tuners. As quickly as possible after that the government will push the transition from analog simulcasting to digital-only. Once the transition to digital is complete, older television sets will have to be equipped with converter boxes. CBS sent all of its 2001-2002 prime-time programming in digital, although not all of its affiliates were broadcasting in digital. ABC offered 60 percent of its prime-time programming in digital. NBC and Fox are only beginning the transition. High-quality, high-definition, digital content on television, combined with high-speed broadband Internet access in the home, and new compression techniques, could cause television programming to be just as vulnerable to digital piracy as music CDs are to Internet-shared mp3 files. Because commercials will have more impact in digital versions, the decline in broadcast television advertising could slow down as advertisers seek more attention-grabbing commercials.

Virtual Product Placement.   Virtual product placement will emerge as a viable advertising vehicle. UPN first pioneered virtual product placement on a 1999 rerun of "Seven Days" when a computer inserted a can of Coca-Cola, a bottle of Evian, a Kenneth Cole handbag, and a Wells Fargo Bank sign into the program. Brown Williams, the chairman of Princeton Video, which pioneered this technology, said that virtual product placement offered much more value to a program. Program producers and networks can sell the space over and over again, not only in first run, but it can also be sold in syndication, and there can be a different class of products every year. In the future, there is nothing to stop

Archie Bunker from seeming to drink from a can of Budweiser, Jerry Seinfeld from seeming to eat Raisin Bran, or Hawkeye Pierce appearing to munch on a Hershey candy bar, while in subsequent episodes it could be changed to Miller, Fruit Loops, and a Nestle's Crunch bar. According to Princeton Video, each product introduced into a scene via computer sells at about the same price as a 30-second spot in that program.

This technology will increase the complexity of television selling and will require more technical expertise, which creates opportunities for those of you who are technically sophisticated.

Radio's Digital Conversion.   Radio's digital conversion will increase the value of radio broadcasting and create new revenue streams for stations. Two commercial-free, satellite–delivered, subscription radio services, XM Radio and Sirius, are making inroads into radio listening habits. XM Radio predicted that it would have a million subscribers by the end of 2003, and General Motors plans to offer satellite radios in 75 percent of its 2004 models. While both Sirius and XM continue to struggle financially, the future of broadcast radio is clearly digital, although it may be a terrestrial-delivered technology, rather than one coming from satellites.

AM and FM stations are beginning a conversion to digital using an in-band, on-channel system developed by iBiquity. The conversion to digital radio is taking longer than that of television because the technical and economic structure challenges in radio are far greater. In the United States, every television station has a coverage area essentially equivalent to every other television station. Because of this equality, most television station owners were not threatened by a transition to a new digital band. But because radio evolved as local, regional, and super-regional services, and as both an AM and FM medium, a transition to a single digital audio broadcast band has proved unworkable. Larger stations see no reason to give their smaller competitors the equivalent of a boost in power, and smaller radio stations balk at the financial costs of moving to digital transmission. As a compromise, iBiquity has developed an in-band/on-channel simulcast technology allowing current radio broadcasters to stay at the same frequency, or spot on the AM or FM dial, but embed a digital signal into their broadcast. The technology is not foolproof yet, especially for night-time AM, but it promises that AM stations will be able to broadcast FM-quality signals and FM stations will achieve CD-quality sound. Both will be able to offer new wireless data services as well (hidden within their audio broadcast transmission), and each will be completely static- and fade-free. Consumer receivers went on sale in mid-2003 under the brand name HD Radio. HD Radios, in addition to offering higher-quality audio, will also be able to feature on-demand traffic reports, weather alerts, emergency road condition updates, breaking news bulletins, and program information.

These technological advances indicate that radio will not be left behind in the digital revolution. Even though radio listening has declined somewhat due to Internet-enabled song swapping and listening to mp3 files, improved digital radio signals will slow the declines in terrestrial radio listening and radio will remain a strong, viable local advertising medium. Furthermore, because consolidation has increased the number of sales jobs, radio will continue to have 50 percent more jobs than newspapers, the second medium in terms of number of sales jobs.

Finding or Upgrading a Job

Many of the trends mentioned above will not only affect the way media are sold, but they will also affect how and where to look for a job. In the past, the standard career path for salespeople was to start in a small market and work up over several years to larger markets. However, this process is no longer necessary. In large markets many media organizations hire inexperienced salespeople in sales-support jobs. Many major-market newspapers, trade magazines, broadcast stations, cable systems, and cable interconnects hire people right out of college if they are well-trained and passionate about the medium they are entering.

Whether you decide to start in a small or large market has more to do with where you want to live and with your own degree of confidence, sophistication, and preparation than with the selling demands in a large market, perhaps with the exception of New York, Los Angeles, or Chicago. These top three markets are still difficult (although not impossible) for inexperienced salespeople to break into.

Target a medium in which jobs are available—radio and newspapers. Radio sales jobs are always available in smaller markets and from radio you can move into television or Interactive. Radio provides excellent selling experience for most other media and is a good stepping stone to other media sales jobs. If you want to wind up in a large market, consider seeking a job in smaller towns or suburban areas near the major market of your choice. Try a large market if you have confidence in your ability and if you think you will feel comfortable in a big city; you have little to lose. If you cannot find a job in your medium of choice in a major market, look in smaller nearby markets.

When looking for a media sales job, look for the ad director or sales manager with the best reputation. Ask around, talk to salespeople in different media, and ask who they think is the best sales manager or ad director in the area. It is surprisingly easy to get through to talk to salespeople and to ask their advice on how to go about looking for a job. Try to meet with them face to face if you can. Group-owned media should take precedence over non-group-owned media; the chance for advancement is greater with groups such as Clear Channel or Gannett.

When you are interviewing, make questions about salary and benefits the last on your list and ask about compensation only if the interviewer fails to mention it. Sales managers and ad directors want to hire people who are looking for opportunities, not guaranteed incomes. Learning and growth opportunities should be first on your list of desired company attributes.

Write personalized cover letters. It is a waste of time to send out resumes attached to a blanket "To Whom It May Concern" cover letter. When you seek a job by mail, write a specific letter to the person who will be doing the hiring. In the letter, tell the person why you want to work for his or her company and what you have to offer that is specific to that company. Do some research on the company so you can be specific about what you can do for it; it may be something such as, "I will provide you with the opportunity to train a salesperson from the ground up, to hire someone who has learned no bad habits." Attach a resume to the letter, which states that you will call on a certain date—then, call when you say you will. Be very persistent in your follow-up.

If you want a job in network or with a major-market local television station or a national consumer magazine, you would be well advised to start at an advertising agency as a media buyer, researcher, or planner, rather than beginning in a small market. It is often difficult to make the transition from the pace and style of a small market to the highly competitive, sophisticated, dynamic atmosphere of the top markets.

Selling as a Career

Sales is still one of the best and quickest routes to management because you will learn skills to help you deal with people, you will be engaged in an activity for which the results are measurable, and successful selling will require that you become goal-oriented. Selling is an intrinsically rewarding job involving a great deal of autonomy and creativity. You will receive immediate and constant feedback on how you are doing, and you will have an interesting variety in the people and businesses you call on.

Finally, selling is a challenging and competitive occupation. If you are successful, you will have an exhilarating sense of pride and accomplishment.

Test Yourself

1. What probable effect will the continued trend toward market segmentation have on television, radio, print, and cable?
2. What emerging technology do you believe will cause the greatest changes in media selling?
3. What type of media knowledge will be necessary for cross-platform selling?
4. What social and cultural changes do you believe will have the greatest impact on your career in media selling?
5. Why is media selling an excellent preparation for a position in media management?

References

Matthew P. McAllister. 1996. *The Commercialization of American Culture: New Advertising, Control and Democracy.* Sage Publications.

John Naughton. 2001. *A Brief History of the Future: From Radio Days to Internet Years in a Lifetime.* New York: Overlook Press.

Veronis Suhler. 2002. *Communications Industry Forecast: Historical and Projected Expenditures for 12 Industry Segments.* July.

Endnotes

1. www.starwars.com. April 2003.
2. Jack Myers. 2003. *The Jack Myers Report.* February 6.
3. Mathews, Anna Wilde. 2003. "Clear Channel Battles TV Networks." *The Wall Street Journal.* May 7. p. B6.
4. Gerberding, Joan E. *2001. Gender Analysis Summary.* The Most Influential Women in Radio.
5. Ibid.
6. Jack Myers. 2003. *The Jack Myers Report.* February 7 2003. p. 1.
7. Ibid.
8. *2002 Television Commercial Monitoring Report.* American Association of Advertising Agencies. New York.
9. www.wildtangent.com. February. 2003.

Part VI

Appendixes

Cost-Per-Point Market Ranks

By Charles Warner

Ron Steiner of the Marketing Communications Group conducts an annual study of the difference in the rank position of television markets according to households compared to each market's cost-per-point (CPP) rank. In his first-quarter 2002 study, some markets, in which rate-holding behavior tends to be the norm, rank as many as 23 markets higher in CPP than in household market rank. In other markets, in which rate-cutting tends to be the norm, there is as much as a 25 negative-rank spread. For example, Las Vegas ranks 51st in Nielsen households but ranks 27th in CPP. Rochester ranks 71st in households but ranks 49th in CPP. Green-Bay-Appleton ranks 69th in households but ranks 87th in CPP. Wilkes-Barre Scranton ranks 52nd in households, but ranks 69th in CPP.[1]

These dramatic differences in rank positions reflect not only the pricing policies of the television stations in those markets, but also the stations' expertise in negotiating.

For the latest cost-per-point market rankings go to www.tvsalespro.com or contact Ron Steiner at rsteiner@swcp.com.

For ways to avoid getting into price wars in television markets, also read the paper "Sell for Rate in Television" in the "Papers by Charles Warner" link on www.charleswarner.us.

Endnotes

1. www.tvsalespro.com. February, 2003. Used with permission.

B Customer Satisfaction Survey

By Charles Warner

The Customer Satisfaction Survey that follows was designed for a local radio station in a top-25 market for which a majority of the business was conducted with agency media buyers. However, the survey was sent to agency media buyers and supervisors and to clients—about 60 percent were sent to agencies and 40 percent to clients. The survey was designed to move from general questions to specific ones, so, at the beginning, respondents could not easily identify the medium for which the survey was being conducted. The survey can be adapted for use by a newspaper, magazine, television station or network, MSO, outdoor company, or Interactive company, but care must be taken to follow the general format of moving from general to specific questions and to tailor the questions to the market, the medium, and the selling situation.

Customer Satisfaction Survey

1) I work for an: <u>Advertiser</u> _____ <u>Agency</u> _____
2) Considering the service you get from all of the media, please rate each medium below on the overall service you get from each on a scale from 10 to 1, 10 = Excellent, 1 = Poor.

   a) Newspaper: 10_____1
   b) Radio: 10_____1
   c) Television: 10_____1
   d) Cable: 10_____1
   e) Direct Mail: 10_____1
   f) Outdoor: 10_____1

3) Please list the four best media salespeople who call on you—overall best regardless of media—in rank order (a = Best).

	<u>Name</u>	<u>Employer</u>
a)	_____	_____
b)	_____	_____
c)	_____	_____
d)	_____	_____

4) Please list the four least effective media salespeople who call on you—the ones you like to deal with the least—in rank order (a. = Least Effective).

Name	Employer
a) _____	_____
b) _____	_____
c) _____	_____
d) _____	_____

5) Please list the four best media sales managers in the market—overall best regardless of media—in rank order (a = Best).

Name	Employer
a) _____	_____
b) _____	_____
c) _____	_____
d) _____	_____

6) Please list the four least effective media sales managers in the market—the ones you like to deal with the least—in rank order (a = Least Effective).

Name	Employer
a) _____	_____
b) _____	_____
c) _____	_____
d) _____	_____

7) Considering the services provided to you by the media, please indicate the importance of each of the following when making a media buy. (Extremely Important = 4, Very Important = 3, Somewhat Important = 2, Not Important = 1)

a) A salesperson's knowledge of his/her medium _____
b) The quality of a medium's audience _____
c) The ability of a medium to get results _____
d) A salesperson's follow-through _____
e) Offering promotions or added-value _____
f) Keeping in touch with regular mailings and handouts _____
g) Addressing your advertising goals with good creative ideas _____
h) Having low rates (CPP/CMP), prices _____
i) Helping you take advantage of co-op dollars _____
j) Upper management making calls on you _____
k) High ratings, large circulation _____
l) No preemptions, running what was ordered _____
m) Knowledge of account's marketing goals, strategy _____

8) Please indicate the influence that ratings have on your broadcast media selections. (Extremely Important = 4; Very Important = 3; Somewhat Important = 2; Not Important = 1) _____

9) What radio salesperson would you call first, second, and third if you needed knowledgeable help?

First Salesperson   Station

_____   _____

Second Salesperson   Station

_____   _____

Third Salesperson   Station

_____   _____

10) What television salesperson would you call first, second, and third if you needed knowledgeable help?

First Salesperson   Station

_____   _____

Second Salesperson   Station

_____   _____

Third Salesperson   Station

_____   _____

11) Please rank the following radio stations in terms of which are the easiest overall to deal with. (Rank them 1 through 7; 1 = Best)

	Rank
WAAA	_____
WBBB	_____
WCCC	_____
WDDD	_____
WEEE	_____
WFFF	_____
WGGG	_____

12) Please rank the following radio stations in terms of the most helpful research they provide to you. (Rank them 1 through 7; 1 = Best)

	Rank
WAAA	_____
WBBB	_____
WCCC	_____
WDDD	_____
WEEE	_____
WFFF	_____
WGGG	_____

13) Please rank the following radio stations in terms of how easy their support staffs (accounting, traffic and sales assistants) are to deal with. (Rank them 1 through 7; 1 = Best)

	Rank
WAAA	_____
WBBB	_____
WCCC	_____

WDDD   _____
WEEE   _____
WFFF   _____
WGGG   _____

14) What is your impression of the overall rating trends of the following radio stations? (Check only one column for each station.)

	Going Up	Staying the Same	Going Down
WAAA	_____	_____	_____
WBBB	_____	_____	_____
WCCC	_____	_____	_____
WDDD	_____	_____	_____
WEEE	_____	_____	_____
WFFF	_____	_____	_____
WGGG	_____	_____	_____

15) Please rank the following stations in terms of the overall effectiveness of
their sales efforts. (Rank them 1 through 7; 1 = Best)

	Rank
WAAA	_____
WBBB	_____
WCCC	_____
WDDD	_____
WEEE	_____
WFFF	_____
WGGG	_____

16) Please rank the following stations in terms of your perception of which
have the most effective general managers. (Rank them 1 through 7; 1 =
Best)

	Rank
WAAA	_____
WBBB	_____
WCCC	_____
WDDD	_____
WEEE	_____
WFFF	_____
WGGG	_____

17) Please rank the following stations according to which you most respect.
(Rank them 1 through 7; 1 = Best)

	Rank
WAAA	_____
WBBB	_____
WCCC	_____
WDDD	_____
WEEE	_____
WFFF	_____
WGGG	_____

18) In the space provided below, please write the six things, in order of importance, that you would like from salespeople—how they can serve you best.

What You Want

1. _____

2. _____

3. _____

4. _____

5. _____

6. _____

19) In the space provided below, please write any comments you would like to make about the general effectiveness of media salespeople, or any pet peeves you might have. Remember, the goal of this survey is to evaluate the service you are getting from media salespeople and to improve that service.

Thank you for your cooperation in completing this survey.

How to Write an Advertising Success Case Study

By Charles Warner

Most success letters published by the media regurgitate bland statements about how advertising on a station, publication, or Web site gets results, but there is rarely any useful information about how this wonderful situation came about.

Case studies are much more effective selling tools than advertiser testimonials. They can give specific details on how a station, system, publication, Web site, or network helped solve marketing and advertising problems. Salespeople can use case studies to demonstrate how a medium can marshal its resources and expertise to help customers achieve their specific marketing objectives, and to position themselves as problem solvers. Case studies are also excellent tools for teaching salespeople the important elements of marketing and advertising.

Finally, advertising success case studies are an excellent way to get closer to a customer and reinforce the value of your medium and your service to that advertiser. By working with a customer to create a case study, the customer's commitment and loyalty to you and your company will be solidified and will increase.

Elements of an Effective Advertising Success Case Study

1. **The Marketing Environment**: A good case study describes the marketing environment: short-term and long-term developments and trends in the advertiser's external environment such as changes in regulation, technology, culture, economics, or demographics.
2. **The Competition:** Define the advertiser's main direct and indirect competitors, both current and potential. Competitors should be described in terms of size, growth rate, market share, and primary strategies. Competitors' major strengths and weaknesses should be noted and their positioning statements and advertising strategies should be outlined.
3. **The Marketing Objectives**: State the advertiser's marketing goals, such as, "Increase market share two points" or "Increase weekday traffic by 20 percent" or "Attain a 30-percent share of mind (recall of stated benefits)." Marketing objectives should be stated in hierarchical order and quantified so progress toward them can be measured.
4. **The Marketing Strategy**: Outline the advertiser's primary marketing strategy (segmentation, differentiation, or low-cost producer) and the critical success factors in the execution of their strategy.
5. **The Advertising Objectives**: Delineate the advertiser's advertising objectives, such as, "create awareness" or "reinforce brand loyalty" or "increase store traffic for next weekend's sale by 15 percent over last year" or "increase usage of canned dog food." Some of the advertising objectives can be sim-

ilar to the marketing objectives but they should also be more short-term and media- and campaign-specific. Advertising objectives should be stated in hierarchical order and quantified so progress toward them can be measured.

6. **The Advertiser's Competitive Positioning Statement (advertising objectives put into the plain words of a consumer promise):** Express the advertiser's positioning statement—not just the current slogan, but a positioning theme that makes a definite promise to customers. A positioning statement clearly defines "who we are."

7. **The Problems that Advertising Can Solve:** Lay out the advertising problems from the advertiser's point of view. The problems must be stated in a manner that is objective and not biased to a particular point of view or does not imply an obvious answer.

8. **The Solutions to the Advertising Problems:** Give details about the specific solutions a medium and its salesperson provided for the client:
   A. Creative: Ideas, strategy, and execution.
   B. Media: Strategy, plans, and execution, including merchandising, promotion, vendor support, co-op coordination, research, copy testing, etc. Be sure to include details of the exact schedules purchased, including reach and frequency estimates.

9. **The Results:** Summarize the results of an advertising campaign in specific, measurable terms. The results section answers the questions: "Did the campaign work?" "Were the marketing and advertising objectives achieved?" "Were the results attributable to the advertising campaign?" "Were the results attributable to the medium used?" Graphs and other visual presentations of results greatly increase their impact.

Make sure to secure the client's and agency's permission to use the case. In some cases clients are reluctant to give permission to use their names. They are afraid their competition will get wind of and try to duplicate their success. In such situations, write a case study using fictitious names and organizations and change the conditions slightly to mask the identity of the client. The principles, strategy, and approximate results should remain the same. When salespeople use the fictional case, they should tell prospects, "This case is based on an actual situation, but the real client doesn't want us to use his name—the results were so terrific that he doesn't want his competitors to know about it."

A medium should have at least one case study that demonstrates how it worked as a partner with an agency to solve a client's problem. A medium should also organize an effort to have case studies in several categories.

Advertising success case studies can be written with a client or an agency as the protagonist.

How to Write an Effective Advertising Success Case Study

1. **Keep your audience in mind:** Remember that you are writing for potential advertisers. Keep jargon to a minimum.

2. **Use short-story writing techniques:** A case has flesh-and-blood characters who are intriguing.

3. **Openings:** Grab the reader with people facing their biggest advertising problem. Set up the conflict, the frustration. Remember, clients are most interested in solutions to their advertising problems.

4. **Provide relevant details:** After the opening that sets the situation, give rel-

evant details about objectives, problems, and solutions. Be stingy with numbers; do not give details that are not applicable to the specific problem.

5. **Use as much dialogue as possible**: Make people come alive with dialogue. Straight narrative is boring.

6. **Make the salesperson the hero**: Salespeople should be perceived as marketing consultants; case studies in which they play this role help reinforce this image—salespeople will use case studies more often when they are portrayed as problem-solving heroes.

Case Studies as Teaching Tools

Not only are case studies excellent ways to walk clients through the problem-solving process, but they are also one of the most effective ways to teach salespeople about the marketing and advertising factors involved in designing successful advertising campaigns. Developing case studies is the best way to teach value-added and solutions selling techniques.

If two or three salespeople are given a team assignment of writing a case study for a business category, in the process of developing the case they will not only become experts in that category, but they will also have to learn a great deal about the marketing and advertising process: objectives, strategies, and execution.

Of course, once a team develops a case study for a business category, the next logical step (and one you will find they will take virtually automatically and enthusiastically) is for the sales team to write a well-organized, problem-solving sales presentation for that category.

Thus, case studies teach value-added and solutions selling, marketing and advertising principles, problem-solving techniques, how to position your medium, and how to write presentations. Advertising success case studies are excellent teaching *and* selling tools.

Negotiating and Closing Outline

By Charles Warner

I. Negotiating

> *Rule: Don't negotiate until you've created value and created a differential competitive advantage.*

> *Rule: Don't discuss price until you're ready to negotiate and close.*

A. The Five Elements in the Negotiating and Closing Process
  1. Your Negotiating Approach
     a. Information-Based
        i. Information about your customers and their competitors
        ii. Information about your competitors
        iii. Information about the other side's cultural background
        iv. The attitudes and tactics of the other side
     b. Relationship-Based
     c. Ethical
     d. Flexible
  2. Preparation
     a. Assess the Situation
        i. Balanced concerns
        ii. Relationships
        iii. Transactions
        iv. Tacit coordination
     b. Assess Negotiating Styles
        i. Competitors
        ii. Accommodators
        iii. Narcissists
        iv. Cooperators

        > *Rule: Match the other side's style (cooperative or competitive).*

     c. Identify Interests, Set Objectives, Determine Targets
        i. Identify both side's interests.
        ii. Set MADCUD objectives (Measurable, Attainable, Demanding, Consistent with company goals, Under control of the individual, and Deadlined).

        > *Rule: When selling a perishable product, always set a deadline on your offers.*

        iii. Determine targets

Rule: Make a commitment to your objectives and targets, write them down, and tell someone about them.

    d. Assess Leverage
      i. BATNAs

Rule: Always go into a negotiation with a BATNA.

      ii. Tit-for-tat

Rule: Use tit-for-tat to teach the other side to cooperate.

      iii. Warning

Rule: Never threaten, politely warn instead.

      iv. Bluffs

Rule: If you bluff, use a mixed strategy and occasionally bluff on a random basis.

    e. Estimate the ballpark, commit to walk-aways, and set anchors
      i. Estimate a ballpark
      Rule: Most settlements are close to the mid-point.

Rule: Always go into every negotiation with a commitment to your walk-aways.

Rule: During negotiations, you must focus on your highest legitimate expectations, not your walk-aways.

Rule: Always have a well-thought-out anchor.

    f. Determine Bargaining Tactics
      i. Acceptable: auction, cherry-pick, crunch, flinch, good guy/bad guy, limited authority, nibble, price tag, red herring, silence, split the difference, take-it-or-leave-it, and throw-aways.
      ii. Unacceptable: big bait, blackmail, change of pace, deliver garbage, renege, starvation, threats, and walk-out.

Rule: Never split the difference when it is in the other side's favor or is not close to your HLE; have patience and continue negotiating.

Rule: When faced with unacceptable, unethical bargaining tactics, name them and tell the other side the names so the other side knows you are not fooled.

Rule: Never respond emotionally; respond calmly, politely, and firmly.

3. Maneuvering for Dominance and Control

Rule: The other side only has the power you give it.

    a. Tactics to get you frustrated: interruptions, hurry-up, delay, keep-you-waiting, and bring in the boss.

Rule: Check your ego at the door and don't let your fear or emotions get the better of you; patience always wins.

> *Rule:* Whoever controls the negotiating agenda controls the outcome.

> *Rule:* In order to avoid negotiating on each element individually, package all the elements in a deal so that the prices of the individual elements always add up to more than the package price.

> *Rule:* Negotiate only after you have created value, early in a customer's planning cycle, and well before your imposed deadline.

> *Rule:* Negotiate at the highest level possible—only with the buying decision maker.

> *Rule:* Don't negotiate with your boss present if you can avoid it.

> *Rule:* Negotiate on your own turf if possible.

> *Rule:* Negotiate face to face whenever possible.

> *Rule:* If you have to negotiate on the phone, you be the caller.

4. Bargaining
   a. Warm-up

   > *Rule:* Listen and get information two-thirds of the time, give information only one-third of the time.

   > *Rule:* Get the other side to state what they want at the beginning, and tell them what your issues are—get everything on the table.

   b. Open
      i. Open first?

      > *Rule:* Open first to set an anchor except when you don't know the other side.

      ii. Open optimistically or realistically?

      > *Rule:* When in doubt, open optimistically and have room to come down.

      > *Rule:* You never get anything you don't ask for, so ask for more than you hope to get.

      > *Rule:* When you know the buyer well, open realistically. Corollary: Open realistically when you have no leverage, when in a tacit coordination situation, and when people say they won't negotiate and mean it.

      > *Rule:* Get the bad news out of the way early.

      > *Rule:* Don't include most of the other side's requests in your initial offer.

   c. Frames

   > *Rule:* Always frame all of your offers appropriately.

d. Signaling Leverage

Rule: Confidence is everything; whoever blinks first, loses.

e. Making Concessions

Rule: Never begin with a major concession.

Rule: Don't just concede, try to trade; if you give up something, always try to get something in return.

Rule: Give the first concession on an unimportant issue, and get a concession from the other side.

Rule: Make the other side work hard for everything; they will appreciate it more.

i. Develop an effective concession pattern that signals when you get close to your walk-away.

f. Building Agreement

Rule: Summarize agreements and restate the other side's position on a regular basis.

Rule: Be patient—with patience and hard work in exploring alternatives, you can make the deal better for both sides.

II. Closing and Gaining Commitment

Rule: Expect to close.

Rule: When you walk away, always leave the door open.

1. Trial Closes: The Direct Close, the Assumption Close, the Summary Close, the Silent Close, the Pin-Down Close, and the t–Account Close.

Rule: Use trial closes throughout the negotiating process.

2. Choice Closes: The Choice Close and the Minor Point Close.
3. Clincher Close: Have a big concession in your back pocket and use it at the end to clinch a deal.
4. Last-Resort Closes: The "Make-Me-an-Offer" Close, the "What-Will-it-Take" Close, and the "What-Did-I-Do Wrong" Close.
5. Bad, Never-Use Closes: The Poor-Me Close, the Now-You-See-It-Now-You-Don't Close, and the For-You-Only Close.

Rule: Don't close too aggressively; always keep the relationship in mind.

Rule: When closing, confidence is vital—you cannot signal your fear of losing or need to close fast.

Rule: Have confidence that you can give the other side a "good deal"—their definition of a good deal.

A. Types of Good Deals: Got a low price, got something someone else wanted, got high quality at a reasonable price, got the last one, got a warranty or guarantee, low risk of dissatisfaction, got a discount, got something else thrown in, got a win, feel like they won something important to them, got good results from advertising, or got a good deal compared to other media.

 B. Get Commitment: Social Ritual, Public Announcement, Accountability, Simultaneous Exchange

> ***Rule: Once you get a commitment, say "thank you," shut up, and leave quickly.***

III. Putting It All Together: Create a Negotiating and Closing Plan

> ***Rule: Always rehearse your negotiating and closing plan.***

> ***Rule: After every negotiation, debrief.***

E Negotiating and Closing Planner

By Charles Warner

Account Name: _____ **Decision Maker:** _____

	YOU	OTHER SIDE
Situation:	__Balanced Concerns __Relationships __Transactional __Coordination	__Balanced Concerns __Relationships __Transactional __Coordination
Negotiating Style:	__Competitive __Cooperative	__Competitive __Cooperative

Interests, Objectives:

Interests:	Objectives:	Interests:	Objectives:
1.	1.	1.	1.
2.	2.	2.	2.
3.	3.	3.	3.

Targets:

Targets:	Targets:
__Specific opportunity	__Specific opportunity
__Price	__Price
__Size of order	__Added value
__Share of budget	__Terms

Leverage:
__Favors you
__Favors them

Tactics _____   Tactics _____

BATNAS:

BATNA _____

Ballpark:
HLE

Your HLE _____   Their initial offer _____

Walk-aways: Price, terms, and conditions

Your walk-aways:	Their walk-aways:
1.	1.
2.	2.
3.	3.

Anchor:

Your anchor _____

Bargaining Tactics:

(Good guy/bad guy, e.g.)

Opening:
__You first
__Them first

Frames:

Frames _____   Possible frames _____

Positioning:

Positioning _____   Possible positioning _____
(Benefits Matrix)

Throw-aways:

Throw-aways _____   Potential red herrings _____

Concessions:
(Effective pattern)

Concessions _____

Closes:

Closes _____
(Clincher close, e.g.)

Selling Magazines to Agencies

By Phil Frank

Media buyers are inundated with information. They have more data to consider and understand than ever before. The manner in which they digest this massive amount of information and use it to help make recommendations on which media vehicles they will invest in is very personal. Each magazine buyer's approach is unique.

Buyers do not only have research tools, but also strategy and tactical tools. The best buyers try to balance all of these elements. They are also creative in finding ways to make research work in their favor.

Media buyers and sellers tend to look at an advertising campaign from two different vantage points. Buyers look at a campaign as a composite, trying to satisfy their marketing objectives in a manner that takes good strategy, smart tactics, and their priorities into consideration. Sellers focus just on their magazine, making sure they get their fair share of a budget (and more).

The Buying Process

The buying process consists of three stages: (1) studying data and determining which markets to buy (pre-buy analysis), (2) making a decision, and (3) placing orders (the buy). In studying and determining which markets to buy, a buyer takes many elements into consideration and analyzes them to figure out which magazines are going to be must-buys and which magazines will have to fight to get the business. In this analysis, buyers begin to sense where they have leverage.

Buyers have many tools in the early stages of a buy, and they try to use them to their advantage. Many buyers, particularly in recent years, rely more and more on objective data from syndicated research firms, and often put magazines with the largest reach on their short lists of must-buys. However, experienced buyers consider magazines that add depth and texture to an advertising campaign; they believe these elements can lift the creative execution based on their own subjective interpretations of the market and a magazines' editorial content and environment.

Media buyers have a responsibility to make the best choices and to buy at the lowest rates they can find. The best buyers, however, are able to balance these two priorities and deliver effective advertising recommendations.

Studying the Market

In studying the market, buyers look at many facets of the market and look closely at individual magazines. They look at information from syndicated research on the demographics of each magazine's audience (composition and coverage), as well as any information they can gather on the psychographics of all of the magazines being considered. Additionally, they will try to balance all this objective research with a certain amount of subjectivity.

Demographics

When conducting an analysis of a magazine's demographics, buyers look at two measures: audience composition and coverage of the target audience. Composition is a percentage of a magazine's audience that is in a particular demographic. For example, 67 percent of *Sports Illustrated's* audience is composed of Men 24 to 39. Coverage is more of a quantitative measure of a magazine's audience; it is a percentage of a particular demographic that is reached by a magazine. For example, *Women's Day* reaches 23 percent of Women 25 to 34.

Buyers look at both sets of data and give each magazine a weighted average on composition and coverage. These weighted averages are applied to all magazines being considered, then magazines are ranked according to these weightings. Therefore, a buyer develops a list that shows, based on objective data, which books are strong performers and which magazines are weaker according to the criteria they have selected. The magazines low on the list will be expected to provide aggressive discounts if they want to be included on a buy.

Quantity versus Quality

Buyers who are trying to promote a product, brand, or service to a large audience but also are interested in a particular type of people, want to deliver reach against a large audience but also be sure that they are using magazines that address the interests and tastes of their target audience. A good buyer tries to balance reaching a large quantity of prospects with reaching the highest-quality prospects with a well-thought-out magazine plan.

Psychographics

Strategic buyers further differentiate magazines by looking into the psychographics of the audience they deliver. They try to find a way to match the attitudes, interests, and life-styles of their prospects to a magazine. Psychographics can be loosely defined and broadly applied, thus they tend to be used on a secondary basis in analyzing a market for an upcoming buy.

A marketer who sells a new European car may be trying to find a demographic segment of Adults 25 to 49 with an annual income of more than $75,000 and who are in managerial positions. They may find through research that their customers are also people who like to hike, prepare meals at home more than three times a week, and own pets. Thus, once buyers have ranked books by their demographic performance, they may alter this list based on how books deliver on the psychographics of their audience. Therefore, an epicurean magazine may have low composition and only above-average coverage, but because its editorial carries a lot of recipes for home cooking, it would potentially be considered higher than other magazines with similar demographics.

Beyond conducting these standard analyses, there are differences in how one buyer may study a market versus how another buyer studies it. Some buyers tend to put more weight on these objective data while others are more subjective.

Subjective and Objective Analysis

To complete the exercise of balancing books that deliver quantity and books that deliver quality, a planner has both objective resources, such as syndicated research, and subjectivity that is based on a buyer's awareness of trends.

Buyers look at all the syndicated research they can get their hands on and the objective data has a great deal of influence on the final purchase. However, there are other factors to consider when putting together a must-buy list. These are more subjective aspects that help distinguish a solid plan.

In the area of more subjective considerations, a smart buyer considers factors such as:

- Whether or not a magazine is receiving advertising from a competitor
- If the magazine provides a highly unique and untapped audience
- If the magazine is getting buzz from PR or strong word-of-mouth reference
- Unique opportunities for different creative advertising executions
- Unique editorial (special issues, for example)
- Extraordinary ad positioning opportunities
- The ability to gain positive PR exposure

Setting The Market

Once all the studying is completed, buyers have a sense of what books make sense to be considered and they must now set the market in a way that will make it highly manageable and provide them with several points of leverage. Setting the market is done in a fairly logical manner. Buyers use research data to try to shrink the market by negotiating separately with magazines in different editorial categories, playing one magazine against another and one category against another. For example, a buyer might tell all of the seven sisters (the top seven women's magazines such as *Better Homes and Gardens, Good Housekeeping,* and the *Ladies Home Journal*) that the others are all giving big discounts.

Buying Criteria

Buyers use their research and their judgment to create a first-cut list. The buying criteria used to make these decisions are based primarily on objective research, but with some subjective considerations.

Buying criteria are typically expressed in terms of minimum indices versus a specific target audience. For example, to make the first cut a magazine must deliver, at the minimum, a 130 index in composition and at the minimum a 120 index in coverage against Adults Age 25 to 54, Professional/Managerial, and College Graduate or more. A buyer is now setting the market, and all books that meet the criteria are able to participate in the later rounds of negotiations.

Segmenting the Market

Next, buyers take the shortened list of magazines and begin to divide it into smaller sections to continue to set the market. This phase is initiated by buyers so they can better compare and contrast magazines that have similar characteristics in either an editorial category or key audience delivery.

For example, buyers segment the market so three or four large-scale business books or four or five of the women's service books are grouped together for comparison. They often create spreadsheets for a quick glimpse at how the competition looks in each segment. The key elements they compare include:

- Composition Index
- Composition Index Rank inside of a segment
- The weight or value that composition holds in their evaluation process
- Coverage Index
- Coverage Index Rank inside of this segment
- The weight or value that coverage holds in their evaluation process

- Efficiency (CPM)
- CPM Rank
- The weight or value that CPM holds in their evaluation process
- Final weighted rank

Weighting a factor simply means assigning a value of how important it is in the evaluation process. When creating this spreadsheet, the weights for each element of comparison are expressed in a percentage, and when all the weights are added together they should equal 100 percent.

Depth of Buy in a Segment

As buyers set the market they can estimate what pricing will come in from the market and begin to make preliminary estimates on how many books they actually will end up buying in the final version of the plan.

The factors that weigh on this decision are based on some of the following elements: editorial differentiation, efficiency, out-of-pocket costs, and strategic importance in reaching the target audience.

In the end, a buyer decides whether or not to buy one or two publications, or two of three publications in a segment, which is vitally important for the buyer to tell sellers, because a buyer's decision determines how aggressive sellers will need to be in negotiations.

Managing a Budget

Finally, buyers put one more twist into setting the market, and that is how they will manage their budget. This often comes down to strategic priorities and the objective of the advertising. Should this budget support a promotion and create very broad reach over a short period of time or does it need to convey a more intricate message over a longer period of time? This is where the marketing side of the buyer's mind comes into play.

In addition, advertising tactics help buyers decide how to manage their budgets. Will they launch with a high-impact, multi-page creative, then sustain their presence with smaller and smaller units, or will their entire campaign be composed of a series of fractional pages running in a variety of magazines? These considerations leave the buyer with some decisions that can be made further into the negotiating process.

Making the Buy

Entering the more competitive rounds of negotiations that ultimately lead to some sellers winning the business and some going home empty-handed, buyers and sellers become very tactical. Buyers often begin to slowly release some pieces of information that they have been holding onto that will make or break a seller's proposals.

Buying Tactics

Smart buyers hold their cards very close to their chests, releasing just enough information to have the market stay as competitive as possible. Often, one seller can dictate the entire direction of a segment and not receive the business in the end. If a buyer sees a seller starting to substantially drop prices, the buyer makes this known to the seller's competition to see how they respond. Often, sellers trump each other and set a new bottom to the market. A smart seller realizes what is happening and will assess if buyers are simply riding the downward spiral or if they would settle early with one or two books that submit the best and final offers.

As a media director in 1993 I witnessed a segment of magazines compete for my business for three consecutive years. The segment contained three publications that were close in audience composition and coverage. One magazine had a unique editorial posture that gave it an advantage, although I was not going to disclose that early in negotiations.

All three magazines submitted their first proposals and they offered aggressive discounts. All of the proposals ended up with very competitive CPMs. All of the magazines were told of their standings after this first round. One of the magazines took its discount much, much deeper than I expected and totally caught the others by surprise. The other two responded and deepened their discounts, but not as deep as their aggressive competitor.

I told the first book that the other two had responded with deeper discounts; I did not offer too many specifics, but said that once again the competition had tightened up. The first magazine dropped its rates again, now putting its discount at a level I had never witnessed before in this segment.

I gave the other two books word of this second move by their competitor and neither one bit. They realized that the other book was willing take the business at a loss and they would not go there. They said they were done negotiating, having offered their best and final rates.

In the end, I had to tell the book that went with the deepest discount that they had over-discounted, and if they were willing to drop their price so far, I could no longer see value in their product. The other two books realized that they had to respond to the first move, but not the second.

For me, as the buyer, I knew I was not going to buy the lowest-discounted book, but it had allowed me to gain leverage and drive the price lower in the other two books.

Tie Breakers

Tiebreakers come into play when, after several rounds of negotiations, the competition is so tight that it is hard for buyers to make a decision. Therefore, buyers must look to elements of a proposal other than audience strength and price.

Tiebreakers that may be considered: which ad positions are promised (covers, opposite TOC, or far forward), the strength of marketing extensions, or the relationship a buyer has with a seller. It is rare that a buyer ends up negotiating with two books and having a dead heat, but it is not unheard of, and the intangibles, such as relationships, become very important—they are tiebreakers.

In the final analysis, after buyers have thoroughly examined all of the objective data, applied expert subjective judgment about editorial environment, and have negotiated aggressively, in a tie-breaking situation the secret of success is not to look into the minds of buyers but into their hearts.

Writing Copy

By Charles Warner

Every ad or commercial should have four major appeals or powers, according to ERISCO (Emotional Response Index System Company), a research firm specializing in testing advertising copy:[1]

1. *Stopping power,* which is an ad's ability to grab attention immediately.
2. *Holding power,* which is the ability to keep attention throughout the body of the message.
3. *Going-away power,* which is the ability to leave the listener, viewer, reader, or user with a memorable image or impression of the main selling point.
4. *A promise* about the product.

Stopping Power

The elements that produce *stopping power* should grab attention and be dramatic and related to the major selling point. Attention grabbers not related to the main idea in an ad or commercial can be counterproductive and confuse the issue. Consumers might remember the attention-grabber rather than the product name.

Holding Power

Holding power is necessary to get the main selling message across. The selling message, or content, must be stated in terms of benefits to the consumer. It must lead up to and connect to a specific or implied promise about the product that satisfies a pressing consumer need or want. Holding power combines the concepts of interest and desire in the AIDCA model.

When writing radio or television commercials, repeat a store's or product's brand name frequently throughout the commercial. This information is an important part of an ad's content and it makes sure the viewer or listener remembers the advertiser. Commercials should use simple language and short, uncomplicated sentences to get the message across. There is not time to build a long, difficult, logical argument for a product (print does this well), and viewers and listeners are unlikely to follow it anyway. Keep to a simple style; read the copy out loud and have someone else read it to you as well. Does it sound comfortable? Does it create the mood and elicit the emotional response you want?

Commercials are best when they are written to appeal to consumers' emotional needs. People tend to buy what they *want* and not necessarily what they *need* in a practical sense. To connect between needs and emotions, commercials must create an emotional involvement and an attitudinal harmony with the product and stimulate an emotional response.

There are four basic emotional appeals, according to ERISCO: money, affection, status, and security. Like leverage, each of these four appeals has two sides, positive and negative. The positive side is the desire to have more of the appeal; the negative side is the fear of losing it or the threat of not having it.[2]

Money.   Virtually everyone wants more of it and feels insecure about being without it. People also want to get money with as little effort as possible. The word *free* has the strongest appeal of any word in advertising. Following are other powerful words associated with money:

Positive	Negative
Bargain	Expensive
Profit	Deficit
Economical	Extravagant
Savings	Loss

Affection.   The desire for love, friendship, attention, belonging, and sex is common to all people. The affection appeal is almost as strong as the money appeal and, for some, even stronger. Fears involved in the affection appeal are as strong, if not stronger, than desires for affection. The attention-holding element in the affection appeal is more in the *promise* than in the *fulfillment*. Affection is a particularly strong appeal for young people.

Positive	Negative
Attraction	Rejection
Understanding	Misunderstanding
Friendship	Dislike
Love	Hate

Status.   Status is the recognition appeal. It reflects the feeling many people have about being perceived as important. The status appeal can be quite powerful, as people seek approval and appreciation for their work, appearance, attitudes, and actions.

Positive	Negative
Advancement	Demotion, stagnation
Superior	Inferior
Exclusive	Common, run-of-the-mill
Suave	Sloppy
Beautiful	Ugly

Security.   Security is the emotional appeal of self-preservation. Generally, the older people get, the more important security is to them.

Positive	Negative
Comfort	Pain, discomfort
Family, together	Alone, isolated
Healthy	Sick
Time-saving	Time-wasting
Secure, safe	Vulnerable

Going-Away Power

Ads with *going-away power* stay in people's minds. The memorable aspect of a commercial should be related to the main selling point.

The Promise   To be effective, all advertising must contain a future promise: "Get clothes whiter than ever before," "Builds strong bodies twelve ways," "The ultimate driving machine." Even retailers who are promoting a sale can include a promise in their commercials: "Up to 40 percent off on all items," "Best savings of the year," "No credit refused." The promise is the benefit to the consumer, and the best way to present it is to link it strongly to the advertiser's name: "Wal-Mart—Always the lowest prices."

When you write advertising for customers, craft it to make sure it has stopping power, holding power, and going-away power. Make sure it has at least one strong emotional appeal. Emotional appeals have two dimensions, positive and negative—people want it or fear losing it. And finally, all good advertising has a strong promise—explicit or implied. Always include a powerful promise when you write advertising.

Endnotes

1. Charles Warner and Joseph Buchman. 1991. *Broadcast and Cable Selling,* 2nd Edition. Belmont, CA.: Wadsworth Publishing. p. 263. Adapted from ERISCO (Emotional Response Index System Company) promotional material.
2. Ibid.

Index